Guide to Global Real Estate Investment Trusts

Guide to Global Real Estate Investment Trusts

Eleventh Edition

Edited by

Stefano Simontacchi
Ilona McElroy
Rosaleen Carey

Published by:
Kluwer Law International B.V.
PO Box 316
2400 AH Alphen aan den Rijn
The Netherlands
E-mail: lrs-sales@wolterskluwer.com
Website: www.wolterskluwer.com/en/solutions/kluwerlawinternational

Sold and distributed by:
Wolters Kluwer Legal & Regulatory U.S.
7201 McKinney Circle
Frederick, MD 21704
United States of America
E-mail: customer.service@wolterskluwer.com

Printed on acid-free paper.

ISBN 978-94-035-4613-1

e-Book: ISBN 978-94-035-4643-8
web-PDF: ISBN 978-94-035-4653-7

Printed in the Netherlands.

Editors

STEFANO SIMONTACCHI

Stefano Simontacchi is the President of BonelliErede, where he gained vast experience in both domestic and international real estate transactions and in structuring real estate collective investment vehicles.

He obtained his PhD at the Faculty of Law of Leiden University, the Netherlands, where, since 2000, he has been lecturing in international taxation for the Adv. LLM organized by the International Tax Center Leiden. In addition, he has lectured in taxation and international taxation for many years at several other universities and Master's programmes. In 2015, Stefano became an independent member, as representative of the International Tax Center Leiden, of the EU Joint Transfer Pricing Forum. Stefano Simontacchi is also the author of several publications and articles. His book *Taxation of Capital Gains under the OECD Model Convention: With Special Regard to Immovable Property* was published in 2007 by Kluwer Law International.
E-mail: stefano.simontacchi@belex.com

ILONA McELROY

Ilona McElroy is PwC EMEA Real Estate Tax Leader and a partner in Ireland's asset management tax practice. Ilona specializes in providing tax consultancy services to the real estate sector and has been very active in the space of international acquisitions of Irish real estate, advising on the structuring of a large number of deals through the use of REITs, limited partnerships, property companies, ICAVs, and section 110 companies.

Domestically, Ilona is a member of the tax steering group of the Irish funds industry association and the chairperson of the recently formed Irish Real Estate Funds (IREF) working group, which focuses on liaising with the Department of Finance and Revenue on IREF legislation. Ilona is a member of the Department of Finance audit committee and also acts as the main tax advisor to the Irish Institutional Property (IIP) industry group.

Ilona provides corporate tax structuring services to a number of high-profile clients in the Irish real estate sector.

Ilona has a first-class LLM from Trinity College, Dublin and is a member of the Irish Taxation Institute. Ilona also sits on the projects committee of the Foundation for Fiscal Studies.

E-mail: ilona.mcelroy@pwc.com

ROSALEEN CAREY

Rosaleen Carey is a director in our asset management tax and real estate practice in Dublin, Ireland. She has extensive experience in advising real estate fund structuring solutions for international and domestic clients.

Rosaleen on a day-to-day basis advises on the tax implications arising from large-scale real estate acquisitions and disposals, including providing detailed tax due diligence reports along with the tax and legal requirements. Rosaleen has significant experience in working in transactional-based deals in relation to making and managing investments and returning value to shareholders in a tax-efficient manner.

Rosaleen has a Bachelor of Common Law and German and is an associate of the Irish Institute of Taxation.

E-mail: rosaleen.carey@pwc.com

Contributors

FABRIZIO ACERBIS

Fabrizio Acerbis is tax partner and chairman of the managing committee of TLS Associazione Professionale di Avvocati e Commercialisti.

Fabrizio Acerbis' professional experience includes tax advice to a large number of financial institutions in respect of corporate taxation and international structuring. His professional experience also includes regulatory aspects and requirements to be met under the Italian Civil Code.

E-mail: fabrizio.acerbis@pwc.com

JORDAN ADELSON

Jordan Adelson is a director currently on tour in PwC's National Professional Services – Accounting Services Group, a group that focuses on global consultations with domestic and international clients and engagement teams on a wide range of technical accounting matters. Jordan focuses primarily on real estate, leasing, consolidation and various transactional-related accounting issues. He is also actively involved in following standard-setting projects (i.e., leasing, consolidation, etc.) and authoring industry and firm through leadership. In his role, Jordan directly assists and serves clients in the real estate industry on accounting issues and complex transactions.

Prior to his tour in the Accounting Services Group, Jordan was a member of the New York real estate assurance practice of PwC from October 2009 to June 2018. His clients included both public and private REITs, large institutional real estate investment advisors and funds, real estate owners/developers and residential/commercial property managers. Jordan is also the co-creator and editor of *Current Developments for the Real Estate Industry*, a nationally distributed publication providing perspective on the latest market and economic trends, regulatory activities and legislative changes affecting the real estate industry, as well as informed views on the most current developments in operations, business strategy, taxation, compliance and financing.

Jordan has a Bachelor of Science in Accounting and a Master's in Accounting and Information Analysis from Lehigh University, is a licensed Certified Public Accountant, and is a member of the American Institute of Certified Public Accountants.
E-mail: jordan.y.adelson@pwc.com

BARAN AKAN

Baran Akan is a tax director at PwC Turkey. He has been with the firm for twenty years and has gained experience in various fields, especially in real estate taxation and international tax planning for multinational companies. He is working as a senior advisor rendering tax audit consultancy and international tax planning services, both to international investors and to respectable local companies.
E-mail: baran.akan@pwc.com

MARIO ALBERTO GUTIERREZ

Mario Alberto Gutierrez is an international tax services partner with PwC Mexico specializing in corporate and international taxes. He has more than fifteen years of professional experience; he joined PwC Mexico City's office in September 2005. Mario Alberto's advisory activities focus on legal and tax structures for international transactions involving the US and Mexican tax laws, dispute resolution, optimization of Mexican income tax, alternative minimum tax and employee profit-sharing. Mario Alberto has assisted a number of clients in evaluating Mexican migration, debt financing and cost comparison issues in global restructurings involving changes in business models. During his professional career, Mario Alberto has participated in international tax for the consumer products industry, real estate companies, individuals and limited liability partnerships, as well as interpreting and developing efficient international solutions in the Mergers and Acquisitions environment.

Mario Alberto was assigned to PwC USA (New York) for two years, where he was the project leader in charge of implementing reorganization processes in several multinational groups with subsidiaries in Mexico, such as cross-border redeployment by a multinational enterprise of functions, assets and/or risks.

Mario Alberto is a Certified Public Accountant who graduated from the UNAM and holds a postgraduate international taxation qualification from the ITAM. He has attended different national and international tax courses in Mexico and the US and has written for several tax-specialized publications, among others, *International Tax Review* and *World Bank's Doing Business* editions. He is also a member of the International Tax Committee of the Mexican National Institute of Accountants.
E-mail: mario.alberto.gutierrez@pwc.com

MARIO ALBERTO ROCHA

Mario Alberto Rocha is a partner of the Legal Area of PwC in Mexico City. He is an Attorney-at-Law with a Master's in International and European Business Law in Spain and has postgraduate certifications in Mexico, the US and Europe related to Antitrust, Intellectual Property, Energy Law, Internet Law, among others.

Mario joined PwC in January 2001, and he has expertise in commercial law, M&A, cross-border transactions, real estate, intellectual property, antitrust, government, corporate governance and legal risk analysis. During his tenure at PwC, Mario collaborated on diverse projects involving restructurings of corporate groups, mergers, acquisitions and unwinding of multinational companies and governmental entities.

Mario is a member of the National Association of Corporate Attorneys (ANADE), a speaker in business forums and an author of legal publications.
E-mail: mario.alberto.rocha@pwc.com

EKATERINA ALEKSOVA

Ekaterina Aleksova is a senior manager in PwC Bulgaria. She works in the corporate income tax team and is involved in tax structuring projects and tax assignments, including various cross-border transactions. She is a member of PwC real estate and transfer pricing network. Ekaterina holds a Master's in Business Taxation from Osnabrück University, Germany, and a Master's in Finance from the University of National and World Economics, Sofia, Bulgaria.
E-mail: ekaterina.aleksova@pwc.com

JULANNE ALLEN

Julanne Allen is a Principal in PwC LLP's National Tax Service practice, and in that role, she advises REITs and brings her unique perspective from her time at the Internal Revenue Service (IRS) to help REITs navigate the complicated myriad of rules that they are required to follow.

Julanne began her career working at a large international law firm where she advised clients on a myriad of tax issues relating to the formation and operation of REITs and real estate funds. After several years of advising clients on tax matters, she entered the public sector, where she brought her practical knowledge and business understanding to the IRS' Office of Chief Counsel.

While at the IRS, she drafted, reviewed, and commented on most REIT issues addressed in published guidance, private letter rulings, and taxpayer conferences. She authored the regulation defining real property for REIT qualification purposes as well as many seminal private letter rulings addressing REIT tax and compliance matters. After many years of working in the public sector, she joined PwC, where she synthesizes her experience representing and advising clients with her unique understanding of the IRS' outlook.

Julanne has a Master of Laws in Taxation from New York University School of Law, graduated from the Catholic University of America School of Law, *magna cum laude*, and earned her BBA and BA from the College of William and Mary.
E-mail: julanne.allen@pwc.com

EDUARDO ALVES DE OLIVEIRA

Eduardo Alves De Oliveira is the PwC partner responsible for the Financial Services industry and Real Estate in Brazil. Eduardo is experienced in Brazilian and international tax, advising large banks, private equity funds, venture capital funds and multinational corporations on structuring, mitigating tax risk and improving their tax strategy. He has gained his experience working in São Paulo, Brazil and Boston, US. With twenty years at PwC, Eduardo has extensive experience working with financial institutions and investment managers to develop innovative fund, hedging and deal structures for foreign investors in the Brazilian financial market.

Eduardo holds a Bachelor's in Law from Mackenzie University, in Accounting from the University of São Paulo (USP), a Master's in Accounting and Business/Management from the University of São Paulo (USP) and a PhD in Tax and Accounting from the University of São Paulo (USP).

Eduardo is the author of books related to the financial industry, among them 'Taxation – Current Topics' and 'Economic Availability of Fair Value'.

E-mail: eduardo.alves@pwc.com

ERSUN BAYRAKTAROĞLU

Ersun Bayraktaroğlu is a tax partner and territory real estate leader of PwC Turkey. He has been a tax practitioner for about thirty-five years and has been providing advisory services to several domestic and international clients in the real estate area for years. He obtained his Master of Arts in Economics at Western Michigan University in the USA. Mr Bayraktaroğlu is the author of several articles in business dailies and real estate magazines. Also, he is a speaker in several domestic and international panels, discussions and conferences and a lecturer in several seminars on tax issues.

E-mail: ersun.bayraktaroglu@pwc.com

ORSOLYA BOGNÁR

Orsolya Bognár is working as a senior manager at PwC Hungary's corporate tax department. She joined the Budapest office in 2013. Orsolya is an economist with a major in Accounting and also holds a Bachelor's in Law. She is a certified accountant and an ACCA member since 2015. Orsolya mainly deals with corporate income tax matters of large Hungarian and international clients with a focus on real estate taxation, and she is often involved in international tax structuring projects.

E-mail: orsolya.bognar@pwc.com

CARLOS BRAVO

Carlos Bravo is Director of the TLS Tax Team in Madrid and is a member of the International Real Estate Tax Network of PwC, having over seventeen years of experience in leading transactional works, particularly for real estate investment funds and private equity houses on complex deals.

Carlos started his professional career at Garrigues, a Spanish law firm, and joined PwC in 2005. While working for PwC, he was involved in establishing part of the Real Estate Tax business team.

He has a great deal of experience in the real estate sector, with deep knowledge of the SOCIMI regime, serving both national and international clients. He provides tax services to (listed) real estate companies, asset managers and construction companies. This includes mergers, contributions and assisting clients in setting up regional-, country- or property-specific real estate investment funds, among others.

Carlos holds a Bachelor's in Law (Granada University) and a Master's in Taxation (Garrigues Study Centre).

E-mail: carlos.bravo.gutierrez@pwc.com

JOSHUA CARDWELL

Joshua Cardwell is the leader of the Australian Real Estate Tax practice. Joshua advises a broad spectrum of institutional real estate clients in respect of inbound and outboard investments, funding raising, M&A transactions and reorganizations. Joshua has been extensively involved with the Property Council of Australia's lobbying in respect of many recent tax change proposals.

E-mail: josh.cardwell@pwc.com

JENNIFER CHANG

Jennifer Chang is a partner in the Tax–Financial Services division of PwC Malaysia. Jennifer's experience includes advising clients on tax matters relating to income tax, real property gains tax, stamp duty, service tax, applicable tax incentives, double tax treaties as well as structured finance and international tax. She works with industry players in the financial services industry and has been involved in numerous presentations and has often done lobbying for tax incentives on financial services products and clients, including unit trust and fund management, closed-end funds, REITs, securities borrowing and lending, bonds, offshore banking, leasing, Islamic Finance and so on. She is a regular speaker at public seminars on the taxation of the financial services industry, including Islamic banking, asset-backed securitization, REITs, international tax and Labuan.

E-mail: jennifer.chang@pwc.com

JONATHAN CLEMENTS

Jonathan Clements leads the UK Real Estate Tax Network of PwC LLP.

He specializes in the provision of property taxation advice to a broad spectrum of clients, including Real Estate Investment Trusts (REITs), property investors (both direct and via indirect vehicles) and real estate funds.

E-mail: Jonathan.clements@pwc.com

DAVID CUELLAR

David Cuellar is the lead partner of Tax and Legal Services of PwC in Mexico; previously, he performed as the lead of the international tax services practice in Mexico. He is a specialist in Mexican international tax planning and structuring and has helped several multinational companies in expanding their operations into Mexico. David is also the leader of the PwC Mexico Real Estate Tax practice and forms part of the global Real Estate Tax network. He has more than fifteen years of experience in structuring operations for foreign companies doing business in Mexico.

David was seconded to PwC UK for over three years, where he was in charge of the firm's Mexican Tax Desk for Europe, the Middle East and Africa, based in London. He graduated *summa cum laude* from the Escuela Bancaria y Comercial, receiving two degrees, one as a Certified Public Accountant and the other in Business Administration. He is also a Tax Professor and is in charge of the tax department at his alma mater.

David has authored a number of articles in several tax magazines, including *International Tax Review*, *Tax Business Magazine* and *Tax Notes International.*
E-mail: david.cuellar@pwc.com

BHAIRAV DALAL

Bhairav Dalal is the Real Estate Sector Leader and Partner in the tax & regulatory practice. He has varied experience in advising Indian and multinational groups in the areas of real estate, infrastructure and private equity. Over the last twenty years, his focus has been transaction and tax advisory services specializing in the real estate sector.

Bhairav has also advised real estate companies on complex projects involving investment structuring and group restructuring. Given his experience, he has been extensively involved in the REIT/InvIT discussions in the industry and regulators as well. He has handled diverse assignments in the transaction and corporate restructuring space, involving the following:

- Developing real estate fund structures and consummating their investments.
- Redevelopment Projects (including SRA's & Society redevelopment projects).
- Infra space such as bid structuring, private equity funding, and restructuring for Singapore BT listing. M&A and inbound advisory.

Bhairav was also a part of the team advising the two large REIT offerings and a recent secondary acquisition in India.

Bhairav is a graduate of Commerce from the University of Mumbai and is a member of the Institute of Chartered Accountants of India since 2002. He regularly speaks on real estate-related topics before various forums and contributes to articles and interviews for several newspapers, magazines and business news channels.
E-mail: bhairav.dalal@pwc.com

SERGE DE LANGE

Serge de Lange (1974), a tax partner in the real estate group of PwC in Amsterdam, is leading the real estate/real assets group of PwC in the Netherlands. He studied Dutch Tax Law (LLM) at the University of Amsterdam and started his career in 1999. In 2007, he obtained his Master's in Real Estate (MRE) at the University of Amsterdam. Serge provides tax advisory services to real estate investors and asset managers investing and divesting in real estate, advising on tax optimization of corporate structures including internal or external refinancing, advising in respect of mergers and acquisitions and assisting clients set up the regional, country- or property-specific real estate investment funds. Areas of expertise include corporate income tax, real estate transfer tax and REITs. Serge often speaks at real estate seminars on various topics in the Netherlands and has contributed as an author to real estate journals and publications.
E-mail: serge.de.lange@pwc.com

DANIELE DI MICHELE

Daniele Di Michele is a tax partner of TLS Associazione Professionale di Avvocati e Commercialisti, Italian leader for real estate tax services of PwC Tax and Legal Services.

He regularly advises several multinational players on all Italian tax aspects for their Italian recurring and extraordinary operations concerning their real estate business.

E-mail: daniele.di.michele@pwc.com

PHILIPPE EMIEL

Philippe Emiel is an Of Counsel in the PwC Societe d'Avocats real estate group and lawyer of the Hauts-de-Seine Bar. He is also a Member of the Board of Directors of the Hauts-de-Seine Bar. He has numerous years of experience advising international investment funds within the scope of their real estate investments in France with regard to investment tax structuring, sell-side and buy-side tax due diligence. He also frequently works on assignments of externalization of property assets and restructuring of property portfolios and also advises clients in the creation of real estate vehicles: SCPI, OPCI and REITs.

E-mail: philippe.emiel@avocats.pwc.com

ADAM FEUERSTEIN

Adam Feuerstein, a principal in the Washington National Tax Services practice, is PwC LLP's National Real Estate Tax Technical Leader. Adam's experience includes a broad cross-section of product types and owners, including real estate investment trusts (REITs), real estate investment funds, institutional investors, sovereign wealth funds and tax-exempt entities. Prior to joining PwC, Adam was a partner at a large international law firm where he worked for over a decade advising REITs and other clients on a variety of tax matters. Adam's experience covers the life cycle of public and private REITs from formation to operation and through liquidation, including due diligence and structuring for mergers and acquisitions of REITs. Adam has served as an adjunct professor at the Georgetown University Law Center and the Villanova University Law School and is co-author of the treatise on REITs in RIA's Catalyst series. Adam graduated from Harvard Law School, *cum laude*, has a Master's in Public Policy from Harvard University's John F. Kennedy School of Government and received his BS with honours from Cornell University.

E-mail: adam.s.feuerstein@pwc.com

DAVID GERSTLEY

David Gerstley is a partner with PwC in the New York office with twenty years of experience serving audit and non-audit clients in the asset management and real estate industry. He works on both public and private REITs, works with asset managers, developers and institutional investors and has extensive experience with real estate investment transactions, including acquisition due diligence, REIT conversions, mergers & acquisitions and initial public offerings. David has been a consultant in PwC's

National Office in the SEC Services Group, where he consulted with clients in the real estate industry on matters of accounting, auditing and financial reporting. David also assists clients with capital raising activities, including initial public offerings, quarterly and annual reports, SEC comment letters and comfort letters.

David received a Bachelor of Science in Accounting from the Sy Syms School of Business of Yeshiva University, New York, US. He is a CPA licensed in New York and New Jersey and is a member of the New York State Society of Certified Public Accountants and the American Institute of Certified Public Accountants.
E-mail: david.gerstley@pwc.com

KEN GRIFFIN

Ken Griffin is a partner in the Toronto office of PwC and is a member of the Real Estate and Private Company Services groups. Ken provides advice on Canadian income tax issues to private companies and their shareholders in a variety of industries. He focuses, in particular, on the real estate sector and in this area also works with public REITs, pension funds and domestic and foreign investment funds. Ken's experience includes structuring new investments – both domestic and cross-border – advising clients on tax reorganizations and shareholder estate planning matters and handling tax issues regarding the use of partnerships, joint ventures, trusts and other ownership and financing arrangements.

Ken graduated from the University of Waterloo, Ontario with a Bachelor of Mathematics and is a Chartered Professional Accountant. Ken is a member of the Joint Committee of Taxation of the Canadian Bar Association and the Chartered Professional Accountants of Canada.
E-mail: ken.griffin@pwc.com

ADAM HANDLER

Adam Handler is a tax partner with PwC's Tokyo office, where he specializes in structuring inbound real estate investments. Adam has over thirty-seven years of experience in the real estate industry, including transactions involving REITs, partnerships, sovereign wealth funds, fund structuring and investments, and public companies.

Prior to joining PwC in Tokyo, Adam spent twenty years as a principal with PwC in the United States, where he was the leader of its real estate tax consulting practice in its Washington National Tax Service.

Education

He graduated from Yale University with a Bachelor of Chemistry, *summa cum laude*, and he is a Phi Beta Kappa society member with a distinction in Chemistry.
He obtained J.D. from Stanford Law School.

Bar Memberships

He is a member of the State Bar of California, US District Court for the Central District of California, and US Tax Court.
E-mail: adam.m.handler@pwc.com

ALEX HOWIESON

Alex Howieson is a partner in the Toronto office of PwC. Alex works closely with Canadian and foreign REITs, and domestic and international private equity funds investing in Canadian and foreign real estate. Alex has significant experience advising clients on acquisitions, and dispositions, financing, joint venture arrangements, and mergers and acquisitions.

Alex is a Chartered Professional Accountant and received a Bachelor of Commerce from the University of Toronto.

E-mail: alex.t.howieson@pwc.com

LEE JAE-DOK

Lee Jae-Dok is a tax director who worked in the PwC Korean office for seventeen years, including the period of secondment in PwC Singapore in 2009 and 2010.

He was involved in various advisory projects from the international tax and regulatory perspective for foreign clients making investments into Korean assets, including real estate and financial products. He also was involved in the structuring service to maximize the cash flow in a tax-efficient manner for cross-border transactions.

During his secondment in PwC Singapore, he advised foreign clients to make investments in Korea using the Singapore platform.

E-mail: jae-dok.lee@pwc.com

GERGELY JUHÁSZ

Gergely Juhász is a tax partner who joined PwC in 2007. He holds a degree in Economics with a major in Finance and is also a Certified Tax Advisor. He specializes in corporate income taxation, taxation of the real estate industry and international tax structuring and as such, he is a member of PwC's International Tax Structuring Network. He is also the Hungarian country leader of EUDTG, PwC's pan-European network of EU tax law experts.

E-mail: gergely.juhasz@pwc.com

GRÉGORY JURION

Grégory Jurion is a tax partner and is working in PwC Belgium's Financial Services and Real Estate team since 2001.

He has broad experience in advising on international and domestic tax restructuring and is a tax adviser to a number of real estate funds, REITs and developers. In most of Grégory's assignments, he plays a European coordination role covering foreign investments in Belgium and within the European Union, coupled with real estate advisory practice.

His work qualification is a Bachelor's in Law *cum laude* from the University of Louvain-la-Neuve (Belgium) and a Master's in Law from Solvay Business School (Belgium). He is also a member of the Belgian Institute of Tax Consultants.

Grégory has written a number of articles on tax and has spoken on the subject at in-house and external conferences.

E-mail: gregory.jurion@pwc.com

TOMOHIRO KANDORI

Tomohiro Kandori has extensive experience in both domestic and cross-border finance transactions. His practice focuses mainly on real estate finance and asset finance. He has advised clients on a wide variety of transactions including real estate acquisition, development, and sale, as well as investment into and financing of real properties in Japan. He has represented domestic and foreign investors, including investment funds, financial institutions, investment managers, and developers from the United States, Europe and Asia. He has also represented lenders in numerous structured finance transactions and in restructuring distressed investment projects.

Prior to joining PwC Legal Japan, Tomohiro worked for more than fifteen years at one of the largest law firms in Japan. He also worked as in-house counsel for a global financial institution at its London branch.

He received his LLB from the University of Tokyo and his LLM from the School of Law, University of California, Berkeley.

He is a member of the Dai-ichi Tokyo Bar Association (2002).

E-mail: tomohiro.kandori@pwc.com

HANNA KIM

Hanna Kim is a manager in PwC Korea's Global Tax Services Group.

Prior to joining PwC Korea, he worked at the PwC LA office for eight years, advising global asset managers/institutional investors investing in the US.

E-mail: hanna.k.kim@pwc.com

SUNG YEOL KIM

Sung Yeol Kim is a senior associate in PwC Korea's Corporate and International Tax team. Prior to joining PwC Korea, he worked in PwC Atlanta office for two years providing US income tax compliance and income tax provisions to privately held businesses and high net worth individuals.

E-mail: sungyeol.s.kim@pwc.com

LENNON LEE

Lennon Lee is a tax partner with PricewaterhouseCoopers Singapore Pte. Ltd ('PwC Singapore'), and he leads the financial services tax practice in PwC Singapore. He is part of the real estate and hospitality (REH) team in PwC Singapore.

With close to twenty-five years of experience in practising Singapore and international tax, Lennon has been involved in many international advisory projects and assignments across a whole spectrum of industries. He advises financial institutions, government-linked entities, high net worth individuals, family offices, fund management houses, real estate developers, REIT managers, and listed companies on various Singapore and cross-border tax and regulatory implications arising from investment, development and management of real estate globally.

In addition, he manages the China tax practice in Singapore and advises corporates on both inbound and outbound investments involving China. In particular, he has been involved in the listing of a few China-sponsored REITs in Singapore.Lennon is an active speaker for various industry conferences and seminars organised by financial institutions, business organizations and government agencies, and has contributed articles to various publications. He is on the board of directors of the Tax Academy of Singapore.

E-mail: lennon.kl.lee@pwc.com

MIKKO LEINOLA

Tax Partner Mikko Leinola co-leads PwC Finland's Financial Services tax and legal practice. Mikko specializes in advising major Finnish and international institutional investors in their direct and indirect real estate investments. In addition, Mikko is regularly assisting Finnish and Nordic fund managers in setting up and operating real estate funds investing in Finnish and Nordic real estate. He is a frequent speaker in seminars. Mikko is a Master of Laws from the University of Turku.

E-mail: mikko.leinola@pwc.com

DAMYAN LESHEV

Damyan Leshev has co-authored the chapter on Bulgaria while working at Tsvetkova Bebov and Partners, one of the major Bulgarian business law firms, which cooperates on an ongoing basis with the PwC network. He works in the financial services law team and specializes in capital markets law. He holds a Master's in Law from the Faculty of Law of the University of National and World Economy, Sofia, Bulgaria and a Bachelor's in Accounting and Control from the same university.

E-mail: damyan.leshev@tbp.bg

LIM MAAN HUEY

Lim Maan Huey is a tax partner with the Financial Services group of PwC Singapore, and she leads the real estate tax practice of the firm. She has over eighteen years of experience in working with global and local clients in the financial services industry on tax consulting and compliance matters. She previously worked in the New York firm of PwC US, advising private fund clients on international tax matters.

Maan Huey works with clients in family offices, hedge funds, private equity, real estate, retail funds and sovereign wealth funds. She has tax advisory experience in many aspects, including operational tax compliance and procedural issues, permanent establishment issues for funds and fund managers, set-up of funds and fund management operations, use of Singapore-domiciled investment/fund structures, cross-border investments as well as restructuring and mergers and acquisition transactions.

She is involved in the tax working committee of the Singapore Chapter of the Alternative Investments Management Association and the tax working committee of the Investment Management Association of Singapore.

E-mail: maan.huey.lim@pwc.com

CINDY MAI

Cindy Mai is a director currently on tour at PwC's National Quality Organization – Accounting Services Group, specializing in the new lease standard and complex accounting issues and transactions related to the real estate industry.

Prior to her tour, she was a director of PwC's New York real estate assurance practice, and her clients included both public REITs and private real estate investment funds.

She has experience working on real estate funds reporting at fair value, as well as historical GAAP, REIT compliance, SEC reporting, Sarbanes-Oxley 404 compliance, etc.

From 2005 to 2013, she worked in PwC's Guangzhou Office, where she provided a broad range of assurance services, including annual audits, IPO transactions and bond offerings for leading real estate development companies in China, whose shares were listed on The Stock Exchange of Hong Kong Limited.

Cindy received an MBA from Fordham University's Gabelli School of Business in 2015. She is a licensed Certified Public Accountant in New York, New Hampshire and China. She is also a CFA charter holder.

She has in-depth knowledge of US GAAP, China GAAP and IFRS.
E-mail: qiyan.mai@pwc.com

SAMULI MAKKONEN

Tax Partner Samuli Makkonen co-leads PwC Finland's Financial Services tax and legal practice. Samuli advises banks, insurance companies, pension institutions and investment funds on all aspects of Finnish and international tax law. Samuli's practice focuses on asset management, fund structuring (including private equity funds, real estate funds, and hedge funds), complex financing transactions and financial products, including structured finance and derivatives. He has written several articles in the field of taxation of financial instruments and investment management and is a frequent speaker in seminars in this field. Samuli is a Master of Laws from the University of Helsinki and a Bachelor of Science (Econ) from the Helsinki School of Economics.
E-mail: samuli.makkonen@pwc.com

KYLE MANDY

Kyle Mandy is Head of National Tax Technical at PwC South Africa. As part of that role, he is responsible for formulating PwC's position on matters of tax policy and tax design. Kyle has over twenty years of experience in tax and has advised numerous large corporates on all aspects of tax, including with respect to mergers and acquisitions, debt and capital markets, capital gains tax, international tax, share incentive schemes and dispute resolution.
E-mail: kyle.mandy@pwc.com

JAVIER MATEOS

Javier Mateos is a qualified attorney. He received a Bachelor's in Law from Universidad Pontificia de Comillas-ICADE and a Master's in Political Sciences from Universidad

Complutense de Madrid. He is a legal partner at PwC. He joined PwC in 2014 after working in different leading Spanish and English law firms. He specializes in major transactions involving mergers, reorganizations, tender offers, corporate LBOs, securities issues and public offerings, and regulatory matters concerning listed companies. He regularly advises on major M&A deals and is actively involved in real estate transactions (overall, in SOCIMIs).
E-mail: javier.mateos.sanchez@pwc.com

KEVIN NG

Kevin NG is a partner in the Toronto-based Financial Services Tax Group and leads the Canadian Tax Reporting & Strategy Practice as well as the Private Equity/Pensions Tax Practice.

With more than twenty-five years of experience in the investment and financial services industry, Kevin is focused on providing practical tax solutions for asset management, real estate, banking, and capital markets organizations.

Kevin began his career with PwC, and after eleven years in the assurance and tax practice, Kevin joined a Canadian public company as its Director, Taxation and ultimately took on the role of Vice President, Taxation. During a thirteen-year span in the industry, Kevin acquired significant practical experience in a wide range of areas, including investment product development, real estate and real estate investment products, mergers and acquisitions, financing strategies, executive compensation and general corporate tax planning.
E-mail: kevin.ng@pwc.com

EVELYNE PAQUET

Evelyne Paquet is a director within PwC Belgium's Financial Services and Real Estate team.

Evelyne has broad experience in providing tax advice on international and Belgian tax restructuring. She is a tax adviser to a number of real estate funds, REITs and developers. She is assisting clients in the due diligence process of real estate companies, including review of tax clauses in purchase agreements, etc. Evelyne also frequently negotiates tax rulings with the Belgian ruling commission on the tax treatment of restructuring activities.

She obtained her Master's in Economics – specialization in finance at the HEC, Liège (Belgium) in 2001 and Master's in Taxation at the ESSF, ICHEC, Brussels (Belgium) in 2003.
E-mail: evelyne.paquet@pwc.com

TAEJIN PARK

Taejin Park is a tax partner of the tax transaction structuring team, which is part of PwC Korea's Financial Services Group, and especially specialized in real estate transaction structuring advisory.

He has over nineteen years of experience in providing tax transaction structuring advisory services for international clients. He mainly deals with clients who make cross-border and international real estate transactions.

He has extensive experience in real estate transactions made by several core funds, opportunistic funds or investment banking based in the US, Europe and Asia.

The clients include sovereign wealth fund, Angelo Gordon, Invesco, AEW, M&G, GIC, Ascendas, Carlyle, etc.

E-mail: taejin.park@pwc.com

ARIEF ROELSE

Arief Roelse (1990) studied Dutch Notarial Law (LLB and LLM) and Tax Law (LLM) at the Radboud University of Nijmegen. He has a background in Dutch corporate law, contract law and financial market regulations and combines this knowledge with his expertise to advise national and international clients in the financial services industry, including investment funds, investment managers and (institutional) investors. He specializes in structuring and establishing investment funds, as well as advising on topics relevant to investment teams or investors, such as (co-)investment arrangements, liquidity, exits, (fund) governance, regulations and marketing and AIFMD-related topics. During the course of his career, he advised clients on cross-border (re-)structurings, mergers and acquisitions, initial and follow-on public offerings and corporate governance.

E-mail: arief.roelse@pwc.com

ANTONIO SÁNCHEZ

Antonio Sánchez is a tax lawyer and tax partner at PwC. Antonio holds a Bachelor of Laws from Universidad Complutense de Madrid, Spain. He joined PwC Spain in 1996 and became a partner in 2007. He has also worked as an in-house tax advisor for two major companies in the construction and telecom sectors. He currently leads the Spanish tax practice for construction, engineering and real estate. He is working with the top companies within the real estate, engineering and construction industries, including national and international real estate investment funds, institutional and private, domestic and foreign investors, providing local and international tax services. Antonio is a usual lecturer in postgraduate and executive programmes and seminars with regard to taxation for construction and real estate.

E-mail: antonio.sanchez.recio@pwc.com

ANISH SANGHVI

Anish Sanghvi is a partner in Price Waterhouse & Co LLP's tax & regulatory team and has over twenty years of experience working with international consulting firms.

He advises sovereign funds, pension funds, private equity funds, domestic clients on Indian and international tax, inbound investment advisory and corporate tax with a focus on infrastructure and real estate sectors. He advises them on a number of activities, including putting investment structures in place, entering into joint ventures, undertaking business reorganizations and conducting tax due diligence. He also advises clients on exchange control regulations, corporate and other regulatory laws. Anish also led the team which was advising a large REIT offering in India.

He has a wide experience in advising infrastructure and real estate clients on:

- structuring buyouts and divestitures;
- migration to REIT/InvIT including evaluating their readiness;
- structuring joint development agreements and EPC contracts;
- restructuring their groups and M&A transactions to create profit extraction strategies, value enhancements, etc.

He is a chartered accountant and commerce graduate.
E-mail: anish.sanghvi@pwc.com

BIRIM SARAN

Birim Saran is a senior tax manager at PwC Turkey. She has been with the firm for more than ten years and has been providing tax advisory services to several domestic and international clients in the real estate area.
E-mail: saran.birim@pwc.com

JEROEN ELINK SCHUURMAN

Jeroen Elink Schuurman (1968) studied Dutch Tax Law at the University of Leiden. As a tax partner of PwC, he is also the Global Real Estate Tax Leader of PwC. In the past, he led the real estate group of PwC in the Netherlands. In 2000, he achieved a Master's in Real Estate (MRE) at the University of Amsterdam. He is a frequent lecturer and has published articles in the field of real estate and taxation. Jeroen has more than twenty-five years of experience in advising clients on their Dutch and international real estate investments and developments. Among Jeroen's clients are many institutional investors, asset managers and development companies.
E-mail: jeroen.elink.schuurman@pwc.com

KWOK KAY (KK) SO

KK joined PwC Hong Kong in 1985, transferred to Melbourne, Australia in 1988 and returned to Hong Kong in 1992. Over the years, KK has accumulated extensive experience in providing advice on real estate and infrastructure projects. KK's real estate clients include real estate funds, listed and private real estate groups, institutional investors, and family offices. He is also the tax advisor to a number of REIT projects involving real estate in Hong Kong, Mainland China and other jurisdictions. During his professional career, KK has held various positions, including Chairman of the Executive Committee of the Taxation Faculty of Hong Kong Institute of Certified Public Accountants and PwC's Asia Pacific Real Estate Tax Leader.
KK graduated from the Chinese University of Hong Kong with an MBA. He is an associate of the Institute of Chartered Accountants in Australia and the Hong Kong Institute of Certified Public Accountants. He is also a fellow of the Association of Chartered Certified Accountants in the UK.
E-mail: kk.so@hk.pwc.com

UWE STOSCHEK

Uwe Stoschek joined PwC in 1994. He has a Bachelor's in Law from the Free University of Berlin and is both Attorney-at-Law (Rechtsanwalt) and a Certified Tax Consultant

(Steuerberater). He has been a Tax Partner with PwC from 2000 until 2021, currently serving as Senior Advisor and Director. Uwe was PwC's Global, Real Estate Tax Leader for fifteen years until 2021, and for five years held the position of Real Estate Industry Leader EMEA. He is a member of the EPRA (European Public Real Estate Association) Tax Board which plays an important role in the European REIT market. He has also been a member of the tax committee of INREV, the European organization for non-listed funds for many years. Furthermore, Uwe supports German industry associations, such as ZIA. He was also a member of the Consultative Working Group (CWG) of the European Securities and Markets Authority's (ESMA) Investment Management Standing Committee (IMSC) from 2013 to 2017.

Uwe specializes in national and international investment funds' tax issues as well as real estate for German and non-German open-end and closed-end funds, institutional and private, German and foreign investors. He has advised many international opportunity funds in designing, establishing and implementing their German investments.

Moreover, Uwe has special expertise in advising German and foreign REITs. He is also a frequent speaker on issues related to the Alternative Investment Fund Managers Directive (AIFMD).

E-mail: uwe.stoschek@pwc.com

HIROSHI TAKAGI

Hiroshi Takagi is a tax partner at PwC Japan. Hiroshi joined PwC in 2001, and he specializes in J-REIT and real estate investment funds. He has extensive experience assisting offshore investors (including Luxembourg and Singapore funds and Australian listed property trusts) in investing in Japanese real estate using *Tokumei Kumiai* (TK) and *Tokutei Mokuteki Kaisha* (TMK) structures.

Hiroshi graduated from the University of Tokyo and the University of Chicago, and he is a Certified Public Accountant in Japan and the US, as well as a licensed tax accountant in Japan.

E-mail: hiroshi.takagi@pwc.com

STEVE TYLER

Steve Tyler is a tax partner in PwC LLP's Atlanta office. He focuses on the taxation of real estate companies, including private and public REITs and other real estate owners and investors. He has focused on tax-efficient structuring of real estate transactions and ownership structures for US and non-US investors as well as tax-exempt institutions. He advises public and private REITs on investment structures, ongoing REIT qualification, partnership arrangements, cross-border transactions, debt workouts, and mergers and acquisitions.

Steve received a Bachelor's in Accounting and a Master's in Taxation from the University of North Texas. He is a licensed, Certified Public Accountant in New York, Texas and Georgia and is a member of the AICPA and NAREIT.

E-mail: steve.tyler@pwc.com

MAYA VAN BELLEGHEM

Maya van Belleghem is a senior manager within the Financial Services Legal and Regulatory team of PwC Belgium.

She is a former member of the Brussels and Luxembourg bars and specialized in banking, financial law and asset management regulation. She focuses on the regulatory aspects of financial services and on asset management operations.

Maya assists domestic and international clients on the regulatory, corporate and compliance aspects of the structuring, formation, organization, marketing and management of investment vehicles with a strong focus on structuring and organizing private equity and real estate investment funds.

Maya is frequently involved in negotiation with the competent regulatory authorities in Belgium in relation to the registration or listing of regulated investment funds. Throughout her career, Maya gained significant experience in investment management, both in Belgium and abroad.

E-mail: maya.van.belleghem@pwc.com

CHRIS VANGOU

Chris Vangou is a partner in the Toronto office of PwC and is a member of the Canadian Real Estate Tax Practice. Chris is primarily involved in providing advice to public and private real estate companies, REITs and tax-exempt funds. He has extensive experience advising real estate clients in the area of tax planning for acquisitions, divestitures, partnership and joint venture arrangements, financings and investments in and out of Canada. His clients are involved in land and commercial development, infrastructure projects and the ownership of offices, shopping centres, hotels and residential properties.

Chris is a Chartered Professional Accountant and a graduate of the University of Toronto. He is a member of the Tax Committee of the Real Property Association of Canada. Chris has presented at various conferences and seminars.

E-mail: chris.vangou@pwc.com

VASSILIOS VIZAS

Vassilios Vizas is a partner of PwC in Athens. His expertise lies in taxation of the financial services sector, real estate and private equity, as well as international tax structuring. He obtained his LLM in Banking and Financial Law from the University of London and LLM and LLB from the University of Athens. He is a member of the Athens Bar and a number of professional organizations including the International Fiscal Association.

Vassilis is also the author of several publications and articles in the Greek press, including 'Tax treatment of Real Estate Mutual Funds and Investment Companies', in *Synigoros Law Journal*, Issue 23/2001, as well as a number of international publications sponsored by PwC.

He is also the author of a book called 'The GAAR in Greek Law – Scope and Limitations', published in January 2017.

E-mail: vassilios.vizas@gr.pwc.com

DAVID VOSS

David Voss is a tax partner in PwC LLP's New York office. He focuses on the taxation of real estate investors, including public and private REITs, real estate funds and inbound real estate investors, including sovereign wealth funds and other institutional investors. He advises investors and investment sponsors with respect to tax-efficient ownership structures and real estate transactions for US and non-US investors as well as tax-exempt institutions. He advises public and private REITs on investment structures, ongoing REIT qualification matters, partnership arrangements, cross-border transactions, and mergers and acquisitions.

David has a BA from Manhattanville College and a JD from Emory University School of Law. He is a member of the New York State Bar and a licensed Certified Public Accountant in New York.

E-mail: david.m.voss@pwc.com

TOM WILKIN

Tom Wilkin is PwC LLP's US REIT Leader. Tom has over thirty years of experience serving clients in the real estate industry, including public/private real estate investment trusts (REITs), real estate investment advisory firms, opportunity funds, hotel operators, commercial developers and residential homebuilders, as well as extensive transactional real estate investment and acquisition due diligence experience in connection with both property and corporate M&A transactions. Over the span of his career, Tom has been responsible for some of PwC LLP's most complex real estate engagements with a significant focus on public transactions.

In addition to directly serving our traditional real estate clients, Tom also leads our 'Real Estate Life Cycles' initiative, Real, which is designed to help us seamlessly deliver our ever-broadening range of real estate-related services to meet emerging client needs for both our traditional real estate clients and significant users of real estate. These services go way beyond traditional audit and tax services. They also focus on difficult or emerging areas such as non-traditional REIT conversions/IPOs/spin-offs, mortgage REITs and products like single-family rentals.

Tom has a Bachelor's from Tulane University, Louisiana, and an EMBA from Columbia University, New York City.

E-mail: tom.wilkin@pwc.com

JACKY WONG

Jacky Wong is an assurance partner of PwC. Jacky is the Hong Kong and Macau Institutional Clients Business Unit Leader, and the Hong Kong REITs Leader. Jacky has over twenty years of experience in serving real estate and infrastructure companies. Over these twenty years, he has led various initial public offering projects, merger and acquisition projects; privatization projects and complex restructuring projects. He is currently the lead client service partner of various leading REITs and real estate companies listed on the Hong Kong Stock Exchange. Jacky has worked in both PwC Hong Kong and PwC US.

Jacky obtained his Bachelor's in Accounting and Finance from the University of Hong Kong and obtained his Bachelor's and Master's in Law from universities in the UK. He is currently a PhD student in Economics. He is a Chartered Financial Analyst (CFA) of the CFA Institute, a Chartered Accountant (CA) of the Institute of Chartered Accountants of Wales and England, and a Certified Public Accountant (CPA) of the Institute of Certified Public Accountants of Hong Kong.

E-mail: jacky.wong@hk.pwc.com

FREDY YATRACOU

Fredy Yatracou joined PwC in March 2002 as a Senior Manager of the Tax & Legal (TLS) Department and currently is the leader of the Tax FS services and responsible for the Tax Real Estate sector.

She is a specialist in corporate income taxes and international taxation. She has been engaged in a large number of projects, involving transactions in the Financial Sector, focusing on Mergers and Acquisitions tax advice, complex finance raising arrangements and corporate restructurings. She has more than twenty years of experience in advising Greek-based multinational companies in their international and local tax affairs.

Fredy has been involved in various projects in all aspects of tax issues concerning companies in the real estate and hospitality sector, REITs, Real Estate funds, Real Estate developers, NPL Real Estate structures. etc.

Fredy holds an LLB from the University of Athens and an LLM in European and International Trade Law from the University of Leicester – UK.

She is a lawyer registered with the Athens Bar Association.

E-mail: fredy.yatracou@pwc.com

Summary of Contents

Summary of Contents

Table of Contents

Canada
Chris Vangou, Ken Griffin, Kevin Ng & Alex Howieson

List of Abbreviations

AFO	Adjusted Funds from Operations
AFM	Financial Market Authority
AFS	Australian Financial Services
AIF	Alternative Investment Fund
AIFM	Alternative Investment Fund Manager
AIFMD	Alternative Investment Fund Managers Directive
AIM	Alternative Investment Market
AMC	Asset Management Company
ASIC	Australian Securities and Investment Commission
ASX	Australian Stock Exchange
AVD	Ad Valorem Stamp Duty
BEPS	Base Erosion and Profit Shifting
BMV	Mexican Stock Exchange
BITT	Banking and Insurance Transaction Tax
BSD	Buyer's Stamp Duty
BT	Business Trust
CAD	Cash Available for Distribution
CGT	Capital Gains Tax
CEB	Certified Evaluator's Body
CIT	Corporate Income Tax
CITA	Corporate Income Tax Act
CIV	Collective Investment Vehicles
CMB	Capital Markets Board
CNBV	Commission of Banking and Securities
CVM	Commission Comissão de Valores Mobiliários
CMC	Capital Market Committee

DOT	Declaration of Trust
DTT	Double Tax Treaty
ECI	Effectively Connected Income
EEA	European Economic Area
EGM	Extraordinary General Meeting
ERISA	Employee Retirement Income Security Act
FAD	Funds Available for Distribution
FBI	Fiscale Belegginginstelling
FFO	Funds from Operations
FIBRAS	Fideicomisos de Infraestructura de Bienes Raices
FIC	Foreign Investment Committee
FII	Fundo de Investimento Imobiliário
FIRPTA	Foreign Investor in Real Property Tax Act
FSC	Financial Supervision Commission
FSMA	Belgian Financial Services and Markets Authority
FTC	French Tax Code
GAAP	Generally Accepted Accounting Principles
GREIT manual	Guidance on Real Estate Investment Trusts
GST	Goods and Services Tax
HoER	Holder of Excessive Rights
HMRC	Her Majesty's Revenue and Customs
HRMC	HM Revenue & Customs
IFRS	International Financial Reporting Standards
IAS	International Accounting Standards
IBA	Industrial Building Allowance
ICG	The Informal Consultative Group on the Taxation of Collective Investment Vehicles and Procedures for Tax Relief for Cross-Border Investors
I.R.C.	Internal Revenue Service
IM	Information Memorandum
IRAS	Inland Revenue Authority of Singapore
IRES	Imposta sul Reddito delle Società
IRAP	Imposta Regionale sulle Attività Produttive
IRS	Internal Revenue Service
ISE	Istanbul Stock Exchange
ITA	Income Tax Act
IRO	Inland Revenue Ordinance of Hong Kong
KLSE	Kuala Lumpur Stock Exchange
KOSDAQ	Korea Securities Dealers Association
LMV	Ley del Mercado de Valores
MAS	Monetary Authority of Singapore

M&A	Merger & Acquisitions
MFFO	Modified Funds from Operations
MFT	Mutual Fund Trust
MIS	Managed Investment Schemes
MITA	Malaysian Income Tax Act
MLTM	Ministry of Land Transport and Maritime Affairs
MSC	Multimedia Super Corridor
MTA	Mercato Telematico Azionario
NAV	Net Assets Value
NFFO	Normalized Funds From Operations
NOL	Net operating loss
NTA	Net Tangible Assets
OECD	Organisation for Economic Co-operation and Development
OECD MC/OECD Model	OECD Model Tax Convention on Income and Capital OECD Commentary/Commentaries on the Articles of the OECD Model Tax Commentary Convention on Income and Capital (version incorporating the changes of 2005)
UN Model	United Nations Model Double Taxation Convention between Developed and Developing Countries (version 2001)
US Model	United States Model Income Tax Conventions (version 15 November 2006)
OECD Report 2007	OECD Discussion Draft on the tax treaty issues related to REITs
OECD CIV Report 2009	OECD Report of the Informal Consultative Group on the Taxation of Collective Investment Vehicles and Procedures for Tax Relief for Cross-Border Investors on the Granting of Treaty Benefits with Respect to the Income of Collective Investment Vehicles
OEICs	Open-Ended Investment Companies
PAIF	Property Authorized Investment Fund
PDS	Product Disclosure Statement
PEA	Plan d'Epargne en Actions
PFG	Property Fund Guidelines
PID	Property Income Distribution
PIF	Property Investment Fund
RE	Responsible Entity
REIF	Reserved Alternative Investment Fund
REMIC	Real Estate Mortgage Investment Conduit
REIT	Real Estate Investment Trusts
REICA	Real Estate Investment Company Act

REITA	REIT Act
REMF	Real Estate Mutual Funds
RNV	National Registry of Securities
RPGT	Real Property Gains Tax
SA	Societe Anonyme
SC	Securities Commission
SEA	Securities and Exchange Act
SEC	Securities and Exchange Commission
SEHK	Stock Exchange of Hong Kong Limited
SFA	Securities and Futures Act
SGX	Singapore Stock Exchange
SFC	Securities and Futures Commission
SICAFI	Société d'investissement à Capital Fixe Immobilière
SIF	Special Investment Fund
SIIC	Société d'Investissement Immobilier Cotée
SIINQ	Società di Investimento Immobiliare Non Quotata
SIIQ	Società di Investimento Immobiliare Quotata
SPV	Special Purpose Vehicle
SSD	Special Stamp Duty
TAP	Taxable Australian Property
TBA	Trust Business Act
TRS	Taxable REIT Subsidiary
TSE	Tokyo Stock Exchange
TSX	Toronto Stock Exchange
TFEU	Treaty on the Functioning of the European Union
UCITS	Undertakings for Collective Investments in Transferable Securities
UPREIT	Umbrella Partnership REIT
VAT	Value Added Tax
WHT	Withholding Tax
YA	Year of Assessment

Preface

Following the US example, many countries have introduced a special set of rules and regulations that apply to vehicles aimed to invest in immovable property (so-called Real Estate Investment Trusts (REIT) regimes). Presently, there are more than thirty REIT regimes globally, the majority of which were enacted over the last fifteen years.

What has made the REIT idea become such a globally accepted concept without any global institution having instructed countries to do so?

The compelling idea always was to make attractive investments in different professionally managed real estate asset types accessible to both institutional and private investors with lower amounts available to invest. At the same time, liquidity through stock markets, transparency and governance to the highest standard is gained. All funds are available for real estate investments with no additional liquidity requirements. The investor achieves pure real estate exposure. REITs are all about the quality of management and real estate cash flows converted into regular dividends. In addition, today's highly specialized analysts provide high-end international market transparency through key performance indicators designed for REITs accompanied by indices all over the globe for this sector, thereby making it a unique product.

REITs have started to invest internationally, and REITs shares are being marketed globally directly or through REITs funds or other products. Investors want to diversify their real estate portfolio in the global real estate markets. Cross-border M&A activity has emerged.

As a result, increasing globalization and the related cross-border legislation and providing a deep analysis of the regulatory and tax laws for the REITs, investors, lawmakers and flows of capital resources make it likely that more and more cross-border investments will be made both in and by foreign REITs. Thus, in time, the role played by REITs will continue to grow in importance and will become even more important in the future. However, REITs are not excluded from tax evasion and harmonization initiatives like from the Organisation for Economic Co-operation and Development (OECD) and within the European Union and thus have to adapt to changes.

Yet, despite all these developments, very little attention has been devoted in the international literature to this topic and, in particular, to the tax profiles arising from: (i) cross-border investments made by REITs, and (ii) cross-border investments in REITs. This is most likely due to the diversity of the regimes and the extreme complexity of the subject matter.

In light of the increasing importance given to the subject, this manuscript aims at contributing to a comprehensive analysis of the existing REIT regimes. The primary focus has been to build a fundamental knowledge of the most important available REIT legislation and provide a deep analysis of the regulatory and tax laws for the REITs, investors, lawmakers and finance authorities.

This book is divided into two main parts. The first part is a general report providing: (i) a summary of the twenty-five selected REIT regimes with a critical outline of the main differences among them, and (ii) a critical and in-depth analysis of the tax treaties' aspects of REITs, including OECD recommendations. The second part comprises country chapters providing a comprehensive analysis of the selected REIT regimes by focusing on regulatory law and tax law.

The idea that inspired the manuscript was to provide a guide that is comprehensible and accessible to the business community, yet at the same time comes complete with an adequate level of critical analysis.

The real challenge in the future for the authors is to continuously monitor the evolution of the market and regulatory framework in order to constantly update and expand the scope of the book, which – as intended by the publisher and authors – should become one of the main sources of information for the market.

The manuscript was completed in May 2022. We would very much welcome any feedback, comments or criticism.

The authors wish to express their gratitude to Ilona McElroy and Rosaleen Carey, PwC Ireland, for coordinating and reviewing this edition of the Guide to Global Real Estate Investment Trusts and Federico Aquilanti, Bernardo Leoni, Caterina Marchello and Michela Rubbi BonelliErede, for their valuable remarks on the general report.

General Reports

STEFANO SIMONTACCHI

Stefano Simontacchi is the President of BonelliErede, where he gained vast experience in both domestic and international real estate transactions and in structuring real estate collective investment vehicles.

He obtained his PhD at the Faculty of Law of Leiden University, the Netherlands, where, since 2000, he has been lecturing in international taxation for the Adv. LLM organized by the International Tax Center Leiden. In addition, he has lectured in taxation and international taxation for many years at several other universities and Master's programmes. In 2015, Stefano became an independent member, as representative of the International Tax Center Leiden, of the EU Joint Transfer Pricing Forum. Stefano Simontacchi is also the author of several publications and articles. His book *Taxation of Capital Gains under the OECD Model Convention: With Special Regard to Immovable Property* was published in 2007 by Kluwer Law International.
E-mail: stefano.simontacchi@belex.com

General Reports

Stefano Simontacchi

§1.01 BACKGROUND AND CONTEXT

[A] Introduction

[1] *Scope of the General Report*

Real Estate Investment Trusts (REITs) have become increasingly popular as investment **1**
vehicles. Furthermore, increasing globalization and the related cross-border flow of
capital resources make it likely that more and more cross-border investments will be
made both in and by foreign REITs. Despite this, very little attention has been devoted
in the international tax literature to the systematic analysis of: (i) investments in REITs,
and (ii) investments made by REITs in relation to tax treaties. This is in all likelihood
due to the extreme complexity of the subject matter. This is all the more true if one
considers that different legal forms may fall under the label of REIT and that the
application of tax treaties to some of these legal forms (i.e., partnerships, trusts and
mutual funds) is a matter of controversy.

In 2007, the Organisation for Economic Co-operation and Development (OECD) issued **2**
a discussion draft on the tax treaty issues related to REITs ('OECD Report'),[1] on the
basis of which changes have been made in the 2008 OECD Commentary.[2] This
confirms the great interest in the issue being examined here.

The purpose of this General Report is to provide a comprehensive analysis of **3**
International REIT regimes, with particular attention to the implications for tax treaty
application. This general report is divided into two main parts. Sections §1.01 through

---

1. See OECD, *Tax Treaty Issues Related to REITs – Public Discussion Draft*, Paris, 30 Oct. 2007.
2. For the modifications introduced in 2008, *see also*, OECD, *The 2008 Update to the OECD Model Tax Convention*, Paris, 18 Jul. 2008 and OECD, *Draft Contents of the 2008 Update to the Model Tax Convention*, Paris, 21 Apr. to 31 May 2008. In the absence of any indication of the year of publication, reference is made to the 2014 OECD Model Tax Convention and to the 2014 OECD Commentary. Where treaty articles are mentioned, reference is made to the 2014 OECD Model Tax Convention (unless a different specific reference is added).

§1.03 contain a comparative survey of the various REIT regimes covered by the national reports.[3] Despite the differences in the solutions endorsed in the various countries, an effort is made to discern – with no pretence of being exhaustive – some common patterns. This analysis covers both: (i) the regulatory framework and (ii) the tax regime.

4   Section §1.04 analyses in detail the treaty regime applicable to: (i) cross-border investments made by REITs, and (ii) cross-border investments in REITs (addressing the tax regime applicable to both REIT distributions and gains derived from the alienation of interests in REITs).

5   For the purposes of this general report, the term 'REIT regimes' refers to the countries covered by the national reports.

[2]   REIT Definition

6   Following the United States (US) experience, many countries introduced special tax regimes generally providing for taxation at the investor's level only; that is, taxation of immovable property vehicles is generally excluded. The investment may be held in different legal forms, such as a corporation, partnership, trust or contractual or fiduciary arrangement. Irrespective of the specific legal form, these investment vehicles are referred to as 'REITs'.

7   The term 'REIT regime' is used to refer to the entire set of rules and regulations that apply to REITs. In this respect, REIT regimes are usually considered to be tax regimes. However, these are also characterized by regulatory requirements and restrictions governed by company law. There are countries where the emphasis is more on tax law (e.g., Italy, the United Kingdom (UK) and the US), countries where the emphasis is more on company law (e.g., Hong Kong and Malaysia) and countries where a specific REIT regime is not even codified (Australia and the Netherlands). Irrespective of these different legislative solutions, the term 'REIT regime' is used to make reference to the entire set of rules and regulations characterizing a certain regime.

[3]   History

8   Presently, there are more than thirty REIT legislations in the world, the majority of which were enacted over the last decade. The oldest REIT regimes in each geographical area are:

---

3. The national reports cover the following countries: Australia, Belgium, Brazil, Bulgaria, Canada, Finland, France, Germany, Greece, Hong Kong, Hungary, India, Ireland, Italy, Japan, Malaysia, Mexico, the Netherlands, Singapore, South Africa, South Korea, Spain, Turkey, the United Kingdom and the United States.

(a) America: US (1960).
(b) Europe: the Netherlands[4] (1969).
(c) Oceania: Australia (1971).
(d) Asia: Singapore (1999).
(e) Africa: South Africa[5] (2002).

The origin of REITs can be traced back to the 1880s[6] when US investment trusts were   **9**
used not only to invest in immovable property but also to invest in movable property.
In the 1935 *Morrissey v. Commissioner*[7] decision, US Supreme Court ruled that
investment trusts were taxable as corporations, that is at the level of the investment
vehicle. One year after this landmark case, a specific provision was inserted in the
Internal Revenue Code[8] to provide for an exemption at the vehicle level (i.e., taxation
at the investor level) for stock and bond investment funds. No rule was enacted to deal
with immovable property investment trusts. Only in 1960, due to the increase in
demand for immovable property investment funds, President Eisenhower signed REIT
Act,[9] providing for a preferential tax regime that applied only to trusts.[10] This can be
considered the first modern REIT regime. The purpose of the act was: (i) to grant REIT
investors the same tax treatment to which they would be subject if they had invested
directly in immovable property, and (ii) to finance immovable property development.
This regime was confined to passive investments in immovable property and, thus,
REITs were not allowed to directly manage or operate their own assets.

[B]   REIT Market

REIT global market had its peak in 2007; indeed, between January 2002 and June 2007,   **10**
REIT global market capitalization grew to USD 829 billion. In 2008, REIT industry faced
the impact of the recent economic downturn, in particular suffering from the global
credit freeze and the subprime mortgage crisis. The total global market capitalization
of listed REITs decreased from USD 829 billion (June 2007) to USD 430 billion (June
2009). Since the first months of 2009, the global REIT market has seemed to be
recovering. In particular, the total market capitalization of listed REITs reached USD

---

4. The Fiscal Investment Institution regime (*Fiscale Belegg?nginstelling*) introduced in 1969 is
   applicable also to passive portfolio investment other than real estate investments.
5. In 2002, collective investment schemes regimes, applicable also to REIT, have been introduced.
   With effect from 1 May 2013, a formalized REIT Regime commenced in South Africa.
6. William A. Kelley Jr, *Real Estate Investment Trust Handbook*, 2nd edn (1990), at 2.
7. 294 U.S. 344 (1935).
8. Revenue Act 1936, Pub. L. No. 740, ss 48 and 49 Stat. 1648. These provisions as amended are
   codified in I.R.C. ss 851–855.
9. Pub. L. No. 86-779, s. 10(a), 74 Stat. 998.1004.
10. In 1956 President Eisenhower voted favourable legislation approved by the Congress for the
    following reasons: (i) the analogy between REITs and regulated investment companies is
    inappropriate since the latter, unlike REITs, receive previously taxed income; and (ii) the
    Treasury would be deprived of substantial revenues.

600 billion (June 2010) and US FTSE NAREIT[11] Equity REIT Index climbed (from March 2009 to June 2010) by 133.84%. This trend was confirmed by the situation up to July 2011, when the total market capitalization of listed REITs reached USD 815 billion. In 2012, the market increased up to USD 942 billion, with a significant increase in the market capitalization of US REITs (+45%).

11   US is the biggest REIT market, considering both the number of REITs (200) and their market capitalization (EUR 939). US-listed REITs represent 64.84% of the global REIT market capitalization. Other large REIT markets are Australia, Canada, France, Japan, Singapore and UK[12] (*see* Table 1).

Table 1   REIT Markets in September 2021

REIT Regime	Year Enacted	Number of REITs[13]
Australia	1985	43
Belgium	1995	17
Brazil	1993	120
Bulgaria	2004	39
Canada	1994	44
Finland	2010	–
France	2003	27
Germany	2007	7
Greece	1999	4
Hong Kong	2003	10
Hungary	2011	2
India	2014	3
Ireland	2013	3
Italy	2007	3
Japan	2000	64
Malaysia	2002	17
Mexico	2004	15
The Netherlands	1969	5
Singapore	1999	33
South Africa	2013	30
South Korea	2001	15
Spain	2009	75

---

11. National Association of Real Estate Investment Trusts.
12. In Finance Act 2013 and 2014, the Government has introduced further amendments in relation to UK REITs investing in other UK REITs. The measure allows the income from UK REITs investing in other UK REITs to be treated as income of the investing REIT's tax-exempt property rental business, and REITs shareholders to be ignored when considering 'close' status. Please refer to s. §1.01[C] of the United Kingdom chapter.
13. *See* EPRA Global REIT Survey, 2021.

REIT Regime	Year Enacted	Number of REITs[13]
Turkey	1995	33
UK	2007	54
US	1960	198

§1.02   REGULATORY FRAMEWORK

[A]   Introduction

To qualify for the favourable REIT regime, investment vehicles must satisfy a number   **12**
of requirements. These are generally contained in the following sources:

(a) REIT law (which may be found in both tax law and company law);
(b) company,[14] trust or other law applicable to the legal form under which REIT
    is organized;
(c) stock exchange regulations (for listed REITs); and
(d) banking and financial investment rules.

In this respect, the application of REIT regimes is usually subject to authorization (or   **13**
at least to a regulated election procedure) and the investment vehicle is typically
supervised by competent financial authorities, acting in the interest of the investors
(this also implies specific reporting and accounting requirements).

The following sections analyse the main specific requirements/restrictions provided   **14**
for REIT regimes:

(a) entity form requirements;
(b) capital requirements;
(c) investor requirements;
(d) investment restrictions;
(e) listing requirements;
(f) distribution requirements; and
(g) other requirements.

Failure to meet the above-mentioned requirements could lead to: (i) financial penalties,   **15**
and/or (ii) loss of REIT status.

---

14. The term 'company law' is used for the field of law concerning companies and other business
    organizations.

[B]   Entity Form Requirements

16   To be eligible for REIT regime, the investment vehicle usually has to be organized under prescribed legal forms. The following legal forms are typically required:

(a) unit trusts (e.g., Australia, Canada, Greece, Hong Kong, India, Japan, Malaysia, Mexico, Singapore and the US);

(b) corporations (e.g., Belgium, Bulgaria, Finland, France, Germany, Greece, Hungary, Ireland, Italy, Japan, the Netherlands, South Korea, Spain, Turkey, the UK and the US);

(c) partnerships (e.g., France and the US); and

(d) funds (e.g., Brazil and the Netherlands).

17   The majority of REIT regimes allow one single legal form (e.g., Australia, Belgium,[15] Brazil, Bulgaria, Canada, Finland, France, Germany, Hong Kong, Hungary, India, Italy, Malaysia, Singapore, South Africa, South Korea, Spain, Turkey and the UK). There are, however, a number of REIT regimes (e.g., Greece, Japan, the Netherlands and the US) where more than one legal form is permitted. For example, Greece, Japan, South Africa and the Netherlands accept two different legal forms, while in the US[16] any legal entity taxable as a domestic corporation[17] (e.g., corporation, limited partnership, limited liability company and trust) is eligible for REIT regime.

18   It is important to underline that in all cases, the legal form chosen is characterized by limited liability. This is consistent with the nature of REITs as widely held investment vehicles; that is, the unlimited liability of investors would be inconsistent with their status (of persons not actively involved in the assets' management) and would jeopardize the attractiveness of the investment.

19   Most REIT regimes are usually available to vehicles organized under domestic law exclusively. Only four countries (France, Italy, the Netherlands and Singapore) allow – if certain conditions are met – vehicles organized under foreign law to opt for the domestic REIT regime. In particular, the Netherlands regime applies to foreign vehicles organized under legal forms that are comparable with domestic legal forms eligible for the Netherlands REIT regime. Under the Singaporean REIT regime, foreign vehicles are eligible where: (i) the domestic law under which the foreign vehicle is organized grants investors the same level of protection granted by Singaporean law; (ii) REIT has

---

15. Even though Belgian REITs can only be incorporated as public limited liability companies, the Belgian Companies and Associations Code allow to incorporate public limited liability companies with the specific features of a partnership limited by shares. Moreover, Art. 14(2) of RREC Law (law of 12 May 2014 on RREC) has recently been amended by the Law of 28 Apr. 2020, in order to clarify that RRECs may also be set up under the form of a public limited liability company with a sole director.

16. The vast majority of REITs are organized as trusts or corporations.

17. Taxation as a domestic corporation is available under the so-called check the box option.

appointed a Singaporean representative; (iii) REIT manager meets specific requirements; and (iv) REIT and its manager comply with Singaporean rules. In order to be eligible for the French REIT regime, foreign vehicles must be listed on a regulated market pursuant to European regulations.[18] In Italy, REIT regime is also extended to permanent establishments of companies resident in the European Union (EU) or in European Economic Area (EEA) states included under the Italian 'white list', to the extent the permanent establishment carries on eligible business.

The legal form under which REITs are organized has an impact, among other things, on the following key issues: **20**

    (a) REIT legal personality;
    (b) legal ownership of the assets;
    (c) character of the distributed income;[19] and
    (d) REIT treaty entitlement (in conjunction with the applicable tax regime).[20]

For example, REITs organized as corporations are, by definition, legal owners of the relevant assets, while in the case of trusts or mutual funds (which do not have legal personality), the relevant assets are held by the investment vehicle but are legally owned by the trustee (or by the custodian) for the benefit of the investors, or even deemed to be co-owned by REIT investors (e.g., Greece). **21**

[C] Capital Requirements

[1] Introduction

REIT regimes may require the fulfilment of minimum capital obligations in order to ensure a sufficient level of investor protection. These requirements consist of either a minimum level of capital or a maximum level of leverage. **22**

[2] Minimum Level of Capital

The minimum capital requirement generally depends upon REIT's legal form (the requirement provided for by company law) or upon the status of the listed entity (the requirement provided for by stock exchange regulations). **23**

In the case of REITs organized as corporations, most of the company laws provide for minimum capital requirements. The case is different where REITs take the form of a **24**

---

18. BOI-IS-CHAMP-30-20-10-20200701 n° 10.
19. *See* s. §1.03[B][2][a].
20. *See* s. §1.04[C][3].

trust (e.g., Australia, Hong Kong, Mexico, Singapore and the US) or a mutual fund (the Netherlands) where no minimum capital is generally required.[21]

25   In addition, stock exchange regulations usually set specific capital requirements for listed investment vehicles that depart (being generally higher) from the ones set by the relevant company law. For example, in Italy despite the minimum capital set by company law for a joint-stock corporation amounting to EUR 50,000, a REIT must have a minimum capital equal to EUR 40,000,000 in accordance with the stock exchange regulations. Furthermore, Australian REITs are not subject to any capital requirements according to domestic trust law; however, in the case of listing on the stock exchange REITs are subject to minimum capital requirements.

[3]   Maximum Level of Leverage

26   A number of REIT regimes (e.g., Belgium, Bulgaria, Finland, Germany, Hong Kong, Hungary, Ireland, Malaysia, South Africa, the Netherlands and Singapore) provide maximum leverage thresholds to safeguard investors from excessive debt financing. Generally, such requirements are constructed in such a way that the total indebtedness may not exceed a portion of REIT assets (either total assets or immovable assets). To distinguish the level of leverage in relation to different assets (usually much higher for immovable property), certain countries (e.g., the Netherlands) apply the test to immovable assets and a second test to other assets. Some countries (e.g., Belgium) also supplement the asset test with an income test providing that the interest on debts may not exceed a certain percentage of operational and financial income. Finally, there are some regimes providing an income test. In this respect, under the UK REIT regime an interest cover ratio is provided (i.e., income cannot be less than 1.25 times the interest cost).

[D]   Investor Requirements

27   REITs are intended to be collective investment vehicles: hence, most REIT legislation includes provisions requiring a widely held status, that is, of investor requirements. Under some legislation (e.g., France), exceptions are provided for in the case of investors qualifying as collective investment vehicles; that is, the widely held status is considered to be satisfied at the second tier of ownership (typical is the case of a REIT investing in another REIT). Few regimes (such as Australia, Brazil, Greece, Hong Kong, Malaysia[22] and South Africa) do not have investor requirements.

---

21. Malaysian REIT regime and Indian REIT are an exceptions: for the former even though REIT takes the form of a unit trust, a minimum initial capital of MYR 500 million (approximately USD 119.63 million) is required; for the latter, a minimum initial capital of INR 5,000 million (approximately USD 66.83 million) is required.
22. In Malaysia, certain limitations on acquisitions by foreign interests apply. Please refer to s. §1.02[A][2] of the Malaysian chapter.

Investor requirements can be grouped into the following main categories: **28**

(a) minimum number of investors (e.g., Canada, Japan, India, Ireland, Singapore, Spain and the US);
(b) minimum interest owned by institutional investors;
(c) maximum interest owned by a single investor or by investors acting in concert (e.g., Finland, France, Germany, Hungary, India,[23] Ireland, Italy, Japan, the Netherlands, South Korea and the UK);
(d) maximum interest owned by a limited number of investors (e.g., the US);
(e) minimum interest owned by investors not individually exceeding a maximum interest threshold (e.g., France, Germany, Italy and Singapore); and
(f) minimum interest held by founders (e.g., Turkey).

A number of REIT regimes apply a combination of different investor requirements. For   **29**
example, under the Italian legislation, the conditions under (d) and under (f) must both be met. Table 2 summarizes the restrictions of each country.

Table 2   Investor Requirements

REIT Regime	Investor Requirements
Australia	No requirement
Belgium	At least 30% of the interest must be 'publicly held'
Brazil	Specific requirements for funds applying for tax exemption[24]
Bulgaria	– No more than 50 founders
Canada	Minimum of 150 investors each of whom holds not less than one 'block of units' that has an aggregate fair market value of not less than CAD 500
Finland	A single investor must own less than 10% of REIT's share capital
France	– A single investor may not hold more than 60% of capital and voting rights – At the time of election, 15% of the capital and voting rights must be held by investors, who individually own less than 2%
Germany	– 15% of the interest must be widely held (25% at the time of IPO) – A single investor may not own 10% or more of the interest or the voting rights
Greece	No requirements
Hong Kong	No requirements

---

23. Except from sponsors or unless an approval from 75% of the unitholders by value is obtained.
24. Please refer to s. §1.02[A][2] of the Brazilian chapter.

REIT Regime	Investor Requirements
Hungary	– At least 25% of the interest must be 'publicly held' – The holders of the public shares may not own more than 5% of the total share – Credit and Insurance investors may not hold more than 10% of the voting rights
India	– Depending on the amount of post-issue capital, different percentages must be 'publicly held'[25] – Minimum number of subscribers to the initial public offer should be 200 at the time of public offer (other than sponsors, its related parties and associates of REIT) – Maximum subscription from any investor other than sponsors, its related parties and its associates shall not be more than 25% of the total unit capital or unless an approval from 75% of the unitholders by value is obtained
Ireland	– Minimum of 6 investors – A single corporate shareholder may not own 10% or more of the shares/voting rights
Italy	– At least 25% of the interest must be 'widely held' – A single investor may not own more than 60% of the voting rights and profit participation rights
Japan	No requirements[26]
Malaysia	No requirements[27]
Mexico	No requirements
The Netherlands	(a) Public REIT: – Taxable corporate entities may not hold more than 45% of the interest – Individuals may not hold more than 25% of the interest (b) Private REIT: – Individuals/non-taxable corporate entities/listed REITs must hold at least 75% of the interest – Single individuals may not own more than 5% of the interest
Singapore	At least 25% of the interests have to be held by at least 500 public investors for listing
South Africa	No requirements
South Korea	An investor may not own more than 50% of the interest

25. That is: (i) if < INR 16,000 million, 25% or INR 2,500 million should be publicly held; (ii) if INR 16,000 million < INR 40,000 million, INR 4,000 million should be publicly held; (iii) if > INR 40,000 million, at least 10% should be publicly held.
26. There are no restrictions applying to investors in a J-REIT under the ITL. However, the tax law provides conditions regarding the unitholders in a J-REIT that need to be satisfied in order for the J-REIT to qualify for dividend deductibility (please refer to s. §1.02[A][2] of the Japanese chapter). Moreover, conditions are foreseen to be listed on Japanese stock exchanges.
27. Limitations for foreign interest apply. Please refer to s. §1.02[A][2] of the Malaysian chapter.

REIT Regime	Investor Requirements
Spain	– At least 25% of its voting share capital duly allocated to public
Turkey	– Founders owning more than 10% of the interests must meet some requirements (e.g., sufficient financial capacity)
UK	A single corporate investor may not own more than 10% of the interest and at least 35% must be owned by members of the public
US[28]	– At least 100 investors – Five or fewer individuals[29] may not hold more than 50% of the interest

[E]   Investment Restrictions

REIT regimes were developed to promote investments in immovable property (or **30** immovable property rights) and are mainly aimed at deriving rental income. Accordingly, all countries provide restrictions on REIT activity and REIT investments.

[1]   REIT Activity

Some countries restrict the scope of REIT activities by excluding or limiting not only **31** activities unrelated to immovable property but also certain immovable property activities such as: (i) trading activity (e.g., Australia, Germany and the Netherlands) and/or (ii) land development activity (e.g., Belgium,[30] Bulgaria, the Netherlands, Singapore and South Korea). In some countries, REITs may, however, indirectly carry on the prohibited activities through subsidiaries (e.g., the Netherlands) or by setting up stapled arrangements (e.g., Australia and Singapore).

Other countries allow REITs to undertake certain activities not consisting of immovable **32** property investments, but only if auxiliary to the core business activity. Two alternative tests are used to assess the auxiliary nature of these activities:

(a) *income test* (e.g., Canada, Finland, Germany, India, Ireland,[31] Italy, Spain, the UK and the US). The test requires that a REIT derives most of its total annual proceeds from its core activity (generally rental income from immovable

---

28. Beginning with a REIT's second taxable year.
29. A limited group of tax-exempt entities, e.g., private foundations, are treated as individuals for this purpose.
30. Belgium is mentioned as a country where REITs cannot construct buildings itself or have them constructed in view of selling them prior, after or within a period of five years after construction; for more information please refer to s. §1.02[F][5] of the Belgium chapter.
31. At least 75% of the income and 75% of the market value of the assets of REIT must relate to assets of property rental business of REIT.

property).[32] To avoid burdensome and complex determinations, the application of this type of test is generally based on proceeds; that is, those derived from the core activity should represent at least a certain percentage (usually more than 75%) of the annual proceeds. Some REIT regimes may list as eligible proceeds other types of proceeds, such as:

    (i) dividends from qualified immovable property companies (e.g., Italy and Spain);

    (ii) gains from disposal of immovable property (e.g., Canada); and

    (iii) mortgage interest (e.g., Canada).

(b) *asset test* (e.g., Brazil, Canada, Finland, France, Germany, Hong Kong, Hungary, India,[33] Ireland, Italy, Malaysia, Mexico, Singapore, South Korea, Spain, UK and US[34]). The asset test requires that REITs invest the majority of their funds in eligible investments, mainly immovable property. Some countries confine the definition of eligible investments to domestic immovable property (e.g., India) or to immovable property used for deriving rental income (e.g., France, Italy, Hong Kong and the UK). Other countries define eligible investments more broadly to include:

    (i) government bonds (e.g., Canada, Mexico[35] and the US);

    (ii) mortgage loans (e.g., the US);

    (iii) cash (e.g., Canada, South Korea and the US);

    (iv) interests in qualified immovable property companies (e.g., Brazil, Canada, Hungary, India, Italy, South Korea, Spain and in the case of other REITs US).

33 Frequently, in the case of entities controlled by REITs, for the purposes of the asset tests, the immovable property of the entities being participated in is consolidated at REIT level (e.g., Germany).

[2]   REIT Investments

34 Some countries also provide restrictions on the type of immovable property investments. The main restrictions of this kind are the following:

---

32. The United States also treats mortgage interest income and gains on real property and mortgages as qualifying income.
33. At least 80% of the value of a REIT to be in completed and rent-generating real estate, with a lock-in period of three years from the purchase date. For more information please refer to s. §1.02[4] of the Indian chapter.
34. At least 75% of the value of a REIT's total assets must be represented by real estate assets including mortgage loans and interests in mortgages secured by real property, shares in US REITs, debt instruments of publicly offered REITs, personal property (where the fair market value of the personal property under the lease is less than 15% of the total fair market value under the lease) stock or debt attributable to the investment of certain new capital for the one-year period after REIT received new capital, cash and cash items, and US Government securities.
35. The Mexican REIT regime requires the non-eligible assets to be limited to government bonds or debt instruments issued by Mutual Funds.

(a) *minimum level of diversification* (e.g., Belgium, Greece, Hungary, India, Spain and the UK). This requirement is aimed at diversifying REIT investments in order to minimize the overall risk. Such restrictions may require that:

    (i) a single investment in an immovable property may not exceed a predetermined percentage (between 20% and 40%) of total investments; or

    (ii) REIT is obliged to invest in a minimum number of immovable properties.

(b) *limitation on investment in foreign immovable property* (e.g., Bulgaria, Germany, Greece and Turkey). Investment in foreign immovable property may alternatively be:

    (i) forbidden (e.g., India);

    (ii) limited to a maximum amount (e.g., Greece and Turkey). For example, Greek REITs may invest in foreign immovable property situated outside EEA, if the value of the property does not exceed 20%[36] of their total investments; Turkish REITs may invest in foreign immovable property up to 49% of their portfolio value;

    (iii) allowed under other conditions (e.g., Bulgaria,[37] Germany). For example, German REITs may invest in foreign immovable property only if under the law of the situs state, a REIT (or vehicle comparable to a REIT) that is resident therein would be allowed to invest in such property.

(c) *limitation on investments in certain types of immovable property* (e.g., Germany,[38] India, Malaysia[39]). Some countries do not allow REITs to invest in certain kinds of immovable property. For example, in Germany REITs may not invest in residential immovable property; and

(d) *limitation on investments in subsidiaries* (e.g., Australia, Belgium, Bulgaria, Germany, Mexico and the US). REITs are generally allowed to own subsidiaries, except in Mexico. Australian REIT subsidiaries are subject to the same investment restrictions as their REIT parent; in Belgium, REITs have to hold, directly or indirectly, at least 25% of the shares in their real estate companies;[40] in Bulgaria, REITs may not invest more than 10% of their registered capital in service companies; in Germany, immovable property owned by REIT subsidiaries characterized as real estate corporations must be situated abroad; and in the US, not more than 25% of a REIT's assets may be securities in taxable REIT.

---

36. Twenty per cent for Real Estate Investment Companies (REIC), 10% for Real Estate Mutual Funds (REMF). For more information, please refer to s. §1.02[F][5] of the Greek chapter.
37. Bulgarian REITs may invest in immovable property located in other EU member state only if such possibility is explicitly reflected in the REIT's Article of Association and its prospectus.
38. This restriction applies only to residential properties constructed before 1 Jan. 2007.
39. Among the others, the restriction applies to the acquisition of vacant land and property development. For more information please refer to s. §1.02[F] of the Malaysian chapter.
40. For more information please refer to s. §1.02[F][5] of the Belgian chapter.

[F]   Listing Requirements

35   Listing on a stock exchange facilitates REITs in raising funds from investors and also grants investors higher transparency and protection due to several reporting requirements generally provided for by stock exchange regulations and to the supervisory activity performed by the competent authorities.

36   In several countries listing is a mandatory requirement for REIT status election (e.g., Belgium – unless for REIT subsidiaries/institutional REIT – Bulgaria, Finland, France, Germany, Greece,[41] Hong Kong, Hungary, India, Ireland, Italy,[42] Singapore,[43] South Africa, Spain, Turkey and UK). Other countries do not condition the election for REIT regime upon the listing of the vehicle (e.g., Australia, Japan, Malaysia, Mexico, the Netherlands and the US).

37   Except for Hong Kong – the countries that do not require listing are the ones where REITs are organized in the form of trusts or funds. This may depend on the need for maintaining the flexibility that characterizes such investment vehicles and that may be jeopardized by the additional regulatory requirements provided for in the case of listing. Countries where REITs may be organized only in the form of corporations always require listing on the stock exchange.

38   Under some REIT regimes where listing is mandatory (e.g., Finland, Germany, Hungary, Italy, Spain and UK), listing on a foreign stock exchange is also possible. Where REIT regime is also available to vehicles organized under foreign law (e.g., Singapore), the requirement of listing on the domestic stock exchange is imposed on REITs (both domestic and foreign).

39   The listing process takes, on average, at least four months, and requires authorization from the relevant stock exchange authorities. In addition, listed REITs are subject to: (i) supervision of the competent authorities and (ii) the reporting requirements provided by the stock exchange regulations.[44] Table 3 summarizes the listing requirements applicable to the various REIT regimes.

---

41. The mandatory listing is provided only for Greek REITs structured as corporations. Greek REITs must file an application for its listing on the Athens Stock Exchange within two years of its incorporation. The Capital Market Commission may decide to extend the annual deadline for listing in the stock market for up to a total of thirty-six months subject to an application for extension being filed by REIT and demonstration that a force majeure or unfavourable market conditions prevented listing. If a REIT is not accepted to the Athens Stock Exchange, then the Capital Market Commission will revoke its operation licence.
42. As a temporary tax benefit, Italian small-medium companies (i.e., up to 50 million turnover and 250 employees) which start the listing process and are admitted to listing in regulated exchanges from 1 Jan. 2018 to 31 Dec. 2020 are granted of a tax credit, up to EUR 500,000, equal to 50% of the advisory costs suffered, in the same period, for the listing (e.g., legal and tax advice, due diligences analyses, etc.). This tax benefit has been extended to year 2021 and, finally, to 31 Dec. 2022. However, for year 2022 the tax credit is capped to EUR 200,000.
43. Mandatory in order to benefit from the preferential tax regime.
44. *See* s. §1.02[H].

Table 3   Listing Requirements[45]

REITs Regime	Listing Requirement	Average Duration for Listing Process
Australia	No	At least six months
Belgium	Yes	Approximately six months
Brazil	No	Not available
Bulgaria	Yes	Not available
Canada	Yes	Not available
Finland	Yes	Not available
France	Yes	At least six months
Germany	Yes	From four to six months
Greece	Yes	Not available
Hong Kong	Yes	At least two months
Hungary	Yes	From six to nine months
India	Yes	Not available
Ireland	Yes	From two to six months
Italy	Yes	From five to nine months
Japan	No	One year
Malaysia	No	At least six months
Mexico	No	At least six months
The Netherlands	No	At least four months
Singapore	Yes	At least three weeks
South Africa	Yes	From nine to thirteen weeks
South Korea	Yes	At least four months
Spain	Yes	From six to nine months
Turkey	Yes	Not available
UK	Yes[46]	At least six months[47]
US	No	At least six months

[G]   Distribution Requirements

The majority of REIT regimes impose a yearly obligation to distribute a significant **40** portion of REIT profits to investors. This type of requirement is clearly related to the single layer of the tax regime that characterizes such investment vehicles; that is, only

---

45. Canada does not require a REIT to be listed, but SIFT rules generally only apply to listed entities.
46. There is however a proposed relaxation of the listing requirement, due to take effect for accounting periods beginning on or after 1 Apr. 2022, where at least 70% of the REITs ordinary shares are directly or indirectly owned by one or more of certain institutional investors. Please refer to s. §1.02[A] of the United Kingdom chapter.
47. It takes generally around six months to obtain a listing on the Main Market of the LSE. In respect of REITs listed on exchanges other than the LSE, this may vary. In addition, following changes due to take effect from April 2022, not all REITs will need to be listed.

the investors are subject to tax and thus an obligation to distribute profits aims at securing income taxation on an accrual basis (avoiding/limiting any deferral effect). Surprisingly, even countries where the income is taxed at REIT level (e.g., Belgium, Hong Kong and Spain) provide mandatory distribution requirements. This is an indication that the distribution requirement is also driven by financial/regulatory purposes in that it is aimed at ensuring investors a regular flow of income.

41 The mandatory distribution generally varies from 70% to 90% of the income that is eligible for exemption at REIT level. Thus, where the exemption applies only to a certain type of income, the distribution requirement only refers to such income, and does not apply to other types of income ordinarily taxable in the hands of REITs (e.g., France, Italy). For example, where capital gains derived from the alienation of immovable property are subject to ordinary taxation at REIT level, distribution requirements do not apply to the gains (e.g., Italy). Tracing rules become relevant where losses from the non-eligible activity partially offset profits derived from the eligible activity, thus diminishing the distributable profit. In some countries such as Italy, the distribution obligation is rolled over to the following year.

42 In countries where a dividend deduction effectively exempts distributed income from taxation at REIT level, the mandatory distribution is determined either as a percentage of taxable income (e.g., US) or as a percentage of distributable profits (e.g., Japan and South Korea).

43 In the case of REITs controlling subsidiaries owning immovable property, the distribution requirement at the top-tier REIT level may be determined on a consolidated basis (e.g., UK) (*see* Table 4).

Table 4   Distribution Requirements

REIT Regime	Distribution Requirements	Timing
Australia	No mandated distribution requirement but distribution required to avoid income being taxed at REIT level	Annually
Belgium	80% corrected net result[48]	Annually
Brazil	95% of the realized cash profits	Each semester
Bulgaria	90% net profits	Until the end of the following business year[49]
Canada	No mandated distribution requirement – in order to avoid taxation of undistributed income, income is distributed each year	Annually

48. It is the net profit realized during the accounting year excluding non-cash results and capital gains realized on real properties under certain conditions and reduced by the amounts corresponding to the net decrease of their debts during the financial year.
49. When certain additional requirements are met, REITs may distribute semi-annual dividends.

REIT Regime	Distribution Requirements	Timing
Finland	90% net profits	Annually
France	95% eligible income	Annually
Germany	90% net profits	Until the end of the following business year
Greece	50% net profits	Annually
Hong Kong	90% net profits	Annually
Hungary	The expected dividends[50]	Annually
India	90% net distributable cash flow	Every six months
Ireland	85% of property income	Annually
Italy	70% eligible income	Annually
Japan	90% net profits	Annually
Malaysia	90% taxable income	Annually
Mexico	95% taxable income	Annually
The Netherlands	100% taxable income	Within eight months after the end of the fiscal year
Singapore	90% eligible income	Annually or semi-annually or quarterly
South Africa	75% taxable income	Annually
South Korea	90% net profits	Depends on the Articles of Association
Spain	80% of profits derived from rental income and ancillary activities, 50% of eligible capital gains, 100% of profits derived from dividends received from other REITs, qualifying subsidiaries and collective investment institutions	Within six months
Turkey	There is no minimum profit distribution requirement	No obligation
UK	90% eligible income	Within twelve months
US	90% ordinary taxable income	Annually, including certain distributions paid in the following year

---

50. Which is 90% of the distributable profit unless the free cash's and cash-equivalents' sum is lower than such amount.

[H]   Accounting and Reporting Requirements

44   REITs may be subject to the following additional regulatory obligations:

(a) *Accounting.*[51] Almost all the countries (e.g., Belgium, Canada, Finland, Germany, Greece, Hong Kong, Hungary, Italy, Mexico, the Netherlands, Singapore, South Africa, Spain, Turkey and the UK) require the use of International Financial Reporting Standards or Generally Accepted Accounting Principles.

(b) *Reporting requirements.* Non-listed REITs have to file annual reports (including the statutory accounts, reports on the activities performed during the financial period and any further information required) with the competent authorities. Listed REITs are subject to stock exchange regulations that require further reporting obligations, some of which are tailored to REITs. The most common reporting requirements for listed REITs are the following:
- quarterly (and/or semi-annual) financial statements;
- annual financial statements;
- periodical information on the investment activity;
- disclosure of daily/periodical net assets value;
- disclosure of investments; and
- disclosure of information related to particular events (e.g., M&A, distributions, business acquisitions and redemption of interests).

[I]   Election/Authorization

45   REIT regimes that have a predominantly tax nature (e.g., Finland, France, Germany,[52] Italy, the Netherlands, Spain, the UK and the US) usually require an election for REIT status. In such countries, the election is mainly exercised through:

(a) written notice to the competent tax authorities (e.g., Finland, France, Germany, Hungary, Ireland,[53] Italy, South Africa, Spain, and the UK); or
(b) making an election on the tax return (e.g., the Netherlands and the US).

46   Besides the tax election, other authorizations may be required by the relevant market/financial authorities. For example, under the Italian regime, where listing is

---

51. The accounting requirements play an important role in those REIT regimes where the mandatory distribution requirement is based on the net profits (Bulgaria, Canada, Germany, Greece and Hong Kong).
52. In Germany, the election is needed for pre-REIT, which is a stock corporation that aims for G-REIT status.
53. No conversion charge will apply for an existing company converting to a REIT. However, a company that converts to a REIT will be deemed for CGT purposes to have sold its assets at market value, on the day of conversion, immediately before becoming a REIT and reacquired them on becoming a REIT thus creating a CGT liability on any gains at that point.

mandatory, a REIT must obtain authorization from the relevant market authorities for listing on the stock exchange. The relevant market authorities grant the authorization after they have verified that all the market regulations and REIT regime requirements have been fulfilled.

Under other REIT regimes, where the emphasis is more on company law, REIT status **47** may be obtained through an authorization from financial authorities (e.g., Belgium, Hong Kong and Malaysia). The authorization depends on filing certain documentation, such as:

(a) Articles of Association;
(b) governance model;
(c) financial plan;
(d) a detailed list of the assets owned by REIT;
(e) appraisals of the real estate; and
(f) financial statements of past years (where available).

Furthermore, REIT regimes where REIT is managed by an asset management company **48** (e.g., Japan) or a trustee (e.g., Australia) may require that the management company or trustee have a specific licence.

Once REIT status has been obtained, REIT (and the asset management **49** company/trustee where existing) is then subject to the supervisory activities of the competent financial/market/tax authorities.

[J] REIT Within the Scope of AIFMD

At the level of the EU, the Parliament recently established the Directive on Alternative **50** Investment Fund Managers 2011/61/EU (AIFMD) that entered into force on 21 July 2011. In accordance with section 66(1) AIFMD, all EU Member States shall adopt and publish the laws, regulations and administrative provisions to comply with the Directive until 22 July 2013. AIFMD provides a legal framework and establishes common requirements governing the authorization and supervision of Alternative Investment Fund Managers (AIFM).

It is currently under discussion whether AIFMD applies to listed REITs. In that case, **51** REITs and their managers are subject to extensive regulations, that are licence requirements, certain disclosure obligations, depositary requirements, defined investment policy, etc. Therefore, the main question of interpretation referred to Article 4(1)(a) AIFMD, which defines the preconditions of an Alternative Investment Fund (AIF).

In accordance with Article 4(1)(a) AIFMD, 'AIFs' means collective investment under- **52** takings, including investment compartments thereof, which:

   (a) raise capital from a number of investors, with a view to investing it in accordance with a defined investment policy for the benefit of those investors; and

   (b) do not require authorization pursuant to Article 5 of Directive 2009/65/EC.

53 Furthermore, ESMA[54] and the European Commission interpret Article 2 AIFMD ('Scope') as follows:

> The question whether or not a listed real estate investment company is excluded from the scope of the AIFMD depends on whether or not it falls under the definition of an 'AIF' in Article 4(1)(a). Real estate companies cannot be excluded as such a priori, each situation needs to be valued on its own merits, based on substance, not on form.

54 Since neither the European Commission nor ESMA excludes REITs from the scope of AIFMD, each vehicle needs to be analysed to whether it meets the criteria of the definition of an AIF, in particular, whether the articles or by-laws or rules impose a defined investment policy to be followed by the management. As of today, following the implementation of AIFMD directive in the Member States, it appears that in most EU countries, REITs are not in the scope of AIFMD or the impact of the directive and its applicability to REITs are still unclear. REIT industry requires a consistent application of AIFMD in all EU territories.

§1.03   DOMESTIC TAXATION[55]

[A]   Taxation of REITs

[1]   Tax Accounting

55 As already mentioned, to achieve neutrality between direct investments in immovable property and investments through REITs, most countries levy tax at the investors' level only. Therefore, the common thread of virtually all REIT regimes is that of exempting income at REIT level, such exemption being attained in various ways. A few other countries, conversely, do apply tax on REITs while exempting investors upon distribution. However, the common purpose of the above-mentioned approaches aims always to provide for a single taxation level just as it is in the case of direct taxation.

56 The following are the main systems in force:

---

54. The European Securities and Markets Authority (ESMA) is an independent EU Authority that contributes to safeguarding the stability of EU's financial system by ensuring the integrity, transparency, efficiency and orderly functioning of securities markets, as well as enhancing investor protection; for further details, please refer to www.esma.europa.eu and final report 'Guidelines on Key Concepts of the AIFMD' of ESMA.
55. Please refer to Table 6 for a summary of the taxation systems (both at a REIT level and at the investor level) in force in several countries.

(a) exemption (e.g., Belgium,[56] Bulgaria, Finland, Germany, Hungary, India, Malaysia, the Netherlands and Turkey);
(b) flow-through (e.g., Australia and Canada);
(c) dividend deduction (e.g., Japan, Singapore,[57] South Africa, South Korea and the US);
(d) exemption for eligible income (e.g., Brazil, France, Ireland, Italy,[58] Spain and the UK);
(e) taxation on NAV (e.g., Greece); and
(f) ordinary taxation (e.g., Hong Kong).[59]

The exemption method (e.g., Belgium, Bulgaria, Finland, Germany, Hungary, India, **57** Malaysia, the Netherlands and Turkey) commonly requires the distribution of most of the income earned during the year, so that income taxation is not deferred. The exception is the Turkish regime where there is no minimum profit distribution requirement which may lead to a deferral of taxation. In the Netherlands, a 0% rate regime achieves, de facto, the same result as an exemption method.

As a consequence, the first category of REIT regimes implies the following tax **58** consequences: prima facie REIT itself is generally a person liable to tax and not fiscally transparent; where certain requirements are met, either the tax rate is equal to zero or the taxable base is tax-exempt. Both mechanisms lead to the same result: no tax liability should arise at REIT level. Since in the above-mentioned cases, REIT is an autonomous entity for taxation purposes, the income distributed is, thus, generally classified as dividend income and taxed accordingly. However, the income can also be deemed to be rental at the investor level depending on the applicable domestic income characterization.

Similarly, the flow-through system is generally granted under the condition that the **59** unitholder is presently entitled to REIT profits based on the trust deed (compared to the exemption method). In this category of REIT regimes, a REIT, generally, is not an entity liable to tax. At the investors' level, income retains the same character as the underlying income derived by REIT and it is taxed according to the treatment provided for the underlying income.

---

56. A particular system of taxation applies in Belgium, where the taxable base is mainly limited to non-deductible expenses and abnormal or gratuitous benefits received. Under the implementation of the Anti-Tax Avoidance Directive (ATAD), starting from the financial year 2019, a 30% EBITDA limitation rule is introduced (*see* the country report on Belgium for further details).
57. Applicable only to eligible income and subject to a tax ruling obtained from the tax authorities.
58. Where the Italian REIT regime is elected by qualified foreign REITs with reference to their Italian permanent establishments performing the eligible activity as main business, instead of the exemption the income derived by the permanent establishment from such activity is subject to substitute taxation. The substitute tax replaces the withholding tax system provided for distributions of exempt income made by Italian REITs.
59. Taxation (in the form of a property tax) applies at REIT level if Hong Kong immovable property is directly held by REIT. However, REIT generally holds immovable property through special purpose vehicles. In that case, profits tax is levied at the special purpose vehicle level and the subsequent dividend distribution to REIT is tax-exempt.

60   The dividend deduction system implies that dividends paid to an investor are tax-deductible at REIT level. This system may lead to full tax exemption at REIT level if the entire income is distributed. This system is generally associated with distribution requirements with respect to most of the REIT profits. Under the dividend deduction system, income that is not distributed is ordinarily taxed at REIT level. Even though the income is effectively tax-exempt at REIT level, REIT still remains liable to tax for any non-distributed funds. With reference to the dividend deduction system, in October 2015, OECD released the final version of Action 2 of BEPS[60] 'Neutralising the Effects of Hybrid Mismatch Arrangements' ('Action 2').[61] 'Recommendation 1.5 – exceptions to the rule – states that even though dividend deduction is likely to give rise to a mismatch in the tax outcomes "in order to preserve its tax neutrality, a jurisdiction may grant an investment vehicle, such as a mutual fund or real estate investment trust (REIT), the right to deduct dividend payments." The payment of a deductible dividend, which is likely to give rise to a mismatch in tax outcomes, will not generally give rise to a hybrid mismatch under Recommendation 1 provided any resulting mismatch will be attributable to the payer's tax status rather than the ordinary tax treatment of dividends under the laws of that jurisdiction [...].' This clarification constitutes an exclusion from the definition of hybrid financial instruments for the dividend deduction under REIT tax regime.[62]

61   Some countries apply exemption only to eligible income (distribution requirements are generally provided for) and ordinary taxation to other types of income. The exemption for eligible income method is usually associated with an asset test and/or income test requirements (such a system may result in full exemption at REIT level where REIT carries out only eligible activities). Taxing principles applicable for REIT regimes providing for exemption apply accordingly to this regime for the eligible income.

62   In Greece, REITs are subject to a special tax rate on the net average asset value of REIT. Taxation at REIT level is coupled with an exemption at the investor level.

63   Where REIT is subject to ordinary taxation (e.g., Hong Kong), distributions are generally exempt at the investor level.

64   In certain cases (e.g., Malaysia and Mexico), where the conditions for achieving favourable tax treatment at REIT level are not met (e.g., Malaysia) or not all the income is distributed to the investors (e.g., Mexico), the taxes paid by REIT are creditable (so-called indirect tax credit) by investors against taxes levied on subsequent distributions (*see* Table 5).

---

60. Base Erosion and Profit Shifting.
61. *"Neutralising the Effects of Hybrid Mismatch Arrangements, Action 2"*, Final Report (2015), OECD/G20 Base Erosion and Profit Shifting Project.
62. For more information please refer to p. 44 and example 1.10 in p. 202 of Action 2.

Table 5   REITs Taxation

REIT Regime	Fiscal Nature of REIT	Treatment of the Income on REIT Level	Treatment of Investor	Income Class on the Investor Level
(a) Tax exemption	Person liable to tax	Tax exemption or 0% rate	Liable to tax	Dividend or domestic law characterization (e.g., rental income)
(b) Flow-through	Transparent for tax purposes	None, since transparent entity	Liable to tax	Various income classes possible, however, generally income from immovable property (mainly rental income)
(c) Dividend deduction	Person liable to tax	Regular taxation but deduction of dividend paid from the taxable base possible	Liable to tax	Dividend
(d) Exemption for eligible income	Person liable to tax	Exemption for eligible income	Liable to tax	Dividend unless different domestic characterization
(e) Taxation on NAV	Person liable to tax	Special tax on NAV	Tax-exempt	None
(f) Ordinary taxation	Person liable to tax	Regular taxation	Tax-exempt	None

In conclusion, different routes are taken by various countries to achieve, with respect **65** to REIT income, the same outcome: a single tier of taxation, which, in most cases, occurs at the investors' level. The interaction of such wide-ranging approaches, combined with the different legal forms in which a REIT may be organized, gives rise to complexities in cross-border scenarios. Therefore, special focus still shall be given to the fiscal nature of REIT as investment vehicle, since the fact of whether REIT is a person liable to tax or a flow-through entity becomes crucial for:

(a) classification of the income for national and bilateral purposes (*see* section §1.03[B][1] below) and more important;

(b) tax treaty considerations in and via cross-border REIT investments (*see* section §1.04[C] below).

[2]   Determination of the Taxable Income

Countries applying an exemption system generally have no need to calculate taxable **66** income at REIT level (e.g., this is seemingly the case in Bulgaria and Germany). In contrast, all other countries do require computation of the taxable income at REIT level (save for Greece where a special tax on REIT NAV is applied). Approaches to taxable income determination may vary among countries:

(a) application of ordinary corporate income tax rules (e.g., Hungary, Italy, Japan[63] South Africa, Spain, the Netherlands, the UK[64] and the US). Deviations from ordinary tax rules may apply to specific items of income earned by a REIT;

(b) application of individual income tax rules (e.g., Australia and Canada); and

(c) application of special REIT rules (e.g., Belgium).

67 As to tax loss carry-forward by a REIT, losses are generally allowed to reduce future REIT taxable income. Countries applying a flow-through system (e.g., Australia and Canada) do not allow losses to be offset against other investors' income so that such losses will only be available to offset future REIT taxable income in subsequent years. REIT regimes providing for exemption of eligible income (e.g., Italy) do not generally allow cross-offsetting of taxable income between the eligible business and the ordinary one.

[3]   Taxation of Income from Subsidiaries

68 REIT regime is not generally extended to REIT subsidiaries with certain notable exceptions, e.g.:

(a) in Belgium, Hungary, Italy, France, Spain and the Netherlands, qualified domestic subsidiaries may avail themselves of REIT regime;

(b) in the UK, the concept of a REIT group is applied, and REIT subsidiaries benefit from an exemption for eligible income. The exemption applies to UK subsidiaries for rental income derived from immovable property, wherever held, while for non-UK subsidiaries, the exemption applies only to income from UK-located immovable property; and

(c) in the US, wholly owned subsidiaries, both domestic and foreign (except for a 'taxable REIT subsidiary'), are not treated as separate entities for tax purposes, so their assets, liabilities, and items of income are treated as those of REIT.

69 As mentioned, profits of a REIT subsidiary are generally subject to the particular tax rules for REITs at the 'participating' REIT level; countries applying the exemption for

---

63. For the exception to the ordinary corporate income tax rules, please refer to s. §1.03[B][1][b] of the Japanese chapter.
64. A REIT is exempt from corporation tax on sales of shares in UK property-rich companies (i.e., which derive at least 75% of their value from UK land). There are also further relaxations in the rules contained in Finance Bill 2021–2022 which are due to take effect in April 2022.

eligible income systems (e.g., Italy and France) do categorize dividends paid from qualifying subsidiaries out of exempt profits as eligible income.

[4]   *Taxation of Foreign Income*

REIT regimes do not generally discriminate between foreign investments and domestic   **70**
ones (i.e., foreign income is treated at par with domestic income). A peculiar case is that of Hong Kong, which, while applying an ordinary taxation system for REIT income, does not tax foreign income in the application of a pure territorial system of taxation (i.e., foreign income is completely disregarded).

However, double taxation issues may arise in connection with source country taxing   **71**
rights over REIT income derived from direct or indirect investment in situs state immovable property (*see* Figure 1).

Thus, relief for source country taxation becomes crucial for avoiding (or alleviating)   **72**
double taxation. In case where income is not taxed at REIT level, relief in REIT residence state may not be enjoyed. Various remedies may be considered to obviate such a problem. Foreign taxes may be:

   (a) creditable at the investor level (e.g., Australia, Canada, Germany,[65] Japan);
   (b) creditable at REIT level (e.g., Italy and Spain);
   (c) refundable at REIT level (e.g., Korea); or
   (d) deductible at REIT level (e.g., the Netherlands).

For REIT regimes that exempt eligible income only, foreign taxes on foreign-source   **73**
eligible income may be offset against taxable income. In Italy, for example, the foreign tax credit relating to properties of the exempt business may be used to offset taxes levied on taxable income. In the dividend deduction systems, it is normally possible to use the entire foreign tax credit against retained profit (if any).

Double taxation may arise even where the income is not taxed at REIT level and REIT   **74**
residence country applies as the relief method the exemption instead of the credit method.

The way the foreign taxes are dealt with in REIT residence state creates a disincentive   **75**
to invest in a foreign jurisdiction, in that foreign investments may be subject to a higher overall tax burden. In this respect, EU non-discrimination issues may come into play when it comes to the treatment in REIT residence states of taxes levied abroad.[66]

---

65. Under certain conditions only.
66. *See* R. Cornelisse et al., *Proposal for a Uniform EU REIT Regime – Part 1*. European Taxation (2006), at 6.

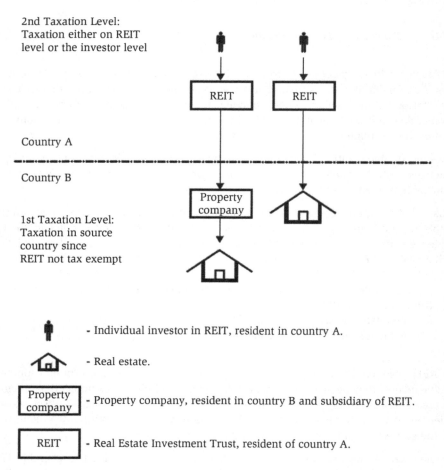

Figure 1   Direct Versus Indirect Investment

- Individual investor in REIT, resident in country A.

- Real estate.

- Property company, resident in country B and subsidiary of REIT.

- Real Estate Investment Trust, resident of country A.

76   Peculiar to Australia[67] is a tax treatment where the exemption of foreign-source income is even extended to investors by a tracing rule that avoids any discrimination.

[5]   *Other Taxes*

77   Taxes such as value added tax (VAT), transfer taxes, registration taxes and net worth taxes generally apply to REITs. In this regard REITs are not an exception to ordinary rules. However, certain countries provide exceptions tailored to REITs, for example:

---

67. This exemption applies only to non-resident investors.

(a) in Belgium, contributions to REITs, in cash or in kind, are exempt from proportional registration duties (only the fixed duty of EUR 50 will in principle be due);

(b) in Greece, immovable property purchased by a REIT is not subject to transfer tax. From 2014 onwards, REITs are subject to the Uniform Tax on the Ownership of Real Estate Property;

(c) in Italy, REITs are subject to 'mortgage-cadastral' tax at a reduced rate;

(d) in Hungary, a reduced transfer tax applies to the acquisitions of real estate property by REIT;

(e) in Japan, REITs are subject to registration tax and acquisition tax at a reduced rate;

(f) in the US, some states have disallowed the deduction for dividends paid by captive REITs, which are, therefore, taxed at the local level;

(g) in Malaysia, the transfer of immovable property made to REITs is exempt from stamp duty;

(h) in Turkey, agreements signed by REITs for the acquisition and disposal of immovable property are exempt from stamp duty.

[6]   *Entry/Exit in REIT Regime*

Certain REIT regimes require the payment of taxes upon election for REIT regime. The **78** charge may take the form of either an exit tax upon exiting the ordinary regime or of an entry tax upon electing the new regime.

Entry/exit taxes may be applied either to: **79**

(a) all assets owned by the electing entity (e.g., Belgium, Germany, the Netherlands and the US); or

(b) immovable property and rights used within the eligible business (e.g., France, Italy).

Entry/exit taxes are generally levied on capital gains computed on the immovable **80** property market value. In certain cases, an entry/exit charge is applied to the immovable property market value (and not to inherent gains).

Entry/exit taxes, if any, are generally applied at favourable rates which may take the **81** form either of a: (i) reduction of ordinary rates (e.g., Belgium)[68] or (ii) substitute tax (e.g., Italy).

---

68. More specifically, as regards the applicable tax rate, the taxable basis should be divided between the result realized during the accounting period up to the liquidation, which is taxed at the standard corporate income tax rate of 25% (since the assessment year 2021, related to the taxable period starting at the earliest on 1 Jan. 2020), and the latent capital gains and the tax-free reserves, which are taxed at 15% (since the financial year 2020).

82   In certain cases (e.g., Germany and Italy),[69] taxes are imposed on capital gains deriving from transfers of immovable property to a REIT. Favourable conditions may be provided in the form of application of a substitute tax (e.g., Italy for in-kind contributions).

[B]   Taxation of Investor

[1]   General Taxation

83   Investors may derive from a REIT income, generally depending on the legal form and the fiscal structure of REIT, characterized as follows:

  (a) current income:
   –   dividends;
   –   original or deemed rental income.[70]
  (b) capital gains:
   –   disposal of interests in a REIT;
   –   disposal of underlying assets of a REIT.[71]

[2]   Current Income

[a]   Income Characterization

84   Current income from a REIT is generally characterized as a dividend following the widespread employment among the countries of REIT corporate structure.

85   In some countries, the character of the underlying income (i.e., income earned by REIT) influences the character of the income earned by REIT investors. In this respect, Australia applies a pure flow-through system; that is, income at the investors' level retains in full the same character as income earned by REIT. In the US, dividends paid out from gains deriving from dispositions of US interests in immovable property are labelled 'capital gain dividends' and are treated differently from ordinary dividends.

86   Conversely, in other countries such as Mexico and the UK, income from a REIT is taxed as income from immovable property in the hands of the investor. As the UK applies an exemption for eligible income system, this 'deeming provision' applies to distributions out of eligible income only.

---

69. Mexico allows deferral of tax on capital gains arising from the disposal of immovable property to a REIT until such property is sold by REIT or the interest in REIT is disposed of.
70. Due to the operation of the flow-through system, Canada and Australia impose tax on resident investors on the attributable share of REIT taxable income irrespective of actual distribution.
71. May occur due to the operation of the flow-through system.

[b]   *Resident Investors*

Taxation of current REIT income generally depends on whether the investor is an   **87**
individual (outside the course of a business) or a corporate investor. For individual
investors, REIT regimes may alternatively provide for:

(a) final withholding tax (e.g., Belgium, Brazil, Bulgaria, Germany, Hungary,
Italy and Japan);[72]

(b) application of personal income taxation (e.g., Finland, France, Ireland,
Japan,[73] the Netherlands,[74] Spain, Turkey,[75] the UK[76] and the US);[77]

(c) exemption (e.g., Greece,[78] Hong Kong and Singapore).

Certain countries (e.g., Germany, Italy and Singapore) tax income from a REIT   **88**
differently, if units are held as business assets.

The tax treatment of corporate investors is generally pretty straightforward as current   **89**
income from a REIT is taxed according to corporate income tax rules applied to
ordinary corporations (e.g., Australia, Brazil, Canada, Germany, Hungary,[79] France,
Ireland, Italy, Japan, Mexico, the Netherlands, Singapore, Spain, the UK and the US),
or exempt (e.g., Greece,[80] Hong Kong).

Any withholding tax levied on the distribution of REIT income is generally creditable at   **90**
the corporate investor level (e.g., Belgium, Brazil, Germany, Italy and Japan). Countries that provide dividend exemption on qualifying shareholdings do not usually
extend the application of such beneficial treatment to REIT distributions since dividends received from a REIT are not pre-taxed at REIT level as intercompany dividends
are.

---

72. In case the investor opts for the 'non-reporting' method. In Japan, individual investors may opt
for different regimes. For more information please refer to s. §1.03[B][1][a] of the Japanese
chapter.
73. In case the investor opts for the 'aggregate' method.
74. A non-final 15% withholding tax applies to REIT distributions.
75. There is a distribution requirement of half of the dividends received from a REIT which is then
taxed at progressive rates.
76. A withholding tax applies to income that is characterized as income from immovable property;
relief is available for this withholding tax as a credit against higher rate tax.
77. US individual investors are taxed on ordinary dividends received from a REIT at graduated tax
rates but are eligible to deduct 20% of the income for an effective tax rate of 29.6%.
78. A special solidarity contribution may apply to individual investors who are Greek tax resident.
79. Based on the general rules, dividend income received is corporate income tax exempt.
80. Further distributions by the receiving company are subject to a 22% taxation on distributed
profits. For more information please refer to s. §1.03[B][1][a] of the Greek chapter.

[c]   Non-resident Investors

91   The tax treatment of REIT income in the hands of non-resident investors may act as a deterrent to attract foreign investments in a domestic REIT. REIT regimes do not generally discriminate between non-resident corporate and individual investors.

92   When deciding whether to invest in a foreign REIT, investors should carefully consider the following variables:

(a)   taxation in REIT country of residence;
(b)   taxation in the investor's residence country;
(c)   relief for source country tax; and
(d)   application of tax treaty (REIT's country, the investor's country and the source country).

93   The issues (b) through (d) fall outside the scope of this section, which focuses on taxation in REIT country of residence exclusively. As to the issue under (a), the tax treatment of non-residents investors may be reduced to the following:

(a)   withholding tax on distributions (e.g., Australia, Belgium,[81] Brazil, Bulgaria, Canada, Finland, France, Germany, Hungary,[82] Ireland, Italy, Japan, Malaysia, Mexico, the Netherlands,[83] Singapore, South Korea, Spain, the UK and the US);[84] and
(b)   exemption (e.g., Greece, Hong Kong, Hungary[85] and Turkey).

94   Any withholding tax applicable pursuant to REIT country of residence's domestic legislation may be reduced by virtue of an applicable tax treaty. However, due to the particular nature of a REIT, the application of treaties to REITs is debatable (*see* section §1.04 below).

---

81. Where applicable.
82. Only to individuals.
83. Applied only to investors holding a substantial interest and creditable against Dutch income tax.
84. Different rules apply for capital gain dividends.
85. Only to legal entities.

Table 6 Overall Taxation of Current Income

REIT Regime	Taxation Current Income at REIT Level	Taxation Current Income Resident Investors	Taxation Current Income Non-resident Investors
Australia	Flow-through status	– Corporate: taxed at a 30% rate on REIT distributions – Individual: taxed at rates up to 47% on REIT distributions	– Corporate: taxed at a 30% rate on REIT distributions[86] – Individual: taxed at a progressive rate starting from 32.5% on REIT distributions[87]
Belgium	Lump-sum taxable basis	– Corporate: taxed at 25% rate unless participation exemption applies to dividends – Individual: subject to 30%[88] withholding tax on dividends	– Corporate: exempt (to the extent that the dividend distributed does not stem from Belgian-source dividends) – Individual: as a corporate investor
Brazil	Eligible income is exempt	– Corporate: ordinary taxation – Individual: 20% withholding tax on distributions as a general rule. Under certain conditions exempt	– Corporate: 15%/20% withholding tax on distributions – Individual: as a corporate investor

86. Withholding tax rate will be 15% for distributions to non-residents by a Managed Investment Trust (but if the investor is resident in a country that does not have an exchange of information agreement with Australia, the rate of the withholding tax will be 30%).
87. Withholding tax rate will be 15% for distributions to non-residents by a Managed Investment Trust (but if the investor is resident in a country that does not have an exchange of information agreement with Australia, the rate of the withholding tax will be 30%).
88. A reduced withholding tax rate of 15% on dividend distributed is applicable from 1 Jan. 2017 for dividends distributed by RRECs investing at least 60% of their assets in healthcare property. This threshold has recently been increased to 80% and applies to dividend distributions made by RRECs as from 1 Jan. 2022.

REIT Regime	Taxation Current Income at REIT Level	Taxation Current Income Resident Investors	Taxation Current Income Non-resident Investors
Bulgaria	Exempt	– Corporate: ordinary taxation – Individual: 5% withholding tax on dividends	– Corporate: 5% withholding tax on dividends – Individual: as a corporate investor
Canada	Flow-through status	– Corporate: taxed at corporate rates – Individual: taxed at a progressive rate (top marginal rate in Ontario is 53.53%) on REIT distributions	– Corporate: 25%/15% withholding tax on REIT distributions[89] – Individual: as a corporate investor in REIT distributions
Finland[90]	Exempt	– Corporate: taxed at corporate rate (20%) – Individual: taxed at 30%/34% rate	– Corporate: 20% final withholding tax[91] – Individual: 30% final withholding tax[92]

89. Withholding tax rates subject to treaty reduction.
90. The Finnish withholding tax legislation was changed with effect from 1 Jan. 2021 onwards. In short, the application of a tax treaty requires that the custodian or the payer of a dividend provides the Tax Administration with the information on the final recipient of the dividend. The tax at source for dividend is increased to 35%, if the final recipient information is not provided. Assuming the final recipient information is provided, the withholding tax rate is similar as described above. Furthermore, since 1 Jan. 2021, dividend withholding tax may be withheld directly at the applicable tax treaty rate in case of dividends paid to nominee-registered shares. One of the requirements for allowing treaty relief at source is that the payer of the dividend or the custodian must be registered with the Finnish Tax Administration's custodian register in order to receive the benefit.
91. With effect from 1 Jan. 2021, the dividend withholding tax may be withheld directly at the applicable tax treaty rate in case of dividends paid to nominee-registered share if certain requirements are met. As of 1 Jan. 2021, the withholding tax rate is 35% instead if the final recipient information related to the dividends is not provided.
92. With effect from 1 Jan. 2021, the dividend withholding tax may be withheld directly at the applicable tax treaty rate in case of dividends paid to nominee-registered share if certain requirements are met. As of 1 Jan. 2021, the withholding tax rate is 35% instead if the final recipient information related to the dividends is not provided.

REIT Regime	Taxation Current Income at REIT Level	Taxation Current Income Resident Investors	Taxation Current Income Non-resident Investors
France	Eligible income is exempt	– Corporate: profits derived from the ancillary activities are taxed at the rate of 25% or 25.825% if additional contribution applies; dividends received by an institutional investor from the tax-exempt part of a listed SIIC[93] are subject to CIT at the standard rate of 25% or 25.825% if additional contribution applies[94] – Individual: dividends received from SIIC shares (either the tax-exempt or the taxable sector) are subject to a 30% flat tax (comprised of a 12.8% personal income tax and 17.2% social contributions)[95]	– Corporate: 25% withholding tax dividends – Individual: 12.8% withholding tax (plus social contribution)[96]

93. Société d'Investissement Immobilier Cotée.
94. The domestic parent-subsidiary regime does not apply to these dividends.
95. Upon an election made by the taxpayer, dividends received from listed SIIC shares are subject (after the deduction of a 40% allowance applicable only to the dividends distributed out of the taxable sector of the listed SIIC) to personal income tax at progressive rates (ranging from 0% to 45%/increased, in certain cases by the 3% to 4% exceptional tax on high taxpayers) and to 17.2% social contributions (out of which 7.2% are tax-deductible from the personal income tax basis).
96. 75% when the dividend is received by a non-resident (corporate or individual) established in a non-cooperative state or territory.

REIT Regime	Taxation Current Income at REIT Level	Taxation Current Income Resident Investors	Taxation Current Income Non-resident Investors
Germany	Exempt	– Corporate: subject to CIT (15.8%) and trade tax (from 12.5% to 17%) on dividends – Individual: taxed on a progressive rate up to 45% plus trade tax (from 7% to approx. 20%) on dividends, if units in a REIT are part of business assets; flat taxation at 26.4% if units of a REIT are part of private assets	– Corporate:[97] 15.8% withholding tax on dividends – Individual: 26.4% withholding tax on dividends
Greece	Taxed at 10% of European Central Bank rates plus 1% on NAV	– Corporate: exempt – Individual: exempt[98]	– Corporate: exempt – Individual: exempt
Hong Kong	Taxed at a 16.5% rate[99]	– Corporate: exempt – Individual: exempt	– Corporate: exempt – Individual: exempt
Hungary	Exempt	– Corporate: exempt – Individual: 15% personal income tax	– Corporate: exempt – Individual: 15% withholding tax on dividends

97. Taking into account a two-fifth claim of withholding tax available for foreign corporation, *see* Chapter Germany, s. §1.03[A][3].
98. A special solidarity contribution may apply to individual investors who are Greek tax resident. Moreover, if the owner is a Greek company, further distribution of the relevant dividend income by such company may result in a 22% (reduced from 24% to 22% from the fiscal year 2021 onwards by virtue of Law 4799/2021) taxation imposed on distributed profits.
99. A REIT authorized as a collective investment scheme is exempt from Hong Kong Profits Tax, but subject to Hong Kong Property Tax (at 15% of the net assessable value of such real estate). However, if REIT holds real estate in Hong Kong indirectly via special purpose vehicle, which is the standard practice, such special purpose vehicles are subject to Profits Tax (at a rate of 16.5%) in respect of the profits derived from the real estate. Under the two-tier profits tax system which is effective from the year of assessment 2018/2019, the first HKD 2 million of assessable profits of REIT will be taxed at 8.25% (i.e., half of the normal tax rates), regardless of REITs. The remaining assessable profits will be subject to the original rate of 16.5%.

REIT Regime	Taxation Current Income at REIT Level	Taxation Current Income Resident Investors	Taxation Current Income Non-resident Investors
India	Exempt[100]	– Corporate:[101] (a) Income tax on dividends received from REIT: exempt and no taxes are required to be withheld by REIT if the special purpose vehicles distributing such dividends to REIT have not opted for the concessional tax regime;[102] (b) Income tax on distributions received from REIT:- interest income should be chargeable to income tax in the hands of the unitholder being resident at the applicable rates. REIT is required to withhold tax at the rate of 10%;- rental income should be chargeable to income tax in the hands of the unitholder at the rates applicable to such unitholder. REIT is required to withhold tax at the rate of 10% – Individual: same treatment of corporate investor	– Corporate: interest income received by a non-resident unitholder is subject to withholding at the rate of 5%; rental income received by a non-resident unitholder is subject to withholding at the rates in force, who may be allowed to take treaty benefits if available. Taxes withheld by REIT should be available as credit on such income. – Individual: same treatment of corporate investor

100. Any other income, different from: (i) dividend income from SPV; (ii) interest income from SPV; and (iii) rental income from property held directly by REIT should be taxed at a rate of 30% (plus applicable surcharge). Dividend income received by REIT from an SPV continues to be exempt in the hands of REIT. Further, it has been clarified that dividend distributions by an SPV to a REIT should not be subject withhold tax.

101. Specific rules apply for Income tax on units received in exchange of shares of SPV and on sale of such units; Income Tax on Units Received in Exchange of Assets (Other Than Shares of SPV) and Dividend/Bonus stripping. For further information please refer to s. §1.03.B of the Indian Chapter.

102. If SPV distributing the dividends has opted for concessional tax rate under the new regime, the exemption shall not apply and REIT would be required to withhold taxes at the rate of 10% plus applicable surcharge and cess, irrespective of a lower tax rate under the relevant tax treaty.

REIT Regime	Taxation Current Income at REIT Level	Taxation Current Income Resident Investors	Taxation Current Income Non-resident Investors
Ireland	Eligible income is exempt	– Corporate: taxed at 25% rate on dividend, with some exceptions – Individual: income tax on distributions at their marginal rates plus USC and PRSI	– Corporate: 25% withholding tax for property income dividends – Individual: 25% withholding tax for property income dividends
Italy	Eligible income is exempt	– Corporate: taxed at 24% rate dividends paid out of eligible income[103] – Individual: for individuals in their private capacity 26%[104] withholding tax on dividends paid out of eligible income; for individuals in their business capacity ordinary taxation applies to 58.14% of dividends' amount	– Corporate: 26% withholding tax on dividends paid out of eligible income – Individual: same treatment of corporate investor on dividends paid out of eligible income

103. From the tax period 2017, Italian banks and financial institutions, different from assets and investments management companies, and Italian branches of similar foreign institutions are subject to a corporate tax surcharge of 3.5%.
104. Until the end of tax period 2017, the 26% final withholding tax was applicable if the relevant interest did not exceed 2% of the voting rights or 5% of SIIQ's capital (20% of the voting rights or 25% of the capital in case of distributing SIINQ's) – tested on a twelve-month basis; conversely, dividends distributed to more than 2% voting owners or more than 5% capital owners (in case of SIINQs, respectively, 20% and 25%) were subject to ordinary individual income tax with a 41.86% exemption (this exempt portion applies to dividends paid with profits earned following the tax period 2016, which were subject to IRES at 24%; for tax periods from 2008 to 2016, with profits subjected to IRES at 27.5%, the dividends exempt portion amounts to 50.28%) and no withholding tax had to be levied. The former regime will temporarily apply to dividend distributions resolved until 31 Dec. 2022 and executed out from profits earned until the tax period 2017.

REIT Regime	Taxation Current Income at REIT Level	Taxation Current Income Resident Investors	Taxation Current Income Non-resident Investors
Japan	Taxed at 31.46% corporate tax on a taxable basis (dividend deduction applies)[105]	– Corporate: 15.315% withholding tax on dividends – Individual: 20% – 20.315% withholding tax on dividends[106]	– Corporate: taxed at a 15.315% rate on dividends[107] – Individual: 15.315% withholding tax on dividends
Malaysia	Exempt[108]	– Corporate: taxed at a 24% rate on dividends[109] – Individual: 10% withholding tax on dividends	– Corporate: 24% withholding tax on dividends[110] – Institutional investors: 10% withholding tax on dividends[111] – Individual: 10% withholding tax on dividends
Mexico	Taxed at 30% on retained income[112]	– Corporate: taxed at a 30% rate on REIT distributions – Individual: as a corporate investor	– Corporate: taxed at a 30% rate on REIT distributions – Individual: as a corporate investor

105. Additional factors can increase the total tax rate to approximately 35%.
106. The ordinary rate is 20%. Under the Specific Restoration Tax Law, a Restoration Surtax of 2.1% is added to the withholding tax, thus raising WHT rate from 20% to 20.315%. This Restoration Surtax applies to dividend payments for the period from 1 Jan. 2013 through 31 Dec. 2037.
107. Withholding tax rates subject to treaty reduction.
108. If REIT distributes less than 90% of its total taxable income, REIT is subject to corporate income tax on its total taxable income. The regular corporate income tax rate is currently at 24%.
109. With effect from YA 2020, resident companies with paid-up capital of MYR 2.5 million and below and gross income from sources consisting of a business not exceeding MYR 50 million for the basis period for that year of assessment are subject to a tax rate of 17% for the first MYR 600,000 chargeable income, with the balance of chargeable income taxed at the normal corporate tax rate, currently at 24%.
110. Applies where tax has not been levied at REIT level.
111. Applies to distributions that have not been taxed at REIT level.
112. The 30% tax rate applies only to the undistributed amounts and if the taxable income of REIT in a year is higher than the amount distributed to the unit holders by 15 March of the following year.

REIT Regime	Taxation Current Income at REIT Level[113]	Taxation Current Income Resident Investors	Taxation Current Income Non-resident Investors
The Netherlands	Taxed at 0% rate[113]	– Corporate: taxed at a 25.8% rate on dividends – Individual: (i) if substantial interest, taxed at 25% tax rate or (ii) if non-substantial interest, income is subject to capital yield tax[114]	– Corporate: taxed at 15% withholding tax creditable against income tax (if any). Substantial interest holders are subject to 25.8% income tax – Individual: taxed at 15% withholding tax creditable against income tax (if any). Substantial interest holders are subject to 26.9% income tax
Singapore	Specified income[115] is exempt where distributed	– Corporate: taxed at a 17% rate on dividends – Individual: exempt[116]	– Corporate: 10% withholding tax on dividends – Individual: exempt

113. Subject to the election of the Fiscale Beleggingsinstelling (*FBI*) if the latter terminates the entity is subject to a corporate income tax rate of maximum 25.8% (2022, a reduced 15% corporate income tax rate applies to profits up to and including EUR 395,000). Furthermore, per 1 Jan. 2022 the Netherlands is to levy a conditional withholding tax against a 25.8% rate (being the highest CIT rate) on outgoing interest and royalty payments to affiliated entities in countries which levy no tax on profits or at a statutory rate of less than 9%, countries on EU list of non-cooperative jurisdictions or in abusive situations. In addition to this new conditional withholding tax a new conditional withholding tax on dividend payments to aforementioned jurisdictions has been announced per 2024.
114. The tax is based on a notional yield calculated on the basis of three ascending fixed percentages: 1.82% on assets with a total value of EUR 0 to EUR 50,650 (an exemption for capital to an amount of EUR 50,650 applies); 4.37% on assets on a total value of EUR 50,651 to EUR 962,350; and, finally, 5.53% on assets with a total value exceeding EUR 962,351. The notional yield is taxed at a flat rate of 30%.
115. For a more detailed definition of 'specified income' please refer to s. §1.03[B][1][b] and s. §1.03[A][1][b] of the Singaporean Chapter.
116. Individuals who hold units as trading assets or through a partnership in Singapore are subject to income tax on the gross amount of the distribution from REIT. These gross distributions are taxed at the Unitholder's applicable income tax rates, ranging from 0% to 22% (and up to 24% for personal income derived for the YA 2024). Whether the distributions received by the Unitholders are considered to be trading income or investment income is a question of fact, determined by IRAS after a review of the personal circumstances.

REIT Regime	Taxation Current Income at REIT Level	Taxation Current Income Resident Investors	Taxation Current Income Non-resident Investors
South Africa	Income after deduction for dividends paid is taxed at 28%	– Corporate: distributions are taxed at 28% – Individual: distributions are taxed at an individual's marginal tax rate (as if income was directly received[117])	– Corporate: distributions are subject to dividend withholding tax at 20% unless reduced by an applicable double tax agreement – Individual: subject to dividend tax
South Korea	Taxed at 11% (on the first KRW 200 million), at 22% (on the taxable income ranges from KRW 200 million to KRW 20 billion), 24.2% (on the taxable income ranges from KRW 20 billion to KRW 300 billion) and 27.5% (on taxable income exceeding KRW 300 billion) corporate tax on taxable basis (dividend deduction applies for CR-REIT and P-REIT, if 90% distribution requirement met)	– Corporate: taxed at 10% (on the first KRW 200 million), at 20% (on the taxable income ranges from KRW 200 million to KRW 20 billion), 22% (on the taxable income ranges from KRW 20 billion to KRW 300 billion) and 25% (on taxable income exceeding KRW 300 billion) corporate tax – Individual: 15.4% withholding tax if the dividend is lower than KRW 20 million; otherwise subject to ordinary income tax ranging from 6.6% to 46.2% on dividends	– Corporate: taxed at 22% withholding tax on dividends – Individual: as a corporate investor

---

117. The trusts are taxed at a different rate.

REIT Regime	Taxation Current Income at REIT Level	Taxation Current Income Resident Investors	Taxation Current Income Non-resident Investors
Spain	Exempt on eligible income, non-eligible income taxed according to ordinary rules	– Corporate: taxed at a 19% rate on dividends (taxation on eligible income at the level of REIT is creditable) – Individual: taxed standard 19% withholding	– Corporate: taxed according to ordinary rules and treaty provision – Individual: as a corporate investor
Turkey	Exempt	– Corporate: taxed at a 20% rate on dividends[118] – Individual: taxed at a progressive rate from 15% to 40% on 50% of the dividends[119]	– Corporate: 0% withholding tax on dividends – Individual: as a corporate investor
UK	Eligible income is exempt	– Corporate: taxed at a 19% rate on dividends paid out of eligible income[120] – Individual: taxed at a progressive rate of up to 45% on dividends paid out of eligible income	– Corporate: taxed at 20% withholding tax on dividends paid out of eligible income – Individual: same treatment as a corporate investor on dividends paid out of eligible income

118. Dividends received from REICs by corporate investors are subject to a 25% rate for 2021 and 23% for 2022.
119. Where the dividend is lower than a certain threshold, the shareholder is not required to declare the income.
120. However, CIT rate will be rising to 25% from April 2023.

REIT Regime	Taxation Current Income at REIT Level	Taxation Current Income Resident Investors	Taxation Current Income Non-resident Investors
US	Income after deduction for dividends paid is taxed at graduated rates to a maximum effective rate of 21%; state and local taxes may also apply (rates vary and tax regimes may not follow the federal rules)	– Corporate: taxed at 21% – Individual: ordinary dividends taxed at graduated rates up to 37%;[121] capital gain dividends taxed at 20% (plus 3.8% of surtax)	– Corporate: ordinary dividends taxed at a flat rate of 30%; capital gains taxed at a flat rate of 21%.[122] – Individual: ordinary dividends taxed at a flat rate of 30%; capital gain dividends taxed at 21%. – Capital gain dividends from publicly traded REITs: treated as ordinary dividends to a non-resident holding up to 10% of a class during the previous year

121. US individuals are eligible to deduct 20% of the income for an effective tax rate of 29.6%.
122. Although there is some uncertainty regarding whether withholding is required for capital gain distributions not attributable to dispositions of US real property interests.

[3]   Capital Gains

[a]   Resident Investors

95 Taxation of capital gains from the disposal of a REIT interest may vary depending on the nature of the investor, that is individuals (outside the course of a business) or corporate investors. For individuals, REIT regimes may alternatively provide:

(a) ordinary taxation (e.g., Australia, Canada,[123] Finland, France, Hong Kong,[124] Hungary, Ireland, the Netherlands,[125] South Africa, Spain, the UK and the US);[126]

(b) exemption (e.g., Belgium,[127] Bulgaria[128] and Singapore);[129]

(c) withholding tax (e.g., Brazil and Germany);[130] and

(d) flat rate (e.g., Italy[131] and Japan).

96 The tax treatment of corporate investors is the following:

(a) ordinary taxation (e.g., Australia, Belgium, Brazil, Canada,[132] Finland, France,[133] Germany, Hungary,[134] Italy,[135] Japan, the Netherlands, Singapore,[136] Spain, the UK and the US);[137]

---

123. Tax applies to a reduced tax base.
124. Tax applies only to investors carrying out a business or trade in REIT interests.
125. Dutch resident individuals who do not hold a substantial interest (for a more detailed description of the meaning of 'substantial interest' please refer to s. §1.03[B][1][a][i] of the Dutch Chapter) are subject to the capital yield tax.
126. Ordinary taxation applies to short-term capital gains. Long-term capital gains are eligible for a 20% rate of tax.
127. Exemption applies if the disposal occurs within the boundaries of a normal management of a private patrimony. Capital gains derived by individuals holding directly or indirectly at least 25% of the interest in REITs are taxable, if they are sold to interest-holders resident outside EEA.
128. Exemption applies providing the sale takes place on a Bulgarian, EU/EEA-regulated market of securities.
129. Exemption applies if the investor does not carry out any business and trade in REIT interests.
130. Unless the shareholder owns more than 1%; in such a case the ordinary taxation applies.
131. Individual investors, acting in their private capacity, are subject to a 26% substitute tax regardless of the interest held. Before 1 Jan. 2019, only individual investors whose interest did not exceed 2% of the voting rights or 5% of SIIQ's capital were applied the flat rate 26%. Otherwise, they were subject to the ordinary individual income tax.
132. Tax applies to a reduced tax base.
133. A reduced rate is applicable where the interests have been held for at least two years and qualify as participating shares for accounting purposes.
134. Effective from 1 Jan. 2018, no minimum participation threshold has to be met in order to benefit from the Hungarian participation exemption regime but the acquisition has to be reported to the tax authority within seventy-five days, and the disposal has to happen at least one year following the acquisition of the shares.
135. From the tax period 2017, Italian banks and financial institutions, different from assets and investments management companies, and Italian branches of similar foreign institutions are subject to a corporate tax surcharge of 3.5%.
136. Singapore does not impose tax on capital gains.
137. Ordinary taxation applies to short-term capital gains. Long-term capital gains are eligible for a 20% rate of tax.

(b) exemption (e.g., Bulgaria[138] and Greece);[139] and

(c) flat rate (e.g., Germany).[140]

The relevant preferential regimes applicable (if any) for capital gains (e.g., participa- **97** tion exemption) are generally not applicable for capital gains arising from a disposal of interests in REITs (e.g., Germany, Italy and the Netherlands). This is due to the lower or nil taxation levied at REIT level on ordinary income. In some countries, ordinary taxation is levied on a reduced taxable base (i.e., Australia).

[b] *Non-resident Investors*

Capital gains derived by non-resident investors and arising from the disposal of **98** interests in a foreign REIT are treated under domestic legislation as follows:

(a) ordinary taxation (e.g., Australia,[141] Finland,[142] Germany,[143] Spain and the US);[144]

(b) exemption (e.g., Canada,[145] Greece, Hungary, Italy,[146] Japan,[147] the Netherlands,[148] Spain[149] and the UK);[150] and

(c) withholding tax (e.g., Brazil, Ireland and France).[151]

---

138. Exemption applies providing the sale occurs on a Bulgarian, EU/EEA-regulated securities market.
139. Irrespective of whether the seller is an individual or a legal entity, in case of selling listed shares a transaction duty of 0.2% applies.
140. Unless the shareholder owns more than 1%; in such a case the ordinary taxation applies.
141. CGT applies only at certain conditions.
142. Only in case more than 50% of REITs' assets are directly held property located in Finland.
143. In case the investor holds more than 1% interest in REIT.
144. *See* Table 6. Also subject to withholding tax regime.
145. However, the Canadian regime provides for certain circumstances where the taxation is due.
146. For investors owning less than 2% of voting rights, or less than 5% of REIT capital. Where such conditions are not met, capital gains are subject to the 26% substitute tax. For more information, please refer to s. §1.03[B][1][b] and s. §1.03[B][2][b] of the Italian Chapter.
147. The exemption applies unless the corporation is classified as a real estate holding company. Also, where the investor does not hold more than 5% interest (in the case of a listed REIT), or 2% interest (in the case of an unlisted REIT), if these thresholds are exceeded, capital gains are taxed at a flat rate.
148. Where the investor does not own a substantial interest in REIT (i.e., more than 5% of REIT interests), otherwise the Dutch corporate income taxation (max rate 25.8%) is applied for corporate investors and a tax rate of 26.5% is applied to individual investors.
149. Under certain conditions.
150. Until April 2019, capital gains realized by individual and corporate non-UK resident investors were not generally subject to UK CGT but may have been subject to tax under the laws of their own country. Since April 2019 onwards, the disposal of shares in a UK REIT by a non-UK resident individual investor has been within the scope of UK CGT as a result of the 2019 immovable property gains rules.
151. Under certain conditions.

99 Application of the relevant tax treaties may restrict REIT state (*see* section §1.04 below).

[C]   Taxation of Foreign REITs

100 In this section, a foreign REIT is not considered to be a foreign entity joining the domestic REIT regime of another country, but an entity joining a REIT regime in its domestic country and investing in another country where a REIT regime exists.

101 In this regard, the taxation of foreign REITs may be analysed by taking the following approaches:

(a) REIT income.
(b) REIT distributions.

102 REIT preferential tax rules usually apply only to domestic REITs (except in the Netherlands). The reason for denying the recognition of the tax-exempt nature to foreign REITs is to prevent tax erosion in the state of source. This may constitute a limit for attracting foreign capital. In this regard, income earned by foreign REITs is ordinarily treated according to the domestic rules provided for the type of income derived (generally income from immovable property).

103 Furthermore, REIT regimes are not applicable even to foreign REIT permanent establishments, except in a few cases (e.g., Italy).

104 Distributions by foreign REITs to resident investors are generally taxed in accordance with the ordinary tax rules. However, some countries (e.g., Belgium[152] and Germany) explicitly deny the application of any preferential regime (e.g., participation exemption) to foreign REIT distributions in order to avoid tax-exempt income at the distributing entity level being taxed at the investor level under a preferential regime. Finally, there are some countries (e.g., Mexico) where if the foreign REIT is resident in a preferred tax regime country or receives passive income, the vehicle is considered transparent for tax purposes.

---

152. The exclusion of the participation exemption does not apply in case the by-laws of the foreign real estate company assimilated to a Belgian RREC (as defined in Belgian tax law) state that annually at least 80% of the net revenue will be distributed to the shareholders, to the extent that the revenue stems from dividends meeting the subject-to-tax condition or from capital gains on shares qualifying for the participation exemption.

[D] Taxation of Foreign REITs and EU-Law Considerations

[1] Introduction

Tax and regulatory treatment of REITs are not harmonized within the EU since Member **105** States are sovereign regarding direct taxes. Taxation powers of each Member State are, however, restricted by the six fundamental freedoms of Community Law. Important development regarding the compatibility of tax exemption on REIT level in the light of EU laws took place on 12 May 2010. After a long-debated question of whether European REIT regimes can be tax-exempt without running the risk of state aid, the European Commission announced – in case of a Finnish REIT – that a general tax exemption of REIT vehicles is not regarded as illegal state aid.[153]

One must however acknowledge that REIT regimes – as they are most commonly **106** drafted today – have several features that may be in conflict with the above-mentioned EU freedoms.

To provide an exhaustive illustration of all EU compatibility issues that current REIT **107** regimes may trigger goes beyond the scope of this book; however, it is worth mentioning at least some of the main issues.

In general, discrimination issues can take place both at investor level and at REIT level. **108**

As regards investor level, it is worth mentioning that the EU discrimination issue could **109** mainly arise in two situations. The first occurs where a European REIT regime taxes income earned by investors resident in other EU countries in a more burdensome way than the income earned by domestic investors. EU Court of Justice has already stated that a similar treatment of non-resident investors is in breach of the free movement of capital.[154] The second situation occurs when a European country taxes income distributed by domestic REITs and income distributed by REITs organized under the law of other EU countries differently. In such a case, the different taxation discourages residents from investing cross-border. In this respect, the EU Court of Justice has already stated that a similar treatment of resident investors is in breach of the free movement of capital.[155]

As stated previously, EU compatibility issues may arise not only with reference to **110** investors but also with regard to REITs directly. In this respect, it is worth mentioning that an EU discrimination issue at REIT level may mainly arise in two situations. First, the discrimination arises from the fact that several EU REIT regimes are not applicable to REITs organized under the law of other European countries and/or to permanent establishment of European entities. This situation may constitute a breach of EU

---

153. U. Stoschek & T. Kröger, *European REITs Weather Forecast – Sunny, with Some Clouds*. Global REIT Survey Supplement, September 2010, www.epra.com/media/EPRA_REIT_Survey_Supplement.pdf. For Finnish developments, *see* Finland, Ch. 1.01.[B].
154. *See, e.g.*, Case C-379/05 (so-called Amurta case).
155. *See, e.g.*, Case C-139/02 (so-called Manninan case).

fundamental freedoms.[156] Also, the way the foreign investments undertaken by a domestic REIT are treated under a REIT regime may turn out to be a disincentive to invest in a foreign jurisdiction, in that foreign investments are restricted or suffer a higher overall tax burden. In this respect, EU non-discrimination issues may arise when it comes to the treatment of taxes levied abroad in REIT residence states.[157] The second discrimination against foreign investments may even derive from the restriction, provided by certain REIT regimes, to invest in real estate situated abroad.

111 In recent years, EU Commission has started infringement procedures against a number of European REIT regimes (e.g., Belgium, Estonia and Italy). In light of this and of ECJ[158] case law experience, EU Member States have begun aligning their domestic REIT regime with EU fundamental freedoms. In this respect, it is important to remark that in 2009, Italy, in reaction to the infringement procedure, extended its REIT regime to Italian permanent establishments of companies resident in EU or EEA included in the Italian whitelist, carrying out eligible activities.

112 Therefore, the challenge for EU Member States enforcing REIT regimes is finding the right balance between safeguarding the right to levy tax on income from domestic properties and respecting EU freedoms.

[2]   Current Developments

113 In the recent past, some proposals were made on how to improve legal and fiscal framework of REIT regimes within the EU.[159] In this respect, the proposed Mutual Recognition Principle, introduced by European Public Real Estate Association (EPRA), is based on a harmonized legal framework laid down in an EC Communication according to which Member States allow REIT treatment to foreign REITs where certain investment and non-investment minimum criteria in both establishment and investment country are met.

114 The suggested EPRA approach in respect of cross-border taxation aims to combine both the flow-through character of a REIT and the prevention of the situs state taxation rights by:

(a) Single Country approach (taxation only in REIT country and subsequent allocation of such tax to the various situs countries).
(b) Situs Country approach (taxation by each situs country with a tax credit on investor level).

---

156. *See, e.g.*, Case 270-83 (so-called Avoir fiscal case) and Case C-307/97 (so-called Saint Gobain case).
157. *See* R. Cornelisse, et al., *Proposal for a Uniform EU REIT Regime – Part 1*. European Taxation (2006), at 6.
158. Court of Justice of the European Union.
159. *See Ibid.*, at 3 and www.epra.com/media/EPRA_European_REITs_Discussion_Paper.pdf.

Both approaches provide, especially, the following advantages in cross-border invest- **115** ments:

(a) REIT tax exemption;
(b) one-level of taxation;
(c) avoidance of double taxation; and
(d) fair allocation of tax revenues.

§1.04 TAX TREATY ISSUES

[A] Preliminary Remarks

The analysis of the tax treaty issues is based on both the 2017 OECD Model and the **116** 2017 OECD Commentary. However, most of the comments are valid also as regards the previous OECD Models.

Indeed, most of the clarifications contained in the 2017 OECD Commentary stem from **117** the 2007 OECD Report and the 2009 OECD CIV Report, which had already been included in the 2008 OECD Model and the 2010 OECD Model, respectively.

Moreover, the 2017 OECD Commentary provides useful guidance also as concerns the **118** interpretation of Double Tax Agreements (DTAs) based on previous OECD Models (with the exception, of course, of the comments concerning OECD Model provisions that were added or significantly amended in subsequent versions of OECD Model, as happened in 2017).

Cross-border investments in REITs, as well as cross-border investments by REITs, may **119** give rise to international juridical double taxation and thus call for the analysis of the applicability of tax treaties to income (and gains) derived by investors and to income (and gains) derived by REITs. The starting point for the analysis is OECD Model and OECD Commentary thereon. Specific treaty practices are also considered where relevant. OECD Report is the first official OECD document on tax treaty issues related to REITs and led in 2008 to changes in OECD Commentary on Articles 6, 10, 13 and 23.

The following sections analyse the main treaty issues related to REITs: **120**

(a) the definition of REIT for treaty purposes;
(b) the tax regime applicable to REITs' cross-border investments;
(c) the tax regime applicable to REIT distributions;
(d) capital gains derived from the disposal of interests in REITs; and
(e) cross-border income of REITs.

[B]   Definition of REIT for Treaty Purposes

121   Albeit the term 'REIT' is frequently used in many systems, legal forms and the related tax regime vary widely among countries. This clearly prevents identification of an exhaustive general definition for treaty purposes. The common patterns of REITs should thus lead to a general definition, which, however, may need to be adjusted on a case-by-case basis (i.e., in the specific bilateral treaty).

122   In line with this conclusion, OECD Report outlines that a REIT definition can only be given on a bilateral basis:[160]

123   Definition of REIT:

> 31. A first design issue is how to define a REIT for purposes of the above rules. The Working Party concluded that given the differences in domestic law concerning the structure and features of REITs, this should be dealt with bilaterally. For the purpose of the above provisions, countries would therefore be expected to include in their bilateral conventions specific definitions of REITs that would allow the application of these provisions to their own REITs. Such definitions may, for example, make reference to the relevant domestic provisions that define REITs for domestic tax purposes.

124   The introduction in the OECD Commentary of paragraphs dealing with the treaty regime applicable to REITs required OECD to outline at least the key features relevant to distinguish REITs from other vehicles. Thus, in the context of the 2008 amendments, a tentative definition of REIT (the same used by OECD to define the scope of the 2007 OECD Report)[161] was inserted in OECD Commentary:[162]

> A REIT may be loosely described as a widely held company, trust or contractual or fiduciary arrangement that derives its income primarily from long-term investment in immovable property, distributes most of that income annually and does not pay income tax on the income related to immovable property that is so distributed. *The fact that the REIT vehicle does not pay tax on that income is the result of tax rules that provide for a single-level of taxation in the hands of the investors in the REIT* (emphasis added).

125   The first few lines make it clear that the definition is not intended to be exhaustive. The rationale behind the insertion of such a definition seems to be the identification of the common patterns that characterize REITs:

(a) widely held investment vehicles with different legal forms;
(b) deriving income primarily (not exclusively) from long-term investments in immovable property;
(c) distributing annually most (not all) of the immovable property income; and

---

160. *See* para. 31 of OECD Report.
161. *See* para. 3 of OECD Report.
162. *See* para. 67.1 of OECD Commentary on Art. 10.

(d) not paying taxes on the investment income for reasons of a single level of taxation in the hands of the investors.

This definition being discussed here is contained in OECD Commentary on Article 10. **126** A reference to REITs is contained in OECD Commentary on Articles 6, 10, 13, 23 and 29. One may wonder why the definition of REITs is contained in OECD Commentary on Article 10 and not – for example – in OECD Commentary on the first article of OECD Model mentioning REITs (i.e., Article 6). It is likely that the decision was taken to deal with the definition in OECD Commentary on the provision the interpretation of which was considered to be more relevant to REITs' treaty regime (i.e., Article 10).

It would have been, however, preferable to include the tentative definition in OECD **127** Commentary on Article 3 with the additional recommendation to countries to insert a specific definition in Article 3. This solution seems more in line with the structure of OECD Model, in that Article 3 is the provision containing the definitions of terms used in the treaty.

[C]   Tax Regime Applicable to REITs' Cross-Border Investments

[1]   Introduction

Most of the regulatory and tax laws with respect to REITs allow foreign qualifying **128** investments (e.g., investments in immovable property situated in other countries or investments in foreign immovable property companies). In the case of cross-border investments, the source state (i.e., situs state in the case of immovable property) generally asserts jurisdiction to tax over the income derived therefrom. Tax treaties following OECD Model attribute primary taxation rights to the situs state in the case of both income from immovable property and gains derived from the alienation of immovable property.

In the case of cross-border investments made by REITs the following main issues have **129** to be tackled:

(a) definition of the person entitled to the income, who is the person that should invoke the application of the treaty between its residence state and the source state (investors vis-à-vis REIT); and
(b) treaty entitlement of REITs; that is, is it possible for a REIT to invoke the application of the treaty in force between the State under which laws REIT is organized and the source State?

[2]   *Definition of the Person Entitled to the Income (Investors Vis-à-Vis REIT)*

130   The definition of the person entitled to the income derived by a REIT is a key interpretational issue to determine which is the applicable treaty (if any). The legal form of REIT and the relevant domestic tax provisions represent the starting point of the analysis.

[a]   *Legal Form*

131   In the case of REITs organized as a contractual or fiduciary arrangement, investors should be deemed to be the owner of the income, which is directly attributed to them. The same is true in the case of REITs organized in the form of trust or partnerships with a flow-through tax regime.

132   As a general rule, paragraph 2 of Article 1 of the 2017 OECD Model stipulates that the income derived by or through an entity or arrangement that is treated as wholly or partly fiscally transparent under the tax law of either Contracting State shall be considered to be income of a resident of a Contracting State, but only to the extent that the income is treated, for purposes of taxation by that State, as the income of a resident of that State.[163]

133   This paragraph – by referring to entities that are 'wholly or partly' treated as fiscally transparent – covers not only partnerships but also other non-corporate entities.[164,165]

134   As clarified by the 2017 OECD Commentary, this paragraph not only serves to confirm the conclusions of OECD Partnership Report but also extends the application of these conclusions to situations that were not directly covered by the report.[166] With respect to REITs, whether they can be regarded as transparent entails a detailed analysis of their features.

135   For example, if an obligation is imposed on a trust under its deed to distribute all (or substantially all) income deriving from a fixed share (as is the case for REITs), then there would be strong arguments to support extending the conclusions reached by OECD Partnership Report to REIT trusts by applying Article 1(2) of the 2017 OECD

---

163. *See* paras 22–48 of the 2017 OECD Commentary on Art. 1.
164. *See* para. 4 of the 2017 OECD Commentary on Art. 1.
165. This paragraph will ensure, for example, that treaty benefits are available to an investor in a non-CIV fund as long as the non-CIV is treated as transparent by the State of residence of that investor so that the investor is taxed directly on its share of the income derived through that non-CIV. It will therefore ensure that treaty benefits are granted in these circumstances while addressing the two tax policy concerns identified in para. 14 of the Report on Action 6, i.e., that non-CIV funds may be used to provide treaty benefits to investors that are not themselves entitled to treaty benefits and that investors may defer recognition of income on which treaty benefits have been granted (*see* para. 10 of the 2016 OECD Public discussion draft on 'Treaty entitlement of non-CIV funds').
166. *See* para. 4 of the 2017 OECD Commentary on Art. 1.

Model (or the conclusion reached by the Partnership Report as far as DTAs based on previous OECD Model are concerned) to REIT trust.

In that case, income could be said to flow through to the unit-fund holders and paid to **136** them (or derived by them) in the sense that such terms must be interpreted in a treaty context.[167] Where REITs are organized in the form of corporations, the person entitled to the income is generally REIT.

[b]   Tax Regime

Despite the legal form and the legal entitlement to the income, the peculiarity of REITs **137** seems to be the tax regime, which amounts to a de facto exemption at the vehicle level justified by taxation at the investors' level. One may thus wonder whether in some cases the applicable tax regime leaves room to argue for tax transparency of the vehicle. The answer is not straightforward and in many cases seems to be in the negative since generally the favourable regime only applies if certain distribution requirements are met and distributions have a single characterization differing from the types of income derived by REIT.

In conclusion, in light of the tax regimes applied to REITs, it seems possible to argue **138** that in most cases, REITs are the persons entitled to the income and, thus, the relevant taxpayer for treaty purposes.

[3]   REIT Treaty Entitlement

Article 1 of OECD Model provides that the 'Convention shall apply to persons who are **139** resident of one or both of the Contracting States.' Therefore, a REIT is treaty entitled if the following requirements are satisfied:

- (a) it qualifies as a 'person' according to the definition of Article 3; and
- (b) it qualifies as a 'resident of a contracting state' according to the definition of Article 4.

[a]   Definition of 'Person'

Article 3(1) provides a definition of 'person', followed by the definition of 'company': **140** For the purposes of this Convention, unless the context otherwise requires:

---

167. The meaning of the attribution term 'paid to' is analysed in Stefano Simontacchi, *Taxation of Capital Gains under the OECD Model Convention. With Special Regard to Immovable Property* (2007), at 270 and 271.

(a) the term 'person' includes an individual, a company and any other body of persons;

(b) the term 'company' means any body corporate or any entity that is treated as a body corporate for tax purposes.

141   OECD Commentary on Article 3 states that the definition of the term 'person' contained in subparagraph (a) has to be interpreted in a very wide sense:

> The definition of the term 'person' given in subparagraph a) is not exhaustive and should be read as indicating that the term 'person' is used in a very wide sense (cf. especially Articles 1 and 4). The definition explicitly mentions individuals, companies and other bodies of persons. From the meaning assigned to the term 'company' by the definition contained in subparagraph b) it follows that, in addition, the term 'person' includes any entity that, although not incorporated, is treated as a body corporate for tax purposes. Thus, e.g. a foundation (foundation, Stiftung) may fall within the meaning of the term 'person'. Partnerships will also be considered to be 'persons' either because they fall within the definition of 'company' or, where this is not the case, because they constitute other bodies of persons.

142   When dealing with the treaty entitlement of REITs, OECD Report does not expressly mention the definition of 'person', but only bases the analysis on the definition of 'resident'. Certainly, REITs organized under the legal form of corporation qualify as 'persons'. The same conclusion applies to partnerships, which can be safely included in the definition of 'person' either because they fall within the definition of 'company' or, where this is not the case because they constitute other bodies of persons. Less immediately clear seems to be the case of REITs organized in the legal form of trusts and funds.

143   The characterization of trusts as treaty persons has on the one hand always been debated but as yet no unanimous conclusion has been reached on this issue. On the other hand, since a trust is merely a bunch of legal relationships among the various 'persons' involved (i.e., trustee, beneficiaries, grantor), one may question whether it can be characterized as an individual, a company or any other body of persons. Along the same lines, trusts seem also to be excluded from the definition of 'company', which makes reference to 'body corporate' and to 'entity'.

144   As already noticed, OECD Commentary on Article 3 observes that the definition of the term 'person' is not exhaustive and should be read as indicating that the term 'person' is used in a very wide sense[168] and that the term 'company' covers any body corporate and any other taxable unit which is treated as a body corporate according to the tax laws of the Contracting State in which it is organized. Thus, even if Article 3(1)(b) makes reference to 'any entity', by using the term 'taxable unit' the Commentary seems to provide a broad interpretation of the term 'entity', thus attributing relevance to the tax status, despite the legal form. Therefore, trusts seem to may be considered for tax

---

168. *See* para. 2 of OECD Commentary on Art. 3.

treaty purposes either as entities, where treated as a body corporate for tax purposes or as bodies of persons. In addition, one should also consider that common law countries do in fact recognize the existence of a person in a trust relationship and that this generally coincides with the trustee.[169] The same line of reasoning should lead to the inclusion of funds within the scope of treaty persons.

The approach given by OECD with reference to collective investment vehicles seems to **145** be broader than the one taken in respect of REITs. In 2009, OECD issued a discussion draft on the granting of treaty benefits with respect to the income of collective investment vehicles ('OECD CIV Report'),[170] on the basis of which changes have been made in the 2010 OECD Commentary.[171] OECD CIV Report addresses the characterization as a person of CIVs structured as trusts and concludes that the answer depends upon the tax treatment of the trust in the state in which it is established; that is, if the state where the trust is set up views it as a taxpayer, then there are grounds for arguing that a taxpayer is also a person. The relevant passage of OECD CIV Report reads as follows:[172]

> Under the domestic tax law of most common law countries, the trust, or the trustees acting collectively in their capacity as such, constitutes a taxpayer. Accordingly, failing to treat such a trust as a person would also prevent it from being treated as a resident despite the fact that, as a policy matter, it seems logical to treat it as a resident when the country in which it is established treats it as a taxpayer and a resident. The fact that the tax law of the country where the trust is established would treat it as a taxpayer would be indicative that the trust is a person for treaty purposes. In practice, it seems that few countries have denied benefits to CIVs in the form of trusts solely on the grounds that the trust is not a person.

In light of this conclusion, a very similar passage was included in the 2010 OECD **146** Commentary.[173] Unfortunately, there is no further guidance on this point. In relation to funds, the same OECD CIV Report points out that funds set up as contractual arrangements should not be considered, in prima facie, a 'person' for the purposes of the Convention. The relevant passage of OECD CIV Report reads as follows:[174]

---

169. In this respect, it cannot be denied that some common law countries do have a treaty policy according to which a clause is inserted in tax treaties clarifying that the term 'person' does include a trust (though admittedly those countries, e.g., the United States, observe that such an inclusion only has the purpose of clarification as the term 'trust' is intended to fall within the scope of OECD Model definition of the term 'person').
170. *See* OECD, *The Granting of Treaty Benefits with Respect to the Income of Collective Investment Vehicles – Public discussion draft*, Paris, 9 Dec. 2009, adopted (with slight changes) by OECD Committee on Fiscal Affairs on 23 April 2010.
171. For the modifications introduced in 2010, *see also* OECD, *The 2010 Update to the Model Tax Convention*, Paris, 22 Jul. 2010 and OECD, *Draft Contents of the 2010 Update to the Model Tax Convention*, Paris, 21 May 2010.
172. *See* para. 26 of OECD CIV Report.
173. *See* para. 24 of the 2017 OECD Commentary on Art. 1.
174. *See* para. 25 of OECD CIV Report.

in the absence of specific provisions, a CIV that is treated merely as a form of joint ownership, and not as a person, under the tax law of the State in which it is established clearly would not constitute a person for purposes of tax treaties.

147   A fund is referred to in OECD CIV Report as a case of so-called joint ownership: unit-holders' investments are managed by a manager on a collective basis and a custodianship arrangement is generally provided with regard to the managed assets. Prima facie, therefore, a clear-cut distinction between a trust and a fund is hard to draw. Both seem to be fundamentally constructed as contractual arrangements, and tax treaty considerations should take this into account. Within the EU, confirmation of such a conclusion comes from EU directives governing UCITS,[175] where funds and trusts are treated at par, from a purely legal standpoint, since in essence, they are the collective management of savings realized by means of contractual relationships.

[b]   *Definition of 'Resident of a Contracting State'*

> For the purposes of this Convention, the term 'resident of a Contracting State' means any person who, under the laws of that State, is liable to tax therein by reason of his domicile, residence, place of management or any other criterion of a similar nature, and also includes that State and any political subdivision or local authority thereof as well as a recognised pension fund of that State.[176] This term, however, does not include any person who is liable to tax in that State in respect only of income from sources in that State or capital situated therein.[177]

148   Once we have ascertained whether we are dealing with a person for treaty purposes, we have to turn to the question of whether such person is liable to tax. Liability to tax implies being liable to comprehensive taxation by reason of various criteria, for example, domicile, residence and the like (any other criterion of a similar nature) that denote a close personal attachment of that person to a certain jurisdiction.

149   OECD Commentary clarifies this very point as follows:[178]

> Paragraph 1 refers to persons who are 'liable to tax' in a Contracting State under its laws by reason of various criteria. In many States, a person is considered liable to comprehensive taxation even if the Contracting State does not in fact impose tax. For example, charities and other organizations may be exempted from tax, but they are exempt only if they meet all of the requirements for exemption specified in the tax laws. They are, thus, subject to the tax laws of a Contracting State. Furthermore, if they do not meet the standards specified, they are also required to pay tax. Most States would view such entities as residents for purposes of the Convention (*see*, for example, paragraph 1 of Article 10 and paragraph 5 of Article 11).

---

175. Undertakings for Collective Investments in Transferable Securities.
176. Expression inserted in 2017. The definition of 'recognized pension fund' is provided by Art. 3(1)(i) of the 2017 OECD Model.
177. *See* Art. 4(1) of the 2017 OECD Model.
178. *See* paras 8.5 and 8.6 of OECD Commentary on Art. 4.

In some states, however, these entities are not considered liable to tax if they are   **150**
exempt from tax under domestic tax laws. These states may not regard such entities as
residents for purposes of a convention unless these entities are expressly covered by
the convention. Contracting States, taking this view, are free to address the issue in
their bilateral negotiations.

OECD Commentary is of most importance with respect to the issue at stake, in   **151**
particular when it deals with CIVs, which could be deemed liable to tax for treaty
purposes although in fact no tax is actually imposed since, provided it meets all
requirements for exemption specified in the law, CIV is exempt.[179] An exemption,
therefore, does not result per se in the person not being liable to tax, to the extent the
exemption is not conceived as a flat or unconditional exemption but is subject to
certain requirements being cumulatively fulfilled (i.e., tax is due if the requirements are
not met).[180]

As pointed out in previous sections, the guidance deriving from the 2007 OECD Report   **152**
was confirmed by the 2017 OECD Model.

With regard to the preferential treatment accorded to REITs by domestic legislation,   **153**
such legislation may, for example, provide for:

(a) exemption at REIT level;
(b) exemption for eligible income only; or
(c) REIT taxation on non-ordinary basis.[181]

It seems that in these cases a REIT may be deemed to be liable to tax within the   **154**
meaning of OECD Model and as clarified in the Commentary. In the cases mentioned
under (a), exemption never takes the form of a flat and unconditional exemption but is
generally accorded only if certain conditions are cumulatively met. With regard to REIT
regimes under (b), it must be noted that the exemption is generally not conceived as a
subjective exemption but rather as an objective one and it is moreover available only
if certain conditions are met. Finally, the cases under (c) pose greater problems than
the two preceding ones. However, they should also lead to REIT having liability to tax
for treaty purposes; however, a case-by-case analysis is necessary to this end (e.g., the
Belgian REIT may be safely considered to be liable to tax; systems like the Greek one
are, conversely, more problematic).

Generally, therefore, REITs qualifying as treaty persons should also be considered to be   **155**
liable to tax for tax treaty purposes in that REIT tax-favourable regimes are generally
applicable only if certain requirements are met and in some cases, they are only applied
to eligible income. In light of the variety of different tax regimes (deduction, exemption,
partial exemption, flow-through, etc.) and the different legal forms, it is difficult to

---

179. *See* para. 26 of the 2017 OECD Commentary on Art. 1.
180. *See* para. 8.11 of the 2017 OECD Commentary on Art. 4.
181. Reference is made to Belgium, which applies ordinary income tax on a special income tax
     basis, and Greece, which applies a special tax, in lieu of income tax, on the net asset value.

draw a definitive and uniform conclusion: each case must be analysed separately in light of the applicable treaty.

[c]   *Recent Developments*

156 The 2017 OECD Model introduced a detailed limitation of benefits (LOB) clause according to which a resident of a Contracting State is not entitled to the benefits of the Convention unless it constitutes a 'qualified person'.

157 The detailed LOB provides for a list of qualified persons that includes also certain CIVs. The 2017 OECD Commentary clarifies that a proper definition of CIV should be included in paragraph 2 of Article 29.[182]

158 Indeed, because the investment decisions of CIVs are typically not dictated by their beneficiaries, these investment vehicles do not raise the same treaty-shopping concerns as entities such as private companies. For that reason, special exceptions to LOB rule have been developed for CIVs.[183]

159 The definition of 'CIV' should be drafted based on how CIVs are treated in the Convention[184] and how they are used and treated in each Contracting State.[185] In this respect, with regard to REITs, the 2017 OECD Commentary refers to the guidance of OECD Report 2007.[186]

160 Moreover, paragraph 14 of Action 6[187] indicated that further work was needed for the issues related to the treaty entitlement of fund vehicles that do not qualify as CIVs within the meaning of OECD CIV Report since it was not possible to reach the same conclusion reached for CIV funds.

161 On 24 March 2016, a public discussion draft dealing with the treaty entitlement of non-CIV funds was released, with commentators invited to suggest new examples to illustrate the application of the Principal Purpose Test (PPT) rule to common types of arrangements or transactions entered into by non-CIV (including REITs not falling under the definition of CIVs) that do not raise treaty-shopping concerns or allow inappropriate granting of treaty benefits.

162 On 22 April 2016, the comments received on the public discussion draft were published on OECD's website. On the basis of these comments, on 6 January 2017 OECD released a new public discussion draft 'Discussion Draft on non-CIV examples', aiming to clarify

---

182. *See* sub-para. g) of the 2017 OECD Commentary on Art. 29.
183. *See* question and answer No. 47 of FAQ – BEPS 2015 Final Report.
184. *See* paras 22–48 of the 2017 OECD Commentary on Art. 1.
185. *See* para. 55, footnote 1, of the 2017 OECD Commentary on Art. 29.
186. *See* para. 55, footnote 2, of the 2017 OECD Commentary on Art. 29.
187. Paragraph 14 of BEPS Action 6 states that 'there is a need to continue to examine issues related to treaty entitlement of non-CIV funds to ensure that the new treaty provisions that are being considered adequately address the treaty entitlement of non-CIV funds [...]'.

the application of PPT rule to CIVs discussed in the examples related to non-CIV funds in paragraph 14 of the Commentary on PPT rule.

On 3 February 2017, OECD published the comments received on the discussion draft **163** from which it seems that the application of PPT rules to non-CIVs still requires further clarification.

Finally, the 2017 OECD Commentary included the example on the application of PPT **164** rule in relation to a real estate fund's investment.[188]

The detailed LOB clause was not included in the Multilateral Instrument (MLI). MLI is **165** a key element for the actual and timely implementation of BEPS project. OECD resolved that MLI was not an appropriate instrument for the implementation of the detailed LOB rule including a definition of 'qualified person'. MLI thus adopted a simplified LOB without expressly including CIVs (and/or REITs) among the definition of 'qualified person'.

Without a provision that automatically qualifies REITs as 'qualified persons', the **166** entitlement of REITs to the Convention must be assessed on the basis of the other provisions of Article 7 of MLI (e.g., the equivalent beneficiaries provision, or the demonstration to the satisfaction of the competent authority that neither the establishment, acquisition or maintenance of REIT in question nor the conduct of its operations had as one of its principal purposes the obtaining of benefits under the Convention).[189]

[d]   Final Remarks

When dealing with vehicles that despite their diverging legal forms are subject to a **167** common (or similar) tax regime, a clear distinction needs to be made conceptually between: (a) the interpretation of the existing wording of OECD Model and (b) the adoption of a treaty policy decision.

This distinction is needed to avoid confusion about the interpretation of treaty terms **168** (these cannot be broadened in some cases and narrowed in other cases) and to secure consistency. It would seem to be very difficult to derive a common treaty regime applicable to corporations, trusts, partnerships and funds simply by the interpretation of the current wording of OECD Model. As a consequence, the starting point should be the acknowledgement of the need for the introduction of a treaty policy requiring the characterization of a REIT as a person (a resident person) in Article 1 or in Article 3.

This approach, obviously, introduces a relevant new principle into the game: that is, **169** the tax regime on the basis of which a vehicle is treated prevails over the legal form of such vehicle.

---

188. *See* para. 182, example M, of the 2017 OECD Commentary on Art. 29.
189. *See* Art. 7, paras 11 and 12, of MLI.

[D]   **Tax Regime Applicable to REIT Distributions**

[1]   Treaty Characterization of REIT Distributions

170   REITs are widely held investment vehicles that: (i) derive income primarily from long-term investments in immovable property and (ii) do not usually pay income taxes on such income (the majority of which must be distributed to the investors) due to tax rules providing for a single level of taxation in the hands of the investors.

171   Domestic laws may characterize REIT distributions to non-resident investors in different ways:

    (a) as dividends;
    (b) as income from immovable property;
    (c) as other types of income (ordinary income or investment income); or
    (d) as income maintaining the characterization of the income derived by REIT (flow-through regimes, under which income is mainly income from immovable property).

172   The issue thus becomes the treaty characterization of the payment, that is the definition of the applicable distributive provision. Articles 6 and 10 are the treaty provisions that most likely will cover REIT distributions. Article 13 (the scope of which is analysed in more detail in the section on capital gains) may become relevant where a flow-through regime applies and capital gains derived by REITs keep such a characterization in the hands of the investors. Article 21 is a catch-all provision and may become applicable where REITs are organized in the form of a trust and the distribution is characterized as a type of income not covered by any other provision of OECD Model.

173   After a brief analysis of the scope of Articles 6 and 10, the specific cases of REITs organized in the form of corporations and of REITs organized in the form of trusts are dealt with in the following sections.

[a]   Scope of Article 6

174   Article 6(1) and 6(2) reads as follows:

    1. Income derived by a resident of a Contracting State from immovable property (including income from agriculture or forestry) situated in the other Contracting State may be taxed in that other State.
    2. The term 'immovable property' shall have the meaning which it has under the law of the Contracting State in which the property in question is situated. The term shall in any case include property accessory to immovable property, livestock and equipment used in agriculture and forestry, rights to which the provisions of general law respecting landed property apply, usufruct of

immovable property and rights to variable or fixed payments as consideration for the working of, or the right to work, mineral deposits, sources and other natural resources; ships, boats and aircraft shall not be regarded as immovable property.

Article 6(1) attributes primary taxation rights to the situs state on income from **175** immovable property. Since 1977, Article 6(1) has a bilateral reach, in that its scope is limited to cases where the person deriving income from immovable property is resident in one Contracting State and the immovable property is situated in the other Contracting State. Hence, the provision is not applicable to income derived from immovable property situated in the residence state or in a third state. The limitation of the scope of Article 6(1) is in line with the other provisions of OECD Model dealing with immovable property, that is Articles 13(1) and 22(1).

The formula chosen by OECD Model to define the term 'immovable property' in Article **176** 6(2) consists of a general renvoi rule supplemented by a specific list of assets and rights, which are either included or excluded from the definition. The general rule, instead of stating the guidelines to be followed in defining immovable property, simply refers the issue to the domestic law of the state in which the property is situated.

REIT distributions may thus fall within the scope of Article 6 in two main cases: **177**

(1) the domestic law under which REIT is organized defines the interest in REIT (shares, quotas, units or rights) as immovable property; or

(2) the domestic law under which REIT is organized characterizes for tax purposes REIT as a mere flow-through vehicle, attributing to the investors the various items of income derived through the vehicle. In this case, income from immovable property derived by REIT may maintain its characterization in the hands of the investors (the treaty characterization also depends on the way in which the state of residence of the investors views REIT, that is, as transparent or non-transparent).[190]

[b]   *Scope of Article 10*

Article 10(1) and 10(2) reads as follows: **178**

1. Dividends paid by a company which is a resident of a Contracting State to a resident of the other Contracting State may be taxed in that other State.
2. However, dividends paid by a company which is a resident of a Contracting State may also be taxed in that State according to the laws of that State, but if the beneficial owner of the dividends is a resident of the other Contracting State, the tax so charged shall not exceed:
   (a) 5 per cent of the gross amount of the dividends if the beneficial owner is a company which holds directly at least 25 per cent of the capital of the

---

190. For more details, *see* OECD Partnership Report, Paris, 1999 (in particular *see* examples, 6, 17 and 18).

company paying the dividends throughout a 365-day period that includes the day of the payment of the dividend (for the purpose of computing that period, no account shall be taken of changes of ownership that would directly result from a corporate reorganisation, such as a merger or divisive reorganisation, of the company that holds the shares or that pays the dividend);

(b) 15 per cent of the gross amount of the dividends in all other cases.

179 Article 10[191] applies to 'dividends' paid by a company which is a resident of a Contracting State to a resident of the other Contracting State. Article 10(2) attributes limited primary taxation rights to the source state (i.e., the State where REIT is organized). Therefore, to fall within the scope of Article 10, a REIT distribution must satisfy the following main requirements:

(a) REIT qualifies as a 'company' according to the treaty definition; and
(b) the distribution falls within the scope of the definition of dividend contained in Article 10(3).

180 Therefore, where REITs organized in the form of trusts or fiduciary and contractual arrangements do not qualify as companies, distributions fall outside the scope of Article 10.

181 The definition of dividends is contained in Article 10(3):

The term dividends as used in this Article means income from shares, 'jouissance' shares or 'jouissance' rights, mining shares, founders' shares or other rights, not being debt-claims participating in profits as well as income from other corporate rights which is subjected to the same taxation treatment as income from shares by the laws of the State of which the company making the distribution is a resident.

182 The definition of the term 'dividend' as used in Article 10 is syntactically divided into three parts:

(1) income from shares, 'jouissance' shares or 'jouissance' rights, mining shares, founder's shares; or
(2) income from other rights, not being debt-claims participating in profit; as well as
(3) income from other corporate rights which is subjected to the same taxation treatment as income from shares by the laws of the State of residence of the distributing company.

---

191. *See* para. 8 of the 2017 OECD Commentary on Art. 10 with respect to the applicability of Art. 10, para. 2 to a dividend paid by a resident company of one State to a shareholder resident of the same State and attributable to a PE that the shareholder has in the other State.

The wording of Article 10(3) outlines the precise relationship between the three parts **183** of the definition:[192]

(a) the use of the expression 'other rights not being debt claim participating in profits' in part (2) implies that: (i) also the examples enumerated in part (1) cannot be debt-claims participating in profit and that (ii) such a limitation is not applicable to part (3);

(b) the expression 'other corporate rights' contained in part (3) makes clear that all the rights covered by the three parts of the definition must be 'corporate rights'; and

(c) the recourse to domestic law applies only to part (3).

The term 'corporate rights' is not defined and thus recourse has to be made to Article **184** 3(2). According to Vogel, the context indicates that corporate rights must entitle the owner not only to a share in the current profit but also (at least) to a share in the liquidation proceeds of the company.[193] The point is to ascertain whether the right of an investor in a trust may be considered to be a corporate right. Certainly, in the case of REITs, such a right usually not only entitles the investor to a share of both ordinary distributions and liquidation proceeds but also grants the investors rights equivalent to those of a corporate shareholder. This is guaranteed by the regulatory provisions that – in countries with the legal forms of both the corporation and the trust – grant the same set of rights to the investors in both types of REIT.

It is unlikely that when the term 'corporate right' was used, reference was also made to **185** rights of a 'unit trust holding'. One should, however, consider that this becomes an interpretational issue only in cases where the trust falls within the definition of 'company'. In these cases, a broad interpretation of the term 'corporate right' seems to be justified.

[2] REITs Organized in the Form of Corporations

In the case of REITs organized in the form of corporations, distributions should fall **186** under the scope of Article 10, and thus be characterized as dividends. Article 10 attributes limited primary taxation rights to the source state (i.e., the state under whose laws REIT is organized).

A particular case may be the one where the interest in REIT is defined by domestic law **187** as immovable property. In such cases distributions – even if made by corporations – seem to fall within the scope of Article 6. Thus, the same item of income may fall within the scope of two distributive provisions (Articles 6 and 10), thus giving rise to a conflict

---

192. *See* Klaus Vogel, *Klaus Vogel on Double Taxation Conventions: A Commentary to the OECD, UN and US Model Conventions for the Avoidance of Double Taxation on Income and Capital: with Particular Reference to German Treaty Practice* (1997), at 649, m.no 185.
193. *See* Klaus Vogel, n. 187, at 650, m.no 188.

of qualification. As a consequence of such conflict of qualification, double taxation arises where, on the one hand, the situs state taxes the income pursuant to the application of Article 6 so that its taxing right is not limited, and, on the other hand, the country of residence of the investor characterizes the income as dividends and gives the relief accordingly (i.e., credit method pursuant to the provision of Article 23A(2)). In such a case, the tax credit method however applies not to the tax liability actually occurred in the source state (due to Article 6) but only to the extent provided in Article 10 (reduced tax rate).

188   A particular case is the one in the UK where REITs are organized in the form of corporations. In this case, distributions by REITs are characterized for tax purposes as income from immovable property, but the shares of REITs are not characterized as immovable property. Thus, UK domestic tax authorities (HMRC) have taken the position that, despite the domestic characterization, the legal characterization of income from shares prevails at the treaty level.

[3]   REITs Organized in the Form of Trusts

189   Where a REIT organized in the form of a trust qualifies as a 'company' under the treaty, there are grounds for the application of Article 10 to trust distributions. This is the position taken by the US (except for the part of distributions relating to capital gains).

190   Article 10 is, however, not applicable to REITs organized in the form of trusts or contractual or fiduciary arrangements falling outside the scope of the definition of 'company'. In such cases, the applicable treaty regime varies depending upon (a) the legal form of REIT and (b) the applicable domestic tax regime. In the case of a flow-through regime, the distribution may retain the characterization of the income derived by REIT. For example, in Australia, the entire income/gains derived by a REIT retain the original characterization in the hands of the investors. In contrast, in Canada, REIT distributions retain the original characterization in the hands of resident investors while they are re-characterized as distribution from a unit trust in the hands of foreign investors (in Canadian treaty practice a distribution by a trust seems to fall within the scope of Article 21). In Mexico, REIT distributions are characterized as income from immovable property; therefore it is likely that in such a case Article 6 applies.

191   In the case of REITs organized in the form of trusts or contractual or fiduciary arrangements, the treaty regime – in accordance with Article 1, paragraph 2, of the 2017 OECD Model – also depends upon the way the country of residence of the investors views the foreign REIT, that is transparent versus opaque. Timing mismatches or even the inapplicability of the relevant treaty may occur.

[4]   *Treaty Policy Considerations*

In light of the different possible legal forms and tax regimes that characterize REITs, **192** many interpretational issues have to be solved to determine which treaty provision is applicable to REIT distributions. In addition, on the basis of the current version of OECD Model, it is difficult to argue that one provision is applicable to all REIT distributions, irrespective of the legal form of REIT. Thus, OECD Report concludes that the only feasible solution is to act at treaty policy level:[194]

> The Working Party therefore went beyond a strict legal analysis based on existing provisions of tax treaties to try to articulate a tax treaty policy that would be generally applicable to REITs.

This conclusion implies the solution of the key policy issue in the case at stake, that is **193** the relevance of the economic purpose of a legal structure versus the relevance of the legal structure itself. OECD has clearly opted in favour of the first one. On the one hand, this position achieves consistency among the treaty regimes applicable to similar investment vehicles, despite their legal form. This is also in line with the approach taken by the relevant authorities for regulatory purposes, in that it would make no sense to subject investment vehicles to different regulatory requirements just because of the legal form.

On the other hand, however, the disregard for the legal form raises the dilemma of **194** drawing the borders between cases that have to be addressed on the basis of the legal structure and cases that deserve a special treaty policy departing from the 'ordinary' approach. A mismanagement of this delicate equilibrium would inevitably jeopardize OECD Model framework of reference, that is its status as a model.

Having taken the decision to draft a uniform treaty regime for REIT distributions, in **195** order to define which is the most appropriate regime to be applied, we must carefully consider whether the treaty characterization may be affected by the following three issues:

(1) the nature of REIT as a widely held (public) investment vehicle;
(2) the immovable property type of income derived by REIT; and
(3) the absence of taxation at the vehicle level.

The most critical aspect of approaching such a dilemma is that the final position taken **196** should not only be consistent with the current treaty policy but also be laying grounds for future policy and interpretational positions. One may wonder whether the time has come to reconsider the structure of OECD Model in light of economic developments, instead of trying to stretch it on a case-by-case basis with the risk of losing the main path.

---

194. *See* para. 20 of OECD Report.

Recently, the OECD adopted the Global Anti-Base Erosion (GloBE) Rules to provide for a coordinated system of taxation intended to ensure large multinational enterprise (MNE) groups pay a minimum level of tax on the income arising in each of the jurisdictions where they operate. The OECD proposal is essentially based on a top-up tax on profits arising in a jurisdiction whenever the effective tax rate, determined on a jurisdictional basis, is below the minimum rate.[195]

In fairly general terms, the GloBE Rules apply to the so-called Constituent Entities that are members of an MNE Group that has annual revenue of EUR 750 million or more in the consolidated financial statements of the ultimate parent entity (as defined by Article 1.4. of GloBE Model Rules; 'UPE') in at least two of the four fiscal years immediately preceding the tested fiscal year.[196] However, there are some Entities that are defined as 'Excluded Entities', which are not subject to the GloBE Rules.[197]

As regards the 'Excluded Entities' the GloBE Rules enclose, *inter alia*, the 'Investment Fund[198] that is an Ultimate Parent Entity'[199] and the 'Real Estate Investment Vehicle[200] that is an Ultimate Parent Entity'.[201]

As clarified by the Commentary to the GloBE Rules, 'As with Investment Funds, a Real Estate Investment Vehicle that is the UPE of an MNE Group is an Excluded Entity [...] While in many cases, these investment vehicles would qualify as Excluded Entities by virtue of being Investment Funds, in certain cases Real Estate Investment Vehicles may not be subject to the necessary regulation or managed by investment fund management professionals to satisfy [...] [certain] requirements terms [...] of the

---

195. OECD (2021), *Tax Challenges Arising from the Digitalisation of the Economy – Global Anti-Base Erosion Model Rules (Pillar Two): Inclusive Framework on BEPS*, OECD, Paris.
196. *Ibid.*, para. 1.1.1., Art. 1.1. Scope of GloBE Rules.
197. *Ibid.*, para. 1.1.3., Art. 1.1. Scope of GloBE Rules.
198. Under the GloBE Rules an Investment Fund is defined as 'an Entity that meets all of the criteria set out in paragraphs (a)–(g) below:
    (a) it is designed to pool assets (which may be financial and non-financial) from a number of investors (some of which are not connected);
    (b) it invests in accordance with a defined investment policy;
    (c) it allows investors to reduce transaction, research, and analytical costs, or to spread risk collectively;
    (d) it is primarily designed to generate investment income or gains, or protection against a particular or general event or outcome;
    (e) investors have a right to return from the assets of the fund or income earned on those assets, based on the contributions made by those investors;
    (f) the Entity or its management is subject to a regulatory regime in the jurisdiction in which it is established or managed (including appropriate anti-money laundering and investor-protection regulation); and
    (g) it is managed by investment fund management professionals on behalf of the investors.'.
199. OECD (2021), *Tax Challenges Arising from the Digitalisation of the Economy – Global Anti-Base Erosion Model Rules (Pillar Two): Inclusive Framework on BEPS*, OECD, Paris, para. 1.5.1. (e), Art. 1.5. Excluded Entity.
200. Under the GloBE Rules a Real Estate Investment Vehicle is defined as 'an Entity the taxation of which achieves a single level of taxation either in its hands or the hands of its interest holders (with at most one year of deferral), provided that that person holds predominantly immovable property and is itself widely held.'.
201. OECD (2021), *Tax Challenges Arising from the Digitalisation of the Economy – Global Anti-Base Erosion Model Rules (Pillar Two): Inclusive Framework on BEPS*, OECD, Paris, para. 1.5.1. (f), Art. 1.5. Excluded Entity.

Investment Fund definition. Accordingly Real Estate Investment Vehicles are also identified under the GloBE Rules as a separate category of Excluded Entity [...].'[202]

In this respect, the EPRA (European Public Real Estate Association) stated that 'EPRA's Public Affairs department together with partner associations in Europe and globally provided expertise to the Pillar Two Rules and the exclusion for REITs comes as just one out of a list of six excluded entities, showcasing the specific understanding the listed real estate industry with its strong REITs sector has achieved among the OECD framework.'[203]

Thus, from the REIT industry standpoint, it will be very important to follow the next developments on the GloBE Rules.

[a]   The Nature of Widely Held (Public) Investment Vehicle

REITs are vehicles in which a person invests in order to derive a flow of income. This **197** is all the more true since most of the REIT regimes require a significant portion of the income to be distributed annually. In a widely held investment vehicle – generally – investors do not have any control over the properties held by the vehicle, nor do they have an influence on the management of the investments. One may argue that – from a financial investment perspective – there is no difference whether a person invests in shares of public companies, in quotas of investment funds, in bonds or in REITs. In all these cases, an investor just expects a financial return on the capital employed.

The argument is certainly financially sound, but it highlights a critical policy issue, that **198** is the relevance of the subjective perspective of taxpayers for the purpose of determining the appropriate treaty regime. Along the same lines, one may thus argue that distributive rules should be revisited to accommodate this new perspective.

[b]   The Immovable Property Type of Income Derived by REITs

It has always been thought that there is a close economic connection between **199** immovable property and the situs state.[204] On the basis of the situs rule, exclusive or primary taxation rights have to be attributed to the situs state on income/gains and on capital relating to immovable property. In all OECD Models and their predecessors, the situs rule is followed in provisions dealing with the taxation of: (i) income from

---

202. OECD (2022), *Tax Challenges Arising from the Digitalisation of the Economy – Commentary to the Global Anti-Base Erosion Model Rules (Pillar Two)*, OECD, Paris, Chapter 10, para. 144.

203. EPRA statement on the exclusion of REITs from Global Anti-Base Erosion (*GloBE*) rules under Pillar Two, Brussels, 21 Dec. 2021.

204. *See*, para. 1 of OECD Commentary on Art. 6, which states: 'para. 1 gives the right to tax income from immovable property to the State of source, that is, the State in which the property producing such income is situated. This is due to the fact that there is always a very close economic connection between the source of this income and the State of source. [...]'. For more details on the situs principle and on its history, *see*, among others, Stefano Simontacchi, *Taxation of Capital Gains under the OECD Model Convention with Special Regard to Immovable Property* (2007), at 201 et seq.

immovable property; (ii) gains derived from the alienation of immovable property and (iii) capital represented by immovable property. Article 5 of OECD Estate and Gift Tax Model also attributes primary taxation rights to the situs state on immovable property forming part of an estate or a gift.

200   The same 2007 OECD Report mentions that:[205]

> The starting point of that policy analysis was that the State in which the immovable property is located should have the primary, unlimited, right to tax that income. This has been a fundamental and consistent feature of provisions based on the OECD Model Tax Convention for a long time and whilst alternative views were briefly discussed, it was quickly concluded that this approach should not be challenged.

> The real policy question, however, is whether a distribution from a REIT should be considered to be income from immovable property or income from investing in a security.

201   In this respect, one cannot ignore that in 2003 OECD introduced Article 13(4), which attributes primary taxation rights to the situs state on gains derived from the alienation of shares deriving more than 50% of their value from immovable property situated in this state. The provision aims at achieving equality in the treaty regimes for the direct and indirect alienation of immovable property. In this sense, Article 13(4) is aimed at applying to gains deriving from the alienation of shares in an immovable property company the same treaty regime that would have been applicable had the underlying immovable property been disposed of. OECD Commentary points out:[206]

> By providing that gains from the alienation of shares deriving more than 50 per cent of their value directly or indirectly from immovable property situated in a Contracting State may be taxed in that State, paragraph 4 provides that gains from the alienation of such shares and gains from the alienation of the underlying immovable property, which are covered by paragraph 1, are equally taxable in that State.

202   Would the, de facto, characterization of shares of immovable property companies as immovable property (for capital gains tax (CGT) purposes) lead to the characterization of REIT distributions as income from immovable property rather than income from other types of investment? The answer seems to be in the negative for the following main reasons:

(a) even if Article 13(4) is drafted as an autonomous distributive provision, the application of which is not limited to abusive situations, there is no doubt that

---

205. *See* para. 21 of OECD REIT Report.
206. *See* para. 28.3 of OECD Commentary on Art. 13. *See also* para. 23 of OECD Commentary on Art. 13.

Article 13(4) has an anti-abuse goal: that is, to prevent rule shopping through the use of legal entities as interposed owners of immovable property;[207] and
(b) the same distributions made by the immovable property companies falling within the scope of Article 13(4) are not re-characterized as income from immovable property but ordinarily, remain within the scope of Article 10.

[c]   *The Absence of Taxation at the Vehicle Level*

The issue here is whether the fact that income distributed from REITs generally has not suffered income taxation at the vehicle level should impact on the applicable treaty regime. In other words, the problem at stake is the limitation of taxation rights of the source state in cases where the source state (i.e., REIT state of residence) did not collect any tax on the income derived by the vehicle. **203**

OECD Report provides the following answer:[208] **204**

> It was noted, however, that there is a fundamental difference between a REIT distribution and other dividends since other dividends represent the after-tax distribution of income that has already been taxed in the country of residence of the company and/or in the country where the profits of that company arose. REIT distributions, on the other hand, represent income that has not been subjected to residence-based taxation at the entity level. To the extent that the treaty treatment of dividends takes account of the corporate level taxation, which seems clear in the case of the lower rate applicable to substantial inter-corporate shareholdings, it could therefore be argued that a different treatment is warranted for REIT distributions. There are, however, other circumstances in which a reduced rate of withholding tax is applied notwithstanding that there is no underlying corporate tax. This would be the case with respect to interest on bonds, which is another type of security where there is no underlying corporate level tax (since interest is deductible) and in respect of which tax treaties generally provide for an even lower rate of tax than that applicable to dividends. REIT distributions are, of course, more of the nature of a return on equity than on debt. Even in the case of dividends, however, the treaty rules applicable to the income from portfolio investment usually provide for lower source taxation than on income from direct investment in immovable property, probably because the most practical, and usual, way of collecting tax from portfolio investment is through a withholding tax on the gross return that does not take account of the investment expenses of the investor (e.g. leverage costs).

There is no doubt that OECD Model also provides for a limitation of the source taxation rights in cases where the income is gross (i.e., not taxed at the source level), as, for example, in the case of interest. In any case, the applicability of Article 10 is not made conditional on a subject-to-tax requirement at the distributing company level, so that **205**

---

207. For more details on the purpose and nature of Art. 13(4), *see* Stefano Simontacchi, *Taxation of Capital Gains under the OECD Model Convention with Special Regard to Immovable Property* (2007), at 318 et seq.
208. *See* para. 25 of OECD Report.

technically – assuming the application of Article 10 is the policy answer – no problems should arise from the absence of effective taxation at the vehicle level.

206   The real policy issue, however, relates to the fact that the income not subject to tax at the vehicle level is income from immovable property and that the source state is, in most cases, the situs state. The consequence of limiting or excluding taxation rights of the source state is that the situs state would not collect income tax on income from immovable property or only collect it to a very limited extent.

[d]   Recent Developments

207   Provisions could be included in a tax treaty in order to deny the application of specific treaty provisions with respect to income benefitting from regimes that satisfy the criteria of a general definition of 'special tax regimes'.[209] In principle, the term 'special tax regime' means any statute, regulation or administrative practice in a Contracting State with respect to a tax[210] that meets specific conditions.[211,212]

208   According to Proposal 1 of BEPS Action 6, 'special tax regime' should not apply to any legislation, regulation or administrative practice:

> vii) that facilitates investment in widely-held entities that hold real property (immovable property), a diversified portfolio of securities, or any combination thereof, and that are subject to investor-protection regulation in the Contracting State in which the investment entity is established.

209   With regard to the application of this exemption to REIT as noted by EPRA[213] in the comments provided for the revised discussion draft on Action 6, if the final version of LOB clause will retain the requirement of the investor-protection regulation, there is the risk that some REITs would not qualify for this exclusion from the definition of special tax regime.

210   The 2017 OECD Commentary argues that the provisions on 'special tax regimes' should not apply to persons the taxation of which achieves a single level of taxation in the hands of either the person or the person's shareholders (with at most one year of deferral) and that hold predominantly immovable property.[214]

211   Among other developments of BEPS project, it is worth mentioning that, on 12 December 2016, OECD released an updated version of Action 4 'Limiting Base Erosion Involving Interest Deductions and Other Financial Payments Action 4 – 2016 Update Inclusive Framework on BEPS', which includes guidance on the design and operation

---

209. *See* para. 85 of the 2017 OECD Commentary on Art. 1.
210. As described by the Contracting States in the given Convention.
211. The conditions are to be defined by the Contracting States in the given Convention.
212. *See* para. 86 of the 2017 OECD Commentary on Art. 1.
213. *See* the comments of EPRA on pp. 133 and 134: http://www.oecd.org/ctp/treaties/public-comments-revised-beps-action-6-follow-up-prevent-treaty-abuse.pdf.
214. *See* para. 86, point (iv), letter D) of the 2017 OECD Commentary on Art. 1.

of the group ratio rule. The updated version contains a further layer of technical detail to assist countries to implement the group ratio rule in line with the common approach without changing the conclusion agreed upon in Final Action 4 of 2015.

Among the target rules provided in Chapter 9, Action 4 proposes the introduction of a   **212** new definition of 'related parties' and 'structured arrangements' for the application of these limitation rules:

> 179. Two persons will be treated as acting together in respect of ownership or control of any voting rights or equity interests if they meet any of the following conditions:[...]
>   The ownership or control of any such rights or interests is managed by the same person or group of persons. In respect of any taxpayer that is a collective investment vehicle (CIV), if the investment manager can establish to the satisfaction of the tax authority from the terms of the investment mandate and the circumstances in which the investment was made that two funds were not acting together in respect of the investment, then the interests held by those funds should not be aggregated under this part of the 'acting together' test.
>
> 180. For these purposes a CIV is any vehicle which is widely held, holds a diversified portfolio of securities and is subject to investor-protection regulation in the country in which it is established. It is left to countries to determine the types of vehicles which would meet this definition. For example, countries may consider certain types of CIVs to be widely held if their shares or units are listed for quotation on a stock exchange or can be readily purchased or sold by the public (i.e., the purchase or sale of shares or units is not implicitly or explicitly restricted to a limited group of investors). However, a country may apply a different test to determine whether a CIV is widely held.

[5]   Changes to the 2008 Commentary Regarding REIT Distributions

As already mentioned, the fundamental question that OECD had to address is whether   **213** income from a REIT should retain its character of income from immovable property (or of capital gains on immovable property), that is the nature of the underlying income, or whether it should instead be deemed to be income from a security (a security having the mixed character of a bond and of a share). OECD took a fairly straightforward and pragmatic approach to the taxation of distributions of REITs: Article 10 should be the applicable provision regardless of the legal form of REIT.

OECD, however, introduces a differentiation between small and large investors. While   **214** a small investor has no control over the immovable property acquired by REIT and cannot be viewed as having made an investment in the underlying immovable property, the case is different for a large investor, which may be properly seen as holding the investment in a REIT as 'a substitute for a direct investment in the underlying property of the REIT'.[215]

---

215. *See* para. 67.3 of OECD Commentary on Art. 10.

215   OECD argues that, from a treaty policy perspective, it is thus fair to treat a small investor as if he had invested in shares and to tax him accordingly: hence, the solution put forward by OECD is that of taxing the small investor as a portfolio equity investor with the consequent attribution of limited taxation rights to the source state.

216   The same does not hold true in the case of a large investor in respect of which, OECD argument goes, the dividend article should not provide any limitation to source (situs) state taxation, thus achieving the same treaty regime that would have been applicable in the case of application of Article 6 or Article 13(1).

217   If OECD countries were to agree with OECD view according to which REIT distributions are covered by Article 10 of OECD Model, then a provision worded along the lines of the one that follows should replace the current Article 10(2) of OECD Model:

> 2. However, such dividends may also be taxed in the Contracting State of which the company paying the dividends is a resident and according to the laws of that State, but if the beneficial owner of the dividends is a resident of the other Contracting State (other than a beneficial owner of dividends paid by a company which is a REIT in which such person holds, directly or indirectly, capital that represents at least 10 per cent of the value of all the capital in that company), the tax so charged shall not exceed:
> (1) 5 per cent of the gross amount of the dividends if the beneficial owner is a company (other than a partnership) which holds directly at least 25 per cent of the capital of the company paying the dividends (other than a paying company that is a REIT);
> (2) 15 per cent of the gross amount of the dividends in all other cases.

218   The provision makes it clear that the limitation to a 15% rate of source taxation applies only to investors holding less than 10% of the capital of a REIT. In the case of interests equal to or higher than 10%, distributions would thus be covered by the first sentence of Article 10(2) with no limitation to source state taxation.

219   OECD Report also states that where the state of residence of the investor applies the exemption method it seems reasonable to apply the credit method to distributions received by small investors and to maintain the exemption method for distributions received by large investors that have suffered unlimited taxation in the source state.[216] A change in the Commentary on Article 23 has also been introduced to take this issue into account.[217]

220   As described in section §1.03[B][2] above, many REIT regimes characterize income distributed by REITs as dividends. Therefore, OECD income characterization for REITs' distributions seems to be in line with the common domestic law characterization. What differs from the domestic characterization is the different treatment provided for the investors based on the participation amount. Indeed, REIT distributions to large investors are characterized as dividends but are de facto treated as income from

---

216. *See* para. 43 of OECD Report.
217. *See* para. 31 of OECD Commentary on Art. 23.

immovable property (i.e., REIT state is not restricted). This difference impacts directly the allocation of taxation rights.

In this respect, the following results arising from the proposed OECD approach can be **221** outlined:

    (a) in both cases (i.e., large investor and small investor) Article 10 applies since income REIT distribution is characterized as dividend for tax treaty purposes;
    (b) in both cases it can be assured that the source state can tax the relevant income;
    (c) in case of REIT distribution to large investors, REIT state is not restricted.

As a consequence, the proposed mechanism seems to be coherent with both single- **222** level taxation and securing taxation rights of the source state. The peculiarity arising from this approach results from the treatment of large investors. In this case, allocation of taxation rights reverses from the country of residence of the investor to the source state so that the taxation of the latest remains unlimited. In other words, dividend payments are liable to unreduced domestic tax rate of the source country.

What the amendments to OECD Commentary fail to address is how the new dividend **223** article in OECD Model should be applied whenever REIT incorporation state applies an eligible income approach, that is only income deriving from certain qualifying activities carried on by REIT benefit from the exemption at REIT level. If this were the case, straightforward application of the new dividend article would lead to excluding altogether from the reduced treaty rate dividends paid by a resident REIT to a large investor notwithstanding the fact that the dividends may have been paid out of fully taxed REIT profits (profits deriving from non-eligible REIT activities). Hence, the ordinary dividend tax treaty provision should be fully applicable in respect of those dividends. However, from the way the new provision is drafted, such differentiation does not seem feasible. It is arguable, however, that it will be up to the Contracting States during treaty negotiations to amend the proposed treaty provision so as to take into account the fact that REIT dividends may be paid either from fully taxed profits or from eligible (and thus generally exempt) profits. For example, Article 11 of the 2008 France-UK treaty makes a distinction (for large investors) between the regime applicable to the distribution of eligible income (attribution of primary taxation rights to the source state) and the regime applicable to the distribution of taxed income (attribution of limited primary taxation rights to the source state).

One may wonder whether the distinction between small and large investors really has **224** sufficient grounds from a tax treaty policy angle. The equation of interests in REITs with investments in immovable property for large investors is highly debatable as, in many cases, decisions of REITs should not likely be influenced by investors possessing more than 10% (where the applicable REIT legislation allows such interest-holding) in the value of REIT capital. Such a view completely disregards the intrinsic value (surrounded in most cases by a consistent regulatory framework) of the role of the management of collective investment vehicles. OECD is aware of these criticisms and expressly allows member countries to vary such a percentage on a bilateral basis during treaty negotiations (along the same lines OECD countries may wish to distinguish among distributions whenever national legislation provides for rules discerning distributions of rental income and distributions of REIT capital gains).[218]

225   The Commentary acknowledges that the new provision would leave out of its scope 'distributions' made by REITs that do not qualify as a resident of a Contracting State for not being liable to tax by reason of domicile, residence or any other similar criteria attracting worldwide taxation. In such a case the proposed dividend article should be amended as follows:[219]

(1) Dividends paid by a company which is a resident, or a REIT organized under the laws, of a Contracting State to a resident of the other Contracting State may be taxed in that other State.

(2) However, such dividends may also be taxed in, and according to the laws of, the Contracting State of which the company paying the dividends is a resident or, in the case of a REIT, under the laws of which it has been organized, but if the beneficial owner of the dividends is a resident of the other Contracting State (other than a beneficial owner of dividends paid by a company which is a REIT in which such person holds, directly or indirectly, capital that represents at least 10% of the value of all the capital in that company), the tax so charged shall not exceed:

(a) 5% of the gross amount of the dividends if the beneficial owner is a company (other than a partnership) which holds directly at least 25% of the capital of the company paying the dividends (other than a paying company that is a REIT).

(b) 15% of the gross amount of the dividends in all other cases.

226   The Commentary also suggests a new provision to be added to Article 10(2) to also cover REITs organized in the form of a trust or of contractual or fiduciary arrangement that cannot be subsumed under OECD Model definition of company:[220]

> For the purposes of this Convention, where a REIT organized under the laws of a Contracting State makes a distribution of income to a resident of the other Contracting State who is the beneficial owner of that distribution, the distribution of that income shall be treated as a dividend paid by a company resident of the first-mentioned State.

> Under this additional provision, the relevant distribution would be treated as a dividend and not, therefore, as another type of income (e.g. income from immovable property or capital gain) for the purposes of applying Article 10 and the other Articles of the Convention. Clearly, however, that would not change the characterization of that distribution for purposes of domestic law so that domestic law

---

218. *See* para. 67.4 of OECD Commentary on Art. 10.
219. *See* para. 67.6 of OECD Commentary on Art. 10.
220. *See* para. 67.7 of OECD Commentary on Art. 10.

treatment would not be affected except for the purposes of applying the limitations imposed by the relevant provisions of the Convention.

[E]   Capital Gains Derived from the Disposal of Interests in REITs

Cross-border gains derived from the alienation of interests in REITs are generally taxed **227** by both the state of residence of the investor and the state under whose laws REIT is organized. These gains fall within the scope of Article 13. In theory, gains derived from the alienation of interests in REITs may be covered by Article 13(1), Article 13(4) or Article 13(5).[221] While both Article 13(1) and Article 13(4) attribute primary taxation rights to the situs state, Article 13(5) attributes exclusive taxation rights to the residence state.

[1]   Article 13(1)

Article 13(1) reads as follows: **228**

> Article 13(1)
>
> Gains derived by a resident of a Contracting State from the alienation of immovable property referred to in Article 6 and situated in the other Contracting State may be taxed in that other State.

The scope of Article 13(1) is limited to gains derived from the alienation of immovable **229** property 'referred to in Article 6'. Article 6(2) provides:

> Article 6(2)
>
> The term 'immovable property' shall have the meaning which it has under the law of the Contracting State in which the property in question is situated. … .

As already mentioned in section §1.04[D][1][a] above, the formula chosen by OECD **230** Model to define the term 'immovable property' consists of a general renvoi rule supplemented by a specific list of assets and rights, which are either included or excluded from the definition. The general rule, instead of providing the guidelines to be followed in defining immovable property, simply refers the issue to the domestic law of the state in which the property is situated. Recourse to the domestic law of the situs state is, however, limited by the second part of Article 6(2): that is, independently of what may be determined by domestic law of the situs state, Article 6(2) provides:

   (a) a list of assets and rights that must be regarded as immovable property (hereinafter 'the positive list'); and

---

221. The applicability of Art. 13(5) instead of Art. 21 to gains outside the bilateral reach of Art. 13(1) is analysed in detail in Stefano Simontacchi, *Taxation of Capital Gains under the OECD Model Convention. With Special Regard to Immovable Property* (2007), at 206 et seq.

(b) a list of assets that must not be regarded as immovable property (hereinafter 'the negative list').

231 Article 13(1) may thus turn out to be applicable to gains derived from the alienation of interests in REITs where: (i) REIT is organized in a non-corporate form and as a consequence of a flow-through regime REIT is viewed as transparent by the state of residence of the investors and (ii) the interest in REIT is defined as immovable property.

232 The case under (i) may become rather complex where REIT has investments in different states, thus giving rise to the possible application of multiple treaties for the same gain.

233 In cases where the interest in REIT is defined as immovable property, the relevant interpretational issue becomes the definition of the state where the property is situated. In fact, to define immovable property, Article 6(2) refers to the law of the state where the property is 'situated'. Neither Article 6 nor OECD Model, however, defines what the term 'situated' means, that is when an asset may be considered situated in a certain state. In the absence of a definition, Article 3(2) is applicable and, thus, the term will have the meaning that it has under the law of the state applying the treaty, unless the context otherwise requires. In this case, the problem then becomes to ascertain whether the context appears to be sufficiently defined so as not to allow any leeway for applying domestic rules.

234 In relation to immovable property physically connected to the soil and non-movable, the meaning of the term 'situated' can only be the indication of the place where such property is physically located, thus not allowing any leeway for applying domestic rules. Nevertheless, difficulties may arise in the case of property that, even though defined as immovable property by Article 6(2), is: (i) physically movable from one place to another or (ii) intangible. This, for example, is the case for property accessory to immovable property and of rights connected to immovable property. Where such types of immovable property are situated must then be ascertained. In particular, the following problems have to be addressed: (i) the definition of where movable or intangible property is situated and (ii) the definition of the moment at which the place where the property is 'situated' has to be determined.

235 A difficult case is the one of property the definition of which as immovable property depends on the renvoi to the law of the situs state. Article 6(2) provides that such property is immovable property if it is so defined by the law of the Contracting State where the property is situated.[222] Thus, in such cases, the term 'situated' has to first be defined to determine the applicable law; this will then determine whether the property is immovable property or not. If two states claim that the property is situated therein,

---

222. The same should apply with regard to 'rights to which the provisions of general law respecting landed property apply' since it seems reasonable to assume that the reference is intended to be to the general law of the situs state.

a conflict of laws in the definition of the property may come into existence. The following may clarify the issue.

Mr Alpha, resident of R State, owns some units of Beta, a REIT organized under the **236** laws of R State in the form of a trust and investing in immovable property situated in S State. The following figure illustrates this scenario:

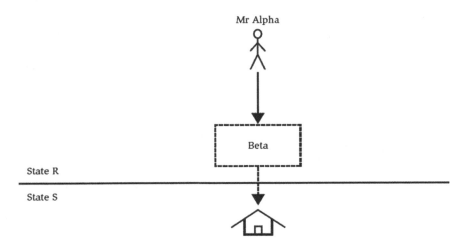

Two alternative situations may be considered: **237**

(1) both states consider the asset as situated therein, but only one state considers the asset to be immovable property:
   – the domestic law of R State defines the fund units in Beta as movable property situated in R State (the state under whose law Beta has been organized); and
   – the domestic law of S State defines the fund units in Beta as immovable property situated in S State (the state where the underlying immovable property is situated); or

(2) both states define the asset as an immovable property situated therein:
   – the domestic law of R State defines the fund units in Beta as an immovable property situated in R State (the state under whose law Beta has been organized); and
   – the domestic law of S State defines the fund units in Beta as immovable property situated in S State (the state where the underlying immovable property is situated).

This example demonstrates that two possible conflicts may arise; the first one relates to **238** the definition of immovable property, and the second one relates to the determination of the situs state. Given the fact that 'situated' is an undefined term, Article 3(2) is applicable. It is, however, worth noting that if recourse has to be systematically made to the domestic laws of the state applying the treaty, the rationale for Article 6(2) would disappear. Such a consideration constitutes a crucial aspect of the context, which would limit the adoption of domestic law definitions. If the property is bound to physically immovable property, then the conclusion in the previous section remains applicable, in that the context should lead one to conclude that the property is situated where the related physically immovable property is situated. In the other cases, the positive and negative lists in Article 6(2) may serve as a guideline for the definition of immovable property. In the limited cases where the context does not provide a clear indication, then the definition provided in the law of the state applying the treaty should be used. Paragraphs 32.132.7 of OECD Commentary on Article 23 aim to solve exactly the type of conflicts of characterization outlined under (1) and (2): that is, conflicts arising from differences in the domestic laws.[223] Paragraph 32.3 reads as follows:

> Where, due to differences in the domestic law between the State of source and the State of residence, the former applies, with respect to a particular item of income or capital, provisions of the Convention that are different from those that the State of residence would have applied to the same item of income or capital, the income is still being taxed in accordance with the provisions of the Convention, as interpreted and applied by the State of source. In such a case, therefore, the two Articles require that relief from double taxation be granted by the State of residence notwithstanding the conflict of qualification resulting from these differences in domestic law.

[2]   Article 13(4)

[a]   Purpose and Nature of Article 13(4)

239   The 2003 OECD Model has introduced an entirely new paragraph in Article 13, which deals with the alienation of shares deriving more than 50% of their value from immovable property situated in a Contracting State:

> Article 13(4)
>
> Gains derived by a resident of a Contracting State from the alienation of shares deriving more than 50 per cent or their value directly or indirectly from immovable property situated in the other Contracting State may be taxed in that other State.

---

223. Paragraph 32.5 of OECD Commentary on Art. 23, after having given an example, reads as follows:

> Such conflicts resulting from different interpretation of facts or different interpretation of the provisions of the Convention must be distinguished from the conflicts of qualification described in the above paragraph where the divergence is based not on different interpretations of the provisions of the Convention but on different provisions of domestic law.

Immovable property company provisions[224] are found in several of the model conven-   **240**
tions drafted before the 2003 amendment of OECD Model: the 1980 and 2001 UN
Models, the 1981 and 2006 US Models and the 1987 Intra-Asian Model. In addition, a
large number of the treaties currently in force include an immovable property company
provision.

Article 13(4) attributes primary taxation rights to the situs state on gains derived from   **241**
the alienation of shares deriving more than 50% of their value from immovable
property situated in this state. The attribution of taxation rights provided for in Article
13(4) is not in any way connected to the existence of an immovable property provision
in the law of the state where the immovable property is situated. Hence, states that tax
capital gains derived by non-resident persons from the alienation of shares in companies (for whatever reason) will no longer be prevented from taxing such gains by
Article 13(5) if the alienated shares derive more than 50% of their value from
immovable property situated in their territory. Thus, the provision in question clearly
goes beyond merely solving a possible conflict of interpretation where there are
domestic anti-abuse sourcing rules.

As already mentioned in section §1.04[D][4][a] above, the provision aims at achieving   **242**
equality in the treaty regimes for the direct and indirect alienation of immovable
property; that is, Article 13(4) is aimed at applying to gains deriving from the alienation
of shares in an immovable property company the same treaty regime that would have
been applicable had the underlying immovable property been disposed of. OECD
Commentary points out:[225]

> By providing that gains from the alienation of shares deriving more than 50 per
> cent of their value directly or indirectly from immovable property situated in a
> Contracting State may be taxed in that State, paragraph 4 provides that gains from
> the alienation of such shares and gains from the alienation of the underlying
> immovable property, which are covered by paragraph 1, are equally taxable in that
> State.

Article 13(4) stems from the domestic sourcing provisions in force in a number of states   **243**
and from the related treaty practice, which is also reflected in several of the model
conventions other than OECD Model. In each case, immovable property company
provisions have an anti-abuse aim. Article 13(4) clearly has an anti-abuse goal: that is,
to prevent rule shopping through the use of legal entities as interposed owners of
immovable property. The 1989 OECD Tax Treaty Override Report, in commenting on
similar (domestic) provisions, confirms this by stating that 'the overriding measure is

---

224. Companies the shares of which derive more than 50% of their value directly or indirectly from
     immovable property (or, as the case may be, fulfil a comparable requirement in a treaty or
     domestic provision) will be referred to as 'immovable property companies'. Domestic and
     treaty provisions similar to Art. 13(4) will be referred to as 'immovable property company
     provisions'.
225. *See* para. 28.3 of OECD Commentary on Art. 13. *See also* para. 23 of OECD Commentary on Art.
     13.

clearly designed to put an end to the improper use of its tax treaties'.[226] In light of the above, one may say the following:

(a) the introduction of Article 13(4) in OECD Model was targeted at preventing a rule-shopping tax planning tool that had already been addressed by a number of states in their treaty practice;

(b) the purpose of Article 13(4) is to put the alienation of shares in immovable property companies and the alienation of the underlying immovable property on an equal footing, from a treaty regime perspective; and

(c) Article 13(4) is drafted as an autonomous distributive provision, the application of which is not limited to abusive situations (i.e., an assessment of the abusive intent of the transactions is not a requirement for application of the provision).

[b]   *Applicability of Article 13(4) to Disposals of Interests in REITs*

244   In the case of REITs organized in the form of corporations the conditions for the application of Article 13(4) are generally met and, thus, primary taxation rights are attributed to the situs state, this being the state where the relevant property is situated (in most of the cases this is the state under whose laws REIT is organized).

245   In this respect some issues arise, which are also discussed by OECD Report:

(a) the scope of Article 13(4) is confined to the alienation of shares;

(b) no difference is made between small and large investors;

(c) a double exemption may arise from the application of Article 13(4).

246   The following sections analyse these issues and some other relevant issues concerning Article 13(4).

247   Article 13(4) was significantly amended in the 2017 OECD Model in order to address issues deriving solely from the provision introduced in 2003. Most of the DTAs currently in force are based on previous versions of OECD Model.[227] The following sections first analyse the 2003 version of the provision, with a specific section then dealing with the 2017 provision.

[i]   Scope: Gains Derived from Alienation of Shares

248   The scope of Article 13(4) is limited to gains derived from the alienation of shares having certain characteristics (i.e., deriving more than 50% of their value from immovable property situated in a Contracting State). The context appears to be

---

226. *See* OECD, *Tax Treaty Override*, Paris (1989), para. 32.
227. However, Art. 9 of MLI resembles Art. 13(4) of the 2017 OECD Model.

sufficiently defined so as not to allow any leeway for applying domestic rules on the definition of 'shares'. In fact, the term 'shares' is also used by Article 10(3) of OECD Model. Moreover, OECD Commentary thereon clearly states that 'shares' means 'holdings in a company limited by shares (joint-stock company)'.

From the above, it follows that the scope of Article 13(4) does not encompass: (i) **249** interests in entities other than joint-stock companies or (ii) interests in joint-stock companies other than shares.

[ii]   Exclusion of Interests in Other Entities

Confirmation of the fact that 'shares' have to be interpreted narrowly can be gleaned **250** from OECD Commentary on Article 13(4). It discusses a broad version of the provision for states wanting to extend the rule to interests in 'other entities, such as partnerships or trusts' deriving their value from immovable property:[228]

> Gains derived by a resident of a Contracting State from the alienation of shares or comparable interests deriving more than 50 per cent of their value directly or indirectly from immovable property situated in the other Contracting State may be taxed in that other State.

In the case of application of Article 13(4) to REITs organized in the form of corpora- **251** tions, no valid reason seems to be capable of being invoked not to apply the same provision to REITs organized in other forms as well. In this respect, the alternative wording for Article 13(4) proposed by OECD Commentary in order to broaden its scope seems to be too restrictive to achieve the aims set out by the same Commentary. The use of the term 'comparable interest' significantly limits the scope of the provision and will very likely generate conflicts of interpretation. For example, it is questionable whether an interest in a trust is 'comparable' to a share in a joint-stock company. It would have been preferable to use either a narrower definition of the type of interest covered by the provision or a more general reference such as 'interest in other entities'. The immovable property company provisions in the 2001 UN Model and in the 1981 and 2006 US Models also cover gains derived from the alienation of interests in entities such as partnerships, trusts or estates. Also, in the treaty practice of states where REITs are (or at least can be) organized in the form of partnerships or trusts, the scope of the immovable property company provisions frequently includes gains derived from the alienation of interests in these other types of entities.

[iii]   Exclusion of Other Interests in Joint-Stock Companies

A share representing a portion of the capital is not the only interest an investor may **252** hold in a joint-stock company. As a consequence, the alienation of any other interest in

---

228. *See* para. 28.5 of OECD Commentary on Art. 13(4).

an immovable property joint-stock company falls outside the scope of Article 13(4). This holds, for example, for gains derived from the alienation of a silent partnership right, the alienation of a profit-participating loan, or the alienation of other hybrid instruments related to an immovable property company that may entitle the owner to rights similar to a shareholder's rights. These gains are, then, covered by Article 13(5), which attributes exclusive taxation rights to the residence state; that is, the situs state is prevented from taxing the gains. It is also questionable whether Article 13(4) covers the alienation of part of the rights relating to the shares, such as usufruct, bare ownership or the right to subscribe to an increase of capital of the company. Another issue concerns the alienation of contractual rights related to the shares, such as an option to purchase the shares for a certain price. In fact, the value of the option is economically dependent on the relationship between the strike price and the value of the shares.

253 Under the domestic law of certain countries, gains derived from the alienation of an interest other than a share in an immovable property company may give rise to taxation. For example, under US law, non-resident persons are subject to tax on gains derived from the alienation of any interest (other than as a creditor) in an immovable property holding company.[229] The US has a treaty practice that does not prevent the application of such provisions. By referring to domestic law for the definition of the scope of the provision, the 2006 US Model avoids any possibility of conflict. Only a few Canadian treaties take this issue into account. They alternatively refer to 'shares or comparable interest' or to 'shares or other rights'.[230]

[iv]   Absence of a Minimum Threshold

254 Article 13(4) applies even to the alienation of a single share representing a minuscule portion of the capital of the immovable property company. Thus, for purposes of Article 13, any share in an immovable property company is, de facto, characterized as a fraction of the underlying immovable property and, thus, primary taxation rights on gains derived from its alienation are attributed to the situs state. This kind of approach may penalize transactions and structures that have not been set up to circumvent the treaty regime applicable to the alienation of immovable property. The following illustrates this: an individual investor resident in R State who: (i) purchases a few shares in a large company (e.g., the shares of which are listed on a stock exchange) deriving more than 50% of their value from immovable property situated in S State and (ii) subsequently sells these shares and derives a gain. It is disputable whether applying a treaty regime similar to the one for the alienation of the underlying immovable property to such a gain is in line with the anti-abuse origin of Article 13(4). OECD Commentary seems to acknowledge the issue related to the broad scope of the provision on two occasions: (i) when it leaves the door open to the restriction of Article

---

229. *See* I.R.C. s. 897(c)(1)(A)(ii).
230. *See, e.g.*, the following treaties: Art. 13(1)(b) of Canada France (1975); and Art. 13(1)(b) of Canada-Papua New Guinea (1987).

13(4) to cases where the alienated shareholding does not exceed certain thresholds,[231] and (ii) when it points out that states are free to exclude from the scope of Article 13(4) gains derived from the alienation of shares of companies that are listed on an approved stock exchange of one of the Contracting States.[232]

In the aggregate, with regard to the alienation of shares, OECD Commentary, since the **255** introduction of Article 13(4), considers (among other things)[233] the following possible limitation to the provision's scope:

> (1) *non-substantial shareholdings.* Paragraph 28.6 of the OECD Commentary on Article 13(4) points out that:
>
> ... Another change that some States may agree to make is to restrict the application of the provision to cases where the alienator holds a certain level of participation in the entity.

The anti-avoidance origin of the provision requires that the taxpayer plays an active **256** role in the re-characterization of the transaction in question. A non-substantial shareholder is, after all, likely to be a passive investor who did not participate in the structure from which he is nonetheless benefiting. In addition, the idea that the alienation of shares by a non-substantial investor amounts to an alienation of the underlying immovable property is debatable. In brief, the dilemma that the Contracting States have to solve is whether the benefit of the rule-shopping structure has to be disregarded as such, or whether Article 13(4) should aim at hitting only taxpayers who have more likely played an active role in the structuring and/or whose participations more effectively represent the underlying immovable property. Neither US law nor Canadian law limits the immovable property company provision to substantial shareholdings as such. However, even though none of the model conventions limits the scope of the immovable property company provision to the alienation of substantial shareholdings, certain treaties have restricted the scope of the immovable property company provision on this point:[234]

> (1) *listed shares.* The OECD Commentary on Article 13(4) provides:[235]
>
> Also, some States consider that the paragraph should not apply to gains derived from the alienation of shares of companies that are listed on an approved stock exchange of one of the States. ... .

The reason for the exception for listed shares clearly lies: (i) in the unlikelihood that **257** listed companies were set up to avoid taxation in the situs state through an indirect alienation planning tool and (ii) in the certainty that this is not the case for non-substantial investors who buy and sell shares on the stock exchange. In this respect,

---

231. *See* para. 28.6 of OECD Commentary on Art. 13.
232. *See* para. 28.7 of OECD Commentary on Art. 13.
233. The Commentary also makes reference to corporate reorganizations and to investments made by pension funds.
234. *See, e.g.,* many of the treaties concluded by Canada.
235. *See* para. 28.7 of OECD Commentary on Art. 13.

the exception could be limited to investors that do not exceed a certain threshold of participation (i.e., a level that would allow them to influence the business decisions of the company).

258   The limitation of the exception to shares listed on an approved stock exchange of a Contracting State seems inconsistent with the structure of Article 13(4), which does not require the immovable property company to be resident in a Contracting State. It thus would have been preferable to refer to approved stock exchanges of whichever state. For example, both US and *Canadian* domestic laws contain an exception providing for the non-taxability of gains derived from the alienation of shares of immovable property companies that are listed on an approved stock exchange (including foreign stock exchanges) unless certain thresholds of participation are exceeded. Several treaties exclude gains derived from the alienation of listed shares from Article 13(4), albeit none of the model conventions do.[236]

[v]   2017 OECD Model

259   The new version of OECD Model released in November 2017 provides for a new wording of Article 13(4):

> Gains derived by a resident of a Contracting State from the alienation of shares or comparable interests, such as interests in a partnership or trust, may be taxed in the other Contracting State if, at any time during the 365 days preceding the alienation, these shares or comparable interests derived more than 50 per cent of their value directly or indirectly from immovable property, as defined in Article 6, situated in that other State.

260   This new wording provides for:

> (a) a broader scope of the provision covering also 'comparable interests such as interests in partnership or trust';
> (b) an anti-abuse clause, covering also situations where, at the time of the sale of the interests, the prevalence of the value of the immovable properties is not met. Indeed, as outlined by paragraph 28.5 of the 2017 OECD Commentary, 'this change was made in order to address situations where assets are contributed to an entity shortly before the sale of the shares or other comparable interests in that entity in order to dilute the proportion of the value of these shares or interests that is derived from immovable property situated in a Contracting State'.

261   From the above, it follows that Article 13(4) extends its scope to cover also: (i) gains from the alienation of interests in other entities, such as partnerships or trusts, that did

---

236. *See, e.g.*, many treaties concluded by Canada and many of the other treaties containing an immovable property company provision.

not issue shares, as long as the value of those interests was derived principally from immovable property; and (ii) situations where the shares or comparable interests derive their value primarily from immovable property at any time during the 365 days preceding the alienation as opposed to at the time of the alienation only.

In any case, OECD points out that Contracting States are free to negotiate broader or narrow clauses regarding Article 13(4).[237]   **262**

[vi] 2007 OECD Report

Following the recommendations of OECD Report, the 2008 Commentary introduced the following new paragraphs, as amended by the 2017 OECD Commentary,[238] to address the case of interests in REITs: **263**

(1) Finally, a further possible exception relates to shares and comparable interests in a REIT (*see* paragraphs 67.1–67.7 of the Commentary on Article 10 for background information on REITs). While it would not seem appropriate to make an exception to paragraph 4 in the case of the alienation of a large investor's interests in a REIT, which could be considered to be the alienation of a substitute for a direct investment in immovable property, an exception to paragraph 4 for the alienation of a small investor's interest in a REIT may be considered to be appropriate.

(2) As discussed in paragraph 67.3 of the Commentary on Article 10, it may be appropriate to consider a small investor's interest in a REIT as a security rather than as an indirect holding in immovable property. In this regard, in practice, it would be very difficult to administer the application of source taxation of gains on small interests in a widely held REIT. Moreover, since REITs, unlike other entities deriving their value primarily from immovable property, are required to distribute most of their profits, it is unlikely that there would be significant residual profits to which the capital gain tax would apply (as compared to other entities). States that share this view may agree bilaterally to add, before the phrase 'may be taxed in that other State', words such as 'except shares or comparable interests held by a person who holds, directly or indirectly, shares or interests representing less than 10 per cent of all the shares or interests in an entity if that entity is a REIT'.

(3) Some States, however, consider that Article 13, paragraph 4 of the 2017 OECD Model was intended to apply to any gain on the alienation of shares or similar interests in an entity that derives its value primarily from immovable property and that there would be no reason to distinguish between a REIT and a publicly held entity with respect to the application of that paragraph, especially since a REIT is not taxed on its income. These States consider that as

---

237. *See* para. 28.6 of the 2017 OECD Commentary on Art. 13.
238. *See* paras 28.10, 28.11 and 28.12 of the 2017 OECD Commentary on Art. 13(4).

long as there is no exception for the alienation of shares or similar interests in entities listed on a stock exchange (*see* paragraph 28.7 of 2017 OECD Commentary), there should not be a special exception for interests in a REIT.

264 As outlined by OECD Report, no general consensus was reached in the Working Party about the application of Article 13(4) to REITs and, in particular, about the distinction between small and large investors. OECD had already argued in favour of such a differentiation in the case of distributions (different thresholds for source taxation in Article 10). This does not, however, automatically imply that the same reasoning also holds with reference to Article 13(4). Indeed, when Article 13(4) was introduced a clear position was taken with reference to the applicability of the provision: (i) to small investors and (ii) to listed companies. Consistency is needed in the position on these issues; that is, there do not seem to be enough grounds to differentiate REITs from other types of immovable property companies.

[c]   *Direct or Indirect Derivation of Value*

265 REITs are generally allowed to invest in interests in companies/entities characterized by an immovable property business. One of the issues that come into play to ascertain the applicability of Article 13(4) is the definition of the immovable property that is relevant for the value test. The provision makes clear that indirect derivation of value is also relevant.

266 Inclusion of the indirect derivation of value from immovable property is consistent with the anti-abuse origin of the provision. Indeed, in the absence of this addition, it would have been easy to circumvent the application of Article 13(4) by interposing a company between the shareholder and the company owning the immovable property. The most renowned example of the crucial role of the 'indirect' derivation of value can be found in the Australian *Lamesa* case,[239] where the interposition of a company between the foreign shareholder and an Australian immovable property company allowed the gains derived by the foreign shareholder to fall outside the scope of the immovable property company provision in the Australia-Netherlands treaty.

267 Clearly, the provision's broad coverage has an impact on how the requirement relating to the value of the shares is determined in practice. The valuation may be particularly complicated in the case of an alienation of shares of a top holding with a chain of subsidiaries resident in different states. OECD Commentary does not provide any guidance with regard to the method to be applied in taking into account an indirect derivation of value. Nevertheless, in the absence of any further guidance, the only feasible solution seems to consist of a two-step process (hereinafter 'proportional consolidation'):

---

239. *See Federal Commissioner of Taxation v. Lamesa Holdings BV* (1997), 77, F.C.R., 597. For comments, *see*, among others, R. Vann, [2005], at 144 et seq.; M. Kobetsky, [2005], at 236 et seq.; I.V. Gzell, [1998], at 528 et seq.; R. Krever & J. Chang, [1997], at 1187 et seq.

(a) a proportional consolidation of all the companies (entities) involved in the company the shares of which are alienated (following the accounting standards for drafting a consolidated balance sheet); and

(b) the determination of the properties from which the shares derive their value on the basis of the consolidated situation mentioned under (a).

Under such an approach: (a) the value of the properties owned by the various **268** companies (or entities) in which a participation is held is attributed proportionately to the shares alienated with respect to the level of participation, and (b) all the rules and exceptions applicable in order to verify the fulfilment of the condition are applied with regard to all the companies (entities) involved. From a practical standpoint, the process is far from simple and may very well create conflicts of interpretation. This is particularly true for the consolidation process, which also takes into account non-recorded properties and which must be based on the market value of the properties. The process may be further complicated where the standard accounting principles to be applied are not the same in the Contracting States.

Taking into account value indirectly derived from non-substantial participations is an **269** interesting point and warrants further discussion. For example, if directly or indirectly a company has a 1% investment in another company, should the property of the latter company be taken into account? In light of: (i) the purpose of the provision being discussed and (ii) the complexity of a consolidation process, the answer is that a non-substantial participation may be considered to be movable property, regardless of the nature of the underlying property.

As an alternative to the solution chosen by OECD Model, the loophole concerning the **270** indirect derivation of value may be closed by defining the shares of an immovable property company (or interest in other entities) as immovable property situated where the relevant property is situated. This is, for example, the solution incorporated in the 1981 US Model and in some treaties.[240] In the case of a two-tier group, the process (hereinafter 'separate determination') should thus consist of the following two steps:

(1) applying the value test separately to each of the subsidiaries (or entities in which a participation is held); and

(2) application of the value test at the holding company level (whose shares are being alienated) by considering the market value of the participations held in the subsidiaries (or entities) either as movable property (if the entity did not meet the value test under (1)) or as immovable property (if the entity did meet the value test under (2)).

---

240. Article XIII of the 1976 Canada-Spain treaty – after providing that gains from the disposal of shares in an immovable property company and interest in an immovable property partnership or trust may be taxed in the situs state – includes for the first time a provision intending to serve as a 'loophole closer', which defines as 'immovable property' for the purpose of the paragraph the same shares of an immovable property company (and interests in an immovable property partnership or trust). *See also* D.G. Broadhurst, [1978], at 322 et seq.

271   In the case of multi-tier groups, the above-mentioned steps have to be performed tier by tier. There are also intermediate solutions that use both methods. For example, US law provides, on the one hand, for a proportional consolidation for controlled companies and for interests in partnerships, trusts and estates, while, on the other hand, it provides for the separate determination for non-controlled companies.[241]

272   As already mentioned, the indirect derivation of value is provided for by Article 13(4) to prevent the use of avoidance structures by the interposition of a company between the immovable property company and the owner of the shares. This having been said, one should not forget that the other side of the coin is that Article 13(4) may lead to a multiple attribution of taxation rights to the situs state where: (i) the company owning the relevant immovable property is controlled through a chain of companies, each of which controls one of the others; and (ii) more than one company in the chain satisfies the requirement of Article 13(4) of the relevant treaty with the situs state, as the result of the control of the immovable property company. In such cases, gains derived by the alienation of the shares in each company of the chain satisfying the requirement would be taxable in the situs state.

   [d]   *Compatibility of the Value Test with the Purpose of the Provision*

273   The attention paid by OECD to REITs and to the applicability of Article 13(4) to gains derived from the alienation of interests in REITs may represent a good opportunity for OECD to revise the value test, which seems to be inconsistent with the purpose of the provision.

274   Article 13(4) – and thus the equation of the treaty regime applicable to direct and indirect alienations of immovable property – applies if the shares being alienated derive more than 50% of their value from immovable property situated in a Contracting State. Article 13(4) postulates the following:

   if a company mainly derives its value from immovable property situated in a certain state, then:

   (a)   the alienation of the shares of the company amounts, de facto, to an alienation of the underlying property; and
   (b)   gains derived from such an alienation are mainly attributable to the immovable property situated in that state.

275   Consequently, the provision attributes primary taxation rights on gains derived from the alienation of the shares to the state where the relevant immovable property is situated (since it considers that such gains are sourced there). It is thus necessary to ascertain whether the value test is an economic indicator appropriate to achieve the aim of this provision. The consistency of the value test with the purpose of Article 13(4)

---

241. *See* s. 897(c)(4) and s. 897(c)(5).

must be analysed at two different levels: (i) requirements for its application and (ii) the attribution of taxation rights.

The fundamental principle underlying the entire OECD Model is that the attribution of taxation rights stems from the substantive economic nexus of the income or capital. At first sight, the value of property would thus not appear to be the appropriate economic factor for the attribution of taxation rights in the context of capital gains taxation. In fact, a value test would seem more appropriate for taxes on capital than for capital gains taxation. Where gains are derived from the alienation of shares in an immovable property company, the attribution of primary taxation rights to the situs state is consistent with the purpose of the provision only to the extent that such gains reflect unrealized gains on immovable property situated in the situs state, that is gains that would have fallen under Article 13(1) in the event of the direct alienation of the property. From an anti-abuse standpoint, 'rule shopping' may penalize the situs state in the attribution of taxation rights only to the extent that gains falling within the scope of Article 13(5) reflect unrealized gains on immovable property situated in its territory. **276**

It follows that the provision should be applied subject to the condition that there are unrealized gains attributable to the immovable property situated in the situs state. Applying this principle would, however, be extremely complicated from a practical point of view. In fact, in order to ascertain the unrealized gain attributable to each property, it would be necessary to determine not only the value attributable to the company's property but also the tax basis related to each property. From the situs state's perspective, this could be achieved in the case of property located there, but it would become rather complex in the case of property situated elsewhere (especially when a foreign company has title to the property). **277**

In light of the above, the value test – even though economically not the most appropriate one – would seem to represent the most feasible solution from a practical viewpoint. In fact, the additional efforts necessary to apply a test based on unrealized gains would not be justified in view of the limited purpose of the requirement. However, a practical solution like this one will lead to significant adverse consequences, unless an appropriate remedy is offered in order to define the extent of application of the provision. **278**

As already pointed out, the value test is easier to apply than an unrealized gains test. Thus, the value test may continue to be used to determine the applicability of Article 13(4). However, if the provision is applicable, an additional unrealized gain test should limit the attribution of taxation rights to the source state, to the extent of unrealized gains deriving from immovable property situated in that state. Under this additional rule, the source state would be given taxation rights not exceeding those that would have been attributed to that state under Article 13(1), where there is a direct alienation of immovable property situated in that state. A possible amendment of Article 13(4) is the following: **279**

Article 13(4)

Gains derived by a resident of a Contracting State from the alienation of shares deriving more than 50 per cent or their value directly or indirectly from immovable property situated in the other Contracting State may be taxed in that other State to the extent of the amount of the [net] unrealised gains relating to immovable property situated in the latter State proportionally attributable to the shares alienated.

[e]   *Obtaining Information and Collecting Taxes*

280   Article 13(4) does not contain a requirement with regard to the residence of the immovable property company. When such a company is not resident in the state where the relevant immovable property is situated, a problem arises in obtaining information and collecting taxes. The situation is further complicated when the company is not resident in the residence state (where the person alienating the shares is resident), but rather in a third state. This problem – which in the first instance has to do with the domestic sourcing rule and then with the application of the treaty – can be split into four levels:

(1) obtaining information about the application of the value test;
(2) obtaining information about the occurrence of an alienation;
(3) obtaining information necessary to determine the amount of the gain; and
(4) collecting taxes.

281   As already mentioned, collecting all the information necessary to apply the value test can be rather complex. Even assuming that a treaty with an exchange of information article is in force between the situs state and the state where the company is resident, the complexity of the monitoring activity that would have to be done (continuously) by both states would be likely to render the use of such an instrument meaningless. Complex ownership structures with several entities resident in different states would make the task almost impossible.

282   This is very likely one of the main reasons why countries such as the US exclude gains derived by non-residents from the alienation of shares in foreign companies from the scope of the immovable property company provision even though the shares derive their entire value from immovable property situated in its territory.[242] To mitigate such problems, domestic law may, for example, contain:

(a) presumptive mechanisms through which, if certain minimum requirements are met, a foreign company owning immovable property situated in the territory of the state is assumed to fulfil the condition for the application of the

---

242. In fact, US sourcing rules provide for the taxation in the United States of gains derived from the alienation of shares of US immovable property companies only. *See* I.R.C. s. 897(c)(1)(A) (ii).

domestic immovable property company provision (unless proof to the contrary is provided). In this way, the burden of proof is, de facto, shifted to the taxpayer. Nevertheless, it should be emphasized that, in the case of non-substantial investors, the taxpayer itself may have difficulty obtaining all the relevant information. In any case, the question then boils down to the application of the treaty, and may lead to cumbersome mutual agreement procedures; or

(b) obligations for the foreign company to provide, on a yearly basis, certain information regarding its property (e.g., value, nature and location) and its shareholders (e.g., identity, address, number of shares held). On the one hand, the source state, being the situs state of the immovable property owned by the company, can easily require the company to fulfil such an obligation. On the other hand, the system would probably become ineffective if there is a chain of companies (i.e., when the alienation relates to shares in a company different from the one owning directly the relevant immovable property).

In addition, it is hard for the situs state: (i) to become cognizant of the fact that a taxable **283** event has occurred, and (ii) to obtain the information necessary to determine the amount of the taxable gain that has to be taken into account. Certainly, once the source state is aware that the shares of the foreign company satisfy the value test, an exchange of information procedure may solve both of the above problems.

The last problem is the collection of taxes. This may be burdensome if the foreign **284** taxpayer does not have any other interests in the source state. The tax system of the residence state of the alienator may also play a part with regard to the regime applicable to capital gains and to the relief method chosen to avoid international juridical double taxation. In fact, for exemption systems, there is a big incentive for the taxpayer to evade the tax due in the source state. However, in states with credit systems, if the taxes paid in the source state are entirely creditable against the taxes due in the residence state, there is no economic incentive for the taxpayer to avoid payment of taxes in the source state. The same cannot be said if the taxes paid in the source state are not (or are not entirely) creditable against the taxes due in the residence state, since in such a case the payment of the taxes in the source state would increase the overall tax burden.[243]

From a source state perspective, two factors may be considered: (i) location of the **285** immovable property, and (ii) joint liability of the purchaser. Even the location of the immovable property does not seem to protect the source state from tax evasion. In theory, a state cannot have a lien on the immovable property, since the owner of this property (the foreign company) is not the taxpayer that owes income taxes. The source state may take advantage of the conflict of interest existing between seller and

---

243. In the case of the exemption of capital gains in the residence state, no credit would likely be given. In the case of a tax burden in the residence state that is lower than the taxes paid in the source state, only a partial credit would likely be granted, with the effect that at the end the real tax burden is the one incurred in the source state.

purchaser, by providing for joint liability for the purchaser for the taxes owed by the seller. For example, Canadian law contains a withholding tax and clearance requirement system the key element of which is the onus put on the purchaser of the shares, even though this is a foreign resident. Under this system, the purchaser of the shares has to levy a withholding tax on the gross amount of the purchase price of the shares (to be remitted to the Canadian tax authorities), unless the alienator provides the purchaser with a clearance certificate issued (upon request) by the Canadian tax authorities. To obtain the certificate, the seller has either to pay or to provide acceptable security in relation to his tax liability. Obviously, such a measure is more effective where the purchaser is a resident of the source state. Moreover, in the case of a treaty-protected purchaser, the possibility of collecting taxes from it is questionable. US law has a substantially similar system with regard to the alienation of shares in a US immovable property company. A similar system seems to apply in Mexico.

[f]   Double Exemption

286 If the residence state is an exemption country, the newly introduced provision leads to a double exemption on the gain where the situs state does not subject to tax gains falling within the scope of Article 13(4). OECD Commentary acknowledges this issue and provides a possible solution for avoiding, on a bilateral basis, double non-taxation:[244]

> Since the domestic laws of some States do not allow them to tax the gains covered by paragraph 4, States that adopt the exemption method should be careful to ensure that the inclusion of the paragraph does not result in a double exemption of these gains. These States may wish to exclude these gains from exemption and apply the credit method, as suggested by paragraph 35 of the Commentary on Articles 23 A and 23 B.

287 OECD Report also highlights this problem in relation to REITs where the exemption usually granted at the vehicle level puts a particular emphasis on this problem:[245]

> It was also noted that allowing source taxation of such gains could result in a double exemption if the State of source did not exercise this taxing right and the State of residence of the investor was an exemption country (that problem, which is inherent to paragraph 4 of Article 13, is described in paragraph 28.9 of the Commentary on that Article).

[F]   Cross-Border Income of REITs

288 In a global financial world, REITs' market for investments is not confined to the country under whose laws REIT is organized. REITs thus also invest in foreign

---

244. *See* para. 28.12 of OECD Commentary on Art. 13.
245. *See* para. 41 of OECD Report.

countries and derive foreign-source income. At the same time, usually, countries do not extend the application of REIT domestic regimes to foreign REITs (except for – under certain conditions – France, the Netherlands and Singapore).

REITs mostly derive rental income that falls within the scope of Article 6 or gains from **289** the alienation of immovable property that falls within the scope of Article 13(1). Both these treaty provisions attribute primary (unlimited) taxation rights to the situs state.

The main issue then becomes to ascertain the possibility of recovering the foreign taxes **290** suffered on the investments made abroad. The following example represents a valid starting point for the analysis of the above-mentioned issues.

Facts: Alpha and Beta are REITs organized in the corporate form under the laws of R **291** State:

(a) Alpha and Beta are residents of R State for the purpose of the application of the R-S treaty.
(b) Investors in both REITs are all residents of R State.
(c) No investor holds 10% or more of the capital of any of the two REITs.
(d) Under the laws of R State, a REIT is exempt on income and each year must distribute 100% of the income derived.
(e) Alpha owns one immovable property situated in R State and derives 100% of rental income per year.
(f) Beta owns one immovable property situated in S State and derives 100% of rental income per year.
(g) R State taxes REIT distributions by means of a final withholding tax of 15%.
(h) S State taxes rental income by means of a final withholding tax of 20%.
(i) To avoid international juridical double taxation, R State applies the exemption method.
(j) The R-S treaty follows OECD Model and includes the alternative provisions on REITs contained in OECD Commentary.

The following figure illustrates this scenario: **292**

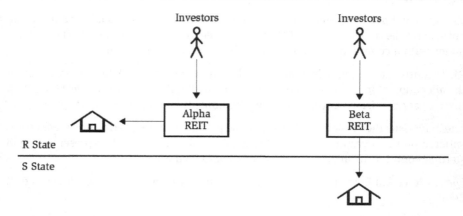

Article 6(1) of the R-S treaty provides that S State may tax the rental income derived from immovable property situated in S State. R State may tax but must grant relief under Article 23 of the same treaty. Even if R State were a credit country, there would have been no recovery of taxes collected by S State, due to the absence of taxable income in the hands of Beta. The following table contains a summary of the tax burden suffered by the investors of the two REITs:

	Alpha REIT	Beta REIT
Rental Income	100	100
S State tax on rental income [20%]		(20)
Net profit	100	80
Distribution	100	80
R State tax on distribution [15%]	(15)	(12)
Investors net income	85	68
Total tax suffered	(15)	(32)

293   The example makes clear that source taxation on income may represent a substantial obstacle to REITs' cross-border investments. Three main issues deserve further analysis:

    (1) relief from double taxation;
    (2) extension of the domestic REIT regime to foreign REITs; and
    (3) applicability of Article 24(3).

[1]   *Relief from Double Taxation*

294   When dealing with cross-border investments, the solution of taxing the income only at the level of the investors may not achieve the result of avoiding double taxation. In most countries, REIT is the person entitled to the income and, thus, the exemption granted at the vehicle level makes it difficult to recover foreign tax. In fact, exemption or credit is granted at REIT level, while taxes are collected at the investor level.

As a matter of fact, not all of the described REIT regimes provide for single-level **295** taxation if cross-border investments are concerned and thus are not in line with the general approach of a REIT as an investment vehicle.[246] Consequently, there might be situations, especially in cross-border investments, where REIT appears disadvantageous compared with other investment vehicles like funds or comparing with direct investments.

OECD Report states that it would be appropriate and consistent with the rationale of **296** REIT regime that the country under whose laws REIT is organized grants relief from source taxes despite the exemption of REIT:[247]

> Since, however, the REIT will not pay residence State tax on that income to the extent that it is distributed, this will create difficulties with respect to the application of domestic and treaty provisions for the relief of double taxation. The Working Party considered that, as a general rule, it would be appropriate, as a policy matter, for a State to allow relief of double taxation for any source tax that has been levied on the REIT even if the residence State imposes tax on the investors rather than on the REIT itself. Where the domestic law of a country does not provide for the flow-through of relief, the Working Party considers that that country should try to find a way to provide such relief.

The most straightforward way of achieving such a result is to provide for the **297** flow-through of relief to the investors. In the case of a country applying the credit method, this would mean granting the credit to the investors upon distribution (this is, for example, the solution endorsed in the Netherlands and Japan). In the case of a country applying the exemption method, this would mean establishing a tracing rule and exempting REIT distributions in the hands of the investors to the extent these are made from foreign-source income (this was, for example, the solution endorsed in Malaysia[248]).

OECD notes that where domestic law does not provide for the flow-through of relief, **298** countries should find a way to provide for relief on taxes paid abroad by REIT on foreign-source income. No additional guidance is added to identify what such alternative methods for granting relief may be.

In the case of countries applying the credit method, one possibility seems to be the **299** granting of a credit in the hands of REIT, irrespective of its exempt status. In the case of REITs benefiting from the exemption on the eligible income only, the rule should allow the credit to be used to offset taxes due on non-eligible income (this is, for example, the solution endorsed in Italy). In the case of REITs exempted in relation to

---

246. *See* s. §1.03[A][1].
247. *See* para. 16 of OECD Report.
248. Prior to 1 Jan. 2022, foreign-sourced income earned by a REIT was exempted in Malaysia. With effect from 1 Jan. 2022, the exemption of foreign-sourced income received in Malaysia is only applicable to a person who is a non-resident.

all types of income, the rule should grant the possibility for REITs to ask for a refund. In the case of countries applying the exemption method, the only way would seem to be to depart from such methodology and to grant a credit to REIT for foreign tax.

300   The implementation of OECD Report in the Commentary does not contain anything about the application of the relief. This is a policy type of issue that a state should carefully consider in light of all the relevant issues. This may also become a reciprocal concession that countries may make in the context of a double tax treaty to encourage reciprocal cross-border investments.

301   The case is different in the few countries where REITs are organized in the form of trusts and a flow-through imputation of income is provided for by domestic law (Australia and Canada). In these cases, not only the income but also the relief for foreign taxes are passed through to the investors with the result of not jeopardizing foreign investments.

302   This is also in line with OECD's position on the application of tax treaties to partnerships. The Commentary on Article 23 states:[249]

> to the extent that the State of residence flows through the income of the partnership to the partner for the purpose of taxing him, it must adopt a coherent approach and flow through to the partner the tax paid by the partnership for the purposes of eliminating double taxation arising from its taxation of the partner.

[2]   Extension of Domestic REIT Regime to Foreign REITs

303   The extension of the domestic REIT regime to foreign REITs would certainly remove the obstacles to cross-border investments. The main problem with such scenarios is the difficulty in finding a solution that permits taxation by the source state without jeopardizing REIT rationale. OECD Report envisages three main alternative approaches:

(1) levying source tax at the time REIT distributes the income;
(2) deeming the foreign REIT to be a domestic REIT for treaty purposes; and
(3) deeming the foreign REIT to have a permanent establishment.

[a]   Subsequent Withholding Tax

304   Under this approach, the source state exempts income from domestic immovable property derived by a foreign REIT but applies a tax (by means of withholding) on the distribution of that income to the investors of the foreign REIT. The following critical issues should be considered:

---

249. *See* para. 69.2 of OECD Commentary on Art. 23.

- this solution requires the traceability of the income derived from immovable property in the source state, which may be extremely complex and burdensome;
- it would become rather complex to determine the appropriate tax rate if a difference between small and large investors applies;
- collection may become rather difficult and burdensome, especially where investors are resident in third countries;
- a specific treaty provision is probably needed to cover such a case. This means that to be applicable this solution calls for a modification of all the relevant treaties; and
- a similar taxation would be prevented by Article 10(5), dealing with the extraterritorial taxation of dividends; that is, an exception to such a provision has to be inserted.

[b]   *Deeming the Foreign REIT to Be a Domestic REIT*

Under this approach, the source country will levy tax on a 'deemed' distribution that   **305** would take place between a 'deemed domestic REIT' and the foreign REIT. This distribution would be treated in accordance with the provisions of Article 10 as proposed by the Commentary. The following critical issues should be considered:

- a specific treaty provision is probably needed to cover such a case. This means that to be applicable this solution calls for a modification of all the relevant treaties;
- a decision needs to be taken about which is the applicable treaty rate, that is whether the foreign REIT should be treated as a small investor or as a large investor; and
- problems relating to the relief from double taxation would likely arise.

[c]   *Deeming the Foreign REIT to Have a Permanent Establishment*

The last approach is similar to the second approach, in that it makes use of deeming   **306** provisions. The idea is to deem the existence of a permanent establishment of the foreign REIT in the source country, to which the relevant income is connected. The source state would then apply a tax on the deemed distribution of such income to the head office (i.e., the foreign REIT).

The following critical issues should be considered: **307**

- a specific treaty provision is needed to cover such case. This means that to be applicable this solution calls for a modification of all the relevant treaties;
- situs state taxation would be prevented by Article 10(5) dealing with the extraterritorial taxation of dividends; that is, an exception to such provision has to be inserted; and

– it would become rather complex to determine the appropriate tax rate if a distinction between small and large investors applies.

[d]   Conclusion

308   In all three OECD approaches, the income derived by a foreign REIT in the source country is dealt with under Article 10 OECD, which is consistent with the treatment provided for REIT distributions. However, all the solutions put forward seem – at least at this stage – to present too many major problems to be seriously considered. In light of this, it may be useful to explore alternative approaches based on the application of different treaty provisions.

309   In this respect, it is worth mentioning that some REIT regimes (e.g., Italy) allow the application of specific rules to permanent establishments of foreign companies engaged in eligible activities. Such REIT regimes tax the income derived by the permanent establishments consistent with REIT distributions. This approach seems to address the main concerns regarding the three OECD approaches: (a) to safeguard the situs principle (the source country is not restricted by Article 10(5)); (b) to extend REIT regimes to foreign entities; (c) to apply existing treaty provisions (the relevant treaty provision is either Article 6 or Article 7); (d) no traceability is required; and (e) to apply the standard domestic collection for non-residents. However, the above-mentioned solution (a) assumes that under the source country REIT regime, it is not possible to obtain any tax deferral (which is generally the case due to the mandatory distribution requirement); otherwise, the direct taxation of the permanent establishment may become a more burdensome regime, and (b) does not allow the application of different taxation of small investors.

310   This approach seems suitable even for cases where the foreign REIT does not derive its foreign income from a permanent establishment. This result may be achieved by providing the same level of taxation applied to distribution to investors in local REIT to eligible income derived therein by foreign REIT.

[3]   Applicability of Article 24(3)

311   One may wonder whether Article 24(3) may be interpreted as requiring the extension of the domestic REIT regime to permanent establishments of foreign REITs. Article 24(3) provides:

> The taxation on a permanent establishment which an enterprise of a Contracting State has in the other Contracting State shall not be less favourably levied in that other State than the taxation levied on enterprises of that other State carrying on the same activities. This provision shall not be construed as obliging a Contracting State to grant to residents of the other Contracting State any personal allowances, reliefs and reductions for taxation purposes on account of civil status or family responsibilities which it grants to its own residents.

OECD Report concludes that a permanent establishment of a foreign REIT is not 312 comparable to a domestic REIT, in that domestic REITs are exempted because of the subsequent taxation of the investors upon distribution and this second layer of taxation is not possible in respect of foreign REITs:[250]

> The Working Party concluded that such an interpretation should be rejected and noted that extending the benefit of an exemption granted to a domestic REIT (the distributions from which would be taxed) to such a permanent establishment would result in an undue advantage for the foreign REIT since the distributions of that REIT could not similarly be taxed, in particular because of paragraph 5 of Article 10, by the State where the permanent establishment is located. As explained in paragraph 20 of the Commentary on Article 24:

> [...] the wording of the first sentence of paragraph 3 must be interpreted in the sense that it does not constitute discrimination to tax non-resident persons differently, for practical reasons, from resident persons, as long as this does not result in more burdensome taxation for the former than for the latter. In the negative form in which the provision concerned has been framed, it is the result alone which counts, it being permissible to adapt the mode of taxation to the particular circumstances in which the taxation is levied.

OECD's position is certainly well founded, but there seems to be room for further 313 analysis of the issue. The final interpretation of the applicability of Article 24(3) also depends on the specific tax regime applicable and on the conditions and requirements provided for by the relevant domestic law.

---

250. *See* para. 54 of OECD Report.

Australia

JOSHUA CARDWELL

Joshua is the leader of the Australian Real Estate Tax practice. Joshua advises a broad spectrum of institutional real estate clients in respect of inbound and outboard investments, funding raising, M&A transactions and reorganizations. Joshua has been extensively involved with the Property Council of Australia's lobbying in respect of many recent tax change proposals.
E-mail: josh.cardwell@pwc.com

Australia

Joshua Cardwell

§1.01 BACKGROUND

[A] Key Characteristic

There are no specific Real Estate Investment Trusts (REIT) rules in Australia. Austra-   **1**
lian REITs are trusts that can be listed or unlisted. REITs are not taxable entities (i.e.,
they have a 'flow-through' tax status) provided they meet certain requirements. Most
importantly, REIT must distribute all of its income annually and the business activities
of REIT must be passive in nature such that REIT is not a Public Trading Trust (*see*
section §1.02[A][2] below). Australian REITs can be sector-specific (e.g., industrial,
office, etc.) or diversified funds. In this report, the term 'REIT' has been used for both
listed and unlisted property trusts. This report only considers REITs that are Managed
Investment Schemes (MISs) as defined in the Corporations Law (*see* section §1.02[C]
below).

[B] History of REIT

The Australian REIT market has a history dating back to 1971 when the first REIT was   **2**
listed on the Australian Stock Exchange (ASX). REITs were historically externally
managed until the late 1990s when stapled entities emerged (*see* section §1.02[A][1][b]
below). Stapled entities are typically internally managed but this is not always the case.
Many entities are stapled so that investors can obtain exposure to investments that
would not be allowed for a trust that wants to retain flow-through status (e.g., property
development). In 1998, MIS rules were introduced into the Corporations Law. MIS
rules govern investment vehicles in Australia, including REITs. A REIT can either be an
unregistered MIS or a registered MIS. In 2008, new withholding tax (WHT) rules were
introduced for a REIT that qualifies as a Managed Investment Trust (MIT) (*see* section
§1.03[A][3] below).

3   From 1 July 2016, certain MITs were able to elect to apply the Attribution MIT (AMIT) tax regime with effect from 1 July 2016. Where a trust elects into the AMIT regime, then a key outcome is that the trust will not be subject to the existing present entitlement rules in Division 6 of the Australian Tax Act but instead will be subject to the specific attribution rules contained in the AMIT regime.

[C]   REIT Market in Country

4   The Australian REIT market is very large, established and sophisticated with approximately 50% of Australian investment-grade properties securitized. This has made it difficult for REITs to acquire new property and resulted in a large push in the early 2000s by Australian REITs to acquire international real estate. REITs have historically had an annual income yield of between 5% and 10%. Apart from distributions, REITs have also offered the opportunity for capital growth. As of 31 December 2021, there were forty-six listed REITs on ASX with a market capitalization exceeding AUD 172 billion.

§1.02   REGULATORY ASPECTS

[A]   Legal Form of REIT

[1]   Corporate Form

[a]   General

5   An Australian REIT is a trust governed by general trust law. Broadly, trust law includes requirements for the trustee to act in the best interests of beneficiaries, to act honestly and to exercise the same prudence and diligence as ordinary persons would exercise in carrying on their own business. A trust is not a separate legal entity or person, but, broadly, it is a set of obligations accepted by a person (the trustee) in relation to property (the trust property), where such obligations are exercised for the benefit of another person (the beneficiary). The obligations of the trustee, and the rights of beneficiaries, are typically set out in writing in the trust deed. The trust deed is a very flexible document. However, it must still adhere to certain requirements in order to access MIT and AMIT regimes.

6   While there are many types of trusts, an Australian REIT is typically a unit trust. That is, all the income and capital entitlements of the trust are fixed in accordance with the trust deed and those entitlements are unitized. That is, the income and/or capital entitlements of a beneficiary (or unitholder) are determined by reference to the units they hold and the rights attaching to those units (per the trust deed). Similar to a shareholder's liability in a company, a unitholder's liability is also limited, although the law is not explicit on this.

The trustee of an Australian REIT will be the legal owner of the trust property. The   7
custody of the assets may however be undertaken by a custodian who typically also
provides reporting services for the manager of REIT.

Overall, an Australian REIT will be in legal form, the same as other Australian trusts.   8
A typical Australian REIT structure will include a series of wholly owned sub-trusts,
with each sub-trust housing similar types of assets.

[b]   Stapled Entities

Stapled entities are a common feature of the Australian real estate investment market.   9
In the case of listed property trusts, the majority of Australian REITs are now in the
form of stapled entities, involving two, and often more than two, entities in a stapled
arrangement. Stapled entities are also commonly used for many infrastructure-type
investments.

In the case of unlisted property trusts, stapled structures are less common but are used 10
where fund managers diversify from pure core property investment into opportunistic
type investments.

Stapling occurs when two or more different securities are contractually bound together   11
in a manner so that they cannot be traded separately. The stapling itself is implemented
by means of a contractual arrangement, usually in the form of a stapling deed. Terms
of stapling deeds may vary, but in essence, their effect is to prevent the securities
(shares, units) of the entities subject to the stapling deed from being traded separately.
This is then reflected in the constituent documents of the underlying entities which
provide that their securities may not be traded separately.

For legal and tax purposes, separate securities retain their individual legal character   12
and they continue to be treated separately for income tax purposes. Accordingly, for
example, if a stapled security consists of shares in a company and units in a unit trust,
then the rights and obligations of the security holder as a shareholder in the company
continue and similarly, the rights and obligations as a unitholder and hence beneficiary
of the unit trust continue.

Stapled structures, when first used, were generally a company stapled to a trust.   13
Practice for newly created staples has moved towards stapling two or more trusts
together. The principal reason for this is not tax-related but rather to do with
restrictions that apply to companies under corporate law, which do not exist for trusts.
Historically, this was related to the ability of trusts to distribute cash even when there
are no profits (which a company was until very recently precluded from doing). Also,
the directors of the trustee of each trust are appointed by the trustee rather than
unitholders. Therefore, the trustee can retain more control over who its directors are.

The emergence of stapled entities has allowed REITs to retain 'flow-through' tax status   14
in relation to the holding of investment properties but at the same time allowed for
internalization of management and also for diversification of investment exposure to

other property-related services such as development. That is, the 'taxable' side of the staple undertakes non-investment activities while the 'flow-through' side of the staple invests in real estate.

15   A comprehensive reform package was enacted in late 2018 (with some transitional rules over seven to fifteen years) relating to the taxation of 'stapled structures', the types of income that can be derived by MITs, the financing of these investments and a statutory rule in respect of sovereign immunity.

[2]   Investment Restrictions

16   There are no specific investment restrictions imposed on a REIT. However, where a trust, including an Australian REIT, is a Public Trading Trust under Division 6C of Part III of the *Income Tax Assessment Act 1936 (the Act)*, the trust will effectively be treated as a company for many (but not all) income tax purposes. In particular, the trust (or more correctly the trustee) will be assessed to tax at the corporate tax rate on its taxable income. Distributions from such trusts will be assessable in the hands of the unitholders in the same way as dividends are assessable in the hands of shareholders. In other words, under the Public Trading Trust provisions, the trust is in many, but not all, ways effectively taxed as a company and therefore will lose its 'flow-through' status.

17   Under the relevant provisions, an Australian REIT will be a Public Trading Trust in relation to a year of income where all of the following four conditions are satisfied:

> (1)   the trust is a public unit trust;
> (2)   the trust is a trading trust;
> (3)   the trust is a resident unit trust or a Public Trading Trust in a year preceding the relevant year of income; and
> (4)   the trust is not a corporate unit trust (which also effectively taxes a trust as a company).

18   It is important to note that the test is a year-by-year test. An entity may be a Public Trading Trust in one year and not in another, depending upon the factual tests above as applied in the year.

19   Generally speaking, when examining the potential application of the Public Trading Trust provisions in the context of Australian REITs, that are listed or unlisted (and offered to the public), it is condition (2), the trading trust issue, that is most relevant. An Australian REIT will be a trading trust if at any time during an income year it carries on a 'trading business' or controls the affairs and operations of another person who carries on a trading business.

20   A trading business is defined to mean a business that does not consist wholly of eligible investment business. An eligible investment business is defined to mean either of:

(a) investing in land for the purpose, or primarily for the purpose, of deriving rent;
(b) investing or trading in any or all of the following:
    (i) secured or unsecured loans (including deposits with a bank or other financial institutions);
    (ii) bonds, debentures, stock or other securities;
    (iii) shares in a company, including shares in a foreign hybrid company (a defined term);
    (iv) units in a unit trust;
    (v) futures contracts;
    (vi) forward contracts;
    (vii) interest rate swap contracts;
    (viii) currency swap contracts;
    (ix) forward exchange rate contracts;
    (x) forward interest rate contracts;
    (xi) life assurance policies;
    (xii) a right or option in respect of such a loan, security, share, unit, contract or policy;
    (xiii) any similar financial arrangements.
(c) investing or trading in financial instruments (not covered by paragraph (b)) that arise under financial arrangements (other than certain excepted arrangements).

Most relevant for an Australian REIT will be paragraph (a) – investing in land for the **21** purpose, or primarily for the purpose, of deriving rent. On the simplest level, a REIT that invests in land for the purpose of deriving rent will be carrying on an eligible investment business. On the other hand, if a REIT were to invest in land for the purpose of developing the land for sale at a profit, this would not be an eligible investment business.

However, the practical application of paragraph (a) of eligible investment business is **22** not so simple given the complexity of the transactions involving land in the real world.

The term 'land' takes its ordinary meaning. For example, it will include an interest in **23** land such as a leasehold interest. It also includes buildings and fixtures that are attached to the land. As a general rule, income attributable to chattels held by a REIT will not qualify as income derived from investing in land for the purpose of deriving rent. This view is based on the proposition that, unlike fixtures and fittings, chattels are not attached to the land and therefore do not form part of the land.

While the term 'rent' is not defined in Division 6C or any other part of the Act, it has **24** generally been accepted that in its ordinary meaning, it is 'a sum of money which the tenant has contracted to pay to the landlord for the use of the premise let'. Rent should also include amounts attributable to fixtures and fittings. This is because fixtures and fittings form an integral part of land and will therefore fall within the definition of land.

25 While the intention of the provisions is to exclude certain types of activities from Division 6C, the practical application of these provisions has created significant uncertainty and confusion – in particular, the attempts to reconcile a practical application of the rules with the original intent of the legislature.

26 Historically the Commissioner of Taxation did not treat a unit trust as a trading trust provided the trust predominately carried on an eligible investment business and any income from ineligible activities was relatively insignificant or incidental. This was a rather haphazard approach, not particularly consistent with the written law, but gave results that were commercially sensible, and probably results that were consistent with the original intent and purpose of the laws when introduced. In 2008, the Public Trading Trust provisions were modified to update the provisions and codify the Commissioner's concession. Included in the modifications is a rule that treats chattels as forming part of the land in certain circumstances. Also included are certain safe harbour rules to allow for a REIT to earn some non-rental income without becoming a Public Trading Trust. Trading income is still not tolerated, however.

27 The Public Trading Trust rules will also apply to an Australian REIT if at any time during the year of income the trustee controlled, or was able to control, the affairs and operations of another person carrying on a trading business. The rationale for including this control test is to provide a safeguarding provision against arrangements to circumvent the operation of the Public Trading Trust provisions by having activities that would constitute a trading business of a public unit trust carried on by an associate. By taking income from an associate in the form of eligible investment income (i.e., a dividend), the trustee could otherwise ensure that the relevant trust did not qualify as a trading business and so avoid the operation of the Public Trading Trust provisions.

28 While the term 'control' is not defined, the control requirement seems to refer to control over the management of a trading business. On this basis, it would seem that, in the case of a company, one way to exercise control of the affairs and operations of the company in carrying on its trading business would be through control of the board of directors.

29 At the simplest level, the only relevant issue will be whether the Australian REIT can control the majority voting rights at a general meeting of an entity carrying on a trading business. However, in the absence of any guidance in the relevant provisions but in light of decided cases and comments from the Commissioner of Taxation, a wider concept of control should be applied. This would include control of the board of directors and also extend to concepts of control involving the ability to restrain others from a decision. For example, a holding of exactly 50% voting control while not enough to control in a positive sense is in the view of the Australian tax authorities enough to control in a negative sense by preventing others from making decisions.

[B]   Regulatory Authorities

Trusts are unregulated vehicles. However, a REIT that is an MIS (in particular, a **30** registered MIS) must satisfy certain Corporations Law requirements. These require- ments are regulated by the Australian Securities and Investment Commission (ASIC).

[C]   Legislative and Other Regulatory Sources

In Australia, there are no special legal or regulatory requirements that need to be **31** satisfied in order to establish a REIT. However, broadly speaking, REITs offered to twenty or more persons or that are required to issue a Product Disclosure Statement (PDS) when issuing units must be registered with ASIC as an MIS.

In brief, registration as an MIS requires an Australian REIT to adopt certain rules and **32** regulations in the Corporations Law, including the following:

(a) Appointment of a Responsible Entity (RE) who has the dual role of trustee and manager of the scheme. MIS law requires RE to be licensed and imposes extensive duties on RE, including the duty to act honestly, exercise reasonable care and diligence and treat each member equally.
(b) Each MIS must have a Constitution. A Constitution is a trust deed that must contain certain requirements including powers of RE in dealing with or investing the scheme property, complaints resolution and winding up of the scheme.
(c) Preparation of a compliance plan which sets out the measure which RE is to apply in operating MIS to ensure compliance with MIS law and the scheme's constitution.
(d) If less than half the directors of RE are external directors, RE is required to have a compliance committee.

These requirements deal with governance and disclosure and currently have no impact **33** on the tax treatment of the trust as a 'flow-through' entity (except for an MIS that qualifies as an MIT, in which case special WHT rules will apply – refer to section §1.03[A][3] below).

Where a REIT that is required to be registered as an MIS is not registered, ASIC, a **34** unitholder of REIT or RE, can apply to the Court to have REIT wound up.

[D]   Exchange Controls and Reporting Requirements

ASX has detailed rules that must be complied with if a REIT is listed. Broadly, the rules **35** include the following requirements:

(a) Ongoing Disclosure Requirements. Subject to certain exceptions, if a REIT becomes aware of any information regarding it that a reasonable person would expect would have a material impact on REIT's unit price, REIT must inform ASX.

(b) Provide reports for the financial year (audited) and half-year (subject to a review) prepared from the financial statements of REIT.

(c) Lodge REIT's annual report with ASX.

(d) Announce distributions and record date.

[E]   Registration Procedures

[1]   Preparatory Measures

36   To register an MIS, RE must be a registered Australian public company and hold an Australian Financial Services Licence (AFSL) authorizing RE to operate the scheme. The licensing rules are very detailed, but, broadly speaking, the following are the main requirements:

(a) ASIC will consider the good fame and character and the expertise and ability of RE. In making this assessment, ASIC will take into account the nature of the proposed scheme.

(b) RE must meet certain net tangible assets (NTA) requirements.

(c) RE must maintain appropriate professional indemnity insurance and insurance against fraud by the officers of RE.

37   As a rule of thumb, an RE should allow for at least three months for ASIC to grant an AFSL. In the context of establishing an MIT, it is commonplace for a REIT to utilize a third-party trustee service provider that holds a valid AFSL to satisfy this requirement. Alternatively, if REIT is also outsourcing its investment management activities, to the extent the appointed investment manager also holds a valid AFSL, this requirement can be satisfied.

[2]   Obtaining Authorization

38   To register an MIS, the following must be lodged with ASIC:

(a) An application form with the appropriate fee.

(b) A copy of REIT's constitution.

(c) A copy of REIT's compliance plan.

(d) A statement signed by the directors of RE confirming that REIT's constitution and compliance plan comply with the Corporations Law.

A scheme will not be registered unless (or until) RE has an AFSL.   39

[3]   Other Requirements for the Establishment of a REIT That Is a Registered MIS

The Formation of a REIT is a relatively simple process. The Constitution for REIT is   40
prepared and lodged with ASIC upon registering REIT as an MIS.

[4]   Obtaining Listing Exchanges

[a]   Costs

The costs associated with a listing will depend on several factors such as whether the   41
associated capital raising is underwritten. As a general rule though, RE should allow for
between 6% and 10% of funds raised.

[b]   Time

The time required to list a trust will depend on several factors including the size and   42
complexity of the transaction, the state of the market and how quickly funds are
received from investors. As a general rule though, RE should allow for at least six
months for any listing.

[F]   Requirements and Restrictions

[1]   Capital Requirements

Unlike a corporation, a REIT does not have capital requirements. A REIT can also very   43
easily return capital or distribute assets to unitholders. In order to list on ASX, however,
a REIT must meet either a minimum NTA or market capitalization threshold.

[2]   Marketing/Advertising

A listed REIT is required to issue a PDS when it seeks to list or raise equity. PDS sets out   44
the terms of the transaction, provides information as to REIT and its RE, includes
various experts' reports, includes financial information and also information on the
real estate owned by the trust. PDS must be lodged with ASIC and ASX.

An unlisted REIT is required to issue an Information Memorandum (IM) when it seeks   45
to raise equity. IM is similar to a PDS and must be lodged with ASIC.

[3]   Redemption

46   There are no strict redemption restrictions for REITs. Therefore, redeeming units is a simple process that is effectively governed by REIT's constitution. Where REIT is listed, ASX listing rules for redemptions need to be considered.

[4]   Valuation of Shares/Units for Redemption and Other Purposes

47   Units are redeemed in accordance with the requirements of the Constitution. Typically, the Constitution requires units to be redeemed at their net asset value.

[5]   Investment Restrictions

48   There are no investment restrictions for a REIT. As noted in section §1.02[A][2] above though, if a REIT wants to retain 'flow-through' status for tax purposes, its investments must satisfy the Public Trading Trust provisions.

[6]   Distribution/Accumulation

49   There are no distribution or accumulation restrictions for a REIT. However, in order to maintain its 'flow-through' tax status and to ensure that the trustee is not subject to tax on REIT's taxable income, the unitholders of an Australian REIT must be presently entitled to all of REIT's income at year-end. The term 'income' is not defined in the Tax Laws, but it is taken to mean the income of a REIT in accordance with its Constitution. Australian REITs typically distribute their income on at least an annual basis, and listed trusts typically distribute on a quarterly or semi-annual basis. In order for REITs to benefit from concessional WHT rates under the withholding MIT rules in respect of distributions to certain non-resident unitholders, the taxable income of REIT must be distributed to the unitholders within three months after year-end in the form of a so-called Fund Payment. AMIT rules allow an allocation of the income to the unitholders being sufficient to trigger the unitholders' tax liability, including the concessional MIT WHT rates, without the need for actual cash distributions. In order to access AMIT regime, additional requirements must be satisfied and additional compliance obligations must be satisfied each year. Further, a non-arm's length rule for MITs: the trustee will be liable to pay tax at 30% on the amount of income that is derived and is deemed to be 'non-arm's length income'.

[7]   Reporting Requirements

There are no formal reporting requirements for a REIT unless it is an MIS in which case **50** the Corporations Law requirements will need to be satisfied. Broadly, an MIS is required to lodge its annual report with ASIC.

RE is also required to lodge its audited financial reports and compliance plan audit **51** report with ASIC together with the audit of its AFSL.

Where REIT is listed, it must meet ASX reporting requirements (*see* section §1.02[D] **52** above).

[8]   Accounting

A REIT that is an MIS is required to prepare audited financial statements in accordance **53** with Australian International Financing and Reporting Standards. A REIT that is listed is also required to prepare half-year financial statements which must be subject to a review by REIT's auditors.

§1.03   TAXATION

[A]   Taxation of REIT

[1]   Trust Income Taxation

[a]   Tax Accounting

The taxation of REIT taxable income is in most instances at the unitholder level. **54** Provided certain conditions are met, the unitholders will be taxed on REIT's taxable income and the character of income, gains and other distributions by REIT will flow through to the unitholders.

The two key conditions that must be satisfied for 'flow-through' treatment of an **55** Australian REIT are annual distribution of income (*see* section §1.02[F][6] above) and it is not a Public Trading Trust (*see* section §1.02[A][2] above).

Importantly, this allows an Australian REIT to distribute income before the imposition **56** of taxes and effectively flow-through tax preferences such as depreciation. Distributions of tax preferences are effectively treated as capital distributions for tax purposes. Tax on such distributions may be deferred until such time as the units are disposed of, or the distributions of tax preferences exceed the cost base of REIT units. This is why they are called tax-deferred distributions.

Retaining flow-through status for a REIT is critical because REIT stock is valued by the **57** market on a pre-tax basis. If REIT were to pay tax, its distributions would be reduced by the tax paid. This would adversely impact REIT's stock price. Tax-deferred distributions are also valued but typically only by retail investors.

[b]   *Determination of Taxable Income*

58   A REIT calculates its taxable income on the same basis as an Australian resident individual. A REIT's taxable income includes its net rental income and deductions for costs such as management fees, interest and land taxes.

59   A tax deduction should be available for interest expenses incurred in connection with loans used to acquire the income-yielding property. There are however some anti-avoidance provisions that need to be considered. Australian tax law contains no specific gearing limits for unit trusts. The general Thin Capitalization rules may apply however to effectively impose a gearing limit where the property trust is controlled by non-resident unitholders or is an outbound investor. Broadly, under the Thin Capitalization rules, a trust's total debt cannot exceed 60% of its adjusted net assets. Note that transfer pricing rules may also need to be considered in relation to interest rates on loans and loan terms. Australia has also recently introduced anti-hybrid mismatch provisions that must also be considered.

60   A REIT can claim depreciation for depreciable assets. There are specific rules that apply to the depreciation of buildings. Building depreciation is based on the original construction cost which is not reset on acquisition to market value and is generally claimed over forty years on a straight-line basis (or twenty-five years for some buildings). Broadly, buildings can only be depreciated where construction commenced after the following dates:

(a) 21 August 1979 for buildings located in Australia (the exact date will depend on the type of building).
(b) 21 August 1990 for buildings located outside Australia.

61   Structural improvements can also be depreciated where the construction commenced after 26 February 1992.

62   Tax losses incurred by an Australian REIT cannot be distributed to its unitholders. Revenue losses can be carried forward and may be offset against future assessable income and capital gains of the trust. Capital losses must be carried forward and may be offset only against future capital gains of the trust.

63   The utilization of prior-year revenue losses is subject to the trust loss rules. Broadly, an Australian REIT must satisfy the 50% stake test during the relevant period in order to utilize prior-year revenue losses. The 50% stake test requires continuity of majority beneficial ownership of the income and capital rights of the trust during the relevant trust loss period. In general, a trust must satisfy the 50% stake test during the period commencing at the start of the income year the loss was incurred and ending at the end of the income year in which the loss is to be utilized. If the Australian REIT cannot satisfy the 50% stake test, an alternative same business test may be utilized. However, this is only available for listed trusts (and their wholly owned sub-trusts).

There are no trust loss rules applicable to Australian REITs in order to utilize prior-year **64** capital losses.

[c] *Taxation of Income from Taxable/Non-taxable Subsidiaries*

In order to retain 'flow-through' tax status, a REIT cannot control a subsidiary that **65** would result in REIT being a Public Trading Trust. It is for this reason that most REIT subsidiaries are also trusts that invest in rental properties. A trust subsidiary is taxed in the same way as a REIT (i.e., on a 'flow-through' basis). Therefore, a trust subsidiary is typically not taxable in its own right. Rather, REIT is required to include the income from the trust subsidiary in its taxable income. Unitholders of REIT pay tax on the taxable income of REIT (*see* section §1.03[B][1][a] below).

With the emergence of investment by REITs in foreign real estate, some REITs now **66** have corporate subsidiaries (e.g., a Luxembourg company or US REIT). Dividends paid by a subsidiary company are included in the taxable income of REIT.

[d] *Taxation of Foreign Income*

Foreign-sourced income derived by a REIT is included in the taxable income of REIT. **67** Foreign-sourced income retains its character when distributed to unitholders. If REIT has paid tax in the foreign jurisdiction in relation to that income (including WHT), then REIT may be eligible to recognize a foreign tax credit in respect of the tax paid and distribute those credits to unitholders. When foreign income is distributed to non-resident unitholders, no WHT otherwise payable on distribution of taxable Australian income to non-resident unitholders applies.

[2] **Value Added Tax**

Australia has a Value Added Tax (VAT) system with a tax rate of 10%. Where REIT **68** holds a direct interest in the property, REIT should be subject to VAT of 10% in respect of its Australian-sourced rental income. A REIT will also pay VAT on the acquisition of Australian real estate unless it is an acquisition of a going concern. If VAT is payable in respect of an acquisition, it should be creditable but transfer taxes will be paid on VAT inclusive purchase price. A REIT should generally be eligible for a credit for VAT paid. There are however notable exceptions, for example where the property is held through sub-trusts. In these circumstances, REIT holding the units in the sub-trusts will not be entitled to recover VAT in full as the costs relate to a financial supply. In which case, a reduced credit for VAT paid may be available.

[3]   Withholding Taxes

69   All Australian-sourced income of a REIT distributed to non-resident unitholders will be subject to WHT. The same applies to distributions of capital gains relating to Taxable Australian Property (TAP), TAP being either direct interests in land or indirect interests, being interests of 10% or more in entities whose gross assets are represented to 50% or more by interests in Australian land.

[a]   Trust Distributions (Non-MIT)

70   In regard to non-MITs, the trustee WHT is generally 30% or, where the income is distributed to individuals or foreign trusts, the marginal personal tax rate (in case of non-resident trusts being unitholders at the highest marginal tax rate of 45%).

[b]   MIT Distributions

71   Where REIT satisfies the definition of an MIT (refer below) the concessional MIT WHT rate of 15% applies unless the investor is resident in a country that does not have an exchange of information agreement with Australia, in which case the rate of WHT will be 30%. Where the capital gain is a discount gain, WHT is applied to the gross capital gain, that is before applying the 50% discount concession. The 'stapled securities' legislative changes increase the 15% MIT rate to 30% for certain types of income, including that from agricultural land, most residential properties and certain non-controlled investments.

72   MIT WHT is effectively a final tax. Accordingly, non-resident taxpayers cannot claim any concessions and/or tax deductions and are not due a refund for any tax withheld in excess of their taxable income after such deductions.

73   Broadly, a trust will be an MIT if the following conditions are satisfied:

  (a) The trust has the relevant connection with Australia.
  (b) The trust must meet certain regulatory requirements, including being an MIS.
  (c) The trust must meet certain widely held requirements. Broadly, a retail fund must be listed or have at least fifty members and a wholesale fund must have at least twenty-five members. For this purpose, special tracing rules apply. There is also an additional concessional test if REIT is a registered MIS (known as the '25/60 rule').
  (d) The trust is not a trading trust (refer to §1.02[A][2] above).
  (e) A substantial proportion of the trust's investment management activities in relation to certain Australian assets is undertaken in Australia.
  (f) The trust satisfies certain closely held restrictions.
  (g) The trustee or manager has an appropriate AFSL.

For a REIT which does not qualify as an MIT, the relevant withholding rate will be as   **74**
follows:

    (a) Non-resident individual: individual marginal tax rate, currently commencing
        at 32.5%.
    (b) Non-resident company: corporate tax rate, currently 30%.
    (c) Non-resident trustee: highest individual marginal tax rate, currently 45%.

This WHT is not a final tax.   **75**

[4]   *Other Taxes*

Transfer taxes of up to 13.5% of the higher of market value or consideration paid may   **76**
be liable on the transfer of property or transfer of units in unlisted property trusts
(depending on the ownership of the units and state in which the real estate is located).
There is no transfer tax on the transfer of listed trust units.

Land tax is an annual tax assessed to the owner of the land. While the imposition of   **77**
land tax varies from state to state, it is generally levied on the unimproved value of
land. Land tax is generally payable where the value of land exceeds certain thresholds.
The rate of tax varies from state to state but could be as high as 4%.

[5]   *Penalties Imposed on REIT*

Given that a REIT is typically not a taxpayer, there are generally no material income tax   **78**
penalties that are imposed on a REIT. Penalties can however be imposed in respect of
VAT and transfer taxes. Further, non-compliance penalties may be imposed under MIT
or AMIT regimes if the trustee fails to comply with all compliance obligations required
under each regime.

[B]   Taxation of the Investor

[1]   *Private Investors*

[a]   *Taxation of Current Income (All Income Derived from REIT in Holding
      Phase)*

Residents

Resident unitholders are liable to pay tax on the full amount of their share of the taxable   **79**
income (including capital gains) of a REIT in the year in which they are presently
entitled to the income of REIT. A unitholder's share of the taxable income of REIT for
the year ended 30 June must therefore be included in the unitholder's assessable

income for the financial year ended on that date. This applies irrespective of whether the actual distribution of the income from REIT is paid in a subsequent year.

80   Distributions from REIT may include various components, the taxation treatment of which may differ. Taxable distributions from a REIT may include both foreign-sourced income and gains (e.g., from properties located overseas) and Australian-sourced income and gains. Distributions from an Australian REIT may also include a tax-deferred component, capital gains tax (CGT) concession component, a capital gain component and a foreign tax credit component.

81   Tax-deferred amounts are generally attributable to returns of capital, building allowances, depreciation allowances and other tax timing differences. It is the practice of the Commissioner of Taxation to treat tax-deferred amounts as not assessable when received unless and until the total tax-deferred amounts received by a unitholder exceed the unitholder's cost base of REIT units. For CGT purposes, tax-deferred amounts received reduce the unitholder's cost base of REIT units and therefore affect the unitholder's capital gain/loss on disposal of those units.

82   Where a capital asset that is owned by the Australian REIT for at least twelve months is disposed of, the trust may claim a 50% CGT discount on the capital gain realized upon disposal of that asset. CGT concession component of a distribution by REIT will represent CGT discount claimed by the trust in respect of asset disposals. CGT concession component is not assessable when received by unitholders. Where a REIT distribution includes a CGT concession component, there will be no reduction to the cost base of the trust units held by a unitholder.

83   The capital gain component of a REIT distribution must be included in the unitholder's calculation of their net capital gain. Where the distributed capital gain includes a discount capital gain component, the unitholder is required to 'gross up' that component by the discount applied by REIT (i.e., 50%). The nominal capital gain (i.e., the whole amount of the gain prior to discounting) is then included in the calculation of the unitholder's net capital gain (*see* section §1.03[B][1][b] below).

84   Unitholders may be entitled to a foreign tax credit for foreign taxes paid by a REIT. The credit is applied against the Australian tax payable on foreign-sourced income of REIT or other income subject to foreign tax.

85   The amount of the foreign tax credit available to a unitholder will generally be equal to the lesser of:

    (a) the Australian tax payable by the unitholder on foreign-sourced income and other income subject to foreign tax; or

    (b) the unitholder's share of the foreign tax paid by REIT.

Non-residents

Non-resident unitholders are subject to Australian tax on their share of REIT's taxable **86** income that is attributable to sources within Australia. Foreign-sourced income can flow through an Australian REIT to a non-resident unitholder tax-free. Distributions to non-residents are subject to WHT (*see* section §1.03[A][3] above).

Stapled Security Holders

An investor in a stapled REIT may appear to be buying a single security and receiving **87** a single stream of investment returns.

However, the taxation reality is that the investor is acquiring two (or more) securities, **88** and upon disposal is similarly disposing of two (or more) securities. In addition, the income stream is not a single stream of payments, but typically will consist of a flow of dividends from a company, together with a separate and distinct flow of distributions from one or more unit trusts. Further, differences can arise in the character of these distinct investment returns. For example, dividends may be franked or unfranked, and trust distributions may consist of numerous separate components such as a tax-deferred component, a capital gains component, a CGT discount component, etc.

While typically stapled securities will make a single distribution, which may be made **89** quarterly, half-yearly or annually, the payment in fact represents the combined payment of a dividend together with the payment of one or more trust distributions. There are important differences in the character and timing of recognition of these different components.

The dividend is assessable to the investor at the time the dividend is paid by the **90** company. In relation to the final dividend payment, it is typically made in respect of the year ended 30 June but is paid in, say, the following August. The trust distribution (or distributions) paid at the same time, that is in August, will be in respect of entitlement arising on the previous 30 June.

The implications are that the dividend must be included in the later year's assessable **91** income and hence tax return, while the trust distribution component must be included in the earlier year's assessable income and hence tax return.

  [b]   *Taxation of Capital Gains (From Disposal of REIT Units)*

Residents

The disposal of a REIT unit will have CGT implications for the unitholder. Broadly, the **92** unitholders must include any capital gain or loss on the disposal in the calculation of their net capital gain or loss for the year. A unitholder will derive a capital gain on the disposal of REIT unit to the extent that the capital proceeds on disposal exceed CGT cost base of the unit. A unitholder will incur a capital loss on the disposal of a REIT unit to the extent that the capital proceeds on disposal are less than CGT reduced cost base of the unit. The cost base of each unit will be reduced by any tax-deferred distributions or returns of capital made by REIT in respect of that particular unit.

93   All capital gains and capital losses arising in a year, including distributions of capital gains by REIT (*see* section §1.03[B][1][a] above), are added together to determine whether a unitholder has derived a net capital gain or incurred a net capital loss in that year.

94   If a unitholder derives a net capital gain in a year, this amount is, subject to the comments below, included in the unitholder's assessable income. If a unitholder incurs a net capital loss in a year, this amount is carried forward and is available to offset capital gains derived in subsequent years.

95   If the unitholder has held REIT units for twelve months or more at the time of disposal and there is a capital gain, a discount factor will be available to that unitholder. The discount factor for individuals is 50%. The capital gain on the units is initially reduced by any other capital losses of the unitholder. If a net capital gain arises, it may be reduced by the relevant discount factor.

Non-residents

96   A non-resident will generally only be subject to tax on capital gains which relate to TAP. Broadly, TAP includes land and buildings situated in Australia and where a non-resident holds 10% or more of the units in interposed entities, where more than 50% of the value of the interposed entity's assets are attributable (directly or indirectly) to Australian real property. Therefore, where a non-resident owns less than 10% of the units in an Australian REIT, the disposal of the units in that trust should not be subject to Australian tax.

97   There are non-resident CGT WHT rules which impose a 12.5% WHT on the purchase of land or interests in land from non-residents (subject to an AUD 750,000 *de minimus*). If a non-resident disposes of the listed REIT units, there is an exemption from these withholding obligations for 'on-market' transactions. Otherwise, the purchase will have to withhold 12.5% of the gross purchase price for the sale of land or indirect interests in land unless the seller:

(a)   provides an exemption certificate obtained from the Australian Tax Office (ATO) in respect of the sale; or
(b)   for indirect interests in land only – provides a declaration that the relevant interest is not TAP.

98   Non-residents are not entitled to the 50% capital gains discount available to certain resident investors.

99   We have discussed these rules in further detail above.

[2] *Institutional Investors*

[a] *Taxation of Current Income (All Income Derived from REIT in Holding Phase)*

Institutional investors are taxed the same as private investors in respect of REIT **100** distributions.

[b] *Taxation of Capital Gains (From Disposal of REIT Units)*

Institutional investors are taxed the same as private investors in respect of capital gains **101** except that the discount rate for institutional investors is 50% for trusts, 33.33% for complying superannuation entities and nil for companies. For non-resident institutional investors, the 50% discount rate is not available.

[3] *Penalties Imposed on Investors*

There are no material income tax penalties that are imposed on investors unless the **102** investor understates the taxable income allocated to them by REIT in respect of an income year.

[C] Tax Treaties

[1] *Treaty Access*

Australia has a large treaty network. Whether a REIT is eligible for treaty relief is **103** ultimately dependent on the particular treaty. There is uncertainty when considering certain treaties, particularly with civil law countries where trusts are not recognized. More recent treaties contain specific Collective Investment Vehicles provisions which can also apply to REITs. The Australia–Germany treaty has specific provisions which treat a collective investment vehicle subject to certain conditions as a resident individual of a Contracting State for the purposes of the Treaty (refer to Article 4(4) of the new Australian German Double Tax Treaty, signed on 15 November 2015). These provisions would apply to an Australian REIT where the relevant conditions are satisfied (such as REIT being listed and owned to 75% by Australian residents).

[2] *WHT Reduction*

There is no WHT reduction for distributions by an Australian REIT under the relevant **104** treaties, including the more recent treaties. Typically, most REITs are MITs. MITs have already afforded a concessional WHT rate of 15% and thus there is no further reduction permitted under the treaties.

[D]   Exit Tax/Tax Privileges/Concessions

105 There are no specific exit tax concessions. The treatment of capital gains is discussed in section §1.03[B][1][b] above.

[E]   Taxation of Foreign REITs

[1]   *Taxation of Foreign REIT Holding Assets in Country*

106 A foreign REIT will be subject to income tax in Australia in respect of rental income derived from Australian real estate. The rate of tax will depend on the nature of REIT, but if it is a company, it will be at 30%.

[2]   *Taxation of Investors Holding Shares in Foreign REIT*

107 Australian investors holding shares in a foreign REIT will generally be taxed in Australia on distributions from that REIT and also in respect of capital gains on the disposal of REIT shares.

Belgium

GRÉGORY JURION

Grégory Jurion is a tax partner and is working in PwC Belgium's Financial Services and Real Estate team since 2001.

He has broad experience in advising on international and domestic tax restructuring and is a tax adviser to a number of real estate funds, real estate investment trusts (REITs) and developers. In most of Grégory's assignments, he plays a European coordination role covering foreign investments in Belgium and within the European Union, coupled with real estate advisory practice.

His work qualification is a Bachelor's in Law *cum laude* from the University of Louvain-la-Neuve (Belgium) and a Master's in Law from Solvay Business School (Belgium). He is also a member of the Belgian Institute of Tax Consultants.

Grégory has written a number of articles on tax and has spoken on the subject at in-house and external conferences.

E-mail: gregory.jurion@pwc.com

EVELYNE PAQUET

Evelyne Paquet is a director within PwC Belgium's Financial Services and Real Estate team.

Evelyne has broad experience in providing tax advice on international and Belgian tax restructuring. She is a tax adviser to a number of real estate funds, REITs and developers. She is assisting clients in the due diligence process of real estate companies, including review of tax clauses in purchase agreements, etc. Evelyne also frequently negotiates tax rulings with the Belgian ruling commission on the tax treatment of restructuring activities.

She obtained her Master's in Economics – specialization in finance at the HEC, Liège (Belgium) in 2001 and Master's in Taxation at the ESSF, ICHEC, Brussels (Belgium) in 2003.

E-mail: evelyne.paquet@pwc.com

MAYA VAN BELLEGHEM

Maya is a senior manager within the Financial Services Legal and Regulatory team of PwC Belgium.

She is a former member of the Brussels and Luxembourg bars and specialized in banking, financial law and asset management regulation. She focuses on the regulatory aspects of financial services and on asset management operations.

Maya assists domestic and international clients on the regulatory, corporate and compliance aspects of the structuring, formation, organization, marketing and management of investment vehicles with a strong focus on structuring and organizing private equity and real estate investment funds.

Maya is frequently involved in negotiation with the competent regulatory authorities in Belgium in relation to the registration or listing of regulated investment funds. Throughout her career, Maya gained significant experience in investment management, both in Belgium and abroad.

E-mail: maya.van.belleghem@pwc.com

Belgium

Grégory Jurion, Evelyne Paquet & Maya van Belleghem

§1.01 BACKGROUND

[A] Key Characteristics

The real estate investment trust (REIT) regime in Belgium was introduced as a specific 1
form of an investment company, the *Société d'Investissement à Capital Fixe Immobil-ière* (SICAFI) or *Vastgoedbeleggingsvennootschap met Vast Kapitaal* (VASTGOEDBE-VAK), which is a closed-ended undertaking for collective real estate investments. A parallel regime to the existing SICAFI was introduced in 2014 with the Regulated Real Estate Company (RREC) (*société immobilière réglementée*/SIR or *gereglementeerde vastgoedvennootschap*/GVV). Contrary to SICAFI, RREC is a commercial-operational and listed company that should not qualify as an undertaking for collective investment and should hence not be caught by the alternative investment funds and their managers (AIFM) Law (as defined below).

Provided certain regulatory requirements are met, the Belgian Financial Services and 2
Markets Authority (FSMA) can grant an RREC/SICAFI licence to a new or an existing company. A company that has obtained RREC/SICAFI licence is subject to corporate income tax, but its taxable basis is very limited.

[B] History of REIT

Although the legal basis for investment companies, such as SICAFIs, was created by the 3
Law of 4 December 1990 related to financial operations and financial markets (repealed and replaced by the Law of 3 August 2012 on undertakings for collective investment in transferable securities complying with the conditions of European Directive 2009/65/CE and on securitization undertakings – UCITS Law – and by the Law of 19 April 2014 on AIFM Law), it took until 1995 to introduce the regulatory framework for REITs in Belgium.

4　The Royal Decree of 10 April 1995 (SICAFI I) put in place a regulatory framework that balanced investment flexibility providing security to the investor. The introduction of SICAFI was inspired by the emergence of foreign REITs (such as US REIT or the Dutch FBI (Fiscale Belegginginstelling)) that allowed real estate investments through more transparent structures. SICAFI was enacted to promote real estate investments by private individuals in a relatively safe and tax-favourable environment.

5　The Royal Decree was slightly amended by the Royal Decree of 10 June 2001 ('SICAFI II Reform' – increase of the debt-to-asset ratio from 33% to 50% to remain competitive with some foreign REITs) and more substantially by the Royal Decree of 21 June 2006 ('SICAFI III Reform'). Besides loosening the investment and the leverage restrictions and increasing the debt-to-asset ratio to 65%, SICAFI III Reform has made international financial reporting standards (IFRS) mandatory for both consolidated and statutory accounts of SICAFIs.

6　Following European instigated changes to the legal framework of collective investment vehicles and the evolution of the financial markets, amendments were necessary in order to keep SICAFI as a flexible investment vehicle whereby the investors are protected. Therefore, the Belgian legislator, in close cooperation with the stakeholders of the Belgian SICAFI and real estate sector, decided to replace the Royal Decrees of 10 April 1995 and 21 June 2006 with the Royal Decree of 7 December 2010 ('SICAFI IV Reform').

7　The most important novelty of SICAFI IV Reform was the introduction of a regulatory framework for 'institutional SICAFIs'. An institutional SICAFI is a real estate investment vehicle which, contrary to a public SICAFI, does not offer its shares to the public, but exclusively to institutional or professional investors (e.g., credit institutions, insurance companies, large companies exceeding certain thresholds). The Royal Decree of 7 December 2010 describes the safeguards which must be put in place to ensure the institutional or professional character of their investors. The legislator has decided that an institutional SICAFI must be under the exclusive or joint control of a public SICAFI since the institutional SICAFI is merely intended as a tax attractive vehicle allowing a public SICAFI to realize specific projects with third parties, i.e., other institutional or professional investors (including public partners under public-private partnership). The regulatory framework of the institutional SICAFI aims at protecting the ultimate investors in the public SICAFI (i.e., retail investors).

8　Besides aligning SICAFI regime with the changed legal framework for collective investment vehicles, SICAFI IV Reform provided more flexibility to attract funding. It allows a SICAFI explicitly to issue other securities than shares (such as convertible bonds), and henceforth a SICAFI can increase its share capital through an accelerated procedure without application of the normal preference rights provided that existing shareholders receive an irreducible allotment right upon distribution of the new shares.

Furthermore, SICAFI IV Reform also increases investor protection (strengthening **9** the conflict of interest rules and of the mortgage and debt restrictions, increasing the independence of the real estate expert and of the management, expanding the responsibility of the promoters, especially in respect of the minimum free float) and no longer requires the appointment of a depository.

Following the entering into force of European Directive 2011/61/EU on alternative **10** investment fund managers (AIFMD) and its Belgian implementing law (AIFM Law), SICAFI sector argued that, particularly for real estate investment companies, the additional framework of alternative investment funds (AIFs) does not provide any added value and does not correspond to the economic reality of SICAFIs. In addition, other regulations such as European Market Infrastructure Regulation (EMIR) (Regulation (EU) No. 648/2012 of the European Parliament and of the Council of 4 July 2012 on (over-the-counter) OTC derivatives, central counterparties and trade repositories) would severely and inadequately impact SICAFIs.

Further to the request of the sector and in line with legislative initiatives in neighbour- **11** ing countries, the Belgian legislator adopted the Law of 12 May 2014 on RREC ('RREC Law') and the implementing Royal Decree of 13 July 2014 on RREC ('RREC Royal Decree'). RREC Law and RREC Royal Decree introduced a separate REIT regime in Belgium, next to the real estate investment fund (REIF) of SICAFI. Consequently, since May/July 2014, Belgium has had two different regimes for structuring real estate investments: REIF regime and REIT regime.

RRECs are listed companies subject to supervision of FSMA and to various restrictions **12** in terms of leverage, risk diversification and distribution requirements, in a similar way as SICAFIs are today. However, since RRECs are not REIFs such as SICAFIs, they fall outside the scope of AIFMD and AIFMD Law. RREC is not an undertaking for collective investment with a defined investment policy acting in the interest of investors, but a commercial company having a commercial purpose and acting within the limits of its corporate object. As such, RREC is not falling under the definition of an AIF and, hence, is under the scope of AIFMD and AIFM Law. RREC regime is open to existing SICAFIs (which position themselves commercially and operationally as genuine commercial-operational companies, putting real estate at the disposal of users, and which would hence need to convert into RRECs) as well as to other qualifying real estate companies which meet the various conditions imposed by RREC Law and RREC Royal Decree (e.g., in terms of the type of activities, shareholding structure, eligible assets).

From a regulatory perspective, SICAFIs and RRECs are two different statuses (i.e., REIF **13** and REIT), but from a tax point of view, the regime of such two vehicles is quite similar. The tax regime applicable to SICAFIs was formerly governed by the Law of 4 December 1990 related to financial operations and financial markets, but it is currently incorporated into the Belgian Income Tax Code. RRECs can also benefit from the same special tax regime as SICAFIs. Public and institutional RREC/SICAFI are subject to corporate income tax, although the tax base is not determined based on their accounting result but on a lump sum basis. The alignment of the tax treatment of a public and an institutional SICAFI already dates back to December 2008, but the possibility for institutional SICAFI to benefit from the advantageous tax regime remained, however, theoretical until the introduction of the regulatory framework for institutional SICAFI by the Royal Decree of 7 December 2010.

14 In addition to the existing REIF regime of SICAFI, a new REIF regime was adopted in November 2016: the specialized REIF (*fonds d'investissement immobilier spécialisé*/'*gespecialiseerd vastgoedbeleggingsfonds* commonly called FIIS). This regime is governed by the Royal Decree of 9 November 2016 on specialized REIFs, as published in the Belgian Official Gazette on 18 November 2016 (FIIS Royal Decree). It entered into force on 28 November 2016. Contrary to the public SICAFI, this new REIF is exclusively reserved for professional and institutional investors. The regulatory requirements for FIIS are less stringent than for SICAFI or RREC. For instance, an FIIS has no legal obligation for public issuance/admission to listing on a regulated market of its shares and is not directly supervised by FSMA (a registration with the Ministry of Finance suffices). Additionally, FIIS benefits from flexible regulatory requirements, such as the absence of limits on leverage or the absence of diversification requirements. Contrary to RREC, FIIS will qualify as an AIF, although it can benefit from certain exemptions. Recently, the Law of 2 May 2019 containing various financial provisions (the 'Law of 2 May 2019') has amended AIFM Law and amongst some other provisions applicable to FIIS.

15 The main amendments made by the Law of 2 May 2019 related to:

- (i) the new possibility for joint ventures and club deals to opt for FIIS regime;
- (ii) the minimum share capital requirement (which is no longer EUR 1.2 million, but the minimum capital requirements provided by the Belgian Companies and Associations Code (BCAC), e.g., for public limited liability company, EUR 61,500);
- (iii) some derogations to BCAC which will no longer be applicable to FIIS;
- (iv) the clarification that the Belgian Ministry of Finance is competent to monitor the compliance of FIIS with the provisions of AIFM Law and FIIS Royal Decree. In that respect, new tools are provided to the Belgian Ministry of Finance.

16 Consequently, since November 2016, Belgium has had three different types of vehicles for structuring real estate investments: two REIF regimes (SICAFI and FIIS) and one REIT regime (RREC). Since the present book focuses on REIT regimes, the following sections will exclusively comment on the characteristics of the Belgian RRECs.

[C]   REIT Market

17 Currently, FSMA has granted authorization to seventeen public RRECs and fourteen institutional RRECs (7 February 2022). Next to RRECs, there are approximately 160 registered FIIS in Belgium (7 February 2022). Although the legal framework of SICAFI regime remained in place, in practice, no SICAFIs are registered and active anymore.

The Belgian RRECs represent a market capitalization of more than EUR 13 billion. The **18** majority of RRECs are mainly active in the office building market. Some RRECs specialize in investments in retail, logistics or residential real estate (including senior housing). Furthermore, as companies are looking for solutions to optimize the return on their real estate, RRECs are becoming more interesting vehicles.

[D]   Recent Reforms

Previously, a REIT could be incorporated as either (i) a public limited liability company **19** (*'société anonyme'*/*'naamloze vennootschap'*) or (ii) a partnership limited by shares (*'société en commandite par actions'*/*'commanditaire vennootschap op aandelen'*). BCAC has recently been amended and restated. The legal form of partnership limited by shares has been abolished. Consequently, a REIT can only be incorporated as a public limited liability company. However, BCAC allows incorporating public limited liability companies with the specific features of a partnership limited by shares.

Over the past few years, RREC regime has been discussed and reviewed at political **20** level. In this respect, a law amending RREC Law has been adopted by the Belgian Federal Parliament on 22 October 2017. The changes proposed by this law are related to, amongst other things (i) the extension of the permitted RREC activities to the infrastructure sector, (ii) the abolition of the current obligation for public RRECs to have sole or joint control of the companies in which they hold shares (new minimum participation conditions are however introduced), (iii) the possibility for individuals to hold securities issued by an institutional RREC under certain conditions and (iv) new rules on the maximum debt ratio. In addition, an RREC with a social purpose has been introduced. Next to these amendments to RREC Law, a royal decree amending RREC Royal Decree has been adopted on 23 April 2018. Consequently, the amended RREC regime entered into force on 17 May 2018.

RREC Law has also been amended by the Law of 2 May 2019 to permit RRECs to raise **21** capital in cash through the technique called Accelerated Book Building. This technique allows the raise of capital in cash without having to allocate a preferential subscription right or irreducible allocation right to existing shareholders. Thus, this amendment allows easier and faster access for an RREC to invest in the capital markets.

Article 14(2) of RREC Law has recently been amended by the Law of 28 April 2020, in **22** order to clarify that RRECs may also be set up under the form of a public limited liability company with a sole director (*'société anonyme administrée par un administrateur unique'*/*'naamloze vennootschap die door een enige bestuurder wordt bestuurd'*).

§1.02   REGULATORY ASPECTS

[A]   Legal Form of REIT

[1]   Corporate Form

23   As part of the regulatory framework and the above-mentioned reform of BCAC, only public limited liability companies ('*société anonyme*'/'*naamloze vennootschap*') are eligible for RREC licence. These entities are corporate bodies and have a separate legal personality according to Belgian corporate law.

24   RREC regime is open to both existing and new companies. Registration of an existing company as an RREC by FSMA is to be considered as liquidation for corporate income tax purposes, and an 'exit tax' has to be paid (except in case an existing company with SICAFI licence intends to become an RREC). *See* section §1.03[D] below.

25   As there is an explicit residency requirement, only Belgian companies can obtain the Belgian RREC licence and, hence, benefit from RREC tax regime.

[2]   Investment Restrictions

26   The promoters of RREC, i.e., the persons controlling RREC, have to ensure that at least 30% of the shares in RREC are held by the public. In other words, RREC must have a minimum *free float* of 30%. Persons acting together with the promoters or persons associated with the promoters are not deemed to be a part of the public.

27   Whereas this obligation used to be an initial free float commitment, RREC Law and RREC Royal Decree have made the commitment permanent: the promoters have to ensure a free float of at least 30% from the first year after having obtained RREC licence. Furthermore, the persons who qualify as promoters at the moment RREC has obtained its licence will keep this qualification for at least three years and as long as they have not complied with their obligations. Therefore, even though they no longer have control over RREC, they will remain liable as long as, amongst others, the free float does not amount to at least 30%.

28   In principle, the promoters can freely choose how to comply with this obligation, but, as the means used should reasonably allow the promoters to reach and maintain the minimum 30% free float, the shares are usually made available to the public via listing the shares on a stock exchange (*see* section §1.02[D] below). As such, listing is done on the Euronext Brussels exchange; their market rules should also be taken into account.

29   Next to this free float requirement, there are no restrictions whatsoever as to the type of investors in an RREC or their country of residence.

30   For institutional RRECs, however, only professional or institutional investors ('*investisseurs éligibles*'/'*in aanmerking komende beleggers*') or natural persons investing at least EUR 100,000 can own shares or instruments issued by institutional RRECs. Before the reform of RREC regime in 2017, an institutional RREC needed to be exclusively or jointly controlled by a public RREC. Further to that reform, more than 25% of the share capital of an institutional RREC must be held by an RREC.

[B]   Regulatory Authorities

RRECs and institutional RRECs are subject to authorization ('*agrément*'/'*vergunning*')   **31** and supervision by FSMA. The supervision of institutional RRECs is however limited compared to the supervision on RRECs. The statutory accounts of the institutional RREC are only subject to supervision to the extent that this is necessary for the supervision of the consolidated accounts of RREC. Furthermore, the relation between the institutional RREC and its shareholders which are not RRECs is outside the scope of supervision by FSMA, unless it is required for the consolidated supervision on RREC.

FSMA is a public institution. Its mission consists in directing public offerings, super-   **32** vising the financial markets and controlling public investment funds and, together with the National Bank of Belgium (NBB), financial institutions. FSMA is responsible for protecting the consumers or retail investors of financial services. To perform these tasks, FSMA has the authority to request information and to investigate the books and any other relevant documents at the premises of an RREC.

FSMA plays an important role in the life of an RREC. It not only verifies whether a   **33** company meets the conditions to obtain RREC licence but also supervises RREC's continued compliance with the prescribed legal and regulatory rules and intervenes when necessary to protect retail investor's and market's integrity.

After having obtained its RREC licence, an RREC has to continuously inform FSMA to   **34** allow the latter to play its supervisory mission and tasks. Such information require-ments include, for instance, any changes in the elements and content of the application file that has to be submitted by to FSMA in view of getting RREC authorization, as well as potential conflicts of interest. Furthermore, some contemplated changes require prior authorization by FSMA, such as amending the articles of association of an RREC or appointing new directors of an RREC.

[C]   Legislative and Other Regulatory Sources

The general regulatory framework for RRECs is enacted in the Law of 12 May 2014 (as   **35** previously defined as RREC Law) and the Royal Decree of 13 July 2014 (as previously defined as RREC Royal Decree), as both amended from time to time. RREC Law lays down the general principles with respect to the registration and the operation of RRECs and institutional RRECs and the supervisory role of FSMA.

The tax rules applicable to an RREC including its taxable basis and the exit-tax rules are   **36** set forth in the corporate income tax section of the Belgian Income Tax Code.

37   Furthermore, since an RREC has to offer its shares to the public, a number of other regulations are applicable, such as, amongst others, the Prospectus Regulation (EU) 2017/1129 and the Law of 11 July 2018 on the public offering of investment instruments and the admission of investment instruments to trading on regulated markets, and the Royal Decree of 14 November 2007 regarding the obligations of issuers of financial instruments that are admitted to trading on a regulated market (implementing different directives into Belgian legislation including Directive 2004/25/EC on takeover bids and the so-called Transparency Directive 2004/109/EC), as amended from time to time.

38   Moreover, RRECs and institutional RRECs are subject to BCAC to the extent that the specific regulatory framework does not provide for deviating rules. RRECs and institutional RRECs being commercial companies usually falling outside the definition of AIF should not be subject to the provisions of AIFMD and of AIFM Law.

[D]   Exchange Controls and Reporting Requirements

39   To get listed, RREC, usually in cooperation with an investment services provider, such as a credit institution, a placement agent, an investment bank or an investment firm, will prepare the listing prospectus and the listing application that will be submitted to FSMA (and to Euronext Brussels). After the approval, the shares of RREC can be listed on the stock exchange.

40   Once listed, a company agrees to comply with certain requirements in terms of transparency and financial disclosure. It has to inform its investors of any event that may have an impact (even slightly) on the value of its shares. Furthermore, an RREC has to file annual and semi-annual reports which have been audited by the Euronext Market Undertaking, which approved the listing. Finally, whenever a shareholder of RREC reaches certain shareholding thresholds (5%, 10%, 15% and every further bracket of 5%), RREC has to make this information publicly available. Please note that these thresholds can vary (to a certain extent) depending on the articles of association of RREC.

[E]   Licensing Procedures

[1]   Preparatory Measures: Application File

41   To obtain RREC or institutional RREC licence, a company must submit a request for authorization (commonly called 'application file') with FSMA. The request for authorization has to include a detailed file which demonstrates that the company meets the requirements to be licensed as RREC or institutional RREC and which details the programme of activities of the future (institutional) RREC.

It should contain at least the following elements: **42**

- the (draft) articles of association of RREC;
- a list of the persons who are affiliated or associated with RREC and the shareholders' agreements which may have been concluded by the shareholders of RREC;
- the composition of the corporate bodies of RREC as well as the identity of the statutory auditors of RREC;
- the identity (curriculum vitae and a recent extract from the police records) of all persons involved in the management of RREC;
- evidence that the managers or executive directors of RREC and the directors who are not involved in the management have, amongst others, the required professional reliability, the required expertise, appropriate experience and required independence;
- proof that the board of directors is made of directors allowing an appropriate management of the company's activities (*see* section §1.02[F][5][a] below) and is composed of at least three independent directors (within the meaning of Article 7:87, §1 of BCAC);
- a description of the management structure and of the accounting, financial, administrative and technical organization of RREC in view of the envisaged activities of RREC and the requirements of the law with respect to the authorized activities (*see* section §1.02[F][5][a] below); and
- a financial plan for the first three financial years as from registration, containing in particular (i) prospective balance sheets and profit and loss accounts; (ii) a minimum investment budget allowing to meet the described strategy during the aforementioned period; (iii) an inventory of the real estate properties already held by the company, and other relevant real estate properties, together with the information required to prove that it meets the requirements of the law; and (iv) the justification that RREC and its subsidiaries meet the criteria with respect to the authorized activities (*see* section §1.02[F][5][a] below).

In addition to the above, the application file for an RREC should also include the   **43**
following information (i) the identity of the promoters of RREC; (ii) a list of the independent real estate valuation experts; (iii) the template agreement to be concluded with the real estate valuation experts; (iv) the commitment of the company to trade its shares on a stock exchange at the latest within one year after registration (except when the shares are already traded on a stock exchange prior to the request for authorization); (v) the confirmation of the commitments of the promoters (e.g., the continued commitment to have a 30% free float); (vi) the identity of RREC that has control over the institutional RREC; and (vii) the identity of the institutional RREC's shareholders, and the shareholders' agreements which may have been concluded by the shareholders.

[2]   Obtaining RREC Licence

44   FSMA grants the licence to RREC or institutional RREC provided it meets the requirements imposed by RREC Law and by RREC Royal Decree and provided that the articles of association are in line with these requirements.

45   When FSMA officially decides that RREC or institutional RREC meets all the licensing requirements, the company is considered as an RREC or an institutional RREC and is registered on the list of (institutional) RREC published on the website of FSMA (www.fsma.be).

[a]   Licence

46   To be licensed, the company applying for RREC licence has to prove that it meets all the requirements.

47   RREC thus has to prove, amongst other things, that:

- it has the eligible legal form (public limited liability company) with a share capital of at least EUR 1.2 million which is fully paid up;
- its statutory seat and its head office are located in Belgium;
- it has been incorporated for an undefined period of time;
- it is managed in line with the corporate purpose (contrary to a SICAFI, which is managed in the sole interest of its shareholders/investors);
- it has its own management structure and an administrative, accounting, financial and technical organization which enables it to carry out its activities in line with the authorized activities (*see* section §1.02[F][5][a] below);
- as introduced by RREC Law and RREC Royal Decree, its corporate bodies are solely composed of natural persons who have the requested professional reliability and an appropriate experience (application of the 'fit & proper' rules by FSMA);
- as introduced by RREC Law and RREC Royal Decree, its effective management ('*dirigeants effectifs*'/'*effectieve leiders*') is entrusted to at least two natural persons; and
- it has organized a suitable internal control procedure and integrity policy to ensure compliance with the corporate, legal and regulatory requirements.

48   For a company applying for (institutional) RREC licence, reaching the management and organizational requirements may be challenging. Therefore, RREC and its subsidiaries can delegate their portfolio management to a related company specialized in property management, provided a number of conditions are met.

49   An RREC must also rely for the valuation of its real estate on one or more independent real estate experts who have the required professional reliability, the appropriate expertise and organization. Since real estate also includes shares in affiliated real estate companies (such as institutional RRECs), the real estate held by these companies is also to be appraised by the real estate expert(s) of RREC so that the legislator deemed it unnecessary to impose this requirement on institutional RRECs.

In order to guarantee the independence of the real estate expert, such expert may not **50** have any ties with the promoters of RREC and his remuneration may not be related to the value of the real estate held by RREC and its subsidiaries.

Furthermore, a double rotation system should be observed in appointing the real estate **51** expert(s). First, the expert may only be appointed for a renewable term of three years. Second, after having appraised a property for three consecutive years, the same expert may not appraise that same property for the next three years ('cooling-off period'). When the real estate expert is a legal person, these restrictions only apply to the natural persons representing the real estate expert, provided that the expert demonstrates that these individuals are functionally independent.

RRECs have to observe specific rules for the determination of the fixed and variable **52** remuneration of directors and managers and the disclosures thereof in the reports to the shareholders.

During the analysis of the file, FSMA can request any additional information which it **53** deems necessary to conduct the assessment of the request for authorization.

[b]   Articles of Association

The articles of association of an RREC have to contain a number of specific stipulations. **54**

Annex A to RREC Royal Decree contains the minimum stipulations which should be **55** included in the articles of association of an RREC. Some of these stipulations only apply to institutional RRECs.

[3]   Obtaining Listing on a Stock Exchange

The overall costs for obtaining an exchange listing can be estimated to range between **56** 3% and 6% of the funds raised, but vary from case to case and strongly depends on the amount of capital raised on the market. These costs include regulatory authorities' fees, Euronext stock exchange fees, consulting fees (real estate, legal, tax, accounting, technical, communication), notary fees, publication and printing costs.

The initial public offering process, from the preparation to the actual listing, takes **57** approximately five to seven months (minimum). The time to obtain regulatory authorization takes at least four to eight months, knowing that FSMA takes its decision within three months from when the application file is considered complete.

[F]   Requirements and Restrictions

[1]   Capital Requirements

58   An RREC must have a fully paid-up share capital of at least EUR 1.2 million. However, obtaining a listing on the Euronext stock exchange requires an additional market capitalization. RREC must establish an investment budget plan allowing it to meet the risk diversification criteria within two years after a certain threshold is exceeded.

[2]   Marketing and Advertising

59   In the application file of RREC, the promoters have to commit themselves to ensure that 30% of the voting shares are held publicly within one year after the authorization as RREC. A dual listing on Euronext Brussels and on another European stock exchange is possible.

60   The listing of RREC's shares has to be preceded by the publication of a prospectus. The prospectus has to contain sufficient information to enable the public to make a well-informed decision, taking into account the characteristics of the transaction. All marketing materials for the offering of the shares, including the prospectus and related documents, have to be approved a priori by FSMA.

61   To protect investors, the prospectus should contain a number of specific disclosures to the public investors, including, amongst others (i) a description of the risk diversification criteria of RREC and (ii) the promoters' commitment to reimburse the investors the invested amounts, including fees and costs, in case the total equity funds are lower than the funds mentioned in the investment budget.

[3]   Redemption

62   The redemption of its own shares by RREC is allowed, provided the requirements and constraints imposed by BCAC have been met.

63   Note, however, that an RREC may not redeem its own shares at the request of a shareholder. This is mainly due to the fact that an RREC lacks liquid assets to fund a redemption since its assets mainly consist of real estate.

[4]   Valuation of Shares for Redemption

64   The valuation of the shares is important for the reporting requirements and for the share transactions carried out by RREC, such as redemption of existing shares and issuance of new shares.

At the end of each financial year, an independent real estate expert values the real **65**
estate property, including relating rights in rem, option rights and leasing rights owned
by RREC or by real estate companies in which RREC holds interests, including an
institutional RREC. The assets which have been leased and which have to be accounted
for as receivables under IFRS are excluded from this valuation. This valuation is
binding as regards the drafting of the statutory and consolidated annual accounts of
RREC (*see* section §1.02[F][8] below). Furthermore, the expert updates the total
valuation at the end of the first three quarters of the subsequent financial year based on
the market evolution and the specifics of the real estate properties concerned.

In case of an issuance of new shares, listing of additional shares or redemption of **66**
shares other than through the stock exchange, the expert has to make a new valuation
which, although not binding, should be used by RREC to justify the valuation of the
issuance or acquisition price. No new valuation is needed if the shares are issued
within four months after the latest valuation or actualization thereof if the independent
real estate expert confirms that no new valuation is required.

[5]   *Investment Restrictions*

[a]   *Authorized Activities*

RREC has a strategy of long-term real estate holding. In RREC Law and RREC Royal **67**
Decree, a definition of the authorized activities of an RREC and of an institutional RREC
has been introduced. Those activities are exclusively the activities of making real estate
assets available for its users, either directly or via a participation in a company,
provided the actual value does not exceed 20% of the consolidated assets of RREC,
holding real estate in:

- shares in public SICAFIs;
- participations in foreign AIFs investing in real estate which are registered with
  FSMA;
- participations in AIFs investing in real estate which are established and
  registered in another Member State within European Economic Area (EEA)
  which are not registered with FSMA but are subject to similar regulatory
  control as for public SICAFI;
- shares in REITs subject to the legislation of another Member State within EEA;
  and
- listed real estate certificates ('*certificats immobiliers*'/'*vastgoedcertificaten*').

Since the recent RREC regime reform, RRECs are also authorized to: **68**

(1) directly or indirectly ensure, potentially together with third party(ies) and/or
     using the ability to outsource these activities, the development, establish-
     ment, management, operation of (i) installation and storage facilities for the

transportation, distribution or storage of electricity, gas and non-fossil fuels; (ii) facilities for the transport, distribution, storage or purification of water; (iii) facilities for the production, storage and transportation of energy; and (iv) incinerators and landfills, including related goods;

(2) directly or indirectly conclude, potentially together with third party(ies), with a public contracting authority:

- DBF (Design, Build, Finance) long-term agreements.
- DB(F)M (Design, Build, (Finance) and Maintain) long-term agreements.
- DBF(M)O (Design, Build, Finance, (Maintain) and Operate) long-term agreements.
- Certain types of public procurement long-term agreements.

69 In the framework of making real estate assets available, RRECs can in particular carry out any activity related to the construction, rebuilding, renovation, development, acquisition, disposal, management and operation of real estate assets.

70 For the purposes of RREC Law and of RREC Royal Decree, real estate assets currently include amongst others (i) real estate properties and rights in rem, excluding forestry, agriculture and mining; (ii) shares with voting rights in other real estate companies, jointly or exclusively controlled by RREC; (iii) options rights on real estate; (iv) shares in (institutional) RRECs (the latter requires a joint or exclusive control); (v) real estate certificates; and (vi) immovable leasing rights or similar rights as defined under IFRS.

71 The definition of real estate assets has been modified. It now includes shares of Belgian REIFs. Also, the joint or exclusive control on (institutional) RRECs is not necessary anymore. A minimum interest of 25% is required.

72 The articles of association of an RREC may authorize the investment in other assets. Investments in securities which are not considered to be real estate as defined above are allowed to the extent that they are temporary or of minor importance (to be verified on a consolidated basis) and that they are listed on a regulated market. Such investments need to be explained, detailed and justified in the annual reports. Furthermore, RREC can invest in instruments hedging the financial risk related to real estate financing and management. These investments cannot be speculative.

73 Further to the recent RREC regime reform, two RRECs will be authorized to invest/hold together and/or to set up together subsidiaries or joint-venture. Merger, joint-venture or restructuring between RRECs is now facilitated.

[b]   Control over Subsidiaries

74 The control over subsidiaries has been revamped by the recent RREC regime reform. RREC Law and RREC Royal Decree contain a set of rules regarding investments by an RREC in affiliated companies (called 'perimeter companies' or '*sociétés du* *périmetre'/'perimetervennootschap'*) when they do not hold (directly or indirectly) all the shares representing the entire share capital of the real estate company.

The requirement for an RREC to control, directly or indirectly, its real estate compa- **75** ny(ies) has been repealed. Under the new regime, an RREC has to hold, directly or indirectly, at least 25% of the shares in its real estate company(ies). To ensure RRECs keep a sufficient operational role and supervise sufficiently its perimeter companies, the fair market value of the non-controlling participation an RREC holds in perimeter companies cannot exceed 50% of the consolidated asset value of RREC.

[c] Diversification Requirements

An RREC must diversify its assets in order to adequately spread the investment risks **76** between the geographical area, the investment type and the category of tenant.

In principle, a maximum of 20% of the consolidated assets can be invested in one or **77** more real estate assets which can be considered to constitute a single risk for RREC. Under certain circumstances (for a maximum of two years or in case it would be of the interest of the shareholders or in case it is justified considering the specific nature or size of the investment), FSMA can allow RREC to deviate from this rule, subject to further conditions, such as a maximum consolidated indebtedness of 33%.

[d] Restricted Activities

Some activities cannot be performed by RREC. An RREC nor any perimeter company or **78** subsidiaries may act as a mere property developer ('*promotion-vente'/'bouwpromotie'*); i.e., its activity – excluding transactions on an ancillary basis – may not consist in constructing buildings itself or having them constructed in view of selling them prior, after or within a period of five years after construction.

An RREC may not grant loans to or provide guarantees to companies other than from **79** RREC to its subsidiaries and vice versa. The mortgages or guarantees granted in the framework of the financing of real estate acquisitions may not exceed 50% of the total real estate portfolio value and 75% of the value of the concerned real estate.

RREC and its subsidiaries can engage as a lessee in a lease transaction. However, in the **80** hands of RREC, the net investment relating to a lease agreement whereby RREC has not been granted an option right may not exceed 10% of RREC's assets at the moment of closure of the lease agreement. RREC can act as a lessor if authorized by the articles of association. Leasing activities with an option right can be exercised as an auxiliary activity only. There is no limitation on leasing real estate assets with an option right if such real estate assets are intended for general interest purposes, including social housing and education.

[e]   *Debt Restrictions*

81   RREC's statutory and consolidated debt ratio cannot exceed 65% of its statutory and consolidated assets.

82   Variations in the fair market value of the real estate as such do not trigger non-compliance with this rule, provided that RREC is below the threshold of 65% within two years. In case the 65% threshold is exceeded for more than two years, a general shareholders' meeting should discuss and decide on the possible dissolution of RREC.

83   When the debts exceed 50%, RREC must establish a financial plan indicating how it will avoid exceeding 65% in the future. This plan must be audited by the statutory auditor of RREC.

84   Furthermore, RRECs' annual financial charge cannot be higher than 80% of the total operational and financial income.

[6]   Distribution

85   A minimum of 80% of the corrected net result of an RREC and an institutional RREC, reduced by the amounts corresponding to the net decrease of their debts during the financial year, must be distributed to its shareholders by means of dividends.

86   The corrected net result is the net profit realized during the accounting year, excluding non-cash results (e.g., write-offs, variations in the fair market value of the real estate) and capital gains realized on real properties to the extent that the amount of the capital gain will be reinvested in qualifying assets within four years. The part of the capital gain that is not reinvested within this period of time is added to the corrected net result for the following accounting period.

87   However, this obligation can only be carried out to the extent that the dividend distribution respects the boundaries imposed by BCAC. Indeed, as a consequence of the dividend distribution, the net assets of a Belgian limited liability company or a partnership limited by shares may not drop below its paid-up capital increased with the reserves which are not available for distribution. RREC Royal Decree defines in its annexes which reserves should be taken into account since RRECs have a specific reporting scheme (*see* section §1.02[F][7] below). Upstreaming cash (dividends) from an institutional RREC to RREC is easier than from a normal real estate company as the former is subject to IFRS and not to Belgian Generally Accepted Accounting Principles (GAAP).

88   The dividend distribution by an (institutional) RREC is restricted due to the debt-to-assets ratio of RREC. The debt-to-assets ratio should be considered on both statutory and consolidated bases (unless RREC holds the entire share capital of its subsidiaries). When the debt-to-assets ratio of an RREC exceeds 65% or would as a consequence of the dividend distribution exceed the said threshold, an RREC may not distribute any dividend and an institutional RREC, whose share capital is not entirely held by an RREC (directly or indirectly), may only conditionally distribute a dividend.

An RREC must reserve the amount which it would have distributed in the absence of **89** this restriction as well as the dividends received from institutional RRECs (in order to allow the latter to distribute a dividend). RREC can only use this reserve for repayments necessary to decrease the debt-to-assets ratio below 65%. The balance of this reserve may afterwards be distributed as a dividend.

An RREC may also decide to give investors the choice to receive a dividend in shares **90** rather than in cash.

[7] Reporting Requirements

RREC and institutional RRECs are subject to reporting requirements mentioned in **91** BCAC, such as the deposit with NBB of the annual statutory and consolidated accounts together with the annual report as drawn up by the board of directors and the auditor's report.

RREC Law and RREC Royal Decree prescribe that an RREC also has to publish an **92** annual and a half-year reports containing at least the (detailed) elements which have been mentioned in Annex B of RREC Royal Decree. It includes, for example, an inventory of the assets, an overview of the transactions, inventory value of shares, information on investment markets, composition of real estate portfolio, vacancy, hedging policy, justification of transactions whereby there is more than 5% difference between actual price and the real estate expert valuation, remuneration of real estate experts and auditors. The information on the institutional RREC controlled by RREC is included therein so that the legislator has only imposed this obligation on RREC.

Since an RREC is a listed company, it is also subject to the reporting obligations **93** mentioned in the Royal Decree of 14 November 2007 regarding the obligations of issuers of financial instruments that are admitted to trading on a regulated market. Generally speaking, the issuers have to put the required information available to the public in order to ensure the transparency, integrity and proper functioning of the market. Furthermore, the listed company must publish its annual report within four months after the end of the financial year and the half-year report as soon as possible and, in any event, within three months after the first six months of the financial year. Such publication must be done so that it is easily accessible. RREC must also publish the reports on its website.

[8] Accounting

The statutory account and the consolidated accounts (if any) of an RREC and of an **94** institutional RREC are to be prepared and approved according to IFRS. A specific reporting scheme is provided for by RREC Royal Decree.

95 Under IFRS, real estate investments have to be recorded in the books at 'fair market value'. This fair market value is the price that a well-informed third party would pay for the real estate, after deduction of the transfer taxes. The amount of these transfer taxes is dependent on the type of transfer, the buyer and the geographical location of the real estate property.

96 The Belgian Asset Managers Association issued guidelines in 2006 as to the amount of transfer taxes which can be deducted depending on the fair market value of the real estate:

- value below EUR 2.5 million: registration duties are estimated at 10% (real estate located in the Flemish Region) or 12.5% (real estate located in the Brussels Capital or Walloon Region);
- value exceeding EUR 2.5 million: registration duties are estimated at 2.5%.

97 In 2016, a panel of valuers and the *Belgian REIT Association* jointly decided to have an update of this calculation prepared in accordance with the methodology applied in 2006. The panel of valuers concluded that the above guidelines should be maintained. The rate will be reviewed every five years or when the fiscal context would change considerably.

§1.03   TAXATION

98 As all of the former SICAFIs have converted to an RREC, we will hereinafter describe the tax regime of an RREC which is mainly the same as the one applicable for a SICAFI unless otherwise stated.

[A]   Taxation of REIT

[1]   Corporate Income Tax

99 Public, as well as institutional RRECs, are subject to corporate income tax, but they benefit from a special tax status. However, when a public RREC holds simultaneously participation in institutional RRECs and normally taxed Belgian real estate companies with the aim of taking advantage of tax arbitrage, the general anti-abuse provision may be applied.

[a]   Tax Accounting

100 Under general Belgian tax rules, no specific tax accounting is needed since the corporate income tax is determined based on the accounting result under Belgian GAAP. Although an RREC is subject to corporate income tax at 25% (as from the assessment year 2021, related to the taxable period starting at the earliest on 1 January

2020), the taxable result is determined alternatively compared to regular companies subject to the corporate income tax. RREC is taxed on a lump sum rather than on a profits basis (*see* section §1.03[A][1][b] below).

[b]   *Determination of Taxable Income*

The taxable income of an RREC is limited to (i) the abnormal or benevolent advantages   **101** received, (ii) the non-deductible expenses (excluding the reductions in value on shares and capital losses realized on shares) and the secret commission tax, which can be due on certain fees that are not correctly reported to the tax authorities.

Advantages are abnormal in case they are not in line with what is customary and   **102** benevolent in case they have been granted without any compensation. Therefore, in case the transactions of an RREC do not reflect open-market conditions (i.e., as if the transaction was with a third party), RREC has received or granted an abnormal or benevolent advantage. The advantages received constitute an element of the taxable basis of an RREC.

A 30% EBITDA (earnings before interest, taxes, depreciation, and amortization)   **103** limitation rule is introduced in the financial year 2019. Under the implementation of the Anti-Tax Avoidance Directive, a fixed ratio rule is applicable which states that the 'exceeding borrowing costs' are only tax deductible up to the higher of (i) 30% of the 'tax-adjusted EBITDA' of the company or (ii) EUR 3 million. RREC is however excluded from the application of the 30% EBITDA limitation rule.

Regional taxes, such as office space tax, are not deductible for tax purposes, and   **104** constitute a large part of the taxable basis of an RREC. The immovable withholding tax, which is the main property tax in Belgium, is however considered a deductible expense.

The corporate income tax that has been provisioned for accounting purposes is a   **105** non-deductible expense. There is some discussion about whether the provisioned tax is to be included in the taxable basis of an RREC. In this respect, the Belgian Supreme Court decided with respect to (the former) Belgian Coordination Centers (whose (minimal) taxable basis was identical to the taxable basis of an RREC but based on another legal provision) that the provisioned tax due is not to be included in the taxable basis of the entity to avoid a tax-on-tax situation. However, according to the position of the tax authorities and recent lower case law, this position regarding Belgian Coordination Centres cannot by analogy be applied for an RREC, resulting in a tax-on-tax situation for RRECs. On 20 October 2016, the Belgian Constitutional Court rendered a decision confirming the non-discriminatory character of the inclusion of the corporate income tax expenses/provisions as a disallowed expense in the corporate income tax return of an RREC. This was again confirmed in June 2017 by the Antwerp Court of Appeal. In September 2019 the Court of Cassation confirmed this position.

106   There is also discussion in doctrine about whether or not the withholding tax on interest and dividends received should be included in the taxable basis of a SICAFI. Since the assessment year 2014, however, withholding tax on Belgian dividends received is no longer creditable by SICAFI/RREC and the position of the tax authorities is hence that the withholding tax on Belgian dividends must no longer be included in the taxable basis of a SICAFI/RREC.

107   An RREC is also subject to secret commission tax of 100%, which is due on certain fees that are not correctly reported to the tax authorities on form 281.50 and relating summary statement 325.50. The rate is further limited to 50% in case it can be demonstrated that the beneficiary of the income is a legal entity, or that the hidden profits are recorded in later financial accounts (this second option, related to the recording of the hidden profits in the financial accounts, has been abolished as from the assessment year 2021, related to the taxable period starting at the earliest on 1 January 2020), to the extent the taxpayer has not been informed (in written) on the ongoing tax audit. The secret commission tax does not apply in case it can be demonstrated that the beneficiary properly has declared the income. Further, in case the income was not properly declared by the beneficiary, no secret commission tax is levied if the beneficiary is identified at the latest within two years and six months following 1 January of the tax year concerned. The secret commission tax is not to be considered a non-deductible expense, and it should not be added to the taxable basis of RREC. Since the assessment year 2021 related to the taxable period starting at the earliest on 1 January 2020, the secret commission tax charge is to be considered a non-deductible expense.

108   As an RREC is taxed on a lump sum basis, no deductions such as dividend received deduction can be used to offset against the above-mentioned taxable items.

[c]   *Taxation of Income from Taxable/Non-taxable Subsidiaries*

109   The interest and dividend income received by RREC from its subsidiary are not taxed in Belgium. However, if the interest rate received exceeds an open-market interest rate, the difference is considered to be an abnormal or benevolent advantage received by RREC and added to the taxable basis of the latter.

110   As regards the treatment of the withholding taxes on the dividend distributions or interest payments made by the subsidiary to its RREC parent, *see* section §1.03[A][3] below.

111   The capital gains realized by n RREC on the disposal of the shares in its subsidiary are not included in its taxable basis.

[d] Taxation of Foreign Income

Foreign income is not included in the Belgian taxable basis of an RREC (taxable basis **112** is lump sum based, *see* section §1.03[A][1][b] above). It may however be taxed in the source state.

[2] **Value Added Tax**

[a] VAT Status of REIT

The Value Added Tax (VAT) status of an RREC depends on its outgoing supplies of **113** services to its subsidiaries or to the tenants of the real estate assets.

RREC can render support and management services to its subsidiaries. Such services **114** will be subject to VAT and will entitle RREC to recover input VAT on costs linked to the services rendered.

For real estate assets directly owned, RREC will receive rental incomes. In Belgium, **115** rental income is generally exempt from VAT with several exceptions. Therefore, RREC will often generate VAT-exempt revenues with no input VAT deduction.

That said, in January 2019, the Belgian government adopted a new law allowing opting **116** for the application of VAT on commercial rent for real estate assets build after 1 October 2018.

In practice, RREC will normally apply the direct cost allocation methodology for VAT **117** deduction. This means, for example, that the costs will be allocated to a specific building and VAT deduction will be determined based on the income (VAT exempt or not) generated by that building. For the overheads, a percentage of VAT deduction will be determined, for instance, based on the turnover subject to VAT and VAT exemption.

[b] Management of REIT and of the Real Estate Assets

Even if RREC is not considered a fund from a regulatory point of view, the management **118** of an RREC is VAT exempt according to Article 44, §3, 11° Belgian VAT Code (VAT exemption relating to the management of special investment funds).

In this respect, the services rendered to RREC must be analysed in order to determine **119** whether they fall within the scope of that VAT exemption.

Distinction Between Financial/Administrative Management and Property Management

In the case 'Fiscale Eenheid X' C-595/13, the Court of Justice of the European Union **120** ruled that the management of property funds that are subject to specific state supervision benefits from VAT exemption for fund management services. However, the management of the real estate assets (e.g., property management) is not covered by VAT exemption, as it is not specific to the activity of a special investment fund.

121   A distinction must therefore be made between the financial and administrative management and the management of real estate assets.

122   In the same vein, the Belgian ruling commission indicated[1] that financial and administrative management services are exempt from VAT but that tasks relating to the actual operation of the immovable property are not VAT exempted. It concerns in particular services relating to:

   – project monitoring and development;
   – commercialization of the immovable property, including the negotiation and conclusion of letting agreements (e.g., lease and/or rights in rem) with users;
   – the actual management of the immovable property, including the negotiation and conclusion of letting agreements;
   – analysing the opportunity for additional investments, repairs and maintenance, as well as closing down the contracts necessary for their implementation.

123   The contractual framework with RREC manager, property manager and other services suppliers should be assessed to determine if the services rendered to RREC benefit from VAT exemption or not.

[3]   Withholding Taxes

[a]   Interest Income Received by a REIT

124   Interest payments are in principle subject to a 30% withholding tax.

125   The Belgian tax law provides, however – under certain conditions – for a withholding tax exemption for interest payments received by a professional investor being defined as a Belgian resident company, which should also be applicable on interest payments made to an RREC.

126   RRECs should be able to benefit from a general exemption from Belgian withholding tax on movable income other than Belgian dividends (i.e., including interest). This exemption is subject to the formal condition to provide the debtor with a certificate confirming that the revenue relates to assets owned by RREC. Furthermore, to claim the exemption, the permanence condition should be met. RREC has to be the owner of the interest-bearing security during the entire period the interest corresponds to. The debt instruments have to be registered during the entire taxable period with the issuer

---

1. Decision 2017.948 dated 23 May 2018.

in case of registered securities. Dematerialized securities have to be registered with a clearing institution located in EEA or a recognized account-holder.

The Belgian Minister of Finance has confirmed that if the interest payments have been **127** subject to withholding tax, the latter is creditable (and refundable) in proportion to the period during which RREC has had full ownership of the interest-bearing security.

[b] Dividend Income Received by a REIT

Dividends paid by a Belgian company to an RREC are in principle subject to a 30% **128** withholding tax.

Since the withholding tax treatment of domestic dividends has been aligned to the **129** Parent-Subsidiary Directive as implemented in Belgian tax law, RREC can benefit from a withholding tax exemption on the dividends received from a Belgian company, provided that RREC has a participation of at least 10% in the share capital of the distributing company for an uninterrupted period of at least one year (or in case of commitment to keep such minimum participation during at least one year).

If Belgian dividends received by an RREC have been subject to withholding tax, the **130** latter is no longer creditable (nor refundable) in the framework of RREC's corporate income tax return (since the assessment year 2014).

[c] Dividend Distributed by a REIT

Withholding tax on dividends paid by an RREC amounts to 30%. **131**

A reduced withholding tax rate of 15% on dividends distributed is applicable since 1 **132** January 2017 for dividends distributed by RRECs investing at least 60% of their assets in health care property. This threshold has recently been increased to 80% and applies to dividend distributions made by RRECs as of 1 January 2022.

Dividends distributed by RRECs may benefit from certain Belgian domestic withhold- **133** ing tax exemptions:

Dividends distributed to certain non-resident investors

Since 1 July 2016, a withholding tax exemption in principle applies to dividends distributed by an RREC to non-resident investors (i.e., any foreign private person or legal entity who does not use its shares to carry out a professional activity in Belgium). This exemption applies to the extent that the dividends distributed do not stem from Belgian-source income, i.e., dividends distributed by Belgian companies or real estate located in Belgium. The exemption on dividends remains nevertheless applicable via a look-through approach in case they stem from dividends distributed by other Belgian RRECs or by Belgian funds (e.g., SICAFI, REIF, any other Belgian UCITS or AIFM fund) in so far that the redistributed dividends do not stem from Belgian-source income. To this end, a breakdown should be provided by the RREC in order to determine to which extent the withholding tax exemption should apply.

Dividends distributed to certain non-Belgian pension funds

Non-Belgian pension funds benefit, under certain conditions, from a general exemption of dividend withholding tax, including on dividends distributed by an RREC (*see* section §1.03[B][2][a] below).

Dividends distributed to a Belgian tax resident company holding a 'substantial' participation in the RREC could benefit from an exemption under the Parent-Subsidiary Directive.

Indeed, for dividends distributed by an RREC to a Belgian tax resident company, an exemption of withholding tax would be available, provided that the Belgian company has a participation of at least 10% in the share capital of the distributing company for an uninterrupted period of at least one year (or in case of commitment to keep such minimum participation during at least one year).

[4] Other Taxes

134 From the year following their registration with FSMA, RRECs are subject to an annual tax on their net asset value to the extent that their shares are held by Belgian shareholders. The tax rate amounts to 0.0925% for public RRECs and 0.01% for qualifying institutional RRECs. RRECs must annually file prior to 31 March a return and declare their net asset value as per 31 December of the previous year.

135 The contributions in cash or in kind (e.g., real estate) made to an RREC benefit from an exemption from proportional registration duties. Only the fixed duty of EUR 50 will in principle be due. However, to the extent that the contribution in kind is remunerated by any other means than with newly issued shares (e.g., by the assumption of the corresponding debt), proportional registration duties will be due since the contribution will be partially considered to be a sale, triggering 10% or 12.5% registration duties depending on the type and location of the contributed real estate (i.e., Flemish Region, Walloon or Brussels Capital Region) unless this contribution qualifies as a branch of activity.

[5] Penalties Imposed on REIT

136 RRECs are generally subject to the same penalties for infringing tax provisions (corporate income tax, VAT, etc.) as any other taxable entity.

[B]   Taxation of the Investor

[1]   Retail Investors

[a]   Taxation of Current Income (All Income Derived from REIT in Holding Phase)

An RREC does not pass through its income to investors; it distributes its profits to investors via a dividend. As regards the withholding taxes/tax exemption for dividends distributed by an RREC, *see* section §1.03[A][3] above.   **137**

The tax treatment of a dividend paid by an RREC to a private investor depends on the legislation of the country where the investor resides. In Belgium, the withholding tax, if any, on the dividends received by private individuals or by legal entities (not subject to corporate income tax) is the final tax, so that no dividend income is declared (unless opted for globalization of income).   **138**

Please note that capital gains realized by a Belgian resident individual (i) upon redemption of own shares, (ii) upon the complete or partial distribution of the net assets, or (iii) upon transfer for valuable consideration of the shares in a so-called Undertaking for Collective Investment in Transferable Securities are treated as interest subject to Belgian income tax at a rate of 30% provided certain conditions are met. This specific rule is applicable *inter alia* when the investment company (or sub-fund) invests for more than 25% – since 1 January 2018, this threshold has been reduced to 10% – in interest-bearing assets.   **139**

Since an RREC is an investment company that benefits from a regime that deviates from the common corporate income tax regime, the dividend distributed by an RREC to a corporate investor can in principle not benefit from the participation exemption and is fully taxable in the hands of the Belgian tax resident company shareholder at 25% (since the assessment year 2021, related to the taxable period starting at the earliest on 1 January 2020).   **140**

The participation exemption can in principle not be applied to dividends distributed by an RREC to Belgian tax resident companies.   **141**

However, since July 2016, in case the dividends (i) stem from real estate located in a European Union (EU) state other than Belgium or with whom Belgium has concluded a double tax treaty including an exchange of information clause and (ii) have been subject to the Belgian (non-resident) corporate income tax or a similar non-Belgian tax (which does not deviate from a normal income tax regime), the participation exemption can be applied.   **142**

Furthermore, the participation exemption can also be applied provided the articles of association of RREC state that annually at least 80% of the net revenue will be distributed to the shareholders to the extent that the income stems from dividends   **143** meeting the taxation condition or from capital gains that qualify for the participation exemption.

[b]   Taxation of Capital Gains (From Disposal of REIT Shares)

144   Capital gains realized by a Belgian private individual from the disposal of public RREC shares are not subject to tax so long as the gain is realized within the boundaries of a normal management of private assets.

145   However, capital gains are taxable (at 16.5%, unless opted for globalization of income) if realized by a private individual or a legal entity (not subject to corporate income tax) on the transfer of shares in a Belgian tax resident company such as an RREC to a non-resident company or governmental body outside EEA to the extent the transferor, alone or together with his relatives as defined by law, have directly or indirectly held at any time in the five years preceding the transfer at least 25% of the shares.

146   In the unlikely event that shares in RREC are held in the framework of a professional activity, then any capital gains realized upon disposal are taxable in the hands of the individual at the applicable progressive rates.

147   Capital gains realized on the disposal of RREC shares held by corporate investors are taxable at 25% (since the assessment year 2021, related to the taxable period starting at the earliest on 1 January 2020), to the extent that the subject-to-tax condition for the participation exemption is not met. For more details, *see* section §1.03[B][1][a] above.

[2]   Institutional Investors

148   Retail and institutional investors are in principle taxed on the income derived from an RREC in the same way, irrespective of whether the income is dividend distributions or capital gains.

[a]   Taxation of Current Income (All Income Derived from REIT in Holding Phase)

149   *See* section §1.03[B][1][a]. However, specific tax benefits are available to certain institutional investors in an RREC. As an example, certain non-resident pensions may claim a withholding tax exemption for the dividends received from an RREC if they are exempt from income taxes in their country of residence.

[b]   Taxation of Capital Gains (From Disposal of REIT Shares)

150   *See* section §1.03[B][1][b] above.

[3]   Penalties Imposed on Investors

No specific penalties apply.   **151**

[C]   Tax Treaties

[1]   Treaty Access

Based on Article 4 of the Organisation for Economic Co-operation and Development   **152**
(OECD) Model Tax Treaty, an RREC should be eligible for treaty protection as it can be
considered to be a resident for tax treaty purposes. An RREC is subject to corporate
income tax in Belgium be it that the taxable basis is significantly reduced (notional tax
basis). Note, however, that treaty access is determined on a case-by-case basis.

[2]   WHT Reduction

The Belgian RREC legislation does not impose a maximum holding participation on   **153**
RREC shareholders. Therefore, withholding tax reductions are generally available
provided the minimum participation requirements for withholding tax reductions laid
down in Article 10 OECD Model Tax Treaty are met.

[D]   Exit Tax/Tax Privileges/Concessions

When an existing company obtains RREC status, it is deemed to be liquidated for tax   **154**
purposes. This means that the latent capital gains and the tax-free reserves also become
taxable. As regards the applicable tax rate, the taxable basis should be divided between
the result realized during the accounting period up to the liquidation, which is taxed at
the standard corporate income tax rate of 25% (since the assessment year 2021, related
to the taxable period starting at the earliest on 1 January 2020), and the latent capital
gains and the tax-free reserves, which are taxed at 15% (since the financial year 2020).

In case an existing company is merged or (partially) split into an RREC, the above-   **155**
described exit tax equally applies for tax purposes, including the split of the taxable
basis for the application of the reduced tax rate.

Since 1 July 2016, if an existing company contributes real estate properties into an   **156**
RREC remunerated solely with newly issued shares, the above-described exit tax also
applies to the latent capital gains (no reduced rate however on the transfer of tax-free
reserves). Up to 1 July 2016, capital gains triggered by a contribution of real estate into
an RREC were taxable at the standard corporate income tax rate of 33.99% (corporate
income tax rate applicable before the last corporate income tax reform whereby the rate
was reduced to 25%) in the hands of the corporate transferor.

157   Capital gains triggered by a sale of real estate to an RREC are taxed at the standard corporate income tax rate of 25% (since the assessment year 2021, related to the taxable period starting at the earliest on 1 January 2020) in the hands of the corporate transferors. In case a contribution is made by a private individual or a legal entity (not subject to corporate income tax), the capital gains realized by the latter persons are not taxable if the property was held for more than five years (transfer of land and building) or for more than eight years (transfer of land without a building) if realized within the boundaries of a normal management of private assets.

158   The conversion of a SICAFI, REIF (in French: FIIS; in Dutch: GVBF) or a non-listed Belgian private equity fund (*PRICAF/PRIVAK*) into an RREC does not trigger the exit tax.

159   Under the liquidation regime when an existing company obtains RREC licence, the liquidation bonus (i.e., the positive difference between the fair market value of the assets and the paid-up capital of the existing company) benefits from a withholding tax exemption. In case of a merger or (partial) split, the liquidation bonus is in principle subject to 30% withholding tax, unless in case of a lower treaty rate or under the conditions of the Parent-Subsidiary Directive as implemented in Belgian law.

[E]   Taxation of Foreign REITs

[1]   *Taxation of Foreign REIT Holding Assets in Belgium*

160   Based on Article 6 of the OECD Model Tax Treaty, the income derived by a foreign REIT from real estate located in Belgium is taxable in Belgium. The foreign REIT is taxed at 25% (since the assessment year 2021, related to the taxable period starting at the earliest on 1 January 2020) on its Belgian real estate income as if it is a regular company subject to Belgian non-resident corporate income tax. Interest expenses are deductible if they are at arm's length and the beneficiary of the interest payments does not benefit from a regime that is noticeably more advantageous.

161   EU discrimination issues with respect to the fundamental freedoms could arise as Belgian tax legislation treats foreign REITs with real estate located in Belgium less favourably than Belgian REITs with Belgian real estate as only the latter can benefit from the significantly reduced notional tax basis described under section §1.03[A] above.

[2]   *Taxation of Investors Holding Shares in Foreign REIT*

162   Dividends received by individual Belgian investors holding shares in a foreign REIT are taxable. Individuals pay Belgian tax of 30% on the dividend received (unless opted for globalization of income), without credit for foreign withholding tax paid (unless a treaty reduction applies).

Dividends received by a Belgian company from a foreign REIT are in principle not **163**
eligible for the participation exemption assuming the distributing REIT company is
subject to a tax regime that is deviating from the Belgian common tax regime. Belgian
tax law explicitly excludes the participation exemption for dividends distributed by a
foreign real estate company assimilated to a Belgian RREC (as defined in Belgian tax
law).

However, in case the dividends (i) stem from real estate located in an EU state other **164**
than Belgium or with whom Belgium has concluded a double tax treaty including an
exchange of information clause and (ii) have been subject to the Belgian (non-resident)
corporate income tax or a similar non-Belgian tax (which does not deviate from a
normal income tax regime), the participation exemption can be applied.

Furthermore, the participation exemption can also be applied provided the articles of **165**
association of the foreign REIT state that annually at least 80% of the net revenue will
be distributed to the shareholders to the extent that the revenue stems from dividends
that meet the taxation condition or from capital gains qualifying for the participation
exemption.

Brazil

EDUARDO ALVES DE OLIVEIRA

Eduardo is a PwC partner responsible for the Financial Services industry and Real Estate in Brazil. Eduardo is experienced in Brazilian and international tax, advising large banks, private equity funds, venture capital funds and multinational corporations on structuring, mitigating tax risk and improving their tax strategy. He has gained his experience working in São Paulo, Brazil and Boston, US. With twenty years at PwC, Eduardo has extensive experience working with financial institutions and investment managers to develop innovative fund, hedging and deal structures for foreign investors in the Brazilian financial market.

Eduardo holds a Bachelor's in Law from Mackenzie University, in Accounting from the University of São Paulo (USP), a Master's in Accounting and Business/Management from USP and a PhD in Tax and Accounting from USP.

Eduardo is the author of books related to the financial industry, among them 'Taxation – Current Topics' and 'Economic Availability of Fair Value'.

E-mail: eduardo.alves@pwc.com

Brazil

Eduardo Alves de Oliveira

---

§1.01 BACKGROUND

[A] Key Characteristics of REIT

In Brazil, an investment vehicle for real estate endeavours is called a Fundo de **1** Investimento Imobiliário – Real Estate Investment Fund (FII). These funds are always closed end. Shares of these funds should be registered before by the Brazilian Securities and Exchange (Commission Comissão de Valores Imobilia'rio (CVM)). FII can invest in real estate properties (logistic, commercial or residential) or securities linked to any real estate asset or receivables.

[B] History of REIT in Country

FII was first authorized in 1993. **2**

Despite the current political and economic scenario in Brazil, the country is still an **3** attractive destination for investment in Real Estate Investment Trust (REIT), especially for foreign investors, due to the depreciation of national currency and tax incentives available.

[C] REIT Market

As of June 2020, there were FIIs in operation in Brazil, with approximately BRL 132 **4** billion in net assets, representing 2% of the equity in the Brazilian Funds industry.[1]

---

1. Data according to *Brazilian Association of Financial and Capital Market Entities* (Associação Brasileira das Entidades dos Mercados Financeiro e de Capitais – ANBIMA).

5 FIIs portfolios can be compared to Equity REITs – consisting basically of real estate assets (some financial investments are allowed to grant liquidity to the fund). Mortgage and Hybrid REITs do not necessarily create a parallel with the Brazilian system.

6 The main objective of statement last amendments (Normative 472/08 of CVM) was to update the discipline of real estate funds in order to bring them close to the other funds regulated by CVM and at the same time, make the rules more flexible in its formation and in its functioning. A relevant growth in the amount of operations in the real estate market using investment funds can be noticed in the past years, mostly through FII and through Participation Investment Fund (FIP).

7 From a regulatory point of view, it is possible to understand that FII is the most similar vehicle if compared to REITs.

8 Note that there is no further consideration of 'FIP' in this chapter.

§1.02   REGULATORY ASPECTS

[A]   Legal Form of REIT

[1]   Corporate Form

9 FII is not a legal person but is entitled to assume certain rights and obligations on its behalf.

[2]   Investment Restrictions

Unitholder Requirements

10 In order to avoid the use of FII as a tax planning instrument, FIIs may not invest in a real estate which has as developer, builder or partner, a quotaholder or FII which holds solely or with related parties more than 25% of FII quotas, or it will be taxed as a corporation for income tax purposes. Unitholders may be persons or legal entities, in Brazil or abroad.

11 If FII applies for the tax exemption benefit, all the unitholders have to be Brazilian individuals, there have to be a minimum of fifty investors and no investor can own more than 10% of FII nor be entitled to receive more than 10% of FII earnings.

[B]   Regulatory Authorities

12 FII is regulated and controlled by CVM. FII must be formed and managed by institutions duly authorized by CVM, which must exclusively be financial institutions with investment portfolios, real estate assets, credit portfolios or other financial instruments.

Requirements for the financial institution: **13**

- must obtain the due register for FII formation;
- must register the units' offering and distribution;
- must register the constitution of such an FII in the registered office of acts and bonds.

CVM must approve the following events: **14**

- adjustments to FII's regulations;
- issuing of new units;
- indications/substitutions of the person responsible for trust's management;
- mergers, spin-offs or liquidations;
- units' secondary emissions.

Loss of status rules would subject FII's net income to a 34% corporate tax. **15**

[C]   Legislative and Other Regulatory Resources

FII regime is governed by Federal Law 8.668/93, amended by 9.779/99, 11.196/05 and **16** 12.020/09, and subsequently issued Regulations CVM 205/94, 206/94, CVM 389/03, 418/05, CVM 472/08, CVM 554/14, CVM 571/15, CVM 580/16, CVM 604/18.

CVM regulation of FII is detailed in CVM Instruction 472/08 and amendments. **17**

[D]   Exchange Controls and Reporting Requirements

Up to 2008, there were prohibitions for any type of Brazilian Fund, including, FII, to **18** invest abroad; such rules were amended and therefore it is now possible for Brazilian Funds to invest abroad. While the rule has been made more flexible for general funds, FIIs are still prohibited from investing overseas capital raised in the country.

CVM must approve some of FII's acts as indicated in section [B]. **19**

[E]   Registration Procedures

[1]   Preparatory Measures

Basically, preparatory procedures to register FII shares should follow the same rules **20** applicable to any other type of investment fund.

Before the process of offering FII shares, it is mandatory to obtain the registry issued by **21** CVM.

22   The request for registry should be presented with documents, such as request for public offering; by-laws of the fund; indication of an independent auditor; indication of the administrator of the fund and others. Upon submission/presentation of the documents and information herein mentioned, CVM will automatically grant in ten days the registration of the fund.

23   Once the registration is granted, a request must be filed including information and documents such as: Distribution Agreement, Liquidity Agreement, Appraisal of Economic Situation of the Company, Risk Factors, Financial Statements, By-laws, among others.

24   Upon submission/presentation of the documents and information herein mentioned, CVM has a twenty days term for approving public offerings. Distributions may be subject to a simpler approval procedure if destined solely for professional investors (restricted offerings).

25   Lastly, the contribution to capital of FII should be preferably proceeded in Brazilian Reals; however, whether established in the By-laws, it is possible to contribute in assets or with rights related to assets.

26   In case of a contribution in kind, there should exist an appraisal validating the amount contributed.

27   By-laws should establish a minimum amount to be contributed to FII. In case this amount cannot be reached, the other shareholders should contribute the amount established according to By-laws. In the case of first distribution of shares, this event can cause the termination of FII.

[2]   Obtaining Authorization

28   *See* section §1.02[E][1] Preparatory Measures above.

[3]   Other Requirements for the Incorporation of the Company

29   Not Applicable.

[4]   Obtaining Listing Exchanges

[a]   Costs

30   Not Applicable.

[b]   Time

Not Applicable.   **31**

[F]   Requirements and Restrictions

[1]   Capital Requirements

No minimum initial capital requirement exists. The capital is divided into units and   **32**
must be all paid for. The payment of capital may be in the form of real estate or usufruct
rights that must first be market-value evaluated. All units must be paid for within the
term determined under By-laws; otherwise, the capital must be proportionally returned
to investors.

[2]   Marketing/Advertising

Not applicable.   **33**

[3]   Redemption

FII does not allow investors' redemption of units, so units can only be sold in the open   **34**
market through the Stock Exchange or over the counter. The term of FII may or may
not be predetermined (must be established in FII's by-laws). In the case where the term
is not determined, a unitholder has no other means of realizing the value of the units
unless there is a unanimous decision of all the unitholders to return capital.

The fund manager though can consider redeeming part of the capital if that is not   **35**
necessary within the fund prior to the liquidation.

[4]   Valuation of Shares/Units for Redemption and Other Purposes

Not Applicable. *See* section §1.02[F][3] Redemption above.   **36**

[5]   Investment Restrictions

The REIT must be invested only in financial fixed income/securities and derivatives   **37**
regarding hedging of its own assets.

[6]   Distribution/Accumulation

Operative Income

38   At least 95% of the realized cash profits must be distributed each semester (30 June and 31 December).

Capital Gains

39   Only gains which the investors realize through the disposal of their shares.

40   When FII sells one of the assets of its portfolio, the gain is distributed as profit to the quotaholders.

[7]   Reporting Requirements

41   Total Net asset value (NAV) and NAV per share must be reported on a daily basis.

42   Monthly reports have to include the trial balance, statement of the composition and diversification of the fund's portfolio and a statement that includes details of the account balance and the transactions during the period.

43   Annually, FII has to report its audited financial statements.

[8]   Accounting

44   Financial statements must be audited and published.

§1.03   TAXATION

[A]   Taxation of REIT

[1]   Corporate Income Tax

[a]   Tax Accounting

45   Revenue from real estate activities is tax-exempt in FII's portfolio, regardless of whether that income is ordinary income or capital gains. The portfolio itself is not taxable including financial income arising from real estate activity (real estate receivables, real estate funds' shares and other fixed-income real estate bonds) (*see* section §1.03[A][3] Withholding Taxes below), except variable income.

[b]   Determination of Taxable Income

Solely the assets invested into financial investments (variable income) will trigger   **46**
taxable income in FII's portfolio (*see* section §1.03[A][3] Withholding Taxes below).
Additionally, if FII invests in a real estate which has as developer, builder or partner a
quotaholder or FII which holds solely or with related parties more than 25% of FII
quotas, it will be taxed as a corporation for income tax purposes and, as such, income
will be subject to taxation.

A recent administrative decision by the Federal Revenue has established that if an FII   **47**
invests in quotas of other FIIs, the revenues arising from such investment, as well as
the sale of such investments, would trigger taxable income in FII's portfolio. Although
this decision represents solely the position of the Federal Revenues (and therefore,
does not represent a position of legal or administrative tax authorities), it should be
considered as a risk in respect of the taxation of FIIs investing in the FII quotas
(shares/units).

[c]   Taxation of Income from Taxable/Non-taxable Subsidiaries

Profits from a Brazilian subsidiary of an FII are taxable at the subsidiary level, and   **48**
dividends will be tax-free in FII portfolio.

[d]   Taxation of Foreign Income

Not applicable at portfolio's level in Brazil.   **49**

[2]   Value Added Tax

Not applicable.   **50**

[3]   Withholding Taxes

Revenue from non-real estate investments is subject to withholding income tax. The   **51**
tax is 15%–22.5% on a cash basis over the variable income investments. There is an
exemption for certain fixed-rate instruments arising from real estate activity (real estate
receivables, real estate funds' shares and other fixed-income real estate bonds).

[4]   Other Taxes

No other taxes are levied on FII.   **52**

[5]   **Penalties Imposed on a REIT**

53   Not applicable.

[B]   **Taxation of the Investor**

[1]   *Private Investors*

[a]   *Taxation of Current Income (All Income Derived from REIT in Holding Phase)*

54   Final withholding income tax of 20% over units' revenue.

55   Pursuant to Federal Law 11.196/05, individual unitholders may be exempt from the withholding income tax if:

- units have been negotiated in the stock market;
- there are at least fifty unitholders.

56   This exemption is not applicable to individuals with more than 10% participation in the units or FII's revenues.

[b]   *Taxation of Capital Gains (From Disposal of REIT Shares)*

57   Individual investors are subject to a final withholding income tax of 20% on capital gain from the disposal of FII interests. If sold via Exchanges, there is no tax if the amount of gain realized by the investor is less than BRL 20,000 (around USD 5,228) per month.

58   Foreign investors are subject to withholding income tax of 15% on capital gains from the disposal of FII interests. There is no taxation if the interest is sold through the Exchanges, and the investor is not a resident in a tax haven jurisdiction.

[2]   *Institutional Investors*

[a]   *Taxation of Current Income (All Income Derived from REIT in Holding Phase)*

59   Withholding income tax of 20% over units' revenue can be offset with the tax due by corporates at the end of the period.

60   Corporate investors are subject to a withholding income tax of 20% on FII revenue. The tax can be offset with tax due on portfolio's gains.

[b]   *Taxation of Capital Gains (From Disposal of REIT)*

Corporate investors are subject to income tax and social contribution tax on income **61** from the disposal of FII interests. The combined rate is 34%.

Foreign investors are subject to withholding income tax of 15% on capital gains and no **62** taxation if the shares are sold through the Exchanges and considering an investor no resident in a tax haven jurisdiction.

Foreign investors located in tax havens are subject to the same treatment provided to **63** local investors (20% withholding income on capital gains).

[3]   *Penalties Imposed on Investors*

Not applicable.   **64**

[C]   Tax Treaties

[1]   *Treaty Access*

Tax treaties do not impose a benefit condition once compared to the ones offered to **65** foreign investors.

[2]   *WHT Reduction*

See section §1.03[B][1][a] Taxation of Current Income and §1.03[B][1][b] Taxation of **66** Capital Gains above.

[D]   Entry Tax/Tax Privileges/Concessions

The Tax on Financial Operations for Foreign exchange Operation of the Entrance **67** reaches 0% in the acquisition of FII.

[E]   Taxation of Foreign REITs

[1]   *Taxation of Foreign REIT Holding Assets in Country*

Taxation of foreign REITs depends on whether the assets in Brazil are owned directly **68** or indirectly (e.g., through a Special Purpose Vehicle or an FII). The tax burden can vary from 15% to 34%.

[2]   *Taxation of Investors Holding Shares in Foreign REIT*

69 Brazilian investors owning shares in foreign REITs are subject to a tax of 15% on capital gains realized from the disposal of REIT interests. As of 2017, taxation rates on the disposal of foreign REITs will be subject to a progressive rate ranging from 15% to 22.5%, depending on the gains.

70 Earnings from the holding are taxed monthly. The rate of tax varies from 0% to 27.5%, depending on the amount received.

Bulgaria

DAMYAN LESHEV

Damyan Leshev has co-authored the chapter on Bulgaria while working at Tsvetkova Bebov and Partners, one of the major Bulgarian business law firms, which cooperates on an ongoing basis with the PwC network. He works in the financial services law team and specializes in capital markets law. He holds a Master's in Law from the Faculty of Law of the University of National and World Economy, Sofia, Bulgaria and a Bachelor's in Accounting and Control from the same university.
E-mail: damyan.leshev@tbp.bg

EKATERINA ALEKSOVA

Ekaterina Aleksova is a senior manager in PwC Bulgaria. She works in the corporate income tax team and is involved in tax structuring projects and tax assignments, including various cross-border transactions. She is a member of the PwC real estate and transfer-pricing network. Ekaterina holds a Master's in Business Taxation from Osnabrück University, Germany, and a Master's in Finance from the University of National and World Economics, Sofia, Bulgaria.
E-mail: ekaterina.aleksova@pwc.com

Bulgaria

Damyan Leshev & Ekaterina Aleksova

§1.01   BACKGROUND

[A]   Key Characteristics

The Bulgarian real estate investment trust (REIT) is a public joint-stock company, a **1** closed-end fund, which invests in real estate and raises funds through the issuance of securities. Bulgarian REITs are regulated under the Special Purpose Investment Companies and Securitisation Companies Act (the 'Act'). The Act was promulgated on 12 March 2021 and replaced the previous Special Purpose Investment Companies Act (SPICA). A REIT can carry out its activities lawfully only if licensed by the Bulgarian Financial Supervision Commission (FSC) (the 'Commission').[1]

[B]   History of REIT

The adoption of SPICA[2] (replaced by the Act) in 2003 aimed to stimulate further growth **2** of the real estate market in Bulgaria (and the investment markets overall). Most REITs were established in 2005, 2006 and 2007 under the regime of the then-existing SPICA. Most REITs are established for an indefinite period of time, while there is a possibility of REITs being term funds. As of 14 February 2022, there are fifty-three REITs operating in the Republic of Bulgaria.

---

1. This is an oversight authority independent of the government, which supervises the financial markets, except for the banking sector which is supervised by the Bulgarian National Bank.
2. As for SPICA, in addition to REITs, the Act regulates special purpose investment companies investing in accounts receivables ('securitization of receivables'). Except for the eligible investment assets (real estate or receivables), the rules applicable to both types of special purpose investment companies are generally the same.

[C]   REIT Market

3   The majority of REITs are diversified, and they invest in a wide variety of real estate transactions. However, there are also specialized funds, which invest only in agricultural land.

4   As of 14 February 2022, seventeen REITs are listed on the Main Market of the Bulgarian Stock Exchange – Sofia. Other REITs are listed on the less liquid Bulgarian Alternative Stock Market.[3]

5   The total market capitalization of the actively traded seventeen Bulgarian REITs, i.e., those listed on the Main Market, as of the end of January 2022 was BGN 1,047,816,661 (approximately EUR 535,740,152).

6   BG REIT,[4] the specialized stock exchange index for REITs, rose by 14.22% between 15 February 2020 and 14 February 2022.[5]

§1.02   REGULATORY ASPECTS

[A]   Legal Form of REIT

[1]   Corporate Form

7   REIT is a public closed-end joint-stock company which invests in real estate. Under Bulgarian law, REITs are qualified as undertaking collective investments (*see* section §1.02[E][1] below for information on the formation of the company). REITs are managed and represented under the one-tier system of management by a Board of Directors. Their Articles of Association have to contain some REIT-specific provisions. A REIT can neither reorganize itself into another type of company nor change its scope of business unless it explicitly withdraws from its licence.

[2]   Investment Restrictions

8   No more than fifty founders may establish a REIT.

---

3. As of 14 Feb. 2022, the SPV market in Bulgaria consists of fifty-three REITs, including special purpose investment companies investing in securitization of receivables. These SPVs were listed on the Bulgarian Stock Exchange – Sofia, the more liquid on the main (regulated) market, the less liquid on the Bulgarian Alternative Stock Market, called BaSE Market.
4. BG REIT is an index based on the free-float-adjusted market capitalization and covers seven issues of common shares of special investment purpose companies that operate in the field of securitization of real estates and/or land, i.e., REITs, with the greatest market value of the free-float and market capitalisation, which meet certain additional requirements.
5. The statistical information is published on the website of the Bulgarian Stock Exchangewww.bse-sofia.bg.

[B]   Regulatory Authorities

The competent authority is the Bulgarian FSC – refer to footnote 1. The FSC issues   9
licences for REITs, authorizes their prospectuses, and oversees the activities of REITs
as issuers of securities and as licensed entities. The FSC also supervises REIT service
companies. REITs need FSC permission to amend their Articles of Association, change
the depository bank for the outsourcing of activities to a service company, and
reorganize or terminate.

[C]   Legislative and Other Regulatory Sources

The legal regime of REIT is set out, particularly in the following domestic laws and   10
regulations:

- Special Purpose Investment Companies and Securitisation Companies Act.
  The Act defines the process of investing in real estate assets indirectly, that is
  through investment in the shares of REIT, as 'securitization' of real estate.
- FSC Act.
- Public Offering of Securities Act.
- Act on the Activity of Collective Investment Schemes and Other Undertakings
  for Collective Investments.
- Ordinance No. 11 of 3 December 2003 of the FSC on the Licenses for
  Performance of Activities as a Regulated Market, Market Operator, for Orga-
  nization of Multilateral Trading Facility, for Performance of Activities as an
  Investment Intermediary, an Investment Company, a Management Company,
  a Special Purpose Investment Company, National Investment Fund, Person
  Managing Alternative Investment Fund, and data reporting service provider.
- Ordinance No. 2 of 9 November 2021 on the Initial and Subsequent Disclosure
  of Information upon Public Offering of Securities and Admission of Securities
  to Trading on a Regulated Market.
- Regulation (EU) 2017/1129 of the European Parliament and of the Council of
  14 June 2017 on the prospectus to be published when securities are offered to
  the public or admitted to trading on a regulated market, and repealing
  Directive 2003/71/EC ('Prospectus Regulation').

The ordinances listed above are adopted by the FSC under the authority to adopt   11
ordinances delegated to the FSC. The FSC also issues instructions to clarify specific
laws and regulations.

[D]   Exchange Controls and Reporting Requirements

Listing is mandatory for Bulgarian REITs (*see* section §1.02[F][1] below).   12

13   REITs have reported obligations as undertaking for collective investments under the Act on the Activity of Collective Investment Schemes and Other Undertakings for Collective Investments. REITs are required to publish the following information in their quarterly, semi-annual and annual reports:

- information on the share of assets which REIT has assigned to third persons for use against consideration compared to the total amount of securitized assets;
- information about the sale or the purchase of new assets whose value exceeds 5% of the value of the securitized assets;
- information on the measures undertaken to meet the requirements of the Act;
- some other information specified in FSC's ordinances;
- REITs which hold an interest in a service company must also present information on the activity of the relevant service company in their semi-annual and annual reports. In addition, REITs holding interest in a service company should disclose in their quarterly financial data information on the equity interest in such company;
- REITs which hold an interest in a special purpose vehicle (SPV) must also present information on the activity of the relevant SPV in their semi-annual and annual reports. In addition, REITs holding interest in an SPV should disclose in their quarterly financial data information on the equity interest in such company; and
- information on the real estate possessed on the territory of other EU Member States, per relevant countries.

14   REITs are not subject to any special foreign exchange control requirements, but according to Bulgarian law, local companies must report information on foreign transactions to the Bulgarian National Bank.

[E]   Registration Procedures

[1]   Preparatory Measures

15   A REIT is established at a constituent meeting at which its shares are subscribed. The founders may not be more than fifty.

[2]   Obtaining Authorization

16   Not later than six months from the date of its entry into the commercial register, the prospective REIT is required to submit to the FSC an application for the issuance of a licence allowing the prospective REIT to perform activities as a REIT. Pursuant to the Act, the application must include a prospectus for a mandatory capital increase through public offer of shares and admission to trading on a regulated market (in relation to the resolution for the initial capital increase adopted by the constituent meeting of REIT; *see* section §1.02[F][1] below).

The FSC issues a licence and authorizes the prospectus within a month of the receipt of the application or where additional data and documents are required (which the FSC can request once only), within fifteen days of receipt of such additional materials.   **17**

[3]   *Other Requirements for the Incorporation of a Company*

REIT's corporate name must include the indication, 'joint-stock special purpose investment company'.   **18**

A REIT comes into existence upon its registration with the commercial register.   **19**

[4]   *Obtaining Listing Exchanges*

[a]   *Costs*

REITs are required to obtain a listing on a regulated market at the time of the mandatory share capital increase (*see* section §1.02[F][1] below). The rights related to the capital increase must be listed first. The cost of listing is minimal.   **20**

[b]   *Time*

Not later than thirty business days from the issuance of the specific licence, REIT must notify the regulated market whereon REIT shares shall be offered. The notification must specify the date on which the rights offering shall start, the terms for subscription and information on the nominal and issue value of the shares to be subscribed. According to recent amendments in the Public Offering of Securities Act, REIT must apply for registration of its shares for listing with the special register of the FSC within seven days after the registration of the capital increase, following the rights offering, in the Commercial Register and to apply for listing within two business days after the registration with the register of the FSC.   **21**

[F]   **Requirements and Restrictions**

[1]   *Capital Requirements*

The capital of a REIT subscribed at its incorporation may not be less than BGN 500,000. The capital must be paid in full before REIT is incorporated through the registration with the commercial register. The contributions to the initial capital may not be in kind.   **22**

23   The shares of a REIT must be book-entry securities even before they are listed.[6] A REIT may not issue preferred shares with multiple votes.

24   Upon the incorporation of a REIT, the constituent meeting is obliged to pass a resolution for an initial capital increase that is a minimum of 30% of the initial share capital (i.e., at least BGN 650,000 if REIT was incorporated with the minimum legally required capital). The capital increase has to be by way of issuance of shares of the same class as those subscribed at the constituent meeting. The founding shareholders do not have pre-emption rights in the initial capital increase.

25   The initial capital increase can be performed only on the basis of a prospectus authorized by the FSC. The first capital increase is to be effected through the issuance of rights entitling the holders to take part in the subscription of the increase. One right is issued for each share. Rights, and consequently the shares issued in the increase, must be listed.

26   The monetary funds of a REIT and securities owned by a REIT are to be entrusted for safekeeping to a depository bank which performs all payments for the account of the REIT.

[2]   *Marketing/Advertising*

27   No special rules apply to the marketing of REITs, but REITs have to comply with all rules on the dissemination of information applicable to public companies. In general, REIT prospectus has to contain the information and meet the requirements provided for in the Prospectus Regulation and the Public Offering of Securities Act (general rules) and the Special Purpose Investment Companies and Securitisation Companies Act (special rules). In particular, marketing should be done in a way which does not breach the rules against market abuse.

[3]   *Redemption*

28   REITs are closed-end: their shares are not subject to the statutory right of redemption. In practice, REITs in Bulgaria do not issue redeemable shares.

[4]   *Valuation of Shares/Units for Redemption and Other Purposes*

29   Not applicable.

---

6. Registers for book-entry securities are currently kept by the Central Securities Register, maintained by Central Depository AD, which is a company held by the various market participants and the State.

[5]   *Investment Restrictions*

REITs are entitled to invest in: **30**

- real estate and limited property rights in real estate, construction works and improvements, with the purpose of providing the property for management, letting out, leasing and selling the property;
- mortgage-backed bonds admitted to trading on a trading venue in an EU Member State (up to 10% of their own funds);
- service companies for their own needs (up to 10% of their own funds);
- REITs may invest their free cash in securities, issued or guaranteed by an EU Member State and in bank deposits in banks, which are authorized to perform activities in such Member State. REITs may invest in such assets within six months after the registration of any capital increase within the relevant registries;
- SPVs specialized in the acquisition of real estate and limited property rights and construction works (up to 30% of its total assets and provided that REIT exercises control over the respective SPV). Certain additional requirements apply to SPVs, which are eligible investments by REITs; and
- other REITs (up to 10% of its total assets).

The total amount of investments (save for these mentioned in the fourth point above, within the period specified therein) in assets specified above cannot exceed 30% of the REIT's assets.

REITs may not acquire real estate which is the subject of a legal dispute. Any real estate **31** acquired must be located in the territory of Bulgaria or other EU Member State (the possibility to make real estate investments located in other EU Member State must be explicitly reflected in the REIT's Articles of Association and its prospectus). The SPVs, in which REITs can make investments, may in turn invest in real estate located in Bulgaria or other EU Member States (including other state parts of the European Economic Area).

REITs may not guarantee obligations of other persons, save for bank loans provided to **32** a subsidiary SPV (preliminary approval of the general meeting of shareholders of the respective REIT is necessary) or provide loans or borrow money from persons other than banks.

Moreover, a REIT may not perform directly the activities relating to management and **33** maintenance of acquired real estates, performance of constructions and improvements thereon, or, respectively, collection of amounts resulting from acquired receivables. These have to be outsourced to one or more companies ('service companies'). REITs may themselves invest in service companies under certain restrictions and with certain limitations.

[6]   Distribution/Accumulation

34 REITs in Bulgaria are income – rather than growth-generating investments. REITs must distribute at least 90% of their adjusted accounting profits for the respective financial year as dividends, which are payable within twelve months after the end of the financial year. Adjustments to the accounting profit aim to eliminate the effects of accounting entries which are not related to cash flows. When certain additional requirements are met, REITs may distribute semi-annual dividends.

35 REITs may not increase their capital with bonus shares, that is, through capitalization of distributable earnings.

36 As joint-stock companies, Bulgarian REITs are required by the Commercial Act to maintain a reserve fund.

[7]   Reporting Requirements

37 *See* section §1.02[D] above.

[8]   Accounting

38 Prior to acquiring real estate, REITs are required to assign the valuation of the property to one or more qualified experts (with the purpose of avoiding conflicts of interest, there are certain restrictions concerning the experts). According to the Act, the prices at which a REIT acquires real estate may not be considerably higher, and the prices at which it sells real estate may not be considerably lower than the expert valuation unless there are exceptional circumstances. In this case, the persons who manage and represent REIT must explain their actions in the next regular report.

39 The real estate held by REIT must be valued at the end of each financial year, or in case of a change of more than 5% in the index of the prices of real estate or in the inflation index determined by the National Statistical Institute. Such valuation must be presented in the financial reports of REIT in accordance with the requirements of accounting legislation.

40 REITs follow International Financial Reporting Standards in their reporting.

§1.03 TAXATION

[A] Taxation of REIT

[1] Corporate Income Tax

[a] Tax Accounting

REITs established under the Act are taxable entities but they are exempt from corporate **41** income taxation. They are legally obliged to distribute at least 90% of their profits (distribution profits) as dividends. The dividends distributed by REITs are subject to taxation at the level of the unitholder.

[b] Determination of Taxable Income

REITs in Bulgaria are not subject to corporate income tax and do not adjust their **42** financial statements for tax purposes.

[c] Taxation of Income from Taxable/Non-taxable Subsidiaries

REITs are legally restricted from owning a subsidiary company, except that REITs may **43** invest:

- up to 10% of their registered capital in service companies (i.e., companies which manage and control REITs);
- up to 30% of their total assets in SPVs specialized in acquisition of real estate and limited property rights and construction works provided that REIT exercises control over the respective SPV. Certain additional requirements apply to SPVs, which are eligible investments by REITs; and
- up to 10% of their total assets in other REITs.

Any dividends REIT receives from the service company, SPV or the other REIT, are not **44** taxable to REIT and are distributed as profits to the investors in REIT.

[d] Taxation of Foreign Income

REITs are legally restricted to investing only in Bulgaria. They cannot have foreign- **45** sourced income.

[2]   Value Added Tax

46   If the seller is registered for Bulgarian value added tax (VAT) purposes, there will be a 20% VAT for the purchase of regulated land plots and the buildings/parts thereof that qualify as 'new buildings' (i.e., buildings whose use permit was issued less than five years ago). The purchase of land (other than regulated land plots, i.e., building land plots), buildings that are not new and parts thereof, as well as their adjacent land, is exempt from VAT. However, the seller may decide to treat the sale as a VAT-able supply.

47   The renting out of buildings by REIT for business purposes or holiday use is a VAT-able transaction. If VAT-able turnover from such rent reaches BGN 50,000 for a period of twelve consecutive months, REIT will have to register for Bulgarian VAT purposes and start charging VAT on the rent invoiced after VAT registration.

48   Both renting out buildings or parts thereof for residential purposes and renting out land are VAT exempt, but if REIT is VAT registered, it may decide to charge VAT on the value of the rental payments.

49   If REIT deducts VAT charged on the acquisition of real estate, that real estate would also be used for VAT-exempt supplies within a period of twenty years, and REIT may become obliged to adjust part of the deducted VAT.

50   If REIT is VAT registered in Bulgaria, and REIT sells regulated land plots and new buildings/parts thereof, it should charge 20% VAT. The tax base is the price of the property increased by transfer tax, a 0.1% registration fee and notary fees if the tax and the fees are paid and requested by the supplier. The sale of land (other than regulated land plots) and old buildings/parts thereof is a VAT-exempt transaction, for which VAT may be optionally charged.

[3]   Withholding Taxes

51   *See* section §1.03[B] below.

[4]   Other Taxes

52   The transfer of real estate is subject to a transfer tax from 0.1% to 3.0% on the higher of the purchase price or the statutorily determined tax value of the real estate. The exact rate of the transfer tax is determined by the municipality in which the property is located. Generally, the tax is paid by the buyer unless otherwise agreed. In case the buyer of the real estate is located abroad, the seller should pay the transfer tax.

53   There is a 0.01%–0.45% annual real estate tax levied on the higher than the gross book value and the statutorily determined tax value of the real estate (except agricultural land and forests) held by REIT. The exact rate of real estate tax is determined by the municipality in which the property is situated. Specific higher real estate tax rates were introduced in the legislation as of 1 January 2019 (e.g., in the range of 0.5%–0.7% for certain property located in touristic resorts); however, these were later announced as counter-Constitutional by the Constitutional Court.

A garbage collection fee determined by each municipality is collected for the real estate **54** situated in the municipality. The fee is not a tax, but it is generally assessed in conjunction with the real estate tax. It is expected that in 2024, new rules for the calculation of garbage collection fees will come into force. Under these rules, the amount of the fee due should be determined in accordance with the actual volume of the garbage. However, the exact methodology of fee calculation is still under discussion.

[5]   Penalties Imposed on REITs

Because REITs are not subject to corporate income tax, penalties cannot be imposed on **55** them for corporate income tax non-compliance. REITs may be penalized if they do not comply with their VAT, transfer tax, real estate tax and garbage collection fee obligations. The penalties for infringements of VAT regulations are the most severe. Moreover, if REIT does not meet the capital requirements, it will not be registered or will be dissolved.

[B]   Taxation of the Investor

[1]   Private Investors

[a]   Taxation of Current Income (i.e., All Income Derived from REIT in Holding Phase)

A final withholding tax of 5% is levied on the gross amount of dividends distributed by **56** REIT to a Bulgarian or a non-resident individual.

Non-resident individuals can lower or eliminate the withholding tax on dividends **57** under the provisions of an applicable Double Tax Treaty (DTT). See section §1.03[C][2] below.

[b]   Taxation of Capital Gains (From Disposal of REIT Shares)

Capital gains from the sale of the shares in REIT by resident and European **58** Union/European Economic Area (EU/EEA) resident individuals are exempt from tax if the sale was made on a Bulgarian, EU/EEA regulated market of securities. The disposal of shares on these markets by non-EU/EEA residents, as well as the disposal on other markets by resident and non-resident individuals, would trigger a 10% tax on the capital gain. The taxable gain is the difference between the acquisition price and the sales price of the shares.

59 Non-resident individuals can lower or eliminate the tax on capital gains from the sale of shares under the provisions of an applicable DTT. The application of DTT is subject to the same conditions as for the withholding tax on dividends.

[2]   Institutional Investors

[a]   *Taxation of Current Income (i.e., All Income Derived from REIT in the Holding Phase)*

60 Dividends distributed by REITs are included in the taxable income of a resident institutional investor and are subject to corporate income tax at a rate of 10%.

61 Under the Bulgarian tax legislation, there is a 5% withholding tax on dividends distributed by REITs to a non-resident institutional investor. No Bulgarian withholding tax is due if the investor is an EU/EEA tax resident.

[b]   *Taxation of Capital Gains (From Disposal of REIT Shares)*

62 Capital gains from the disposal of shares in REIT (i.e., the difference between the acquisition price and the sales price of the shares) by a resident institutional investor are exempt from taxation if the disposal of the shares is done on a Bulgarian, EU/EEA regulated market. If the sale is made on other markets, the capital gains are included in the taxable income of the company and are subject to 10% corporate income tax.

63 Similarly, capital gains from the disposal of shares in REITs by a non-resident institutional investor are exempt from taxation if the disposal of the shares is done on a Bulgarian, EU/EEA regulated market. If the sale is made on other markets, the capital gains are subject to a 10% withholding tax on the difference between the acquisition price and the sales price of the shares.

64 The withholding tax can be reduced or eliminated by following the applicable DTT procedure.

[3]   Penalties Imposed on Investors

65 There are no specific tax penalties for investors in REITs under the Bulgarian tax legislation. REIT investors are subject to the general corporate income tax and personal income tax penalties for non-compliance.

[C]   Tax Treaties

[1]   Treaty Access

Bulgaria has a large treaty network with more than sixty countries around the world.   **66**
However, pursuant to the legal restrictions established by the Act, a REIT cannot have
foreign source income in respect of which to apply a favourable DTT regime (*see*
section §1.03[A][1][d] above).

If the respective treaty provides for a lower rate for income payable by a REIT to a   **67**
foreign resident, such relief may be applied. However, it should be noted that there are
some legal restrictions on the transactions which may be entered into by local REITs,
and accordingly, the items of income which could be payable to a foreign resident are
limited.

[2]   WHT Reduction

An advance clearance procedure for DTT relief must be followed if the income accrued   **68**
to the foreign recipient exceeds BGN 500,000 (EUR 255,646) for the calendar year.

If the accrued income is less than BGN 500,000, DTT can be applied directly by the   **69**
foreign recipient. For direct application of DTT relief, the non-resident must give REIT
a tax residence certificate and a declaration of beneficial ownership of the income.

[D]   Exit Tax/Tax Privileges/Concessions

There are no specific exit tax regulations in respect of REITs.   **70**

[E]   Taxation of Foreign REITs

[1]   Taxation of a Foreign REIT Holding Assets in Country

There are no specific rules regarding the taxation of foreign REITs under the Bulgarian   **71**
tax legislation. The general tax rules apply to them.

A foreign REIT is subject to a 10% withholding tax in Bulgaria in respect of rental   **72**
income derived from Bulgarian real estate and capital gains from the sale of Bulgarian
real estate. Generally, no tax treaty exemption is available in respect of such items of
income.

If a foreign REIT has a permanent establishment in Bulgaria and is allowed for offering   **73**
as a collective investment scheme in the country, it is exempt from corporate income
tax. If the foreign REIT has a permanent establishment in Bulgaria and is not allowed

for offering as a collective investment scheme, the income attributable to the permanent establishment is subject to 10% corporate income tax.

74   Further, depending on its activities in Bulgaria, the foreign REIT may need to register for Bulgarian VAT purposes.

[2]   Taxation of Investors Holding Shares in a Foreign REIT

75   Bulgarian individual investors holding units in a foreign REIT are taxed in Bulgaria on gross dividends received from the foreign REIT at a rate of 5%.

76   Capital gains from the sale of the units of a foreign REIT are included in the annual taxable income of the investor and are subject to personal income tax at a flat rate of 10%. If the transaction has been made on an EU/EEA regulated market, then the income is not taxable.

77   Dividends distributed by a foreign REIT to a Bulgarian institutional investor are included in the taxable income of the company unless REIT is an EU/EEA tax resident.

78   Capital gains realized by Bulgarian institutional investors from the sale of units of the foreign REIT are subject to 10% corporate income tax unless the transaction has been made on an EU/EEA regulated market.

Canada

CHRIS VANGOU

Chris is a partner in the Toronto office of PwC and is a member of the Canadian Real Estate Tax Practice. Chris is primarily involved in providing advice to public and private real estate companies, Real Estate Investment Trusts (REITs) and tax-exempt funds. He has extensive experience advising real estate clients in the area of tax planning for acquisitions, divestitures, partnership and joint-venture arrangements, financings and investments in and out of Canada. His clients are involved in land and commercial development, infrastructure projects and the ownership of offices, shopping centres, hotels and residential properties.

Chris is a Chartered Professional Accountant and a graduate of the University of Toronto. He is a member of the Tax Committee of the Real Property Association of Canada. Chris has presented at various conferences and seminars.
E-mail: chris.vangou@pwc.com

KEN GRIFFIN

Ken is a partner in the Toronto office of PwC and is a member of the Real Estate and Private Company Services groups. Ken provides advice on Canadian income tax issues to private companies and their shareholders in a variety of industries. He focuses, in particular, on the real estate sector and in this area also works with public REITs, pension funds and domestic and foreign investment funds. Ken's experience includes structuring new investments – both domestic and cross-border – advising clients on tax reorganizations and shareholder estate planning matters and handling tax issues regarding the use of partnerships, joint ventures, trusts and other ownership and financing arrangements.

Ken graduated from the University of Waterloo, Ontario with a Bachelor of Mathematics and is a Chartered Professional Accountant. Ken is a member of the Joint Committee of Taxation of the Canadian Bar Association and the Chartered Professional Accountants of Canada.
E-mail: ken.griffin@pwc.com

KEVIN NG

Kevin is a partner in the Toronto-based Financial Services Tax Group and leads the Canadian Tax Reporting & Strategy Practice as well as the Private Equity/Pensions Tax Practice.

With more than twenty-five years of experience in the investment and financial services industry, Kevin is focused on providing practical tax solutions for asset management, real estate, banking, and capital markets organizations.

Kevin began his career with PwC, and after eleven years in the assurance and tax practice, Kevin joined a Canadian public company as its Director, Taxation and ultimately took on the role of Vice President, Taxation. During a thirteen-year span in the industry, Kevin acquired significant practical experience in a wide range of areas, including investment product development, real estate and real estate investment products, mergers and acquisitions, financing strategies, executive compensation and general corporate tax planning.

E-mail: kevin.ng@pwc.com

ALEX HOWIESON

Alex is a partner in the Toronto office of PwC. Alex works closely with Canadian and foreign REITs, and domestic and international private equity funds investing in Canadian and foreign real estate. Alex has significant experience advising clients on acquisitions, and dispositions, financing, joint-venture arrangements, and mergers and acquisitions.

Alex is a chartered professional accountant and received a Bachelor of Commerce from the University of Toronto.

E-mail: alex.t.howieson@pwc.com

Canada

Chris Vangou, Ken Griffin, Kevin Ng & Alex Howieson

§1.01   BACKGROUND

[A]   Key Characteristics

Since 2007, Canada's income tax legislation has contained a specific set of rules that   **1**
apply to listed Real Estate Investment Trusts (the 'REIT Rules'). The REIT Rules were
introduced as an exception to new provisions dealing with specified investment
flow-through entities (i.e., certain publicly traded trusts and partnerships) (the 'SIFT
Rules'). Entities subject to the SIFT Rules are subject to tax ('SIFT tax') in a manner
similar to that of public corporations, and they are not entitled to the flow-through tax
treatment that is generally available to trusts and partnerships. In their legal form,
REITs are mutual fund trusts (MFTs). Those that qualify as REITs under the REIT Rules
are not subject to the SIFT Rules and are subject to the flow-through tax regime
applicable to MFTs provided they meet certain requirements. Most importantly, the
REIT must distribute all of its income annually, and the activities of the REIT must be
passive in nature.

The majority of REITs are sector-specific (e.g., residential, office, retail, etc.). Others   **2**
are involved in more than one sector. There are also unlisted or private REITs that are
not subject to the REIT Rules and that can be involved in a broader range of activities
through controlled partnerships and corporations. Private REITs, which usually have
at least 150 investors, are generally not subject to tax so long as they distribute 100%
of their taxable income annually. Similar to listed REITs in other countries, Canada's
REITs generally provide predictable cash distributions and opportunities for capital
appreciation. This chapter only considers REITs that are subject to the REIT Rules – i.e.,
listed REITs.

[B]   **History of REIT**

3   The first modern Canadian public REIT was formed in 1993, with the REIT market reaching a reasonable size in the late 1990s. Prior to that time, there had been a few publicly traded REITs, but the vast majority of listed real estate enterprises were structured as taxable corporations. As discussed in more detail below, the REIT Rules that became law in 2007 severely restrict the nature of activities that a qualifying REIT may carry on either directly or indirectly. As of 1 January 2011, the SIFT Rules apply to all listed MFTs. The initial application of the SIFT Rules was deferred, in general, until 2011 for listed MFTs that were in existence on 31 October 2006, the day that the intention to introduce the SIFT Rules was announced by the Federal Government. A number of the listed MFTs that, prior to 2011, referred to themselves as REITs, no longer qualified for exemption from SIFT tax under the REIT Rules due to the nature of the activities that they carried on. However, some non-qualifying REITs were restructured before 2011 to bring themselves into compliance with the REIT Rules.

[C]   **REIT Market**

4   The listed REIT market in Canada is small compared to the total market capitalization of the Toronto Stock Exchange (TSX), Canada's principal stock exchange. As of 21 January 2022, there were thirty-eight TSX-listed MFTs that referred to themselves as REITs, with a market capitalization of approximately CAD 98 billion. Listed real estate corporations had a market capitalization of approximately CAD 14 billion on the same date. There were also at least one listed MFT that referred to itself as a REIT on TSX Venture Exchange (TSX-V), with a market capitalization of approximately CAD 268 million.[1]

§1.02   REGULATORY ASPECTS

[A]   **Legal Form of REIT**

[1]   Corporate Form

5   A Canadian REIT is a trust governed by general trust law. For income tax purposes, it is an 'MFT'. Broadly, trust law includes requirements for the trustee(s) to act in the best interests of beneficiaries, to act honestly and to exercise the same prudence and diligence that ordinary persons would exercise in carrying on their own business. A trust is not a separate legal entity or person, but it is a set of obligations accepted by the trustee in relation to the trust property, where such obligations are exercised for the benefit of the beneficiary. The obligations of the trustee, and the rights of beneficiaries,

---

1. Source of data on 21 Jan. 2022 is derived from the 21 Jan. 2022 version of the Daily Market Indicator, produced by RBC Capital Markets Real Estate Group.

are typically set out in writing in the declaration of trust (DOT). The DOT is a very flexible document.

In order to qualify as an MFT, a Canadian REIT is structured as a unit trust. That is, all **6** the income and capital entitlements of the trust are fixed in accordance with the DOT and those entitlements are unitized. The income and/or capital entitlements of a beneficiary (or unitholder) are determined by reference to the units they hold and the rights attaching to those units (per the DOT). Although there is some uncertainty under common law, certain provincial statutes provide that a unitholder's liability is limited in a manner similar to that of corporate shareholders.

A unit trust may be either open-ended or closed-ended. Most Canadian REITs are **7** structured as open-ended unit trusts as there are certain restrictions applicable to closed-ended unit trusts.

A typical Canadian REIT structure generally includes a limited partnership that holds **8** the assets of the REIT.

[2]   Investment Restrictions

Certain unitholder and distribution requirements must be met in order for the Canadian **9** REIT to qualify as an MFT. There must be at least 150 unitholders, each holding not less than one block of units with a fair market value of at least CAD 500. Further, there must be a lawful distribution in a province to the public of units of the trust, or a class of units of the trust must be qualified for distribution to the public. Finally, the REIT cannot be established or maintained primarily for the benefit of non-residents

[B]   Regulatory Authorities

As listed entities, REITs are subject to the rules of the stock exchange on which they are **10** listed as well as the rules of provincial securities regulators.

[C]   Legislative and Other Regulatory Sources

Listed REITs are governed in accordance with Canadian trust law and their DOT. They **11** must also comply with the requirements of the relevant securities legislation and stock exchange rules, as well as the Income Tax Act (Canada).

[D]   Exchange Controls and Reporting Requirements

The listing requirements of TSX, Canada's major exchange, provide minimum require- **12** ments for:

- annual or forecasted earnings or revenue;
- annual pre-tax cash flow, net tangible assets, working capital;
- the number of freely trading public shares/units;
- the market value of freely trading shares/units;
- the number of public shareholders/unitholders; and
- the number of shares to be held by each shareholder/unitholder.

13 In the context of a REIT, these listing requirements generally are not burdensome. While most REITs are listed on TSX, smaller REITs may be listed on TSX-V. Listing a REIT on TSX-V has fewer listing and reporting requirements. The focus of this document is on REITs listed on TSX.

14 Reporting requirements for a listed REIT come from TSX and the securities regulators of the provinces in which the REIT units are registered for distribution. There are two types of reporting requirements, namely periodic filings and event-driven filings.

15 The periodic filings include:

- quarterly financial statements together with a management discussion and analysis or 'MD&A';
- annual financial statements together with MD&A;
- annual report;
- annual information form;
- management information circular;
- annual CEO and CFO Certification;
- distribution declaration;
- corporate governance disclosure; and
- security-based compensation arrangement disclosure.

16 The event-driven filings include:

- material information;
- material change;
- business acquisition;
- insider trading;
- rights offerings and other securities issues;
- grants of options;
- normal course issuer bids;
- redemptions of units; and
- capital reorganizations.

17 Canada has a web-based or electronic filing system called SEDAR. Generally, the information referred to above is filed on SEDAR and is accessible by the public through the website: www.sedar.com.

[E]   Registration Procedures

[1]   Preparatory Measures

Not applicable.   18

[2]   Obtaining Authorization

There is no registration or authorization necessary to operate an MFT as a REIT.   19

[3]   Other Requirements for the Establishment of a Trust

The formation of a trust is a relatively simple process. A trust may be established upon   20
the execution of the DOT.

[4]   Obtaining Listing Exchanges

[a]   Costs

Original listing fees for TSX range between CAD 10,000 and CAD 200,000, as deter-   21
mined by the market value of the REIT at the point of listing. During the life of the
listing, there are additional fees for certain transactions such as property acquisitions,
public offerings and private placements. As well, there is an annual sustaining fee
payable after the first year of the listing.

[b]   Time

The time required to list a REIT will depend on several factors, including the size and   22
complexity of the transaction, the state of the market and how quickly funds are
received from investors.

[F]   Requirements and Restrictions

[1]   Capital Requirements

In order to list on TSX, a REIT must have at least 1 million free trading public units,   23
CAD 4 million held by public unitholders and 300 public unitholders each holding a
board lot. If the operations of the REIT have a track record, the minimum NTA
requirement is CAD 2 million. If the REIT is merely forecasting profitability, it will
require a minimum NTA of CAD 7.5 million.

[2]   Marketing/Advertising

24   A listed REIT is required to issue a prospectus when it seeks to list or raise equity. The Prospectus sets out the terms of the transaction, provides information about the REIT, includes various experts' reports, if applicable, and includes financial information and information on the real estate owned or to be owned by the REIT. The Prospectus is filed with the relevant provincial securities regulator(s).

[3]   Redemption

25   Although REIT units are almost always disposed of through the exchange, most REITs also provide a redemption procedure to establish open-ended status and avoid certain investment restrictions otherwise imposed on closed-end REITs by the income tax rules. Redemptions are typically permitted at the end of each month for a redemption price that usually represents a discount on the trading price of the units. Further, the REIT typically has the discretion to limit the amount of cash that it will pay out on redemptions in any month.

[4]   Valuation of Shares/Units for Redemption and Other Purposes

26   Units are redeemed in accordance with the requirements of the DOT. As noted above, the DOT typically provides for units to be redeemed at a discount to the trading price.

[5]   Investment Restrictions

27   There are a number of investment restrictions imposed on a REIT by virtue of its status as an MFT and a REIT. An MFT can only invest its funds in property (other than real property or an interest in real property), or acquire, hold, maintain, improve, lease or manage any real property (or interest in real property) that is capital property of the REIT, or a combination of such activities. Further, the REIT Rules impose a number of conditions which must be satisfied in order to qualify as a REIT in a taxation year. These rules require that:

> (a) at each time in the taxation year, the total fair market value at that time of all non-portfolio properties held by the REIT that are qualified REIT properties must not be less than 90% of the total fair market value of all non-portfolio properties owned by the REIT. Qualified REIT properties include real property that is capital property, eligible resale property, securities of certain subsidiary entities that manage the real or immovable property of the REIT, certain nominee entities, and certain property ancillary to the earning of rental income and capital gains by the REIT from its real or immovable property);

(b) not less than 90% of the REIT's gross REIT revenue for that taxation year must be from rent from real or immovable properties, interest, dispositions of real or immovable properties that are capital properties, dividends, royalties, and dispositions of eligible resale properties;

(c) not less than 75% of the REIT's gross REIT revenue for that taxation year must be from rent from real or immovable properties, interest from mortgages or hypothecs on real or immovable properties, and dispositions of real or immovable properties that are capital properties;

(d) the REIT must, throughout the taxation year, hold real or immovable properties that are capital properties, eligible resale properties, and cash and certain government-guaranteed debt with a total fair market value that is not less than 75% of the REIT's equity value; and

(e) investments in the REIT t must be publicly listed or traded on a stock exchange or other public market.

Also, the DOT may place restrictions on the type of investments that a particular REIT can make. **28**

Eligible resale property, as mentioned above, permits REITs to hold non-capital real or immovable property in circumstances where this property is contiguous to and ancillary to the holding of a real or immovable property (which may be capital or eligible resale) held by the entity or its affiliates. **29**

Gross REIT revenue, which is applicable for both the 90% and 75% tests, means the total of all amounts that are received or receivable in a taxation year by the entity in excess of the cost to the entity for any property disposed of in the taxation year. Accordingly, amounts such as recaptured depreciation will be excluded from this definition. **30**

The REIT Rules provide that for the purpose of determining gross REIT revenue of an entity, (the 'parent entity') for the purposes of the revenue tests, gross REIT revenue received from certain subsidiary entities (the 'source entities') will have the same character in the parent entity that it had in the source entities. **31**

[6]   *Distribution/Accumulation*

In order to maintain its 'flow-through' status for tax purposes and to ensure that the REIT is not subject to tax on its taxable income, all taxable income of the REIT must be paid or become payable to its unitholders at least annually. REITs typically make cash distributions to unitholders, on a monthly or quarterly basis. These distributions usually exceed the amount of any income that is required to be allocated to unitholders. **32**

[7]   Reporting Requirements

33   In addition to audited financial statements, quarterly financial statements which may or may not be reviewed by the auditor, and MD&A, REITs generally provide their unitholders information relating to funds from operations, adjusted funds from operations, adjusted cash flow from operations, and distributable income.

34   *See* section §1.02[D] above for additional reporting requirements.

[8]   Accounting

35   The annual financial statements of REITs and other publicly listed companies must be audited and prepared in accordance with International Financial Reporting Standards as issued by the International Accounting Standards Board. These audited financial statements must be filed on SEDAR and provided to TSX and securities regulators. Generally, the quarterly financial statements are reviewed by the REIT's auditor.

§1.03   TAXATION

[A]   Taxation of the REIT

[1]   Corporate Income Tax

[a]   Tax Accounting

36   In general, a REIT's taxable income is taxed in the hands of the unitholder, not the REIT. Assuming the REIT qualifies as a REIT under the REIT Rules and it distributes 100% of its income to its unitholders, the REIT itself will not be subject to tax. Units of listed REITs derive a significant part of their value from the amount of the annual distributions that they make. Consequently, an important objective for all REITs is to ensure that they are not subject to income tax, which would reduce cash available for distribution.

37   Most often, distributions made to unitholders are greater than a REIT's taxable income because non-cash deductions are taken into account in the determination of taxable income. Non-cash deductions include, for example, tax depreciation and the amortization of the costs of issuing securities or debt. Amounts distributed to unitholders in excess of a REIT's taxable income generally reduce the unitholders' tax cost of their REIT units and are referred to as a return of capital. Taxes on these excess distributions are effectively deferred until unitholders dispose of their REIT units.

[b]   Determination of Taxable Income

A REIT determines its taxable income on the same basis as a Canadian resident **38** individual. Income from investments, including net rental income, is reduced by expenses incurred for the purpose of earning income. Such expenses include reasonable interest on money borrowed to acquire property, tax depreciation, property taxes in excess of amounts recovered from tenants, amortization (over a period of five years) of the costs incurred in connection with the issue by the REIT of debt and/or units, trustee fees, and other costs associated with the maintenance and operation of a public REIT.

Tax depreciation on buildings is calculated on a declining balance basis at the rate of **39** 4% (or 6% for Canadian non-residential buildings constructed after 19 March 2007), subject to a 50% reduction in the full tax depreciation rate in the first year in which the building becomes available for use. The costs of additions to buildings and replacements of building components that are capital in nature are added to the tax cost for depreciation purposes. Eligible property acquired after 20 November 2018 and available for use before 2028 may qualify for accelerated tax depreciation during the year in which the property becomes available for use. Eligible property that becomes available for use before 2024 may qualify for the application of 1.5 times the full tax depreciation rate to the cost of the additions. Eligible property that becomes available for use between 2024 and before 2028 may qualify for the application of the full tax depreciation rate to the costs of additions in the year in which the property becomes available for use. A REIT cannot claim tax depreciation to the extent that such a claim would create a loss for tax purposes.

Operating tax losses realized by a REIT cannot be passed through to investors. Rather, **40** they can be carried back three years and forward for twenty years to be deducted in the calculation of the REIT's taxable income in those years.

One-half of a capital loss realized by a REIT can be carried back three years or forward **41** for an indefinite period to be set off against the one-half of the capital gains that were included in taxable income in those years.

[c]   Taxation of Income from Taxable/Non-taxable Subsidiaries

A Canadian REIT cannot have a corporate subsidiary that is exempt from tax. **42** Consequently, income earned by corporate subsidiaries is subject to tax at the corporate level. If the appropriate designations are made by the REIT, dividends paid by corporate subsidiaries to a REIT retain their character in the REIT and are distributed to REIT unitholders along with REIT income from other sources. In general, income earned by flow-through vehicles such as partnerships and trusts that are subsidiaries of a REIT is included in the computation of the REIT's income, which in turn is distributed to unitholders.

[d]   Taxation of Foreign Income

43 Foreign-sourced income derived by a REIT is included in the taxable income of the REIT. If properly designated, such income retains its character when distributed to unitholders. Generally, foreign taxes paid by the REIT or a flow-through subsidiary, in respect of the foreign-sourced income, are available as a foreign tax credit, and the credits are allocated to unitholders.

[2]   VAT

44 Canada's VAT-type system is known as the Goods and Services Tax (GST) and in provinces that have harmonized their sales tax with the Federal Government, the Harmonized Sales Tax (HST). GST, at the current rate of 5% (in Ontario, the current rate of HST is 13%), is levied on supplies of most goods and services in Canada. Generally, businesses that make taxable supplies must register and collect GST/HST on their sales, and may claim a refund or credit for GST/HST paid on their purchases. Earning rental income from the supply of commercial rental real estate is subject to GST/HST. However, rents charged from the supply of residential rental real estate are generally exempt from GST/HST, and any GST/HST paid by an owner of residential rental property on the purchase of supplies or services made in connection with the residential rental property cannot be recovered through any refund or credit mechanism.

[3]   Withholding Taxes

45 A non-resident REIT unitholder is subject to Canadian withholding tax at the rate of 25% on any distributions of income or taxable capital gains paid or credited to such unitholder, which may be reduced under some of Canada's double-tax treaties. Distributions of amounts other than income and taxable capital gains are subject to 15% withholding tax where a REIT's value is derived primarily from Canadian real estate. This 15% tax could be fully or partially recoverable, upon filing a special Canadian tax return, to the extent that the non-resident unitholder realizes a loss from a subsequent disposition of the REIT units.

[4]   Other Taxes

46 A REIT may be subject to land transfer taxes on purchases of real property in Canada. The rate of tax depends on the province, territory or city in Canada where the property is located. Presently, the city of Toronto, in the Province of Ontario, imposes the highest rate of transfer tax – 4% (combined provincial and city rates) on the value of commercial property.

Owners of real property are generally subject to annual property taxes. In many cases, **47** a portion of the property taxes is recovered from tenants of commercial properties.

[5]   Penalties Imposed on REIT

Income tax penalties are generally not imposed on a REIT where all of its income is **48** distributed to its unitholders. Penalties can be imposed on a REIT for failure to withhold taxes on distributions to non-residents and for a failure to remit taxes, which are withheld, to the tax authorities. In addition, penalties can be imposed in connection with failure to pay GST/HST, land transfer taxes and annual property taxes.

Failure to comply with the REIT Rules will result in the REIT being subject to tax under **49** the SIFT Rules. Further, a loss of MFT status will result in a number of adverse consequences for both resident and non-resident investors.

[B]   Taxation of the Investor

[1]   Private Investors

[a]   *Taxation of Current Income (i.e., All Income Derived from REIT in Holding Phase)*

Residents

A resident REIT unitholder is generally required to include in income the portion of the **50** net income, including net taxable capital gains (50% of the capital gains of the REIT) that is paid to such unitholder. Provided the appropriate designations are made by the REIT, net taxable capital gains, taxable dividends from Canadian corporations and foreign source income that is paid to unitholders will effectively retain their character in the hands of the resident unitholders. Other income, for example, rental income, does not retain its character but is treated as property income to the investors. Unitholders may be entitled to a foreign tax credit for foreign taxes paid by a REIT. For an Ontario resident, the top combined federal/provincial marginal tax rate for 2022 for ordinary income (including foreign source income) is 53.53% and for eligible dividends, the top rate is 39.34%.

The non-taxable portion of net capital gains (50% of a capital gain) that is paid to a **51** resident unitholder is not included in the current income of the resident unitholder, and the distribution does not reduce the tax cost of the resident investor's units. Other amounts distributed to resident unitholders in excess of the REIT's taxable income for the year (generally referred to as returns of capital) are not immediately taxable, but instead reduce the resident unitholders' tax cost of their units, which increases the capital gain on a disposition of the unit. Further, the resident unitholder realizes a capital gain in the year when such other distributions cause the tax cost of the units to become a negative amount.

Non-residents

52   In Canada, non-resident unitholders are generally subject only to the withholding taxes referred to in section §1.03[A][3] above on current distributions paid to them whether they are derived from Canadian or foreign sources.

[b]   *Taxation of Capital Gains (From Disposal of REIT Units)*

Residents

53   A resident unitholder will generally realize a capital gain (or capital loss) on the disposition of a unit equal to the amount by which the proceeds of the disposition exceed (or are less than) the total of the resident unitholder's tax cost and any reasonable costs of disposition. For the purposes of determining the tax cost to a resident unitholder when a unit is acquired, the cost of the newly acquired unit will be averaged with the tax cost of all of the units owned by the resident as capital property immediately before that acquisition.

54   One-half of any capital gains realized by a resident unitholder is included in the resident unitholder's income as taxable capital gains. One-half of any capital loss realized by a resident unitholder on a disposition of units may generally be deducted only from taxable capital gains of the resident unitholder in the year of disposition, in the three preceding taxation years or in any future taxation years. As noted above, the top marginal tax rate for 2022 for a resident of Ontario is 53.53% resulting in an effective tax rate of 26.76% (i.e., one-half) on capital gains.

Non-residents

55   Generally, a non-resident unitholder will not be subject to Canadian tax on any capital gain realized on the disposition of REIT units unless the units are taxable Canadian property to the non-resident. The REIT units will be taxable Canadian property if the non-resident, either alone or together with persons with whom the non-resident does not deal at arm's length, owns 25% or more of the issued units of the REIT at any time during the sixty-month period immediately preceding the disposition (the 'lookback period') and at that time more than 50% of the fair market value of the units was derived directly or indirectly from Canadian real or immovable property, options in respect of, or interest in, such property. Under a number of Canada's double-tax treaties, the lookback period is eliminated. A capital loss realized by a non-resident on a disposition of REIT units that are taxable Canadian property can be deducted against capital gains realized by the non-resident from dispositions of taxable Canadian property in subsequent taxation years or in the preceding three taxation years.

If non-resident unitholders realize a loss on the disposition of their REIT units, **56** regardless of the status of the units as taxable Canadian property, they may be able to fully or partially recover the 15% withholding tax referred to in §1.03[A][3] upon filing a special Canadian tax return.

[2]   Institutional Investors

[a]   Taxation of Current Income (i.e., All Income Derived from REIT in Holding Phase)

Residents

Resident taxable institutional investors that hold REIT units are taxed in the same **57** manner as private investors discussed in section §1.03[B][1] above.

Resident institutional investors that are exempt from Canadian tax, such as pension **58** funds, are not subject to Canadian tax on income from any source received from a REIT.

Non-residents

Non-resident institutional investors (either taxable or exempt) are subject to the same **59** Canadian taxation on REIT distributions as private investors discussed in section §1.03[B][1] above.

[b]   Taxation of Capital Gains (From Disposal of REIT Units)

Residents

Taxable institutional investors are taxed in the same manner as private investors in **60** respect of capital gains realized on the disposition of REIT units. Exempt resident institutional investors are exempt from Canadian tax on any capital gains arising on the disposition of REIT units.

Non-residents

All non-resident institutional investors (taxable or exempt) are subject to the same **61** rules as private non-resident investors in respect of gains from the disposition of REIT units.

[3]   Penalties Imposed on Investors

Generally, the only income tax penalties that are imposed on investors in connection **62** with the ownership of REIT units arise if the investors understate the REIT income allocated to them or the gain realized on the disposition of the units.

[C]   **Tax Treaties**

[1]   Treaty Access

63   Canada has a large treaty network. Any relief to be granted to a non-resident REIT unitholder will depend entirely on the relevant treaty.

[2]   WHT Reduction

64   Any withholding tax reduction will depend on the particular treaty. For example, under Canada's treaty with the United States of America, the rate of withholding tax on the income portion of distributions made to US residents is reduced from 25% to 15%.

[D]   **Exit Tax/Tax Privileges/Concessions**

65   Where a trust that does not qualify as a REIT under the REIT Rules commences to qualify as a REIT under those Rules, there is no deemed or actual disposition of the trust property and, therefore, no liability for income tax. In general, tax-deferred transfers of property to a REIT are not permitted, although a tax-deferred transfer may be made to a corporation or partnership in the REIT structure. In addition, there are rules providing for tax-deferred exchanges of property in the course of a tax-deferred merger of REITs.

[E]   **Taxation of Foreign REITs**

[1]   Taxation of Foreign REIT Holding Assets in Country

66   A foreign REIT will be subject to Canadian tax on income arising from its activities conducted in Canada in respect of real property located in Canada. If the foreign REIT is carrying on business in Canada, then it will be subject to Canadian income tax at rates similar to those for Canadian residents. Canadian net income of a foreign REIT is determined in accordance with Canadian rules as modified by the relevant tax treaty, if any. If the activities conducted in Canada are passive, then the foreign REIT will be subject to Canadian withholding tax at the rate of 25% on its gross rents in connection with directly owned Canadian rental property. Alternatively, the REIT can elect to be taxed on its net income. Capital gains from the disposition of Canadian real property owned by a foreign REIT are almost always subject to Canadian taxation. Foreign REITs may also own Canadian real property indirectly through a Canadian corporation. Income and taxable capital gains would be subject to tax at the Canadian corporate tax rate, which is 15% plus the provincial rate which ranges from 8% to 16%. After-tax dividend distributions from the Canadian corporation (excluding returns of capital) are subject to 25% withholding taxes, which may be reduced under Canada's tax treaties.

[2]   *Taxation of Investors Holding Shares in Foreign REIT*

Except for tax-exempt investors, Canadian residents are taxable in Canada on their   **67**
worldwide income determined in accordance with Canadian law. This generally
includes taxation of the income portion of distributions from a foreign REIT if the REIT
is a trust, or all or a portion of a dividend received from a REIT that is a corporation. In
certain circumstances, it may also include deemed income in respect of a foreign REIT.
Capital gains realized by a taxable Canadian resident on the disposition of units or
shares of a foreign REIT are subject to Canadian income tax.

Finland

SAMULI MAKKONEN

Tax Partner Samuli Makkonen co-leads PwC Finland's Financial Services tax and legal practice. Samuli advises banks, insurance companies, pension institutions and investment funds on all aspects of Finnish and international tax law. Samuli's practice focuses on asset management, fund structuring (including private equity funds, real estate funds, and hedge funds), complex financing transactions and financial products, including structured finance and derivatives. He has written several articles in the field of taxation of financial instruments and investment management and is a frequent speaker in seminars in this field. Samuli is a Master of Laws from the University of Helsinki and a Bachelor of Science (Econ) from the Helsinki School of Economics.
E-mail: samuli.makkonen@pwc.com

MIKKO LEINOLA

Tax Partner Mikko Leinola co-leads PwC Finland's Financial Services tax and legal practice. Mikko specializes in advising major Finnish and international institutional investors in their direct and indirect real estate investments. In addition, Mikko is regularly assisting Finnish and Nordic fund managers in setting up and operating real estate funds investing in Finnish and Nordic real estate. He is a frequent speaker in seminars. Mikko is a Master of Laws from the University of Turku.
E-mail: mikko.leinola@pwc.com

Finland

Samuli Makkonen & Mikko Leinola

§1.01   BACKGROUND

[A]   Key Characteristics

A Finnish Real Estate Investment Trust (FIN-REIT) is a Finnish-listed corporate entity **1** that is exempt from corporate tax provided that certain requirements are met, for example:

- it invests mainly in residential properties;
- it has a maximum of 80% debt-to-asset ratio; and
- it distributes at least 90% of annual profits as dividends.

Dividend distributions by a FIN-REIT are fully subject to tax for the Finnish dividend **2** recipient.

[B]   History of REIT

The possibility to set up a Finnish-regulated real estate investment fund was introduced **3** with effect on 1 March 1998 by the Finnish Act on Real Estate Funds (1173/1997, REF Act). However, no such real estate funds have been set up, mainly due to the fact that such real estate funds referred to in the REF Act have been subject to regular corporate tax rules and therefore fully subject to corporate tax.

However, after a lengthy lobbying effort by the industry, a tax exemption for such real **4** estate fund, governed by the said REF Act, was introduced with effect from 1 January 2009 by the Finnish Act on Tax Incentives for certain Limited Companies Carrying on Residential Renting Activities (299/2009, FIN-REIT Act). Despite the objections from the market participants, the tax exemption was only extended to real estate funds investing in residential property.

5   The introduction of the FIN-REIT Act was however subject to a state aid notification to the European Commission. On 12 May 2010, the Commission announced that such tax exemption is not regarded as illegal state aid. However, the Commission considered that a provision allowing FIN-REITs to use up to 30% of their annual profits to create tax-exempt reinvestment reserves would constitute incompatible aid. Following the Commission's concerns, the Finnish authorities made the commitment not to put into force this provision.

6   Due to the notification procedure and the consequent amendments made to the FIN-REIT Act, as a result, the FIN-REIT Act entered into force on 17 November 2010 with retroactive effect from 1 January 2010.

7   Hereinafter, FIN-REIT refers to real estate funds regulated by the REF Act and where the FIN-REIT Act is applicable.

[C]   REIT Market

8   Currently, there are no FIN-REITs in the market.

§1.02   REGULATORY ASPECTS

[A]   Legal Form of REIT

[1]   Corporate Form

9   A FIN-REIT must be a public limited company incorporated in Finland.

[2]   Investment Restrictions

10   In order for FIN-REIT to obtain a tax-exempt FIN-REIT status (i.e., exemption from Finnish corporate taxation in accordance with the FIN-REIT Act), the FIN-REIT must be subject to the provisions of the REF Act. Therefore, the investment restrictions set forth by the REF Act are relevant. However, in practice, the FIN-REIT Act provides for more specific restrictions. Therefore, such investment restrictions described in the FIN-REIT Act have been discussed in the following.

11   In accordance with the FIN-REIT Act, the tax exemption must be granted upon application in case certain conditions are met (*see* section §1.02[E][1]). Relating to investment restrictions, such conditions include:

   – the FIN-REIT does not carry on any other activities than renting of property and certain ancillary activities, such as property administration and maintenance and cash management. Property development on its own account is permitted;

– at least 80% of the total assets of the company must comprise residential real property (as defined in the relevant legislation), shares in an apartment housing company (i.e., a residential mutual real estate company), or shares entitling the shareholder to possess residential premises in such other mutual real estate company, which solely carries on holding and controlling of real estate and the buildings located on the real estate (measured using financial statements). In general terms, a mutual real estate company is a company the shares of which entitle the shareholder to possess (and lease out) the premises owned by the mutual real estate company (*see* section §1.03[A][1][b]); and

– the FIN-REIT does not hold any other assets than property, equipment required by its ancillary activities and liquid funds (as defined in the relevant legislation). The company may not, except for shares in mutual real estate companies, hold any shares in subsidiary companies.

Furthermore, penalty tax charges (*see* section §1.03[A][5]) may be payable by the **12** FIN-REIT, if:

– less than 80% of the net income (excluding capital gains) is derived from renting residential property; or

– the FIN-REIT sells assets and certain conditions are not met with respect to said disposals; or

– at the record date, a shareholder owns 10% or more of the share capital.

In practice, such penalty tax charges may obviously have an impact on the investment **13** strategy.

[B]   Regulatory Authorities

FIN-REITs are subject to the supervision of the Finnish Financial Supervisory Authority **14** (FIN-FSA) in accordance with the REF Act, the Finnish Act on Alternative Investment Fund Managers (162/2014, AIFML) and the Finnish Securities Markets Act (746/2012). Moreover, the Finnish tax authorities review FIN-REIT's compliance with the requirements of the FIN-REIT Act.

[C]   Legislative and Other Regulatory Sources

FIN-REITs are subject to the general rules for public limited companies in accordance **15** with the Finnish Companies Act (624/2006). Moreover, FIN-REITs are also subject to the applicable rules of, for example, the REF Act, the Finnish Securities Markets Act, the Finnish Accounting Act (1336/1997) and the Finnish Auditing Act (1141/2015). FIN-REITs are regarded as alternative investment funds within the meaning of the AIFML.

[D]   Registration Procedures

[1]   Obtaining Authorization

16   A FIN-REIT, as an alternative investment fund, must be managed by an authorized or registered alternative investment fund manager. In addition, pursuant to AIFML, the FIN-FSA must approve the FIN-REIT's letter of commencement of marketing before the FIN-REIT may begin its public marketing activities and before it may accept funds from the public.

17   An application for FIN-REIT status must be filed with the Finnish tax authorities. FIN-REIT status must be granted to the Finnish limited company under the conditions set forth in the FIN-REIT Act (*see* section §1.02[E][1]).

[2]   Obtaining Listing

18   According to the FIN-REIT Act, one condition for tax exemption is the fact that the FIN-REIT's shares must be listed on a regulated market or have been upon application admitted to trading on a Multilateral Trading Facility (MTF) in the European Economic Area (EEA).

[E]   Requirements and Restrictions

[1]   Requirements Set Out by FIN-REIT Act

19   In order for a FIN-REIT to obtain a tax-exempt FIN-REIT status (i.e., exemption from Finnish corporate taxation in accordance with the FIN-REIT Act), the following requirements must be fulfilled in accordance with the FIN-REIT Act:

- the FIN-REIT does not carry on any other activities than renting of property and certain ancillary activities, such as property administration and maintenance and cash management. Property development on its own account is permitted;
- at least 80% of the total assets of the company must comprise residential real property (as defined in the relevant legislation), shares in an apartment housing company (i.e., a residential mutual real estate company), or shares entitling the shareholder to possess residential premises in such other mutual real estate company, which solely carries on holding and controlling of real estate and the buildings located on the real estate (measured using financial statements). In general terms, a mutual real estate company is a company the shares of which entitle the shareholder to possess (and lease out) the premises owned by the mutual real estate company (*see* section §1.03[A][1][b]);

- the FIN-REIT does not hold any other assets than property, equipment required by its ancillary activities and liquid funds (as defined in the relevant legislation). The company may not, except for shares in mutual real estate companies, hold any shares in subsidiary companies;
- the FIN-REIT's total liabilities may not exceed 80% of the total assets (measured using (consolidated) financial statements);
- each shareholder must hold less than 10% of the share capital of the company; and
- the REF Act must apply to the company, hence it must be subject to the supervision of the FIN-FSA.

The following additional conditions for FIN-REIT status apply as of the beginning of the   **20**
first tax year as a FIN-REIT:

- the FIN-REIT must distribute at least 90% of its net income (excluding unrealized gains) unless the Finnish Companies Act restricts the company's possibility to distribute dividends (e.g., if the amount of unrestricted equity is not sufficient or there are solvency reasons for restricting the amount of distribution);
- the FIN-REIT's shares must be listed on a regulated market or must be upon application admitted to trading on an MTF in the EEA. However, upon application to the Finnish tax authorities, this requirement may be disapplied during the first two tax years as a FIN-REIT;
- the FIN-REIT does not make distributions in any other form than as dividends; and
- the FIN-REIT or its mutual real estate company subsidiaries have not been involved in transactions the purpose of which is deemed to be tax avoidance.

[2]   Capital Requirements

The share capital of a FIN-REIT must amount to at least EUR 5 million in accordance   **21**
with the REF Act.

[3]   Investment Restrictions

A FIN-REIT is limited to the investments and activities as defined in the legislation (*see*   **22**
sections §1.02[A][2] and §1.02[E][1] above).

[4]   Reporting Requirements

FIN-REITs are subject to the general reporting requirements that apply to public limited   **23**
companies and the reporting requirements in accordance with the REF Act, the AIFML and the Finnish Securities Market Act. Despite FIN-REIT's tax exemption, it is obliged

to file a tax return. In the tax return, the FIN-REIT must provide information on whether it meets the requirements necessary to remain eligible for the tax exemption.

[5]   Accounting

24   General accounting rules in accordance with the Finnish Accounting Act apply to FIN-REITs. Please note that public limited companies, whose securities are admitted to trading in a regulated market in an EEA state, are obliged to prepare consolidated International Financial Reporting Standards financial statements in Finland.

§1.03   TAXATION

[A]   Taxation of REIT

[1]   Corporate Income Tax

25   A FIN-REIT is tax-exempt.

[a]   Conversion Charge

26   In case an existing company applies for FIN-REIT status, all assets held by a company converting to FIN-REIT status are revalued to market value for Finnish tax purposes. A conversion charge equalling the in-force corporate income tax rate (currently 20%) is levied on the unrealized gains on all assets held on the day of conversion. The conversion charge can upon application be spread over three years from the year of conversion to FIN-REIT status.

[b]   Taxation of Income from Subsidiaries

27   A FIN-REIT may not hold any shares in subsidiary companies except for shares in mutual residential real estate companies and other mutual real estate companies. These subsidiaries do not benefit from FIN-REIT's tax exemption and are therefore subject to the general taxation rules. However, in practice, generally the mutual real estate companies do not pay tax because their taxable income is typically nil. This is briefly discussed in the following.

28   Shareholders of mutual real estate companies are entitled to possess (and lease out) the premises owned by the mutual real estate company. If the premises possessed by virtue of the mutual real estate company's shares are leased out by the shareholder, the shareholder directly receives the lease income and pays the mutual real estate company a maintenance fee to cover the costs of the mutual real estate company. The maintenance fee is taxable for the mutual real estate company. However, the mutual

real estate company's net taxable income is typically nil, as the amount of taxable maintenance fees is set to the level of the mutual real estate company's tax-deductible items.

[c]   Taxation of Foreign Income

A FIN-REIT is tax-exempt for Finnish corporate tax purposes. This covers also **29** foreign-source income. Since a FIN-REIT is a tax-exempt entity, it is not entitled to obtain a credit on taxes paid (including withholding tax) in a foreign jurisdiction.

[2]   Value Added Tax

Finland has a value added tax (VAT) system with a standard rate of 24%. Where a **30** FIN-REIT holds a direct interest in domestic residential real estate or is the shareholder of a Finnish residential Mutual Real Estate Company, the rental income is VAT exempt. In return, a FIN-REIT is not eligible for input VAT credit for its purchases.

Under certain conditions, it is possible for a FIN-REIT to opt for VAT liability as a lessor. **31** In this case, the FIN-REIT will include VAT on the rent charge and be entitled to benefit from input VAT credit for the part of the activities subject to VAT. Opting for VAT liability concerns only the lease of premises to VAT-registered persons who use the leased premises for taxable business activities subject to VAT.

[3]   Withholding Tax

Distributions to Finnish resident individuals are subject to tax prepayment (*ennakon-* **32** *pidätys*) withheld at source.

Distributions to foreign shareholders are also subject to withholding tax. General **33** withholding tax rate is 15%/20%/30%. A tax treaty may reduce the withholding rate.

The Finnish withholding tax legislation was changed with effect from 1 January 2021 **34** onwards. In short, the application of a tax treaty requires that the custodian or the payer of a dividend provides the Tax Administration with the information on the final recipient of the dividend. The tax at source for dividends is increased to 35% if the final recipient information is not provided. Assuming the final recipient information is provided, the withholding tax rate is similar to that described above.

Furthermore, since 1 January 2021, dividend withholding tax may be withheld directly **35** at the applicable tax treaty rate in case of dividends paid to nominee-registered shares. One of the requirements for allowing treaty relief at source is that the payer of the dividend or the custodian must be registered with the Finnish Tax Administration's custodian register in order to receive the benefit.

[4]   Other Taxes

36   FIN-REITs are only exempt from corporate income tax. With regard to other taxes, general rules apply.

37   For example, a transfer tax of 4% is levied on the direct transfer of real estate property, and a transfer tax of 2% on the transfer of shares in real estate companies (tax is calculated on 'transfer base', as defined in the Transfer Tax Act).

[5]   Penalties Imposed on REIT

38   The following penalty tax charges may be imposed on a FIN-REIT:

(1) Where less than 80% of the net income (excluding capital gains) is derived from renting residential property, a penalty tax charge of 20% will be levied on the FIN-REIT on the shortfall in the income from renting of residential property.

(2) Disposals of property result in the taxation of the capital gain (tax levied will be equal to the applicable corporate income tax rate, which is 20% in 2022) unless the following requirements are met:

(a) the FIN-REIT disposes of less than 10% of its real estate assets during a tax year (measured using balance sheet values);

(b) the real estate assets disposed of by the FIN-REIT have been held for at least five years; and

(c) at least five years have elapsed from a comprehensive refurbishment (as defined in the legislation) of the buildings when the real estate assets in question are disposed of by the FIN-REIT.

(3) Where a dividend is distributed to a shareholder holding 10% or more of the shares in the FIN-REIT, a penalty tax charge equal to the applicable corporate income tax rate (20% in 2022) will be levied on the FIN-REIT on the amount equivalent to the dividend paid to such shareholder.

39   Finally, as a general rule, failure to meet any of the conditions for FIN-REIT status (*see* section §1.02[E][1]) could result in the loss of the status. However, the fact that a shareholder holds 10% or more of the shares in the FIN-REIT does not justify the tax authorities to cancel the FIN-REIT status (in such a case, a penalty tax charge becomes payable as described above).

40   If a FIN-REIT fails to meet the conditions for FIN-REIT status, the tax authorities will generally set a reasonable time limit for the FIN-REIT to correct the situation, unless it is certain that the requirements will not be fulfilled. However, if the tax authorities consider that the FIN-REIT has made arrangements with the sole or main purpose of tax avoidance, the decision concerning the authorization for FIN-REIT status will be cancelled in any case.

[B]   Taxation of the Investors

[1]   *Private Investors*

[a]   *Taxation of Dividend*

Resident Private Individuals

Dividends distributed by a FIN-REIT to Finnish resident private individuals are capital **41** income fully taxable at a 30% to 34% rate. The FIN-REIT must withhold tax prepayment at source on dividends paid to Finnish individuals and pay such tax to the Tax Administration. Such prepayment will be credited against tax payable by the individual.

Non-resident Private Individuals

Under domestic law, dividends distributed by a FIN-REIT to a non-resident recipient **42** will be subject to withholding tax at source (rate currently 30%), subject to the applicable tax treaties. Treaty relief can be claimed *ex ante* or retrospectively.

With effect from 1 January 2021, the dividend withholding tax may be withheld **43** directly at the applicable tax treaty rate in case of dividends paid to nominee-registered shares if certain requirements are met. As of 1 January 2021, the withholding tax rate will be 35% instead if the final recipient information related to the dividends has not been provided.

[b]   *Taxation of Capital Gains (From Disposal of REIT Shares)*

Resident Private Individuals

Capital gain on the disposal of shares in a FIN-REIT is taxable under normal capital **44** gains tax rules taxable at a 30% to 34% rate in Finland.

Non-resident Private Individuals

Under domestic law capital gain on the disposal of shares in a FIN-REIT could be **45** subject to tax at 30%/34% in case more than 50% of the FIN-REIT's assets are directly held property located in Finland, subject to the applicable tax treaties. In practice, it can be expected that the disposal of shares in a FIN-REIT should typically be outside the scope of Finnish capital gains tax, as it is likely that a FIN-REIT will own the real estate via so-called mutual real estate companies (*see* section §1.03[A][1][b]) rather than directly.

*[2]   **Corporate Investors***

[a]   Taxation of Dividend

Resident Corporate Investors

46 Dividends distributed by a FIN-REIT to Finnish corporate investors are fully taxable at the applicable corporate income tax rate (20% in 2022).

Non-resident Corporate Investors

47 Under domestic law, dividends distributed by a FIN-REIT to a non-resident recipient will be subject to withholding tax at source (rate currently 20%), subject to the applicable tax treaties. Treaty relief can be claimed *ex ante* or retrospectively.

48 With effect from 1 January 2021, the dividend withholding tax may be withheld directly at the applicable tax treaty rate in case of dividends paid to nominee-registered shares if certain requirements are met. As of 1 January 2021, the withholding tax rate is 35% instead if the final recipient information related to the dividends is not provided.

[b]   Taxation of Capital Gains (From Disposal of REIT Shares)

Resident Corporate Investors

49 Capital gain on the disposal of shares in a FIN-REIT is taxable under the normal capital gains tax rules taxable at a 20% (in 2022) corporate tax rate.

Non-resident Corporate Investors

50 Under domestic law, capital gains on disposals of shares in a FIN-REIT could be subject to tax at the corporate income tax rate (20% in 2022) in case more than 50% of the FIN-REIT's assets are directly held property located in Finland, subject to the applicable tax treaties. In practice, it can be expected that the disposal of shares in a FIN-REIT should typically be outside the scope of the Finnish capital gains tax, as it is likely that a FIN-REIT will own the real estate via so-called mutual real estate companies rather than directly.

France

PHILIPPE EMIEL

Philippe Emiel is an Of Counsel in the PwC Societe d'Avocats real estate group and lawyer of the Hauts-de-Seine Bar. He is also a Member of the Board of Directors of the Hauts-de-Seine Bar. He has numerous years of experience advising international investment funds within the scope of their real estate investments in France with regards to investment tax structuring, sell-side and buy-side tax due diligence. He also frequently works on assignments of externalization of property assets and restructuring of property portfolios and also advises clients in the creation of real estate vehicles: SCPI, OPCI and REITs.
E-mail: philippe.emiel@avocats.pwc.com

France

Philippe Emiel

---

§1.01   BACKGROUND

[A]   Key Characteristics

Since 2003, a specific tax regime has been offered to listed Real Estate Investment Trust   **1**
(REIT) or *Société d'Investissement Immobilier Cotée* (SIIC) under Article 208, C of the
French Tax Code (FTC).

The regime is applicable upon election to companies listed on a French-regulated   **2**
market or under certain conditions on a foreign market, whose share capital is superior
or equivalent to EUR 15 million, whose corporate purpose is the acquisition or
construction of buildings with a view to their demise, and/or the direct or indirect
holding of stakes in companies having this identical corporate purpose.

This regime is also applicable, upon election, to French subsidiaries of SIICs liable for   **3**
Corporate Income Tax (CIT), as long as they are held directly or indirectly up to 95 %
at least by a SIIC or by several SIICs or jointly by one or several SIICs and *Société de
Placement à Prépondérance Immobilière à Capital Variable* (SPPICAVs) and that they
have a main corporate purpose identical to that defined above. At the time of the
election for this tax regime, an exit tax at the rate of 19 % is assessed on any latent gain
existing in SIIC real estate assets or on the shares of their tax transparent subsidiaries
(the payment of this exit tax is spread over a four-year period).

Companies that elect to be taxed under this special tax regime are exempt from CIT on   **4**
the following income provided that the distribution requirements are met:

- Taxable profits derived from rental income on condition that they are distributed up to the minimum amount of 95 % before the end of the fiscal year
  following their realization.
- Capital gains resulting from the assignment of properties, certain real rights,
  rights attached to a real estate financial lease, shares of companies liable for
  CIT having elected for the regime and shares of partnerships on condition that

they are distributed up to the minimum amount of 70% before the end of the second fiscal year following their realization.

– Dividends paid by a subsidiary having elected for the regime, or a SIIC, a foreign company subject to an equivalent SIIC status, a SPPICAV to another SIIC holding at least 5% of the share capital and voting rights of its subsidiary for at least two years on condition that they are fully distributed before the end of the fiscal year following the distribution.

[B]   History of SIIC

5   SIIC tax regime was introduced by Finance Bill for 2003.[1] It has constantly been amended by nearly all the subsequent budget acts.

6   'SIIC 2'[2] boosted the attractiveness of the regime, creating a favourable merger regime and a favourable regime for contribution of real estate assets to SIIC. 'SIIC 3'[3] has added new conditions of eligibility and exemption for SIIC regime, widened the regime (intra-group sales) and extended SIIC 2 regime. 'SIIC 4'[4] has extended SIIC 3 regime to sales of shares in real estate-oriented companies and situations of exemptions of dividends and has created new conditions for shareholders, setting forth anti-abuse provisions (an anti-captive provision and an 'anti-Spanish' route provision). 'SIIC 5'[5] has extended the scope of SIIC regime and has modified rules applicable to exit from SIIC regime.

7   Amendatory Finance Bill for 2009[6] has modified conditions for the election of SIIC regime of the foreign companies and has facilitated the implementation of partnerships between SIIC and SPPICAV through subsidiaries electing for the tax exemption regime. Amendatory Finance Bill for 2010[7] has extended the application of SIIC 3 regime.

[C]   SIIC Market

8   Given the favourable tax regime, the French 'SIIC' market is well established. As of 31 December 2019,[8] SIICs represented EUR 77.8 billion of market capitalization.

9   As of 31 May 2020, there were twenty-four SIICs in France, including several Pan-European REITs. Several French-listed SIICs are among the largest REITs in Europe

---

1. Finance Bill for 2003 n° 2002-1575 dated 30 Dec. 2002.
2. Finance Bill for 2005 n° 2004-1484 dated 30 Dec. 2004.
3. Amendatory Finance Bill for 2006 n° 2006-1771 dated 30 Dec. 2006.
4. Finance Bill for 2008 n° 2007-1822 dated 24 Dec. 2007.
5. Finance Bill for 2009 n° 2008-1425 dated 27 Dec. 2008.
6. Amendatory Finance Bill for 2009 n° 2009-1674 dated 30 Dec. 2009.
7. Amendatory Finance Bill for 2010 n° 2010-165 dated 29 Dec. 2010.
8. IEIF website as of 11 Feb. 2022.

(e.g., Unibail-Rodamco, Klépierre and Gecina). Very few non-French listed companies (all of them from the European Union (EU)) have opted for the regime.

§1.02 REGULATORY ASPECTS

[A] Legal Form of SIIC

As listed entities, SIICs must be incorporated under the legal form of a *Société Anonyme* **10** (joint-stock company) or any other legal form of company which is eligible for listing (e.g., *Société en Commandite par Actions*).

The share capital of SIIC must be divided into shares which must be listed on a **11** French-regulated market or on a foreign market pursuant to European regulations.[9]

Therefore, the benefit of SIIC regime is granted to EU-listed companies and non-EU- **12** listed companies as well.

French subsidiaries that are at least 95% owned by a SIIC or by several SIICs or jointly **13** by one or several SIICs and SPPICAVs can also elect for SIIC regime provided that they fulfil certain conditions. No corporate form requirement is imposed on these subsidiaries.

[B] Regulatory Authorities

Like any other companies listed on a French-regulated market, listed SIICs are under **14** the control of the French *Autorité des Marchés Financiers* (AMF), the authority supervising the French Financial Market.

[C] Legislative and Other Regulatory Sources

The French regime is a pure tax regime governed by FTC, mainly sections 208 C and **15** 219 IV. The French Tax Authorities (FTAs) issued administrative guidelines for SIIC regime.[10]

Should SIIC be considered an Alternative Investment Fund (AIF) and be subject to **16** Alternative Investment Fund Manager (AIFM) regulations?

Both SIICs and investment funds are quite similar. However, it is necessary to **17** understand SIICs' activities and, in particular, their investment policies in order to establish that SIICs do not fall within the scope of AIFM:

---

9. BOI-IS-CHAMP-30-20-10-20200701 n° 10.
10. Administrative Guidelines BOFiP BOI-IS-CHAMP-30-20-20190327.

- As in all listed companies, the French SIIC management has developed industrial policies (strategies for growth and expansion). However, it is not considered an investment policy as defined by the Alternative Investment Fund Managers Directive. Requirements regarding the shareholders are aligned for both SIIC and listed companies.
- SIICs are eligible for a specific tax regime in order to boost the real estate business and stimulate real estate funding.
- SIICs act on their own behalf and manage held assets in order to increase the value of the assets.
- SIICs shareholders do not invest based on a defined investment policy (i.e., SIICs are not Undertakings for Collective Investments in Transferable Securities (UCITS)). The shareholders are involved in industrial projects carried out by the management company.

18   Consequently, SIICs are not subject to AIFM regulations.

[D]   Exchange Controls and Reporting Requirements

19   Listed SIICs must comply with the same reporting obligations required for listed companies.

[E]   Registration Procedures

[1]   Preparatory Measures

20   There are no preparatory measures applicable.

[2]   Obtaining Authorization

21   Except for non-French listed companies, there is no authorization procedure to become a SIIC. In order to be taxed under SIIC regime, eligible entities are only required to elect for it. The election is valid for as long as the company meets the requirements of the regime.

22   An eligible SIIC parent company may elect for SIIC regime within the first four months of each financial year. The election letter must be filed to the competent tax office for the parent company with a list of subsidiaries which have also been elected. This list of subsidiaries must be updated once a year, at the time of the annual corporate tax return.

23   If a subsidiary wishes to elect for SIIC regime, it must identify its parent company and file the election letter with the competent tax office accordingly.

The election changes a company's tax regime and election causes a partial cessation of **24**
business. Accordingly, the listed parent company and its electing subsidiaries must file
a specific cessation tax return.

The election is irrevocable. Once completed and filed, it is not possible to waive the **25**
election without adverse tax consequences. The election is a global election, meaning
that it applies to all properties and shares in qualifying partnerships.

[3]   Other Requirements for the Incorporation of a Company

There are no other requirements in connection with the incorporation of a SIIC **26**
company.

[4]   Obtaining Listing Exchanges

[a]   Costs

Legal fees, bank fees, AMF fees and Euronext fees must be paid to list the shares. The **27**
quantum of fees varies depending on the size of the company and the number of shares
listed.

[b]   Time

It usually takes between six and twelve months to establish the listing files and to **28**
obtain approval to list the shares.

[F]   Requirements and Restrictions

[1]   Capital Requirements

The share capital of the listed SIIC must equal at least EUR 15 million. The regulatory **29**
rules do not impose specific gearing limits; however, from a tax perspective, it is
recommended to respect the new French thin capitalization rules which remain
applicable to the net financial expenses relating to the taxable sector (*see* below
§1.03[A][1][b]).

[2]   Investment Restrictions

Any investor (whether individual or corporate) other than a SIIC or a group of investors **30**
other than SIICs acting together cannot hold, directly or indirectly, more than 60% of

the share capital and voting rights of the listed parent company. This requirement has to be fulfilled continuously.

31   At the time SIIC election is made, at least 15% of the share capital and voting rights must be held by investors who individually own (directly or indirectly) less than 2% of the share capital and voting rights of the listed SIIC. This requirement has to be fulfilled continuously.

[3]   Marketing/Advertising

32   Any company that wants to list its shares must prepare and make available a prospectus, which has to be approved by AMF.

[4]   Redemption

33   The redemption or buy-back of listed shares is possible; however, it is strictly regulated.

[5]   Valuation of Shares/Units for Redemption and Other Purposes

34   The value of shares in listed SIICs is determined through the regulated market on which the shares are listed.

[6]   Restrictions of Activities

35   The main activities of SIIC must be the acquisition or construction of buildings with a view to their demise and/or the direct or indirect holding stakes in companies having this identical corporate purpose. This activity may be performed either in France or abroad. Income from these principal activities is tax exempt under certain conditions ('exempted sector').

36   SIICs can also perform, as an accessory, other activities (e.g., real estate dealer, property management or development). Income from these ancillary activities is, however, fully taxable ('taxable sector'). Qualifying ancillary activities include the following:

–   Financial leasing of properties (*crédit-bail immobilier*) entered into effect before 2005[11] if the net book value of the portfolio of properties does not exceed 50% of the gross asset value of the company. This also applies to

---

11. Financial leasing contracts entered in effect or purchased after 1 Jan. 2005 are a qualifying activity eligible to SIIC regime.

entities that leased properties under a financial lease and granted a sublease to tenants.

– Real estate development or brokerage provided that the gross book value of the relevant assets does not exceed 20% of the total gross asset value of the company. To calculate this threshold, the value of properties subject to financial leases is not taken into account. If the real estate development or brokerage is performed through subsidiaries, then the book value of the shares held in these subsidiaries and current-account receivables are taken into account for the computation of the 20% threshold.

The French Tax Administrative Guidelines provided that these ratios had to be **37** respected continuously throughout each financial year. However, since 1 July 2020, the French Tax Administrative Guidelines have been amended and now provide that these ratios no longer have to be complied with on a continuous basis during the financial year but must be complied with, for each financial year covered by the option, at the end of the sixth month following the opening and at the closing date of the financial year. Thus, for fiscal years corresponding to the calendar year, these ratios must be complied with on 30 June and 31 December.[12]

A SIIC may carry out directly or indirectly activities abroad. In that case, the benefit of **38** SIIC regime in France is limited to the activity that would be taxable in France. Accordingly, if income from directly held properties that are located abroad is not exclusively taxable in the country where the properties are located (based on the provisions of a double tax treaty, if any), SIIC tax exemption applies to such properties. A company may elect to exclude these properties from SIIC regime. Such election is definitive and income derived from the excluded properties will be subject to CIT (i.e., it will fall within SIIC taxable regime).

SIIC regime may apply to profits derived through subsidiaries, provided that these **39** entities (i) have an activity identical to a SIIC activity (including ancillary activities), (ii) are liable to French CIT and (iii) are 95% at least owned (directly or indirectly) by a SIIC or by several SIICs or jointly by one or several SIICs and SPPICAVs.

SIIC regime may apply to the parent's shares in a partnership, provided such partner- **40** ship has a corporate business purpose similar to that of a SIIC. If the partnership engages in qualifying activities, there is no percentage participation requirement.

[7]   *Distribution/Accumulation*

To benefit from the tax exemption for profits derived from the exempted sector, listed **41** SIICs and qualifying 95% French subsidiaries must distribute at least:

---

12. BOI-IS-CHAMP-30-20-10-20200701 n° 360.

- 95 % of the profits derived from the demise of the buildings or sublease of real estate properties financed through a financial lease. These profits must be distributed before the end of the tax year following the year during which they are realized.
- 70 % of the capital gains resulting from the sale of buildings, of certain real estate rights, of rights attached to a real estate financial lease, of shares of companies liable for CIT having elected for the regime and shares of partnerships held by SIICs or one of their subsidiaries having elected for SIIC regime. Capital gains must derive from transactions with an entity with which SIIC has no ties of dependence.[13] These capital gains must be distributed before the end of the second fiscal year following the year during which they are realized.
- 100 % of dividends paid by a subsidiary having elected for the regime, or a SIIC, a foreign company subject to an equivalent SIIC status, a SPPICAV to another SIIC holding at least 5 % of the share capital and voting rights of its subsidiary for at least two years. These dividends must be distributed in the financial year following the one during which the dividends are received.

[8]   Reporting Requirements

42   Like any other French companies, listed SIICs and qualifying 95 % French subsidiaries of listed SIICs must file standard annual CIT returns with FTAs.

[9]   Accounting

43   Listed SIICs must complete annual accounts under French Generally Accepted Accounting Principles.

§1.03   TAXATION

[A]   Taxation of SIIC

[1]   Corporate Income Tax

[a]   Exit Tax

44   The election of the regime entails immediate taxation at the rate of 19 % of latent capital gains on:

---

13. For the purpose of this exemption, two companies are deemed to have ties of dependence where (i) one of them holds directly or indirectly more than 50 % of the share capital of the other one; or (ii) one of them has the decision-making authority of the other one; or (iii) both of them are placed under the control of the same entity as defined in (i) or (ii).

– buildings held directly or indirectly by a SIIC and its subsidiaries liable for CIT electing for the regime; and
– shares of partnerships (tax transparent companies) held by a SIIC and its subsidiaries liable for CIT electing for this regime.

The portion subject to the exit tax is determined by reference to the tax value of the real **45** estate assets or of the shares of the partnership.

One-quarter of the exit tax is required to be paid on 15 December of the fiscal year of **46** the election and one-quarter is payable at the latest on 15 December of each three subsequent fiscal years.

[b]   Determination of Taxable Income

Exempted Sector

The following incomes, derived from the principal activities of SIICs, are exempted **47** from CIT under the condition that the distribution requirements defined above are met:

– Profits derived from the demise of the buildings or sublease of real estate properties financed through a financial lease.
– Capital gains resulting from the sale of buildings, of certain real rights, of rights attached to a real estate financial lease, of shares of companies liable for CIT having elected for the regime and shares of partnerships held by SIICs or one of their subsidiaries having elected.
– Dividends paid by a subsidiary having elected for the regime, or a SIIC, a foreign company subject to an equivalent SIIC status, a SPPICAV to another SIIC holding at least 5% of the share capital and voting rights of its subsidiary for at least two years.

The transfer of real estate assets from a SIIC to a subsidiary in which SIIC owns at least **48** 95% of the share capital, together with a SPPICAV, may be realized under tax neutrality.

The sale of properties among members of the same group may benefit from an **49** exemption under certain conditions; however, the tax basis remains the same. For example, when non-depreciable assets such as land are sold, no tax is crystallized and the acquirer takes over the seller's base cost. Any capital gain upon the subsequent sale is computed from the rolled-over base cost, which will increase the 70% distribution obligation.

When depreciable assets are sold among members of the same group, no tax is **50** crystallized and the acquirer inherits a stepped-up basis. However, the gain must be recaptured in the tax-exempt income which will increase the distribution obligation.

Taxable Sector

51 Profits derived from the ancillary activities are within the scope of the taxable sector. They are taxed at the rate of 25 % from 1 January 2022 or 25.825 % if additional contributions apply.

52 Taxpayers must provide documentation to support the corporate tax calculation if requested by FTAs.

Allocation of Expenses

53 FTA provides for specific rules concerning the allocation of expenses common to both the taxable sector and the exempted sector. The principle is the exclusive and total allocation when possible, to one or the other sector. If not possible, the common expenses are allocated based on a specific ratio.

General Limitation of Net Financial Expenses (EU Anti-Tax Avoidance Directive (ATAD I))

54 Since January 2019, according to Article 212*bis* of FTC, the deductibility of the net financial expenses would be limited to the highest of either EUR 3 million or a 30 % 'tax' Earnings before interest, taxes, depreciation, and amortization of the company, reduced respectively to EUR 1 million or a 10 % in the case where the company is thinly capitalized. With regard to SIICs, these rules only apply to the net financial expenses relating to the taxable sector.[14]

Rules Governing the Use of Carried-Forward Tax Losses

55 Tax losses carried forward are available to offset EUR 1 million plus 50 % of the current taxable income exceeding that amount. The tax losses that cannot be offset in a given year are still eligible to be carried forward and offset future taxable profits. Those rules should apply to SIIC and its subsidiaries.

[c]   *Taxation of Income from Taxable/Non-taxable Subsidiaries*

56 Taxable income realized by SIICs from tax-transparent subsidiaries is exempt from CIT. Dividends received from qualifying 95 % French subsidiaries are also exempt from CIT. CIT exemption for dividends is conditioned on compliance with the required dividend distribution regulations.

---

14. BOI-IS-BASE-35-40-10-10-20200513 n°10.

[d]   Taxation of Foreign Income

SIIC tax exemption applies to income from directly held properties located abroad if the   **57**
properties are not exclusively taxable in the country in which the properties are located
according to the applicable tax treaty. Income from foreign properties can be taxable if
an election is made to exclude the properties from SIIC regime.

[2]   Value Added Tax

There are no specific Value Added Tax (VAT) rules for SIICs. Therefore the standard   **58**
VAT rules are applicable.

The rental of non-furnished office or commercial premises is not subject to French   **59**
VAT. Nevertheless, the rental of non-furnished offices or commercial premises could
be subject to VAT at the standard rate of 20% under a special VAT election made with
FTAs.

Conversely, the rental of furnished office or commercial premises is automatically   **60**
subject to French VAT at the standard rate of 20% (i.e., there is no need to elect for
VAT).

The rental of residential properties is exempt from French VAT (without any possibility   **61**
of electing French VAT).

The same rules apply if the properties are held by a subsidiary of SIIC.   **62**

Input VAT incurred by SIICs (or by subsidiaries of SIICs) is recovered under the   **63**
standard rules.

[3]   Withholding Taxes

Under French domestic tax rules, dividends paid by a French SIIC to a non-French tax   **64**
resident are subject to French withholding tax (WHT) at a rate of:

- – 12.8% when the dividend is received by an individual (plus social contribution);
- – 25% for the dividends received by a non-French company; or
- – 75% when the dividend is received by a non-resident (corporate or individual)
  established in a non-cooperative state or territory.

Pursuant to section 119*ter* of FTC, dividends paid by French companies to a non-French   **65**
Parent Company (resident in the EU country, Iceland or Norway) are WHT exempt
under certain conditions (i.e., the distributed profits have to be subject to CIT at
standard rate).

66   As French SIICs are partly tax-exempt, the WHT exemption should not apply to distribution of dividends from the results of the tax-exempt sector, whereas the exemption of WHT provided by Article 119*ter* of FTC should apply to dividends distributed from the results of the taxable sector.[15]

67   Meanwhile, under tax treaties, the rate of the WHT can be reduced. However, in the event the double tax treaty qualifies a resident as a person liable to tax, a recent French court decision tends to deny the benefit from the treaty if the person is not effectively taxed in one of the other Contracting States.[16]

68   No French WHT is levied when dividends are paid by French SIICs to French tax residents (companies or individuals). Nevertheless, dividends paid by a SIIC or an elected qualifying subsidiary from its exempt sector to a French UCITS, *Organisme de placement collectif en immobilier* or *Société d'Investissement à Capital Fixe* (fixed-capital Investment Company) or to a non-French AIF are subject to a WHT at the rate of 15%.

[4]   Other Taxes

[a]   Transfer Duty

69   Concerning the shares or interest in French *unlisted* real estate subsidiaries or partnerships, the acquisition is subject to registration duties at a rate of 5% based on the sale price indicated in the sale agreement (or fair market value if higher).

70   As of 1 August 2012, the transfer of French SIIC shares documented by a written deed executed in France or outside of France is subject to transfer duties at a rate of 0.1%.

71   However, where SIIC has a market capitalization of more than EUR 1 billion, the registration duties above mentioned are replaced by a financial transaction tax of 0.3% which is computed on the same basis as the registration duties.

72   Registration duties and financial transaction tax are due by the purchaser of the shares.

[b]   Specific Corporation Tax at a 20% Rate

73   Anti-abuse measures levied a 20% tax on dividends paid by a SIIC to domestic or foreign shareholders under certain circumstances.

74   The tax becomes due if:

– the beneficiary of the dividends is a French or foreign taxpayer other than an individual;

---

15. BOI-RPPM-RCM-30-30-20-10-20190703 n° 60.
16. CE, 9 Nov. 2015, n° 370054.

- the taxpayer holds directly or indirectly, at the moment of the payment, 10% or more of the financial rights in the French SIIC;
- the taxpayer is either exempt from any CIT on dividends or subject to tax at a rate lower than two-thirds of the standard French CIT rate.

This anti-abuse provision (the 'anti-Spanish' route provision) was enacted because **75** SIIC dividends paid to French corporations are fully subject to CIT, whereas SIIC dividends paid to a Spanish parent company may not have been subject to any tax in France and Spain.

This 20% tax is presented as an autonomous tax but it is assessed and collected as CIT. **76** FTA has stated that this tax cannot be reduced under a tax treaty. The compatibility of the 20% tax with EU legislation and existing tax treaties will have to be evaluated.

[5] Penalties Imposed on SIIC

If a parent company or a qualifying subsidiary that has elected SIIC status does not **77** meet the minimum distribution obligations, the favourable tax regime is denied for the financial year during which the distribution shortfall appears. If FTA conducts a tax audit and then reassesses the exempt profits, the reassessed amount is usually fully taxable as it would not have been distributed in accordance with the minimum distribution obligations. The excess exempt profits are not taxable if excess distributions of exempt profits were previously made.

If the listed parent company no longer fulfils the conditions of SIIC regime (e.g., one of **78** its shareholders holds more than 60% of its share capital or voting rights), the rental income and capital gains are fully taxable for the financial year in which the loss of status occurs. It should also be stressed that if the loss of status occurs within ten years after the initial election, the capital gains, having been subject to exit tax at the level of SIIC, will be subject to additional taxation at the standard CIT rate, from which will be deducted the exit tax paid on entering this regime. With respect to the latent capital gains acquired during the exemption period, they are taxed at the rate of 25%. The basis of the 25% taxation should be the sum of the unrealized capital gains and losses relating to all assets and rights eligible for the exemption regime, less than one-tenth for each calendar year spent under the exemption regime.

In addition, the loss of status causes the reinstatement in the taxable income for the financial year of the portion of distributable income within the meaning of the first paragraph of Article L 232-11 of the French Commercial Code, existing at the closing date of the year of disposal and corresponding to a portion of the income previously exempt under the SIIC regime. This should in principle correspond to net positive reserves not yet distributed.

If an elected qualifying subsidiary no longer fulfils the conditions for SIIC regime, the **79** benefit of the leasing profits and gains exemption is lost for the financial year in which the loss of status occurs. A strict interpretation of the French tax law should lead to the conclusion that the other penalties are not applicable to the SIIC subsidiary.

80   In case of a merger of two SIICs, or an acquisition of one SIIC by another SIIC, the exemption regime remains valid as long as the distribution conditions are fulfilled by the acquirer. In the case of an acquisition, the target must remain subject to SIIC regime, as a subsidiary for the remaining ten-year period from its own election as a SIIC parent.

[B]   Taxation of the Investor

[1]   *Private Investors*

[a]   *Taxation of Current Income (All Income Derived from SIIC in Holding Phase)*

81   Finance Bill for 2012 has modified the tax treatment of dividends paid by SIICs to private investors.

Plan d'Epargne en Actions (PEA) Investment Scheme

82   Previously, private investors, who are French tax residents, used to hold listed SIIC shares through the favourable investment scheme. The dividends received from these shares were tax exempt provided that all PEA income and share disposals were reinvested in PEA for a minimum five-year period.

83   As of 21 October 2011, private investors cannot hold listed SIIC shares through the favourable PEA. However, for the shares registered on a PEA prior to 21 October 2011, dividends received remain exempt under the same conditions.

French Personal Income Tax

84   For listed SIIC shares not registered on a PEA prior to 21 October 2011, dividends received from SIIC shares (either the tax-exempt or the taxable sector) are subject, as o 1 January 2018, to a 30% flat tax (comprised of a 12.8% personal income tax and 17.2% social contributions).

85   Upon an election made by the taxpayer, dividends received from listed SIIC shares are subject (after the deduction of a 40% allowance applicable only to the dividends distributed out of the taxable sector of the listed SIIC) to personal income tax at progressive rates (ranging from 0% to 45%/increased, in certain cases by the 3% to 4% exceptional tax on high taxpayers) and to 17.2% social contributions (out of which 6.8% are tax-deductible from the personal income tax basis).

86   Dividends paid by listed SIICs to non-French tax resident individuals are subject to a 12.8% French WHT.

[b]   Taxation of Capital Gains (From Disposal of SIIC Shares)

As of 1 January 2018, capital gains derived from the disposal of listed SIIC shares are **87** subject to a 30% flat tax (comprised of a 12.8% personal income tax and 17.2% social contributions).

For capital gains derived from the disposal of listed SIIC shares acquired or subscribed **88** before 1 January 2018, an election can be made by the taxpayer so that said capital gains are subject to personal income tax at a progressive rate (0%–45%) and benefit from an allowance (50% or 65% if shares have been held at least two years or at least eight years). Social contributions of 17.2% must be added.

Under French domestic tax rules, capital gains realized by a non-resident private **89** investor on the disposal of listed SIIC shares are exempt if the investor holds directly or indirectly less than 10% in the French SIIC. If the non-resident private investor holds directly or indirectly more than 10% in the French SIIC, the capital gain is subject to a French WHT of 19% and 17.2% social contributions.

[2]   Institutional Investors

[a]   Taxation of Current Income (i.e., All Income Derived from SIIC in a Holding Phase)

Dividends received by an institutional investor from the tax-exempt part of a listed SIIC **90** are subject to CIT at the standard rate of 25%[17] or 25.825% if additional contribution applies. The domestic parent-subsidiary regime does not apply to these dividends.

The same tax regime applies to dividends received by an institutional investor from the **91** taxable part of a listed SIIC. However, if the institutional investor held at least 5% of the shares of SIIC, the dividend-received benefits from the domestic parent-subsidiary regime apply, and there is a 95% dividend exemption.

Any reduction in the share capital or the distribution of share premiums will be treated **92** as a tax-free return, provided that all reserves (excluding the legal reserve) and retained earnings have been previously distributed.

Under French domestic tax rules, dividends paid by French SIICs to non-French tax **93** residents, including dividends paid to a non-resident institutional investor, are subject to a French WHT at the rate of 25%.[18]

---

17. *Ibid.*, p. 9.
18. *Ibid.*, p. 10.

[b]   Taxation of Capital Gains (From Disposal of SIIC Shares)

94   Capital gains realized by institutional investors upon the disposal of listed SIIC shares are subject to:

- the standard CIT rate as mentioned above;
- the specific long-term capital gain tax rate of 19% (or 19.63% including the additional contribution).

95   To qualify for the lower long-term capital gain rate, the shares must have been held for at least two years and the shares must qualify as participating shares for accounting purposes, which means that the investor must hold at least a 5% interest in SIIC.

96   Under French domestic tax rules, capital gains realized by a non-resident institutional investor on the disposal of SIICs shares are also subject to a WHT calculated under the same domestic rules (i.e., basis and rate) that applies for the determination of CIT if the non-resident institutional investor holds directly or indirectly more than 10% in the French SIIC and is a resident in an EU country or another state party to the agreement on the European economic area which has concluded with France a convention on administrative assistance to combat tax evasion and avoidance. In all other cases, the WHT should be calculated at the rate of 25%.[19] No WHT should be levied if the non-resident institutional investor holds directly or indirectly less than 10% of the French SIIC.

97   This WHT is not definitive and is credited towards CIT due on the same capital gain.

[3]   Penalties Imposed on Investors

98   There are no penalties imposed on SIIC investors.

[C]   Tax Treaties: Treaty Access and Withholding Reductions

[1]   Treaty Access

99   France has a large treaty network. FTA does not clearly allow non-French companies to benefit from the treaty provisions with respect to capital gains realized on the disposal of shares in French SIICs or with respect to dividends received from French SIICs.

---

19. *Ibid.*

[2]   WHT Reduction

WHT on dividends may be reduced or exempted by applicable tax treaties. However, **100** FTA does not consider EU Parent-Subsidiary Directive applicable to French SIICs or dividends from the tax-exempt sector.

France fully supports the recent Organisation for Economic Co-operation and Devel- **101** opment (OECD) paper on REITs, which advocates substantial renegotiations of tax treaties to secure a minimum right for source countries to tax REIT income. France has already begun to negotiate new REIT-specific provisions in its tax treaties.

[D]   Exit Tax/Tax Privileges/Concessions

By making the election for SIIC CIT exemption regime, the listed SIIC (or the qualifying **102** 95% French subsidiary of a SIIC) is no longer subject to CIT. As a result, SIIC or its subsidiary exits from CIT regime and has to pay a 19% exit tax assessed on latent capital gains on real estate properties and on interests in qualifying real estate partnerships. The exit tax is payable over four years and in four equal instalments. There is no exit tax on latent capital gains on other assets. However, the tax basis of these other assets is rolled over. Any tax losses carried forward are deductible from the exit tax charge and the remaining losses are cancelled.

[E]   Taxation of Foreign REITs

[1]   Taxation of Foreign REIT Holding Assets in Country

If a foreign REIT has not been elected for SIIC regime in France, it will be subject to the **103** standard rate of 25% or 25.825% if an additional contribution applies on all income (rental income and capital gains) derived from real estate assets held directly in France.

On capital gains derived upon disposals, a 25%[20] WHT will be due that will be **104** deductible from CIT due with regard to such a capital gain.

[2]   Taxation of Investors Holding Shares in Foreign REIT

French investors holding shares in a foreign REIT will be taxed in accordance with the **105** provisions of applicable tax treaties.

---

20. *Ibid.*

[F]   Taxation of Foreign REITs

[1]   ATAD II

[a]   Anti-hybrid Rules (ATAD II)

106   The 2020 Finance Act implemented into French law the rules derived from Directive EU/2017/952 of 29 May 2017 essentially focusing on double deductions and deduction without inclusion situations that would apply not only between the EU Member States but also in situations involving third countries.

107   These new rules apply to FYs starting on or after 1 January 2020, except for those related to reverse hybrids, which will apply to FYs starting on or after 1 January 2022.

108   The new rules would apply between 'associated entities' as defined under French law with two main direct and indirect thresholds (25% and 50% of voting rights, share capital, or rights to profits) and would apply depending on the type of hybrid mismatch at stake (e.g., 50% for reverse hybrid). It also includes a provision covering persons acting jointly with another person in order to be considered an associated entity.

109   The new rules tackle hybrid mismatches that arise from (i) double deduction, (ii) deduction without inclusion, or (iii) from the interaction between associated entities as well as between two or more permanent establishments of the same entity, whether located in EU or in a third country.

110   Pursuant to ATAD II rules, a payment made by a French entity should not be tax-deductible in France when the double deductible or the deduction/non-inclusion is due to the hybrid nature of either (i) the instrument or (ii) the entities.

111   It results from the above that the non-taxation of French-sourced interest at the level of the related beneficiary, due to its tax-exempt status in its jurisdiction, should not in itself trigger the application of ATAD II rule.

112   ATAD II rule should not apply automatically to the income received by a SIIC. However, ATAD II should be applicable to the taxable sector of SIIC under the conditions of ordinary law.

[2]   DAC 6

113   EU Council Directive No. 2018/822, known as DAC 6, was adopted on 25 May 2018 by EU Council. It is the result of work carried out by the European institutions in conjunction with those of OECD. Member States had to transpose the Directive by 31 December 2019 at the latest. In France, this transposition has been carried out by ordinance supplemented by a decree, FTAs' guidelines and technical specifications.

The objective of DAC 6 regulation is to provide EU Member States' tax administrations **114** with knowledge of *cross-border arrangements* that could be considered *potentially aggressive from a tax point of view*.

DAC 6 applies to cross-border tax arrangements, which meet one or more specified **115** characteristics (hallmark categories A to E), and which concern either more than one EU country or an EU country and a non-EU country.

In principle, hallmarks must follow the reporting rules according to their general or **116** specific category. For example, some hallmarks (categories A, B and some of category C) are to be reported only if they meet the tax 'main benefit test'.

The main reporting obligation to FTAs is borne by intermediaries located in France **117** (promoter intermediary, service provider intermediary) and in some specific cases directly by the taxpayer.

The reporting obligation must be carried out within thirty days after the reportable **118** cross-border arrangement (i) is made available for implementation, (ii) is ready for implementation, or (iii) when the first step in its implementation has been made, depending on which event occurs first. With respect to intermediaries, they are required to report within thirty days of the day on which they provided assistance or advice within an operation falling within the hallmarks of DAC 6.

Failure to comply with the French DAC 6 reporting obligation will be subject to a fine **119** of up to EUR 5,000 (EUR 10,000 in the event of a repeat offence in the current and the previous three calendar years).

The provisions of DAC 6 entered into force in France on 1 July 2020. However, **120** cross-border arrangements whose first phase was implemented between 25 June 2018 and 1 July 2020 were to be declared by 31 August 2020 at the latest. However, a six-month optional postponement on DAC 6 reporting was adopted by the Council of EU. Each country had the possibility to choose between postponing or not. France decided to postpone. Thus, the declaration was postponed for six months as follows:

- From 1 January 2021: declaration of arrangements within thirty days.
- 31 January 2021: declaration of the arrangements for the period from 1 July 2020 to 31 December 2020.
- 28 February 2021: declaration of the arrangements for the period from 25 June 2018 to 30 June 2020.

For SIIC purpose, the mere fact that these companies are tax exempt should not make **121** it possible to consider that any cross-border transaction involving a SIIC is a reportable arrangement. A case-by-case analysis would be required to consider whether the arrangement implying a SIIC is reportable.

Germany

UWE STOSCHEK

Uwe Stoschek joined PwC in 1994. He has a degree in Law from the Free University of Berlin and is both Attorney-at-Law (Rechtsanwalt) and a Certified Tax Consultant (Steuerberater). He has been a Tax Partner with PwC from 2000 until 2021, currently serving as Senior Advisor and Director. Uwe was PwC's Global, Real Estate Tax Leader for fifteen years until 2021, and for five years held the position of Real Estate Industry Leader EMEA. He is a member of the European Public Real Estate Association Tax Board which plays an important role in the European Real Estate Investment Trust (REIT) market. He has also been a member of the tax committee of INREV, the European organization for non-listed funds for many years. Furthermore, Uwe supports German industry associations, such as ZIA. He was also a member of the Consultative Working Group of the European Securities and Markets Authority's Investment Management Standing Committee from 2013 to 2017.

Uwe specializes in national and international investment funds' tax issues as well as real estate for German and non-German open-end and closed-end funds, institutional and private, German and foreign investors. He has advised many international opportunity funds in designing, establishing and implementing their German investments.

Moreover, Uwe has special expertise in advising German and foreign REITs. He is also a frequent speaker on issues related to the Alternative Investment Fund Managers Directive.

E-mail: uwe.stoschek@pwc.com

Germany

Uwe Stoschek

§1.01 BACKGROUND

[A] Key Characteristics

German Real Estate Investment Trusts (G-REITs) are stock corporations that must be **1** listed on an organized stock market in Germany, in a Member State of the European Union (EU) or in another Contracting State to the Agreement on the European Economic Area (EEA). G-REITs are income tax exempt provided that certain requirements are met. Primarily, G-REIT must distribute at least 90% of its income annually and meet certain asset, yield structure and share ownership requirements. G-REITs cannot own German residential property constructed before 2007.

Pre-REIT (Vor-REIT) is the precursor to G-REIT. Pre-REITs are stock corporations that **2** aim for G-REIT status. In contrast to G-REITs, pre-REITs are subject to corporate income and trade tax.

[B] History of REIT

G-REIT was introduced in 2007. At that time, most of the major industrial countries **3** already had a REIT regime. The introduction of G-REIT was forced by the German real estate industry, which felt that Germany needed to keep up with the establishment of REIT regimes in other EU countries like France, the Netherlands and the United Kingdom (UK).

In 2008, the upper house of the German Parliament passed – within the Annual Tax Bill **4** 2009 – certain amendments to REIT Act (REITA). The amended REITA provides relief from double taxation of REIT dividends derived from foreign properties and taxable subsidiaries.

German real estate organizations were lobbying for further amendments to REITA in **5** order to remedy certain structural deficits of G-REIT (e.g., acceptance of residential property as an investment object)[1] and they succeeded to a limited extent. Pre-REITs got one year more time to transform into a REIT – the application for admission as a REIT has to be applied within three years after registration as a pre-REIT, and under certain circumstances, the time limit can be extended twice for one year in each case.[2]

[C]   REIT Market

6 The initial phase of G-REIT has been difficult due to the weak market environment and significant regulatory changes in the real estate and investment market. As of June 2018, three REITs were listed in RX REIT Index of the German Stock Exchange.

§1.02   REGULATORY ASPECTS

[A]   Legal Form of REIT

[1]   Corporate Form

7 The only legal form that is permissible for a G-REIT is a stock corporation (*Aktiengesellschaft*). Both the statutory seat in accordance with the corporate articles and the place of management must be in Germany.

[2]   Investment Restrictions

8 At least 15% of the shares must be freely available to the public (free-float), and the holders of these shares must each hold less than 3% (small investor rule). At the moment of listing, 25% of the shares must be freely available. The German Securities Trade Act (Wertpapierhandelsgesetz) and REITA provide complex supervision of share ownership. Thus, both G-REIT and the German Federal Financial Supervisory Authority (Bundesanstalt für Finanzdienstleistungsaufsicht – BaFin) must be notified by G-REIT shareholders if a shareholder attains, exceeds or falls below certain shareholding thresholds. G-REIT is obliged to annually (31 December) report the free-float quota to BaFin.

9 A single shareholder is not allowed to hold directly 10% or more in G-REIT as this would allow the shareholder to unify more than 10% voting rights. The shareholding requirement does not apply to indirect shareholdings so that indirectly one investor is allowed to hold more than 10%.

---

1. Cf. Annual report of Deutsches Aktieninstitut 2010, pp. 21–22, 28 with reference to the position paper to the reform of REIT Act (DAI together with ZIA, DVFA, BFW, 23 Apr. 2010).
2. Cf. BGBl. Part I Nr. 30 of 25 Jun. 2011, p. 1173, Art. 11 and s. 10(2) REITA.

[B]   Regulatory Authorities

Compliance with REITA is reviewed within the annual statutory audit (*see* section **10** §1.02[F][7] below). In addition, the German tax authorities review compliance with the requirements of REITA.

Since G-REITs must be listed on an organized stock market in Germany, the EU or the **11** (EEA, G-REITs are subject to stock exchange supervision by BaFin or other stock exchange supervisory authorities.

[C]   Legislative and Other Regulatory Sources

G-REITs are subject to the general rules for stock corporations, that is the German Stock **12** Corporation Act and the German Commercial Code. Moreover, due to their listing, G-REITs are subject to the German Securities Trading Act.

Where REITA provisions diverge from the general stock rules for corporations, the **13** more specific REITA rules take precedence over the more general stock rules.

The Alternative Investment Fund Manager Directive (AIFMD Directive 2011/61/EU) **14** came into force on 22 July 2013 with the German Capital Investment Code (*Kapitalan-lagegesetzbuch – KAGB*). KAGB applies for Alternative Investment Funds (AIF) as defined in Article 4(1)(a) of Directive 2011/61/EU respectively under section 1(1) KAGB. An AIF is defined as a collective investment undertaking, including investment compartments thereof, which raise capital from a number of investors, with a view of investing it in accordance with a defined investment policy for the benefit of those investors. This means that a G-REIT may basically qualify as AIF in accordance with that definition and there is no general exemption to exclude G-REIT from the scope of KAGB. For BaFin, G-REIT may be subject to KAGB and it depends from case to case if a G-REIT may be exempt.[3] BaFin also refers in this context to the European Commission and cites *inter alia* 'Each structure should be considered on its own merits based on substance, not on form.'[4] Regarding G-REIT all legal requirements of section 1(1) sentence 1 KAGB must be met to qualify as an investment fund. A G-REIT may be exempt from the scope of KAGB if it qualifies as an operating company (*operativ tätiges Unternehmen*) or as an entity without defined investment strategy (*festgelegte Anlagestrategie*).[5]

---

3. Cf. the interpretation issued by BaFin on the scope of application of KAGB and to the term 'investment fund' – reference number Q 31 – Wp 2137-2013/0006 dated from 14 Jun. 2013 and last amended on 10 Dec. 2014, II 2, p. 6.
4. *Ibid.*, fn 17 with reference to the European Commission, FAQ to AIFMD, ID 1171, 'Definition of an AIF'.
5. Cf. the interpretation issued by BaFin on the scope of application of KAGB and to the term 'investment fund' – reference number Q 31 – Wp 2137-2013/0006 dated from 14 June 2013 and last amended on 10 Dec. 2014, II 1 and 2, p. 6.

15   Pursuant to section 2 paragraph 1 n° 14 lit. b of the German restricted asset regulation (*Anlageverordnung*), a G-REIT is an eligible asset allocable to the real estate quotes of the restricted asset of German Solvency I small insurance companies and pension funds.

[D]   Exchange Controls and Reporting Requirements

16   G-REITs are subject to certain obligations arising from admission to a stock exchange, including:

- ad hoc disclosure requirements regarding insider information;
- provision of reports for the financial year and half-year prepared from the audited accounts of G-REIT;
- announcement of the convening of the shareholders' meeting; and
- disclosure of the free-float quota.

17   Additional obligations may apply; for example, companies listed on the Prime Standard of the German Stock Exchange must fulfil further transparency requirements.

[E]   Registration Procedures

[1]   *Preparatory Measures*

18   The registration (with the Federal Central Tax Office) of pre-REIT first merely requires the following:

- stock corporation;
- corporate seat in Germany.

19   G-REIT status requires that the corporate name contains the term 'REIT-Aktiengesellschaft' or 'REIT-AG' and the corporation has to be registered in the commercial register. Typically, an existing real estate stock corporation is already registered in the commercial register. Therefore G-REIT applicant needs only to change its name.

20   For the registration of a G-REIT, the following main requirements should be met:

- stock corporation with a minimum nominal capital of EUR 15 million;
- statutory and management seat in Germany;
- licence to trade on an organized stock market in Germany, in a Member State of the EU or in another Contracting State to the Agreement on the EEA;
- to observe the conversion period in section §1.01[B]above;
- restriction of G-REIT's nature and purpose as described in section §1.02[F][5] below;

- minimum free-float quota of 25% in G-REIT shares at the moment of listing (*see* section §1.02[A][2] above);
- direct shareholding of the shareholders of less than 10% (*see* section §1.02[A][2] above); and
- compensation clause within G-REIT's articles of association regarding share-holders with a shareholding of less than 3% in case of termination of the tax-exempt G-REIT status (*see* section §1.03[A][5] below).

[2]   *Obtaining Authorization*

There is no specific authorization apart from the registration described above (*see*   **21** section §1.02[E][1] above).

[3]   *Other Requirements for the Incorporation of a Company*

To form a stock corporation, the following documents must be filed with the registered   **22** court:

- notarial application form;
- stock corporation's articles of association;
- certificate confirming that the shares were assumed by the constitutors;
- certificate of the appointment of the management board and the board of directors;
- statutory report and audit report concerning the foundation of the stock corporation; and
- certificate confirming that on each share the amount claimed (nominal capital of at least EUR 50,000 in total) was fully paid in and is at the management board's free disposal.

[4]   *Obtaining Listing Exchanges*

[a]   *Costs*

As a general rule, the costs for a listing at the German Stock Exchange are about   **23** 7.5%–9.5% of the gross offering proceeds.

[b]   *Time*

The time required to list G-REIT will depend on several factors, including the size and   **24** complexity of the transaction, the state of the market and how quickly funds are received from investors. As a general rule, initial public offering (IPO) process requires four to six months.

[F]   Requirements and Restrictions

[1]   Capital Requirements

25   The nominal capital of a G-REIT must amount to at least EUR 15 million. All G-REIT shares must be voting shares, and all shares must belong to the same class of shares, that is must have the same profit payout rights.

26   REITA stipulates a limit on debt financing (leverage provision). Thus, G-REIT's equity must not fall below 45% of the immovable property value as shown in the consolidated or the individual financial statements prepared under International Financial Reporting Standards (IFRS).

[2]   Marketing/Advertising

27   According to the German Securities Prospectus Act (Wertpapierprospektgesetz), G-REITs that seek a listing on an organized stock market in Germany must issue a product disclosure statement. The product disclosure statement is subject to approval by BaFin. If G-REIT is listed on a stock exchange in the EU or the EEA, foreign law may require the issuance of a product disclosure statement as well.

[3]   Redemption

28   There is no statutory right to redeem shares in a G-REIT. A G-REIT may buy back its own shares. The share buyback is subject to the general provisions for stock corporations. The share buyback must be approved by a resolution at G-REIT's general meeting.

[4]   Valuation of Shares/Units for Redemption and Other Purposes

29   As aforementioned, there is no statutory redemption right. Therefore, the shares are not valued for redemption purposes.

[5]   Investment Restrictions

30   G-REIT is limited to the following investments and activities.

[a]   *Immovable Property*

G-REITs may acquire, hold, lease, let and dispose of property or property rights in   **31**
domestic and foreign immovable property. The term 'immovable property' includes
real property, legal rights in real property (e.g., hereditary building rights) and
comparable rights under the laws of other states. Foreign immovable property may
only be held indirectly, i.e., via a foreign corporation, via a foreign REIT or an entity
comparable to a REIT being resident in the foreign country.

Existing residential properties located in Germany are non-eligible assets. Existing   **32**
residential properties are defined as mainly (more than 50%) used for residential
purposes and constructed before 1 January 2007.

[b]   *Other Assets*

A G-REIT may hold other assets insofar as the assets are in close connection with   **33**
G-REIT's core activity (e.g., assets that are necessary to manage G-REIT's immovable
property, bank deposits, money market instruments, claims and debts that stem from
the usage or the sale of immovable property).

[c]   *Auxiliary Activities*

Activities that serve the principal activity, such as the management, maintenance and   **34**
advancement of G-REIT's own real estate inventory, are considered allowable auxiliary
activities. In contrast, auxiliary activities that are rendered to third parties may only be
performed by G-REIT service corporations (*see* margin number 38).

[d]   *Real Estate Partnerships*

G-REITs may hold interests in German and foreign real estate partnerships   **35**
(Immobilien-Personengesellschaften). Such partnerships may hold German and foreign real estate. The nature and purpose of real estate partnerships must be limited to
the acquisition, the holding, the letting and the disposal of domestic and foreign
property or property rights in domestic and foreign immovable property, including the
above-described other assets and auxiliary activities. In addition, real estate partnerships may hold interests in other real estate partnerships. From 2024 onwards
partnerships must have legal personality following a revision of the German partnership laws in the year 2021.

[e]   *Corporate General Partners*

36   G-REITs are entitled to hold shares in a German or a foreign corporation that acts as a general partner of a real estate partnership if the shares of the corporation are listed on an organized stock market in Germany, the EU or the EEA. The corporate general partner itself cannot participate in the property of the partnership (i.e., general partner owns a 0% interest in the partnership).

[f]   *Real Estate Corporations*

37   Real estate may also be held through a German or foreign resident real estate corporation (Auslandsobjektgesellschaften). Such corporations must be wholly owned by G-REIT. 90% of the real estate corporation's assets must consist of immovable property. The immovable property must be entirely located outside of Germany and may only be held if, under the law of the foreign country, a REIT (or an entity comparable to a REIT), resident in this country, would be allowed to do so.

[g]   *G-REIT Service Corporations*

38   Sideline occupations (such as facility management, brokerage, project control and development control) rendered to third parties may only be performed by wholly owned German or foreign G-REIT service corporations (REIT-Dienstleistungsgesellschaften).

39   In addition to the aforementioned, G-REITs must fulfil the following asset and yield structure requirements.

[h]   *Asset Structure Requirements*

40   At least 75% of G-REIT's total assets (less the obligation to pay out dividends and allocations to reserves; *see* section §1.02[F][6] below) must consist of immovable property. The asset structure requirements are determined based on the consolidated financial statements under IFRS. If consolidated financial statements do not have to be drawn up, the individual financial statements under IFRS are used. Immovable property held as a financial investment is taken into account at its fair value (International Accounting Standards 40).

41   Shares in real estate corporations do not qualify as immovable property. However, since real estate corporations must be wholly owned by G-REIT, real estate corporations must be consolidated. As real estate corporations are consolidated, their immovable property is taken into account for the determination of the assets structure quota. Interests in real estate partnerships are classified as immovable property by definition of REITA and are taken into account at fair value.

If G-REIT renders services to third parties via G-REIT service corporations, a further **42** threshold must be taken into consideration. The assets of G-REIT service corporations must not exceed 20% of G-REIT's total assets (less the obligation to pay out dividends and allocations to reserves).

[i] Yield Structure Requirements

At least 75% of G-REIT's total sales revenues in a fiscal year must stem from the leasing **43** and letting (including auxiliary activities), or the disposal of real estate property.

Moreover, the total sales revenues generated by G-REIT service corporations may not **44** exceed 20% of G-REIT's total sales revenues in the fiscal year. Both quotas are to be determined under IFRS financial statements.

[j] No Trade in Real Estate

A G-REIT may not trade in real estate. Trading exists if G-REIT and its consolidated **45** subsidiaries' proceeds from the disposal of immovable property in the last five fiscal years (or in the period since G-REIT's formation if it has not existed for five years yet) exceed half of the value of immovable property held on average during that period. The value of the immovable property held on average is to be determined based on the consolidated or the individual financial statements under IFRS. By definition under REITA, real estate partnerships that do not belong to the consolidated group are considered immovable property. Therefore, the fair value of the partnerships is included in the determination of the average value of the immovable property.

[6] Distribution/Accumulation

G-REIT is obliged to distribute at least 90% of its profits. The amount of profit is **46** determined under the German Commercial Code and is reduced for allocations to the reserve for reinvestment purposes. Profits are reduced by accumulated losses brought forward from the previous year, and they are increased by dissolutions of the reserve for reinvestment purposes. For the determination of profits, straight-line depreciation is mandatory.

Up to 50% of capital gains stemming from the disposal of immovable property may be **47** allocated to a reserve for reinvestment purposes. The reserve decreases the distributable profit. The reserve may be invested in real estate property within the following two fiscal years. In case of a transfer, the reserve is deducted from the acquisition or production costs of real estate property acquired or created. If the reserve is not transferred to real estate property within the two-year period, the reserve has to be dissolved, and G-REIT's distributable profit increases.

[7]   Reporting Requirements

48   G-REITs are subject to the general reporting requirements that apply to stock corporations. Therefore, G-REITs have to prepare annual financial statements.

49   In addition to the regular audit of financial statements, the auditor is obliged to review whether the computation of the free-float and the maximum shareholding quota complies with the data reported to BaFin. Moreover, the auditor must determine whether G-REIT adhered to the asset and yield structure requirements, the distribution and the minimum equity requirements and to the prohibition on trading in real estate. For the purpose of the privileged dividend taxation at G-REIT shareholders' level which provides relief from double taxation, the auditor must assess the portion of pre-taxed income (*see* section §1.03[B] below).

50   Despite G-REIT's tax exemption, G-REIT is obliged to file a tax return. In the tax return, G-REIT must provide information on whether it meets the requirements necessary to be tax-exempt. Moreover, G-REIT must report the portion of pre-taxed income in order to enable investors to make use of the privileged dividend taxation (*see* section §1.03[B] below).

[8]   Accounting

51   The asset and yield structure requirements are calculated under IFRS. Therefore, G-REITs are obliged to prepare IFRS financial statements. IFRS applies to the individual financial statement and consolidated financial statements.

52   The provisions of the German Commercial Code and the Stock Corporation Act apply to the determination of distributable profits. Therefore, G-REITs also need to prepare individual financial statements under German Generally Accepted Accounting Principles.

§1.03   TAXATION

[A]   Taxation of REIT

[1]   Corporate Income Tax

[a]   Tax Accounting

53   G-REITs are exempt from corporate income and trade tax. The tax exemption applies retroactively to the start of the financial year in which G-REIT's corporate name is registered in the commercial register.

In order to be exempt from corporate income and trade tax, G-REIT must continuously **54** meet the following requirements:

- restriction of G-REIT's nature and the purpose as described in section §1.02[F][5] above;
- arrangement of the minimum nominal capital and the shares as specified in section §1.02[F][1] above;
- statutory and management seat in Germany;
- licence to trade on an organized stock market in Germany, the EU or the EEA;
- compliance with the free-float quota and the maximum shareholding quota (*see* section §1.02[A][2] above);
- compliance with the assets and yield structure requirements (*see* section §1.02[F][5] above);
- no trade in real estate (*see* section §1.02[F][5] above); and
- compliance with the distribution requirements (*see* section §1.02[F][6] above).

To ensure that appropriate tax revenues are generated at the shareholder level, REITA **55** provides for the aforementioned extensive dividend distribution obligation.

As a tax-exempt entity, G-REIT does not need to prepare special tax accounts. **56** However, elements of tax accounting are necessary to determine the tax status of REIT dividends in the hands of its investors (*see* section §1.03[A][1][b] below).

From a German investment tax perspective, a G-REIT is regardless of the possibility of **57** a material double qualification as an AIF, not an investment fund within the meaning of the German Investment Tax Act (ITA) according to section 1 paragraph 3 n° 5 ITA.

[b]   Determination of Taxable Income

G-REIT's distributable profit is determined under the German Commercial Code (*see* **58** section §1.02[F][6] above).

As a tax-exempt entity, G-REIT has no taxable income. **59**

[c]   Taxation of Income from Taxable/Non-taxable Subsidiaries

Subsidiary Corporations and real estate partnerships do not benefit from G-REIT's tax **60** exemption and are therefore subject to the general taxation rules.

For German income tax purposes, domestic partnerships are treated transparently; that **61** is, income is determined at the level of the partnership and is subsequently attributed to and taxed at the level of the partners. Since G-REITs are corporate income tax exempt, G-REITs may generate income from real estate partnerships without an income tax burden.

62   For trade tax purposes, partnerships are not transparent. Partnerships are subject to trade tax if they maintain a permanent establishment in Germany (e.g., have their place of management in Germany) and they pursue commercial activities or have a commercial structure. As an exception, if a partnership is commercial by structure but only leases and lets real estate on a long-term basis, the partnership may be entitled to make use of the extended trade tax deduction, effectively reducing the trade-taxable income to nil.

63   If both the real estate partnership and G-REIT shareholder are subject to trade tax, and the real estate partnership cannot claim the extended trade tax deduction, a double tax burden will occur. The real estate partnership's profits are subject to trade tax at the partnership level and are included in G-REIT's distributable profits. Due to G-REIT's 90% distribution obligation, these profits also increase G-REIT shareholder's trade-taxable profit. Normally, trade-taxable shareholders may deduct dividend distributions from their trade-taxable profit. However, since G-REIT is a tax-exempt entity, the trade tax deduction does not apply. Therefore, the income is subject to trade tax at a rate of approx. 12.5%–17% (depending on the respective municipality where the permanent establishment is maintained), both at the level of the real estate partnership and at the level of G-REIT shareholder. In certain cases, REITA enables investors to make use of a privileged dividend taxation providing relief from double taxation (*see* section §1.03[B] below). However, the privileged dividend taxation at the investor's level only applies to German corporate income tax and comparable foreign taxes, but not to German trade tax.

64   Real estate corporations may largely only invest in real estate property, and the real estate property must be entirely located abroad (*see* section §1.02[F][5] above). Most double tax treaties assign the taxing right on income from the leasing and letting and the disposal of real estate to the state where the real estate property is located. Therefore, irrespective of whether the real estate corporation is a resident in Germany or abroad, the income from real estate property will be taxed abroad. The dividends distributed by the real estate corporation to G-REIT will regularly be subject to withholding tax (WHT) abroad. Since G-REITs are tax exempt, the foreign tax credit amounts to nil. Whether withholding tax of 15.825% on dividends distributed by a domestic corporation to G-REIT is final or subject to a refund is not entirely clear. G-REIT's distribution obligation includes dividend income received from real estate corporations. The dividends are taxed again when they are distributed to G-REIT shareholders. Therefore, if the real estate corporation distributes its profits to G-REIT, a double tax would occur with respect to the real estate corporation's income. To provide relief from double taxation, REITA, under certain conditions, enables investors to make use of the privileged dividend taxation (*see* section §1.03[B] below).

65   G-REIT service corporations and corporate general partners are subject to standard taxation. If the corporation is a resident in Germany, the corporation is subject to corporate income tax at 15.8% (including solidarity surcharge) and trade tax at approximately 12.5%–17% of its taxable income. Whether withholding tax of 15.825% on dividends distributed by a domestic service corporation or corporate general partners to G-REIT is final or subject to a refund is not entirely clear. If there were a final withholding tax, double tax occurs. REITA, under certain conditions, enables investors to make use of the privileged dividend taxation (*see* section §1.03[B] below).

[d] *Taxation of Foreign Income*

G-REIT is not taxed on foreign income earned, but it may be taxed on that income in other jurisdictions. Since G-REIT is a tax-exempt entity, the foreign tax credit amounts to nil. However, if the foreign taxes are comparable to German corporate income tax, REITA grants relief from double taxation at the level of G-REIT investors under certain conditions (privileged dividend taxation, *see* section §1.03[B] below). **66**

[2] Value Added Tax

Germany has a value added tax (VAT) system with a standard rate of 19%. Where G-REIT or its subsidiaries hold a direct interest in domestic real estate, the rental income is VAT exempt. In return, G-REIT or its subsidiaries are not eligible for input tax relief on services received. Under certain conditions, it is possible to opt for VAT in order to benefit from input tax relief. An option to VAT is possible provided that the real estate property is let to an entrepreneur who uses the property both for his own business and solely for supplies that do not exclude input tax relief. **67**

If the transfer of German real estate property is deemed to be a transfer of an entire business, the transfer is not subject to VAT. A transfer of an entire business occurs if the purchaser may continue the business without noteworthy financial expenditures. Typically, this will be the case if the purchaser enters into the tenancy agreements concluded by the vendor. If a transfer of an entire business does not occur, the transfer of German real estate is still VAT exempt. VAT exemption avoids the double tax burden of VAT and real estate transfer tax. However, an option for VAT is possible if the property is sold to an entrepreneur who acquires the property for his own business. If G-REIT or its subsidiaries intend to lease out property subject to VAT, G-REIT is eligible for input tax relief on the acquisition costs. However, if the circumstances regarding the initial input tax relief change, a correction of input tax relief might occur. **68**

Transfers of corporate shares and partnership interests are also VAT exempt. Again, an option for VAT is possible under certain conditions. **69**

[3] Withholding Taxes

A 26.4% withholding tax (including solidarity surcharge) is levied on dividend distributions by G-REIT. **70**

At the beginning of 2009, the final withholding tax (Abgeltungsteuer) was introduced in Germany. The final withholding tax only applies to resident individual shareholders **71** holding G-REIT shares as private assets. Under the final withholding tax (26.4% on the dividend distributions), resident individual shareholders' income tax will be considered as paid.

72   The German Income Tax Act provides that foreign corporate shareholders can claim a refund of two-fifths of German withholding taxes paid, resulting in a withholding tax of 15.8% (including solidarity surcharge) on dividends distributed by G-REIT. However, most German double tax treaties already provide for German withholding tax rates of 15%.

73   A shareholder that holds at least 10% in G-REIT would (according to most German double tax treaties) normally qualify for the international affiliation privilege, resulting in reduced withholding tax rates. However, the prevailing REITA stipulates that a G-REIT shareholder is not entitled to receive such a privilege.

74   EU-Parent-Subsidiary Directive is not applicable due to G-REIT's tax-exempt status.

[4]   Other Taxes

75   G-REITs are only exempt from corporate income and trade tax. With regard to other taxes, the general rules apply. Real estate transfer tax with rates currently (June 2018) ranging between 3.5% and 6.5% is levied on the direct transfer of real estate property, on the transfer of interests and shares and on certain corporate reorganizations and restructurings.

76   German municipalities levy a yearly land tax on real estate situated in their district. The tax base is the assessed unitary value to which the municipalities apply their local multiplier. The land tax charge is relatively low, deductible for income tax purposes and typically charged to the tenant.

[5]   Penalties Imposed on REIT

77   If G-REITs breach the requirements for tax exemption, REITA provides a detailed catalogue of penalties. Penalty payments are imposed as a first step. The following penalty payments may be assessed:

  – 1%–3% of the amount by which G-REIT's proportion of immoveable assets falls below 75% at the end of a financial year.
  – 10%–20% of the amount by which the gross earnings from letting, leasing, or the sale of real estate property fall below 75%.
  – 20%–30% of the amount by which the distribution falls below 90% of the profit.
  – 20%–30% of the earnings from sideline services if G-REIT or an affiliated real estate partnership renders sideline services to third persons for remuneration.

Material and recurrent breaches may lead to a loss of G-REIT's tax exemption. A loss of **78**
the tax exemption occurs:

(a) with effect from the end of the previous financial year if G-REIT becomes unlisted;
(b) at the beginning of the financial year in which G-REIT trades in real estate;
(c) after the end of the third financial year in case of a breach of the 10% maximum shareholding or the 15% minimum free-float quota over three consecutive financial years. However, this only applies where G-REIT had (or could have had) knowledge of the breach due to G-REIT shareholders' notification. Where a breach is detected, G-REIT can remedy the breach until the end of the subsequent financial year. The corporate articles must contain provisions to compensate minority shareholders (entitled to less than 3% of the voting rights) if G-REIT loses its tax exemption;
(d) after the end of the third financial year if G-REIT fails to comply with the minimum equity requirement over three consecutive financial years;
(e) after the end of the third financial year if G-REIT continuously violates the same requirement, which may lead to a penalty payment (*see* margin numbers 77 et seq.); and
(f) after the end of the fifth year if G-REIT violates different requirements which may lead to a penalty payment (*see* margin numbers 77 et seq.) over five consecutive years.

In case of a loss of the tax exemption, G-REIT becomes liable for tax. Reserves for **79**
reinvestment purposes (*see* section §1.02[F][6] above) that have been set up during
G-REIT's tax exemption are released. The release of reserves increases the earnings and
thus the distributable profit in the first fiscal year of tax liability.

Once the tax exemption has been lost,[6] a new tax exemption cannot be reactivated or **80**
recommenced before the expiry of four years after the loss of the tax exemption.[7]

In addition to the aforementioned, the tax authorities may assess penalties if G-REIT's **81**
tax return is not filed in time. Tax returns must be filed by 31 May of the year following
the year for which taxes are due. This date can be extended upon request.

---

6. Within the meaning of s. 18 REITA.
7. Cf. s. 17(4) REITA.

[B]   Taxation of the Investor

[1]   *Private Investors*

[a]   *Taxation of Current Income (i.e., All Income Derived from REIT in Holding Phase)*

Resident Private Investors Holding G-REIT Shares as Private Assets

82   A final withholding tax applies to investors that hold G-REIT shares as private assets. Under the final withholding tax, dividend distributions are taxed at a rate of 26.4% (including solidarity surcharge). Income tax is considered as settled by the withholding tax.

Resident Private Investors Holding G-REIT Shares as Business Assets

83   Usually, if private investors hold shares in stock corporations as business assets, the partial income procedure applies, and 40% of the distributions on the shares in stock corporations are income tax exempt at the investor level. Since G-REIT is tax-exempt, REITA stipulates that the partial income procedure does not apply to dividend distributions received from G-REITs. Hence, distributions by G-REIT are fully subject to personal income tax (at a progressive rate of up to 45%; withholding tax can be credited) and trade tax (at a rate of 7% to approx. 20% depending on the municipality). There is however a lump sum credit of trade tax against individual income tax to the extent that the payable income tax relates to business income.

84   Distributions may include income from non-taxed German properties held by G-REIT itself or taxed income from foreign properties or taxable subsidiaries. In the latter case, REIT's dividend distribution obligation (90%) and the full tax liability of these distributions at the investor level would result in double taxation. In this case, REITA provides for privileged dividend taxation at the investor level, granting relief from double taxation. Thus, dividend distributions of G-REIT are entitled to the same tax privileges that apply to ordinary dividends, to the extent that REIT distributions stem from pre-taxed income (income which has been taxed with German corporate income tax or a comparable foreign tax). As a result, if the distributions stem from pre-taxed income, dividends are 40% exempt in the hands of the investors.

Non-resident Private Investors

85   Dividend distributions to non-resident shareholders are subject to German withholding tax (*see* section §1.03[A][3] above). Withholding tax is a final tax. The rate might however be reduced due to a double tax treaty.

86   If G-REIT shares are held by a private non-resident investor holding the shares in a German permanent establishment, the non-resident investor will be assessed for income and trade tax under the ordinary provisions that apply to resident private investors holding the shares as business assets with the possibility to credit withholding tax.

[b] Taxation of Capital Gains (From Disposal of REIT Shares)

Resident Private Investors Holding G-REIT Shares as Private Assets

With regard to capital gains derived from the disposal of G-REIT shares held by resident **87** investors as private assets, the following applies:

- if the shareholder did not hold 1% or more of the shares at any time during a five-year period prior to the disposal and the shares were acquired before 1 January 2009, capital gains are only taxable (at the personal income tax rate of up to 47.5% including solidarity surcharge) if the shares are disposed of within one year after acquisition;
- if the shareholder did not hold 1% or more of the shares at any time during a five-year period prior to the disposal and the shares were acquired after 1 January 2009, capital gains are subject to a final tax of 26.4% (including solidarity surcharge) irrespective of the holding period;
- if the shareholder did hold 1% or more of the shares at any time during a five-year period prior to the disposal, capital gains from the sale of the shares are fully subject to personal income tax and solidarity surcharge, irrespective of whether the shares were acquired before or after 1 January 2009. However, there is no trade tax obligation.

Resident Private Investors Holding G-REIT Shares as Business Assets

Capital gains derived by resident private investors from the disposal of G-REIT shares **88** are fully subject to personal income tax if the shares are held as business assets. The partial income procedure (normally exempting 40% of capital gains derived from the disposal of shares in stock corporations) does not apply.

Non-resident Private Investors

Basically, a non-resident shareholder's capital gains from the disposal of G-REIT shares **89** are only subject to German taxation if the shareholder held at least 1% of the shares (directly or indirectly) in G-REIT at any time within the five years preceding the disposal. Double tax treaties regularly assign the taxing right to the state where the shareholder resides. Such double tax treaties would usually provide a non-resident investor with a tax exemption for capital gains in Germany.

In case G-REIT shares are held in a German permanent establishment, the capital gains **90** are subject to German taxation irrespective of the shareholding in G-REIT. Capital gains are subject to income tax at the shareholder's personal income tax rate depending on the total German source income. Income tax on the capital gains is levied within a tax assessment. Moreover, the capital gains are also subject to trade tax.

[2]   Institutional Investors

[a]   Taxation of Current Income (All Income Derived from REIT in Holding Phase)

91 Usually, 95% of the dividend distributions received by resident corporate shareholders on shares held long term in stock corporations are tax-exempt. REITA stipulates that the 95% dividend exemption does not apply to distributions by G-REITs. Thus, dividends distributed by G-REIT to German corporate shareholders are fully subject to corporate income tax (15.8% including solidarity surcharge; withholding tax can be credited) and trade tax.

92 As an exception, if dividends stem from pre-taxed income (see section §1.03[B][1][a], §1.03[B][1][a]), G-REIT's distributions are entitled to the same tax privileges that apply to ordinary dividends; that is, the distributions are 95% tax exempt.

93 Dividend distributions to non-resident shareholders are subject to German withholding tax (see section §1.03[A][3] above). Provided that G-REIT shares are not attributable to a German permanent establishment, withholding tax is a final tax. Withholding tax will amount to 26.4% of the gross amount of dividends (with the possibility to claim a refund of two-fifths). If a double tax treaty is in place, withholding tax may be reduced, and will usually amount to 15% of the gross dividends. According to REITA, both the international affiliation privilege and EU-Parent-Subsidiary Directive do not apply (see section §1.03[A][3] above).

94 If REIT shares are held by a German permanent establishment of the non-resident, the non-resident corporation will be assessed corporate income and trade tax on dividends received in the same manner that resident corporate shareholders are taxed (withholding tax can be credited).

[b]   Taxation of Capital Gains (From Disposal of REIT Shares)

95 If G-REIT shares are directly held by a German corporation, capital gains from the disposal of the shares are fully subject to corporate income tax and trade tax. The 95% capital gain exemption pursuant to section 8b CITA (Corporate Income Tax Act) does not apply.

96 Basically, a non-resident institutional shareholder's capital gains from the disposal of G-REIT shares are only subject to German taxation if the shareholder held at least 1% of the shares (directly or indirectly) in G-REIT at any time within the five years preceding the sale. Double tax treaties regularly assign the taxing right to the state where the shareholder resides. Such double tax treaties would usually provide a non-resident investor with a tax exemption for capital gains in Germany.

In case G-REIT shares are held in a German permanent establishment of the non- **97** resident, the capital gains are subject to German taxation irrespective of the shareholding in G-REIT. Provided that the institutional investors are considered as corporations pursuant to German law, capital gains are subject to corporate income tax and trade tax.

[3] Investors Subject to the German ITA

For German investment tax purposes, G-REIT shares are deemed real estate of a value **98** up to 75% of the value of the shares, where such are held by an investment fund subject to ITA. For such a qualification, section 2 paragraph 9 sentence 6 of ITA requires that the target REIT invests, according to its by-laws or investment rules, 75% of its gross asset value in immovable assets. Furthermore, either the capital gain of the entity must be subject to corporate income tax to a rate of at least 15% without any exemption or distributions to shareholders have to be taxable to a 15% rate at least and the shareholder investment fund is not exempted. As mentioned previously, dividend distributions on G-REIT shares are subject to 15.8% corporate income tax unless they stem from pre-taxed income. Moreover, tax-opaque investment funds subject to Chapter 2 of ITA are also subject to 15% final withholding tax with regard to dividends distributions stemming from incomes pursuant to section 7 paragraph 1 in combination with section 6 paragraph 2 ITA. Thus, in case of a German REIT, only a withholding tax of 0.8% out of 15.8% would be subject to exemption pursuant to section 11 paragraph 1 n° 2 ITA.

This enables Chapter 2 investment funds to allocate G-REIT shares to their real estate **99** quota. Where such German investment fund reaches the minimum real estate fund quota as required in section 2 paragraph 9 sentence 1 of ITA, it can be eligible for a partial tax exemption of 60%.

[4] Penalties Imposed on Investors

Income tax penalties are imposed on investors if the investor understates the taxable **100** income allocated to them by G-REIT in respect of an income year. Moreover, there may be assessed late-filing penalties.

[C]   Tax Treaties

[1]   *Treaty Access*

101   Germany has a large treaty network. Since G-REITs are stock corporations they are eligible for treaty relief. Many treaties provide for special rules dealing with income from REITs.

[2]   *WHT Reduction*

102   If a double tax treaty applies, withholding tax on G-REIT distributions is regularly reduced to 15%. If a shareholder owns more than 10% of G-REIT, and a double tax treaty grants a further withholding tax reduction, the further reduction does not apply (*see* section §1.03[A][3] above). EU-Parent-Subsidiary Directive does not apply.

[D]   Exit Tax/Tax Privileges/Concessions

103   Under certain requirements, the conversion of a taxable stock corporation into a G-REIT before 1 January 2010 and the disposal of real estate to a G-REIT based on a contract concluded after 31 December 2006 and before 1 January 2010 has been privileged under the so-called exit tax. Under the exit tax privilege, 50% of the realized hidden reserves and capital gains have been tax exempt.

104   The exit tax has not been prolonged by the German legislator, so that from 1 January 2010, the disposal of assets to a G-REIT and the conversion of a taxable stock corporation into a G-REIT are subject to the general income taxation rules. The change to the tax-exempt G-REIT status is treated as a taxable liquidation of the prior taxable stock corporation. Therefore, the stock corporation must prepare a closing balance sheet at the end of its final taxable financial year. All assets are reported on the closing balance sheet at fair value, resulting in a realization of hidden reserves for corporate income and trade tax purposes.

105   Irrespective of the exit tax, the disposal of shares in a stock corporation to a G-REIT is subject to the general rules of the partial income procedure and the participation exemption according to section 8b CITA providing for a 95% exemption.

106   The exit tax has also applied to capital gains from the disposal of real estate to a pre-REIT. Pre-REIT status requires the following as per the end of the business year following pre-REIT's year of registration (*see* section §1.02[E] above) and each consecutive year:

  – limitation of pre-REIT's nature and purpose to the nature and purpose of G-REIT (*see* section §1.02[F][5] above);

    – compliance with the assets and yield structure requirements (*see* section §1.02[F][5] above); the assets and yield structure requirements must be verified by an auditor.

Under the current REITA, the exit tax privilege once claimed is denied retroactively if **107** pre-REIT is not registered as a G-REIT within a four-year period from the conclusion of the (exit-tax-privileged) contract between pre-REIT and the seller of the real estate property. The vendor will become subject to taxation if the preferential tax treatment is inapplicable retroactively. The purchaser will be liable for the taxes payable.

[E] Taxation of Foreign REITs

[1] *Taxation of Foreign REIT Holding Assets in Country*

A foreign REIT does not benefit from G-REIT's corporate income and trade tax **108** exemption. Therefore, a foreign REIT's German source income is subject to regular non-resident income taxation in Germany. Provided that the legal structure and the economic position of the foreign REIT are comparable to a German corporation, and the foreign REIT does not have a permanent establishment, the income from the leasing and letting of real estate property is subject to corporate income tax at a rate of 15.8% (including solidarity surcharge). Capital gains from the disposal of real estate will also be subject to corporate income tax at the rate stated above.

If the foreign REIT maintains a permanent establishment in Germany, the foreign REIT **109** will also be subject to trade tax at a rate of approx. 12.5%–17% of its income (depending on the municipality where the permanent establishment is maintained).

[2] *Taxation of Investors Holding Shares in Foreign REIT*

REITA defines foreign REITs as follows: **110**

    – The foreign entity is not domiciled in Germany.
    – More than two-thirds of the foreign entity's assets consist of real estate property.
    – More than two-thirds of the foreign entity's gross yields stem from the letting or the sale of real estate property.
    – The foreign entity is not subject to an investment supervisory in its state of residence.
    – The foreign entity's shares are listed on an organized stock market.
    – The foreign entity's distributions stemming from immovable properties may not be subject to taxation comparable to German corporate income tax.

111   If a foreign entity qualifies as a foreign REIT within the meaning of REITA, distributions are fully taxable to the German investor.

112   If the foreign REIT's distributions stem from pre-taxed income, and the German investor is able to demonstrate that a certain amount of pre-taxed income is contained in the distributions, the privileged dividend taxation applies (*see* margin numbers 84, 92). REITA does not provide further details with regard to the demonstration. In any case, the foreign REIT will have to determine the amount of pre-taxed income and report it to the German investors.

113   Dividends that are received from foreign entities that do not qualify as a foreign REIT within the meaning of REITA are taxed according to the general German tax principles. Basically, distributions of a foreign REIT that do not qualify as a foreign REIT within the meaning of REITA to an inbound corporation may be exempt from corporate taxes in Germany, but 5% of such income will be considered in the tax base for CITA tax purposes. Since the fiscal year 2014, the general corporate tax exemption for income derived from such foreign REIT was changed and the tax exemption will be granted only if the distributed dividends have not reduced the taxable income at the foreign REIT level.

Greece

VASSILIOS VIZAS

Vassilios Vizas is a partner of PwC in Athens. His expertise lies in taxation of the financial services sector, real estate and private equity, as well as international tax structuring. He obtained his LLM in Banking and Financial Law at the University of London and LLM and LLB from the University of Athens. He is a member of the Athens Bar and a number of professional organizations including the International Fiscal Association.

Vassilios is also the author of several publications and articles in the Greek press, including 'Tax treatment of Real Estate Mutual Funds and Investment Companies', in *Synigoros Law Journal*, Issue 23/2001, as well as a number of international publications sponsored by PwC.

He is also the author of a book called 'The GAAR in Greek Law – Scope and Limitations', published in January 2017.

E-mail: vassilios.vizas@ pwc.com

FREDY YATRACOU

Fredy joined PwC in March 2002 as a Senior Manager of the Tax & Legal (TLS) Department and currently is the leader of the Tax FS services and responsible for the Tax Real Estate sector.

She is a specialist in corporate income taxes and international taxation. She has been engaged in a large number of projects, involving transactions in the Financial Sector, focusing on Mergers and Acquisitions tax advice, complex finance raising arrangements and corporate restructurings. She has more than twenty years of experience in advising Greek-based multinational companies in their international and local tax affairs.

Fredy has been involved in various projects in all aspects of tax issues concerning companies in the real estate and hospitality sectors, REITs, Real Estate funds, Real Estate developers, NPL Real Estate structures, etc.

Fredy holds an LLB from the University of Athens and an LLM in European and International Trade Law from the University of Leicester – UK.

She is a lawyer registered with the Athens Bar Association.
E-mail: fredy.yatracou@pwc.com

Greece

Vassilios Vizas & Fredy Yatracou

§1.01 BACKGROUND

[A] Key Characteristics

Greek Real Estate Investment Trusts (REITs) are special purpose entities. Their main   1
activities consist of the investment in real estate assets prescribed by the Greek REIT
law. The Greek REIT law provides for two types of REITs:

(1) those having a corporate legal form (Real Estate Investment Companies
    (REICs)). REICs must obtain a listing on a stock exchange operating in Greece
    (i.e., Athens Stock Exchange);
(2) those having a unit trust form (Real Estate Mutual Funds (REMFs)). REMFs
    are not listed vehicles.

Considerable tax exemptions are the key advantage of the Greek REIT regime.   2
However, the following stringent investment restrictions have held back the development of the Greek REIT:

(a) the lack of ability to invest in real estate subsidiaries (finally allowed);
(b) the severe restrictions on ownership of properties under development;
(c) restrictions on leverage (finally liberalized);
(d) plus the lack of clarity in a number of provisions, mainly with respect to the
    (relatively strict) investment restrictions.

Pursuant to various legislative amendments (L. 4141/5 April 2013, L. 4209/21 Novem-   3
ber 2013, L. 4223/31 December 2013, L. 4261/05 May 2014, L. 4281/8 August 2014),
the respective regime has become even more flexible, but only with respect to REICs.
Nevertheless, L. 4389/2016 has introduced a minimum tax for REICs that significantly
increased their tax leakage. Moreover, L. 4514/2018 (through which MiFID II (Market
and Financial Instrument) Directive has been implemented in the Greek legislative

framework) has introduced certain minor changes relating to the field of the investments that a REIT may invest. In addition, L. 4646/2019 has amended some provisions regarding the taxation of REICs and REMFs.

[1]   History of REIT

4   The Greek REIT law was introduced in December 1999 by L. 2778/1999. The initial version of the law was poorly adapted to the needs of the market, and no REITs were established. The Greek REIT law was amended a few years later. A further second amendment to the law, lifting a number of restrictions (e.g., increases limitations on leverage, allows investments in real estate Special Purpose Vehicles rather than only direct ownership of properties), created a more favourable environment for the establishment of REITs, whereas the latest legislative amendment adopting the applicable regime to the negative economic circumstances in Greece may result in the establishment of more REITs, as it has widened the scope of eligible properties (e.g., residential or touristic developments, land to be used for development).

[B]   REIT Market

5   Greece does not have a large domestic REIT market. Presently, the following REICs are listed on the Athens Stock Exchange: *Trastor REIC* with a market capitalization as of 10 February 2022 of EUR 180.87 million, *Prodea Investments* (i.e., formerly known as NBG Pangaia) *REIC* with a market capitalization as of 10 February 2022 of EUR 2,299.45 billion, *Intercontinental International REIC* whose shares became listed in Athens Stock Exchange in mid-2016 with a market capitalization as of 10 February 2022 of EUR 72.97 million, *Briq Properties REIC* whose shares became listed in the Athens Stock Exchange in July 2017 with a market capitalization as of 10 February 2022 of EUR 77.25 million. Moreover, *Noval Property REIC is also listed on the Athens Stock Exchange.* Additionally, there are currently non-listed REICs, namely *Blue Kedros REIC, Orilina REIC and Trade Estates.* Several other groups, including other banks, construction groups, and public sector companies, have or are currently considering the establishment of REICs. There are no REMFs. In general, the REMF structure is not attractive to investors. As of the date of this report, Greek-listed REICs are considered as traded at a considerable discount to their Net Asset Value (NAV), something that has been surely impacted by the current financial crisis. One of the major REICs in the Greek market, namely Grivalia Properties, was absorbed by Eurobank Societe Anonyme (SA) in 2019.

§1.02   REGULATORY ASPECTS

[A]   Legal Form of REIT

[1]   Corporate Form

REIC is a special type of SA company (a Greek stock corporation). Its exclusive purpose   **6**
is to manage an asset portfolio consisting of real estate (mainly), securities and cash.

REMF, which has a legal form similar to a unit trust, is actually a pool of assets   **7**
comprised of real estate and liquid financial instruments. REMFs are jointly owned by
a number of investors and managed by a management company. The management
company is a special purpose company which must have the form of an SA. REMF is
not a legal entity, and its assets are legally considered co-owned by its investors.

In many aspects, such as investment restrictions and tax benefits, the REMF regime is   **8**
similar to REIC. Since REMFs are not used in the Greek market, the rest of this report
refers mainly to REICs.

[2]   Investment Restrictions

There are no restrictions on the identity of investors in a REIT. However, there are   **9**
significant restrictions on the investments that REIT itself may carry out (please refer to
section §1.02[F][5] below for more details).

[B]   Regulatory Authorities

REICs, REMF and REMF management companies are regulated vehicles, subject to a   **10**
licence granted by the Hellenic Capital Market Committee (HCMC) and the regulator of
the Athens Stock Exchange. Once a REIC becomes listed, it is subject to the regulatory
authority of the respective stock exchange.

HCMC must approve not only the establishment but also any amendment to the   **11**
Articles of Association of REIC or a REMF management company. HCMC also must
approve any capital increase.

[C]   Legislative and Other Regulatory Sources

Law 2778/1999 is the main legislative source for REIT rules. A few decisions of HCMC   **12**
further specify the terms and conditions of licensing and operating a REIT. Furthermore, there is a Ministerial Decision of the Minister of National Economy that sets forth
the ways to value the real estate property of a REIT.

13   REICs and REMF management companies are also subject to the formalities and procedures set out by Greek Corporate Law for SAs (L. 4548/2018 as in force since 1 January 2019).

14   It be noted that the Alternative Investment Fund Managers Directive (AIFMD) has been integrated into the Greek legislation, and in principle applies to Greek REICs and REMFs, although the effect of AIFMD on the currently applicable REIT regime remains open to interpretation.

[D]   Reporting Requirements

15   REITs are obliged to submit to HCMC and/or make available to investors the following documents.

[1]   REIC

16   (a) Prospectus: A prospectus containing detailed information about the application for listing.
        (b) Table of Investments: A semestrial table of investments, which is audited by a certified auditor and is based on the evaluations of the certified evaluator. The table of investments is published on the website of REIC and the stock market exchange on which the latter is listed.

    Subsequent to listing, REICs are subject to the disclosure requirements set by the relevant securities regulation laws.

[2]   REMF

17   (a) Prospectus: A prospectus containing detailed information on REMF.
        (b) Bulletin: A simplified bulletin containing some of the information included in the prospectus.
        (c) Table of investments: A semestrial table of investments, which is audited by a certified auditor and is based on the evaluations of the certified auditor.
        (d) Reports: Semestrial and annual reports.
        (e) Newspapers: REMF publishes in at least two financial newspapers and one political newspaper on a daily basis its NAV, as well as the number of its shares, their value and the acquisition and redemption price thereof.

[E]   Registration Procedures

[1]   Preparatory Measures

Prior to the establishment of a REMF, its management company or a REIC, a special   **18**
licence is required by HCMC. Before it grants a licence, HCMC will evaluate the
business plan of the company and the experience and credentials of the company's
management.

Along with the application for the operation licence, the entities must also submit   **19**
additional information. A REIC must submit a detailed analysis of its investment policy,
including the proposed use of the real estate property in which the company will invest
its funds. REIC must also submit a detailed description of its strategy and the means by
which the company plans to accomplish its strategic goals. A REMF must submit the
following:

   (a) A detailed table of all the assets of REMF.
   (b) A declaration by a financial institution operating in Greece and acting as a
        Custodian of the Mutual Fund.
   (c) The draft regulation of the Fund signed by the management company and the
        Custodian.
   (d) A detailed description of the investment policy and the use of the property in
        which the Fund invests its assets.

[2]   Obtaining Authorization

Provided that all the requirements as to minimum capital, management credentials,   **20**
etc. are fulfilled as set in law, HCMC will grant authorization.

[3]   Other Requirements for the Incorporation of a Company

Apart from the above HCMC-related procedure, the normal process for the incorpora-   **21**
tion of a Greek SA would have to be run through as well. This entails a notarial deed
incorporating the Articles of Association of the company, which is submitted for
approval to the competent corporate registry (such approval being a formality; that is,
registry has no discretion to deny registration).

The law allows for the conversion of a normal Greek SA into a REIC. SA must change   **22**
its Articles of Association by way of a shareholders' decision and limit its scope of
activities to the exclusive activities that a REIC is allowed to perform. Existing REICs
were, in principle, normal SAs that converted to REICs.

[4]   Obtaining Listing Exchanges

23   The listing conditions may depend on the actual exchange where listing is pursued. There are no special rules for REICs in this respect.

[a]   Costs

24   The costs to list the shares on the Athens Stock Exchange depend on the value of shares, as determined by the following scale:

Value of Shares	Percentage on Value
Up to EUR 1,000,000,000	0.04%
EUR 1,000,000,001–EUR 3,000,000,000	0.02%
More than EUR 3,000,000,000	0.00%

[b]   Time

25   Listing must be sought within two years from the formation of REIC, provided that by the time of the listing, at least 50% of the share capital of the company is invested in real estate property. Such deadline may be extended, subject to HCMC's approval, for another thirty-six months. If the company fails to list its shares on a recognized stock exchange operating in Greece (i.e., the Athens Stock Exchange), the Capital Market Committee will revoke its operation licence and REIC will be put in liquidation. In case of a revocation of the operating licence of REIC, any tax benefits and favourable tax regulations provided are repealed as well.

26   Usually, the listing process is completed within several months following the filing of the application. However, the time will depend on several factors, including the size and complexity of the transaction and whether the company is able to provide all the requested documentation and any requested additional documentation for the listing of the shares.

[F]   Requirements and Restrictions

[1]   Capital Requirements

27   For the establishment of a REIC, the company must hold a share capital of at least EUR 25 million, fully payable upon incorporation. The share capital of the company includes cash contributions, securities, other liquid assets and real estate property. The share capital is divided into registered shares.

The share capital of a REMF management company must be at least EUR 2.935 million, **28**
fully payable upon incorporation. Its share capital, divided into registered shares,
should be owned with a percentage of at least 51% by one or more financial institutions
or/and insurance companies or/and companies offering investment services with a
minimum share capital of at least EUR 2.935 million.

[2]   Marketing/Advertising

There are no specific provisions regarding the marketing and advertising of a REIT.   **29**

[3]   Redemption

The redemption of the units of a REMF requires a written application of the unitholder   **30**
to the management company. The redemption price is paid in cash within fifteen days
from the date of the submission of the application.

The law on REICs does not provide for the redemption of shares of a REIC. In theory,   **31**
redemption is possible under the general conditions of Greek Corporate Law. Based on
the Corporate Law, the buy-back of the corporation's own shares is permissible
provided that the following conditions are fulfilled:

    (a) The total nominal value of the shares shall not exceed one-tenth of the paid
        share capital of the company.
    (b) Following the buy-back of shares, the shareholder's equity of the company
        shall not fall below an amount equal to its share capital plus its non-
        distributable reserves.
    (c) The shares must be fully paid up.

The General Assembly of the shareholders must approve any redemption. The General   **32**
Assembly's resolution determines the conditions and terms of the redemption, the total
number of shares to be acquired as well as the duration of the approval, which shall not
exceed twenty-four months.

[4]   Valuation of Shares/Units for Redemption and Other Purposes

REIC's assets are valued at the end of each accounting period. The real estate assets are   **33**
valued by a certified evaluator. A Joint Ministerial Decision of the Minister of Finance
and of National Economy specifies the rules for the valuation of REIC's real estate
assets.

The management company values REMF's assets every three months for a real estate   **34**
property, and, on a daily basis, for the rest of the assets. The management company

appoints a certified evaluator to value the real estate property, and such valuation is binding upon the management company.

[5]   Investment Restrictions

35   The available funds of a REIC or a REMF must be invested only in the following:

(a) Real estate property located in Greece or another European Economic Area (EEA) Member State. In the case of a REIC, more than 80% of REIC's funds must be invested in real estate property. Real estate property is defined as property which may be used for commercial and general business purposes (e.g., hotels, tourist residences, marinas), or the exploitation of residential properties not exceeding 25% of the total real estate investments. Property under development is allowed only to the extent that it is expected to be completed within thirty-six months from the issuance of the respective building permit or acquisition of property and that the budgeted remaining costs do not exceed 40% of the value of the property, which will be evaluated once works are completed. In additionally, REICs may invest in land plots, provided that the respective building permit for the construction of buildings is issued within five years from the acquisition of the plot and on the condition that the value of said plots does not exceed 25% of the total real estate investments of REIC. Real estate property includes subsidiaries, aside from partnerships, held at a percentage of at least 80%, provided that such subsidiaries are engaged exclusively in real estate activities and invest in real estate property in which a REIC may also invest directly, and companies being in a parent-subsidiary relationship with REIC, at least 10% owned, provided that the subsidiary company is engaged in the acquisition, management and exploitation of property and the participation of REIC in its capital forms part of a common business strategy for the development of properties exceeding EUR 10 million in value, as well as participating at a percentage of at least 80% in Undertakings for Collective Investments in Transferable Securities investing in REITs and Alternative Investment Funds provided that said Funds have received an operating licence in a European Union (EU) Member State and are subject to the legislation and supervisory authority in such EU Member State and its assets are invested in real estate. REMFs may invest in subsidiaries held at a percentage of at least 90%, provided that such subsidiaries are engaged exclusively in real estate activities and invest in real estate property in which a REMF may also invest directly.

(b) Money market instruments. Especially for REMF, money market investments should not exceed 10% of the minimum share capital of the management company.

(c) Real estate property in the non-EEA Member States so long as the investments do not exceed 20% of the total real estate investments for REICs and 10% for REMFs.

(d) No more than 25% in properties acquired under financial leasing contracts, provided that each contract individually does not exceed 25% of the total investments of REIC as well. Furthermore, no more than 20% of the total investments in real estate property may consist of properties for which REIT does not hold full ownership.

A REIC can also invest in other movable assets which serve the company's operational **36** needs, provided that such assets, together with the value of any real estate property acquired for the same purpose, do not exceed 10% of the total value of REIC's funds.

The law provides a number of restrictions on the nature of assets in which a REIT may **37** invest, such as the following:

(a) Each individual property in which funds are invested may not exceed 25% of the total investment value of all properties.
(b) Investment in property under development for REICs is allowed only if it is expected that the development will be completed within thirty-six months from the issuance of the respective building permit or acquisition of property and that the budgeted remaining costs do not exceed 40% of the value of the property after development is completed, whereas for REMFs if the development will be completed within a reasonable amount of time and the budgeted remaining costs do not exceed 25% of the total value of the property upon completion. Investment in land plots acquired by REICs for the construction of buildings is permitted provided that the respective building permit is issued within five years from the acquisition of the land and that at the time of acquisition the value of all plots does not exceed 25% of the total value of REICs' investments.
(c) REIT may not invest more than 25% of its net equity in properties acquired under financial leasing contracts, and no individual contract individually can exceed 25% for REICs and 10% for REMFs of the net equity. Furthermore, no more than 20% for REICs and 10% for REMFs of the total investments in real estate property may consist of properties that REIT does not fully own.
(d) Properties and participations in subsidiaries may not be disposed of less than twelve months from the date the properties are acquired, with the exception of residential properties and properties under construction forming part of the assets of REICs.
(e) The acquisition or disposal of real estate property must be preceded by a valuation of the property by a certified evaluator, and the price paid may not deviate (upwards for acquisition or downwards for disposal) more than 5% from the value, as determined by the certified evaluator.

[6]   Distribution/Accumulation

38   A *REIC* is obliged to annually distribute at least 50% of its annual net profits. The Articles of Association may authorize a waiver of the dividend distribution by resolution of the General Assembly for the purposes of either:

   (a) forming a special reserve from profits other than capital gains; or
   (b) converting profits into share capital and issuing free shares to shareholders.

39   Furthermore, the General Assembly may decide to create reserves from capital gains to offset losses incurred from the sale of securities.

40   The net profits of REMF are distributed according to the procedures specified in REMF regulations.

[7]   Reporting Requirements

41   In addition to the specific rules covered by section §1.02[D] above, a REIC has to comply with the same financial reporting requirements that apply to Greek companies (i.e., publication of annual financial statements). More detailed requirements may apply depending on the applicable stock exchange regulations.

[8]   Accounting

42   As a listed company, REIC is obliged to prepare its financial statements in compliance with International Financial Reporting Standards (IFRS). The law on REITs was enacted before the mandatory introduction of IFRS for listed companies, and the law provides a number of rules for the determination of profits of REICs which are not in line with IFRS. However, IFRS should prevail for companies which are listed on the Athens Stock Exchange.

§1.03   TAXATION

[A]   Taxation of REIT

43   The Greek corporate tax legislation has been subject to significant amendments, which however are not fully reflected in L. 2778/1999, as currently in force. In any case, this is not expected to have an impact on the fundamental aspects of REIT taxation.

[1]   **Corporate Income Tax**

[a]   *Tax Accounting*

Law 2778/1999 introduced significant income, transfer, and ownership tax exemptions   **44**
for REICs and REMFs.

REITs are exempt from any income tax, so there are no specific tax accounting rules for   **45**
REITs. However, REITs are subject to a tax imposed on their average NAV (*see* section
§1.03[A][1][b] below). The tax rate is 10% of the intervention interest rate as
determined by the European Central Bank, increased by one percentage unit. The tax
is payable by REIC twice a year within the first fifteen days of the month following the
end of the respective semester.

[b]   *Determination of Taxable Income*

NAV is determined by the semestrial tables of investments, and the tax is imposed on   **46**
the average of the investments as reported in the table of investments. The table of
investments includes a description of each separate real estate property, the contemplated use of the property, its commercial value compared to the 'objective value'
(objective value is a special tax valuation of real estate properties established in
accordance with specific tax rules, and normally serves as minimum tax value for
purposes of real estate transfer transactions), along with any additional information
critical to determining the value of the investments. Properties owned either directly or
indirectly by subsidiary companies are not included in the NAV of REIC for tax
purposes, provided that said properties are indicated separately on the semestrial
tables of investments.

A valuation of the investments is performed at the end of each accounting year by a   **47**
certified evaluator.

If the annual valuation of the property shows an increase in value, such increase is not   **48**
reported in the accounting books, but it is included in a 'revaluation gains table', which
accompanies the financial statements. IFRS provides rules for the recognition of
revaluation gains, which render the above provisions irrelevant in practice for companies that actually publish IFRS accounts.

[c]   *Taxation of Income from Taxable/Non-taxable Subsidiaries*

Dividends distributed from Greek companies to REIC are subject to a 5% dividend   **49**
Withholding Tax (WHT) as of 1 January 2020 and the relevant dividend tax is withheld
by the paying company. In such a case, any dividend WHT imposed on dividend
payments received by REIC is then set off against the above-mentioned, under section
§1.03[A][1][a] tax on NAV.

50   Dividends distributed by REICs are not subject to such WHT.

[d]   Taxation of Foreign Income

51   Foreign source income is exempt from tax in Greece. Foreign tax authorities may tax income derived from real estate situated in foreign countries, by REICs subject to a favourable taxable regime in Greece. It is questionable whether a REIT could credit the foreign income taxes paid against the Greek annual tax liability.

[2]   VAT

52   Pursuant to Value Added Tax (VAT) legislation, REITs are engaged in non-VATable activities, that is property leasing and selling, and REITs do not have the right to deduct their input VAT. Any VAT charged to a REIT constitutes a cost. However, there are cases which could, in theory, result in a REIT having VATable income:

   (i)   By virtue of L. 3427/2005, the initial acquisition of real estate property by an entity subject to VAT is considered as a VATable activity subject to a 24% VAT if the building licence for the property was granted after 1 January 2006. However, based on enacted tax legislative framework, the imposition of VAT will be suspended until 31 December 2022 and real estate transfer tax (RETT) will be levied on all unsold real estate with a construction permit issued from 1 January 2006 onwards, upon relevant application by taxable persons. In December 2021, it has been agreed at the Ministerial level at the Ecofin that the measure of VAT suspension on real property will be extended up to the end of 2024, however not any relevant document has been issued.
   (ii) By virtue of L. 4110/2013, leases of spaces used for the exercise of professional activities, either independently or as part of mixed contracts, may be subject to VAT, by the election of the owner.

[3]   Withholding Taxes

53   Any income from securities and deposits is exempt from WHT. Interest income derived from bond loans is also exempt provided that the respective titles on which the interest is imposed have been acquired thirty days prior to the payment of the interest-bearing coupons. Interest on titles acquired less than thirty days before payment is subject to WHT according to the general income tax rules (normally a 15% WHT withheld by the payer of the interest).

[4] Other Taxes

[a] Real Estate Transfer Tax

The transfer of real estate property to REIC or REMF is exempt from real estate transfer **54** tax, and any other tax or duty in favour of the State or third parties. On the contrary, the transfer of real estate property by REIC or REMF is subject to real estate transfer tax. The transfer tax is imposed:

(a) either on the objective value of the real estate property based on a deemed calculation method (predetermined by the Greek Ministry of Finance based on several factors, i.e., on a specific value per square metre depending on the area where the real estate property is situated, the type of the real estate, i.e., residency, office, factory, plot of land, etc., and other factors, such as the date the building licence was issued and construction details); or

(b) on the value of the real estate property being transferred.

The value is determined by the parties in the transfer agreement. Tax is paid by the **55** buyer at a rate of 3% (increased by a municipality duty of 3%), applicable from 1 January 2014 onwards.

The transfer of assets to a REIC or REMF is not exempt from capital gains tax. However, **56** there are ways that an existing company may use corporate restructuring forms such as mergers, divisions and spin-offs to transfer certain assets into a REIT without incurring taxable capital gains.

[b] Real Estate Tax

Up to 2013, REITs are subject to a 0.1% tax imposed on the objective value of their real **57** estate property. The objective value is the value of the real estate property as determined by specific coefficients provided by the Ministry of Finance. The objective value is normally lower than the market value of the property, depending on the timing of the latest adjustment of such coefficients (The updated objective values, as adjusted by the No. 57732 EΞ 2021/18-05-2021 Decision of the Minister of Finance (Government Gazette vol. B 2375/07-06-2021) have been in force since 1-01-2022.). The real estate tax must be at least EUR 1 per square meter.

From 2014 onwards, REITs are subject to the Uniform Tax on the Ownership of Real **58** Estate Property, taking the form of a principal tax imposed on each real estate property and a supplementary tax on the total value of the real estate property. The Uniform Tax is no longer imposed on the basis of the objective value of real estate property but will be determined on the basis of various factors, according to the final registration of the property at the land registry or ownership title.

59 The principal tax on buildings is calculated by multiplying the square metres of the building by the principal tax ranging from EUR 2–EUR 13/sqm and other coefficients affecting the value of the property (e.g., location, use, flour of the property, etc.).

60 The principal tax on land is calculated by multiplying the square metres of the land by the principal tax ranging from EUR 0.0037–EUR 11.25/sqm and other coefficients affecting the value of the property (e.g., location, use of the property, etc.).

61 In relation to the supplementary tax, said tax is calculated at a standard rate of 0.55% on the total tax value of the rights to property, not self-used. Self-used property is subject to a tax of 0.1%.

Note: To be noted that from 2022 onwards, amendments have been unofficially announced in the calculation of the Uniform Tax on the Ownership of Real Estate Property without being specified yet.

[c]   Stamp Duty

62 Lease payments in Greece are subject to a 3.6% stamp duty – there is no exemption for leases entered into by REITs unless those for which VAT election has been made on the conditions indicated under §1.03[A][2] above.

[5]   Penalties Imposed on REIT

63 Law 2778/1999 specifically stipulates that the company is subject to the same income tax penalties imposed on individual taxpayers.

[B]   Taxation of the Investor

[1]   Private Investors

[a]   Taxation of Current Income (All Income Derived from REIT in Holding Phase)

64 Dividends distributed by REITs are tax-free in the hand of private investors.

65 To be noted, however, that such dividends will be subject to the special solidarity contribution based on a progressive tax scale of up to 10% (for income exceeding EUR 220,000) levied on individuals' income generated in the respective tax year and declared through their respective Greek income tax returns.[1] This applies only to individual investors that are Greek tax residents.

---

1. The special solidarity contribution is calculated based on a progressive tax scale (for the first EUR 12,000 null tax rate, for income EUR 12,001–EUR 20,000 2.2%, for income EUR 20,001–EUR

It is to be noted that for the tax year 2021, all individuals' income is exempt from special solidarity contribution (Article 43A of L. 4172/2013), except for employment income from the public sector and pensions. As clarified in Ministerial Circular E. 2125/2021, it is explicitly mentioned that the above exemption refers to (apart from private sector employment income where an exemption is already in force) income derived from business activities, capital (dividends, interest, royalties and rental income) and capital gains. For the tax year 2022, only employment income from the private sector is exempt from special solidarity contribution (Article 43A of L. 4172/2013); hence dividends distributed by REITs are not exempted and therefore subject to special solidarity contribution.

However, if the owner is a Greek company, further distribution of the relevant dividend **66** income by such company may result in 22%[2] taxation imposed on distributed profits.

[b]   Taxation of Capital Gains (From Disposal of REIT Shares)

Capital gains realized by the transfer of non-listed shares in REICs are exempt from **67** income tax. Any capital gains deriving from the sale of listed shares by individuals are subject to a 15% tax if their participation is more than 0.5% and the shares to be transferred have been acquired from 1 January 2009 and said the transaction is not qualified as a 'business transaction'.

Furthermore, the redemption gains from a REMF unit are exempt from corporate **68** income tax (CIT), but any further distribution may be subject to WHT. Irrespective of whether the seller is an individual or legal entity, in the case of listed shares (i.e., once REIC becomes listed) a 0.2% transaction duty applies.

[2]   Institutional Investors

[a]   Taxation of Current Income (All Income Derived from REIT in Holding Phase)

There are no special tax rules for taxation of institutional investors on income from a **69** REIT. Therefore, what is mentioned in section §1.03[B][1][a] above equally applies in this respect, unless institutional investors enjoy a differentiated tax treatment themselves, depending on their legal form and residence.

30,000 5%, for income EUR 30,001–EUR 40,000 6.5%, for income EUR 40,001–EUR 65,000 7.5%, for income EUR 65,001–EUR 220,000 9% and for income exceeding EUR 220,000 10%).
2. By virtue of Law 4799/2021, CIT rate has been further reduced from 24% to 22% beginning from the fiscal year 2021 onwards.

[b]   Taxation of Capital Gains (From Disposal of REIT Shares)

70 There are no special tax rules for taxation of institutional investors on income from a REIT. Therefore, what is mentioned in section §1.03[B][1][b] above equally applies in this respect, unless institutional investors enjoy a differentiated tax treatment themselves, depending on their legal form and residence.

[3]   Penalties Imposed on Investors

71 There are no specific penalties imposed on investors.

[C]   Tax Treaties

[1]   Treaty Access

72 There are no specific treaty protections for a REIT. REITs are not normal taxpayers subject to income tax, and thus they may not be qualified as tax residents for the application of the Double Tax Treaties. Since a REIT is subject to the special tax on its NAV, in lieu of income tax, it could be argued that a REIT should be treaty-protected. The issue has not been formally addressed by the Greek tax authorities.

[2]   WHT Reduction

73 WHT reduction depends on the provisions and applicability of any Double Tax Treaty (DTT). There are no special rules for Greek REITs.

[D]   Exit Tax/Tax Privileges/Concessions

74 No special rules apply in this respect.

[E]   Taxation of Foreign REITs

[1]   Taxation of Foreign REIT Holding Assets in Country

75 Law 2778/1999 contains no provision regarding REITs established outside Greece, and, therefore, there is no framework for such companies to enjoy the tax benefits of the Law in Greece.

76 A foreign REIT holding assets in Greece will be taxed in the same way as any other foreign legal entity. Pursuant to the Greek Income Tax Code applicable from 1 January

2014 onwards, foreign legal entities seem to be subject to tax in Greece only if maintaining a permanent establishment (PE) in Greece. In this respect, merely the ownership of real estate property in Greece or participation in a Greek subsidiary should not give rise to any PE considerations. However, the exploitation of the real estate property located in Greece gives rise to PE considerations and as such any income arising at the level of the foreign REIT will be considered as business income and be subject to CIT in Greece.

In any case, should the foreign REIT holding assets in Greece be subject to taxation in **77** Greece, the following implications may apply:

(a) CIT at 22% on all profits and capital gains realized by the exploitation of Greek property (plus WHT at 5% on profits distributed abroad in case of subsidiary companies held in Greece and on the condition that such WHT cannot be eliminated under a DTT/EU Parent-Subsidiary Directive. In case of branches, no WHT shall be due upon the remittance of profits to the head office).

(b) An additional annual special real estate tax 15% tax is imposed on any entity holding real estate assets in Greece. Exemption from such tax may be granted if the foreign REIT is supervised by a respective authority in its country of incorporation on the condition that the foreign REIT is not incorporated in a non-cooperative state or meets certain investor disclosure requirements, provided that the investor holds a Greek tax registration number. The disclosure requirements are not as strict if REIT is regulated by an EU regulatory authority. The 15% tax is imposed on the objective value of the property, as determined by the tax authorities.

[2]   *Taxation of Investors Holding Shares in Foreign REIT*

There are no specific rules for the taxation of investors holding shares in foreign REITs. **78** In the absence of any specific rules, the tax treatment will follow the general income tax rules and will thus depend on the legal form of the foreign REIT, and whether the investor is a corporate entity or an individual.

Hong Kong

KWOK KAY (KK) SO

KK joined PwC Hong Kong in 1985, transferred to Melbourne, Australia in 1988 and returned to Hong Kong in 1992. Over the years, KK has accumulated extensive experience in providing advice on real estate and infrastructure projects. KK's real estate clients include real estate funds, listed and private real estate groups, institutional investors, and family offices. He is also the tax advisor to a number of Real Estate Investment Trust (REIT) projects involving real estate in Hong Kong, Mainland China and other jurisdictions.

During his professional career, KK has held various positions, including Chairman of the Executive Committee of the Taxation Faculty of Hong Kong Institute of Certified Public Accountants and PwC's Asia Pacific Real Estate Tax Leader.

KK graduated from the Chinese University of Hong Kong with an MBA degree. He is an associate of the Institute of Chartered Accountants in Australia and the Hong Kong Institute of Certified Public Accountants. He is also a fellow of the Association of Chartered Certified Accountants in the UK.

E-mail: kk.so@hk.pwc.com

JACKY WONG

Jacky Wong is an assurance partner of PwC. Jacky is the Hong Kong and Macau Institutional Clients Business Unit Leader, and the Hong Kong REITs Leader. Jacky has over twenty years of experience in serving real estate and infrastructure companies. Over these twenty years, he has led various initial public offering projects, merger and acquisition projects; privatization projects and complex restructuring projects. He is currently the lead client service partner of various leading REITs and real estate companies listed on the Hong Kong Stock Exchange. Jacky has worked in both PwC Hong Kong and PwC US.

Jacky obtained his Bachelor's in Accounting and Finance from the University of Hong Kong and obtained his Bachelor's and Master's in Law from universities in the UK. He is currently a PhD student in Economics. He is a Chartered Financial Analyst (CFA) of the CFA Institute, a Chartered Accountant CA of the Institute of Chartered

Accountants of Wales and England; and a Certified Public Accountant of the Institute of Certified Public Accountants of Hong Kong.
E-mail: jacky.wong@hk.pwc.com

Hong Kong

Kwok Kay (KK) So & Jacky Wong

§1.01 BACKGROUND

[A] Key Characteristics

In Hong Kong, REITs generally refer to real estate investment trusts authorized by the **1** Securities and Futures Commission (SFC) under the Code on REITs (the 'Code'). Under the Code, a REIT is defined as:

> A collective investment scheme is constituted as a trust that invests primarily in real estate with the aim to provide returns to holders derived from the rental income of the real estate. Funds obtained by a REIT from the sale of units in the REIT are used in accordance with the constitutive documents to maintain, manage and acquire real estate within its portfolio.

In this report, the term 'REIT' is used in reference to REITs authorized by SFC, unless **2** otherwise stated.

The Code sets out the guidelines for authorizing and regulating REITs in Hong Kong. **3** Among these requirements, for a REIT to be authorized by SFC, REIT has to be listed on the Stock Exchange of Hong Kong Limited (SEHK) within a period acceptable to SFC. Accordingly, REITs in Hong Kong are also subject to the Listing Rules of SEHK.

Unlike REITs in some other jurisdictions, REITs in Hong Kong are not transparent for **4** income tax purposes. They are subject to Hong Kong tax on rental income derived from real estate to the extent to which such income is derived from real estate situated in Hong Kong. Such income is subject to either Property Tax or Profits Tax depending on whether the real estate is held directly by a REIT or indirectly via a special purpose vehicle.

[B]   History of REIT

5   In 2002, SFC started deliberating the introduction of REITs in Hong Kong. It was considered that introducing REITs to Hong Kong might broaden the choice of investment products available to the public and reinforce Hong Kong's position as an international finance centre.

6   On 7 March 2003, SFC issued the Consultation Paper on the draft Code on REITs. Public consultation was then conducted, and the Code was published in August 2003.

7   In June 2005, June 2010, April 2013, August 2014 and December 2020, SFC made various amendments to the Code which, among other things, allow REITs to invest in overseas real estate and raise the permitted financial gearing ratio. In December 2020, SFC made certain further amendments to the Code regarding the investment restrictions.

[C]   REIT Market

8   Hong Kong currently has eleven REITs with a total market capitalization of approximately USD 30.25 billion as of 10 February 2022. These REITs invest in different types of real estate, including office buildings, shopping malls, and hotels. Six of these REITs hold real estate predominantly in Hong Kong, while the other five hold real estate primarily in Mainland China (one of which is denominated in Renminbi).

§1.02   REGULATORY ASPECTS

[A]   Legal Form of REIT

[1]   Corporate Form

[a]   General

9   Under the Code, a REIT seeking authorization from SFC is required to be structured in the form of a trust. The trust structure ensures clear segregation of the assets of REIT from any other assets.

10   REIT may hold real estate directly, although the Code requires that special purpose vehicles hold all REIT investments in hotels, recreation parks or serviced apartments. A REIT may also hold real estate indirectly through special purpose vehicles that are legally and beneficially owned by REIT. While it is generally expected that the special purpose vehicles should be wholly owned by REIT, in special and limited circumstances, such as the need to comply with the regulatory requirements in an overseas jurisdiction, majority ownership and control of the special purpose vehicles may be acceptable.

Special purpose vehicles should be incorporated in jurisdictions that have established **11** laws and corporate governance standards that are commensurate with those observed by companies incorporated in Hong Kong. Existing REITs have special purpose vehicles incorporated in overseas jurisdictions such as the Cayman Islands and the British Virgin Islands. In addition, REIT should have no more than two layers of special purpose vehicles, although SFC may allow more layers to be used as certain special circumstances may require.

Special purpose vehicles may also be established for arranging finance for REIT. **12**

The Code also sets out the requirements for REIT to appoint a trustee, a management **13** company, a listing agent, a financial adviser, an auditor, and a property valuer.

[b]   Trustee

The trustee to be appointed by REIT has to be acceptable to SFC. It can be a bank **14** licensed under section 16 of the Banking Ordinance of Hong Kong, a trust company which is a subsidiary of such a bank, or a banking institution or trust company incorporated outside Hong Kong which is acceptable to SFC.

The trustee functions independently from the management company of REIT. The **15** trustee has a fiduciary duty to hold the assets of REIT in trust for the benefit of the investors and to oversee the activities of the management company for adherence to the relevant constitutive documents and compliance with regulatory requirements. The trustee ensures that all investment activities carried out by the management company are in line with the investment objectives and policies of REIT and its constitutive documents and that the investment activities are in the best interests of the investors.

[c]   Management Company

The management company appointed by REIT has to be approved by SFC. It has to be **16** licensed under the Securities and Futures Ordinance of Hong Kong. The management company owes a fiduciary duty to the investors in REIT and should act in the best interests of the investors. It performs all the key functions in relation to the management of REIT, including carrying out the stated investment objectives and policies of REIT. While certain functions may be delegated to third parties, the management company remains fully liable to the investors and the trustee of REIT for the proper performance of the management functions. It should observe high standards of integrity, market conduct, fair dealing and corporate governance, and act within the powers conferred upon it by the constitutive documents of REIT, and in compliance with the Code.

17 REIT may be internally managed by a management company that is owned and controlled by REIT. Alternatively, it may be externally managed by a management company outside REIT.

[d]   *Appointment of Listing Agent and Financial Adviser*

18 REIT has to be listed on SEHK within a period acceptable to SFC. Accordingly, the management company should ensure that there are sufficient resources and expertise to address the requirements of SEHK and comply with its Listing Rules. It should ensure that the initial public offering process is conducted in a fair, proper and orderly manner. The manager appoints a listing agent acceptable to SFC, and such agent prepares REIT as a new applicant for listing, lodges the formal application for listing and all supporting documents with SEHK, and deals with SEHK on all matters arising in connection with the application. Accordingly, the listing agent shall have sufficient experience in respect of communications with SEHK, overall management of the listing process and duties as a sponsor.

19 Where necessary or required by the Code or the Listing Rules, the management company should engage a financial adviser.

[e]   *Auditor*

20 Upon the formation of REIT, the management company appoints an auditor to audit the financial statements of REIT and any special purpose vehicles of REIT. The manager also fills any vacancies in the auditor position. The auditor should have an international name and reputation and should be qualified under the Professional Accountants Ordinance of Hong Kong. The auditor should be independent of the management company, the trustee and any other party concerned.

[f]   *Property Valuer*

21 REIT has to appoint a property valuer. The property valuer should be independent of REIT, the trustee, the management company, and each of the significant investors in REIT. To qualify for the appointment, the property valuer should be a company that:

- provides property valuation services on a regular basis;
- carries on business of valuing real estate in Hong Kong;
- has key personnel who are fellow or associate members of the Hong Kong Institute of Surveyors and who are qualified to perform property valuations;
- has sufficient financial resources at its disposal to enable it to conduct its business effectively and meet its liabilities; in particular, it must have a minimum issued and paid-up capital and capital reserves of HKD 1 million or

its equivalent in foreign currency, and its assets must exceed its liabilities by HKD 1 million or more as shown in the company's last audited balance sheet;
– has robust internal controls and checks and balances to ensure the integrity of valuation reports and that these reports are properly and professionally prepared in accordance with international best practices; and
– has adequate professional insurance to cover its usual risks.

The property valuer values all the real estate held directly by REIT and indirectly via **22** special purpose vehicles, on the basis of a full valuation in accordance with Chapter 6 of the Code. The valuer annually inspects the real estate, building(s), and facilities and produces a valuation report. The inspection and valuation must also be done prior to issuance of new units of REIT, if real estate is acquired or sold by REIT, or in any other circumstances prescribed by the Code. Mandatory rotation of the property valuer is required once every three years.

[2] *Investment Restrictions*

The Code does not impose any specific restrictions that apply to the investors in REITs. **23** Both Hong Kong and overseas investors may invest in REITs.

[B] Regulatory Authorities

SFC is empowered under section 104(1) of the Securities and Futures Ordinance of **24** Hong Kong to authorize collective investment schemes (including REITs), subject to such conditions as it considers appropriate. SFC also monitors REITs to ensure ongoing compliance with the Code.

As REITs are required to be listed on SEHK, they are also subject to the supervision of **25** SEHK. SEHK monitors REITs for ongoing compliance with the Listing Rules.

[C] Legislative and Other Regulatory Sources

The Code on REITs and the Practice Note(s) issued by SFC establish guidelines for **26** authorizing and regulating REITs in Hong Kong.

As REITs are required to be listed on SEHK, they are also subject to the requirements **27** of SEHK and its Listing Rules.

[D] Exchange Controls and Reporting Requirements

The Code and SEHK Listing Rules require the following: **28**

- An up-to-date offering document should be issued when an authorized REIT offers its units to the public. The document contains information necessary for investors to be able to make an informed judgment on the proposed investment.
- A semi-annual report should be issued within two months after the end of the relevant period and an annual report within three months after the end of the relevant year.
- Management should inform unitholders of any material information pertaining to REIT in a timely and transparent manner; and management should seek unitholders' approval for significant transactions, including connected party transactions.
- Any valuation of the real estate of REIT conducted upon request by the trustee should be disclosed to the investors.

[E]   Registration Procedures

[1]   Preparatory Measures

29   In preparation for the authorization of a REIT, qualified parties are appointed as the listing agent, trustee, management company, property valuer, and reporting accountant/auditor of REIT. An offering document is prepared according to the requirements of the Code. The reporting accountant audits the historical financial information of REIT to be included in the offering document. Legal advisors assist the listing agent to undergo legal and financial due diligence on REIT. Legal advisors draft the trust deed for REIT, and the management agreement with the management company. The property valuer values the real estate portfolio of REIT. Tax advisors may be involved in exploring the best structure for REITs. An appropriate distribution policy will also need to be formulated (*see* section §1.02[F][6] below).

[2]   Obtaining Authorization

30   REIT has to complete and submit to SFC REIT's Application Form and Application Checklist. REIT also submits written confirmation of compliance with the Code which is signed by a senior executive or officer of the management company, or their respective legal advisers, for the final version of the offering document and the constitutive documents. SFC evaluates the constitutional and offering documents and authorizes REIT under the Code.

[3]   Other Requirements for the Incorporation of a Company

31   Every REIT in Hong Kong should be structured as a trust. *See* section §1.02[A][1] above.

[4]   Obtaining Listing Exchanges

[a]   Costs

Costs mainly include professional fees, underwriting commission, marketing, printing, **32** brokerage, trading and levy. With reference to listing of the existing REITs, the issuance costs generally amount to approximately 3%–6% of the proceeds raised from the initial public offering.

[b]   Time

The time required for listing a REIT largely depends on the level of compliance of REIT **33** with the Code, the complexity of REIT, and the quality of the listing documents. In general, a straightforward REIT application should take around thirty to thirty-five business days to process, assuming that all relevant information is submitted and the documents are in compliance with the requirements under the Code. Additional time may be needed for the applicant to respond to SFC's requests and comments.

In practice, an applicant should allow at least two to three months after the submission **34** of the listing application form to obtain the approval to list from SFC.

[F]   Requirements and Restrictions

[1]   Capital Requirements

There is no specific requirement as to the minimum capital or market capitalization for **35** a REIT in Hong Kong.

REIT may borrow for financing investment or operating purposes. However, the **36** aggregate borrowing may not, at any time, exceed 50% of the total gross asset value (GAV) of REIT.

[2]   Marketing/Advertising

Advertisements and other invitations to invest in a REIT shall be submitted to SFC for **37** authorization prior to their issue or publication in Hong Kong. No advertisement can be made that is false, biased, misleading or deceptive. Any advertisement or announcement that concerns the trustee should be accompanied by the trustee's written consent. Authorization may be varied or withdrawn by SFC as it deems fit.

Advertisements and marketing materials should have proper risk warning statements, **38** including a reference to the offering document for a detailed discussion of the risk factors of REIT.

[3]   Redemption

39   According to the Circular to Management Companies of SFC-Authorized REITs issued by SFC on 31 January 2008, a REIT may purchase its own units on the exchange, provided that certain requirements stated in the circular are satisfied, for example, approval of the unitholders.

40   Any REIT proposing to repurchase its units shall also comply with the other restrictions and notification requirements applicable to listed companies purchasing their own shares on a stock exchange under Rule 10.06 of the Listing Rules, with necessary changes being made, as if the provisions therein were applicable to REITs.

[4]   Valuation of Shares/Units for Redemption and Other Purposes

41   A management company must not repurchase or redeem any units of its REIT, other than any on-market repurchase effected in accordance with the aforementioned circular.

[5]   Investment Restrictions

42   On 9 June 2020, the SFC issued a Consultation Paper on the Proposed Amendments to the Code on REITs (the 'Consultation Paper') to provide Hong Kong REITs with more flexibility in making investments. On 27 November 2020, the SFC concluded its consultation and published a Consultation Conclusions on Proposed Amendments to the REIT Code. In view of the support received by the vast majority of the respondents, most of the proposals in the Consultation Paper were adopted. The revised REIT Code became effective upon its gazettal on 4 December 2020. The amendments to the Code on Real Estate Investment Trusts ('REIT Code') include (i) allowing REITs to make investments in minority-owned properties subject to various conditions; (ii) allowing REITs to make investments in property development projects in excess of the existing limit of 10% of GAV subject to unitholders' approval and other conditions; (iii) increasing the borrowing limit for REITs from 45% to 50% of GAV; and (iv) broadly aligning the requirements for REITs' connected party transactions and notifiable transactions with the requirements for listed companies, in line with existing policy and practices.

43   A REIT shall primarily invest in real estate. The real estate may be situated in Hong Kong or overseas. At least 75% of the gross asset value of REIT shall be invested in real estate that generates recurrent rental income at all times. REIT may acquire uncompleted units in a non-income generating building provided that the aggregate contract value together with the property development costs of such real estate does not exceed 10% of the gross asset value of REIT at any time. REIT is prohibited from investing in vacant land unless the management company has demonstrated such investment is part-and-parcel of the property development within the investment objective or policy of REIT.

A REIT may, subject to the provisions in its constitutive documents, invest in securities **44** listed on the exchange or other internationally recognized stock exchanges, unlisted debt securities, government and other public securities, and local or overseas property funds (collectively the 'Relevant Investments'), provided that the value of REIT's holding of the Relevant Investments issued by any single group of companies does not exceed 10% of the gross asset value of REIT, the Relevant Investments should be sufficiently liquid which could be readily acquired/disposed of under normal market conditions and in the absence of trading restriction and has transparent pricing, and at least 75% of the gross asset value of a REIT shall be invested in real estate that generates recurrent rental income at all times.

A REIT may hold real estate as a joint tenant or a tenant-in-common provided that REIT **45** holds majority interest and control, and REIT has freedom to dispose of its interest. Subject to certain conditions, REIT may invest in jointly owned properties in which the REIT will not have a majority (more than 50%) ownership and control.

A REIT is required to hold its interest in each property for a period of at least two years **46** unless consent for an earlier disposal is obtained from the investors by way of a special resolution at a general meeting.

If a REIT indicates a particular type of real estate in its name, the REIT has to invest at **47** least 70% of its non-cash assets in such type of real estate.

[6]   Distribution/Accumulation

REIT is required to distribute dividends to unitholders each year in an amount that is **48** not less than 90% of its audited annual net income after tax. The trustee should determine if the distributable net income includes any revaluation surplus or gains on disposal of interests in real estate. It is a common practice for the trust deed to stipulate other items that constitute adjustments to net income for distribution purposes, for example, major non-cash items.

If real estate is held in special purpose vehicles, the special purpose vehicles have to **49** distribute all their income to REIT as permitted by the relevant laws and regulations.

[7]   Reporting Requirements

The management shall keep holders informed of any material information pertaining to **50** the scheme in a timely and transparent manner. The general reporting requirements are set out in section §1.02[D] above.

[8]   Accounting

51   A REIT in Hong Kong has to prepare its audited financial statements in accordance with either Hong Kong Financial Reporting Standards or International Financial Reporting Standards. There is no mandatory requirement for auditors to review the interim financials, although it is a customary practice. The Code prescribes minimal disclosure requirements for financial reports.

§1.03   TAXATION

[A]   Taxation of REIT

[1]   Corporate Income Tax

52   A REIT authorized by SFC as a collective investment scheme is exempt from Hong Kong Profits Tax under section 26A(1A) of the Inland Revenue Ordinance of Hong Kong (IRO). However, if REIT holds real estate in Hong Kong directly, and derives rental income therefrom, such rental income is subject to Hong Kong Property Tax.

53   If a REIT holds real estate in Hong Kong indirectly via special purpose vehicles, such special purpose vehicles are subject to Profits Tax in respect of the profits derived from the real estate. Such special purpose vehicles are generally exempt from Property Tax.

54   Income derived by a REIT or a special purpose vehicle from real estate situated outside Hong Kong and capital gains is generally exempt from Property Tax and Profits Tax.

55   Dividends paid by a special purpose vehicle to another special purpose vehicle are generally exempt from Profits Tax.

[a]   Tax Accounting

56   Property Tax is imposed on the net assessable value of real estate situated in Hong Kong, whereas Profits Tax is imposed on profits arising in or derived from Hong Kong from any trade, business or profession carried on in Hong Kong.

[b]   Determination of Taxable Income

Property Tax

57   Property Tax is charged to the owner of any real estate in Hong Kong at 15% of the net assessable value of such real estate. The net assessable value of real estate includes the net rental income received by REIT after deduction of government rates paid by REIT. A notional deduction of 20% of the net rental income amount is also allowed to cover repairs and other recurrent expenses.

Profits Tax

A special purpose vehicle of a REIT is subject to Hong Kong Profits Tax at 16.5% on **58** profits arising in or derived from its real estate in Hong Kong. Under the two-tier profits tax system which is effective from the year of assessment 2018–2019, the first HKD 2 million of assessable profits of REIT will be taxed at 8.25% (i.e., half of the normal tax rates), regardless of REIT's size or industry. The remaining assessable profits will be subject to the original rate of 16.5%. In computing the taxable profits, the special purpose vehicle may deduct interest expenses incurred on loans used to finance income-producing real estate in Hong Kong, subject to certain conditions. Other expenses incurred in producing the taxable income are also allowed as deductions. However, no deductions are allowed for capital expenditures.

The special purpose vehicle is also entitled to tax depreciation allowances on its **59** buildings and structures (but not the land), and on any plant and machinery installed therein. Accounting depreciation is capital in nature and is not tax-deductible.

Tax losses may be carried forward indefinitely to offset future taxable profits. There is **60** no loss carry-back.

Depending on the amount of deductions and allowances available to offset the rental **61** income, it may be more tax efficient to hold real estate through special purpose vehicles.

[c] *Taxation of Income from Taxable/Non-taxable Subsidiaries*

Dividends from special purpose vehicles are generally exempt from Hong Kong Profits **62** Tax.

[d] *Taxation of Foreign Income*

Hong Kong does not impose any income tax on income derived outside Hong Kong. **63**

[2] **Value Added Tax**

Hong Kong does not impose value added tax. **64**

[3] **Withholding Taxes**

Hong Kong does not impose any withholding tax on interest, dividends or distributions **65** from a REIT.

[4]   Other Taxes

66   Hong Kong Stamp Duty is charged on transfers of real estate in Hong Kong. Unless specifically exempted from the ad valorem stamp duty (AVD), any residential property (except that acquired by a Hong Kong permanent resident who does not own any other residential property in Hong Kong at the time of acquisition) acquired by either an individual or a company will be subject to AVD at a flat rate at 15% of the consideration or value, whichever is the higher.

67   For transfer of non-residential property executed on or after 26 November 2020, AVD will be charged at the maximum rate of 4.25% where the transfer consideration or value of real estate is above HKD 21,739,130. Where shares in a Hong Kong company are transferred, Hong Kong Stamp Duty at the rate of 0.26% applies to the higher of the transfer consideration or the value of the shares (transferor and transferee should each be liable for 50% of the stamp duty, i.e., 0.13% each).

68   Hong Kong Stamp Duty also applies to a lease of real estate in Hong Kong, generally at a rate of 0.25%–1% of the average yearly rent, depending on the term of the lease.

69   With effect from 20 November 2010, unless specifically exempted, any residential property acquired on or after 20 November 2010, by either an individual or a company (regardless of where it is incorporated), and resold or transferred within a specified period of time after acquisition, would be subject to a Special Stamp Duty (SSD). SSD payable is calculated by reference to the stated consideration or the market value, whichever is higher. SSD rates were revised for any residential property acquired on or after 27 October 2012. All parties to a contract are liable to SSD. The below table shows the rates at which Special Stamp Duty is levied when the property in question is resold or transferred within the mentioned timeframe:

Period Within Which the Residential Property Is Resold or Transferred after Its Acquisition	SSD Rates (For Residential Property Acquired on or after 27 October 2012) (%)
6 months or less	20
More than 6 months but for 12 months or less	15
More than 12 months but for 36 months or less	10

70   Hong Kong introduced a Buyer's Stamp Duty (BSD) with effect from 27 October 2012. Unless specially exempted, a purchaser (any individual without Hong Kong permanent residence or any corporation irrespective of its place of incorporation) would be liable to BSD for transfer of residential property on or after 27 October 2012. BSD is charged at 15% on the higher of sales consideration or market value.

[5] Transfer Pricing

The Inland Revenue (Amendment) (No. 6) Ordinance 2018 ('the Amendment Ordi-   **71**
nance') was gazetted on 13 July 2018. The main objectives are to codify the transfer
pricing principles, implement certain measures under the Base Erosion and Profit
Shifting package and align the provisions in IRO (Cap. 112) with international tax
requirements. The key elements of the Amendment Ordinance are enhancements to
double taxation relief provisions, transfer pricing rules and related provisions, transfer
pricing documentation requirements relating to the master file, local file and country-
by-country report, amendments to preferential regimes, including extension of tax
concession to domestic transactions and prescription of thresholds for substantial
activities requirements.

[6] Automatic Exchange of Financial Account Information

The Inland Revenue (Amendment) (No. 2) Ordinance 2019 was gazetted on 1 March   **72**
2019. The legislative framework of Automatic Exchange of Financial Account Information under IRO (Cap. 112) is effective from 1 January 2020 for better aligning the
relevant provision with the requirements promulgated by the Organisation for Economic Co-operation and Development.

[7] Penalties Imposed on REIT

REIT or its special purpose vehicles may be subject to penalties where an offence is   **73**
committed under the tax legislation, for example filing its Property Tax or Profits Tax
returns late.

[B] Taxation of the Investor

[1] Private Investors

[a] Taxation of Current Income (i.e., All Income Derived from REIT in Holding Phase)

In practice, distributions received from a REIT are generally not subject to any Hong   **74**
Kong tax.

[b] Taxation of Capital Gains (From Disposal of REIT Shares)

Gains on disposal of units in a REIT should be exempt from Hong Kong Profits Tax if   **75**
such gains are capital gains.

76 An investor carrying on a trade or business in Hong Kong consisting of the acquisition and disposal of units in a REIT is generally subject to Hong Kong Profits Tax in respect of any gains derived from disposal of the units in Hong Kong. Non-resident investors may be exempt from Profits Tax under the Unified Offshore Fund Exemption Regime, subject to certain conditions.

77 Hong Kong Stamp Duty is chargeable in respect of transfer of REIT Units at 0.26% of the transfer consideration or fair value of the units transferred, whichever is higher (payable by the transferor and transferee at 0.13% each). In addition, a fixed duty of HKD 5 is currently payable on any instrument of transfer of units.

[2]   Institutional Investors

[a]   Taxation of Current Income (i.e., All Income Derived from REIT in Holding Phase)

78 In practice, distributions received from a REIT by an institutional investor are generally not subject to any Hong Kong tax.

[b]   Taxation of Capital Gains (From Disposal of REIT Shares)

79 Gains on disposal of units in a REIT should be exempt from Hong Kong Profits Tax if such gains are capital gains.

80 An institutional investor is taxed on the gains from the disposal of units in a REIT in the same manner that a private investor is taxed.

[3]   Penalties Imposed on Investors

81 An investor may be subject to penalties where an offence is committed under the tax legislation, for example, failure to inform the Inland Revenue Department of its chargeability to Hong Kong Profits Tax.

[C]   Tax Treaties

[1]   Treaty Access

82 As of 8 July 2020, Hong Kong had entered into forty-two comprehensive double tax agreements with its trading partners, including Belgium, Luxembourg, the Mainland of the People's Republic of China, Thailand, Vietnam, Brunei, the Netherlands, Indonesia, Hungary, Kuwait, Austria, the UK, Ireland, Liechtenstein, France, Japan, New Zealand, Switzerland, the Czech Republic, Malta, Portugal, Spain, Canada, Italy,

Jersey, Malaysia, Mexico, Guernsey, Korea, South Africa, the United Arab Emirates, Latvia, Romania, Russia, Qatar, Belarus, Pakistan, Saudi Arabia, India, Finland, Cambodia and Estonia. The availability of treaty relief depends on the contents of the particular agreement and its application to the individual case.

[2]   WHT Reduction

Hong Kong does not impose any withholding tax on interest, dividends or distributions from a REIT.   **83**

[D]   Exit Tax/Tax Privileges/Concessions

There is no exit tax, and are no specific tax privileges and concessions regarding the sale of real estate to a REIT or the conversion of a company into a REIT.   **84**

[E]   Taxation of Foreign REITs

[1]   Taxation of Foreign REIT Holding Assets in Country

If a foreign REIT holds real estate in Hong Kong via a foreign corporation or a resident corporation, the corporation will be subject to Hong Kong Profits Tax in respect of its assessable profits derived from the real estate.   **85**

[2]   Taxation of Investors Holding Shares in Foreign REIT

Investors are exempt from Hong Kong Profits Tax on any offshore income or capital gains derived from or in connection with holdings in a foreign REIT.   **86**

Hungary

GERGELY JUHÁSZ

Gergely is a tax partner who joined PwC in 2007. He holds a degree in Economics with a major in Finance and is also a Certified Tax Advisor. He specializes in corporate income taxation, taxation of the real estate industry and international tax structuring and as such, he is a member of PwC's International Tax Structuring Network. He is also the Hungarian country leader of EUDTG, PwC's pan-European network of EU tax law experts.
E-mail: gergely.juhasz@pwc.com

ORSOLYA BOGNÁR

Orsolya Bognár is working as a senior manager at PwC Hungary's corporate tax department. She joined the Budapest office in 2013. Orsolya is an economist with a major in Accounting and also holds a Bachelor's in Law. She is a certified accountant and an ACCA member since 2015. Orsolya mainly deals with corporate income tax matters of large Hungarian and international clients with a focus on real estate taxation, and she is often involved in international tax structuring projects.
E-mail: orsolya.bognar@pwc.com

Hungary

Gergely Juhász & Orsolya Bognár

§1.01 BACKGROUND

[A] Key Characteristics

Hungarian Real Estate Investment Trusts (REITs) are public listed companies which **1** are registered with the Hungarian national tax authority. REITs must be listed on at least one stock exchange or regulated market operating in the European Union (EU). A REIT may hold and operate its real estate portfolio directly, or, alternatively, through its 100% owned companies (Project Companies). A REIT's core business is limited to investing in and operating real estate; it may, however, engage in a number of services relating to real estate such as leasing and certain real estate development activities.[1] REITs and their Project Companies are exempt from corporate income tax, local business tax, and enjoy a reduced transfer tax rate on acquisition of real properties, provided that certain requirements are met.

Companies (including private companies which are not yet listed) which do not fully **2** qualify for registration as a REIT but meet certain conditions can apply for a conditional preliminary REIT status. They will be registered as REIT qualifiers ('pre-REITs') and operate in the same way as REITs. REIT qualifiers also enjoy the same tax benefits as REITs. REIT qualifiers must ensure full compliance by the last day of the financial year following the financial year in which they were registered on REIT qualifier register.

[B] History of REIT and REIT Market

Traditionally, investments into real estate were made through Project Companies in **3** Hungary. REIT is an investment vehicle in Hungary, which was introduced on 28 July 2011. The Government's aim was to enhance the real estate market in Hungary, and it wished to create a regime similar to the existing European REITs.

---

1. *See* s. §1.02[F][2] Investment Restrictions for a detailed description.

4   The first pre-REIT was registered in 2017, and at the time of preparing this section, only a couple of REITs operate in Hungary.

§1.02   REGULATORY ASPECTS

[A]   Legal Form of REIT

[1]   Corporate Form

5   The only legal form that is permissible for a REIT is a public company limited by shares. They must have a registered seat in Hungary or in any other Member State of the European Economic Area (EEA). REIT has to be listed on a regulated market within EU.

6   There is no specification as to the company form of a Project Company. The wording of the law implies that foreign-registered companies may also qualify for Project Company status.

[2]   Holding Restrictions

7   Upon registration, at least 25% of the shares of REIT must be available to the public for trading (free float). No shareholders of the free float may hold more than 5% of the total shares. This restriction applies to both direct and indirect shareholding. If only the free float of a REIT is listed, shareholders of the free float are required to report their direct and indirect shareholding to REIT on a quarterly basis. If their shareholding exceeds 5%, they are required to dispose of the excess shares and their voting rights are limited to 5% so long as they hold shares in excess of 5%. If the excess is not disposed of within three months, REIT has the right to sell the excess shares on behalf of the shareholder. Investors may include both small investors and large institutional investors, but credit institutions and insurance companies together may not exercise more than 10% of the total voting rights.

[B]   Regulatory Authorities

8   Given that REITs are listed on the stock exchange, their operations are supervised by the Central Bank of Hungary,[2] or, if the listing is done on a stock exchange in another EU Member State, it will be subject to the respective regulatory body of that country.

9   REITs are also subject to supervision by the national tax authority which oversees their compliance with the requirements. If the Tax Authority establishes that the company does not meet the statutory requirements, the company will have to fulfil all the

---

2. The operations of REITs were previously supervised by the Hungarian Supervisory Financial Authority; however, it was merged into the Central Bank of Hungary as of 1 Oct. 2013.

obligations within (in most cases) ninety days. Otherwise, it will be removed from the registry; that is, its REIT/pre-REIT status will be revoked.

[C] Legislative and Other Regulatory Sources

REITs are subject to the general rules for Hungarian-registered companies, that is, the **10** Hungarian Civil Code[3] and the Company Registration Act,[4] while the conditions for REIT status are regulated within REIT Act.[5] Due to their listing, REITs are also subject to the Capital Market Act.[6]

As far as the Alternative Investment Fund Managers Directive is concerned, it was **11** implemented on 15 March 2014 by the amendment of Act XVI of 2014 on the Collective Investment Funds and their Fund Managers. Although the aforementioned Act contains specific rules for real estate funds, REITs are not expressly specified in the regulations, and hence, currently, it is understood that such Act does not apply to REITs.

[D] Exchange Controls and Transparency Requirements

In Hungary, no exchange control mechanisms apply. REITs are subject to the same **12** transparency requirements as normal listed companies (annual and semi-annual reporting, etc.).

[E] Registration Procedures

[1] Preparatory Measures

REIT is subject to various requirements for its operations. Some of these conditions **13** have to be met already upon registration of pre-REIT, while others have to be fulfilled later only.

The main requirements, which have to be fulfilled at the time of registration by a **14** pre-REIT, are as follows:

- company form as a stock corporation (a public company limited by shares);
- complying with the limitation on the business activity which may include exclusively sale, lease, operation of its own real estate, management of real

---

3. Act V of 2013 on the Hungarian Civil Code. Please note that previously Act IV of 2006 on Business Association contained the general rules regarding Hungarian-registered companies; however, this Act was incorporated into the Hungarian Civil Code as of 15 Mar. 2014.
4. Act V of 2006 on Public Company Information, Company Registration and Winding-Up Proceedings.
5. Act CII of 2011 on the Regulated Investment Companies.
6. Act CXX of 2001 on the Capital Market.

estate and asset management (holding). A REIT's activity may include organization of real estate development projects as well;
- it is not under winding up, bankruptcy or liquidation procedure;
- based on the deed of foundation, the management of REIT undertakes to propose to the shareholders on the shareholders meeting to distribute at least 90% of REIT's annual profits (generated from the date of REIT registration) or 90% of the available free cash (whichever is smaller) as expected dividend[7] to the shareholders, which expected dividend – upon its acceptance by the shareholders – has to be paid within thirty trading days from the approval of the annual financial statements;
- it may own shares exclusively in the following types of entities: Project Companies; other REITs; and companies organizing building construction projects or building residential and non-residential buildings as a main activity. In the case of other REITs, REIT's stake may not exceed 10%;
- REIT may not enter into agreements (except for loan agreements with financial institutions) that: (i) limit its right to distribute dividends to its shareholders or (ii) grant purchase option right to third parties over REIT's properties;
- only 10% of its voting rights may be exercised directly by insurance companies and credit institutions;
- it does not have an overdue payment liability towards the tax authorities.

15 If the above conditions are met and the company submits a request to the Tax Authority with the respective documentation, the Tax Authority will register the company with a pre-REIT status. The company will be entitled to the tax benefits and has to comply with the relating liabilities under pre-REIT/REIT status from the registration.

16 For a final REIT status, pre-REIT has to reach full compliance with the following criteria until the last day of the financial year following the financial year of the registration:

- its starting capital amounts to at least HUF 5 billion (approx. EUR 1 3. 9 million) on stand-alone or consolidated basis;
- it issues exclusively ordinary shares, employee stocks and preference shares (with the exception of preference in terms of dividends and preference shares securing veto rights);
- it introduces an ordinary share series amounting to the value of the mandatory free float to the regulated market.

17 The Project Companies have to fulfil similar requirements, as follows:

---

7. In case the total amount of free cash and cash-equivalents of a REIT (free cash and cash-equivalents are defined as current accounts, time deposits, governmental securities issued by an EEA or OECD Member State, bonds issued by international financial institutions and securities that are traded on recognized stock exchanges) does not reach the amount of the expected dividend, at least 90% of the cash and cash-equivalents of a REIT need to be distributed.

- the management of the Project Companies proposes to distribute the expected dividend (which is 100% of the annual profits in this case) as dividend to the shareholder, which expected dividend – upon its acceptance by the shareholders (REIT) – has to be paid within thirty trading days following the approval of the annual financial statements, unless the free cash's and cash-equivalents' sum is lower than such amount;
- the Project Company may not enter into agreements that limit its right to distribute dividends to REIT except agreements with financial institutions;
- the Project Company engages an auditor for which the independence requirements are met;
- the Project Company's debt compared to the value of its real property and investments does not exceed 70%;
- its properties are revaluated at least quarterly.

[2]   Other Requirements for the Incorporation of a Company

A REIT may be established by either setting up a public company limited by shares or **18** transforming an existing company (e.g., a private company limited by shares or a company limited by quotas) into a public company limited by shares. Consequently, it depends on the exact legal method which set of documents has to be submitted to the Court of Registry to incorporate a company which may then apply for a REIT status.

[3]   Obtaining Listing Exchanges

[a]   Costs

As a general rule, the costs for a listing at the Hungarian Stock Exchange may vary **19** depending on the gross offering proceeds.

[b]   Time

The estimated time required to list REIT depends on several factors, including the **20** amount of the offering proceeds, the complexity of the transactions and the timeliness of the reaction of the investors. As a general rule, Initial Public Offering process requires six to nine months.

[F]   Requirements and Restrictions

[1]   Capital Requirements

The nominal capital of a REIT must amount to at least HUF 5 billion (approx. EUR 1 3.9 **21** million) on either a stand-alone or consolidated basis. A REIT can issue exclusively ordinary shares, employee stocks and certain preference share types. A REIT has to have a 25% ratio of public ownership on a regulated market (upon registration, 25% of the entire series of shares should be owned by shareholders holding a maximum of 5% of the total shares, which diversified ownership status has to be maintained in the case of REITs non-entirely listed on a stock exchange). Investors may include both small investors and large institutional investors, but credit institutions and insurance companies should not have directly more than 10% voting right in a REIT.

22   REIT Act stipulates a limit on debt financing (leverage provision). Thus, REIT's debt financing may not exceed 65% of the real property value as shown in the consolidated or the individual financial statements prepared under Hungarian Generally Accepted Accounting Principles (GAAP) or International Financial Reporting Standards (IFRS).

23   REITs may own Project Companies that are one-man companies solely owned by a REIT. Project Companies' debt financing (if they are not involved in consolidation) may not exceed 70% of the real property value.

[2]   Investment Restrictions

24   A REIT is limited to the following investments and activities.

25   REITs have to limit their business activities to the sale, lease and operation of their own real estate, management of real estate, asset management and organization of real estate development projects. Project Companies may also pursue exclusively the above business activities but may not have any participation in any companies.

26   A REIT may have shares exclusively in Project Companies, other REITs and companies organizing building construction projects or building residential and non-residential buildings as main activity. In the case of other REITs, REIT's stake may not exceed 10%.

27   Furthermore, a REIT may hold other assets exclusively (besides the ones directly linked to its operation) in bank deposits at sight, term bank deposits, government securities issued by the Member States of the EEA and Organisation for Economic Co-operation and Development (OECD), debt securities issued by international financial institutions and securities introduced to recognized capital markets. The asset portfolio of a REIT may also include derivative transactions.

28   At least 70% of REIT's total assets must consist of immovable property. Immovable property held as fixed asset is taken into account at its fair value (for more details, please see section §1.02[F][5]). Furthermore, none of the value of the real properties (or shareholding in another REIT) may exceed 30% of the total assets of REIT. The asset structure requirements are determined based on the consolidated financial statements under Hungarian GAAP or IFRS. If consolidated financial statements do not have to be prepared, the stand-alone financial statements are used. Acquisition of a new asset with a value exceeding 10% of the balance sheet total is subject to the preliminary approval of REIT's Supervisory Board.

[3]   Distribution/Accumulation

REIT is obliged to distribute the expected dividends (which is 90% of the distributable **29** profit, unless the free cash's and cash-equivalents' sum is lower than such amount), provided that the shareholders accept such proposal from the management. The amount of profit is determined under Hungarian GAAP or IFRS, as profit after tax. Project Companies must pay the expected dividend to REITs, provided that the shareholders (REIT) accept such proposal from the management.

Both REITs and Project Companies may not conclude any contracts that include any **30** limitations to their dividend payments (except for loan agreements with financial institutions).

[4]   Reporting Requirements

REITs are subject to the general reporting requirements that apply to stock corpora- **31** tions. Therefore, REITs have to prepare and publish audited annual financial statements.

As publicly traded entities, REITs are obliged to disclose information to the public on **32** their financial position and on the general course of their business on a regular basis the same way as normal listed companies.

Despite REIT's tax exemption, REIT is obliged to file a tax return.   **33**

[5]   Accounting

Valuation of real properties to their fair value is mandatory quarterly. The difference **34** between the fair market value and the book value has to be registered in REIT's books at least quarterly under Hungarian GAAP or under IFRS. As a valuation method, the following can be chosen:

- market comparative method;
- yield-based calculation method; or
- replacement cost method.

Decision on the valuation method has to be detailed in the consolidated financial **35** statements, and the chosen method has to be used in later periods. Another method can be chosen only if reasons are detailed in an evaluation expert's opinion.

Project Companies have to perform a mandatory quarterly revaluation based on the **36** above rules, as well.

§1.03   TAXATION

[A]   Taxation of REIT

[1]   *Corporate Income Tax*

[a]   *Tax Accounting*

37   There is no specific tax accounting in Hungary. The basis of the corporate income tax calculation is the pre-tax profit as shown in the annual financial statements prepared according to Hungarian GAAP or IFRS (stand-alone IFRS bookkeeping is obligatory for companies listed on a stock exchange). Then after, such pre-tax profit is modified by certain tax base adjusting items. These tax base adjusting items mainly relate to depreciation, provisions created, disposal of tangibles/intangibles, dividends received, impairment, certain tax base allowances, controlled foreign company (CFC) legislations, transfer pricing rules, and so on.

38   Effective from 1 January 2017, the applicable corporate income tax rate is flat 9%.

[b]   *Determination of Taxable Income*

39   Hungarian REITs (for the purposes of section §1.03, besides regulated real estate investment companies, the term 'REIT' also includes pre-REITs and the Project Companies of the above mentioned) are in principle exempt from corporate income taxation. However, due to certain penalty-like measures and the general anti-avoidance rules, the corporate income tax bases of REITs still have to be calculated.

40   The Hungarian REITs' corporate income tax base is calculated according to the general rules, with the following differences.

41   REITs are not allowed to apply certain tax base adjusting items, most of which relate to tax base allowances. These in particular include:

- utilization of deferred tax losses;
- creation of development reserves;
- tax base allowances related to the disposal of intellectual properties;
- tax base allowances related to royalty income;
- tax base allowances related to research & development; and
- tax base allowances of donations given.

42   To prevent the erosion of tax bases within company groups, REITs are not entitled to apply the corporate income tax exemption (on a pro rata basis) for income earned from those related parties that do not fall under the scope of REIT Act. These are generally foreign entities with the exception of Project Companies, and Hungarian entities that are not REITs. When calculating such income, the general transfer pricing regulations

are applicable, which in particular means that the prices applied in such transactions have to be at arm's length, or the tax bases of the entities affected by such transaction have to be modified accordingly.

[c] *Taxation of Income from Taxable/Non-taxable Subsidiaries*

Hungarian-regulated real estate investment companies and pre-REITs may only hold **43** participations in Project Companies, other regulated real estate investment companies and companies whose main activity is organizing real estate development projects. Out of these possible subsidiaries, only the latter is out of the scope of the Hungarian-regulated real estate investment company regulations and thus are subject to taxation as per the general corporate income tax rules, provided that they are considered Hungarian resident or are considered to be the subject of Hungarian taxation for some other reason (e.g., due to having a Hungarian permanent establishment). The rest may benefit from the corporate income tax exemption as detailed above.

Regarding the income received from the subsidiaries, the rules detailed in section **44** §1.03[A][1][b] apply. Thus, in general, it will not be subject to corporate income taxation. However, there are some exceptions: (i) the income received from such companies whose main activity is organizing or carrying out real estate development projects and which qualify as related companies of REIT receiving the income; and (ii) capital, F/X gains realized on the participation of companies whose main activity is organizing or carrying out real estate development projects, provided that the participation in such company exceeds 10%. These incomes are subjected to corporate income taxation as per the general rules.[8]

In terms of income received from subsidiaries, it has to be noted that based on the **45** general Hungarian corporate income tax rules, dividend received is tax exempt provided that the entity distributing the dividend is not considered to be a controlled foreign corporation (the Hungarian definition of which is in line with the Anti-Tax Avoidance Directive (ATAD) Article 7(2) option (b) provisions).

[d] *Taxation of Foreign Income*

No special rules apply to foreign income. It is subject to the rules described in sections **46** §1.03[A][1][a] to §1.03[A][1][c].

---

8. Please note though that according to the general rules, participations which qualify as reported participation under the Hungarian domestic legislation may qualify for participation exemption, which can give access to tax exemption on capital and F/X gains provided that certain conditions are met.

[e]   *Achieving/Losing REIT Status Mid-Financial Year*

47   Based on REIT Act, it is possible for a company to obtain/lose its REIT status in the course of its financial year without the above resulting in having a financial year end. Although in these cases REITs have to prepare an accounting closing, the corporate income tax regulations do not seem to deal with this issue. Thus, currently, it is unknown how the corporate income tax-exempt tax base has to be calculated in these cases. As the Hungarian REIT regulation has no significant established practice yet, this issue will have to be dealt with in the future practice of the tax authorities.

[2]   Value Added Tax

48   Hungary has a Value Added Tax (VAT) system with a standard rate of 27%. Such VAT system does not provide special rules for REITs. However, based on the general rules, with the exception of newly built buildings and building plots, renting, leasing and selling real estate is exempt from VAT. In return, such activities do not allow for the deduction of input VAT.

49   A taxpayer may opt for VATable treatment of the above transactions. In this case, the input VAT relating to such activities is deductible, but the taxpayer may not return to VAT-exempt treatment within five years following the last day of the calendar year in which it has opted for VATable treatment.

[3]   Withholding Tax

50   Distributions (dividend) to Hungarian resident individuals are subject to the general rules, that is, to 15% personal income tax. No social tax or other tax is payable after the dividend.

51   As per the general rules, foreign resident individuals are also subject to 15% personal income tax withheld at source on distributions made thereto. Such general withholding tax rate may be reduced by an applicable treaty at source or by a refund from the Tax Authority.

52   Distributions to entities are not subject to withholding taxation.

[4]   Other Taxes

53   Besides the corporate income tax exemption, REITs may benefit from favourable local business – and transfer tax rules as per the below.

[a] Transfer Taxes

In general, the transfer tax payable on the acquisition of real estates, property rights **54** related to real estates, and the 75% participation of certain real estate holding companies is 4% up to a tax base of HUF 1 billion (approx. EUR 2.8 million) and 2% for the amount exceeding such threshold, but is capped at HUF 200 million (approx. EUR 55 6,000) per real estate. The tax base of the transfer tax is the real estates' market value (in the case of participation of real estate holding companies, the tax base is the proportionate amount of the company's real estates' market value). In the case of REITs, the above transfer tax rates are uniformly reduced to 2%; however, no cap applies.

[b] Local Business Tax

Subject to the local municipalities' decision, on the basis of their business activities **55** performed in the given municipality's jurisdiction, companies may be obliged to pay up to 2% local business tax calculated on their net sales revenues reduced by the cost of goods sold, the cost of mediated services and material costs (in the cases of the first two deductions subject to certain limitations).[9] REITs on the other hand are exempted from the above local business tax payment obligation.[10]

[5] Penalties Imposed on REIT

As a general rule, failure to meet any of the conditions for REIT status will result in the **56** loss of such status. In such a case, certain taxes that were not paid previously due to the special status have to be paid with penalties.

---

9. In addition to the aforementioned, royalty income is exempted from local business taxation, and certain research and development costs may also be deducted from the tax base. However, REITs typically do not have items like the above in their accounting records. The deduction of the cost of goods sold and mediated services from the local business tax base is limited depending on the total net sales revenues. Up to HUF 500 million net sales revenues, the allowed deduction is 100% of the incurred respective costs; between HUF 500 million and HUF 20 billion net sales revenues, the allowed deduction is the incurred respective costs capped at 85% of the net sales revenues; between HUF 20 billion and HUF 80 billion net sales revenues, the allowed deduction is the incurred respective costs capped at 75% of the net sales revenues; and over HUF 80 billion net sales revenues, the allowed deduction is the incurred respective costs capped at 70% of the net sales revenues.

10. Nevertheless, despite their local business tax exemption, REITs may be subject to 0.3% innovation contribution calculated on the local business tax base. The respective regulation is not straightforward in this respect.

[a]   *Corporate Income Tax*

57   If pre-REIT loses its status without being registered as a regulated real estate investment company, the double of the corporate income tax that was previously not paid
because of REIT status is due.

58   Similarly, if the Project Company of pre-REIT loses its status prior to pre-REIT being
registered as a regulated real estate investment company, pre-REIT is obliged to pay the
double of the corporate income tax that was previously not paid by the Project
Company due to REIT status.

[b]   *Transfer Taxes*

59   If the regulated real estate investment company loses its status prior to the end of the
tax year in which it acquired the property with the reduced transfer tax rate, or if
pre-REIT does not get registered as a regulated real estate investment company, the
double of the difference between the amount of transfer tax calculated as per the
general and the reduced rates has to be paid.

60   If the property was acquired by a Project Company of the regulated real estate
investment company or pre-REIT and later on the latter falls under the above
paragraph, the double of the difference between the amount of transfer tax calculated
as per the general and the reduced rates is levied on the regulated real estate investment
company/pre-REIT, instead of the Project Company. The same rules apply if the Project
Company is wholly or partly alienated prior to pre-REIT being registered as a regulated
real estate investment company.

[c]   *Local Business Tax*

61   If pre-REIT does not get registered as a regulated real estate investment company, the
double of the local business tax that has not been paid by pre-REIT and its Project
Company because of their preferential status is due. In addition, if pre-REIT's Project
Company ceases or is partly/wholly alienated, the double of the local business tax
previously not paid thereby is due.

[B]   Taxation of the Investors

[1]   Private Investors

[a]   *Taxation of Dividend*

62   Dividends distributed by REITs to Hungarian or foreign resident private individuals are
subject to taxation as described in section §1.03[A][3].

[b]   *Taxation of Capital Gains (From Disposal of REIT Shares)*

Resident Private Individuals

Capital gain on the disposal of shares in a REIT is taxable under the general rules in   **63**
Hungary; that is, it is subject to 15% personal income tax and 13% social tax, the latter
of which is capped at approx. EUR 1,750 in 2022.[11] In addition, if certain conditions are
met, exemption from the 13% social tax may be achieved. However, if the shares of
REIT are sold under market conditions with the involvement of a financial service
provider, the capital gain is regarded as controlled capital market transaction. This
means that all the losses of other transactions are deductible, and the income is only
subject to 15% personal income tax.

Non-resident Private Individuals

Based on several double tax treaties – such as the treaty with United Kingdom or   **64**
Germany – the capital gain of shares of such companies that hold mainly Hungarian
immovable property is taxable in Hungary even if the individual is a non-resident.
Thus, based on the residency of the foreign private individual investor, it may be liable
to pay 15% personal income tax.

[2]   Corporate Investors

[a]   *Taxation of Dividend*

Dividend distributions to corporate investors are subject to the general rules. Thus,   **65**
dividend from a REIT is corporate income tax exempt.[12]

Based on the general domestic rules, no withholding tax is applicable to dividend   **66**
distributions made to foreign legal entities and unincorporated associations.

[b]   *Taxation of Capital Gains (From Disposal of REIT Shares)*

Resident Corporate Investors

Capital gain on the disposal of shares in a REIT is taxable under the normal corporate   **67**
income tax rules. Thus, they are subject to corporate income tax, unless the participation exemption rules may apply, which results in no taxation.

---

11. For the purposes of the annual cap of the social tax base, the gross salary and certain other
    income of the individuals also have to be taken into consideration.
12. For the purposes of the outlined tax treatment, it is assumed that REIT is Hungarian resident,
    which is likely to be the case, as there seems to be no point of establishing a Hungarian REIT
    which is considered to be tax resident outside of Hungary based on mind-and-management
    location.

68 Effective from 1 January 2018, no minimum participation threshold has to be met in order to benefit from the Hungarian participation exemption regime, but the acquisition has to be reported to the Tax Authority within seventy-five days, and the disposal has to happen at least one year following the acquisition of the shares[13] (additional acquisitions may also be reported to the Tax Authority).

Non-resident Corporate Investors

69 Provided that REIT is registered on a recognized stock exchange,[14] no Hungarian taxation may arise if the shares thereof are alienated by a foreign resident entity. Further safe-harbour rules may also apply.

[C]   Tax Treaties

[1]   Treaty Access

70 Hungary has a large treaty network. Since Hungarian-regulated real estate investment companies and pre-REITs are companies limited by shares, they are considered to be eligible for treaty benefits.

71 Regarding the Project Companies, if they are established according to Hungarian law, they are also deemed to be eligible for treaty benefits.

72 Nonetheless, eligibility for treaty benefits should be checked on a case-by-case basis to make sure that source countries are of the same opinion.

[2]   WHT Reduction

73 Withholding tax reduction is only an issue when REIT distribution is made to foreign resident private individuals, as in the case of foreign resident entities, no withholding tax applies based on domestic law.

74 The vast majority of Hungary's treaties are concluded based on OECD Model Tax Treaty, and thus the applicable withholding tax rate on dividend distributions is likely to be 15%.

---

13. Again, for the purposes of the participation exemption rules' applicability, REIT is assumed to be Hungarian resident. Otherwise, the CFC rules would also have to be investigated.
14. Recognized stock exchange means exchanges which are recognized as such by the competent supervisory authorities and which meet the following conditions: (i) they function regularly; (ii) they have rules, issued or approved by the appropriate supervisory authorities of the home country defining the conditions for the operation of the exchange, the conditions of access to the exchange, as well as the conditions that shall be satisfied by a contract before it can effectively be dealt on the exchange; and (iii) they have a clearing mechanism whereby futures contracts are subject to daily margin requirements which, in the opinion of the competent supervisory authorities, provide appropriate protection.

[D] **Exit Tax/Tax Privileges/Concessions**

No special rules apply to Hungarian REITs in this regard (with the note that ATAD's **75** exit tax provisions were implemented in the Hungarian legislation effective from 1 January 2020).

India

BHAIRAV DALAL

Bhairav Dalal is the Real Estate Sector Leader and Partner in the tax & regulatory practice. He has varied experience in advising Indian and multinational groups in the areas of real estate, infrastructure and private equity. Over the last twenty years, his focus has been transaction and tax advisory services specializing in the real estate sector.

Bhairav has also advised real estate companies on complex projects involving investment structuring and group restructuring. Given his experience, he has been extensively involved in the Real Estate Investment Trust (REIT)/InvIT discussions in the industry and regulators as well. He has handled diverse assignments in the transaction and corporate restructuring space, involving the following:

- Developing real estate fund structures and consummating their investments.
- Redevelopment Projects (including SRA's & Society redevelopment projects).
- Infra space such as bid structuring, private equity funding, and restructuring for Singapore BT listing. M&A and inbound advisory.

Bhairav was also a part of the team advising the two large REIT offerings and a recent secondary acquisition in India.

Bhairav is a graduate of Commerce from the University of Mumbai and is a member of the Institute of Chartered Accountants of India since 2002. He regularly speaks on real estate-related topics before various forums, and contributes to articles and interviews for several newspapers, magazines and business news channels.
E-mail: bhairav.dalal@pwc.com

ANISH SANGHVI

Anish Sanghvi is a partner in Price Waterhouse & Co LLP's tax & regulatory team and has over twenty years of experience working with international consulting firms.

He advises sovereign funds, pension funds, private equity funds, domestic clients on Indian and international tax, inbound investment advisory and corporate tax with focus on infrastructure and real estate sectors. He advises them to put in place investment structures enter joint ventures, reorganize their business and conduct tax due diligence. He also advises clients on exchange control regulations, corporate and other regulatory laws. Anish also led the team which was advising a large REIT offering in India.

He has a wide experience in advising infrastructure and real estate clients on:

- structuring buyouts and divestitures;
- migration to REIT/InvIT including evaluating their readiness;
- structuring joint development agreements and EPC contracts;
- restructuring their groups and M&A transactions to create profit extraction strategies, value enhancements, etc.

He is a chartered accountant and commerce graduate.
E-mail: anish.sanghvi@pwc.com

India

Bhairav Dalal & Anish Sanghvi

---

§1.01   BACKGROUND

[A]   Key Characteristics

Indian Real Estate Investment Trust (REIT) is an investment vehicle launched by a **1** 'Sponsor' in the form of a trust duly registered with the Securities and Exchange Board of India (SEBI). REITs are required to list and hold rent/income-generating properties in India either directly or through holding company (Hold Co) or Special Purpose Vehicles (SPVs).

Among others: **2**

- REITs must distribute at least 90% of their net distributable cash flows to the unitholders;
- REITs are prohibited from investing in vacant land/agricultural land or mortgages (with certain exceptions); and
- at least 80% of the value of a REIT to be in completed and rent/income-generating real estate, with a lock-in period of three years from the date of acquisition.

REITs have been accorded effective tax pass-through status, whereby certain specified **3** income of REITs is taxable in the hands of the unitholders of REITs – non-residents could avail relief under the applicable tax treaty, if available. There is, however, no specific pass-through for distribution of gains from disposal of property or shares.

[B]   History of REITs

4   REIT Regulations[1] were enacted on 26 September 2014. Post enactment of REIT Regulations, the regulators in discussions with relevant stakeholders in the country including government bodies, investors and real estate developers brought about amendments in REIT Regulations to bring them in line with globally recognized norms, especially with respect to distribution policies, capital requirements, etc.

5   The Reserve Bank of India (RBI) through a series of amendments in its regulatory policy enabled foreign investments under the automatic route in REITs.

6   The pass-through status for REITs was provided under the taxation regime for REITs right from the beginning. However, to make the pass-through status effective, keeping in mind the practical considerations put forward by the stakeholders, further amendments were made to tax law.

7   Such consistent impetus by government to bring REITs to life led to the launch of the first successful REIT listing in India.

[C]   REIT Market

8   There are three REITs listed on the Indian stock exchanges:

(1) The Embassy Office Parks REIT, jointly owned by Blackstone Group LP and Bengaluru-based developer Embassy Property Developments Private Limited, was the first Indian REIT listed on the Indian stock exchange in 2019. Comprising a portfolio featuring seven office parks and four office buildings, during the financial year 2021, the REIT distributed a total of INR 8,975 million (~ USD 120 million) to its unitholders, giving a total return of up to 30% since listing in 2019.

(2) India's second REIT, Mindspace Business Parks REIT, was listed on the Indian stock exchange on 7 August 2020. The initial public offer raised INR 4.5 billion (~ USD 60.17 million) and was subscribed thirteen times. Mindspace Business Parks REIT is jointly owned by K Raheja Corp and Blackstone Group LP, comprising five integrated business parks and five quality independent offices.

(3) Brookfield India REIT, which was listed on 17 February 2021, became the third REIT to be listed on the bourses in India. The INR 38 billion (~ USD 508 million) public issue was subscribed almost eight times.

---

1. Securities and Exchange Board of India (Real Estate Investment Trusts) Regulations, 2014.

The total market capitalization of the three REITs as on 10 February 2022 is ~ INR 600 billion, i.e., ~ USD 8.02 billion.[2]

The Indian REIT market continues to attract global investors. In the years to come, the REIT market could also see a modification in the asset mix to include data centres, warehouses, industrial parks and retail assets, over and above the traditional office space REITs.

§1.02   REGULATORY FRAMEWORK

[A]   SEBI

[1]   *Formalities/Procedure*

A REIT should be registered with SEBI and should be constituted as a trust with its trust   9
deed having the main objective of undertaking activity of REIT in accordance with REIT Regulations. REIT should have a Sponsor, Manager and Trustee.

[a]   *Sponsor to REIT*

Conditions for Eligibility of Sponsor
- No maximum limit on the number of sponsors; concept of 'Sponsor Group'   10
  incorporated to leverage on the capabilities of other group entities in terms of eligibility criteria for being a Sponsor.
- Consolidated net worth of at least INR 1,000 million (~ USD 13.37 million), with each Sponsor's net worth being at least INR 200 million (~ USD 2.67 million).
- Sponsor or its associates to have not less than five years of real estate development or real estate fund management experience.
- Track record of at least two completed projects for a developer Sponsor.

Key Rights and Responsibilities: Sponsor(s) and Sponsor Groups
(1) Setting up a REIT and appointing a Trustee.   11
(2) Transferring or undertaking to transfer assets, interest and rights in the Hold Co/SPV to REIT before allotment of units to applicants.
(3) Declassification of status of Sponsor whose units have been listed for a period of three years shall be permitted upon receipt of an application from REIT, subject to the following conditions:
  -    The unit holding of such Sponsor and its associates taken together shall not exceed 10% of the outstanding units of REIT.

---

2. https://www.moneycontrol.com/stocks/marketinfo/marketcap/bse/construction-real-estate. html.

- The Manager of REIT is not an entity controlled by such Sponsor or its associates.
- The Sponsor or its associates are not fugitive economic offenders.
- Approval of the unitholders (where the number of votes cast in favour is more than the number of votes cast against).

(4) Minimum post-initial public offering (IPO) holding of Sponsor and Sponsor Group to be at least 25%:
- Three-year lock-in period of 25% for post-IPO holding.
- One-year lock-in period for balance post-IPO holding.

[b]   *Manager to REIT*

Conditions for Eligibility of Manager

12
- Minimum net worth (net tangible assets in case the Manager is Limited Liability Partnership (LLP)) of INR 100 million ($\sim$ USD 1.33 million).
- Manager or its associates should have not less than five years of experience in fund management/advisory services/property management in the real estate industry or in the development of real estate.
- Manager to have at least two key personnel having minimum five years of experience in fund management, advisory or property management in the real estate sector or real estate development.
- Manager to have more than half of its directors (members of the governing board in case the Manager is LLP), as independent and not directors or members of the governing board of another REIT.

Key Rights and Responsibilities: Manager

13
- Make the investment decisions with respect to the underlying assets of the REIT, including any further investment or divestment of the assets.
- Ensuring that a REIT's, Hold Co's and SPV's assets have proper legal, binding and marketable titles and agreements.
- Identifying and recommending investment opportunities.
- Complying with the conditions and strategy mandated for the investment.
- Appointing other service providers in consultation with the Trustee.
- Undertaking lease and property management (directly or through agents).
- Ensuring that a REIT's assets are adequately insured.
- Addressing unitholders' grievances and distribution-related issues.
- Ensuring annual audit of a REIT's accounts by an auditor.
- Overseeing developmental activities.
- Providing activity and performance reports on a REIT every three months to its board or governing board.
- Ensuring adequate disclosure and timely submission of documents to the concerned stock exchange.
- Maintaining records pertaining to activities of a REIT for a minimum period of seven years.

[c]   *Trustee to REIT*

Conditions for Eligibility of Trustee
 – Registered with SEBI and not an associate of the Sponsor(s) or Manager.   **14**

Key Rights and Responsibilities: Trustee
 – Appointing a Manager and executing his or her agreement.   **15**
 – Overseeing the Manager's activities and operations and obtaining compliance certificates on a quarterly basis.
 – Reviewing related-party transactions.
 – Obtaining unitholders' approval on specified matters.
 – Ensure that the activity of the REIT is being operated in accordance with the provisions of the trust deed, the prescribed regulations and the offer document; and
 – Shall not invest in units of the REIT in which it is designated as the Trustee.

[2]   *Legal Form and Minimum Initial Capital*

[a]   *Legal Form*

A REIT is to be mandatorily set up as a trust; no other form of entity is permitted.   **16**

[b]   *Minimum Asset Size*

The minimum asset size to meet the requirements of a REIT is INR 5,000 million (~   **17**
USD 66.83 million).

[3]   *Unitholder Requirements and Listing Requirements*

(1) Mandatory listing of units of REIT within three years from the date of   **18**
registration with SEBI. In case of failure to list within three years, it shall surrender its certificate of registration to SEBI and cease operations.
(2) Slabs for minimum public float have been prescribed as below:

If Post-issue Capital Is:	Minimum Public Float Required
INR 16,000 million	25% of the post-issue capital or INR 2,500 million, whichever is higher
INR 16,000 million ≤ INR 40,000 million	Minimum INR 4,000 million
≥ INR 40,000 million	Minimum 10% of the post-issue capital

(3) However, the public float shall be increased to a minimum of 25% of the post-issue capital (where lower pursuant to the above slabs) within a period of three years from the date of listing.

(4) Minimum trading lot of 1 unit and minimum subscription in the range of INR 10,000–15,000.

(5) Minimum number of subscribers to IPO should be two hundred at the time of public offer (other than sponsors, its related parties and associates of REIT).

(6) Maximum subscription from any investor other than sponsors, its related parties and its associates shall not be more than 25% of the total unit capital, unless an approval from 75% of the unitholders by value is obtained.

(7) Units held by existing unitholder for a period of one year or more may be offered to public for sale:
    – Holding period of equity shares, compulsorily convertible securities (from the date fully paid up), interest in Hold Co and/or SPV (against which units of trust were received) to be considered in the calculation of above one year.
    – Above convertibles to be converted to equity shares prior to filing offer document.

(8) Units held by persons other than Sponsor prior to listing to be held for a period of minimum one year post listing.

(9) Foreign investments in REIT regulated by SEBI are permissible under the automatic route as per the exchange control regulations.

(10) Concept of strategic investor was introduced in December 2017 and further amended in June 2020:
    – Strategic investor means Infrastructure Finance Company registered as a Non-banking Financial Company (NBFC), Scheduled Commercial Bank, Multilateral or Bilateral Development Financial Institution, systemically important NBFC, Foreign Portfolio Investors, an Insurance Company registered with Insurance Regulatory and Development Authority, a Mutual Fund who can invest jointly or severally minimum 5% or maximum 25% of total offer size by REIT.
    – Lock-in period – 180 days from the date of listing of public issue.
    – Draft offer document to mention details of strategic investor.
    – Unit Price for strategic investor should be greater than or equal to Public Issue Price. If strategic investor price is less than Public Issue Price, strategic investor has to make additional investment. If strategic investor price is higher than Public Issue Price, no refund would be issued to strategic investor.
    – If public issue fails due to minimum subscription, Strategic Subscription agreement has to be terminated.

[4]   Asset Levels/Activity Test

Restrictions on Activities/Investments Investment permitted in: (1) real estate assets in India (other than vacant land, agricultural land, etc.); (2) securities of SPVs holding permissible real estate assets in India. Investment through a Hold Co is also permitted, subject to conditions	**19**

Asset-Related Conditions

(1) At least 80% of the value of a REIT to be in completed and rent/income-   **20**
generating real estate, with a lock-in period of three years from the
purchase date.

(2) A maximum of 20% of the total value of REITs can be from:
  - under-construction properties with a lock-in period of three years
    after completion and completed but non-rent generating properties
    with a lock-in period of three years from the date of purchase;
  - the listed or unlisted debt of real estate companies (other than
    investment in debt of Hold Co/SPV);
  - mortgage-backed securities;
  - equity shares of listed companies in India, generating at least 75% of
    their operating income from real estate activities;
  - unlisted equity shares of companies deriving at least 75% of their
    operating income from real estate activities (subject to lock-in as
    mentioned above being satisfied where investment in under-
    construction property or completed but non-rent generating property
    is made through unlisted equity shares);
  - government securities.
  - unutilized floor space index and transferable development rights
    with respect to existing investments;
  - cash or money market instruments.

Additional Conditions

(1) Direct holding of real estate assets in India or through an SPV or a two-level   **21**
structure through a Hold Co.

(2) Investment through a Hold Co should be subject to the following require-
ments:
  - Ultimate holding interest of REIT in SPVs to be at least 26%.
  - Other shareholders/partners of the Hold Co/SPV should not restrict
    REIT, Hold Co or SPV from complying with REIT Regulations, and an
    agreement has to be entered into with such shareholders/partners to
    that effect.

   – The Manager, in consultation with the Trustee, shall appoint at least
     such number of nominees on the board of a Hold Co, which are in
     proportion to the interest held in it by the REIT; and/or an SPV,
     which are in proportion to the interest held in it by the Hold Co.
   – In every meeting of a Hold Co and/or SPV, the voting of REIT shall be
     exercised.
(3) Not less than 51% of the consolidated revenue of REIT (other than gain
    arising from disposal of properties), Hold Co and SPV to be from rental,
    leasing and letting out of assets, or incidental revenue.
(4) Investment not permitted in vacant land, mortgages or agricultural land
    (with certain exceptions).
(5) Investment in other REITs or lending (except lending to Hold Co/SPV) is
    not permitted. Investment in debt securities is not considered as lending.
(6) Unitholder's approval required for disposal of a REIT's/Hold Co's/SPV's
    assets or interest in SPV if it exceeds 10% of the value of REIT assets in a
    financial year.
(7) Co-investment permitted subject to conditions.

[5]   Leverage

22 Aggregate consolidated borrowings and deferred payments, net of cash and cash
equivalents (not including refundable security deposits to tenants) of REIT, Hold Co
and SPV(s) are to be capped at 49% of the value of a REIT's assets.

23 Any further net consolidated borrowings and deferred payments of REIT, Hold Co and
SPV(s) higher than 25% of REIT's assets are to be subject to the following:

   – Credit rating (no minimum rating prescribed).
   – Approval of the unitholders (where the number of votes cast in favour is more
     than the number of votes cast against).

[6]   Distribution Obligations

24

Dividend	Timing
Not less than 90% of net distributable cash flows	At least once in every six months

Where distributions are not made within fifteen days of declaration, the Manager
shall be liable to pay interest as prescribed.

(1) Minimum of 90% of the net distributable cash flow of a REIT to be
    distributed to unitholders.
(2) Minimum net distributable cash flows to be distributed by a Hold Co to a
    REIT (subject to provisions of the Companies Act, 2013 and LLP Act, 2008):
    – 100% of cash flows received from SPVs.

– 90% of the balance net distributable cash flows.

(3) An SPV to distribute a minimum of 90% of its net distributable cash flows to a REIT/Hold Co.

(4) A REIT is to distribute at least 90% of the sale proceeds arising from the sale of property or equity shares/interest in a Hold Co/SPV, unless reinvestment is proposed within a period of one year.

(5) Distribution to be undertaken at least once every six months in a financial year.

REITs may take guidance from the following indicative framework for defining and **25** calculating the net distributable cash flows at the Hold Co/SPV and at REIT level.

[a]   *Calculation of Net Distributable Cash Flows at SPV Level*

Description	Amount
Profit after tax as per statement of profit and loss/income and expenditure (stand-alone) (A)	xx
Add: Depreciation and amortization as per statement of profit and loss/income and expenditure	xx
Add/less: Loss/gain on sale of real estate assets	xx
Add: Proceeds from sale of real estate assets adjusted for the following:	xx
– related debts settled or due to be settled from sale proceeds; – directly attributable transaction costs; – proceeds reinvested or planned to be reinvested as per paragraph 18(7)(a) of REIT Regulations.	
Add: Proceeds from sale of real estate assets not distributed pursuant to an earlier plan to reinvest if such proceeds are not intended to be invested subsequently	xx
Add/less: Any other item of non-cash expense/non-cash income (net of actual cash flows for these items) if deemed necessary by the Manager For example, any decrease/increase in carrying amount of an asset or of a liability recognized in statement of profit and loss/income and expenditure on measurement of the asset or the liability at fair value, interest cost as per effective interest rate method, deferred tax, lease rents recognized on a straight-line basis, etc.	xx
Less: Repayment of external debt (principal)/redeemable preference shares/debentures, etc., if deemed necessary by the Manager	xx
Total Adjustments (B)	xx
Net Distributable Cash Flows (C) = (A + B)	xx

[b]   *Calculation of Net Distributable Cash Flows at the Consolidated REIT Level*

27

Description	Amount
Profit after tax as per statement of profit and loss/income and expenditure	xx
(consolidated) (A)	
Add: Depreciation and amortization as per statement of profit and loss/income and expenditure (consolidated)	xx
Add/less: Loss/gain recognized on sale of real estate assets or equity shares or interest in Hold Co/SPV	Xx
Add: Proceeds from sale of real estate assets or equity shares or interest in Hold Co/SPV adjusted for the following: – related debts settled or due to be settled from sale proceeds; – directly attributable transaction costs; – proceeds reinvested or planned to be reinvested as per paragraph 18(7)(a) of REIT Regulations.	xx
Add: Proceeds from sale of real estate assets or equity shares or interest in Hold Co/SPV not distributed pursuant to an earlier plan to reinvest if such proceeds are not intended to be invested subsequently	xx
Add/less: Any other item of non-cash expense/non-cash income (net of actual cash flows for these items) if deemed necessary by the Manager For example, any decrease/increase in carrying amount of an asset or of a liability recognized in statement of profit and loss/income and expenditure on measurement of the asset or the liability at fair value, interest cost as per effective interest rate method, deferred tax, lease rents recognized on a straight-line basis, etc.	xx
Less: Repayment of external debt (principal)/redeemable preference shares/debentures, etc., if deemed necessary by the Manager	xx
Total Adjustments (B)	xx
Net Distributable Cash Flows (C) = (A + B)	xx

[7]   **Penalties/Loss of Status Rules**

28 In case of any default by REIT or parties to REIT or any other person involved in the activity of REIT, the same is dealt with in the manner provided in SEBI (Intermediaries) Regulations, 2008.

[8]   **Related-Party Transactions**

29 Permission is granted subject to the following:

(1) Arm's-length requirement being met.

(2) Specified disclosures made to unitholders and the stock exchange.

(3) Valuation reports or fairness opinions obtained from independent valuer(s) in the case of specified transactions (for instance, buying and selling of assets).

(4) Unitholder's approval required for the following transactions:
   - acquisition or sale of investments/properties from or to related parties (whether directly or through the Hold Co or SPV), the total value of which in a financial year exceeds 10% of total value of REIT; and
   - borrowings from related parties in a financial year exceeding 10% of total consolidated borrowings of REIT, Hold Co and SPV(s).

[9]   *Valuation*

(1) Complete valuation of a REIT (in the prescribed format) to be undertaken   **30** at least once in every financial year.

(2) Valuer to have minimum experience of five years in valuation of real estate.

(3) Valuer not to be an associate of the Sponsor, Manager/Trustee.

(4) Valuation reports received by the Manager to be submitted to the designated stock exchange and unitholders within fifteen days from the receipt of such valuation reports.

(5) Any issue of units to the public and any other issue of units as may be specified by SEBI, full valuation of all REIT assets to be undertaken (a summary of the report to be included in the offer document and the report should not be more than six months old at the time of offer). This shall not apply where full valuation has been undertaken not more than six months prior to such issue, and no material changes have occurred thereafter.

(6) Half-yearly valuation of REIT assets to be conducted for the half-year ending 30 September.

(7) Complete valuation to be undertaken for purchase or sale of property; unitholders' approval is needed if:
   - the acquisition price is more than 110% of the valuation;
   - the sale price is less than 90% of such valuation.

(8) Two-year cooling-off period for the valuer after every four consecutive years of valuation being done of the same property.

(9) Valuer's remuneration not to be linked to the value of the asset.

[10]   *Governance Aspects*

- Unitholders' meetings to be convened at least once every year within 120 days   **31** from the end of the financial year, with the gap between two meetings not exceeding 15 months.
- Generally, a resolution to be considered as passed if unitholders casting votes in favour are more than those casting votes against it.

- Certain specified matters (for instance, change in investment strategy and delisting) require that votes being cast in favour are at least 1.5 times the votes cast against.
- No person (together with persons acting in concert with him), other than Sponsor(s), its related parties and associates, shall acquire units of a REIT exceeding 25% value of outstanding REIT units without approval of 75% of unitholders by value excluding parties to this transaction.
- In case of change in Sponsor or its control, approval of 75% of unitholders by value excluding parties related to this transaction shall be obtained.
- Annual report to be provided to unitholders within three months from the end of the financial year; half-yearly report to be given within forty-five days from 30 September.
- Price-sensitive information as well as that having a bearing on operations or the performance of a REIT to be disclosed to the stock exchange.

[11]   Other Aspects

32
- Multiple classes of REIT units are not permitted.
- No schemes shall be launched under the REIT.
- However, subordinate units carrying inferior rights may be issued to Sponsor(s) and their associates.
- *Parity to* be maintained between unitholders (no preferential voting or other rights among unitholders).

[B]   Exchange Control Regulations

[1]   Foreign Investment Permitted in REIT

33   Persons resident outside India, including Registered Foreign Portfolio Investor (RFPI) and Non-resident Indian (NRI), are permitted to invest in units of REIT. RFPIs have recently been permitted to invest in debt securities issued by REITs, subject to the terms and conditions specified in this regard.

[2]   Sale/Transfer/Pledge of Units in REIT

34   Such investments can be transferred or sold in any manner or redeemed as per SEBI regulations/directions by the RBI.

35   Further, these units could be pledged by the non-resident unitholder to secure credit facilities.

[3]   *Are Investments by REIT Treated as a Foreign Investment?*

Investments by a REIT shall be regarded as indirect foreign investment only if either the   **36**
Sponsor or the Manager[3] is not Indian 'owned and controlled'. If such investments are
treated as foreign investments, they would need to comply with the applicable sectoral
caps and other restrictions.

For this purpose, ownership and control of companies and LLP are to be determined in   **37**
accordance with the regulations prescribed.

[4]   *Procedural Conditions*

The payment for the units of REIT is to be made by an inward remittance through   **38**
normal banking channels, including by debit to a Non-resident Rupee or a Foreign
Currency Non-resident account or by way of swap of shares of SPV. REIT will have to
report foreign investment in REIT to RBI in the prescribed format.

[5]   *Definition of 'Real Estate Business'*

Under the Foreign Exchange Management (Non-debt Instruments) Rules, 2019, 'real   **39**
estate business' had been regarded as a prohibited sector for foreign direct investment.

The definition of 'real estate business' specifically excludes REITs registered and   **40**
regulated under the extant SEBI regulations, from the ambit of 'real estate business'.
This potentially enables REITs to directly buy (and sell) real estate.

§1.03   TAX TREATMENT

[A]   Tax Treatment at REIT Level

[1]   *Income Tax*

Capital Gains from Sale of Securities of SPV	Dividend Income from SPV	Interest Income from SPV	Rental Income from Property Held Directly by REIT	Any Other Income
Income of REIT is taxable at the applicable rates	Income of REIT should be exempt	Income of REIT is not taxable	Income of REIT is not taxable	30%

41

---

3. Sponsor and Manager can be organized in the form of an LLP.

[a]   *Interest Income from SPV*

42   Any income by way of interest received from SPV should be exempt from tax in the hands of REIT and would be liable to tax in the hands of the unitholders. However, REIT is required to withhold tax at the rate of 5% on distribution of such income to a non-resident unitholder (including a foreign company) and at the rate of 10% on distribution of such income to a domestic unitholder.

[b]   *Dividend Income from SPV*

43   Dividend income received by REIT from an SPV continues to be exempt in the hands of REIT. Further, it has been clarified that dividend distributions by an SPV to a REIT should not be subject to withholding tax.

[c]   *Capital Gains*

44   Gains on transfer of the shares in the Hold Co, SPVs, or real estate assets held by REIT should be subject to capital gains tax as summarized below.

45   Listed equity shares:[4]

 – Long-term capital gains[5] above INR 0.1 million are taxable at 10%.
 – Short-term capital gains are taxable at 15%.

46   Others:

 – Long-term capital gains[6] are taxable at 20% (with indexation[7]).
 – Short-term capital gains[8] are taxable at 30%.

[d]   *Rental Income from Property Held Directly by REIT*

47   Rental income received by REIT should be exempt in the hands of REIT. Tenants are not liable to withhold taxes on rental income paid to REIT on the property held directly by REIT. However, REIT would be required to withhold tax at the rate of 10% on distribution of such income to a domestic unitholder, and in case of distribution of such income to a non-resident unitholder (including a foreign company), the withholding shall be at the rates in force.

---

4. Subject to payment of STT on the transaction of acquisition (unless specifically excluded) as well as on sale of the shares of SPV.
5. If held for more than twelve months.
6. If held for more than twenty-four months.
7. Indexation is not applicable on sale of debt securities.
8. If held for up to twenty-four months.

[e]   *Other Income of REIT*

Any other income of REIT would be generally chargeable to tax at the rate of 30% (plus   **48**
applicable surcharge and health and education cess).

[2]   **Registration Duties**

[a]   *Registration Duties*

Stamp duty and registration costs on real estate range between 5% and 15%.   **49**

Stamp duty on issue and transfer of shares are as follows: **50**

Particulars	Stamp Duty (%)
Issuance of shares (physical and electronic form)	0.005
Transfer of shares on non-delivery basis	0.003
Transfer of shares on delivery basis	0.015

There are no specific exemptions available to REITs.   **51**

Stamp duty is levied at the time of registration of the purchase transaction. Rates for   **52**
stamp duty vary between 5% and 15% on real estate transactions, depending upon the
state in which the instrument for transfer is executed. Stamp duty is levied on sale price
or value of the asset as per circle rates, whichever is higher.

Registration of documents recording the transfer of real estate assets in the name of   **53**
purchaser attracts registration fee. Registration fee is a state levy and varies across
states in India.

The following fee structure is applicable to REIT under REIT Regulations: **54**

Fees	REIT
Application Fees	INR 0.1 million
Registration Fees	INR 1 million
Issue Filing Fees	0.1% in case of initial and follow-on offer; and 0.05% in case of rights issue; of the total issue size including intended retention of oversubscription at the time of filing of draft offer document

[B]   Tax Treatment at the Unitholder's Level

[1]   *Income Tax on Dividend Received from REIT*

55   Dividend distributed by REIT shall be exempt in the hands of the unitholders, subject to the condition that the SPV distributing such dividend to REIT has not opted for the lower corporate tax regime (i.e., the 22% tax rate exclusive of surcharge and cess[9]). Furthermore, no taxes are required to be withheld by REITs on distribution of such dividend. However, the said exemption would not be available in the hands of the unitholders in case SPV distributing dividend to REIT has opted for the concessional tax regime, and dividend would be taxable at the rates applicable to the Investor under the Tax Treaty or the domestic tax laws, whichever is beneficial. Further, REIT while making distribution to unitholders would be required to withhold taxes at the rate of 10% plus applicable surcharge and cess. The withholding tax rate shall be 10% irrespective of a lower rate under the relevant tax treaty.

SPV Taxability	Dividend Taxability in the Hands of Unitholder	Withholding Tax Implications
SPV opting for new tax regime	Taxable	10%
SPV not opting for new tax regime	Exempt	Not applicable

[2]   *Income Tax on Distributions Received from REIT*

56   Income received by the investors as distributions from REIT is exempt in the hands of the investors. However, such distributions received from REIT, which are attributable to the interest income accrued to/received by REIT and rental income received from the tenants with respect to the property held directly by REIT, are as follows:

- Interest income should be chargeable to income tax in the hands of the unitholder being resident at the applicable rates. Taxes withheld by REIT as discussed above should be available as credit. Interest income received by a non-resident unitholder should be taxable at the rate of 5%.
- Rental income should be chargeable to income tax in the hands of the unitholder at the rates applicable to such unitholder (a non-resident unitholder may be allowed to take treaty benefits if available on such income). Taxes withheld by REIT as discussed above should be available as credit.

---

9. Taxation Laws (Amendment) Ordinance, 2019 introduced optional concessional tax regime for Indian companies whereby, after satisfying certain conditions, such companies can opt for lower corporate tax rate of 22% plus applicable surcharge and cess.

[3] Income Tax on Units Received in Exchange of Shares of SPV and on Sale of Such Units

Units received in exchange of shares of SPV should not be taxable in the hands of the unitholder at the time of such exchange. However, at the time of disposal of such units by the unitholder, the unitholder would be liable to pay the applicable capital gains tax as explained below. 57

The cost of acquisition of the shares of SPV should be the cost of acquisition for the purposes of computing the capital gains in the hands of the unitholder. The period of holding of the units should be computed from the date of acquisition of the shares of SPV. 58

Tax implications on capital gains on the sale of the units in REIT are discussed below: 59

- Capital gains more than INR 0.1 million[10] on transfer of units listed on a recognized stock exchange in India, held for more than thirty-six months, are taxable at 10% subject to payment of Securities Transaction Tax (STT).
- Capital gains on transfer of units listed on a recognized stock exchange in India, held for up to thirty-six months, are chargeable to tax at the rate of 15% (plus applicable surcharge and health and education cess) subject to payment of STT.
- STT at the rate of 0.1% should be leviable on the transaction value of the sale. Separately, STT at 0.2% should be leviable in the case of sale of unlisted units of REIT by a unitholder which was acquired by way of swapping of shares of an SPV.
- Minimum Alternative Tax (MAT) at the rate of 15% shall be payable on profits arising from the sale of units by resident companies (other than opting for lower corporate tax regime) and non-resident companies.

[4] Income Tax on Units Received in Exchange of Assets (Other Than Shares of SPV)

Units received in exchange of assets or securities (other than shares of SPV) shall be taxable at the time of swap. Long-term capital gains on the swap of assets shall be taxable at the rate of 20% (10% in case of foreign company transferring unlisted securities), and short-term capital gains shall be taxable at the rate of 30% (40% in case of foreign company). 60

---

10. Calculated on an aggregate basis on transfer of equity shares, units of equity-oriented funds and units of other business trusts in a financial year.

[5] Dividend/Bonus Stripping

61 The Finance Bill, 2022 proposes to include units of REITs under the ambit of dividend stripping[11] and bonus stripping[12] provisions.

[6] Tax Treatment in the Hands of the Sponsor

62 As regards the Sponsor, the swap of shares in an SPV for units in a REIT is a transaction exempt from tax. However, at the time of disposal of such units by the unitholder, the unitholder would be liable to pay the applicable capital gains tax. The cost of acquisition of the shares of SPV should be considered to be the cost of acquisition for the purpose of computing the capital gains in the hands of the unitholder. The period of holding of the units should be computed from the date of acquisition of the shares of SPV.

63 However, where units are received in exchange for assets, other than shares in an SPV, the transaction should be chargeable to tax. Where the exchanged assets are held for more than thirty-six months (more than twenty-four months in case of immovable property), the rate of tax is generally 20% (plus applicable surcharge and health and education cess), and held for up to thirty-six months (up to twenty-four months in case of immovable property), the rate of tax is generally 30% (lower rate of 25% may be applicable subject to fulfilment of specified criteria)[13] (plus applicable surcharge and health and education cess).

64 MAT at the rate of 15% (plus applicable surcharge and health and education cess) for Sponsor being a corporate entity would be applicable, if not opting for concessional tax regime. A separate computation mechanism is prescribed for calculation of such MAT which is payable only on disposal of REIT units.

---

11. Dividend stripping – Where any person purchases any specified securities within a period of three months prior to the record date and such person: (i) sells or transfers such securities within a period of three months after such record date, or (ii) such security within a period of nine months after such record date, and (iii) the dividend or income on such securities or unit received or receivable by such person is exempt, then, any loss arising to such person on account of such purchase and sale of securities or unit, to the extent such loss does not exceed the amount of such dividend or income received or receivable, will be ignored for the purposes of computing its income chargeable to tax.

12. Bonus stripping – Where any person purchases any specified securities within a period of three months prior to the record date and such person is allotted additional bonus securities on the basis of holding of the aforesaid securities on the record date, and if such person sells or transfers all or any of the original securities within a period of nine months after the record date while continuing to hold all or any of the additional securities, then any loss arising on account of such purchase and sale of all or any of the securities will be ignored for the purpose of computing its income chargeable to tax,. Further, the loss so ignored would be deemed to be the cost of acquisition of such additional securities as are held by it on the date of sale or transfer of original units.

13. For FY 2021–2022, where the total turnover or the gross receipt of a domestic company in FY 2019–2020 does not exceed INR 4,000 million, lower tax rate of 25% shall apply.

Note: All tax rates quoted in this document are exclusive of a surcharge as may be **65** applicable and health and education cess.

All the tax rates mentioned in the document would have to be increased by applicable **66** surcharge for the financial year 2021–2022 as tabulated below:

	Taxable Income of INR 10 million or above but Below INR 100 Million (%)	Taxable Income Above INR 100 Million (%)
Foreign company	2	5
Indian company	7	12

The total tax and surcharge to be further increased by education cess of 4%. **67**

Ireland

ILONA McELROY

Ilona McElroy is PwC EMEA Real Estate Tax Leader and a partner in Ireland's asset management tax practice. Ilona specializes in providing tax consultancy services to the real estate sector and has been very active in the space of international acquisitions of Irish real estate, advising on the structuring of a large number of deals through the use of REITs, limited partnerships, property companies, ICAVs, and section 110 companies.

Domestically, Ilona is a member of the tax steering group of the Irish funds industry association and the chairperson of the recently formed Irish Real Estate Funds (IREF) working group, which focuses on liaising with the Department of Finance and Revenue on IREF legislation. Ilona is a member of the Department of Finance audit committee and also acts as the main tax advisor to the Irish Institutional Property industry group.

Ilona provides corporate tax structuring services to a number of high-profile clients in the Irish real estate sector.

Ilona has a first-class LLM from Trinity College, Dublin and is a member of the Irish Taxation Institute. Ilona also sits on the projects committee of the Foundation for Fiscal Studies.

E-mail: ilona.mcelroy@pwc.com

ROSALEEN CAREY

Rosaleen Carey is a director in our asset management tax and real estate practice in Dublin, Ireland. She has extensive experience in advising real estate fund structuring solutions for international and domestic clients. Rosaleen on a day-to-day basis advises on the tax implications arising from large-scale real estate acquisitions and disposals, including providing detailed tax due diligence reports along with the tax and legal requirements. Rosaleen has significant experience in working in transactional-based deals in relation to making and managing investments and returning value to shareholders in a tax-efficient manner.

Rosaleen has a Bachelor of Common Law and German and is an associate of the Irish Institute of Taxation.
E-mail: rosaleen.carey@pwc.com

Ireland

Ilona McElroy & Rosaleen Carey

§1.01   BACKGROUND

[A]   Key Characteristics

An Irish Real Estate Investment Trust (REIT) is an Irish tax resident listed company that **1** carries on a property investment business and elects to become a REIT. A principal company of a property investment group listed on a recognized stock exchange can also make a group election to enter the REIT regime.

Ireland introduced legislation in 2013, enabling the introduction of REITs into the Irish **2** market.

At the point of entry to the REIT regime, a REIT's activities are characterized as either **3** 'property rental business' or 'residual business'. The distribution of proceeds arising from the disposal of a rental property is subject to dividend withholding tax (DWT) upon distribution (25% effective 1 January 2020). However, to the extent that the sales proceeds are reinvested in the acquisition of Irish real estate, reinvested in the development or enhancement of a property held in the REIT's property rental business, or distributed to shareholders within two years, the gain arising on the disposal continues to be exempt from tax. The amount which the REIT would be required to distribute may be reduced by the amounts invested in the REIT business in the twelve months preceding the property disposal and by the repayment of debt associated with the property disposed of. Income from other activities comprises the residual business and may be subject to tax. There are limitations on shareholdings, gearing and the nature of a REIT's activities.

The Irish government's intention is that a REIT should replicate direct ownership of **4** property; therefore, while the REIT itself is exempt from corporate or income tax on its rental income, it is required to distribute most of this income (i.e., at least 85%) to its investors. This distribution is called a Property Income Distribution (PID). Shareholders may be chargeable to tax (subject to their tax status and any applicable tax treaty) on the PID; furthermore, the PID may be subject to Irish withholding tax (WHT).

5   Non-residents can dispose of shares in an Irish REIT without giving rise to a charge to Irish capital gains tax (CGT).

[B]   History of the Irish REIT

6   REITs were introduced in Ireland in Finance Act 2013. The first REIT was listed on the Irish Stock Exchange (ISE) on 18 July 2013.

[C]   REIT Market

7   There are currently two REITs established in Ireland.

§1.02   REGULATORY ASPECTS

[A]   Legal Form of REIT

8   The Irish REIT regime is determined by tax legislation rather than through corporate law. An Irish REIT has to be a public limited company that is listed on a recognized stock exchange in the European Union (EU) and is not a close company (a company being under the control of five or fewer participants). While there are a certain number of non-fiscal requirements which have to be met by a REIT in order to preserve its tax status as a REIT, most requirements are based on Irish tax law. Therefore, we will consider both listing and fiscal requirements in this section.

[1]   Corporate Form

9   The legislation allows an Irish REIT to be set up as a single company REIT or a group of companies with a parent company (Group REIT) once all conditions are met. References to REITs below apply equally to group REITs, where applicable.

10 To become an Irish REIT, a company must comply with a series of conditions and give notice to the Irish Revenue Commissioners that it wishes to be treated as a REIT. Some of these conditions are applicable on day one, some at the end of the first accounting period, while the remainder can be satisfied within a period of three years of becoming a REIT.

11 There are no capital requirements, but there is a limitation on the type of shares a REIT can issue, being ordinary shares and non-voting preference shares. It must have only one class of ordinary share.

[2]   Day One Requirements

The REIT (or where it is a Group REIT, the principal company) must be tax resident in   **12**
Ireland and not resident elsewhere and must be a company incorporated in Ireland
under the Companies Acts.

[3]   End of First Accounting Period Conditions

There are a number of detailed conditions which must be satisfied by the end of the   **13**
REIT's first accounting period:

   (i) In order to qualify as a REIT, at least 75% of the aggregate income of the
       REIT must be derived from carrying on property rental business.
  (ii) At least 75% of the aggregate market value of the assets of the REIT must
       relate to assets of the property rental business of the REIT.
 (iii) A REIT is allowed to incur debt, but there are a number of detailed
       restrictions:
       –   An Irish REIT must maintain a property financing cost ratio of at least
            1.25:1 (i.e., the ratio of the aggregate of the property income and the
            financing costs to the financing costs cannot fall below 1.25). Where
            this ratio is not maintained, the REIT shall be subject to corporation tax
            at a rate of 25% on the amount by which the property financing costs
            would have to be reduced to achieve a 1.25:1 ratio. The amount subject
            to corporation tax shall not exceed 20% of the property income of the
            REIT or a Group REIT, as the case may be.
       –   The aggregate of the debt in the REIT must not exceed 50% of the
            aggregate market value of the assets of the business of the REIT.
  (iv) Subject to having sufficient distributable reserves, the REIT must distribute
       by way of property income dividend to its shareholders at least 85% of the
       property income of each accounting period (on or before the tax return
       filing date, which is normally circa nine months from the end of the
       particular accounting period). However, in the case where a REIT makes a
       gain on disposal, the REIT does not have to pay CGT or distribute the
       income on the basis that the gain is reinvested back into the REIT within
       twenty-four months commencing on the date of disposal.

[4]   End of Third Accounting Period Conditions

There are three conditions that should be satisfied by the end of the third accounting   **14**
period in order for the REIT to maintain its tax status.

First, there is a listing requirement.   **15**

16 The REIT's shares must be listed on the main market of a recognized stock exchange in an EU Member State. The ISE has created a listing regime for REITs and has aligned the requirements with those of the Financial Conduct Authority (FCA) Listing Rules in the United Kingdom (UK) so as to facilitate REITs that may seek a dual listing in Ireland and the UK. For a new REIT, there is a grace period of three years for the shares to be trading on the Main Securities Market or other recognized stock exchange.

17 Second, an Irish REIT cannot be a close company. This is a company controlled by five or fewer investors. Where a new REIT is formed, it can be 'close' for the first three years but must satisfy this requirement by the end of a three-year period.

18 Finally, within three years of commencement, the REIT must conduct a property rental business consisting of at least three properties, with no one property accounting for more than 40% of the total market value of the properties constituting the property rental business.

[5]   Investment Restrictions

19 The investment restrictions which a REIT must adhere to are summarized below:

- At least 75% of the aggregate market value of the assets of the REIT must relate to assets of the property rental business of the REIT.
- Within three years of commencement, the REIT must conduct a property rental business consisting of at least three properties, with no one property accounting for more than 40% of the total market value of the properties constituting the property rental business.
- All transactions entered into by the REIT must be undertaken for bona fide commercial reasons and are not a part of any arrangement or scheme of which the main purpose, or one of the main purposes, is the avoidance of liability to tax.

[6]   Investor Restrictions

20 An Irish REIT is penalized if it makes distributions to shareholders with 10% or more of the share capital, distribution or voting rights in the REIT (other than 'qualifying investors') unless reasonable steps were put in place to prevent the making of the distribution to such a person. A qualifying investor includes any Irish pension scheme, life company or charity, the National Asset Management Agency (NAMA) and other specified persons, including regulated Irish funds.

[B]   Regulatory Authorities

In Ireland, the REIT regime is very much a fiscal regime rather than a financial   **21**
regulatory regime, and compliance with the REIT regime is overseen by the Irish
Revenue Commissioners.

As a REIT must be a company whose shares are listed on a recognized stock exchange,   **22**
it is subject to the regulations of the stock exchange on which it is admitted.

[C]   Legislative and Other Regulatory Resources

The REIT legislation is set out in Part 25A sections 705A–705Q of the Taxes Consoli-   **23**
dation Act, 1997.

[D]   Exchange Controls and Reporting Requirements

An Irish REIT must be listed on the main market of a recognized stock exchange in a   **24**
Member State. A recognized stock exchange is defined as a stock exchange that is
regulated by the appropriate regulatory authority of that Member State, and other than
in the case of the ISE has substantially the same level of recognition in that Member
State as the ISE has in Ireland.

There are no exchange control provisions in force in Ireland. Irish REITs can be dual   **25**
listed or solely listed on other stock exchanges, and, as already noted, they are subject
to the rules of the relevant listing exchange(s).

There are no specific reporting requirements for a REIT under the ISE rules; instead, it   **26**
has to adhere to the same requirements as other listed companies. For example, an Irish
company listed on the ISE must:

- meet the ISE's market capitalization requirements;
- publish a prospectus document before listing, which discloses information on
  the REIT's key promoters, the Board of Directors and any investment manager
  appointed, an overview of its financials, business proposition, future outlook,
  risks and other material information;
- publish half-yearly financial information and an annual financial report which
  includes an analysis of its property portfolio;
- disclose relevant material information to the market on an on-going basis,
  including significant transactions, director dealings and related party transactions;
- update the valuation of its property portfolio at least every two years in
  accordance with the standards adopted by the Society of Chartered Surveyors
  in Ireland or an equivalent international body;

- ensure any investment manager appointed to manage the REIT's investments has adequate and appropriate expertise and experience in the management of property investments (at least three years);
- have a Board of Directors, which is independent of any investment manager appointed;
- comply with the corporate governance standards applicable to Irish listed companies.

27   Similarly, an Irish REIT listing on a non-Irish exchange would need to comply with the local regulatory requirements in other jurisdictions.

28   As noted above, for a new REIT, there is a grace period of three accounting periods (up to three years) for the shares to be listed on a recognized stock exchange.

[E]   Registration Procedures

[1]   Preparatory Measures

29   There are two types of registration – existing companies that convert to a REIT and newly listed companies that enter the REIT regime.

30   Before an existing property investment group can convert to a REIT, the company shareholders have to hold an Extraordinary General Meeting (EGM) and approve an amendment to the Articles of Association of the company. The necessary circular, which is submitted to shareholders prior to voting at the EGM, has to be cleared in advance with the Irish Listing Authority.

31   A newly formed company seeking to list as a REIT needs to develop a business strategy and to identify the type and source of property which it will seek to buy with the cash raised on the listing in order to satisfy shareholders that it will perform as a property investment company.

[2]   Obtaining Authorization

32   To become a REIT, an existing company or group of companies or a newly formed company or group of companies has to be sure that they can meet the REIT requirements. No conversion charge will apply for an existing company converting to a REIT. However, a company that converts to a REIT will be deemed for CGT purposes to have sold its assets at market value, on the day of conversion, immediately before becoming a REIT and reacquired them on becoming a REIT, thus creating a CGT liability on any gains at that point.

33   Once in the REIT regime, a REIT has to monitor its activities to ensure that it continues to comply with the REIT legislation. To enter the regime, a written election is made to

the Irish Revenue Commissioners in accordance with section 705E, Taxes Consolidation Act 1997.

The notice has to contain the following: **34**

- – the date from which the REIT regime will apply to that group/company;
- – a statement that the conditions in section 705B(1), TCA 1997 are reasonably expected to be satisfied by the group/company by the end of the accounting period in respect of which the election is made; and
- – in the case of a Group REIT, a list of the members of that Group.

Furthermore, under section 705E(3A) TCA 1997, each time a new member is added to   **35**
the group, a revised notice must be submitted to Revenue.

[3]   Other Requirements for the Incorporation of a Company

The formation of a group/company is a straightforward process in Ireland. If an   **36**
existing company is used as the principal company of a REIT, it may need to be
re-registered as a public limited company, and there are company law capital and
reserves restrictions that need to be met.

[4]   Obtaining Listing Exchanges

[a]   Costs

The fee to list a company is typically calculated on a tiered basis – from EUR 100,000   **37**
(in respect of capital raised up to EUR 250,000,000) to EUR 250,000 (in respect of
capital raised exceeding EUR 1 billion). A EUR 100 million listing would fall in the
range of EUR 100,000. It is based on equity securities issued, so it would also apply to
subsequent rights issues; however, these will be charged at 90% of the scale for initial
admission fees. Annual fees arise based on the nominal value of the securities – from
EUR 7,000 (in respect of capital up to EUR 250 million) to EUR 25,000 (in respect of
capital exceeding EUR 1 billion). The other costs of listing depend on the size and
complexity of the company being listed. The company will need to appoint advisers,
including a sponsor, reporting accountants, legal counsel and potential underwriters,
brokers and property valuers. Sponsors will generally require companies to commission appropriate due diligence.

[b]   Time

It will generally take around two to six months from the appointment of advisers for a   **38**
company to obtain a listing on the Main Market of the ISE.

[F]   Requirements and Restrictions

[1]   Capital Requirements

39   To be listed on the ISE, the company must have a minimum market capitalization with equity of EUR 100 million (unless the exchange agrees otherwise). Other exchanges have different capital requirements.

[2]   Marketing/Advertising

40   All companies looking to list on the ISE must produce a prospectus that includes, *inter alia*, a statement on the sufficiency of working capital, an operating and financial review (for companies with an operating history) and a statement as to whether there has been any significant change since the last published accounts. Property companies must include a valuation report. Investment companies must include information on investment policies. The prospectus has to be approved by the ISE Listing Authority.

[3]   Redemption

41   The redemption or buy-back of listed shares is possible; however, it is regulated.

[4]   Valuation of Shares

42   Shares are typically valued at open market value (i.e., the price which would be agreed between a willing buyer and seller) for redemption purposes.

[5]   Investment Restrictions

43   The REIT is required to meet the following key investment condition:

- within three years of commencement, the REIT must conduct a property rental business consisting of at least three properties, with no one property accounting for more than 40% of the total market value of the properties constituting the property rental business.

44   Furthermore, the REIT has to meet two 'balance of business tests' as follows:

(1) at least 75% of the REIT's assets have to be used in the property rental business; and
(2) at least 75% of the REIT's income has to be derived from the property rental business.

There is also a development restriction that needs to be considered. A corporation tax **45**
charge will arise where a property asset is developed at a cost exceeding 30% of its
market value and sold within three years of completion of the development.

[6]   Restrictions on Investors

An established Irish REIT cannot be a close company (which is a company controlled **46**
by five or fewer investors). Where a new REIT is formed, it can be 'close' for the first
three years.

An Irish REIT is penalized if it makes distributions to shareholders with 10% or more **47**
of the share capital, distribution or voting rights in the REIT (other than 'qualifying
investors') unless reasonable steps were put in place to prevent the making of the
distribution to such a person. A qualifying investor includes any Irish pension scheme,
life company or charity, NAMA and other specified persons, including Qualified
Investor Alternative Investment Funds (QIAIFs).

There are no additional restrictions in respect of non-resident investors. **48**

[7]   Reporting Requirements

REITs listed on the ISE have to file an annual report, a half-yearly report and interim **49**
management statements (quarterly reporting). Preliminary statements are not required, but if companies choose to issue them, they must be agreed upon with the
auditors.

[8]   Accounting

In terms of financial reporting, an Irish REIT prepares accounts in accordance with **50**
International Financial Reporting Standards. The PID is calculated based on the tax
results of the property rental business and therefore uses the accounting standard of the
entity.

[9]   Restrictions on Foreign Assets

There are no restrictions on foreign assets. **51**

[10]   Distribution/Accumulation

At the end of each accounting period (subject to having sufficient distributable **52**
reserves), the REIT must distribute, by way of property income dividend to its

shareholders, at least 85% of the property income of that accounting period (on or before the tax return filing date, which is normally circa nine months from the end of the particular accounting period).

§1.03   TAXATION

[A]   Taxation of the REIT

[1]   *Corporate Income Tax*

53   The distribution of proceeds by an Irish REIT arising from the disposal of a rental property is subject to DWT upon distribution (25% effective 1 January 2020). However, to the extent that the sales proceeds are reinvested in the acquisition of Irish real estate, reinvested in the development or enhancement of a property held in the REIT's property rental business, or distributed to shareholders within two years, the gain arising on the disposal continues to be exempt from tax. The amount which the REIT would be required to distribute may be reduced by the amounts invested in the REIT business in the twelve months preceding the property disposal and by the repayment of debt associated with the property disposed of. Expenses incurred by an Irish REIT not wholly and exclusively for the purposes of its property rental business are chargeable to corporation tax at the 25% rate. An Irish REIT is subject to corporation tax on all other income and gains under the usual Irish taxation rules.

54   A REIT, or the principal company of a Group REIT, must make a statement to Revenue by 28 February in the year following the end of its accounting period, confirming that the conditions necessary for REIT status have been met throughout the accounting period. Where a REIT or Group REIT fails to make a statement or makes an incomplete statement, it will be liable to a penalty of EUR 3,000, and Revenue may treat the company or group as having ceased to be a REIT or Group REIT.

55   If a REIT or Group REIT has breached the relevant conditions set out in the REIT legislation and cannot make the statement, it must notify Revenue of the breach and of the steps taken to rectify it. If within a reasonable time limit imposed by Revenue, a REIT or Group REIT fails to remedy the breach, Revenue may treat the company or group as having ceased to be a REIT or Group REIT.

56   A REIT, or the principal company of a Group REIT, must also file an annual corporation tax return and comply with mandatory e-filing requirements.

57   No conversion charge will apply for an existing company converting to a REIT. However, a company that converts to a REIT will be deemed for CGT purposes to have sold its assets at market value, on the day of conversion, immediately before becoming a REIT and reacquired them on becoming a REIT, thus creating a CGT liability on any gains at that point.

As of October 2019, unrealized property gains which have accrued to a REIT are **58**
brought within the scope of CGT (chargeable to tax at a rate of 33%) if the REIT exits
the regime within fifteen years.

[2]   Value Added Tax

There are no special value added tax (VAT) provisions; a REIT has to comply with **59**
general legislation, case law and practice as it relates to VAT and property. For
example, a REIT can choose to 'opt to tax' (charge VAT on rents) when leasing
commercial property and recover VAT on its letting expenses. Where a REIT buys
residential property to let, it cannot charge VAT to its tenants, and therefore only part
of the VAT cost can be recovered.

[3]   Withholding Taxes

Dividend distributions out of rental income and gains by an Irish REIT (i.e., PIDs) are **60**
normally subject to a WHT of 25%, although certain categories of exempt investors
exist, e.g., pension funds, regulated funds, etc.

Distributions out of taxed income are treated as ordinary dividends, and more **61**
wide-ranging exemptions from WHT may apply.

[4]   Other Taxes

There is no exemption from property rates, employment taxes or stamp duty for a REIT. **62**
Stamp duty is currently levied at a rate of 1% for certain residential property up to EUR
1 million, it is then levied at 2% on the value of the residential property above EUR 1
million. From 20 May 2021, a 10% stamp duty charge applies on the bulk purchase of
houses and duplexes ('relevant residential units'). A residential unit will be considered
a relevant residential unit where it is part of a bulk purchase of ten or more residential
units, or where the buyer has bought at least nine other residential units in the twelve
months preceding the current purchase. Apartment blocks are excluded from this
definition.
     A 7.5% stamp duty rate applies to commercial properties acquired. A 5.5%
refund may be available if the commercial real estate is developed for residential
purposes where certain conditions are satisfied.

[5]   Penalties Imposed on a REIT

There are various penalties that can be levied on a REIT. Some can result in financial **63**
penalties, and others can lead to disapplication or even termination of the REIT regime.

64 A summary is set out below:

- An Irish REIT must maintain a property financing cost ratio of at least 1.25:1 (i.e., the ratio of the aggregate of the property income and the financing costs to the financing costs cannot fall below 1.25). Where this ratio is not maintained, the REIT shall be subject to corporation tax at a rate of 25% on the amount by which the property financing costs would have to be reduced to achieve a 1.25:1 ratio. The amount subject to corporation tax shall not exceed 20% of the property income of the REIT or a Group REIT, as the case may be.
- A corporation tax charge will arise where a property asset is developed at a cost exceeding 30% of its market value and sold within three years of completion of the development.
- An Irish REIT is penalized if it makes distributions to shareholders with 10% or more of the share capital, distribution or voting rights in the REIT (other than 'qualifying investors') unless reasonable steps were put in place to prevent the making of the distribution to such a person. A qualifying investor includes any Irish pension scheme, life company or charity, NAMA and other specified persons, including regulated Irish funds. The REIT is subject to tax on the amount of the dividend paid to a substantial shareholder at a rate of 25%.
- Where a REIT does not meet the 85% distribution requirement, it is subject to tax at a rate of 25% on an amount equal to the amount by which the distribution falls short of the 85% threshold.

[B] Taxation of the Investor

[1] Private Investors

65 Irish resident shareholders in a REIT should be subject to income tax at normal rates on income distributions with credit for DWT (current rate is 25%). Individuals will be taxed at marginal rates of income tax (up to 40%) plus pay related social insurance (PRSI) and universal social charge (USC).

66 CGT at a rate of 33% applies in respect of a gain on the disposal of REIT shares.

[2] Institutional Investors

67 Irish resident corporate investors should be liable to 25% corporate tax on income distributions from a REIT and will be liable to CGT at a rate of 33% on the disposal of shares in a REIT.

[3]   Non-resident Investors

Non-resident investors should not be liable to Irish CGT as a REIT is a publicly listed   **68**
company. However, these investors may be liable to such taxes in their home
jurisdictions. The REIT will apply DWT at the rate of 25% from income distributions to
non-residents, and depending on their country of residence, they may be able to
reclaim some of this DWT under a relevant double taxation treaty. The reduced treaty
rate must be claimed as a refund.

[4]   Penalties Imposed on Investors

There are no penalties levied on investors.   **69**

[5]   Transfer Taxes

Any transfer of shares in a REIT should be subject to 1% stamp duty.   **70**

[C]   Tax Treaties

Revenue accepts that a distribution of a REIT is a distribution of the profits of a   **71**
company, and therefore an investor may be able to make a claim under the dividend
article of a double tax treaty to reduce the WHT. A dividend cannot be paid under a
reduced rate of withholding, and instead, any amount due needs to be formally
reclaimed.

[D]   Exit Tax/Tax Privileges/Concessions

As of October 2019, unrealized property gains which have accrued to a REIT are   **72**
brought within the scope of CGT (chargeable to tax at a rate of 33%) if the REIT exits
the regime within fifteen years.

[E]   Taxation of Foreign REITs

[1]   Taxation of Foreign REIT Holding Assets in Country

There are no special rules for the taxation of foreign REITs, and they are treated like any   **73**
other investor. If the investment vehicle is not an Irish resident, then only the rental
income (net of expenses, finance costs and tax depreciation) is subject to income tax at
20%. Gains derived from Irish source property should also be subject to Irish CGT at a
rate of 33%.

[2]   *Taxation of Investors Holding Shares in Foreign REIT*

74 The taxation of shares in foreign REITs depends on the tax status of the owner. If the owner is an Irish resident individual, the tax applies to the dividend income at the investor's marginal rate of up to 40%, with tax relief for WHTs. Gains on the sale of shares are subject to Irish CGT at 33%. Irish companies are subject to tax on income and gains on the sale of shares at 12.5%/25% depending on the precise circumstances, with relief for WHT and possibly underlying tax. Irish pension funds and charities may suffer local WHT on distributions, but they are not subject to tax on the income in Ireland.

Italy

FABRIZIO ACERBIS

Fabrizio Acerbis is tax partner and chairman of the managing committee of TLS Associazione Professionale di Avvocati e Commercialisti.

Fabrizio Acerbis' professional experience includes tax advice to a large number of financial institutions in respect of corporate taxation and international structuring. His professional experience also includes regulatory aspects and requirements to be met under the Italian Civil Code.

E-mail: fabrizio.acerbis@pwc.com

DANIELE DI MICHELE

Daniele Di Michele is a tax partner of TLS Associazione Professionale di Avvocati e Commercialisti, Italian leader for real estate tax services of PwC Tax and Legal Services.

He regularly advises several multinational players on all Italian tax aspects for their Italian recurring and extraordinary operations concerning their real estate business.

E-mail: daniele.di.michele@pwc.com

Italy

Fabrizio Acerbis & Daniele Di Michele

§1.01 BACKGROUND

[A] Key Characteristics

Following the positive experience of other countries, Italy introduced the *Società di* **1** *Investimento Immobiliare Quotata* (SIIQ), the listed real estate investment company that is similar to Real Estate Investment Trusts (REITs) in other such countries. The SIIQ is not a new type of entity but rather an optional special civil and tax law regime: an ordinary stock corporation that mainly carries on real estate rental activity may make an irrevocable election to be governed by such SIIQ civil and tax law regime. Shares in SIIQ stock corporations must be listed on a stock exchange in the European Union (EU) or in the European Economic Area (EEA).

The SIIQ must be resident in Italy for tax purposes (this requirement is met when the **2** legal office or the place of management or the main purpose is in the Italian territory for the majority of the tax period; in certain circumstances also foreign entities which control and are controlled or managed by Italian subjects are deemed to be Italian tax residents).

However, the SIIQ regime has been afterwards extended to companies resident in the **3** countries of the EU or the EEA included in the Italian white-list (i.e., countries with exchange of information procedures with Italy) with respect to their Italian permanent establishments, to the extent the permanent establishment's main business consists of real estate rental activity.

Unlisted resident stock corporations may also opt for the SIIQ regime provided that **4** they mainly carry on real estate rental activity, and at least 95% of the voting and profit rights in the same are owned by one or more SIIQs. An unlisted stock corporation that elects under the SIIQ regime is called a *Società di Investimento Immobiliare Non Quotata* (SIINQ). In order to qualify as a SIINQ, the controlling SIIQ and the SIINQ have to opt to be treated as a single entity for tax purposes (i.e., tax consolidation regime). The SIINQ is governed by the rules applicable to SIIQs.

5 The SIIQ is exempt from corporate income tax (Imposta sul Reddito delle Società, IRES), which currently applies at a rate of 24%, and regional tax (Imposta Regionale sulle Attivitá Produttive, IRAP), which usually applies at a rate ranging from 3.9% to 4.82%, on any income derived from rental activity and on income from investments in other SIIQs, SIINQs and (starting from 13 September 2014, which is the date of enactment of some amendments to the SIIQ regime) in certain Italian Real Estate Investment Funds (REIFs). The SIIQ's profits are subject to withholding tax (WHT) at a rate of 26% when they are distributed to shareholders (rate reduced to 15% for certain residential rental profits).

6 When the SIIQ regime is applied by a permanent establishment of a foreign company, in lieu of the ordinary corporate income taxation, the annual income derived from the rental activities should be subject to a 20% substitute tax.

7 Upon election for SIIQ status, the basis of the corporation's rental real estate properties and its rental real estate rights is stepped up to fair market value. The built-in gains, net of losses, are favourably taxed at 20%. The tax can be paid, with interest (i.e., the European Central Bank reference rate increased by 1%), over a five-year period. The favourable tax treatment of the step-up only applies if the SIIQ retains the assets for at least three years, and the stepped-up value is recognized for tax purposes only after this term. Alternatively, the company may opt to treat the built-in gains, net of losses, as ordinary business income, and the income is taxed accordingly in the tax period before the election, or in equal instalments in the tax period before the election and in the following four tax periods (in such a case it qualifying as profit from the not exempt business).

8 Unlike Italian REIFs designed primarily for passive investors, the SIIQ regime allows active and strategic investors (in their capacity as shareholders) to exercise control over real estate transactions and strategic management decisions.

[B]   History of REIT

9 The SIIQ regime was introduced, with effect from 30 June 2007, by Law No. 296, dated 27 December 2006 and was then amended by Law No. 244, dated 24 December 2007, by Law No. 166, dated 20 November 2009 and lastly by Law Decree No. 133, dated 12 September 2014 (converted into Law No. 164, dated 11 November 2014).

10 Certain implementation rules were introduced by Ministerial Decree No. 174, dated 7 September 2007 (the 'Implementing Decree'). The Italian tax authorities issued preliminary guidance in November 2007; then, more comprehensive instructions were issued in January 2008 and, after the amendments made by Law Decree No. 133/2014, in September 2015.

11 In the first years of enactment, only very few companies have adopted the SIIQ regime. This may be mainly down to the existence of other more attractive real estate investment vehicles, particularly for small- to medium-sized portfolios. Conscious of this, Law Decree No. 133/2014 (so-called *Sblocca-Italia* Decree) has introduced some changes to the SIIQ regime, with the aim to remove some restrictions in a bid to make it more appealing. Consequently, the interest in SIIQ is increasing.

[C]   REIT Market

The SIIQ market is still at an early stage, and only a few corporations have adopted or   **12** are in the process of adopting the SIIQ regime. However, further to some favourable amendments introduced by Law Decree No. 133/2014, Italian and international real estate players are looking to the SIIQ with more interest.

§1.02   REGULATORY ASPECTS

[A]   Legal Form of REIT

[1]   Corporate Form

Stock corporations ('*Società per Azioni*', '*S.p.A.*') which are resident in Italy for tax   **13** purposes may opt for the SIIQ regime. The option is irrevocable.

[2]   Investment Restrictions

The following shareholding requirements in the SIIQ must be met: (i) no shareholder   **14** shall hold, directly or indirectly, more than 60% (it was 51% until Law Decree No. 133/2014) of the voting rights in the general meeting, and no shareholder shall participate to more than 60% (51% until Law Decree No. 133/2014) in the company's profits; and (ii) at least 25% (35% until Law Decree No. 133/2014) of the shares in the SIIQ shall be held as free float, this meaning that at least 25% of the SIIQ shares have to be owned, at the time of the option for the SIIQ status, by shareholders who each hold, directly or indirectly, no more than 2% of the voting rights in the general meeting and no more than 2% of participation in the company's profits. For this purpose, shares held by pension funds and other investment funds (i.e., undertakings for the invest-ment of saving on a collective basis) have to be taken into account to compute the free float requirement even if exceeding the 2% threshold. Moreover, this free float requirement does not apply to corporations with shares already admitted to the listing. As far as the majority shareholding requirement, if it is overcome following corporate reorganizations or other particular transactions, the SIIQ regime is suspended until the majority shareholding is brought within the stated limit.

The above shareholding requirements have to be met within the end of the first tax   **15** period for which the SIIQ status is opted, with the application of the special regime from the beginning of such period. If within the end of the first tax period only the free float requirement is fulfilled, the majority shareholding requirement may be fulfilled during the following two tax periods, and the special regime starts to apply from the beginning of the tax period during which the requirement is met; meantime, the SIIQ regime is suspended, with the consequent application of the ordinary tax rules, while the favourable tax regimes of real estate properties step-up following SIIQ status election, contributions and acquisitions are temporarily applied, subject to SIIQ regime enactment.

[B]   Regulatory Authorities

16   SIIQs are subject to the supervision of the Bank of Italy and the Italian National Commission for Listed Companies and the Stock Exchange ('Consob').

17   The SIIQ by-laws define the SIIQ's investment policies, the limits on risks concentration, and the maximum admitted leverage.

[C]   Legislative and Other Regulatory Sources

18   The following are the main legal and tax sources governing the SIIQ:

- Law No. 296, dated 27 December 2006 (as amended by Law No. 244, dated 24 December 2007; Law No. 166, dated 20 November 2009 and lastly by Law Decree No. 133, dated 12 September 2014), introducing the SIIQs.
- Ministerial Decree No. 174, dated 7 September 2007 (the 'Implementing Decree'), defining, in particular, the basic regulatory framework, valuation rules and certain tax provisions.
- Regulations issued by Borsa Italiana S.p.A. (the regulator of the Italian Stock Exchange) relating to listing requirements and procedures for the listing in Italian Exchanges, regularly amended and updated.
- Head of Tax Office's Decision, dated 28 November 2007, providing for regulations governing the exercise of the option for the SIIQ regime and approving the relevant application form.
- Tax Authorities' Circular letter No. 8/E, dated 31 January 2008, providing guidance and clarifications on this regime.
- Tax Authorities' Circular letter No. 32/E, dated 17 September 2015, providing guidance and clarifications, particularly on the amendments introduced by Law Decree No. 133/2014.

19   The EU Directive No. 2011/61/EU on Alternative Investment Fund Managers (AIFMD) has been implemented into the Italian legislation by Legislative Decree No. 44, dated 4 March 2014 (in force from 9 April 2014). In this respect, although the definitions of Alternative Investment Fund (AIF) and of Alternative Investment Fund Manager for the purpose of the Directive seem almost wide and may touch some of the features that also it may have, the SIIQ does not seem to fit such definitions, not being properly, from an Italian perspective, an undertaking for collective investment of saving differently than harmonized Undertakings for Collective Investment in Transferable Securities (UCITS); therefore, the SIIQ should fall out of the scope of the Directive.

In any case, Law Decree No. 133/2014 has removed such doubt, stating that the SIIQ **20** is not an undertaking for the collective investment of saving. As a consequence, the SIIQ unlikely qualifies as an AIF and therefore should not be subject to AIFMD regulations.

[D]   Exchange Controls and Reporting Requirements

SIIQs are subject to the same reporting requirements that apply to all entities listed on **21** Italian Exchanges. Those requirements include *inter alia*:

- the publication, in at least one national journal, of the information necessary for the investors/shareholders to exercise their rights. Such information may include notice of the date and time of the shareholders' meetings and data regarding non-exercised option rights in relation to public offers;
- the communication to Borsa Italiana S.p.A. of any equity change, and detailed information on corporate meetings; and
- notification to the market about the investment performed and the applicable restrictions on investments.

In addition, SIIQs are required to communicate to the market: **22**

- the election for the SIIQ status;
- the failure to maintain the requirements necessary to apply the SIIQ regime and the relevant reasons; and
- the interruption of the SIIQ regime.

[E]   Registration Procedures

[1]   Preparatory Measures

In order to be eligible for SIIQ status, a company should be listed on a stock exchange **23** in the EU or in the EEA. SIINQs do not have to be listed. In Italy, the SIIQ's shares can be listed on the 'Mercato Telematico Azionario' (MTA) market or on the 'Mercato Telematico degli Investment Vehicles' (MIV) market.

In general, the following should be filed for the listing of shares on the Italian Stock **24** Exchanges:

- information related to the issuer, including by-laws, shareholders' resolutions approving the listing, offering circular, curricula of the key managers, rating report (if available);

- information related to the instruments to be issued, including a declaration from the issuer that the instruments are freely transferable, authorizations and resolutions approving the instruments, and the estimated number of investors;
- other financial information, including financial statements, consolidated accounts and audit reports from the past three years;
- memorandum on internal auditing, drafted according to the Borsa Italiana S.p.A. standards and indicating the procedures undertaken in order to limit the market risks;
- the latest financial information eventually requested by Borsa Italiana S.p.A.;
- a business plan for the current year, and for the two following years;
- QMAT (Quotation Management Admission Test);
- memorandum on compliance with the Corporate Governance Code in Italian Listed Companies.

25   The requirements and relevant documentation vary according to the market segment the company's shares are to be listed on. For example, for the listing on MIV of 'Real Estate Investment Companies' (to which SIIQs can be assimilated), there is a 'simplified' procedure (for instance, financial statements and audit reports are required for one year only instead of three; QMAT is not needed).

[2]   Obtaining Authorization

26   If the SIIQ will be listed in Italy, the application for the listing admission should be submitted to Borsa Italiana S.p.A. Within two months from the date of the submission of the request, Borsa Italiana S.p.A. should notify the applicant and Consob of its decision to approve or deny the listing. Borsa Italiana S.p.A. may interrupt the two-month period to make one request for additional information. However, Borsa Italiana S.p.A. has extensive authority over the admission process, with the power to potentially add new requirements during the process.

[3]   Other Requirements for the Incorporation of a Company

27   SIIQ incorporation requirements are similar to those of regular stock corporations, with some very limited specific exceptions. For example, the SIIQ's by-laws have to provide for the yearly distribution of at least 70% (it was 85% until Law Decree No. 133/2014) of the net profit deriving directly or indirectly from the rental business (more generally from the exempt business, with some exceptions).

[4]   Obtaining Listing Exchanges

[a]   Costs

Costs of listing vary based on several circumstances, such as the amount of capital   **28**
raised and the market chosen for listing. The average costs range from EUR 0.8 million
to EUR 2 million. As a temporary tax benefit, small/medium companies (i.e., up to EUR
50 million turnover and 250 employees) which start the listing process and are
admitted to listing in regulated exchanges from 1 January 2018 to 31 December 2020
are granted a tax credit, up to EUR 500,000, equal to 50% of the advisory costs suffered,
in the same period, for the listing (e.g., legal and tax advice, due diligence analyses).
This tax benefit has been extended to 2021 and, finally, to 31 December 2022.
However, for 2022, the tax credit is capped at EUR 200,000.

[b]   Time

The time required to list a SIIQ depends on several factors, including the size and   **29**
complexity of the issuer, the market conditions and how quickly the company provides
the documentation required by Borsa Italiana S.p.A. The listing process is usually
finalized in from five to nine months.

[F]   Requirements and Restrictions

[1]   Capital Requirements

For SIIQs, the minimum market capitalization for the listing is equal to EUR 40 million,   **30**
calculated on the basis of the share price times the number of the outstanding shares
(Borsa Italiana S.p.A. can also admit shares with a lower market capitalization when it
deems that such shares will be sufficiently traded). In addition, a minimum free float
of 25% of the capital is required (for 'Real Estate Investment Companies' listed on
MIV). Different parameters may be provided under specific circumstances.

[2]   Marketing/Advertising

SIIQs are subject to the same marketing regulations as other listed entities. When the   **31**
company seeks to list or to raise equity, it has to issue a *Prospetto informativo*
('prospectus'). The prospectus generally provides details of the business and legal and
financial information on the issuer. The prospectus must be approved by Consob.

In addition, corporations are required to nominate a Sponsor for the listing. The   **32**
functions of the Sponsor include:

- provide Borsa Italiana S.p.A. with all the relevant information for the listing process;
- inform the company management about all the obligations and responsibilities associated with the listing process;
- verify the accuracy of the internal audit reports and assist the issuer with the listing procedure.

[3]   Redemption

33 There is no specific rule regarding the redemption ('*recesso*') of SIIQ shares. General redemption rules for stock corporations set forth the conditions and limits under which redemption of stock corporation shares is allowed. For non-listed corporations, in addition to the general rules, redemption rules may be set out by the company by-laws.

34 Usually, a corporation can purchase its own shares in an amount that does not exceed distributable profits and available reserves, as shown in the last approved financial statement. Also, the purchased shares cannot exceed 10% of the share capital. The share buyback is subject to the approval of the shareholders at the general meeting, and the shareholders may impose limits or restrictions on the buyback.

35 The redemption of shares in a listed corporation must be made by means of an OPA (i.e., public purchase offer) or an OPS (i.e., public exchange offer), or according to the specific procedure agreed with the company managing the relevant Exchange (this rule does not apply to some specific cases of share buybacks from employees of the issuer or of the controlled companies). Reporting requirements have to be fulfilled.

[4]   Valuation of Shares/Units for Redemption and Other Purposes

36 *See* section §1.02[F][3] above.

[5]   Investment Restrictions

37 The SIIQ's prevalent activity has to be the real estate rental activity (performed directly or indirectly through interest in certain qualified entities performing such activity). Real estate rental activity is prevalent if the following tests are met:

- Asset test: at least 80% of the assets are rental real estate properties, held in property or pursuant to other real estate rights, shareholdings in other SIIQs, SIINQs and (pursuant to Law Decree No. 133/2014) units into certain REIFs, booked and held as fixed assets (with particular reference to interests into REIFs, they are relevant only if the REIF is invested for at least 80% in real estate properties and rights for the rental activity, interest in real estate companies and other REIFs carrying on the rental activity, SIIQs and SIINQs).

– Profit test: at least 80% of the SIIQ's annual revenues are derived from the aforementioned assets. For the purpose of this test, SIIQ and SIINQ profits that are paid out as dividends from the exempt business (thus deriving from the real estate rental activities) and qualified REIF profits distributions are included. According to Law Decree No. 133/2014, also capital gains derived from the disposal of real estate properties and real estate rights related to the exempt rental business can be taken into account for the purpose of the profit test.

The asset test excludes (i.e., deducts from both the numerator and denominator of the ratio) buildings used as offices by the SIIQ/SIINQ, trade receivables (including Value Added Tax (VAT) credits) derived from the exempt business, loans granted to other entities of the same group and cash. These assets are excluded because they are not directly or solely related to the exempt business activities or to the taxable business. **38**

For the profit test, variations in the inventory value of rental properties under construction are excluded from the 'annual revenues' (i.e., deducted from both the numerator and denominator of the ratio). **39**

[6]   *Distribution/Accumulation*

SIIQs are required to annually distribute at least 70% (it was 85% until Law Decree No. 133/2014) of the net profit derived from the exempt business, available for distribution. In practice, the distribution requirement applies to the net profit derived from profits from the real estate rental business, profits from shareholdings in related SIIQs and SIINQs, and (following Law Decree No. 133/2014) profits distributed by qualified REIFs. Pursuant to Law Decree No. 133/2014, also capital gains, net of related losses, earned from the disposal of the just mentioned assets related to the exempt business and generating exempt profits (i.e., rental real estate, held in property or under other real estate rights, shareholdings into SIIQs and SIINQs and units into certain REIFs), are subject to compulsory distribution for at least 50% of their amount, over the two years following their earning. **40**

If the accounting net profit available for distribution is lower than the net profit from the exempt business, the compulsory minimum distribution is computed on the lower amount. The difference between the net profit from the exempt business and the accounting net profit available for distribution is deemed earned from the subsequent years' accounting net profit from the taxable businesses, and that profit is subject to the minimum distribution obligation. The same 'compensatory' rule applies in case of a loss from the exempt business, which reduces the accounting net profit of the taxable businesses carried out by the SIIQ. **41**

[7]   Reporting Requirements

42 *See* section §1.02[D] above.

[8]   Accounting

43 As listed companies, SIIQs are required to keep their accounts and prepare their financial statements in compliance with the International Accounting Standards (IAS) and the International Financial Reporting Standards (IFRS). Non-listed companies which have opted for the SIIQ status (i.e., SIINQs) have to fulfil the same obligations.

§1.03   TAXATION

[A]   Taxation of the REIT

[1]   Corporate Income Tax

[a]   Tax Accounting

44 SIIQs and SIINQs have to account separately for income from exempt sources and income from other businesses. There are no other specific tax accounting requirements, and the ordinary rules for stock corporations apply.

45 For SIIQs, any income associated with the rental business activity is exempt from IRES and from regional tax (IRAP). Dividends distributed by other SIIQs and SIINQs are similarly exempt, provided that the dividends represent net profit derived from the exempt business. Also, profit distributions from certain qualified REIFs are exempt.

46 In case the SIIQ regime is applied by permanent establishments of foreign companies, the annual income derived from the rental activity should be subject to a substitute tax of 20%.

47 Taking into consideration the 'prevalence' requirements for assets and revenues (*see* section §1.02[F][5] above), SIIQs may carry on activities other than the real estate rental business. However, these activities are subject to ordinary corporate income taxation.

[b]   Determination of Taxable Income

48 Once opted for the SIIQ status, the two following tax regimes apply:

(1) the exempt regime for the qualifying activity (with the exception of permanent establishments of foreign companies which opted for the SIIQ regime); and

(2) the ordinary tax regime for the other activities.

For IRES purposes, the relevant income, exempt or subject to ordinary taxation **49** according to its source, is computed as the difference between the revenues and the costs associated with each activity (adjusted pursuant to the business income taxation rules, as applicable). Costs not directly attributable to a specific activity should be proportionally allocated between the taxable and exempt income.

Tax losses (net operating losses) derived from the exempt activity cannot be used to **50** offset the profits derived from the taxable activity (except for the case of termination of the SIIQ regime). Regardless of the exemption regime, these losses are deemed to offset profits from the exempt business in the following years, pursuant to the ordinary rules regarding the tax loss carry-forward.

As far as IRAP is concerned, the exemption provided for by the SIIQ regime applies to **51** the value of production (i.e., the IRAP taxable base) derived from the rental business (i.e., exempt business). For this purpose, the exempt portion of the value of production (computed by applying the stated tax adjustments to its accounting value) is equal to the amount corresponding to the ratio between: (a) the revenues derived from the exempt business; and (b) the total amount of revenues. With regard to the determination of the ratio, revenues to be taken into account are only those relevant for the purpose of this tax (e.g., rentals are normally subject to IRAP; for subjects other than banks and other stated financial entities, dividends and REIFs profit distributions are generally excluded from IRAP).

[c]   *Taxation of Income from Taxable/Non-taxable Subsidiaries*

Dividends received from SIIQs or SIINQs, paid out from the exempt profits, are exempt **52** in the hands of the recipient SIIQ when the shares in the distributing SIIQs or SIINQs are held as an investment. Profits distributed by certain qualified REIFs are similarly exempt at the level of the recipient SIIQ.

Other dividends, including dividends from related SIIQs or SIINQs paid out from the **53** taxable profits, are taxable under the general rules. Thus, only 5% of the gross dividends collected are subject to IRES (except for dividends earned from shares held for trading, if any, which are fully taxable). Profits distributed by REIFs which do not fulfil the SIIQ asset test are allocated to the taxable business and fully subject to IRES, pursuant to the ordinary rules.

Dividends received from a taxable or non-taxable subsidiary and profits distributed **54** from a REIF are exempt from IRAP.

[d]   Taxation of Foreign Income

55   Foreign income attributable to the rental business is exempt, while foreign income derived from a taxable business is taxable according to the general rules.

56   An Italian tax credit is allowed for foreign taxes paid on income derived from real estate properties located overseas, even if the taxes relate to exempt real estate activities. Ordinary tax rules apply to determine the amount of the credit, as in the absence of the special regime. The tax credit may be used to offset taxes levied on the income from taxable business in the same tax period.

[2]   Value Added Tax

57   With reference to the rental business, there are no specific VAT rules applicable to SIIQs. Accordingly, SIIQ activities are potentially subject to VAT at the ordinary rate (22%, effective from 1 October 2013). In most cases, rental income and certain building transfers are VAT exempt (i.e., falling in the scope of VAT, but with nil VAT in invoice – as banking and financial operations – and limiting the capacity to recover input VAT on purchases). However, in certain circumstances, the application of ordinary VAT can be elected.

58   Contributions of real estate properties to SIIQs are subject to VAT according to ordinary rules. However, contributions of pluralities of real estate properties, rented for their majority, are deemed to constitute going concerns when contributed to a SIIQ, and they do not result in a VAT cost.

[3]   Withholding Taxes

59   Dividends paid by SIIQs to resident individuals acting in their private capacity are subject to 26% (15% for certain residential rental profits) final WHT when paid out from the exempt profits. A 26% WHT ordinarily also applies to dividends that are paid out from the taxable profit to a resident individual investor. In these cases, no further tax applies on this income at the level of the private individual. Until the end of tax period 2017, the 26% WHT was applicable if the relevant interest did not exceed 2% of the voting rights or 5% of the SIIQ's capital (20% of the voting rights or 25% of the capital in case of distributing SIINQ's) – tested on a twelve-month basis; conversely, if the investor owned more than 2% of voting rights or 5% of capital (respectively, 20% and 25% in case of SIINQ), dividends were included in the global annual taxable income, subject to individual income tax according to the ordinary rules, and no WHT had to be levied. The former regime will temporarily apply to dividend distributions resolved until 31 December 2022 and executed out from profits earned until the tax period 2017. *See* section §1.03[B][1][a] below.

Dividends paid out from the exempt profits to resident individuals acting in their   60
business capacity, domestic partnerships and domestic corporations and Italian permanent establishments of foreign entities are subject to a 26% WHT, creditable at the
level of the recipient against the income tax due. Conversely, dividends paid out from
the taxable profits are not subject to WHT and are taxed according to the general rules.

Dividends paid to SIIQs, Italian pension funds and other stated pension schemes,   61
Italian collective investments vehicles (e.g., mutual funds, REIFs, Società
d'Investimento a Capitale Variabile, Società d'Investimento a Capitale Fisso), and
managed savings accounts subject to the substitute tax regime are not subject to WHT.

Dividends paid out to non-residents from the exempt profits are subject to a 26% final   62
WHT (with the exception set out in the 'Institutional Investors' taxation section). The
WHT rate may be reduced under the respective Double Tax Treaties (DTTs) (see
section §1.03[C][2] below). Conversely, the benefits of the EU Parent-Subsidiary
Directive are not available with regard to dividends paid out from exempt profits.

If taxable profit is distributed to non-residents, dividend distributions are subject to   63
domestic WHT at the rate of 26% (with the exception set out in the 'Institutional
Investors' taxation section), which is partially refundable. Reductions may be obtained
under the applicable DTTs. Distributions of taxable profits earned from 2008 onwards,
made in favour of corporate entities that are resident and subject to tax in countries of
the EU or the EEA included in the Italian white-list (which includes non-tax-haven
countries which have an exchange of information procedures with Italy), are subject to
final WHT at 1.2% (it was 1.375% for distributions of profits earned till 2016). Where
subjective and objective conditions are met, the EU Parent-Subsidiary Directive applies
so that no WHT is deducted.

[4]   Other Taxes

In principle, a 'mortgage-cadastral' tax is due at a rate of 4% on non-residential   64
building transfers and contributions (even if subject to VAT); however, when SIIQs are
even one of the parties of the transaction, the 'mortgage-cadastral' tax applies at the
reduced rate of 2%. Where VAT is not applicable, real estate property transfers may be
subject to registration tax at a rate ranging from 2% to 15% (with a minimum amount
of EUR 1,000), plus mortgage and cadastral taxes due in fixed nominal amounts of EUR
50 each (pursuant to the transfer taxes regime in force from 1 January 2014).
Nevertheless, for contributions of pluralities of real estate properties, rented for their
majority, which fall out of the scope of VAT when contributed to a SIIQ because they
are deemed to constitute going concerns, the other main indirect taxes (i.e., registration
tax, mortgage tax, cadastral tax) are due in fixed nominal amount.

Starting from 1 March 2013, a financial transaction tax (FTT) is applicable to, *inter alia*,   65
transfers of shares and similar instruments issued by Italian companies (with a form of
company limited by shares, S.p.A., and companies unlimited by shares, S.A.p.A.),
except for those issued by listed companies with market capitalization lower than 500

million (reference is made to the average market capitalization of the month of November of the previous calendar year), with some stated exclusions. FTT falls due regardless of the residence of counterparts and the place where the transfer is executed and is equal to 0.2% (0.1% for transfers executed in regulated markets and through multilateral trading systems) of the transfer value. FTT is charged to the transferee, with financial intermediaries acting, apart from stated exceptions, as WHT agents.

[5]   Penalties Imposed on REIT

66   SIIQ status is lost if the company does not meet the investment restriction rules (*see* section §1.02[F][5] above) or the distribution rules (*see* section §1.02[F][6] above). In particular, the SIIQ status is lost retroactively to the start of the year in which the asset and the profit tests are both failed, or as of the start of the second year of the three-year period during which one of the tests is not consecutively met (before Law Decree No. 133/2014, the 'grace' period was only two consecutive years). Likewise, failure to comply with the distribution requirement implies the loss of the SIIQ status from the start of the year to which the non-distributed profit refers. Normal tax rules will then apply to the income realized by the company.

67   Once the SIIQ status is lost, any available tax loss associated with the exempt activity may be carried forward and used to offset the taxable income according to the ordinary rules.

68   Administrative tax penalties and criminal penalties may apply to SIIQs and their employees or directors in the same manner that the penalties apply to other taxpayers.

[B]   Taxation of the Investor

[1]   Private Investors

[a]   Taxation of Current Income (i.e., All Income Derived from REIT in Holding Phase)

69   Dividends received from the participation in SIIQs are subject to different tax regimes depending on whether the dividend is a distribution of profits relating to the exempt business or whether the dividend represents a distribution of profits relating to the taxable business (*see also* §1.03[A][3] above).

Dividends Distributed out of the Taxable Income

70   Dividends distributed out of the taxable income, including dividends from pre-SIIQ status, are treated as ordinary dividends. Such taxable income distributed to resident individual shareholders, acting in their private capacity, is subject to a 26% final WHT. Until the end of the tax period 2017, the 26% final WHT was applicable if the relevant interest did not exceed 2% of the voting rights or 5% of the SIIQ's capital (20% of the voting rights or 25% of the capital in case of distributing SIINQ's) – tested on a twelve-month basis; conversely, dividends distributed to more than 2% voting owners or more than 5% capital owners (in case of SIINQs, respectively, 20% and 25%) were subject to ordinary individual income tax with a 41.86% exemption (applicable for tax periods with IRES at 24%) and no WHT had to be levied. The former regime will temporarily apply to dividend distributions resolved until 31 December 2022 and executed out from profits earned until the tax period 2017.

Dividends distributed to resident individual investors acting in their business capacity   **71** are included in the investor's business income and taxed accordingly, regardless of the percentage of their interest, also benefiting from a 41.86% exemption (for tax periods from 2008 to 2016, with profits subjected to IRES at 27.5%, the dividends exempt portion amounts to 50.28%).

Dividends of taxable income distributed to non-residents are subject to final WHT at a   **72** rate of 26% (partially refundable). Reductions may be obtained under DTTs.

Dividends Distributed out of Exempt Income

Dividends of exempt income distributed by the SIIQ to individuals acting in their   **73** private capacity are subject to a 26% final WHT (15% for certain residential rental profits). No further income taxation applies at the level of the individual shareholders.

Dividends of exempt income collected by resident individual shareholders acting in   **74** their business capacity are fully included in their business income (no dividend exemption applies) and taxed accordingly at individual income tax rates. The 26% WHT applied at the source upon the dividends distribution may be credited against the income tax due.

Dividends of exempt income paid by SIIQs to non-residents are taxed in Italy by way of   **75** the 26% final WHT. Reductions may be obtained under DTTs (with regard to the application of DTTs, *see* section §1.03[A][3] above).

[b]   *Taxation of Capital Gains (From Disposal of REIT Shares)*

Capital gains realized by resident individual investors, acting in their private capacity,   **76** are subject to a 26% substitute tax, regardless of the interest held in the SIIQ or SIINQs (this tax regime applies from 1 January 2019; earlier, it was stated for investor's interest not exceeding 2% of the voting rights or 5% of the capital of a listed company, like the SIIQ – 20% of the voting rights or 25% of the capital of a non-listed company, like the SIINQ – tested on a twelve-month basis; otherwise, capital gains were subject to individual income tax at the progressive income tax rates of up to 43%, increased by local surcharges).

77 Capital gains realized by resident individual shareholders acting in their business capacity should be fully included in their business income (no participation exemption applies) and taxed accordingly; that is, they are subject to individual income tax.

78 Foreign individuals are generally treated similarly to resident private individuals; as a result, their capital gains are subject to a 26% substitute tax. However, in case the interest in the SIIQ does not exceed 2% of the voting rights or 5% of the SIIQ's capital – tested on a twelve-month basis – capital gains are exempt pursuant to domestic rule (they are considered as realized out of the Italian territory). For SIINQs, if the interest does not exceed 20% of the voting rights or 25% of the capital, capital gains may be exempt for residents in the white-listed countries (i.e., countries with exchange of information procedures with Italy). Otherwise, if the above thresholds are overcome, as said capital gains derived by foreign individuals are subject to the 26% substitute tax (this tax regime applies from 1 January 2019; earlier, the capital gains from substantial interests were taxed according to the individual income tax rates of up to 43%, without benefiting from any participation exemption). In any case, DTTs should be available to reduce Italian taxation.

[2] Institutional Investors

[a] *Taxation of Current Income (i.e., All Income Derived from REIT in Holding Phase)*

Dividends Distributed out of Taxable Income

79 Resident corporate shareholders and Italian permanent establishments of foreign entities benefit from a 95% dividend exemption. Therefore, only 5% of the gross dividends received are subject to IRES at a rate of 24% (from the tax period 2017, Italian banks and financial institutions, different from assets and investments management companies, and Italian branches of similar foreign institutions are subject to a corporate tax surcharge of 3.5%). However, the 95% dividend exemption does not apply to dividends collected on shares held for trading by entities drawing-up their financial statements under IAS/IFRS. As a general rule, dividends are not subject to the regional tax (IRAP), except for banks and certain other financial institutions, for which 50% of dividends are included in the taxable base of IRAP which, for such entities and with effect from 2011, applies at a rate ranging from 4.65% to 5.57% (from 5.90% to 6.82% for insurance companies, but the taxable amount varies according to the purpose of the investment).

80 Dividends of taxable income distributed to non-resident institutional investors (without a permanent establishment in the Italian territory) are subject to final WHT at source at a rate of 26% (which may be partially refundable). However, distributions of profits earned from 2008 onwards, made to corporate entities, resident and subject to tax in countries of the EU or of the EEA and included in the Italian white-list, are subject to a 1.2% final WHT (it was 1.375% for distributions of profits earned till 2016). Where subjective and objective conditions are met, DTTs, if more favourable, and the EU Parent-Subsidiary Directive apply. However, pursuant to Law No. 178, dated 30 December 2020, from 2021, dividends distributed to foreign investment funds compliant with Directive 2009/65/EC, dated 13 July 2009, and other investment funds whose manager is regulated in compliance with Directive 2011/61/UE, dated 8 June 2011, based in countries of EU and EEA, have become exempt from Italian WHT.

Dividends Distributed out of Exempt Income

Dividends of exempt income collected by resident companies and Italian permanent **81** establishments of foreign entities are fully subject to IRES at a rate of 24% (plus the 3.5% surcharge, when applicable – no dividend exemption applies). The 26% WHT, levied as advance payment upon dividends distribution, is creditable against IRES. Dividends are generally IRAP exempt. For banks and certain other financial entities, 50% of dividends are included in the IRAP taxable base and subject to taxation at a rate which, for such entities and with effect from 2011, ranges from 4.65% to 5.57% (from 5.90% to 6.82% for insurance companies, but the taxable amount varies according to the purpose of the investment).

Dividends paid by SIIQs to non-residents (without a permanent establishment in the **82** Italian territory) are subject to Italian final WHT at a rate of 26%. The WHT rate may be reduced under the applicable DTTs. The benefits of the EU Parent-Subsidiary Directive are not available. However, pursuant to Law No. 178, dated 30 December 2020, from 2021, dividends distributed to foreign investment funds compliant with Directive 2009/65/EC, dated 13 July 2009, and other investment funds whose manager is regulated in compliance with Directive 2011/61/UE, dated 8 June 2011, based in countries of EU and EEA, have become exempt from Italian WHT. This should also apply to dividends distributed under the SIIQ regime.

Dividends Paid to Italian Mutual, Private Equity, Hedge or Other Funds

Dividends paid to Italian mutual, private equity, alternative, pension and real estate **83** funds are included in the fund's profit, which is taxable:

- for pension funds, at fund level through a substitute tax applied to the Net Assets Value annual increase at a rate of 20%;
- for other funds, upon fund profit distribution to unitholders, by way of WHT at a rate of 26%; however, some exemptions or reductions exist.

Due to these specific tax treatments, dividends paid to Italian funds are not subject to **84** WHT at source.

[b]   *Taxation of Capital Gains (From Disposal of REIT Shares)*

85   Capital gains on disposal of SIIQ shares realized by resident companies and Italian permanent establishments of foreign entities are fully subject to IRES at a rate of 24% (from the tax period 2017, Italian banks and financial institutions, different from assets and investments management companies, and Italian branches of similar foreign institutions are subject to a corporate tax surcharge of 3.5% – participation exemption does not apply).

86   As far as IRAP is concerned, capital gains derived from financial instruments are generally exempt for industrial and commercial entities and for certain financial subjects. Conversely, for banks and certain other financial entities, these capital gains are included in the IRAP taxable base and subject to taxation at a rate which, for such entities, ranges from 4.65% to 5.57%, with some exceptions (from 5.90% to 6.82% for insurance companies, but the application of IRAP depends on the purpose of the investment).

87   Foreign investors (other than individuals) without a permanent establishment in the Italian territory are generally treated the same as resident private individuals; as a result, their capital gains are subject to the 26% substitute tax. In case the interest in the SIIQ does not exceed 2% of the voting rights or 5% of the SIIQ's capital – tested on a twelve-month basis – capital gains are exempt pursuant to domestic rule (they are considered as realized out of the Italian territory); for SIINQs, if the interest does not exceed 20% of the voting rights or 25% of the capital, capital gains may be exempt for foreign entities resident in the white-listed countries. Otherwise, if the above thresholds are overcome, as said capital gains are subject to the 26% substitute tax (this tax regime applies from 1 January 2019; earlier, the capital gains from substantial interests were taxed at the standard rate of 24% provided for corporate entities). In any case, DTTs may be available to reduce Italian taxation. However, pursuant to Law No. 178, dated 30 December 2020, from 2021, capital gain from Italian shares disposal earned by foreign investment funds compliant with Directive 2009/65/EC, dated 13 July 2009, and other investment funds whose manager is regulated in compliance with Directive 2011/61/UE, dated 8 June 2011, based in countries of EU and EEA, have become exempt from Italian taxation. This should also apply in the case of SIIQ shares.

88   With regard to Italian pension funds and mutual, private equity, alternative or other funds (including REIFs), capital gains are taxed similarly to ordinary income (20%, 26% or nil).

[3]   Penalties Imposed on Investors

89   SIIQ investors may be penalized for violations of the investor's own tax obligations or in case of fraud or false declarations rendered to the WHT agent.

[C]   Tax Treaties

[1]   Treaty Access

Italy has a large Treaty network. Whether a SIIQ is eligible for Treaty relief is ultimately   **90**
dependent on the particular Treaty and the source country. Although a portion of the
SIIQ income is tax exempt, the foreign source country may consider the SIIQ as an
Italian resident person for Treaty purposes, therefore 'liable to tax' therein and eligible
for Treaty relief. However, no specific guidance has been provided on the matter.

[2]   WHT Reduction

WHT reductions under DTTs concluded by Italy apply to SIIQs' profit distributions,   **91**
paid out not only from the taxable profits but also from the exempt profits, as
confirmed by Law Decree No. 133/2014.

[D]   Exit Tax/Tax Privileges/Concessions

Upon transition to the SIIQ status, all the real estate properties and real estate rights   **92**
related to the exempt business are valued at fair market value ('*valore normale*', to be
intended as a *fair value* according to the rules provided by the applicable IAS/IFRS).
The built-in gains, net of corresponding losses, are deemed to be realized and may be
subject to a substitute tax of 20% ('entry tax'), with a correspondent step-up to the fair
market value of the assets, which is relevant for tax purposes after three years. The
substitute tax may apply in lieu of IRES and IRAP and may be paid, with interest (i.e.,
European Central Bank reference rate increased by 1%), in equal instalments over five
years. The stepped-up values are recognized for tax purposes starting from the fourth
tax period under the SIIQ status; if one or more assets are disposed of before, the net
built-in gains, reduced by depreciation accrued during the SIIQ regime period and
computed on the tax values before the transition, are subject to ordinary taxation, and
the corresponding entry tax paid is creditable against the ordinary taxes due.

In-kind contributions to a SIIQ may benefit from a favourable tax treatment in the   **93**
hands of the contributing subject, provided that the SIIQ retains the assets for at least
three years. In particular, the capital gain realized upon the contribution of real estate
properties and real estate rights to SIIQs (and to SIINQs) may be taxed according to the
ordinary income tax rules or through a 20% substitute tax payable, with interest, over
five years in equal instalments.

In most cases, contributions to SIIQs of pluralities of real estate properties, rented for   **94**
their majority, should not be subject to other material tax costs other than the
above-mentioned taxation in the hands of the contributing entity: these contributions

are outside the scope of VAT; registration tax, mortgage tax and cadastral tax are due on a lump sum basis.

[E]   Taxation of Foreign REITs

[1]   *Taxation of Foreign REIT Holding Assets in Country*

95   A foreign REIT is subject to income tax in Italy on income sourced in the Italian territory. Income is sourced in the Italian territory if the real estate is located therein.

96   Rental income derived by non-resident entities without a permanent establishment within the Italian territory is subject to IRES at 24%, even if such rentals are not actually collected (with some exceptions). A reduction of 5% of the taxable rents is applicable as a flat deduction for expenses related to the rental income. Rental income is not subject to IRAP.

97   If a permanent establishment is created, ordinary business income taxation rules apply. The taxable base is generally determined according to the actual costs and revenues (within limits and under the conditions provided for by the business income taxation rules) relating to the business carried out through the Italian permanent establishment (e.g., depreciation, maintenance expenses, interest expenses, administration expenses, indirect taxes, etc.), and is subject to IRES and IRAP. However, income from residential properties may be taxed, as in the case of the absence of a permanent establishment.

[2]   *Taxation of Investors Holding Shares in Foreign REIT*

98   The Italian tax treatment of income derived from investments in a foreign REIT depends on the tax qualification of such income. If the investment in the foreign REIT qualifies as an investment in an ordinary corporation, income derived from REIT distributions and capital gains realized upon REIT interest disposal are taxable in Italy under the ordinary rules.

Japan

HIROSHI TAKAGI

Hiroshi Takagi is a tax partner at PwC Japan. Hiroshi joined PwC in 2001, and he specializes in J-REIT and real estate investment funds. He has extensive experience assisting offshore investors (including Luxembourg and Singapore funds and Australian listed property trusts) in investing in Japanese real estate using *Tokumei Kumiai* (TK) and *Tokutei Mokuteki Kaisha* (TMK) structures.

Hiroshi graduated from the University of Tokyo and the University of Chicago, and he is a Certified Public Accountant in Japan and the US, as well as a licensed tax accountant in Japan.

E-mail: hiroshi.takagi@pwc.com

ADAM HANDLER

Adam Handler is a tax partner with PwC's Tokyo office, where he specializes in structuring inbound real estate investments. Adam has over thirty-seven years of experience in the real estate industry, including transactions involving REITs, partnerships, sovereign wealth funds, fund structuring and investments, and public companies.

Prior to joining PwC in Tokyo, Adam spent twenty years as a principal with PwC in the United States, where he was the leader of its real estate tax consulting practice in its Washington National Tax Service.

Education

He graduated from Yale University with a Bachelor of Chemistry, *summa cum laude*, and he is a Phi Beta Kappa society member with a distinction in Chemistry.
He obtained J.D. from Stanford Law School.

Bar Memberships

He is a member of the State Bar of California, US District Court for the Central District of California, and US Tax Court.
E-mail: adam.m.handler@pwc.com

TOMOHIRO KANDORI

Tomohiro Kandori has extensive experience in both domestic and cross-border finance transactions. His practice focuses mainly on real estate finance and asset finance. He has advised clients on a wide variety of transactions including real estate acquisition, development, and sale, as well as investment into and financing of real properties in Japan. He has represented domestic and foreign investors, including investment funds, financial institutions, investment managers, and developers from the United States, Europe and Asia. He has also represented lenders in numerous structured finance transactions and in restructuring distressed investment projects.

Prior to joining PwC Legal Japan, Tomohiro worked for more than fifteen years at one of the largest law firms in Japan. He also worked as in-house counsel for a global financial institution at its London branch.

He received his LLB from the University of Tokyo and his LLM from the School of Law, University of California, Berkeley.

He is a member of the Dai-ichi Tokyo Bar Association (2002).

E-mail: tomohiro.kandori@pwc.com

Japan

Hiroshi Takagi, Adam Handler & Tomohiro Kandori

---

§1.01   BACKGROUND

[A]   Key Characteristics

Japanese real estate investment trusts and investment corporations (J-REITs) are   **1**
formed under the Law Concerning Investment Trusts and Investment Corporations
(ITL) to manage investments in specified assets, including real estate. J-REITs are
usually formed as investment corporations and are taxable entities. However, under
special tax measures for J-REITs, a qualifying J-REIT is entitled to a tax deduction for
dividends paid provided that it meets certain statutory requirements, including a
requirement to annually distribute more than 90% of its distributable profit for
accounting purposes. In this chapter, the terms 'J-REIT' and 'investment corporation'
are used interchangeably.

[B]   History of REITs

In September 2001, the first two J-REITs, the Nippon Building Fund Inc. and Japan Real   **2**
Estate Investment Corporation, were listed. As of March 2021, sixty-one J-REITs were
listed on Japanese stock exchanges, with a total market capitalization of approximately
JPY 16.35 trillion. There are also thirty-eight private Real Estate Investment Trusts
(REITs) with a total market capitalization of approximately JPY 2. 46 trillion.

[C]   REIT Market

The J-REIT has been a remarkable success. With ready access to funding from capital   **3**
markets and from non-recourse lending, J-REITs have transformed the Japanese real
estate market.

4   As of March 2021, the Nikkei Average is 29,178, and the Tokyo Stock Exchange (TSE) REIT Index, which is a capitalization-weighted index of all REITs listed on the TSE, is 2,013. Currently, the REIT market in Japan is doing well, but the COVID-19 pandemic is still causing uncertainty and changing the investment environment.

§1.02   REGULATORY ASPECTS

[A]   Legal Form of REITs

[1]   Corporate Form

5   Under the ITL, there are two different types of J-REIT investment vehicles: investment trusts and investment corporations. To date, all listed J-REITs have been formed as investment corporations.

6   An investment corporation is a corporation established primarily to make investments in specified assets, such as real estate and trust beneficiary interests in real estate (*see* section §1.02[F][5] below).

7   Investment corporations issue units similar to shares in ordinary corporations. Holders of the units are called unitholders. Unitholders hold general meetings to select executive officers and auditors. The executive officers conduct the operations of the investment corporation. The auditors investigate the operations conducted by the executive officers. A board of officers monitors the execution of duties by the executive officers and has the authority to dismiss executive officers under certain circumstances.

8   Since investment corporations are merely investment vehicles, they are not permitted to engage in any business other than asset management. Accordingly, investment corporations are prohibited from establishing an office other than a head office or retaining employees. An investment corporation is required to outsource to external entities the following functions:

   (a) *The management of assets.* Investment corporations must delegate the management of their assets to a licensed third-party asset management corporation.
   (b) *The custody of assets.* Investment corporations must delegate the custody of their assets to a third-party custodian corporation that meets the qualifications set forth in the ITL.
   (c) *Other administrative functions.* Investment corporations must delegate other administrative functions to third parties, including:
   - the offering of units or bonds;
   - changes in the register of holders of units or bonds;
   - issuance of certificates representing units or bonds;
   - administration of its organization;

- accounting matters; and
- other matters, as provided in the relevant ordinance.

[2]   Investment Restrictions

There are no restrictions applying to investors in a J-REIT under the ITL. However, the   9
tax law provides conditions regarding the unitholders in a J-REIT that need to be
satisfied in order for the J-REIT to qualify for dividend deductibility. These conditions
are outlined below in section §1.03[A][1][b][i]. In addition, in order for a J-REIT to be
listed, the J-REIT must have a minimum number of investors (at least thousand
unitholders), and the ten largest investors may not together hold more than 75% of the
units.

The investment restrictions applicable to a J-REIT are described in section §1.02[F][5]   10
below.

[B]   Regulatory Authorities

An asset management company is required to obtain two licences from the Ministry of   11
Land, Infrastructure, Transport and Tourism (discussed below). In addition, an asset
management company is required to obtain approval from the Financial Service
Agency (FSA) for registration as a discretionary investment manager under Financial
Instruments Exchange Law (FIEL). A J-REIT is subject to ITL rules, compliance with
which is monitored by the FSA. If a J-REIT lists its units on the TSE, it is required to
comply with the J-REIT listing rules, compliance with which is monitored by the TSE.
Further, if the J-REIT's asset management company is a member of the Investment
Trust Association, it must comply with the Investment Trust Association Rules, the
compliance with which is monitored by the Investment Trust Association.

[C]   Legislative and Other Regulatory Sources

The organization and operation of a J-REIT are generally subject to the following laws   12
and regulations:

- ITL.
- Enforcement Orders of the ITL.
- Enforcement Regulations of the ITL.
- Regulations Concerning the Calculation of Investment Corporations.
- Regulations Concerning the Audit of Investment Corporations.
- FIEL and Regulations thereunder.

If a J-REIT is listed on the TSE, it must comply with the J-REIT listing rules. Under the   13
J-REIT listing rules, the J-REIT's asset management company is required to be a

member of the Investment Trust Association and be subject to the Investment Trust Association rules. The Investment Trust Association Rules concerning REITs and real estate investment corporations cover J-REITs that invest more than half of their assets in real property or asset-backed securities primarily invested in real property.

[D] Exchange Controls and Reporting Requirements

14 A J-REIT that lists its units on the TSE is required to disclose the same information that other listed companies are required to disclose. That information includes the following.

[1] Information Regarding Closing of Accounts

15
- annual financial report (*kessan-tanshin*);
- semi-annual financial report (*chukan-kessan-tanshin*);
- information regarding amendments to the forecasted profit; and
- information regarding amendments to the forecasted distributions.

[2] Information Regarding Investment Corporations

16
- decisions concerning the issue and sale of additional units, unit splits or amalgamations of units;
- the receipt of orders to improve operations; and
- information regarding the asset manager.

[3] Information Regarding Changes in the Level of the Assets under Management

17
- transfers or purchases of assets with a price of JPY 50 million or more as of the end of the latest fiscal period;
- losses equivalent to 3% or more of net assets as of the end of the latest fiscal period as a result of natural disaster/damage; and
- expected profit or loss that differs from the original forecast for the period announced pursuant to the rules of the TSE by 30% or more, or expected distributions that differ from the original forecast by 5% or more.

18 Investment corporations are also required to report on their management and operation.

[E] Registration Procedures

[1] Preparatory Measures

The asset management company is required to obtain a 'Building Lots and Building **19** Transactions Agent License' and a 'Discretionary Transaction Agent License' from the Ministry of Land, Infrastructure, Transport and Tourism. After obtaining these licences, the asset management company must obtain approval from the FSA for registration as a discretionary investment manager under the FIEL. Subsequently, the asset management company may commence incorporating a J-REIT, as described in the next section.

[2] Obtaining Authorization

To establish an investment corporation, an establishment planner, which is generally **20** an asset management company itself, is required to prepare 'by-laws' of the investment corporation, and the planner files the by-laws with the Prime Minister. Once these by-laws have been filed, the investment corporation can issue units to investors.

Upon the issuing of units, the initial unitholders will be informed of the J-REIT **21** executive officer and auditor candidates. These candidates are deemed to be appointed upon the completion of the initial allocation of units. Payment of the investment amount is confirmed by the executive officer at the establishment. The investment corporation is then established by registration, which must occur within two weeks of either the confirmation process being finished or, if convened, a general meeting upon establishment being finished, whichever is later. Once the registration is complete, the investment corporation obtains corporate status. Moreover, to commence its investment activities, the investment corporation must be registered with the relevant local finance bureau of the Ministry of Finance (MoF).

[3] Other Requirements for the Incorporation of a Company

There are no other special requirements for establishing an investment corporation. **22**

[4] Obtaining Listing Exchanges

[a] Costs

The costs associated with establishment and listing depend on several factors, such as **23** the listing exchange and the size of the investment corporation. As a general rule, asset management companies should allow about 5% of funds raised.

[b]   *Time*

24 The time required to establish and list a J-REIT will vary. As a general rule, however, the asset management companies should allow at least one year.

[F]   Requirements and Restrictions

[1]   *Capital Requirements*

25 The minimum share capital of a J-REIT under the ITL is JPY 100 million. Neither the ITL nor tax law provides a leverage limit. However, to qualify for dividend deductibility, borrowings are only allowed from institutional investors (as defined in section §1.03[A][1][b][2]), such as banks and securities companies.

26 Investment corporations are required to maintain a minimum amount of net assets at all times. The minimum amount is set out in the investment corporation's by-laws and must be JPY 50 million or more.

27 Investment corporations are required to promptly notify the director of the relevant local finance bureau of the MoF if their net assets are likely to fall below JPY 100 million. If an investment corporation's net assets fall below JPY 50 million, and they do not recover within a period of three months or more, then, after giving notice to the investment corporation, the director of the relevant local finance bureau of the MoF must revoke the investment corporation's registration.

28 An investment corporation is not permitted to make a distribution to its investors if such distribution would cause its net assets to fall below JPY 100 million.

[2]   *Marketing/Advertising*

29 A listed J-REIT is required to issue an offering document when it seeks to list or raise equity. The offering document sets forth the terms on which an interest in the J-REIT is offered. The offering document provides information on the J-REIT, its business plan and proposed assets and also contains various expert reports and projected financial information. The offering document must be lodged with the TSE or relevant exchange and the FSA.

[3]   *Redemption*

30 Under the ITL, J-REITs may be either open-end or closed-end. Unitholders of an open-end J-REIT are able to require that their units be redeemed at a predetermined price at fixed intervals. Unitholders of a closed-end J-REIT cannot require that their units be redeemed.

[4]   *Valuation of Shares/Units for Redemption and Other Purposes*

To date, all existing listed J-REITs are closed-end funds in the form of investment   **31**
corporations, and unitholders are not entitled to redeem their units.

[5]   *Investment Restrictions*

A J-REIT must invest primarily in specified assets as defined in the ITL. Specified assets   **32**
include but are not limited to securities, real property, leaseholds of real property,
chijo-ken (surface rights), trust beneficiary interests for securities or real property,
leaseholds of land, renewable energy facilities and concessions for public facilities.

Pursuant to the ITL, investment corporations may not enter into transactions that   **33**
obligate the corporation to develop land for housing or to construct buildings.

A J-REIT that lists its units on the TSE may only make investments permitted by the   **34**
TSE's J-REIT listing rules. In this regard, permitted investments include real estate-
related assets, cash and cash equivalents. Real estate-related assets include, but are not
limited to, real estate, trust beneficiary interests for real estate, leaseholds of real
property, leaseholds of land, surface rights and underground rights.

[6]   *Distribution/Accumulation*

A J-REIT must maintain minimum capital requirements as set out in §1.02[F][1] above,   **35**
and it cannot distribute cash or assets if such distribution would cause the J-REIT to
breach those restrictions.

A J-REIT is required to establish a unitholders' capital surplus if: **36**

- the unitholders' capital and capital surplus used for any redemption exceeds
  the total redemption amount for the units; or
- the assumed assets of the non-surviving investment corporation upon a
  merger exceed the amount specified in accordance with the Accounting Rules
  for Investment Corporations.

Under current Corporate Tax Law, a J-REIT must distribute more than 90% of its   **37**
distributable profit for accounting purposes in order to deduct dividends paid to
investors. This requirement is discussed in further detail in section §1.03[A][1][b]
below.

[7]   Reporting Requirements

38   A J-REIT is required to disclose its financial position and operating performance under the FIEL and ITL. For the reporting requirements under the J-REIT listing rules, *see* section §1.02[D] above.

39   Under the FIEL, units of a J-REIT are defined as securities. Accordingly, if the issuance or sale of units of a J-REIT falls under the category of public offering (*boshu*) or public sale (*uridashi*), as defined in Article 2 of the FIEL, the J-REIT is subject to disclosure requirements that apply to primary market transactions and must submit a Security Registration Statement and a Prospectus.

40   If a J-REIT lists its units on the stock market, it is also subject to secondary market disclosure requirements, meaning that it must prepare and disclose an annual report, interim reports, quarterly reports and any extraordinary reports.

41   Under the ITL, a J-REIT must prepare and disclose the following documents:

- balance sheet;
- profit and loss statement;
- asset management report;
- dividend distribution statement; and
- statement of details of accounting documents.

[8]   Accounting

42   A J-REIT is required to prepare financial statements in accordance with the Japanese Regulations Concerning the Calculation of Investment Corporations for each operating period.

§1.03   TAXATION

[A]   Taxation of the REIT

[1]   Corporate Income Tax

[a]   Tax Accounting

43   As noted above, a J-REIT may be structured as either an investment corporation or an investment trust. J-REITs are generally formed as investment corporations. The majority of J-REITs are currently listed. Therefore, this chapter focuses only on the tax treatment for an investment corporation that is listed.

44   Currently, the effective corporate tax rate is approximately 31.46%; however, additional factors can increase the total tax rate to approximately 35%.

As the intended purpose of a J-REIT is to act as an investment and management vehicle **45**
for real estate investments, special rules apply.

A summary of the special rules that apply to J-REITs is outlined in sections **46**
§1.03[A][1][b]; §1.03[A][1][c] and §1.03[A][1][d] below.

[b]   *Determination of Taxable Income*

Dividend Deductibility

The Special Taxation Measures Law (STML) provides that where the following **47**
requirements are satisfied, J-REIT dividends are deductible for corporate tax purposes.

In order to deduct dividends, the J-REIT must satisfy the following requirements: **48**

(1) The J-REIT must be registered under Article 187 of the ITL.
(2) One of the following requirements must be satisfied:
    (a) a public offering of JPY 100 million or more was made at the time of establishment; or
    (b) the units of the J-REIT are held by fifty or more investors at the end of each fiscal period, or 100% of the units of the J-REIT are held by institutional investors ('Institutional Investors') prescribed under Articles 67–15, paragraph 1 of STML.
(3) The offer for investment in the units of the J-REIT must have been made mainly in the domestic market (i.e., the articles of incorporation of the J-REIT must provide that more than 50% of the total outstanding units of the J-REIT have been offered in the domestic market).
(4) The J-REIT must have an accounting period of one year or less.
(5) The J-REIT must not engage in any business other than asset management, must not open any place of business other than its head office and must not hire any employees.
(6) The J-REIT must have outsourced the management of its business to an asset management corporation.
(7) The J-REIT must have outsourced custody of the assets to a custodian.
(8) The J-REIT must not be treated as a family corporation at the end of the fiscal year (a family corporation is defined as a corporation in which a single individual or corporate unitholder (including its related parties) holds 50% or more of the units or certain voting rights of the J-REIT).
(9) The J-REIT must distribute to its unitholders more than 90% of its distributable profit for accounting purposes ('Distributable Profit').

(10) The J-REIT must not hold 50% or more of the equity of another corporation (including *tokumei-kumiai* (TK) contributions). In determining the percentage, shares in corporations held indirectly through TK must be included.[1]

(11) The value of specified assets listed in Article 2(1) of the ITL excluding renewable energy facilities and concessions for public facilities must be more than 50% of the J-REIT's total asset value.

(12) The J-REIT must not have obtained loans from parties other than Institutional Investors.

Special Tax Measures

49 In calculating the taxable income of a J-REIT, certain tax rules that would otherwise apply to a normal corporation are modified under the STML as follows.

Non-application of Dividend Exclusion Rule

50 Generally, a dividend received by a corporation from a domestic corporation (less interest expense attributed to borrowings used to finance the acquisition of the shares in respect of which the dividend was paid) is partly or fully excluded from the recipient corporation's taxable income, provided that the recipient corporation satisfies certain ownership provisions. This rule does not apply to dividends received from a J-REIT; J-REIT dividends do not qualify for exclusion.

Non-application of Reduced Tax Rate for Medium or Small Size Corporations

51 A corporation whose stated capital is JPY 100 million or less at the end of the fiscal year is classified as a medium or small size corporation. Such a corporation is subject to a reduced rate of national tax on its first JPY 8 million of taxable income. However, this reduced rate of tax is not applicable to a J-REIT.

Allowance of Foreign Tax Credits

52 In general, a domestic corporation is entitled to claim a foreign tax credit for foreign taxes paid on its foreign source income, subject to statutory limitations or, under certain circumstances, to exclude dividends from foreign companies from income under Japan's version of the participation exemption.

53 Neither the direct foreign tax credit system nor the participation exemption is available for a J-REIT. Foreign income tax directly paid by a J-REIT is creditable against withholding income taxes imposed on dividends paid by the J-REIT. The amount of credit is limited to the withholding income tax imposed on the dividend.

---

1. Based on a revision of the ITL, a J-REIT can now hold 50% or more of the shares in a foreign special purpose company holding real estate located outside of Japan.

Modifications to the STML

 (a) Special treatment of bad debt reserve for medium or small size corpora- **54**
   tions: For the purposes of calculating the statutory limitation of its bad debt
   reserve, medium and small size corporations may use special rates. These
   rates cannot be used by a J-REIT.
 (b) Non-deductibility of entertainment expenses: Corporations may claim a
   deduction for entertainment expenses, subject to certain limits. A J-REIT
   cannot claim any deduction for entertainment expenses.

 [c] Taxation of Income from Taxable/Non-taxable Subsidiaries

Dividends received by a J-REIT from a taxable or non-taxable domestic corporation are **55**
included in its taxable income and subject to tax.

 [d] Taxation of Foreign Income

Foreign sourced income derived by a J-REIT is included in the taxable income of the **56**
J-REIT. Foreign taxes paid directly by a J-REIT are creditable at the J-REIT investor
level. The amount of the credit cannot exceed the withholding tax liability attributable
to the foreign source income imposed on the dividends distributed by a J-REIT to its
unitholders.

 *[2] **Value Added Tax***

Consumption tax, which is similar to the European Value Added Tax, is generally **57**
imposed on the sale of goods and services in Japan. The consumption tax rate is
currently 10%. An invoicing method will be introduced, although not until 1 April
2023, with transitional measures in place for the three-year and six months' interim.

A Japanese corporation may claim a credit for consumption tax paid depending on its **58**
taxable sales ratio (broadly, the ratio of taxable sales to the sum of taxable sales and
non-taxable sales). The input tax credit is determined based on the percentage using
either the determined taxable revenue method or the attributable method.

The term 'taxable sales' includes rental income from office, commercial and retail **59**
buildings and proceeds from the sale of buildings. The term 'non-taxable sales', in
contrast, includes rental income from residential buildings, proceeds from the sale of
land and interest income.

Any consumption tax paid that is not creditable or refundable is typically deducted in **60**
the fiscal year in which the consumption tax was paid. In the case of a building
acquisition with a taxable sales ratio of less than 80%, the consumption tax paid is
added to the acquisition cost of the building and depreciated over the building's useful

life or accounted for as a deferred consumption tax expense and depreciated over sixty months.

[3]   Withholding Taxes

61   Generally, dividends paid by a J-REIT to its unitholders are subject to withholding tax which must be paid to the relevant tax offices on or before the tenth day of the month following the month of the payment of dividends. *See* section §1.03[B] below for detail.

[4]   Other Taxes

[a]   Acquisition Tax

62   An acquisition tax is imposed upon the acquisition of 'real estate' (defined in local tax law to mean both land and buildings). The tax applies to the acquisition of legal title to real estate, but it does not apply to the acquisition of a trust beneficiary interest in real estate. Acquisition tax will be reduced for a J-REIT if it satisfies certain requirements.

[b]   Registration Tax

63   Registration tax is imposed upon the registration of title to newly acquired real property.

64   According to current practice, it is common for real estate assets to be entrusted. The transfer of a trust beneficiary interest is not characterized as a transfer of the underlying property. Rather, the registration tax rate for the transfer of trust interests (a nominal amount) is applied. Registration tax will be reduced for a J-REIT if it satisfies certain requirements.

[c]   Fixed Assets Tax and Depreciable Assets Tax

65   Land and buildings are subject to a fixed assets tax. Fixed assets tax is imposed on an owner of land and buildings in Japan as of 1 January each year.

66   Depreciable assets are subject to a depreciable assets tax. Depreciable assets are business assets other than land and buildings and include necessary expenses incurred for purchase or acquisition. Each year corporations that own depreciable assets as of 1 January need to file the details of those assets based on the fixed assets ledger by 31 January of that year and make instalment payments for the tax.

[d]   *Business Office Tax*

The twenty-three wards of Tokyo ('Tokyo city'), Osaka city, Nagoya city and certain   **67**
other cities levy business office tax, comprising of a floor space levy and an employee
salary amount levy.

The tax is calculated by self-assessment and paid to the appropriate local tax office in   **68**
the ward in which the principal place of business is located within two months from the
end of the accounting year.

[e]   *Inhabitants Tax*

A J-REIT is subject to inhabitants' equalization tax generally ranging from JPY 70,000   **69**
to JPY 1,210,000 annually, depending on its capital amount. The inhabitants' equalization tax is paid when the corporate tax return is filed, two months after the end of
the fiscal period.

[5]   Penalties Imposed on REIT

If a J-REIT fails to file its tax return or to pay its tax liability by the due date, the J-REIT   **70**
will be subject to a penalty and interest.

[B]   Taxation of the Investor

[1]   Private Investors

[a]   *Taxation of Current Income (i.e., All Income Derived from REIT in*
       Holding Phase)

Japanese Residents

In general, withholding tax is imposed on dividends paid by a J-REIT to Japanese   **71**
individual unitholders and non-Japanese individual unitholders with a permanent
establishment in Japan ('Japanese Individual Investors'). The tax rate is 20%, including a local tax of 5%.

Under the Specific Restoration Tax Law, a Restoration Surtax of 2.1% will be added to   **72**
the withholding tax, thus raising the withholding tax rate from 20.0% to 20.315%. This
Restoration Surtax applies to dividend payments for the period from 1 January 2013
through 31 December 2037. Japan has dividend deduction rules whereby a Japanese
Individual may claim a deduction equal to 6.4% to 12.8% of dividends received. These
rules, however, do not apply to dividends paid by a J-REIT.

73   For income tax purposes, Japanese Individual Investors have the following options:[2]

   (i) Aggregated method: the Japanese Individual Investor aggregates the J-REIT dividend with his or her other income and is subject to income tax at graduated rates. Under the aggregated method, Japanese Individual Investors can credit in full any withholding taxes against their income tax due.

   (ii) Non-reporting method: the Japanese Individual Investor does not report the income on his or her tax return. In this case, the withholding tax is a final tax.

   (iii) Separate tax assessment method: a system of separate taxation whereby capital loss from the transfer of units in a listed J-REIT can be utilized to offset dividend income arising from listed shares, and the balance is taxed at a rate of 20.315% (including the local portion of 5%).

   (iv) NISA (*Nihon* Individual Savings Account) method: dividend income arising from listed shares held in an Exempt Account[3] will be exempted from income tax for five years. To qualify: (a) the Exempt Account must be opened between 1 January 2014 and 31 December 2023; and (b) the acquisition cost of the listed shares held in the Exempt Account is JPY 1.2 million or less per year in total (i.e., the total acquisition cost is capped at JPY 6 million). From 2024, NISA method will be modified and a new method will start.

   (v) Junior NISA (Junior *Nihon* Individual Savings Account) method: dividend income arising from listed shares held in a Junior Exempt Account[4] will be exempted from income tax for five years. To qualify: (a) the Junior Exempt Account must be opened between 1 April 2016 and 31 December 2023; and (b) the acquisition cost of the listed shares held in the account is JPY 0.8 million or less per year in total (i.e., the total acquisition cost is capped at JPY 4 million).

74   Dividends paid to Japanese corporate unitholders and foreign corporate unitholders with a permanent establishment in Japan ('Japanese Corporate Investors') are subject to 15.315% withholding tax. A portion of such withholding tax is creditable against corporate tax payable or, if the amount exceeds the tax due, refundable. The dividend exclusion rule does not apply to dividends paid by a J-REIT (*see* section §1.03[A][1][b][i]).

---

2. Methods listed in paras (ii), (iii), (iv) and (v) do not apply for individuals whose ownership in a J-REIT is 3% or more.
3. The Exempt Account could be opened by a person at least 20 years of age (from 1 Jan. 2023, the account may be opened by a person who will be at least 18 years of age) at the beginning of the year who is a resident of Japan.
4. The Junior Exempt Account could be opened by a person who is under 20 years ago (from 1 Jan. 2023, the account may be opened by a person who will be 18 years of age) at the beginning of the year.

Non-Japanese Residents

Dividends paid to a non-resident unitholder without a permanent establishment in **75** Japan ('Non-resident Investors') are subject to withholding tax. Dividends paid to Non-resident Investors are subject to withholding tax at a rate of 15.315%. This withholding tax rate may be reduced or exempted under applicable tax treaties (*see* section §1.03[C][2] below).

Dividends in Excess of Income

A J-REIT is permitted to make dividend payments in excess of its income ('Excess **76** Payments').[5] The Excess Payments received by unitholders reduce capital without retiring units. Any amount of the Excess Payment which is in excess of the amount equivalent to the reduced capital is deemed a dividend ('Deemed Dividend') and is subject to the same tax treatment as other dividends.

The amount of the Excess Payment after deducting the Deemed Dividend is deemed **77** proceeds on the sale of units. The unitholders should calculate the cost on the sale corresponding to these proceeds. If there is a difference between the revenue and the cost, the unitholders are subject to the same tax treatment on the difference as described in section §1.03[B][1][b] below.

[b]   Taxation of Capital Gains (From Disposal of REIT Units)

Japanese Residents

For Japanese Individual Investors, gains from the sale of units in a J-REIT are treated **78** as 'separate income' and subject to Japanese capital gains tax at a rate of 20% (including the local portion of 5%). Losses from the sale of units in a listed J-REIT can be used to offset gains from the sale of other listed shares derived in the same period. If the losses are greater than the gains in a certain period, the excess portion can be carried forward for the subsequent three years provided certain administrative procedures are followed. In addition, the losses may be used to offset dividend income arising from listed shares, provided that the Japanese Individual Investors elect separate tax assessment as described in section §1.03[B][1][a] above. Where the Japanese Individual Investors elect the NISA method or Junior NISA method, gains from the sale of the listed shares will be exempted from income tax, as described in section §1.03[B][1][a] above. Under the Specific Restoration Tax Law, restoration surtax at a rate of 2.1% on the withholding tax will be withheld from the capital gains for the period from 1 January 2013 through 31 December 2037.

---

5. Under reforms passed in 2015, surplus cash distributions will continue to be treated as profit distributions for tax purposes and accounted for as 'allowance for temporary difference adjustment'.

79   If the unitholder is a Japanese Corporate Investor, capital gains or losses on the disposal of the J-REIT units are included in taxable income and subject to Japanese corporate taxes at normal rates.

Non-Japanese Residents

80   Generally, capital gains arising from the disposal of units in a corporation held by Non-resident Investors are not subject to Japanese income tax unless the corporation is classified as a real estate holding company (REHC).

81   A J-REIT will be classified as a REHC if 50% or more of its gross asset value represents real estate in Japan.

82   The disposal of units in a REHC by Non-resident Investors is subject to capital gains tax if the Non-resident Investor owns more than 5% (in the case of a listed corporation or trust), or more than 2% (in the case of a non-listed corporation or trust) of the units in the REHC as of the end of the fiscal year immediately prior to the year in which the transfer occurs.

83   When determining share ownership, it should be noted that aggregation rules apply. Thus, if the transferor owned units with a group of specially related persons, or through a *Kumiai* (partnership), the 2% and 5% thresholds must be analysed based on the aggregate ownership percentages of the group of specially related persons or the total number of units owned by the *Kumiai*.

84   Consequently, units transferred by Non-resident Investors who hold more than 5% of the J-REIT units as of the testing date should be subject to Japanese capital gains tax. In such case, Non-resident Investors in a J-REIT will need to file a Japanese income or corporation tax return and will be subject to tax at 15.315% (including a 2.1% restoration surtax on income tax from 1 January 2013 through 2037) (for individuals) or 25.59% for fiscal periods beginning on or after 1 October 2019 (for corporate entities) on the capital gain.

[2]   Institutional Investors

[a]   Taxation of Current Income (i.e., All Income Derived from REIT in Holding Phase)

85   There is no special tax treatment for J-REIT dividends to Institutional Investors under Japanese Tax Law. Accordingly, an Institutional Investor is taxed in the same manner as a private investor, as discussed in section §1.03[B][1][a] above. Certain treaties, however, provide reduced rates (or exemptions) for pension funds on J-REIT dividends.

[b]   Taxation of Capital Gains (From Disposal of REIT Units)

There is no special tax treatment for Institutional Investors on capital gains under   **86**
Japanese Tax Law. Accordingly, an Institutional Investor is taxed in the same way as
private investors in respect to capital gains from the disposal of J-REIT units as
discussed in section §1.03[B][1][b] above.

[3]   Penalties Imposed on Investors

If investors fail to meet the filing deadline for a tax return for dividend and capital gain   **87**
or fail to pay the tax liability by the due date, a penalty and interest are imposed.

[C]   Tax Treaties

[1]   Treaty Access

Japan has a large treaty network. Whether a J-REIT is eligible for treaty relief is   **88**
ultimately dependent on the particular treaty.

As of 1 January 2022, Japan had concluded treaties with a number of countries,   **89**
including Australia, Austria, Belgium, Canada, Denmark, Finland, France, Germany,
Ireland, Italy, Korea, Luxembourg, the Netherlands, New Zealand, the People's
Republic of China, Singapore, Spain, Sweden, Switzerland, the United Kingdom, and
the United States.

[2]   WHT Reduction

If certain conditions are met under the applicable tax treaty, a reduced withholding tax   **90**
rate can apply to dividends paid by a J-REIT. It should be noted that to take advantage
of the reduced withholding tax rate, non-resident investors have to file the relevant
treaty forms with the J-REIT for filing with the appropriate tax office prior to the day of
payment.

[D]   Exit Tax/Tax Privileges/Concessions

There are no specific exit tax concessions for the disposal of units in a J-REIT. The   **91**
treatment of capital gains arising from J-REIT unit transfer is discussed in section
§1.03[B][1][b] above.

[E] Taxation of Foreign REITs

[1] *Taxation of Foreign REIT Holding Assets in Country*

92 A foreign REIT will be subject to corporate tax in Japan in respect of rental income derived from Japanese real estate, and a foreign REIT will pay capital gains tax on the disposal of Japanese real estate. The rate of corporate tax depends on the nature of the REIT. The effective tax rate for a foreign company with a permanent establishment in Japan is currently approximately 31.46%; however, additional factors can increase the effective tax rate to approximately 35%. But if it is a foreign company that does not have a permanent establishment in Japan, the tax will generally be 25.59% for fiscal periods beginning on or after 1 October 2019.

[2] *Taxation of Investors Holding Shares in Foreign REIT*

93 Japanese investors holding units in a foreign REIT are taxed in Japan on the dividends from the REIT and on any capital gains realized on the disposal of REIT units.

Malaysia

JENNIFER CHANG

Jennifer Chang is a partner in the Tax–Financial Services division of PwC Malaysia. Jennifer's experience includes advising clients on tax matters relating to income tax, real property gains tax, stamp duty, service tax, applicable tax incentives, double tax treaties as well as structured finance and international tax. She works with industry players in the financial services industry and has been involved in numerous presentations and has often done lobbying for tax incentives on financial services products and clients, including unit trust and fund management, closed-end funds, REITs, securities borrowing and lending, bonds, offshore banking, leasing, Islamic Finance and so on. She is a regular speaker at public seminars on the taxation of the financial services industry, including Islamic banking, asset-backed securitization, REITs, international tax and Labuan.
E-mail: jennifer.chang@pwc.com

Malaysia

Jennifer Chang

§1.01 BACKGROUND

[A] Key Characteristics of REIT

Real Estate Investment Trusts (REITs) listed on Bursa Malaysia are not taxable (i.e., **1** they have a 'flow through' tax status or tax transparency status) provided they meet certain requirements. Where a listed REIT distributes at least 90% of its income, the tax transparency rules will apply so that tax will not be levied at the REIT level. A REIT that is not listed on Bursa Malaysia would not enjoy the above tax transparency treatment.

Malaysian REITs can be sector-specific (e.g., industrial, offices, etc.) or diversified **2** funds. In this report, the term 'REIT' is used for listed and unlisted REITs as well as for Islamic and conventional REITs.

[B] History of REIT

The first property trust fund (PTF) was listed on the Kuala Lumpur Stock Exchange **3** (KLSE) in 1989. In 1997, four PTFs were listed on the KLSE. However, restrictive regulations made these PTFs unpopular with institutional investors. They did not provide for tax transparency, they were subject to Malaysian thin trading volume, and only bank-owned managers were allowed to manage the PTFs.

In early 2005, Malaysia liberalized its PTF framework. PTFs were renamed 'REITs', a **4** more globally adopted term. The new legislation granted tax transparency status to the REIT and liberalized the REIT's borrowing limit to 35% of its asset value. Existing PTFs at that time underwent rebranding exercises to convert to the REIT status and to operate under the new regulations.

Pursuant to the legislative amendments in 2007, the REIT's borrowing limit was **5** increased from 35% to 50% of its asset value and fine-tuning of the tax transparency system was accorded to REITs. Moreover, more favourable withholding tax rates were provided for certain types of investors.

6 The favourable legislative changes led to an increasing number of REITs listed on the Malaysian stock exchange.

7 On 15 March 2018, the Securities Commissions (SCs) of Malaysia issued new guidelines (Guidelines) on REITs and listed REITs to set out requirements for proposal in relation to the listing and quotation of units of a conventional or Islamic REIT on the Main Market of Bursa Securities. In the case of listed REITs, these Guidelines supersede all requirements in previous guidelines issued on REITs and Islamic REITs.

[C]   REIT Market

8 With the average size of Malaysian REITs reaching USD 450 million (MYR 1,400 million), the Malaysian REIT market is small compared to other regional REIT markets like Singapore or Australia, but its breadth and depth continue to develop with the recent and potential progress in the sector. As of 31 December 2021, the biggest REIT in Malaysia is the KLCC REIT which was listed on the main board of Bursa Malaysia in May 2013 and with assets worth approximately USD 4.3 billion (MYR 18 billion) as of December 2021 (audited). With the listing of KLCC REIT in May 2013, Malaysia's largest REIT by asset size, the yield gap between Malaysian REIT and Singapore REIT is expected to narrow down. Continued growth of the REIT market in Malaysia can be attributed to the recent relaxation of the property sector rules and regulations.

9 Historically, REITs have produced an annual income yield of between 4% and 8%. Apart from distributions, REITs have also offered an opportunity for capital growth, with listed REITs performing similar to the wider share market (with less volatility).

10 As of 31 December 2021, Malaysia has eighteen REITs listed on the stock exchange with a total market value of over USD 9.19 billion (MYR 38.44 billion).

§1.02   REGULATORY ASPECTS

[A]   Legal Form of REIT

[1]   Corporate Form

11 Malaysian REIT/PTFs are trusts governed by general trust law. A trust is not a separate legal entity or person. It is a set of obligations accepted by a person (the trustee) in relation to the property (the trust property), in which such obligations are exercised for the benefit of another person (the beneficiary). The obligations of the trustee and the rights of the beneficiaries are typically set out in writing in the trust deed. In addition, the trustee has a legal duty to act in the best interests of beneficiaries, to act honestly and to exercise the same prudence and diligence as an ordinary person would exercise in carrying on their own business.

Malaysian REIT/PTFs are similar to that of a unit trust; that is, all income and capital **12** entitlements of the trust are fixed in accordance with the trust deed, and those entitlements are unitized. Income and capital entitlements of a beneficiary (or unitholder) are determined by reference to the number of units they hold and the rights attached to those units per the trust deed. Similar to a shareholder's liability in a company, a unitholder's liability is also limited, although the law is not explicit on this.

Malaysian REITs are managed by management companies that have to be approved by **13** the SC. The trustee of a Malaysian REIT holds the real estate or properties in a REIT portfolio in trust for the REIT investors.

[2]   *Investment Restrictions*

Approvals from the Economic Planning Unit (EPU) will be required for the following **14** situations:

- – Direct acquisitions of property valued at MYR 20 million and above, resulting in the dilution of Bumiputera interests in the property.
- – Direct acquisitions of property valued at MYR 20 million and above, resulting in the dilution of Government agency in the property.
- – Indirect acquisitions of property by non-Bumiputera interest through the acquisition of shares, resulting in a change of control of a company owned by Bumiputera interest and/or Government agency. This is on the basis that the property held by the company is more than 50% of its total assets, and the property is valued more than MYR 20 million.

Acquisitions which are subject to EPU approval may also be subject to the equity and **15** paid-up capital conditions.

The following type of acquisitions by foreign interest falls under the purview of other **16** relevant Ministries and/or Government Departments:

(a) acquisition of commercial unit valued at MYR 1,000,000 and above;
(b) acquisition of agricultural land valued at MYR 1,000,000 and above or at least five acres in area for the following purposes:
    (i) to undertake agricultural activities on a commercial scale using modern or high technology; or
    (ii) to undertake agro-tourism projects; or
    (iii) to undertake agricultural or agro-based industrial activities for the production of goods for export.
(c) acquisition of industrial land valued at MYR 1,000,000 and above; and

(d) transfer of property to a foreigner based on family ties is only allowed among immediate family members.

[B]   Regulatory Authorities

17 REITs in Malaysia are principally governed by the SC of Malaysia.

[C]   Legislative and Other Regulatory Sources

18 The principal legislation governing the establishment and operation of REITs is the Companies Act of 2016 and the SC Act of 1993, and the Guidelines on REITs and Guidelines for Islamic REIT issued by SC.

[D]   Exchange Controls and Reporting Requirements

19 Non-residents are now free to purchase any ringgit assets and free to repatriate funds from divestments in ringgit assets or profits/dividends arising from the investments. Repatriation, however, must be in a foreign currency other than the currency of Israel.

20 A management company of a listed REIT is expected to prepare an annual report that provides all necessary information to enable unitholders to evaluate the performance of the fund. The report has to contain at least the following:

- fund information;
- report on fund performance;
- manager's report;
- trustee's report;
- Shariah adviser's report (where applicable);
- audited financial statements for the accounting period; and
- auditor's report.

21 The REIT has to notify the SC of specific events, including:

(a) appointment and resignation of directors;
(b) appointment and resignation of chief executive officer;
(c) appointment and resignation of an investment committee member, if any;
(d) appointment and resignation of the Shariah adviser;
(e) appointment of a delegate that is a holder of a Capital Markets Services Licence;
(f) appointment and resignation of the property manager and any delegates;
(g) acquisition of real estates;
(h) disposal of real estates;
(i) foreign markets in which the fund invests in;

(j) a resolution passed (and court confirming where applicable) to terminate/wind up a fund; and

(k) completion of the termination/winding up of a fund.

[E]   Registration Procedures

[1]   Preparatory Measures

To establish a REIT, an application must be made to the SC. Generally, after a   **22**
pre-submission consultation, the applicant submits a property asset valuation to the SC, followed by a complete REIT application and upfront fees. The SC expects a full and complete submission from the applicant. The SC has three months to consider the REIT's submission. Incomplete submissions may cause delays in the application process or can even cause the submission to be returned. Should the applicant receive a favourable response, the applicant is then required to submit an executed trust deed, the registrable REIT prospectus and relevant fees for further processing to the SC.

When successfully registered, the applicant can proceed to list on Bursa Malaysia (the   **23**
stock exchange).

[2]   Obtaining Authorization

In order to obtain the REIT status, the REIT must be registered with the SC. Submis-   **24**
sions required to be made to the SC for registration, lodgement and/or delivery purposes include:

(a) registration and lodgement of deed and supplementary deed of the fund;

(b) registration and lodgement of prospectus and supplementary prospectus of the fund;

(c) lodgement of annual report of the fund and the management company;

(d) delivery of interim report of the fund;

(e) delivery of statistical and compliance returns;

(f) delivery of notices issued or published after the registration of a prospectus;

(g) deposit of information memorandum for excluded offers; and

(h) any other documents as prescribed by the SC from time to time.

[3]   Other Requirements for the Incorporation of a Company

Under the Guidelines, a REIT must be managed and administered by a management   **25**
company approved by the SC under the SC Act, 1993. The management company must:

(a) be an entity incorporated in Malaysia;

(b) (except where the management company is licensed by the SC) be a subsidiary of:
  - a company involved in the financial services industry in Malaysia;
  - a property development company;
  - a property investment holding company; or
  - any other institution which the SC may permit.

(c) have a minimum of 30% local equity; and

(d) be funded with a minimum shareholders' funds of MYR 1 million at all times.

26   The REIT must also appoint a trustee that is approved by the SC. The trustee must:

(a) be a trust company registered under the Trust Companies Act 1949 or incorporated under the Public Trust Corporation Act 1995;

(b) be registered with the SC; and

(c) have a minimum issued and paid-up capital of not less than MYR 500,000.

[4]   Obtaining Listing Exchanges

[a]   Costs

27   Costs associated with a listing will depend on several factors, such as whether the associated capital raising is underwritten or not.

[b]   Time

28   The time required to list a trust will also depend on several factors, including the size and complexity of the transaction, the state of the market, and how quickly funds are received from investors. As a general rule though, REITs should allow for at least six months for a listing.

[F]   Requirements and Restrictions

[1]   Capital Requirements

29   The initial minimum size of a REIT shall be USD 119.63 million (MYR 5 00 million). The prior approval of the trustee and the SC are required for any subsequent issuance/offering of new units of the fund. A listed REIT is required to undertake offering to the general public. Any expenses incurred relating to an offer for sale of units shall be borne by the offeror.

30   The SC has capped a local REIT's gearing at 50%. This means that REITs can only borrow up to half of their total assets.

A trustee of a REIT must have adequate resources, including financial and human **31** resources, to carry on the business of a trustee. In this regard, the REIT Guidelines dictate that the trustee:

(a) must have a minimum issued and paid-up capital of not less than MYR 500,000;
(b) must have adequate human resources with the necessary qualifications, experience and expertise to carry on business as a trustee to REIT; and
(c) must have adequate and appropriate systems, procedures and processes, to carry out its duties and responsibilities in a proper and efficient manner.

[2]   Marketing/Advertising

A listed REIT is required to issue a prospectus when it seeks to list or raise equity. The **32** prospectus sets out the terms of the transaction, provides information as to the REIT and includes various experts' reports, financial information and information on the real estate owned by the trust. The prospectus must be lodged with the SC and Bursa Malaysia.

[3]   Redemption

Listed REITs in Malaysia can be bought and sold on Bursa Malaysia (i.e., the stock **33** exchange) like listed stocks, and investors need to go through a stockbroker to invest in them. Like any listed products on the Exchange, investors should be aware that REITs may trade at a premium or discount to their respective net asset values. Subject to the interest of the unitholders as prescribed by the relevant securities laws, guidelines and rules, buyback by a REIT of its own units is not allowed.

Unlisted REITs in Malaysia, like any other unit trust products, can be bought from or **34** sold to the management company or through other authorized agents. Generally, REITs in Malaysia are structured as closed-end funds, and investors do not normally have the right to require the REIT to redeem investors' interests (in contrast to open-ended mutual funds and unit trusts). Depending on provisions in the trust deed and the prospectus of the REIT, redemption or limited redemption of units in an unlisted REIT is possible.

[4]   Valuation of Shares/Units for Redemption and Other Purposes

Listed REITs are generally valued at their quoted price on the stock exchange. **35**

For unlisted REITs, after the initial offer period, the price of a unit is the Net Assets **36** Value per unit of the fund as at the next valuation point after the request for sale or repurchase of units is received by the management company (forward price).

[5]   *Investment Restrictions*

[a]   *REIT*

37   A REIT may only invest in real estate, single-purpose companies, real estate-related assets, non-real estate-related assets and cash, deposits and money market instruments.

38   At least 50% of the fund's total asset value must be invested in real estate and/or single-purpose companies at all times. The fund's investment in non-real estate-related assets and/or cash, deposits and money market instruments must not exceed 25% of the fund's total asset value.

39   A REIT is prohibited from being involved in the following activities:

(a) Extension of loans or any other credit facilities.
(b) Property development (this restriction does not apply to refurbishment, retrofitting, renovations and extensions carried out on existing real estate within the fund's investment portfolio).
(c) Acquisition of vacant land.

[b]   *Listed REIT*

40   A listed REIT may only invest in real estate, non-real estate-related assets and cash, deposits and money market instruments.

41   At least 75% of the fund's total asset value must be invested in real estate at all times.

42   A listed REIT may also invest in real estate through a lease arrangement, provided that the management company ensure the following:

(a) where the lease relates to a real estate located in Malaysia, the lease must be registered with the land authority;
(b) where the lease relates to a real estate located outside Malaysia, the lease must be registered or recognized by the relevant land authority under a land registry framework equivalent to that of Malaysia;
(c) the listed REIT has the relevant rights, interests and benefits (including the right to sublease) related to the listed REIT's interests as a lessee of the real estate;
(d) the total value of an investment through a lease arrangement, where the real estate having a remaining lease period of less than thirty years must not exceed 25% of the listed REIT's total asset value at the point of listing or acquisition, as the case may be; and

(e) the interests of unitholders of the listed REIT are protected with respect to the risk relating to the listed REIT not being the registered proprietor of the real estate. Legal opinion must be obtained for this purpose.

A listed REIT may invest in real estate where it does not have majority ownership and **43** control provided that the total value of this real estate does not exceed 25% of the listed REIT's total asset value at the point of listing or acquisition and it is in the best interest of unitholders.

A REIT may invest in real estate under construction, provided that: **44**

(a) the arrangement or agreement to acquire the real estate under construction is made subject to the completion of the building with sufficient cover for construction risks;

(b) the arrangement or agreement to acquire the real estate under construction must be on terms which are best available for the REIT and which are no less favourable to the REIT than an arm's-length transaction between independent parties; and

(c) the prospects for the real estate to be acquired upon its completion are reasonably expected to be favourable.

The aggregate investments in property development activities (Property Development **45** Costs) and real estate under construction must not exceed 15% of the REIT's total asset value.

[6]   *Borrowings or Financing Facilities*

A REIT may issue debt securities or Sukuk through a wholly owned special purpose **46** vehicle. Total borrowings of a REIT should not exceed 50% of total asset value.

A REIT may acquire real estate located outside Malaysia subject to the approval of the **47** SC.

[7]   *Distribution/Accumulation*

In order to maintain tax transparency status and to ensure that the trustee is not subject **48** to tax on the listed REIT's taxable income, the listed REIT must distribute at least 90% of its total taxable income at the end of the year of assessment (YA). A REIT may not accumulate a reserve. A REIT which is not listed will not enjoy the tax transparency regime even if it distributes more than 90% of its total income.

[8]   Reporting Requirements

49 The reporting requirements for REITs are detailed in the REIT Guidelines. Broadly, a REIT is required to lodge its annual report with the SC, and where the REIT is listed, it must meet Bursa Malaysia's reporting requirements.

[9]   Accounting

50 A REIT is required to prepare annual audited financial statements in accordance with approved accounting standards. Listed REITs are also required to prepare an interim financial statement which, like the annual audited financial statements, has to be submitted to the SC within two months after the closing period.

§1.03   TAXATION

[A]   Taxation of the REIT

[1]   Corporate Income Tax

[a]   Tax Accounting

51 The Inland Revenue Board of Malaysia has issued Public Rulings in relation to REIT as follows:

- Public Ruling No. 5/2017 'Taxation of Real Estate Investment Trusts/Property Trust Funds'.
- Public Ruling No. 8/2012 'Real Estate Investment Trusts/Property Trust Funds – An Overview'.

52 A listed REIT's income is not to be taxed at the REIT level, provided that at least 90% of its total taxable income is distributed to its investors. If the REIT distributes less than 90% of its total taxable income, the REIT is subject to corporate income tax on its total taxable income. The regular corporate income tax rate is currently at 24%.

53 Since REITs are considered to be unit trusts, certain income is exempt from tax, including interest or discount from the following investments:

(a) any savings certificates issued by the Government;
(b) securities or bonds issued or guaranteed by the Government;
(c) debentures, other than convertible loan stocks, approved by the SC;
(d) Bon Simpanan Malaysia issued by Bank Negara Malaysia;
(e) a bank or financial institution licensed under the Banking and Financial Institutions Act 1989 or Islamic Banking Act 1983; and

(f) bonds and securities issued by Pengurusan Danaharta Nasional Berhad.

The income exempted at the REIT level is also exempt from tax upon distribution to unitholders.   **54**

[b]   *Determination of Taxable Income*

Generally, the taxable income of the REIT consists of rental income, interest (other than   **55**
the interest which is exempt from income tax) and other investment income derived
from or accruing in Malaysia. Rental income from the letting of real property is treated
as business income, and expenses incurred wholly and exclusively in the production of
such gross rental income are deductible against business income. Business deductions
can include management fees, interest and taxes, and the REIT manager's remuneration. Fees paid to the trustee do not qualify for tax deduction. Any business expenses
in excess of business income cannot be carried forward, and they cannot be offset
against other sources of income.

Expenses incurred to set up an entity are not allowed as a tax deduction as these   **56**
expenses are regarded as pre-commencement expenses. However, as an incentive, the
Income Tax (Deduction for Establishment Expenditure of REIT or PTF) Rules 2006
provide that the legal, valuation and consultancy fees incurred for the purpose of
establishing a REIT which is subsequently approved by the SC will be allowed as a tax
deduction when the business of the REIT commences. Costs of obtaining financing
(other than interest), including legal costs and stamp duty on new loan transactions,
are also generally not deductible. Specific tax deductions are given for financing costs
incurred in relation to the issuance of certain Islamic Securities/bonds up to YA 2010.
This incentive has been extended up to YA 2025.

Accounting depreciation of land and buildings does not qualify for a tax deduction.   **57**
Where a building can be classified as an industrial building (e.g., factory, warehouse,
etc.), and it is used for business or is leased to a tenant who uses the premises as an
industrial building, a capital allowance known as Industrial Building Allowance (IBA)
can be claimed against the business or rental income of the building owner. Generally,
the initial allowance is 10%, and the annual allowance is 3% of the building cost. A
REIT that rents out its building will only qualify for IBA if the tenant uses the building
like an industrial building.

The following buildings leased out would not qualify for IBA: **58**

- private hospital;
- nursing home;
- research;
- warehouse for export and imported goods;
- approved service projects;
- hotels;

- airports;
- motor racing circuits;
- school;
- education institution; or
- living accommodation for individuals.

59 Capital allowances may be claimed on qualifying capital expenditures incurred on plant and equipment used in a business of letting property. The initial allowance is 20%, and the annual allowance varies depending on the type of plant and equipment used. The annual allowance rates are as follows:

Office equipment	10%
Furniture and fittings	10%
General plant and machinery	14%
Heavy machinery (including commercial vehicles)	20%
Environmental protection equipment	20%
Computer and information technology assets	20%
Motor vehicles (private passenger car type[1])	20%

60 Expenditure on assets with a life span of not more than two years is allowed on a replacement basis. Certain plants and equipment are eligible for accelerated capital allowances.

61 Capital allowances will be available on qualifying capital expenditures of the REIT. However, any unabsorbed capital allowance for a given YA cannot be carried forward as a deduction against future rental income.

Transfer Pricing

62 The Director General of Inland Revenue is empowered to make adjustments to transactions of goods and services between associated persons, including related companies. The transfer pricing audit framework has been issued by the tax authorities to ensure that controlled transactions comply with the arm's-length principle, the Malaysian tax laws as well as administrative requirements. If any understatement or omission of income is discovered during the transfer pricing audit, a penalty will be imposed. However, a concessionary penalty rate may be imposed in a case where a voluntary disclosure was made.

---

1. Motor vehicles excluding motor vehicles licensed for commercial transportation of goods or passengers are subject to a restriction on the maximum qualifying expenditure:
    (a) new vehicles purchased on or after 28 Oct. 2000 where on-the-road price is MYR 150,000 or less subject to a maximum qualifying expenditure of MYR 100,000; and
    (b) vehicles other than the above is subject to a maximum qualifying expenditure of MYR 50,000.

Taxpayers have to prepare contemporaneous Transfer Pricing Documentation (i.e.,   **63**
either at the point of developing the inter-company transaction or prior to the
submission of the company's tax return). The Detailed Transfer Pricing Rules 2012 and
Advanced Pricing Arrangement Guidelines 2012 were issued on 20 July 2012.

Real Property Gains Tax

Any gains on disposal of real properties or shares in real property companies would be   **64**
subject to the following real property gains tax (RPGT) rates:

Date of Disposal	RPGT Rates		
	Companies Incorporated in Malaysia	Individuals (Citizen & Permanent Resident)	Individual (Non-citizen & Non-permanent Resident) and Companies Not Incorporated in Malaysia
Within three years from the date of acquisition	30%	30%	30%
In the 4th year	20%	20%	30%
In the 5th year	15%	15%	30%
In the 6th year and subsequent years	10%	5% (*)	10%

* RPGT rate reduced to 0% with effect from 1 January 2022.

Where the disposal of property is by a property owner to a REIT approved by the SC,   **65**
exemptions from RPGT and stamp duty have been provided for. This exemption
applies only to acquisitions of properties by an approved REIT. Where the approved
REIT subsequently sells properties, the RPGT and stamp duty exemption would not
apply.

[c]   Taxation of Income from Taxable/Non-taxable Subsidiaries

The tax on a company's profits is a final tax, and the dividends distributed to its   **66**
shareholders are exempt from tax. This would mean that where the dividends received
from a Malaysian Company are single-tier dividends or tax-exempt dividends, no
further tax will be payable by the REIT. Due to tax transparency, single-tier dividend
income or tax-exempt dividend income earned by the REIT will retain its character
when distributed to unitholders so that no withholding tax should apply when it is
distributed to the investors.

[d]   *Taxation of Foreign Income*

67   Prior to 1 January 2022, foreign sourced income earned by a REIT is exempted in Malaysia. With effect from 1 January 2022, the exemption of foreign-sourced income received in Malaysia is only applicable to a person who is a non-resident.

The Ministry of Finance announced on 30 December 2021 that subject to conditions, which will be set out in guidelines to be issued by the Inland Revenue Board (IRB), the following foreign-sourced income received from 1 January 2022 to 31 December 2026 (5 years) will continue to be exempted from Malaysian income tax:

- Dividend income received by resident companies and limited liability partnerships. [currently, it is not clear if REITs would be included under this category].
- All classes of income received by resident individuals, except for resident individuals which carry on business through a partnership.

Pending further clarification from the IRB, this would mean that foreign-sourced income (e.g., dividends, interest, etc.) of a REIT which is received in Malaysia will be subject to tax.

There will be a transitional period from 1 January 2022 to 30 June 2022 where foreign-sourced income remitted to Malaysia will be taxed at the rate of 3% on gross income. From 1 July 2022 onwards, any foreign-sourced income remitted to Malaysia will be subject to Malaysian income tax at the rate of 24%.

Such income from foreign investments may be subject to taxes or withholding taxes in the specific foreign country. The REIT in Malaysia may be entitled for double taxation relief on any foreign tax suffered on the income in respect of overseas investment where the REIT is also subject to tax in Malaysia.

[2]   Goods and Services Tax

68   Effective from 1 September 2018, the Goods and Services Tax has been repealed and replaced by the Sales and Services Tax. Income received by REITs (i.e., rental income, interest income and dividend income) will not be subject to service tax, while expenses incurred by the REIT such as management fees, trustee fees and other administrative and operating expenses will be subject to 6% service tax.

[3]   Withholding Taxes

69   Payments made to non-residents that are deemed to be derived in Malaysia (e.g., interest, royalties, services, contract payments and rental on moveable properties) are subject to withholding tax in Malaysia at the following prescribed rates:

(a) Interest, 15%.

(b) Royalty, 10%.
(c) Contract Payments, 10% + 3%.
(d) Rental, 10%.
(e) Services, 10%.
(f) Other gains or profits 10%.[2]

The rates may be reduced under specific double tax treaties. Malaysia has an extensive **70**
treaty network. Currently, Malaysia has Double Tax Agreements (DTAs) with more
than eighty countries (including restricted DTAs or those pending ratification).

The definition of royalties is expanded to include: **71**

- the use of, or the right to use software;
- the reception of, or right to receive, visual images or sounds, or both,
  transmitted to the public by satellite or cable, fibre optic or similar technology;
- the use of, or the right to use, visual images or sounds, or both, in connection
  with television or radio broadcasting, transmitted by satellite or cable, fibre
  optic or similar technology;
- the use of, or the right to use radiofrequency spectrum specified in a relevant
  licence; and
- total or partial forbearance in respect of the use of, reception of, or the granting
  of the right to use/receive any such property or rights or any such items that
  are covered in the definition of royalty.

At the same time, the definition of a public entertainer is expanded to include: **72**

- a compere, model, circus performer, lecturer, speaker, sportsperson, an artiste
  or individual exercising any profession, vocation or employment of a similar
  nature; or
- an individual who uses his intellectual, artistic, musical, personal or physical
  skill or character in, carrying out any activity in connection with any purpose
  through live, print, electronic, satellite, cable, fibre optic or other medium, for
  film or tape, or for television or radio broadcast, as the case may be.

---

2. The determination of whether a payment made to a non-resident falls under other gains or profits
   is dependent on the facts and circumstances of each case and has been spelt out in the Public
   Ruling No. 1/2010: Withholding Tax on Income under para. 4(f). Briefly, the Ruling indicated that
   other income refers to the following:
   (a) the payment is revenue and not capital in nature;
   (b) the income is not income that falls under para. 4(a) to 4(e) and s. 4A income of the MITA;
   (c) the payment received by the non-resident is in the nature of a miscellaneous income which
       is often casual in nature. Casual income means an occasional income, which is received
       outside the ordinary course of trade or vocation; the payment is for an isolated transaction;
       and there is an absence of repetition of transactions to indicate the commercial nature of
       the transaction.

73 Effective 28 December 2018, the word 'technical' has been removed from the definition of special classes of income. Thus, withholding tax is applicable on advice, assistance or services rendered in connection with management or administration of any scientific, industrial or commercial undertaking, venture, project or scheme, where the services are performed in Malaysia.

74 Malaysia does not impose withholding tax on dividends.

[4]   Digital Service Tax

75 Effective 1 January 2020, a service tax of 6% will be imposed on digital services provided by both local and foreign service providers. Digital services are defined as services that are delivered or subscribed over the Internet or other electronic network and cannot be delivered without the use of IT, and the delivery of the service is substantially automated. This could potentially result in certain service providers charging digital service tax to the REIT, resulting in an increase in cost.

[5]   Other Taxes

76 Stamp duty is imposed on a wide range of documents and transactions. Rates vary with the type of document and amount involved. The stamp duty payable for transfer instruments of real property ranges from 1% to 3% of the market value of the property. The stamp duty payable for transfer instruments for shares is generally 0.3% of the consideration. Instruments of transfer of real property by any person to a REIT approved by the SC are exempt from stamp duty. The sale of property by the REIT is not exempt, and the purchaser has to pay the stamp duty.

77 Generally, the purchase and sale of units in a listed REIT are not subject to stamp duty since the units are traded scripless on the Malaysian stock exchange.

78 A property tax which is referred to as an assessment rate is levied on the gross annual value of the REIT's property, and the tax is payable to the city or town council. Quit rent is a form of land tax and is payable by the REIT to the state land office.

[6]   Penalties Imposed on REIT

79 Non-adherence of the REIT to the SC Act 1993, the SC's Guideline on REITs, Guidelines on Islamic REITs, Guideline on Asset Valuation and various other regulatory requirements could result in various penalties or even the revocation of the REIT status. Most common offences include the failure to give effect to written notices, circulars, conditions or guidelines issued by the SC.

Tax penalties are imposed by the Inland Revenue Board Malaysia for non-compliance   **80**
with tax administration or for understatement of taxes. Offences include the failure to
submit tax returns, submission of incorrect tax returns, and late payment of tax.

[B]   Taxation of the Investor

[1]   *Private Investor*

[a]   *Taxation of Current Income (All Income Derived from REIT in Holding Phase)*

Unitholders pay income tax on their share of the REIT's distributions. Income that has   **81**
been taxed at the REIT level has tax credits attached when subsequently distributed to
the unitholders. Resident unitholders are subject to tax at their own marginal rates on
the distributions. Non-resident unitholders are not subject to any further Malaysian tax
in respect of the distribution received. Where non-resident unitholders are subject to
tax in their respective jurisdictions, depending on the provisions of their country's tax
legislation, they may be entitled to tax credits paid by the REIT, subject to certain
formulae according to their respective jurisdictions.

Where the REIT has not paid taxes on the income due to tax transparency, non-   **82**
corporate investors (particularly resident and non-resident individuals) are subject to
a final withholding tax of 10% up to YA 2025. The withholding tax is a final tax, and
resident individuals and non-corporate investors will not be required to declare the
income received from the REIT in their tax returns.

Where a tax-exempt unitholder receives a distribution of income from a REIT/PTF and   **83**
the distribution of income has been subjected to withholding tax, that unitholder will
be entitled to a tax refund.

[b]   *Taxation of Capital Gains (From Disposal of REIT Shares)*

There is currently no capital gains tax regime in Malaysia. Except for persons seen to   **84**
be dealing in investments, gains received by investors from the disposal of REIT shares
are generally not subject to income tax.

[2]   Institutional Investors

[a]   *Taxation of Current Income (All Income Derived from REIT in Holding Phase)*

Residents

85   Distributions to Malaysian corporate investors are not subject to withholding tax. Instead, corporate income tax will be levied at the corporate investors' level at a rate of 24%. Where tax has already been levied at the REIT level, the distributions made by the REIT of such taxed income will have tax credits attached. Resident corporate unitholders are subject to tax at the prevailing tax rates on the distributions and are entitled to tax credits representing tax already paid by the REIT.

86   With effect from YA 2020, resident companies with paid-up capital of MYR 2.5 million and below and gross income from source or sources consisting of a business not exceeding MYR 50 million for the basis period for that YA are subject to a tax rate of 17% for the first MYR 600,000 chargeable income, with the balance of chargeable income taxed at the normal corporate tax rate, currently at 24%.

Non-residents

87   Where tax has not been levied at the REIT level, foreign institutional investors (i.e., pension funds and collective investment schemes or such other institutions approved by the Minister of Finance) are subject to a final withholding tax of 10% up to YA 2025.

88   Foreign corporate investors are subject to a final withholding tax of 24% on distributions that have not been taxed at the REIT level.

[b]   *Taxation of Capital Gains (From Disposal of REIT Shares)*

89   There is no capital gains tax regime in Malaysia. Except for Financial Institutions or companies dealing in investments, gains received by investors from the disposal of REIT shares are not subject to tax.

[3]   Penalties Imposed on Investors

90   There are no penalties that are applicable to investors.

[C]   Tax Treaties

[1]   Treaty Access

91   Not applicable.

[2] *Withholding Tax Reduction*

The withholding tax rates listed in section §103[A][3] above can be reduced under   **92**
specific double tax treaties. Malaysia has an extensive treaty network. Currently,
Malaysia has DTAs with more than eighty countries (including restricted DTAs or those
pending ratification).

[D]   Exit Tax/Tax Privileges/Concessions

There are no specific exit tax concessions. As mentioned above, there is currently no   **93**
capital gains tax in Malaysia. However, with the reintroduction of RPGT from 1 January
2010, REIT's chargeable gain on disposal of a chargeable asset would be taxed as
follows:

Date of Disposal	RPGT Rates		
	Companies Incorporated in Malaysia	*Individual (Citizen & Permanent Resident)*	*Individual (Non-citizen & Non-permanent Resident) and Companies Not Incorporated in Malaysia*
Within three years from the date of acquisition	30%	30%	30%
In the 4th year	20%	20%	30%
In the 5th year	15%	15%	30%
In the 6th year and subsequent years	10%	5% (*)	10%

* RPGT rate reduced to 0% with effect from 1 January 2022.

[E]   Taxation of Foreign REITs

[1]   *Taxation of Foreign REIT Holding Assets in Country*

A foreign REIT is subject to corporate income tax in Malaysia in respect of rental   **94**
income derived from Malaysian real estate. The current corporate income tax rate is
24%. The tax transparency system does not apply to a foreign REIT.

[2]   ***Taxation of Investors Holding Shares in Foreign REIT***

95 As mentioned above, with effect from 1 January 2022, income received from a foreign REIT would be taxable in Malaysia.

Mexico

DAVID CUELLAR

David Cuellar is the lead partner of Tax and Legal Services of PwC in Mexico; previously, he performed as the lead of the international tax services practice in Mexico. He is a specialist in Mexican international tax planning and structuring and has helped several multinational companies in expanding their operations into Mexico. David is also the leader of the PwC Mexico Real Estate Tax practice and forms part of the global Real Estate Tax network. He has more than fifteen years of experience in structuring operations for foreign companies doing business in Mexico.

David was seconded to PwC UK for over three years, where he was in charge of the firm's Mexican Tax Desk for Europe, the Middle East and Africa, based in London. He graduated *summa cum laude* from the Escuela Bancaria y Comercial, receiving two degrees, one as a Certified Public Accountant and the other in Business Administration. He is also a Tax Professor and is in charge of the tax department at his alma mater. David has authored a number of articles in several tax magazines, including *International Tax Review, Tax Business Magazine* and *Tax Notes International.*
E-mail: david.cuellar@ pwc.com

MARIO ALBERTO GUTIERREZ

Mario Alberto Gutierrez is an International Tax Services Partner with PwC Mexico specializing in corporate and international taxes. He has more than fifteen years of professional experience; he joined PwC Mexico City's office in September 2005. Mario Alberto's advisory activities focus on legal and tax structures for international transactions involving the US and Mexican tax laws, dispute resolution, optimization of Mexican income tax, alternative minimum tax and employee profit-sharing. Mario Alberto has assisted a number of clients in evaluating Mexican migration, debt financing and cost comparison issues in global restructurings involving changes in business models. During his professional career, Mario Alberto has participated in international tax for the consumer products industry, real estate companies, individuals and limited liability partnerships, as well as interpreting and developing efficient international solutions in the Mergers and Acquisitions environment.

Mario Alberto was assigned to PwC USA (New York) for two years, where he was the project leader in charge of implementing reorganization processes in several multinational groups with subsidiaries in Mexico, such as cross-border redeployment by a multinational enterprise of functions, assets and/or risks.

Mario Alberto is a Certified Public Accountant who graduated from the UNAM and holds a postgraduate international taxation qualification from the ITAM. He has attended different national and international tax courses in Mexico and the US and has written for several tax specialized publications, among others, *International Tax Review* and *World Bank's Doing Business* editions. He is also a member of the International Tax Committee of the Mexican National Institute of Accountants.
E-mail: mario.alberto.gutierrez@ pwc.com

MARIO ALBERTO ROCHA

Mario Alberto Rocha is a partner of the Legal Area of PwC in Mexico City. He is an Attorney-at-Law with a Master's in International and European Business Law in Spain and has postgraduate certifications in Mexico, the US and Europe related to Antitrust, Intellectual Property, Energy Law, Internet Law, among others.

Mario joined PwC in January 2001, and he has expertise in commercial law, M&A, cross-border transactions, real estate, intellectual property, antitrust, government, corporate governance and legal risk analysis. During his tenure at PwC, Mario collaborated on diverse projects involving restructurings of corporate groups, mergers, acquisitions and unwinding of multinational companies and governmental entities.

Mario is a member of the National Association of Corporate Attorneys (ANADE), a speaker in business forums and an author of legal publications.
E-mail: mario.alberto.rocha@ pwc.com

Mexico

David Cuellar, Mario Alberto Gutierrez & Mario Alberto Rocha

§1.01 BACKGROUND

[A] Key Characteristics

In Mexico, trusts have been popular vehicles for real estate projects. Mexican trust   **1** schemes are flexible and can be tailored to specific project needs. While most trusts are governed by commercial legislation, the type of trust that resembles a Real Estate Investment Trust (REIT) was originally introduced in Mexico through tax legislation. The trust is known as *Fideicomisos de Infraestructura de Bienes Raices* or FIBRAS (as per its acronym in Spanish), a term that roughly translates as 'Trust for Real Estate Infrastructure'. As a consequence of the Mexican energy reform introduced in 2014 (where many sectors of the energy power generation were opened to private investors before exclusively operated by the Mexican government), the Mexican tax authorities introduced a new variation of REIT for hydrocarbon, electricity and other public infrastructure activities known as FIBRA-E (REIT-E) that would have similar benefits than the regular REIT.

The corporate purpose of a REIT is to engage in real estate construction and leasing,   **2** and REIT-E is mainly to engage in hydrocarbon, electricity and other public infrastructure activities. REIT funding comes from a public offer. In general terms, tax benefits granted in Mexico to REITs and REIT-Es include the deferral of the income tax on the contribution of real estate capital and the exemption from filing estimated monthly income tax payments.

[B] History of REITs

To foster investment in Mexican real estate, the 2005 reforms to the Mexican Income   **3** Tax Law (MITL) introduced the first rules for Mexican REITs. The MITL reforms set forth the requirements for a trust to receive beneficial tax treatment.

4 After further modification of the MITL REIT rules, the Mexican Stock Exchange intensified the promotion of REITs in Mexico. Mexican authorities have stated in public business forums that the legal framework for REITs is complete, and no further amendments will be introduced in years to come.

[C]   REIT Market

5 Quite aware of the success of REITs in foreign markets, Mexican REITs were initially welcomed by Mexican investors. As of early 2022, there are approximately sixteen REITs listed on the Mexican Stock Exchange market, and REITs, in general, are becoming more popular as an alternative to investing in Mexico.

6 Even though REIT-E is a rather recent type of vehicle for Mexican infrastructure investments related to hydrocarbon, electricity and other public infrastructure activities, currently, there are five public REIT-E listed in the Mexican stock exchange market.

§1.02   REGULATORY ASPECTS

[A]   Legal Form of REIT

[1]   Corporate Form

7 Pursuant to the MITL, tax benefits are available to REITs that are structured as trusts (FIBRAS). FIBRAS must have the following trust purpose: the construction or acquisition of properties intended for lease or the acquisition of the right to obtain revenues from such leases, as well as the use of assets to secure financing for activities that fall within the scope of the trust's purpose.

8 Mexico has a civil and commercial law jurisdiction in which the trust structure is defined in the *Ley General de Titulos y Operaciones de Credito* (LGTOC). A trust must be formed as an agreement under Mexican Law. The trust is integrated by three main parties: the settlor, the trustee or fiduciary and the beneficiaries to the trust. The trustee must be a Mexican resident credit institution authorized to act as trustee. The trustee issues certificates of participation that represent a share of the REIT's equity to the beneficiaries, which in certain cases can also be the settlor of the trust. Holders of the certificates are also called unitholders.

9 The by-laws of the trust have to limit the trust purpose to the acquisition or construction of real estate dedicated to leasing, rights over profits derived from real estate leasing and grant financing with mortgages. Mandatory clauses required by the statutory laws which are applicable to stock markets (i.e., corporate governance rules) apply and must comply with banking and securities regulations, but there are no other particular clauses that the trust contract has to include.[1]

[2]   *Investment Restrictions*

At least 70% of the trust estate of the REIT must be invested in real estate properties in   **10**
Mexico destined for lease or the right to obtain income from the lease of such real estate properties, or financings granted for such purposes secured by the respective leased real estate properties and the remainder of such trust estate must be invested in securities issued by the Mexican Federal Government and registered in the Mexican National Securities Registry or debt instruments issued by Mutual Funds.

The properties constructed or acquired by the REIT must be destined for lease and may   **11**
not be sold within a period of four years following the date of construction completion or acquisition thereof, as applicable.

In order to obtain certain tax benefits available for REITs, the trust certificates have to   **12**
be publicly traded. As of 2020, income tax benefits are not available to private REITs, and some rules were included to govern the taxation of deferred gain in the context of private REITs.

[B]   **Regulatory Authorities**

REITs are subject to securities regulations, and their compliance is monitored by the   **13**
Ministry of Finance (SHCP) and the National Commission of Banking and Securities (CNBV). While Mexican stock exchanges (BMV and BIVA) are not formally authorities, they govern the REIT's 'registration' as a public issuer. In practice, they have broad authority to interpret and apply regulations issued by the SHCP and the CNBV.

[C]   **Legislative and Other Regulatory Sources**

REITs have to comply with the following: **14**

- *Ley del Mercado de Valores* (LMV), a law that sets the legal framework for Mexican stock markets.
- *Ley de Títulos y Operaciones de Crédito*, a law that regulates trusts.
- *Ley Federal de Derechos,* a law that annually provides the fees to be paid by a REIT to government agencies and authorities involved in the listing process.
- Internal Rules of Mexican Stock Exchanges (*Reglamentos Interiorer de la Bolsa Mexicana de Valores y Bolsa Institucional de Valores)* contain rules applicable

---

1. *See* s. §1.02[F][5] below.

to the operation of both Mexican stock exchanges. Consequently, any REITs that want to go public needs to be listed at one of the Mexican stock exchanges.
- *Disposiciones de Carácter General aplicables a las Emisoras de Valores*, rules issued by the CNBV which provide detailed information on the requirements to be met by an issuer of titles.
- SHCP and SAT (Ministry of Tax) enact tax decrees and regulations.
- Mexican Central Bank rules may be applicable with regard to specific topics (e.g., credit institutions regulations).

[D]   Exchange Controls and Reporting Requirements

15   Public REITs are subject to the same requirements as other securities issuers. Consequently, REITs submit quarterly and annual reports and report relevant events to the BMV. Reporting is accomplished either directly by the REIT or through the REIT's intermediary. The BMV makes the reported information available to the investors.[2]

[E]   Registration Procedures

[1]   Preparatory Measures

16   Before it can be listed, a public REIT needs authorization from the CNBV to make a public offer (*see* section §1.02[E][2] below). Simultaneously with the registration before the CNBV, the REIT must provide the BMV with the necessary documents to obtain its authorization for listing. Before a REIT can apply for authorization to make an offer, the REIT has to register its certificates with the National Registry of Securities (RNV). To register its certificates, the REIT submits an application and a preliminary prospectus to RNV. This procedure is further explained in the following chapters.

[2]   Obtaining Authorization

17   Once the certificates are registered with the RNV, the REIT's legal representative shall file for the CNBV authorization to make a public offer. In general, the filing must include:

- articles of incorporation (including amendments);
- a preliminary prospectus, to be approved by CNBV in order to become definitive before the public offer is made;
- financial information, such as financial statements audited by an external auditor; and

---

2. For a more detailed description of reporting obligations, *see* s. §1.02[F][7] below.

   – a legal opinion issued by an external independent attorney regarding the REIT's lawful incorporation, subsistence and operation, as well as the validity of the securities it issues.

[3]   Other Requirements for the Incorporation of a REIT

No other requirements are applicable to incorporating a REIT.   **18**

[4]   Obtaining Listing Exchanges

[a]   Costs

CNBV fees for the registration of the securities are variable and depend upon a number   **19** of factors, including the kind of issuer and the type of rights that the security confers to its holders. Currently, the fees may range from USD 1,000 to USD 1,200. BMV and BIVA, as private institutions operating under government authorization, have their own fees for the listing of securities.

[b]   Time

Simultaneous to the registration before the CNBV, the REIT must provide the appli-   **20** cable stock exchange in Mexico with the necessary documents to obtain its listing authorization. CNBV and the applicable stock exchange authorization procedures take place simultaneously. While Mexican laws provide that CNBV has a maximum of three months to authorize or deny a request, the process may take more than six months. If the CNBV or the applicable stock exchange requires further documentation during the application process, it can take longer to obtain the authorization.

[F]   Requirements and Restrictions

[1]   Capital Requirements

There are no specific capital requirements.   **21**

[2]   Marketing/Advertising

The LMV provides several rules regarding advertisement and promotion of securities.   **22** CNBV has to authorize the dissemination of information in connection with the promotion, commercialization or advertising of securities when such information is addressed to the general public.

23   Information disclosed in connection with the public offer of securities must refer to the prospectus, brochures and other authorized documents, and it must be consistent with those documents. The CNBV may order the review, suspension or cancellation of the information if information (regarding advertisement and promotion) was disclosed in breach of the above-mentioned rules.

[3]   Redemption

24   When the trustee distributes to the unitholders (i.e., beneficiaries) an amount in excess of the taxable income of the REIT, the difference is deemed as capital redemption, and the distribution reduces the acquisition cost of the unitholders' certificates. The reduction in acquisition cost affects the amount of gain or loss on a subsequent sale of the REIT certificates.

25   The trustee must keep an account of all the capital redemptions made to the unitholders. The trustee must also provide the unitholders (i.e., beneficiaries) with a statement of any capital redemptions paid to them unless the certificates of the REIT are publicly traded.

[4]   Valuation of Shares/Units for Redemption and Other Purposes

26   In the case of redemption or sale, the tax basis of the REIT participation certificates (units) is determined by dividing their acquisition cost, adjusted for inflation, by the number of certificates held by the seller at the moment of the sale.

27   The acquisition cost of the participation certificates (units) is the amount of cash paid by the unitholder to acquire the units. In cases where the unitholder received the certificates for contributing assets to the REIT, the acquisition cost of the certificates is the value of the assets (as stated in the contribution minutes).

[5]   Investment Restrictions

28   Pursuant to the MITL, a REIT is subject to the following restrictions on investments:

  - The REIT must be incorporated under Mexican Law, and the trustee shall be a Mexican resident credit institution duly authorized for such purposes.
  - The REIT's purpose has to be limited to the construction or acquisition of properties intended for alienation or lease, the acquisition of the right to obtain revenues from such leases, and using its assets to secure financing for these activities.
  - The REIT must invest at least 70% of its equity in real estate or rights derived from real estate. The surplus equity (the other 30%) has to be invested in government bonds or debt instruments issued by Mutual Funds. Such 70%

requirement shall be determined based on the annual average value of the real state, the rights or credits. The value of the real estate shall be determined according to the general rules provided by the MITL.
- The real estate acquired or developed by the REIT must be intended for lease and owned for a period of at least four years after the date on which such real estate was acquired or developed.

[6]   *Distribution/Accumulation*

The REIT has at least once a year and before 15 March to distribute at least 95% of its   **29** prior year's taxable income to its unitholders.

[7]   **Reporting Requirements**

Some of the reports that need to be provided by a REIT as a public issuer of securities   **30** include the following:

- Ongoing reports related to corporate acts, such as resolutions adopted by the directors and unitholders.
- Quarterly reports that contain financial statements and financial information.
- Annual reports with an annual financial statement certified by an external auditor.

[8]   *Accounting*

REITs have to comply with rules related to accounting and reporting in Mexico. These   **31** include the Mexican Generally Accepted Accounting Principles and International Financial Reporting Standards (IFRS) rules; however, it is mandatory for publicly traded companies in Mexico to issue their financial statements in terms of IFRS rules. Companies are obligated to keep their accounting books and records in Mexico. The records must be written in Spanish and financial entries have to be in Mexican Pesos.

[9]   *Trust Registry*

Based on the MITL, REITs shall obtain a registry before the REIT Registry as per rules   **32** issued by SHCP. For these purposes, Tax Miscellaneous Rules state that in order to comply with such obligation, the following requirements shall be met:

(1) The trustee has to issue participation certificates that represent a share of the REIT equity to the beneficiaries.

(2) The participation certificates issued by the trustee have to be publicly traded and shall meet applicable requirements in this regard, including obtaining authorization by the CNBV.

(3) REITs shall obtain a favourable resolution from the SHCP with respect to their tax regime and renew it when applicable.

[10]   REIT Revenue

33   Revenues received by REITs deriving from leases which considerations are dependent upon variable figures or percentages (except with respect to considerations established upon a fixed rate of the sales of the lessee) should be limited to 5% of the annual revenues obtained by such REITs by virtue of their leasing operations.

§1.03   TAXATION

[A]   Taxation of the REIT

[1]   Corporate Income Tax

[a]   Tax Accounting

34   Typically, REIT's income is taxed at the unitholder level. However, if the taxable income of the REIT in a year is higher than the amount distributed to the unitholders by 15 March of the following year, the trustee has to pay a 30% (applicable in 2022) income tax on the undistributed amounts. The tax shall be payable by 30 March. The unitholders may claim a credit for the tax paid if they later receive the funds in a taxable distribution. No income tax is withheld by the trustee on the distribution of the funds.

35   Taxable income of the REIT is determined on an accrual basis (see section §1.03[A][1][b] below).

[b]   Determination of Taxable Income

36   The trustee shall determine the taxable income of the REIT according to the general taxation rules provided in the MITL. Taxable income typically includes income generated by the trust's real estate, goods, rights, receivables and bonds. Revenue derived from granting the temporary use of goods, such as the rent of fixed assets or real property, accrues at the moment the consideration is partially or totally collected, when the consideration becomes payable by the lessor, or at the moment the invoice for the transaction is issued, whichever occurs first.

37   Any deductions claimed by the taxpayer must be directly related to the REIT's business, and fixed assets are depreciated on a straight-line basis. The law provides a

maximum 5% depreciation rate for buildings (land is not subject to depreciation). Based on the Mexican 2020 tax reform, relevant provisions were enacted meant to incorporate fundamentals of the Organisation for Economic Co-operation and Development Base Erosion and Profit Shifting initiative that would be applicable on certain payments made outside Mexico and/or non-Mexican investments.

For income tax purposes, the net income of the REIT is the difference between taxable   **38**
revenues and deductible allowances. Net operating losses incurred in the prior ten years can be deducted from net income to arrive at taxable income.

Non-residents holding Mexican REIT certificates shall consider the withholding made   **39**
by the trustee as a final income tax payment.

The net taxable income is distributed to the unitholders in proportion to their   **40**
ownership in the REIT (as evidenced in the participation certificates).

[c]   *Taxation of Income from Taxable/Non-taxable Subsidiaries*

Mexican REITs are not allowed to have investments in subsidiaries.   **41**

[d]   *Taxation of Foreign Income*

Since taxpayers in Mexico are subject to income tax on their worldwide income,   **42**
foreign-sourced income derived by a REIT is included in the taxable income of the REIT. There is no guidance on whether the unit holders can claim a credit for any foreign tax paid, but the general rules for claiming a foreign tax credit should apply.

[2]   **Value Added Tax**

REITs are subject to the general rules concerning Value Added Tax (VAT).   **43**

VAT represents a one-time tax, payable by the consumer on the following activities: **44**

- alienation of goods;
- rendering of independent services;
- rentals; and
- import of goods and services.

The general VAT rate is 16%.   **45**

The sale of land and residential construction (e.g., houses and dwellings) is exempt   **46**
from VAT, but the sale of commercial buildings is subject to VAT at the general 16% rate. The value of the commercial building plus all amounts charged to or collected from the acquirer (such as other taxes, fees, interest or penalties) is subject to VAT.

47   The rental of residential property is not subject to VAT. Hotel and boarding house rentals are commercial rentals subject to VAT on the amount charged for rent.

48   VAT paid on the acquisition or rental of commercial property ('input VAT') is recoverable by the party paying the tax to the extent that the REIT carries out VAT taxable activities.

49   In order for input VAT to be creditable, the payment to which it relates has to be deductible for income tax purposes, and the VAT has to be clearly stated in the corresponding invoice.

50   All monthly VAT payments are final. The return must be filed by the seventeenth day following the end of every month. VAT payments must be submitted together when filing the monthly return.

51   VAT favourable balances may be credited against future VAT liabilities, or they may be used to offset the tax liabilities arising from other federal taxes. In addition, the REIT is able to request a refund of a favourable VAT balance.

[3]   *Withholding Taxes*

52   The trustee withholds a 30% (for 2022) income tax on distributions to the unitholders. Some unitholders are exempt from income tax withholding (*see* section §1.03[D] below). If the amount of the distribution exceeds the taxable income of the REIT, the difference is as capital redemption (*see* section §1.02[F][3] above), and no income tax is withheld.

53   If the tax on the amount distributed has already been paid by the trustee (*see* section §1.03[A][1][a] above), no withholding is required. The buyer of REIT participation certificates (units) has to withhold tax on the purchase of the units from a foreign investor, when applicable. *See* section §1.03[B][1][b] below.

54   Please note that when the REIT participation certificates are publicly traded, the financial intermediary having custody of the certificates should be the person in charge to withhold the corresponding income tax. Specific rules are given to clarify the information that should be provided by the trustee and the financial intermediary having the custody of the certificates for these purposes.

55   Note that the financial intermediary/trustee is jointly liable with respect to the tax to be paid by the investors.

[4]   *Other Taxes*

56   There is no minimum alternative income tax in Mexico.

[a] Real Estate Transfer Tax

Real Estate Transfer Tax is imposed on the purchaser of real estate. The basis of this tax **57** is the appraised value (performed by a bank or a *cadastre*) or market value (transaction or registered price) of the property, whichever is higher.

The tax rate, as well as the definition of immovable property or real estate, depends on **58** the legislation of the State where the real property is located. The rates imposed by the States generally range from 1% to 5%. Also, please note that in certain States, the Real Estate Transfer Tax may be deferred/exempted upon the contribution of assets into a REIT; however, specific analysis is needed on a case-by-case basis, taking into account the State in which the immovable property is located.

The Public Notary is responsible for remitting the tax. The Notary shall collect the tax **59** from the acquirer at the moment the public deed for the acquisition is signed and must remit it to the corresponding authorities together with the tax return.

[b] Real Estate Property Tax

Real Estate Property Tax is a local tax on ownership of real property. The mechanism **60** to determine it and the tax rate varies depending on the State and the Municipality in which real estate is located.

The owner of the real property is the person liable for the tax. The Real Estate Property **61** Tax is based on the official assessed value or the appraised value of the real estate. In most States, the tax rates are below 1%. However, the effective tax rate may be higher, as the total tax paid is comprised of the tax rate plus a fixed quota. The tax is computed annually and payable bimonthly.

[5] Penalties Imposed on REITs

Under Mexican tax legislation, the trustee and the unitholders are jointly and severally **62** liable for any taxes imposed on the REIT.

Failure to comply with any of the investment restrictions or with the 95% distribution **63** obligation mentioned in section §1.02[F][5] will result in the REIT losing its preferential tax treatment (*see* section §1.03[D] below). Because the tax treatment includes a deferral on the payment of taxes, this can result in the authorities requesting the unpaid tax, adjusted for inflation, along with penalties and surcharges.

[B]   Taxation of the Investor

[1]   Private Investors

[a]   *Taxation of Current Income (i.e., All Income Derived from REIT in the Holding Phase)*

64   Mexican resident unitholders, as well as foreign resident unitholders that have a permanent establishment in Mexico, are taxed at 30% on the total amount of taxable income distributed from the REIT, with no deduction for the income tax withheld by the trustee. The income tax withheld is creditable against the unitholder's income tax liability in the corresponding year.

65   Mexican resident individuals will consider the income received from the REIT as income arising from certificates in immovable property and will accrue the total amount of the taxable income distributed from the REIT, without claiming a deduction for the income tax withheld by the trustee and will be able to claim a credit for an amount equal to the income tax withheld.

66   For non-resident unitholders, the withholding carried out by the trustee is a final income tax payment.

[b]   *Taxation of Capital Gains (From the Disposal of REIT Shares)*

67   Mexican resident unitholders are not subject to Mexican income tax on the gain from the sale of participation certificates in the REIT if the certificates are publicly traded and sold in the recognized Mexican stock market.

68   If the sale of the participation certificates does not meet the criteria for exemption, Mexican residents are taxed on the gain, the difference between the sale price of the certificates and their tax basis. The tax basis of the participation certificates is determined by dividing the acquisition cost (as defined in section §1.02[F][3] above), adjusted for inflation, by the number of certificates issued by the REIT held by the seller at the moment of the sale, regardless of whether the seller is selling all of the certificates.

69   The tax basis calculation is subject to inflationary adjustments as well. The gain arising from the sale of the certificates is subject to tax at the general 30% rate.

70   When the participation certificates (units) are publicly traded and sold in a recognized Mexican stock market, foreign resident unitholders are exempt from Mexican income tax upon the sale of the certificates. If the sale of the certificates does not meet the criteria for exemption, the buyer has to withhold and remit to the tax authorities the income tax related to the transaction. For these purposes, the MITL provides a 10% withholding rate on the gross amount of the sale. No tax is withheld if the foreign resident seller is exempt in its country of residence from income tax on the income arising from the real estate, goods, rights, receivables or bonds that are part of the trust's assets.

[2]   Institutional Investors

[a]   Taxation of Current Income (i.e., All Income Derived from REIT in Holding Phase)

Institutional investors are taxed the same as private investors in respect of REIT   **71** distributions.

[b]   Taxation of Capital Gains (From Disposal of REIT Shares)

Institutional investors are taxed the same as private investors in respect of capital   **72** gains.

[3]   Penalties Imposed on Investors

The trustee and the unitholders are jointly and severally liable for any taxes imposed on   **73** the REIT. *See* section §1.03[A][5] above.

[C]   Tax Treaties

[1]   Treaty Access

Mexico has a large treaty network. Whether a foreign or Mexican REIT is eligible for   **74** treaty relief is ultimately dependent on the particular treaty. It is important to consider that Mexico is part of the Multilateral Convention to Implement Tax Treaty Measures to Prevent Based Erosion and Profit Shifting (MLI) together with over a hundred jurisdictions around the globe. This MLI agreement would add additional requirements to apply tax treaty benefits in Mexico with respect to tax treaties that Mexico has with other jurisdictions that are part of the same convention to the extent that the ratification, acceptance or approval process is also completed in such other jurisdictions. As of 2022, the MLI is not yet in force in Mexico, and it is pending to be approved by the Mexican congress.

[2]   WHT Reduction

Depending on the specific case, a Mexican REIT may be eligible to access treaty-   **75** reduced withholding rates on payments made or received.

[D]   Exit Tax/Tax Privileges/Concessions

76   The specific tax incentives for Mexican REITs include the following:

    (a) Deferral of applicable income tax regarding the contribution of real estate capital in a REIT. In this regard, the unitholders of the REIT should not consider as taxable income the gain of such contribution (sale) until they sell the corresponding certificates, or the REIT sells the real estate contributed by the unitholders. In specific States of Mexico, the Real Estate Tax may also be deferred or even exempt from such tax.

    (b) The deferred gain should be restated by inflation from the moment in which the real estate was contributed to the REIT until the moment in which the certificates or the real estate is sold.

    (c) The REIT is not obliged to file an estimated monthly income tax. Instead, the REIT remits all payments along with its annual return.

    (d) Foreign resident pension funds investing in a Mexican REIT will be exempt from Mexican income tax on the amount related to their investment to the extent such funds are exempt from income tax in their country of residence.

    (e) Other incentives include allowing the REIT benefits when the property is intended for lodging.

[E]   Taxation of Foreign REITs

[1]   *Taxation of Foreign REIT Holding Assets in Country*

77   A foreign REIT that does not have a permanent establishment in Mexico is subject to income tax in Mexico on rental income derived from Mexican real estate. The applicable tax rate is 25% on the gross amount of the rental payment (it may even be 40% if subject to a preferential tax regime).

78   If a foreign REIT has a permanent establishment in Mexico, all the income attributable to it (including rental income and capital gains) is taxable at a 30% rate. Since the permanent establishment is treated as a Mexican taxpayer, it can claim certain deductions related to the activities carried out in Mexico.

    The tax is paid via withholding when the foreign REIT is a Mexican resident or a foreign resident with a Mexican permanent establishment. If the foreign REIT is a foreign resident without a permanent establishment in Mexico, the foreign REIT has to remit the corresponding tax within fifteen days following the payment made to the foreign REIT.

[2] Taxation of Investors Holding Shares in a Foreign REIT

Mexican investors holding shares in a foreign REIT are generally taxed in Mexico on **79** distributions from the foreign REIT, and they are taxed on capital gains from the disposal of their interests in the foreign REIT. In both cases, Mexican investors can claim a credit for the income tax paid in foreign jurisdictions, subject to certain limitations.

On the other hand, Mexican investors would be subject to immediate taxation in **80** Mexico when the income is obtained by the foreign REIT (before it is distributed) in the following cases:

- The REIT is subject to a preferred tax regime and receives passive income[3] for Mexican tax purposes; income should be taxed in Mexico when it is obtained by the REIT. In this regard, a preferred tax regime is an entity or a vehicle that is subject to an effective tax rate lower than 75% of the Mexican income tax rate (specific exceptions may apply if the foreign REIT is located in a broad exchange of information country or in the case of transactions with non-related parties).
- The REIT is a foreign corporate legal entity transparent for tax purposes. For purposes of this rule, the entity would be deemed transparent if it is not a tax resident for income tax purposes in the jurisdiction of its incorporation nor in the jurisdiction in which its effective place of management is situated, and its income is attributable to its members, partners, shareholders or beneficiaries.
- The REIT is a foreign legal figure notwithstanding the taxation regime applicable in the foreign jurisdiction. A foreign figure would include trusts, partnerships, investment funds and any other similar figure to the extent that such vehicle does not have a separate legal personality.

[F] FIBRA-E

[1] Energy Reform and the FIBRA-E

The Mexican Energy Reform, in force as of 2014, opened the Mexican energetic sector **81** to both national and foreign private investors. In this regard, the Mexican Tax Authorities introduced through the Mexican Miscellaneous Tax Regulations (MTR) a new trust investment vehicle model aimed to promote energy and infrastructure-related investments to which they granted a variety of tax benefits, some of which are

---

3. Interests, dividends, royalties, capital gains, negotiable instruments or intangible assets or from derivative financial operations subjacent referred to debt or shares, commissions and intermediation, gains on the transfer of immovable property, revenues from leases, revenues received free of charge and revenues from the sale of goods that are not found physically within the country, territory or jurisdiction of residence or location of a foreign juridical entity or figure, and revenue from services rendered outside said country, territory or jurisdiction are deemed passive revenues for purposes of the CFC Mexican tax rules (i.e., preferred tax regimes).

very similar to the ones applicable to qualifying REITs (described in section D). The trust is known as Fideicomiso de Inversión en Energía e Infraestructura or FIBRA-E (as per its acronym in Spanish) or REIT-E, a term that roughly translates to 'Trust for Energy and Infrastructure Investments'.

[2]   Qualifying Activities

82 The corporate purpose of a REIT-E is to invest in Mexican entities (qualifying entities) which, among other requirements and characteristics, are engaged exclusively in the following activities (or a combination of such activities) as included in the MTR:

(a) Activities included in the Mexican Hydrocarbons Law, as well as activities involving the treatment, blending, processing, conversion and transport of oil products and petrochemicals or any other product derived from oil or natural gas. Some of these activities include refining, sale, transport and storage of oil; process, compress, liquefy, decompress, regasification, transport, storage, distribution and commercialization of gas; transport of petrochemical products through pipelines, as well as storage; generate, transmit and distribute electricity.

(b) Activities such as the transport, storage and distribution of hydrocarbons, even when they are carried on within the perimeter of a contractual area or assignment site, as long as in such a case, the activities are not performed under a contract or assignment would also qualify.

(c) Activities related to the generation, transfer or distribution of electric energy.

(d) Infrastructure projects carried through concessions, service contracts or other contractual schemes, to the extent the aforementioned contracts are celebrated between the public and private sector which are currently under operation and which remaining term is equal or longer to seven years in any of the following concepts: roads, railroads, transport facilities, backbone network communication structure, public security and social rehabilitation facilities, drinking water, drainage system and waste water treatment facilities, ports facilities, maritime terminals, and civil airports.

(e) Managing other Energy and Infrastructure Trusts.

[3]   Corporate Form

83 The FIBRA-E trust must be incorporated as an agreement under Mexican Law, and the trustee must be an authorized Mexican tax resident credit institution, as in the case of the REIT legal form structure included in section A subsection I.

[4]   Requirements and Formalities

The specific requirements and characteristics that should be complied with are the   **84**
following:

- In order to meet the respective exclusive activity status, the Mexican tax
  resident legal entity receiving the REIT-E investment must obtain at least 90%
  of its taxable revenue in the respective tax year from the development of the
  above-mentioned qualifying activities (or a combination of them). Further,
  more than 25% of the average annual accounting value of its non-monetary
  assets must be invested in new assets.
- Moreover, all the shareholders of the Mexican vehicle entity other than the
  FIBRA-E must be legal entities resident for tax purposes in Mexico. This
  requirement should be complied with previously to the acquisition of shares of
  such qualifying entity by the FIBRA-E.
- In addition, an informative filing must be made by the shareholders of the
  Mexican resident entity during the forty-five-day period following the FIBRA-E
  investment by which the Mexican Tax Authorities are informed of such event
  and through which the shareholder's filing it make certain commitments
  related to joint liability. Moreover, the shareholder of the Mexican resident
  entity receiving the investment must establish dispositions in the by-laws of
  the entity through which it is agreed that the legal entity will be making
  distributions to the shareholders, including the FIBRA-E, which are consistent
  with the distribution rules of the FIBRA-E trust. Further, a notice must be
  presented on 15 July of each of the years following the first-mentioned notice
  by the same parties informing the Mexican Tax Authorities that they will
  continue applying the FIBRA-E tax treatment.
- Also, at least 70% of the average annual equity of the FIBRA-E must be
  invested directly in the qualifying Mexican resident legal entities shares, and
  the remnant (if any) must be invested in registered Mexican governmental
  bonds or shares of investment funds managing debt instruments.
- Corporate governance under high standards must be implemented.

[5]   Tax Treatment of the FIBRA-E and Qualifying Entity

- REIT-E would be relieved from filing advance income tax payments and also   **85**
  would be relieved from taxation in regards to the alienation of REIT-E
  certificates to the extent they are traded in a recognized stock market.
  However, as described in prior sections (i.e., section F, subsection 2), unlike a
  REIT, which must maintain its assets directly, the REIT-E will instead hold
  qualifying Mexican entities that own and operate the assets. Note that the
  qualifying Mexican tax resident entities in which the FIBRA-E participates
  would also be relieved from filing monthly income tax returns.
- The trustee of the FIBRA-E would have to determine the taxable income and
  withhold income tax that would be attributable to each holder, taking into

consideration the deduction of deferred expenses resulting from the energy and infrastructure business activities or from the REIT-E's operating expenses. The distributions made to the FIBRA-E trust should not be subject to the additional 10% income tax withholding on dividend distributions applicable to individuals and foreign resident legal entities. In addition, a Capital Contribution Account (CUCA) should be tracked and registered by the trustee. CUCA account would be added by the capital contributions in either cash or kind and will not be subtracted by taxable income distributions. Instead, any distribution exceeding the total amount of the respective taxable year income would be considered capital redemption up to the amount of the aforementioned account until its balance is depleted. Amounts exceeding the CUCA balance would be subject to income tax withholding that would be attributable to each shareholder.

- In order to make it possible for the REIT-E structure not to result in double taxation, the MTR grant tax transparency to the entities held by the REIT-E; in other words, the qualifying entities are treated as if they were part of the trust but subject to the compliance of the several requirements mentioned previously in section 3. In this regard, such entities would be regarded as pass-through entities for Mexican income tax purposes. Distributions made by the qualifying entity should not be subject to the 10% income tax withholding that would normally be applicable to distributions made to non-resident investors.

86 Furthermore, it is important to consider that when a REIT-E acquires the shares of a qualifying Mexican entity for the first time, the fiscal year of such portfolio company would be considered to have ended and a new short fiscal year to which the special REIT-E tax regime would apply will begin on the following day and run until 31 December of the same calendar year. Note that at the moment of the acquisition of shares by the REIT-E, the monetary assets of the qualified portfolio company should not represent more than 5% of its total assets, or otherwise, such monetary assets would be deemed to be proportionally distributed as a reimbursement to its previous shareholders.

87 However, any future transfer of the shares issued by the qualifying Mexican entity that comply with the requirements mentioned before should be audited by a Mexican certified public accountant.

88 In addition to the above, no alienation would deem to exist for the contribution of assets (such as land, fixed assets, and certain intangible assets) by a Mexican tax resident entity to a qualifying Mexican tax resident entity if the following requirements are met:

- In a term no longer than six months after the contribution of the assets, a FIBRA-E acquires at least 2% of the shares of the Mexican resident qualifying entity from the party which contributed such assets to the other Mexican tax resident qualifying entity.

- The consideration received by the Mexican tax resident legal entity contributing the assets consists strictly of shares of the qualifying Mexican tax resident legal entity for the total value of the assets received.
- The Mexican qualifying entity receiving the assets, in fact, fulfils all the conditions and limitations included in the MTR.

The Netherlands

JEROEN ELINK SCHUURMAN

Jeroen Elink Schuurman (1968) studied Dutch Tax Law at the University of Leiden. As a tax partner of PwC, he is also the Global Real Estate Tax Leader of PwC. In the past, he led the real estate group of PwC in the Netherlands. In 2000, he achieved a Master's in Real Estate (MRE) at the University of Amsterdam. He is a frequent lecturer and has published articles in the field of real estate and taxation. Jeroen has more than twenty-five years of experience in advising clients on their Dutch and international real estate investments and developments. Among Jeroen's clients are many institutional investors, asset managers and development companies.
E-mail: jeroen.elink.schuurman@pwc.com

SERGE DE LANGE

Serge de Lange (1974), a tax partner in the real estate group of PwC in Amsterdam, is leading the real estate/real assets group of PwC in the Netherlands. He studied Dutch Tax Law (LLM) at the University of Amsterdam and started his career in 1999. In 2007, he obtained his Master's in Real Estate (MRE) at the University of Amsterdam. Serge provides tax advisory services to real estate investors and asset managers investing and divesting in real estate, advising on tax optimization of corporate structures including internal or external refinancing, advising in respect of mergers and acquisitions and assisting clients set up the regional, country- or property-specific real estate investment funds. Areas of expertise include corporate income tax, real estate transfer tax and REITs. Serge often speaks at real estate seminars on various topics in the Netherlands and has contributed as an author to real estate journals and publications.
E-mail: serge.de.lange@pwc.com

ARIEF ROELSE

Arief Roelse (1990) studied Dutch Notarial Law (LLB and LLM) and Tax Law (LLM) at the Radboud University of Nijmegen. He has a background in Dutch corporate law, contract law and financial market regulations and combines this knowledge with his expertise to advise national and international clients in the financial services industry, including investment funds, investment managers and (institutional) investors. He specializes in structuring and establishing investment funds, as well as advising on topics relevant to investment teams or investors, such as (co-)investment arrangements, liquidity, exits, (fund) governance, regulations and marketing and AIFMD-related topics. During the course of his career, he advised clients on cross-border (re-)structurings, mergers and acquisitions, initial and follow-on public offerings and corporate governance.

E-mail: arief.roelse@pwc.com

The Netherlands

Jeroen Elink Schuurman, Serge de Lange & Arief Roelse

§1.01   BACKGROUND

[A]   Key Characteristics

There are no specific Real Estate Investment Trust (REIT) rules in the Netherlands.   **1**
However, the Netherlands has a regime for collective investment undertakings, the
Fiscale Beleggingsinstelling (FBI), which is comparable to other REIT regimes.

A Dutch private limited liability company, public limited liability company, mutual   **2**
fund or a comparable entity under foreign law can qualify as an FBI. In order to qualify
as an FBI, certain strict conditions must be met. These include shareholder requirements, a profit distribution requirement, an activity test and certain leverage restrictions. The FBI regime is available to both listed and unlisted entities.

A qualifying FBI is subject to corporate income tax (CIT) at a rate of 0%. Dividend   **3**
distributions from a qualifying FBI are generally subject to 15% Dutch dividend
withholding tax.

An FBI may be self-managed if it is in the form of a legal entity. Even a self-managed   **4**
FBI can delegate certain management functions to a separate management company.
Listed FBIs are generally managed internally (self-managed).

The FBI regime is also available to entities whose activities consist of investing in   **5**
securities, warrants, bonds, options, gold, antiques and even in stamp collections, but
this report only covers the FBI that invests directly or indirectly in real estate assets.

The Netherlands also have incorporated in the Dutch CIT laws a special tax regime, the   **6**
so-called Exempt Investment Institution (VBI) regime for open-end and semi-open-end
investment entities. The VBI may only invest in financial instruments and cannot itself
invest in Dutch real estate directly. This report does not include further information on
the VBI since it cannot invest in Dutch real estate directly.

[B]   History of REIT

7   The United States of America (US) and the Netherlands were the first two countries to introduce a tax regime suitable for real estate investments. The US REIT was introduced in 1960, and the FBI regime was introduced in the Netherlands in 1969. The Dutch regime was the first regime similar to a REIT in Europe. In addition to the obligatory annual distribution, FBIs have offered an opportunity for capital growth.

8   The Dutch Government realized that some individuals were not prepared to take risks attached to single capital investments, and the government, therefore, introduced the FBI regime to encourage investments – rather than savings – having a favourable effect on the economic stability and the flow of capital into companies. The FBI regime allows individuals to invest collectively and to hire professional investment managers to optimize the risk-return profile of their investments. In order to place the FBI investors in the same tax position as investors who invest directly, the FBI enjoys a CIT rate of 0% (a de facto full exemption).

9   Since 1969, the FBI regime has been amended from time to time. Recently, due to European competition in the field of investment fund regimes, as well as the European Union (EU) tax law developments, the Dutch Government modernized the FBI regime radically. The new legislation and rules became effective on 1 August 2007. As of 1 January 2010, relief is introduced for the purposes of reducing restrictions on leverage limits for FBIs (*see* section §1.02[F][1] below). The most recent changes relate to permitted activities. Based on law changes per 1 January 2014, the permitted activities are further widened.

[C]   REIT Market

10   The Dutch real estate market is a relatively large and professional market. With two of the world's largest pension funds (with roughly EUR 800 billion assets under management as of December 2021), the Netherlands has a dominant position in Europe and even globally.

11   The FBI regime is increasingly used by investors to hold real estate assets in a tax neutral manner. In 2007, the largest Dutch FBI was taken over (delisted) by a French listed REIT. In addition, two smaller listed FBIs merged in 2011. The second-largest listed REIT was taken private by another French REIT at year end 2014. Today, financial institutions such as pension funds and insurance companies make frequent use of FBIs. Nevertheless, at present, only five real estate FBIs are listed on the Dutch stock exchange, with a market capitalization of approximately EUR 11.1 billion (February 2022).

12   The investments of the listed FBIs are predominantly in the Netherlands, the southern countries of Europe, Turkey, the United Kingdom and countries in the Nordic region. Currently, shares of listed FBIs trade at an average discount of roughly 15%–20% (i.e., the stock price is lower than the underlying net asset value per share), which is a result of the pressure on the stock markets. Apart from the listed FBIs, there are numerous non-listed FBIs that invest in real estate. No record is kept of the estimated property value of the non-listed real estate FBIs, but this was estimated at EUR 20 billion in 2018. A few years ago, the Dutch tax authorities published that 364 FBIs were registered in 2014 with a total asset value (investments) of approximately 260 billion. These numbers include not only FBIs that invest in real estate but also FBI that invest in securities, warrants, bonds, options, etc.

[D] Tax Developments in the Netherlands

[1] Foreign Real Estate Funds Eligible for Dutch FBI Tax Exemption

On 23 November 2018, a Lower Court decided that a German Open-Ended Public Fund **13** was entitled to the FBI regime providing, among others, for a 0% CIT rate on Dutch source real estate income. The Court also ruled that the portfolio investment test (one of the requirements of the Dutch FBI regime) should apply only to the Dutch real estate activities. The German fund held a large portfolio of Dutch real estate investments and was assessed with Dutch CIT on Dutch source real estate income for several years. In the case at hand, the Dutch tax authorities took the position that the German fund was not eligible for the FBI regime as the (German) investors were subject neither to Dutch dividend withholding tax nor to German income tax over the Dutch source real estate income.

According to the Dutch tax authorities, the application of the FBI regime under these **14** circumstances would be contrary to the object and purpose of the Dutch CIT Act (CITA). However, the Lower Court rejected this argument since the requirements for the FBI regime, as laid down in the Dutch CITA, do not require the shareholders of the FBI to be subject to (withholding) tax. The Dutch tax authorities appealed the verdict of the Lower Court. Any developments in this respect have, however, to be monitored closely, given that the case is now under the Court of Appeal.

Furthermore, on 3 September 2021, a Dutch Court of Appeal ruled that under current Dutch tax law a German real estate investment fund (*Publikums-Sondervermögen*) is in principle entitled to the Dutch FBI regime. The Court confirmed that, contrary to the position taken by the Dutch tax authorities, the German fund complies with the current legal form requirement even though no (withholding) tax is effectively levied on the Dutch source real estate income at shareholder level.

Another important judgment of the Court of Justice of the European Union (CJEU) was **15** delivered on 30 January 2020 in relation to the compatibility with EU law of the Dutch FBI regime and particularly the shareholder requirements and the distribution require-ment. In this case, an investment fund under German law (*Publikums-Sondervermögen*), open-ended, listed on the stock exchange, without legal personality, and exempt from profit tax in Germany invested via shareholders in companies based in the Netherlands. The investment fund received dividends from these Dutch-based entities on which a 15% dividend withholding tax was withheld. No Dutch dividend withholding tax will be due if the investment fund has met the FBI criteria.

16   The investment fund had argued in the proceedings before the CJEU that it was difficult to demonstrate that it complied with the shareholders' requirements (refer to the requirements set out later on), as its shares were publicly traded via an electronic trading system and, therefore, was not able to provide information on the identity of its shareholders.

17   The CJEU ruled that the Dutch Supreme Court has to examine whether non-resident investment funds are de facto disadvantaged by the shareholder requirements of the FBI regime. If it appears that the Dutch tax authorities require the same evidence from both resident and non-resident investment funds in order to demonstrate that they comply with the shareholder requirements, the shareholder requirements apply without distinction. If it appears that the Dutch tax authorities impose a stricter burden of proof on non-resident investment funds than on resident investment funds, this difference constitutes an infringement of the freedom of capital movement.

18   With regard to the distribution requirement, the investment fund argued in the proceedings before the CJEU that the legal regime to which it is subject in Germany, in fact, also requires that at least a certain amount of the profits must be distributed to the shareholders. Moreover, not only this minimum profit distribution but also an additional, presumed profit distribution is taken into account for tax purposes. As a result, undistributed profits are effectively subject to taxation at the level of the ultimate investors. Therefore, the investment fund argued that the purpose and scope of this method of profit distribution and taxation are comparable to that of the distribution requirement under the FBI regime.

19   In that regard, the CJEU ruled that the Dutch Supreme Court has to determine whether the purpose and scope of the FBI regime mainly concern the manner of taxation of the shareholder's income in an investment fund (i.e., a fiscally neutral tax treatment for investors in an investment fund). If this is the case, a resident investment fund that actually distributes its profits and a non-resident investment fund whose profits are not distributed but are deemed to be distributed and taxed as such in the hands of the shareholder in that fund must be considered to be in objectively comparable situations. In both situations, taxation is transferred from the investment fund to the shareholder in that fund. To summarize, this judgment brings positive news for foreign investment funds that have filed objections/appeals in the Netherlands up to 2007. In particular, the fact that these funds have not actually distributed their profits to their investors does not automatically make them incomparable with a Dutch FBI. This is because Dutch FBIs are required by law to distribute their profits no later than eight months after the end of the financial year (also refer to the requirements as set out below). The Dutch Supreme Court will now have to give a final judgment, taking into account the CJEU judgment. We still expect further litigation on the compatibility with EU law of the FBI regime as has been in force since 2008. We believe that the CJEU judgment could also be applicable to the current FBI regime. Developments have to be monitored closely.

§1.02 REGULATORY ASPECTS

[A] Legal Form of REIT

[1] Corporate Form

The Dutch FBI regime is a pure tax regime. Therefore, its application does not depend **20** on satisfying regulatory requirements (such as security laws), even though references are made in the tax laws to certain regulatory provisions included in the Dutch Financial Supervision Act (*Wet op het financieel toezicht* or DFSA) in connection with the shareholders' test (*see* section §1.02[A][2] below).

The FBI regime is available to Dutch public limited liability companies (*Naamloze* **21** *Vennootschap* or NV), private limited liability companies (*Besloten Vennootschap* or BV) and mutual funds (*Fonds voor Gemene Rekening* or FGR). The modernization of the FBI regime in the summer of 2007 extended the FBI regime to non-Dutch entities established under the laws of an EU Member State, the islands formally known as the Dutch Antilles (Bonaire, Saint-Eustatius, Saba, Curacao, Saint Maarten) or Aruba. The FBI regime is also available to an entity established in a country that has concluded a tax treaty with the Netherlands if that tax treaty contains a non-discrimination clause. A foreign entity qualifies for the FBI regime if the entity in its corporate form is similar to the corporate form of a Dutch public limited liability company, private limited liability company or mutual fund.

Contrary to many other REIT regimes, the FBI regime does not require listing on the **22** stock exchange. However, the shareholders' conditions may restrict closely held companies from becoming an FBI.

Under Dutch civil law, it is possible to create separate classes of shares/units (A, B and **23** C shares/units, etc.) in a Dutch undertaking. Under certain conditions, entities with capital divided into separate classes of shares qualify for the FBI regime as well.

Public and private limited liability companies have distinct legal personality. As such, **24** they can legally own (real estate) assets, enter into obligations and assume liabilities. A mutual fund has no legal personality. Consequently, it cannot hold the legal ownership of (real estate) assets, enter into obligations and assume liabilities. From a legal perspective, a mutual fund qualifies as a contractual arrangement between each investor, the fund manager and the custodian. A key feature of a mutual fund is the separation between the legal ownership of the investments, mostly held by a custodian, and the entitlement to the proceeds/returns realized on the investments of the fund. The investors provide the capital used for the investments. In return, the investors receive a unit in the fund. The fund manager shall invest the fund's capital and shall manage the assets and liabilities of the fund in accordance with a predefined investment strategy. The legal ownership of the assets and liabilities of the fund is usually held by a separate legal entity. This is in order to ensure that the assets and liabilities of the fund remain separate from the individual investors and the fund manager. Often a separate foundation is used for this purpose. The use of such a separate legal entity is mandatory in the event that the mutual fund falls under the scope of the Alternative Investment Fund Manager Directive (AIFMD).

[2]   Investment Restrictions

25   Shareholder investment restrictions for regulated FBIs are more relaxed than the restrictions that apply to private FBIs. Regulated FBIs are FBIs whose shares/units are admitted to trading on a regulated market, FBIs that are managed by or whose shares/units are offered by a fund manager holding a licence under Article 2:65 or Article 2:69b of the DFSA to offer shares/units in a fund to the public in the Netherlands and FBIs that benefit from the exemption from the licence requirement, in accordance with Article 2:66 subsection 3 or Article 2:69b of the DFSA. With the incorporation of the EU AIFMD in the DFSA, a larger group of fund managers and/or FBIs fall under supervision. Especially for the fund managers and/or FBIs that in the past were considered private, non-regulated, but are now considered regulated FBIs for the application of the shareholder investment restrictions, the ability to raise equity and admit new shareholders becomes easier. For a detailed description of the regulatory landscape in the Netherlands, *see* section §1.02[B] below. The shareholder restrictions for regulated FBIs include the following:

(1) No single entity that is subject to tax on its profits (or the profits of which are subject to tax at the level of the shareholders/participants of such entity) may, together with its one-third or more related entities within the meaning of Article 10a, paragraph 4 juncto paragraph 6 Dutch CITA 1969, own 45% or more of the shares in the FBI. For the purpose of this test, shares on which an entity may vote in the general meeting of shareholders – whether or not on the basis of an agreement with other shareholders – are included in calculating the ownership percentages. This restriction does not apply to participation in an FBI directly or indirectly held by: (i) a regulated FBI and (ii) an investment undertaking as in the meaning of the EU Directive for Undertakings for Collective Investments in Transferable Securities (UCITS).
(2) No individual may hold an interest of 25% or more.
(3) A managing director, as well as more than 50% of the supervisory directors of a regulated FBI, may not be simultaneously managing director, supervisory directors or employees of another entity that holds (together with its one-third or more related entities) an interest of 25% or more in the FBI. This restriction does not apply if such other entity is a regulated FBI.

26   For private FBIs, the following more stringent shareholding requirements apply:

(1) 75% or more of the shares/units in the FBI must be held by:
(a) individuals;

> (b) entities which are not subject to taxation on their profits, or are exempt from tax and the profits of such entities are not subject to tax at the level of the shareholders/participants of such entities; or
> (c) regulated FBIs.
> (2) No individual may hold a substantial interest (a direct or indirect interest of 5% or more) in the private FBI.

In addition to the above-described shareholding requirements, Dutch resident entities **27** may not hold an interest of 25% or more in a regulated or a private FBI through non-resident mutual funds or through non-resident entities with a capital fully or partly divided into shares.

For newly set-up FBIs, it is difficult to meet the various shareholder investment **28** restrictions from the start. Therefore, some relief is published in a decree for newly set-up FBIs in relation to some of the above-described shareholder investment restrictions during the first twenty-four months upon incorporation/formation of the FBI.

Priority shares, entitling holders to a fixed preferential dividend exclusively, and shares **29** with special voting rights are permitted if certain conditions are met.

[B] Regulatory Authorities

The FBI regime is a pure tax regime. Therefore, its application does not depend on **30** satisfying regulatory requirements, even though reference is made to certain regulatory provisions in connection with the shareholders' test (*see* section §1.02[A][2] above).

The Dutch legal framework regulating the access to and the conduct on the financial **31** markets is set out in the DFSA. The DFSA is supplemented by various decrees and guidelines issued by (local and international) supervising authorities. Supervision occurs by the Netherlands Authority for the Financial Markets (*Stichting Autoriteit Financiële Markten* or AFM) and the Dutch Central Bank (*De Nederlandsche Bank N.V.* or DNB). The AFM monitors and supervises the conduct of business, while the DNB primarily monitors and supervises the financial position.

An FBI potentially falls within the scope of the provisions of the DFSA if the FBI **32** qualifies as:

> (1) an issuer of shares/units to the public in the Netherlands or an issuer that has shares/units admitted for trading on a Dutch-regulated market;
> (2) a collective investment undertaking within the meaning of the EU Directive for UCITS; or
> (3) an alternative investment fund (AIF) within the meaning of the AIFMD, whose shares/units are being offered in the Netherlands, which is domiciled in the Netherlands or which is managed by a Dutch fund manager.

33   Since a UCITS invests in financial instruments and may not make a direct investment in (Dutch) real estate, this chapter does not include any further information on FBIs structured as a UCITS. In practice, many funds investing in real estate fall under the AIFMD regime.

34   The implementation of the AIFMD in July 2013 radically changed the fund management industry. Due to the wide scope of the definition 'AIF' in the AIFMD and the fact that this directive also applies in the case offerings are made to professional or qualified investors only, many investment funds that previously fell outside the scope of the regulated environment now find themselves a focus of regulatory attention. The introduction of the AIFMD caused, and will continue to cause, significant modifications to structures, strategies and operations of FBIs that qualify as AIFs and their fund managers. These parties faced a number of challenges in adapting to the new requirements imposed by the AIFMD, particularly in areas concerning the remuneration of identified staff, valuation, risk management, transparency and reporting towards regulators/investors and the appointment of an independent depositary with statutory oversight duties. It is expected that the AIFMD regime will be further advanced and mature during the next years. In this regard, the Directive cross-border distribution of collective investment undertakings 2019/1160 and the Regulation cross-border distribution of collective investment undertakings 2019/1156 entered into force on 1 August 2019. Most of the changes foreseen by the Directive and the Regulation, aforementioned, took effect from 2 August 2021. Broadly, the Directive and the Regulation are aimed at reducing regulatory barriers to cross-border distribution of collective investment undertakings in the EU regulated under the UCITS regime and the AIFMD regime.

35   Under the AIFMD, offers of shares/units made to (professional) investors in the EU, as well as the management of EU-based AIFs, are, in principle, regulated activities for which the fund manager has to obtain a licence. Consequently, the offering of shares/units of FBIs that are non-EU AIFs within the EU is caught by the AIFMD regime. The individual Member States may impose additional obligations in the event that an AIF is offered to retail investors. The Netherlands has done so in the form of the 'top-up retail regime'. In broad terms, the additional requirements of the top-up retail regime relate to investor compliance procedures and the content of the prospectus. An EU-AIF manager with a licence can passport its licence to the other EU Member States through a notification procedure.

36   An FBI is caught by the AIFMD regime if it qualifies as a collective investment undertaking that raises capital from a number of investors, with a view to investing it in accordance with a defined investment policy for the benefit of those investors and is not a UCITS. This applies regardless of whether the AIF is an open-end or closed-end type, whatever the legal form and whether or not shares/units of an AIF are traded on a regulated market.

37   The five Dutch FBIs listed on the Dutch stock exchange (*see* section §1.01[C][11] above) are of the view that they do not qualify as a collective investment undertaking but are genuine enterprises and, as such, do not fall under the AIFMD regime.

The Dutch legal framework provides for the following commonly used regulatory **38** regimes:

(1) First, there is the full regime which entails that the Dutch AIF manager must obtain a licence from the AFM (*see also* section §1.02[E][1] below).

(2) Second, there is a registration regime that applies to 'small' Dutch AIF managers. Under the registration regime, also referred to as the sub-threshold regime, the Dutch AIF manager is compelled to register itself with the AFM and to make certain periodical filings with the AFM and the DNB. However, it is not subject to the ongoing supervision of the AFM.

(3) Finally, in the event that a licensed AIF manager offers shares/units of an FBI-AIF to retail investors in the Netherlands, then the 'top-up retail' regime applies. The 'top-up retail' requirements will have to be complied with unless there is a minimum subscription price of EUR 100,000 per investor or the nominal value of a share/unit amounts to at least EUR 100,000. We note that this regime also applies to non-Dutch AIF FBIs that offer their shares/units to retail or non-professional investors in the Netherlands.

Section §1.02[A][1] above explains that non-Dutch entities may also be eligible to **39** apply the FBI regime. Where shares/units in an FBI that also qualify as a non-Dutch AIF are offered in the Netherlands, this offering must be permitted under the DFSA. The same applies in the event that a licensed Dutch AIF manager intends to manage non-Dutch AIFs. For EU-AIFs, the European passport regime can provide the necessary relief. However, any offerings made of shares/units in non-EU AIFs in the Netherlands must be made in accordance with either the private placement regime or the designated state's regime. These regimes will remain in place until the harmonized AIFMD third-country passport regime becomes available.

[C]   Legislative and Other Regulatory Sources

A Dutch company can simply elect to apply the FBI regime in its CIT return, which is **40** filed after the end of the year (assuming the conditions for application are fulfilled).

[D]   Exchange Controls and Reporting Requirements

The regulatory status of an FBI is decisive for the determination of the applicable **41** reporting requirements. In addition to the requirements set out in the DFSA, Dutch private limited liability companies and Dutch public limited liability companies must also comply with the reporting requirements under corporate law set out in the Dutch Civil Code.

[E]   Registration Procedures

[1]   Preparatory Measures for AIF Managers

42 A fund manager of an FBI that qualifies as an AIF, or in case the FBI is self-managed by the FBI itself, must apply for a licence with the AFM (or an equivalent supervising authority in another EU Member State), unless it falls under the registration regime. In order to obtain a licence, the (prospective) AIF manager must meet certain criteria with respect to:

(1) the suitability of the persons (co)determining the policy;
(2) controlled and sound business operations;
(3) the legal structure and control;
(4) the avoidance of conflicts of interest; and
(5) a minimum equity and solvency position.

[2]   Obtaining Authorization for AIF Managers

43 The application for a licence occurs by submitting completed application forms plus annexes thereto to the AFM. The annexes provide information on the organization of the (prospective) fund manager, its financial position, as well as the suitability of the (co)policymakers. The most recent forms, as well as more specific information on the details to be submitted as part of the application, can be found on the website of the AFM (www.afm.nl).

44 Once licensed, the AIF manager must also inform the AFM of its intention to manage a new AIF or of its intention to offer shares/units in an AIF to investors in the Netherlands. As part of this process, the AIF manager will have to submit the fund documentation, including the private placement memorandum/prospectus, to the AFM.

45 In principle, the AFM has twenty-six weeks to consider an application for a new AIF manager. The AFM is obliged to inform the applicant in the event the process exceeds thirteen weeks. The term for the approval of the marketing of new AIFs is twenty business days.

[3]   Other Requirements for the Incorporation of a Company

46 The incorporation of a Dutch private limited liability company, public limited liability company or mutual fund is a relatively simple process. Dutch limited liability companies and public limited liability companies are incorporated by means of the execution of a notarial deed of incorporation before a Dutch civil law notary. The notarial deed of incorporation contains the relevant company's articles of association, provides for the appointment of the initial members of the management board and supervisory board (if any) and affects the issuance of the shares subscribed for at incorporation. Within a week after its incorporation, the newly established company, as well as the members of the management board and supervisory board (if any), the sole shareholder (if any) and other officers must be registered with the trade register of the Chamber of Commerce.

A mutual fund is a contractual arrangement between each investor, the fund manager   **47**
and the custodian. The relationship between the fund manager, the custodian and each investor is embedded in the terms and conditions of the mutual fund. These terms and conditions contain the agreed principles with respect to, for instance, the investment strategy of the mutual fund, the distribution of proceeds as well as the admission of new investors and the transfer and redemption of units. The establishment of a mutual fund takes place by the adoption of, and in the case of the investors' adherence to, the terms and conditions. A mutual fund does not have to be registered with the trade register of the Chamber of Commerce.

[4]   *Obtaining Listing Exchanges*

[a]   *Costs*

The costs associated with a listing depend on several factors, such as whether the   **48**
associated capital raising is underwritten and the size of the capital raised. As a general rule, an FBI should allow for costs between 3% and 5% of funds raised. This amount includes fees for lawyers, notaries, auditors and tax professionals involved in the listing process.

[b]   *Time*

The time required to list an entity depends on several factors, including the size and   **49**
complexity of the transaction, the state of the market, preparatory work performed by the company and how quickly funds are received from investors. As a general rule, the FBI should allow at least four months for any listing.

[F]   **Requirements and Restrictions**

[1]   *Capital Requirements*

Dutch public limited liability companies must have a minimum share capital of EUR   **50**
45,000. For private limited liability companies, no minimum share capital exists. Both public limited liability companies and private limited liability companies can have a share capital divided into different classes of shares. Each such class can have a different nominal value. In the case of a private limited liability company, it is also

possible to create a class of shares that has no voting rights or a class of shares that is (partially) excluded from profit sharing and/or from distributions of reserves. Furthermore, the articles of association of a private limited liability company may provide that the general meetings of shareholders are held outside the Netherlands. There is no capital duty due in the Netherlands. There are no minimum capital requirements for mutual funds.

51   Moreover, gearing restrictions limit borrowings (both shareholder and third-party loans) to finance investments. Leverage is limited to a maximum of 60% of the tax book value of directly held real estate investments and a maximum of 20% of the tax book value of other investments.

52   The main reason for the leverage restrictions is that, in the opinion of the legislator, high gearing is an indication that the FBI is engaged in activities that go beyond passive investment activities, and such activities are not allowed for the FBI.

53   In back-to-back finance situations, where FBIs attract third-party borrowing that is then loaned to subsidiary companies, the amount of borrowed funds loaned to the subsidiary and the loan receivable from the subsidiary are disregarded for the calculation of the leverage restrictions. Furthermore, the leverage restrictions on FBI investments in subsidiary companies were alleviated. FBIs are now allowed to finance up to 60% of the value of directly held real estate investments and indirectly held real estate investments (shares in subsidiary companies).

54   For the purposes of this legislation, 'subsidiary companies' are companies whose assets generally consist of, on a consolidated basis, 90% or more in real estate assets. FBIs have to hold – together with their one-third or more related entities within the meaning of Article 10a, paragraph 4 juncto paragraph 6 CITA – at least a one-third interest in such subsidiary company.

55   Consolidation for tax purposes can only take place to the extent subsidiaries are included in a 'fiscal unity' or tax consolidation. To form a fiscal unity, the subsidiary entities should also apply to the FBI regime. In this respect, for subsidiaries that are taxed on a consolidated basis with their parent companies, the gearing restriction should be calculated at the level of such fiscal unity only. Loans between entities within a 'fiscal unity' are not considered as borrowings for the purpose of the gearing restrictions. Following court cases of the European Court of Justice and the subsequent implementation of the so-called emergency measures in the Dutch law, the fiscal unity regime is set aside for certain specific tax rules, like for interest limitation. Consequently, the loan between entities within the fiscal unity becomes visible again.

56   Under the gearing restrictions, tax book value means the valuation on the balance sheet for tax purposes. The tax book value can differ from the valuation in the FBI statutory accounts. Because the leverage restrictions are based on the tax book value of the investments, tax depreciation and value impairments of the investments for tax purposes can force the FBI to (partially) redeem the loans in order to obey the leverage restrictions. Based on very old jurisprudence from the Supreme Court, in case of a significant decrease in value, the FBI is obligatorily required to make the impairment

for tax purposes. Although for tax purposes, real estate investments are generally valued at cost price less depreciation rather than market value, in a downturn market, FBIs need to be particularly careful in obeying the leverage restrictions.

[2]   Marketing/Advertising

The marketing requirements applicable to an FBI depend on its regulatory status. If the **57** FBI is an issuer that offers shares/units to the public in the Netherlands or trades on a Dutch-regulated market, such as Euronext Amsterdam, then the prospectus for such offering must be approved by the AFM or an equivalent supervising authority of another EU Member State. The prospectus should be prepared in accordance with the provisions of the EU Prospectus Regulation 2017/1129. An FBI-issuer is *inter alia* exempt from the obligation to prepare a prospectus in the following circumstances:

(1) the aggregate consideration of the offer, when aggregated with the consideration for all other offers of securities issued by the group, throughout the European Economic Area (EEA), over a twelve-month period, is less than EUR 5,000,000 and provided that the conditions described in paragraph [59] are complied with;

(2) an offering to qualified investors only;

(3) an offering to less than 150 persons per Member State, not being qualified investors;

(4) an offering of a subscription price of at least EUR 100,000 per investor;

(5) an offering of shares/units that have a nominal of at least EUR 100,000 each; or

(6) an offering to the public in the EEA having an aggregate consideration of less than EUR 1,000,000 calculated over a twelve-month period.

Where no prospectus is required, any advertisement must include a warning to that **58** effect. In addition, the exemption referred to under (1) above is subject to several specific conditions. First, the AFM should be notified prior to such an offer being made. Second, an information document for investors should be prepared following a predetermined format. Third, unless the offer is made to qualified investors only, the exemption referred to under (1) above is only available to the extent that the offer, advertisements and other documents that contain the prospect of an offer explicitly mention that there is no legal requirement to publish a prospectus approved by the AFM and that the offer is not subject to supervision. This is done through a specific text and picture made available by the AFM. Notwithstanding the above, if an FBI-issuer offers securities pursuant to an exemption to publish the prospectus referred to under (3)–(6) above, a specific text and picture made available by the AFM must be included in the offer, advertisements and other documents that contain the prospect of an offer.

The AIFMD regime also requires that (prospective) investors are provided with certain **59** information on the AIF prior to their decision to invest. This information relates, among others, to the investment strategy, investment restriction and details of the AIF, the risks and costs associated with the AIF and the parties involved in the AIF (e.g., the AIF manager, the depositary, (sub) custodians and the fund administrator).

60 For AIFs that are offered to retail investors under the top-up retail regime, the prospectus must contain a statement of a Dutch auditor in which he/she confirms that the prospectus contains all the information prescribed by law. In addition, (prospective) investors must be provided with a key investor information document that contains a summary of the most important features of the AIF and the investment.

61 A closed-end AIF traded on a regulated market must prepare a prospectus that meets the requirements set by the EU Prospectus Regulation 2017/1129. The information that must be provided to investors under the AIFMD regime should be included either in the prospectus or in a separate document that is made available to (potential) investors at the same time as the prospectus.

62 In the event that an FBI-AIF shall be offered to retail investors under the AIFMD registration regime, all marketing materials and advertisements must state that the fund manager of the FBI-AIF is not licensed or supervised by the AFM.

63 The entry into effect of the Directive cross-border distribution of collective investment undertakings 2019/1160 and the Regulation cross-border distribution of collective investment undertakings 2019/1156 has an impact on the marketing of AIFs in the EU. For instance, the Directive foresees the introduction of a new harmonized 'pre-marketing' regime under the AIFMD. It also requires that placement agents and distributors that carry out any pre-marketing activities must be EU-regulated firms or tied agents. This may require AIFs to review and adjust their distribution (channels). Furthermore, the Regulation *inter alia* also provides for similar standards of marketing communications to EU-AIF managers and UCITS.

[3]   Redemption

64 There are no statutory redemption restrictions for FBIs, as such. Where an FBI takes the form of a Dutch private limited liability company or public limited liability company, the redemption of shares takes place in accordance with the relevant provisions of the offering documents and Dutch corporate law as set out in the Dutch Civil Code. For mutual funds, the redemption of units can take place by the fund manager, pursuant to and in accordance with the terms and conditions governing the mutual fund. If investors can demand the redemption of shares/units, the investment fund qualifies as an open-end fund. In a closed-end fund, investors do not have the right to offer their shares/units for redemption. In general, FBIs investing in real estate are not structured as an open-end fund since real estate investments are not easily converted into cash required to satisfy the redemption payments. Some investment funds address the lack of liquidity by only permitting a redemption of shares/units if there is a matching issue of shares/units. This is the so-called matching principle. When shares/units in an FBI are sold to the entity itself, part of the proceeds is treated as a dividend, subject to dividend withholding tax insofar as the redemption price exceeds the average paid-in capital per share/unit.

[4]   Valuation of Shares/Units for Redemption and Other Purposes

Typically, the fund documentation requires shares/units to be redeemed at their net **65** asset value, whereby the assets and liabilities of the FBI are valued at fair market value. For real estate assets, valuation reports of external evaluators are used.

In the case of an FBI-AIF, the AIF manager must ensure that the net asset value of the **66** shares/units is calculated and disclosed to investors in accordance with the relevant provisions of law and the fund documentation. The AIF manager is generally responsible for ensuring that there are appropriate and consistent procedures in place for a proper and independent valuation of the assets. The valuation and calculation of the net asset value of the shares/units must take place at least once a year. For open-ended AIFs, a valuation and calculation must also be carried out in such frequency as is appropriate to the assets as well as the redemption schedule. For closed-end AIFs, an additional valuation and calculation must be made in the event of any decrease or increase in the capital of the AIF.

[5]   Investment Restrictions

There are no statutory investment restrictions based on Dutch corporate or regulatory **67** laws applicable to issuers or AIFs. Of course, the fund manager must comply with the investment restrictions contained in the fund documentation and the articles of association (if applicable).

However, for an entity to qualify for tax purposes as an FBI, specific investment **68** restrictions are applicable. The statutory purpose of the FBI, as well as the actual activities it performs, must consist solely of passive investment activities (Article 28, section 2, CITA). The FBI is not allowed to carry on a trade or business.

Dutch tax legislation does not define 'passive investment activities' for FBI purposes. **69** Passive investment activities may include lease real estate or investments of a financial nature (such as loan notes, shares or other securities), provided that the investments are held as portfolio investments. To some extent, it is possible to 'actively' manage an investment portfolio without losing FBI status. Such active investment activities can be delegated to professionals who seek to 'maximize' the yield on the investment assets. Those professionals can be employed by the FBI itself or by separate management companies that manage the real estate assets of one or more FBIs. The activities performed by such professionals have to be proportionate to the size and nature of the investment portfolio. However, it is important to avoid the implication that the FBI is actively trading in investment assets.

70 Based on a change of law effective as of 1 January 2014, the permitted activities of the FBI are enlarged. Under these regulations, the FBI is allowed to hold shares in – as well as manage – a taxable service company. As a precondition, the activities of this subsidiary must consist of customary services in relation to the real estate held by the FBI or other affiliated entities. Examples of such services are conference facility, the exploitation of an in-house restaurant or leasing billboards/TV screens placed in or on the real estate. But also thermal storage or the supply of solar energy is under conditions permitted.

71 Furthermore, the FBI is allowed to provide guarantees to third parties – like financial institutions – to secure obligations of subsidiary real estate companies. These activities are considered passive investment activities.

72 In the opinion of the tax authorities, project (re)development falls outside the scope of the FBI's permitted investment activities. According to a decree of the State Secretary of Finance dated 22 February 2001, the activities and risks involved in real estate development cannot be considered passive investments within the FBI regime. While development activities are prohibited, maintenance activities are allowed. Work carried out on real estate assets is considered maintenance if the cost of the work is less than 30% of the property's official fair market value ('WOZ-value') prior to the start of the work. This value is determined by the authorities of the Dutch municipality in which the property is situated.

73 In relation to FBIs, there is no case law yet providing detailed guidance as to whether and to what extent (re)development activities can form part of the investment activities.

74 Impermissible development activity also includes the development of properties for the FBI's long-term investment portfolio. However, based on a recent amendment to the FBI regulations, an FBI is allowed to manage and hold shares in an (non-FBI) entity carrying out real estate development activities for the benefit of the (non-FBI) entity itself, or for the benefit of:

- the FBI as the shareholder in the (non-FBI) entity;
- entities related to the FBI that have FBI status; or
- entities in which the FBI or a related FBI has an interest of at least one-third.

75 This development subsidiary is taxed on its profits at the regular CIT rate of a maximum of 25.8% (2022, a reduced 15% applies to profits up to EUR 395,000). The subsidiary can also develop real estate that is already owned by the FBI in exchange for an arm's-length development fee. The subsidiary has to bear all of the risks of the development activity. In a decree dated 29 November 2019, the Dutch tax authorities have set out their view on an at arm's-length remuneration to be paid by the FBI to its development subsidiary.

76 Besides the investments in Dutch real estate assets and a development subsidiary, the FBI is also allowed to invest in foreign assets. In that case, the FBI is subject to the same investment restrictions. Finally, the FBI may invest through a (foreign) subsidiary company, partnership or mutual fund.

[6] Distribution/Accumulation

An FBI is required to distribute its entire taxable profit (the 'Distributable Amount') **77** within eight months following the financial year end. Tax losses carried forward reduce the taxable profit and the Distributable Amount of the FBI in future years. The amount of the Distributable Amount is calculated in accordance with the standard tax accounting principles, with exceptions especially provided for FBIs. Under International Financial Reporting Standards (IFRS), fair value accounting is leading, whereby for tax purposes, the principles of prudence, reality and simplicity form the basis for recognition of results. Therefore, the Distributable Amount may differ from the net profit in the financial statements.

When calculating the Distributable Amount, the FBI can decide to allocate certain **78** components of its taxable profits into a special reinvestment reserve (for tax purposes), and consequently, these profit components do not have to be distributed. This applies to realized and unrealized gains/losses on securities and realized gains/losses on other investments (like real estate assets).

After having formed a reinvestment reserve, the FBI must annually deduct a certain **79** amount of the expenses relating to the management and administration of the investments from subsequent contributions to the reinvestment reserve. Once the FBI elects to form a reinvestment reserve, the FBI has to continue to allocate all its gains and losses to the reserve.

An FBI can also accumulate a 'rounding-off reserve' for a maximum amount of 1% of **80** its paid-up share capital at the end of the year – including share premium – recognized for tax purposes. If an entity loses its FBI status, the rounding-off reserve must be added to the entity's taxable profits, and it is taxed at the standard CIT rate. The reinvestment reserve does not have to be added to the entity's taxable profits if the FBI regime is lost.

The profit to be distributed by an FBI should be divided equally over all shares. In **81** principle, this condition would seek to preclude the issuance of special classes of shares. However, provided certain conditions are met, it is still possible to form an FBI with separate compartments (e.g., an umbrella fund).

In the event that an FBI is structured as a private limited liability company or a public **82** limited liability company, the distribution of profits is also subject to provisions of Dutch corporate law. Typically, the distribution of profits requires a resolution of either the general meeting of shareholders or the board of directors to that effect. In the case of mutual funds, the terms and conditions contain the agreed principles and procedures on distributions.

[7]   Reporting Requirements

83 As a general rule of law, an FBI in the legal form of a private limited liability company or a public limited liability company is required to publish its annual accounts within eight days after such annual accounts have been adopted by the relevant corporate body. The publication of the annual accounts occurs by filing a copy of the annual accounts together with the management report, the auditor's statement and any other information required by law (together with the 'financial statements') with the trade register of the Chamber of Commerce. If the FBI has shares/units admitted to trading on a regulated market, different publication rules apply. An FBI-issuer must provide a copy of the financial statements to the AFM within five days following adoption. No separate filing with the trade register is required. Publication of the financial statements should occur no later than twelve months after the lapse of the relevant financial year. The term for the preparation of the financial statements depends on the type of legal entity and whether shares/units are traded on a regulated market.

84 In addition to the annual financial statements, an FBI-issuer whose shares/units are traded on a regulated market must also prepare and publish semi-annual financial statements. These must be made public within three months after the lapse of the first six months of the relevant issuer's financial year.

85 Licensed AIF managers, and to a lesser extent fund managers exempted from the AIFMD that are active in the Netherlands, are subject to several ongoing requirements relating to controlled and sound business operations and reporting to the supervising authorities and the investors in the AIFs under their management.

86 For instance, a licensed AIF manager will have to provide a copy of the audited annual accounts accompanied by a directors' report of each EU-AIF under its management and each AIF of which it offers shares/units in the EU to the AFM within four months after the lapse of the financial year. Furthermore, a licensed AIF manager must regularly report to AFM/DNB on the principal markets and instruments in which it trades, as well as on the liquidity, the risk profile and the asset categories of each AIF under its management. This is the so-called Annex IV Reporting.

[8]   Accounting

87 The financial reporting regulatory framework is built around the provisions set out in – mainly – Title 9 of Book 2 of the Dutch Civil Code and is further supplemented by the Dutch Accounting Standards, judicial precedence from the Enterprise Chamber of the Court of Appeal for Amsterdam (de *Ondernemingskamer*), the IFRS and the rules issued by the AFM.

88 In principle, a Dutch FBI should prepare its financial statements in accordance with Dutch Generally Accepted Accounting Principles. However, the Dutch Civil Code permits that financial statements are drawn up in accordance with other approved financial standards, such as IFRS, provided that in that instance, all of the applicable accounting standards are applied. The financial statements must indicate the accounting standards that are applied. An FBI which has shares/units admitted to trading on a regulated market must apply IFRS.

§1.03   TAXATION

[A]   Taxation of the REIT

[1]   Corporate Income Tax

[a]   Tax Accounting

The FBI regime is elected on the CIT return, and the election takes effect at the **89** beginning of the next financial year. The FBI is subject to 0% Dutch CIT, and a CIT return has to be filed each year.

Termination of FBI status is retroactive to the beginning of the financial year in which **90** the entity no longer meets all the requirements for FBI status. However, if the FBI does not comply with its profit distribution obligation, termination of FBI status is retroactive to the beginning of the year in which the relevant profit was made. If FBI status terminates, the entity is subject to a CIT rate of a maximum of 25.8% (2022, a reduced 15% rate applies on profits up to and including EUR 395,000). Based on changes of the law per 1 January 2015, the FBI is required to restate its investments at the market value prior to the entity becoming regularly taxed.

[b]   Determination of Taxable Income

The taxable income of an FBI is calculated the same as the taxable income of a regularly **91** taxed company, with some exceptions especially provided for FBIs. Like ordinary entities incorporated under the laws of the Netherlands, an FBI is deemed to carry out a 'business undertaking' by law, and it is subject to Dutch CIT on its worldwide profit.

For FBIs investing in real estate, taxable profit includes gross income realized on assets **92** less allocable expenses and tax depreciation/impairments. Gross income includes all income from the FBI's investment assets, as well as any results realized on the disposal of those assets. Allocable expenses include repair, maintenance, renovation and similar costs and interest expenses on loans taken out to finance the acquisition of the FBI's assets.

An FBI can depreciate real estate assets with the exception of land in ownership. The **93** depreciation method generally used is the straight-line method. The acquisition costs (including expenses such as registration duties, brokerage fees, notary's fees, architect's fees, transfer tax, and non-recoverable Value Added Tax (VAT)) are the basis for depreciation. The depreciation rate should relate to the expected useful life of the assets and the estimated residual value. As a general rule, 1%–3% depreciation rates are acceptable for commercial properties like office buildings. However, if it can be substantiated, a higher depreciation rate may be applied.

94 Depreciation of immovable property is not allowed when the tax book value (i.e., investment costs less accumulated depreciation) falls below the property's official fair market value for tax purposes ('WOZ-value'). The WOZ-value is determined by the municipal tax authorities on an annual basis. The valuation assumes that the real estate is freehold and free of a lease. As a result, the WOZ-value of commercial real estate will differ from the fair market value.

95 When the market value of the real estate assets falls below the tax book value (i.e., acquisition costs less accumulative depreciations), the FBI can impair the real estate assets. Such impairment is obligatory when the market value is durable and substantially (30% or more) lower than the tax book value.

96 Since the gearing restrictions are directly linked to the tax book value of the investments, tax depreciation and impairments have consequences for the maximum amount of debt funding.

Interest expenses on the debt funding are in principle deductible for Dutch tax purposes, provided the debt qualifies as real debt for tax purposes as well. Certain interest deduction limitation rules prohibit the deduction of interest expenses, although interest expenses in relation to the financing of real estate assets are in principle tax deductible.

Based on the introduction of the Anti Tax Avoidance Directive 1 (ATAD 1), net interest expenses are deductible to the higher of: (i) a threshold of EUR 1 million or (ii) 20% of the taxpayer's tax EBITDA (taxable earnings before interest, tax, depreciation and amortization). Non-deductible interest expenses can be carried forward indefinitely, although such carried forward interest will be forfeited due to a change of the ultimate ownership (30% or more) in the taxpayer. Furthermore, in principle such carried forward interest expenses increase the profitable amount for the calculation of the annual profit distribution of the FBI. Therefore, certain provisions apply for the calculations of the profit distributions, which provisions combat the interaction with ATAD 1 and mitigate adverse consequences of carried forward interest expenses in relation to the profit distribution calculations.

Furthermore, based on the introduction of the Anti Tax Avoidance Directive 2 (ATAD 2), expenses (e.g., interest expenses or other expenses paid to affiliated entities) may be restricted in deduction. ATAD 2 aims to prevent hybrid mismatches and payments to such hybrid entities. Such mismatches may result, for example, due to a difference in tax characterization of an entity or a financial instrument between two countries. This may result in a deductible payment that however is not taxed at the level of the recipient. ATAD 2 prevents double deductions and deductions without inclusions.

97 Capital gains are typically included in the calculation of the gross income of the FBI, and capital losses realized on the sale of FBI property are fully deductible. However, the

FBI may elect to allocate certain gains and losses to a reinvestment reserve (*see* section §1.02[F][6] above).

Tax losses incurred by an FBI can be carried forward for eight years. There is no carry **98** back facility. The tax losses carried forward reduce the taxable profit and the Distributable Amount in future years (*see* section §1.02[F][6] above).

[c]   *Taxation of Income from Taxable/Non-taxable Subsidiaries*

There are no special rules for an FBI with respect to taxation of income from **99** subsidiaries. Irrespective of whether the subsidiary is subject to taxation, dividends received and capital gains or losses realized are included in the calculation of the FBI's taxable profit and Distributable Amount. The FBI is not entitled to a participation exemption.

[d]   *Taxation of Foreign Income*

Foreign source income realized by an FBI is included in the taxable profit and in the **100** Distributable Amount of the FBI. If the FBI pays tax in the foreign jurisdiction in relation to that income, the FBI can reduce the Distributable Amount by the amount of foreign tax paid.

[2]   **Value Added Tax**

The Dutch VAT regulations are comparable to those applicable in the other EU Member **101** States. The Netherlands has a VAT system with rates of 0%, 9% and 21%. The rate of 21% applies to real estate. These regulations and rates also apply to FBIs. The supply of real estate is generally VAT exempt. There are two important exceptions to this general rule. The first exception is that the supply of newly developed or redeveloped land/real estate before, on, or within two years after the day the property was put into use is legally subject to VAT. The second exception is that under certain conditions, parties can jointly opt for a VAT taxed supply of (an independent exploitable part of) the real estate. Such an option can be included in the notarial deed of transfer. The lease of real estate is generally VAT exempt, but parties can, if certain conditions are met, opt for a VAT taxable lease in the lease agreement.

The FBI can recover input VAT on the acquisition, construction and maintenance costs **102** relating to the real estate insofar as the real estate is used for VAT taxable activities (e.g., VAT taxable lease). If the real estate is used for VAT taxable and VAT exempt activities, input VAT can be recovered on a proportional basis.

[3]   *Withholding Taxes*

103 Distributable income paid by an FBI to a Dutch or a foreign shareholder is subject to a 15% dividend withholding tax. Under tax treaties, the percentage may be reduced (*see* section §1.03[C][1] below). If shares in an FBI are redeemed, part of the proceeds is treated as dividends, subject to dividend withholding tax (*see* section §1.02[F][3] above).

104 The reinvestment reserve is considered to be paid-up capital for dividend withholding tax purposes. Consequently, distributions out of the reinvestment reserve are usually not subject to Dutch dividend withholding tax (*see* section §1.02[F][6] above).

105 The Netherlands levies withholding taxes on interest payments of certain hybrid debt instruments that, for tax purposes, are treated as equity. Furthermore, per 1 January 2021, the Netherlands levies a conditional withholding tax against a 25.8% rate (being the highest CIT rate) on outgoing interest and royalty payments to affiliated entities in countries that levy no tax on profits or at a statutory rate of less than 9%, countries on the EU list of non-cooperative jurisdictions or in abusive situations. In addition to this new conditional withholding tax, a new conditional withholding tax on dividend payments to the aforementioned jurisdictions has been announced to come into effect in 2024.

106 Dividends and interest payments received by the FBI may be subject to Dutch dividend withholding tax or foreign withholding tax. FBIs are entitled to credit the Dutch and foreign withholding tax against the obligation to withhold Dutch dividend withholding tax on outgoing dividend distributions. The credit is maximized to 15%.

107 Withholding taxes are, among others, in the centre of EU case law. Recently a number of EU court cases were ruled regarding discriminatory withholding taxes on the basis of free movement of capital (Article 63 Treaty on the Functioning of the European Union (TFEU)). Further developments of EU case law might have an impact on the Dutch tax system in general and, more particular, on the withholding tax treatment of FBIs (including the credit for withholding taxes to FBIs).

108 In addition, in March 2016, the Dutch Supreme Court held that the Dutch dividend withholding tax breaches the freedom of capital to the extent that the tax borne by foreign shareholders in the Netherlands is more burdensome than the personal or CIT, which is borne by their Dutch resident counterparts. These judgments follow the rulings of the EU court. As a result, foreign dividend recipients that actually bear a comparatively heavier tax burden in the Netherlands are from now on eligible for a refund of the excess Dutch dividend taxes levied. The Dutch Supreme Court's decision increases the chances of success on a refund of Dutch dividend withholding tax for foreign investment funds. Comparative calculations must be made on a case-by-case basis. Following this decision, the Dutch law was changed in 2017, and on request and under conditions, certain non-resident shareholders who qualify as the beneficial owner of revenues on which they do not pay personal income tax or CIT in the Netherlands can receive a refund of withheld dividend tax insofar as this levy is higher than the personal income tax or CIT they would owe if they would have resided or been based in the Netherlands.

[4] Other Taxes

The acquisition of legal and/or economic ownership of Dutch real estate is subject to **109** real estate transfer tax. The acquirer has to pay an 8%[1] tax on the higher of: (i) the purchase price or (ii) the fair market value of the real estate at the time of the acquisition. The acquisition or expansion of an interest equal to or exceeding one-third in a real estate company is also subject to the real estate transfer tax. Note that the acquisition of residential real estate is subject to a reduced transfer tax rate of 2%, but this rate only applies to individuals that acquire the residential real estate for their own use.

If the acquisition of real estate takes place within six months of a previous transfer of **110** the same real estate, the taxable basis is reduced by the amount on which real estate transfer tax (or VAT which was not recoverable) was paid on the previous transfer. Various real estate transfer tax exemptions exist. The main exemptions apply to mergers/demergers and internal group reorganizations.

To avoid accumulation of real estate transfer tax and VAT, the acquisition of real estate **111** is not subject to real estate transfer tax if the transfer is subject to VAT (legitimately, not by means of an option request), and the real estate has not been used as a business asset.

The FBI is subject to municipal property tax. This property tax is an annual tax and is **112** split between an owner tax and a user tax (the last only in the case of non-residential property). Tariffs are set by the local council as a percentage of the so-called WOZ-value, which is a property value for tax purposes determined on an annual basis and set by a decree that is open for appeal.

[5] Penalties Imposed on REIT

Penalties can be imposed on the FBI for failure to pay any CIT, VAT, transfer tax or **113** dividend withholding taxes owed. Furthermore, penalties are imposed for not filing or not timely filing tax returns.

---

1. It has been announced that this rate will increase to 9% per 1 Jan. 2023, although there is currently no formal legislation in this regard.

[B] Taxation of the Investor

[1] *Private Investors*

[a] *Taxation of Current Income (All Income Derived from REIT in Holding Phase)*

[i] Resident Individuals

114 Dutch resident individuals who own, alone or together with certain relatives, 5% or more of the shares in an FBI are considered the holders of substantial interest for Dutch personal income tax purposes. Dutch resident substantial interest holders are subject to a flat 25% tax rate on dividends and from an FBI.

115 Dutch resident individuals who own less than 5% of the shares in an FBI are not considered holders of substantial interest. Income from a non-substantial interest in an FBI is subject to capital yield tax, the so-called box 3 income. The tax is based on a notional yield calculated on the basis of three ascending fixed percentages. These percentages have been determined on the basis of relevant market information and investment results and will be reassessed periodically. For 2020 the following percentages will apply:

- 1.82% on assets with a total value of EUR 50,000 to EUR 100,000 (an exemption for capital to an amount of EUR 50,650 applies).
- 4.37% on assets with a total value of EUR 101,300 to EUR 1,013,000.
- 5.53% on assets with a total value exceeding EUR 1,013,000.

116 The notional yield is taxed at a flat rate of 31%. The tax is levied irrespective of the actual positive or negative yield realized. The 15% dividend withholding tax is fully creditable against personal income tax for both substantial interest holders and non-substantial interest holders.

[ii] Non-resident Individuals

117 Non-resident individuals who own 5% or more of the shares in an FBI (substantial interest holders) are subject to tax on FBI dividends at a rate of 26.9%. Some tax treaties limit the right of the Netherlands to levy Dutch income tax on substantial interest income. Non-resident individuals who are not considered holders of substantial interest are not subject to Dutch personal income tax.

118 The 15% (withholding) tax on dividends is credited against Dutch income tax levied (if any) for substantial interest holders.

[iii]   Resident Corporate Investor

Dividends received by Dutch resident corporate investors from an FBI are subject to   **119**
Dutch CIT at the standard rates (25.8% for 2022). In most circumstances, an
investment in an FBI will not qualify for the participation exemption under the CITA.

Dutch corporate investors can credit the Dutch dividend withholding tax paid on   **120**
dividends from an FBI against the CIT due. Any excess withholding tax will be
refunded.

[iv]   Non-resident Corporate Investor

In general, Dutch corporate income taxation (max rate 25.8%) at the level of the   **121**
shareholder will only arise over dividends received if the non-resident investor holds a
substantial interest (5% or more of the shares in an FBI) and if the shares in the Dutch
company are held by the foreign investor with the main purpose (or one of the main
purposes) to avoid the levy of Dutch personal income tax while an arrangement (or
series of arrangements) has been applied which is not based on sound business
motives reflecting the economic reality. As such, the purpose of the shareholding by
the non-resident shareholder must be assessed. If the shares in the FBI are attributable
to an active business carried out by the foreign shareholder, the shares are typically not
considered held with the purpose of avoiding personal income tax. If there are no
private individuals holding a direct or indirect interest in the FBI of 5% or more
(*aanmerkelijk belang*), the foreign shareholding in the FBI should not be considered
held with the purpose of avoiding Dutch personal income tax. Furthermore, Dutch
corporate tax may arise in cases where the shares in the FBI are attributable to a Dutch
permanent establishment of the non-resident shareholder. Tax treaties may limit the
right for the Netherlands to levy Dutch income tax on substantial interest gains. In
addition, the 15% dividend withholding tax may be reduced under tax treaties (*see*
section §1.03[C][2]). It should be noted that the introduction of the Multilateral
Instrument as of 2020 denies treaty benefits in certain cases of abuse.

Non-resident investors with a substantial interest can credit the Dutch dividend   **122**
withholding tax on dividends from an FBI against the CIT liability.

[b]   Taxation of Capital Gains (From Disposal of REIT Shares)

[i]   Resident Individuals

Dutch resident individuals who own a substantial interest in the FBI are subject to a flat   **123**
26.9% tax rate on:

   – capital gains realized on the transfer of shares or profits rights;

– capital gains realized on the transfer of options granting the right to buy shares or profit rights.

124 Dutch resident individuals who do not hold a substantial interest in the FBI are subject to the capital yield tax. Capital yield tax is based on a fictitious return between 1.82% and 5.53% of the value of the shares at a fixed rate of 31% (*see* section §1.03[B][5]). Actual gains or losses are irrelevant.

125 The 15% (withholding) tax on dividends is credited against Dutch income tax levied (if any) for both substantial interest holders and non-substantial interest holders.

[ii]   Non-resident Individuals

126 Non-resident individuals who hold a substantial interest in the FBI are subject to a tax rate of 26.9% on the same basis as resident individuals. Tax treaties may limit the right for the Netherlands to levy Dutch income tax on substantial interest gains. The 15% withholding tax on dividends can be credited against the Dutch tax on substantial interest gains.

127 Non-resident individuals who are not considered holders of substantial interest are not subject to Dutch personal income tax unless attributable to a trade or business in the Netherlands.

[iii]   Resident Corporate Investor

128 Capital gains realized through the sale of shares in an FBI by a Dutch resident corporate investor are subject to Dutch CIT at the standard rates (25.8% for 2022). Capital gains realized by investors subject to Dutch CIT will, in most circumstances, not qualify for the participation exemption under the CITA.

[iv]   Non-resident Corporate Investor

129 In general, Dutch corporate income taxation (max rate 25.8%) at the level of the shareholder will only arise over capital gains realized on the FBI shares if the non-resident investor holds a substantial interest (5% or more of the shares in an FBI) and if the shares in the Dutch company are held by the foreign investor with the main purpose (or one of the main purposes) of avoiding the levy of Dutch personal income tax while an arrangement (or series of arrangements) has been applied which is not based on sound business motives reflecting the economic reality. As such, the purpose of the shareholding by the non-resident shareholder must be assessed. If the shares in the FBI are attributable to an active business carried out by the foreign shareholder, the shares are typically not considered held with the purpose of avoiding personal income tax. If there are no private individuals holding a direct or indirect interest in the FBI of

5% or more (*aanmerkelijk belang*), the foreign shareholding in the FBI should not be considered held with the purpose of avoiding Dutch personal income tax. Furthermore, Dutch corporate tax may arise in cases where the shares in the FBI are attributable to a Dutch permanent establishment of the non-resident shareholder. Tax treaties may limit the right of the Netherlands to levy Dutch income tax on substantial interest gains.

Furthermore, taxation may arise in cases where the non-resident investor is engaged in **130** or participates in a trade or business in the Netherlands to which the FBI's shares are attributable.

Tax treaties may limit the right of the Netherlands to levy Dutch income tax on **131** substantial interest gains.

[2] *Institutional Investors*

[a] *Taxation of Current Income (All Income Derived from REIT in Holding Phase)*

Dutch pension funds are generally exempt from Dutch CIT. Dutch tax-exempt pension **132** funds are entitled to a full refund of the Dutch dividend withholding tax levied on dividend distributions made by an FBI.

EU-resident pension funds that are tax exempt and that are comparable with Dutch **133** pension funds are, under certain conditions, entitled to a full refund of Dutch dividend withholding tax levied on dividend distributions made by an FBI.

As of 1 January 2012, non-EU entities that are tax exempt and resident in a country of **134** which the Netherlands has concluded an agreement for the exchange of information are, under certain conditions, also entitled to a full refund of Dutch dividend withholding tax. This refund relates to portfolio dividends only and refers to Article 63 TFEU. With this amendment, the Dutch tax law is further harmonized with EU tax law.

[b] *Taxation of Capital Gains (From Disposal of REIT Shares)*

Capital gains realized by Dutch and EU-resident pension funds upon disposal of shares **135** in an FBI are not subject to Dutch capital gains tax.

[3] *Penalties Imposed on Investors*

Penalties can be imposed on FBI investors if the investor understates the taxable **136** income derived from the shareholding in the FBI and for late or not filing a tax return.

[C]   **Tax Treaties**

[1]   *Treaty Access*

137   The Netherlands has a large tax treaty network. As an entity resident in the Netherlands, the FBI benefits from the Netherlands tax treaties.

[2]   *WHT Reduction*

138   Depending on the status of the FBI investor, tax treaties may reduce the 15% Dutch dividend withholding tax rate to a lower rate, and in some specific cases, to nil. It should be noted that the introduction of the Multilateral Instrument as of 2020 denies treaty benefits in certain cases of abuse.

139   It is uncertain whether an FBI may invoke the EU Parent-Subsidiary Directive. The Dutch tax authorities maintain that the EU Parent-Subsidiary Directive, as implemented in Dutch legislation, may not be invoked where an FBI (subject to 0% CIT) makes a dividend distribution. Also, in a recent decision, the CJEU judged that an FBI cannot invoke the EU Parent-Subsidiary Directive since an FBI de facto is tax exempt, although it is de jure subject to CIT (against a 0% rate). Therefore, FBIs do not fulfil the subject-to-tax requirement of the EU Parent-Subsidiary Directive. The CJEU ruled that the EU Parent-Subsidiary Directive subject-to-tax requirement lays down a positive criterion ('being subject to tax') and a negative one ('not being exempt from that tax and not having the possibility of an option'). Consequently, the EU Parent-Subsidiary Directive does not merely require that a company should fall within the scope of the tax in question but also seeks to exclude situations involving the possibility that despite being subject to tax, the company is not actually liable to pay that tax. Although FBIs are formally not exempt from tax in the Netherlands, they are practically in a situation in which they are not liable to pay that tax.

[D]   **Exit Tax/Tax Privileges/Concessions**

140   At the end of the year prior to the year that an entity is converted to the FBI regime, all assets are restated at market value. The capital gain resulting from such restatement is subject to tax at the regular CIT rate. Tax-free reserves are added to the taxable income. The exit tax is levied at the ordinary Dutch CIT rates, currently 25.8% (2022).

141   Upon termination of the FBI regime (by non-compliance or voluntarily), the entity becomes subject to the ordinary CIT rules. Based on changes of the law per 1 January 2015, the FBI is required to restate its investments at the market value prior to the entity becoming regularly taxed. As a result, hidden reserves (both positive and negative) built in the investments during the period the entity was taxed under the FBI regime are realized. The realization of the latent capital results is subject to the CIT at a rate of 0%.

[E] **Taxation of Foreign REITs**

[1] *Taxation of Foreign REIT Holding Assets in Country*

Foreign REITs owning real estate assets in the Netherlands are subject to the ordinary   **142**
Dutch CIT regime and tax rates for Dutch source income. Hence, the income and capital
gains realized on the Dutch real estate investment are taxed at a rate of 25.8%. The
basis for the taxable income is the gross income (including capital gains) realized on
the property minus allocable expenses and depreciation.

A foreign REIT is able to apply the FBI regime for its Dutch source income, provided it   **143**
is an entity comparable to a Dutch limited liability company, public limited liability
company or mutual fund, and all other conditions of the FBI regime are met. The main
important conditions are the shareholders' requirements (*see* section §1.02[F][5][c]
above), a profit distribution requirement (*see* section §1.02[F][6] above), an activity
test (*see* section §1.02[A][2] above) and leverage conditions (*see* section §1.02[F][5][b]
above).

[2] *Taxation of Investors Holding Shares in Foreign REIT*

[a] *Individual Investors*

If the individual owns less than 5% of the shares in a foreign REIT, the income derived   **144**
from such a shareholding is subject to the capital yield tax. This means that the income
will be based on a fictitious return between 1.82% and 5.53% of the value of the shares
at a fixed rate of 31% (*see* section §1.03[B][5]). Under this regime, actual income, gains
and losses are irrelevant.

[b] *Corporate Investors*

If the corporate investor owns less than 5% of the shares in a foreign REIT, dividend   **145**
income received and capital gains realized through the investment in a foreign REIT are
subject to Dutch CIT at the standard rates (25.8% for 2022).

The participation exemption may be applicable to a foreign REIT if it fulfils the 'asset   **146**
test'. To qualify for the asset test, the assets of the foreign REIT must consist – on a
consolidated basis – of at least 50% qualifying assets, including real estate. Likewise,
losses resulting from qualifying participation in a subsidiary company are generally not
deductible. In order to apply the participation exemption, the corporate investor should
own 5% or more of the shares in the foreign REIT. Under certain circumstances, losses
incurred upon the liquidation of the subsidiary company are deductible at the holding
company level. Should the participation exemption apply, dividends and capital gains

realized by the shareholder are exempt unless these payments were deductible at the level of the subsidiary.

[c]   *Institutional Investors*

147 Dutch pension funds are exempt from Dutch CIT provided that certain conditions are met. Income received and capital gains realized from a shareholding in a foreign REIT are therefore tax exempt.

Singapore

LIM MAAN HUEY

Maan Huey is a tax partner with the Financial Services group of PwC Singapore, and she leads the real estate tax practice of the firm. She has over eighteen years of experience in working with global and local clients in the financial services industry on tax consulting and compliance matters. She previously worked in the New York firm of PwC US, advising private fund clients on international tax matters.

Maan Huey works with clients in family offices, hedge funds, private equity, real estate, retail funds and sovereign wealth funds. She has tax advisory experience in many aspects, including operational tax compliance and procedural issues, permanent establishment issues for funds and fund managers, set-up of funds and fund management operations, use of Singapore-domiciled investment/fund structures, cross-border investments as well as restructuring and mergers and acquisition transactions.

She is involved in the tax working committee of the Singapore Chapter of the Alternative Investments Management Association and the tax working committee of the Investment Management Association of Singapore.

E-mail: maan.huey.lim@ pwc.com

LENNON LEE

Lennon Lee is a tax partner with PricewaterhouseCoopers Singapore Pte. Ltd ('PwC Singapore'), and he leads the financial services tax practice in PwC Singapore. He is part of the real estate and hospitality (REH) team in PwC Singapore.

With close to 25 years of experience in practising Singapore and international tax, Lennon has been involved in many international advisory projects and assignments across a whole spectrum of industries. He advises financial institutions, government-linked entities, high net worth individuals, family offices, fund management houses, real estate developers, REIT managers, and listed companies on various Singapore and cross-border tax and regulatory implications arising from investment, development and management of real estate globally.

In addition, he manages the China tax practice in Singapore and advises corporates on both inbound and outbound investments involving China. In particular, he has been involved in the listing of a few China sponsored REITs in Singapore.

Lennon is an active speaker for various industry conferences and seminars organized by financial institutions, business organizations and government agencies, and has contributed articles to various publications. He is on the board of directors of the Tax Academy of Singapore.
E-mail: lennon.kl.lee@ pwc.com

Singapore

Lim Maan Huey & Lennon Lee

---

§1.01   BACKGROUND

[A]   Key Characteristics

The Singapore government has made a strong effort to establish the country as a Real   **1**
Estate Investment Trust (REIT) and real estate business trust (BT) hub, and despite its
relatively short history, the Singapore REIT market has matured quickly into one of
Asia's most important markets for listed REITs. A robust and clear regulatory frame-
work guides property fund activities such as those of REITs. A specific tax regime for
REITs provides favourable tax treatment (e.g., allowing flow-through treatment of
Specified Income). Also, REIT-specific tax concessions (e.g., exemption for certain
foreign income) enhance the tax benefits for listed REITs in Singapore.

A property fund may be constituted as a company, a BT or a unit trust governed by the   **2**
Collective Investment Scheme regime. However, only a property fund constituted as a
unit trust under the Collective Investment Scheme regime may enjoy the tax benefits
referred to above. All REITs in Singapore are constituted as unit trusts governed by the
Collective Investment Scheme regime.

Although technically Singapore REITs can be listed or unlisted, all existing REITs in   **3**
Singapore to date are listed entities, given the fact that listing is a mandatory
prerequisite of gaining access to the tax concessions. The REIT can be a stand-alone
entity or a stapled entity, combining both a BT component and a REIT component.

[B]   History of REIT

The REIT regime in Singapore was officially launched in 1999, and the first REIT   **4**
(CapitaMall Trust) was listed on the Singapore Stock Exchange (SGX) in 2002.

Although a relatively late entrant to the global REIT market, the Singapore REIT market   **5**
has witnessed exponential growth in the last few years and has established itself as one

of the largest REIT markets in Asia within a short period of time. The REIT market has grown to forty-four REITs and Property Trusts currently listed on the SGX. The total market capitalization of SGX-listed REITs was approximately over SGD 115 billion as at 31 December 2021.

6 Multiple factors have fuelled the accelerated growth of the Singapore REIT market. On the regulatory front, comprehensive investment guidelines for property funds gave confidence to participants in the REIT industry. The tax regime was also crafted to confer attractive tax concessions to Singapore REITs. Further, the Singapore government is constantly in consultation with key industry participants to improve the regulatory and tax regime for REITs.

[C]   REIT Market

7 The Singapore REIT market started off with mostly REITs that invest in industrial or commercial properties based in Singapore. However, as the pool of investment-grade properties in Singapore became securitized and increasingly limited in availability, owners started to divest their foreign property portfolios into Singapore REITs. BTs and stapled entities are also likely to become increasingly common offerings on the SGX[1] (*see* section §1.02[K] below) in order to enhance the risk profile of the offering.

§1.02   REGULATORY ASPECTS

[A]   Legal Form of REIT

[1]   Corporate Form

8 A REIT is governed by its trust deed, which sets out the responsibilities and obligations of the Trustee and the Manager, as well as the rights and entitlements of the beneficiaries, that is, the Unitholders. The legal title to the REIT's property portfolio is held by the Trustee.

[a]   Manager and Trustee

9 Some of the key responsibilities and obligations of the Manager and the Trustee of a property fund (including a REIT) are set out in the Code on Collective Investment Schemes (the 'Code') and Property Fund Guidelines (PFG) as follows:

---

1. For example, CDL Hospitality Trusts, although the BT component is there only as a lessee of last resort for the time being.

(a) The Manager of the fund has to:
  (i) for a listed fund, be a corporation with a physical office in Singapore, and have minimum shareholders' funds of SGD 1 million;
  (ii) have a resident chief executive officer (CEO);
  (iii) have at least three full-time employees (may include the CEO) who are engaged in the investment management, asset management, financing, marketing and investor relations functions;
  (iv) meet the 'fit and proper' criteria per the Monetary Authority of Singapore's (MAS') Guidelines;
  (v) have more than five years' experience in managing property funds;
  (vi) appoint, with the approval of the Trustee, an adviser with more than five years of experience in investing in and/or advising on real estate; and
  (vii) employ persons with more than five years' experience in investing in and/or advising on real estate.
(b) Commissions or fees paid by the property fund to the adviser cannot be higher than market rates.
(c) The Singapore office has to play a meaningful role in the business activities of the Manager. For a listed property fund, accounting, compliance and investor relations activities have to be performed in Singapore.
(d) The Trustee is obligated to exercise due care and diligence in discharging its functions and duties, including safeguarding the rights and interests of participants.
(e) The trust deed has to provide that the Manager may be removed by way of a resolution passed by a simple majority of participants present and voting at a general meeting.

A stapled structure allows a REIT's real estate holding and management activities to be **10** combined with other non-permissible activities. The non-permissible activities are conducted under a non-REIT entity (e.g., a BT). Such activities may include substantive property development and assuming contingency roles such as that of a lessee of last resort.

A stapling deed contractually binds the separate securities together, and they must be **11** inseparably traded on the SGX as a combined, stapled security. However, the underlying securities continue to be treated as separate entities for tax and legal purposes. Although the stapled structure is recognized by regulators as an allowable listing structure, the Inland Revenue Authority of Singapore (IRAS) has adopted a strict position with regard to the tax treatment of stapled securities. While the REIT component is eligible for REIT-specific tax concessions, the non-REIT component (e.g., BT) is not eligible for such concessions and is taxed under normal tax rules. It is unlikely that the IRAS will allow a BT (investing in real estate) deriving mainly non-taxable supplies to be registered for Goods and Services Tax (GST; Singapore Value Added Tax (VAT)), and they do not grant any GST remission to a BT (investing in real estate) if the BT (investing in real estate) does not make or intend to make any taxable supplies.

[2]   Investment Restrictions

12   The scope of investments that a REIT is allowed to make is restricted to certain classes of 'permissible investments'. *See* section §1.02[F][5] below.

[B]   Regulatory Authorities

13   A REIT constituted in Singapore must be authorized by the MAS, and a foreign constituted REIT must be accorded recognition by the MAS. Both the Manager and Trustee of a REIT constituted in Singapore must be approved by the MAS. In the case of a foreign constituted REIT, its Manager must be licensed or regulated in the jurisdiction of its principal place of business.

[C]   Legislative and Other Regulatory Sources

14   A Singapore REIT, being a property fund, is bound by the rules and restrictions contained in the Code and the *PFG* appended to the Code. Both the Code and PFG are issued by the MAS.

15   A REIT is also liable to comply with the legal requirements set forth under the Securities and Futures Act (SFA).

16   In addition, the Singapore *Code on Take-overs and Mergers* has been extended to include REITs, ensuring that fair and equal treatment is accorded to all Unitholders.

[D]   Exchange Controls and Reporting Requirements

17   A REIT that is listed on SGX is required to observe the listing rules of Singapore Exchange Securities Trading Limited (SGX-ST). To ensure adequate and timely disclosure of information by a REIT, the SGX monitors news reports in the media as well as announcements, financial results and annual reports issued by the REIT.

18   By virtue of being a publicly listed entity, a REIT will need to adhere to the rules in the Listing Manual of the SGX (in particular, Chapters 2 and 4).

19   The rules cover the following areas:

   (a) shareholding spread and distribution;
   (b) quantitative criteria;
   (c) financial position and liquidity;

(d) directors and management;
(e) Articles of Association;
(f) minimum leasehold period;
(g) independence of valuer and valuation report;
(h) conflicts of interest; and
(i) documents to be submitted.

A listed REIT is required to disclose its unit prices quoted on the SGX at the beginning   **20**
and end of the financial year, the highest and lowest unit prices for the year, and the
volume traded during the financial year. The offering prospectus has to disclose the
risks specific to investing in the REIT, including:

(a) diversification;
(b) high gearing;
(c) valuation;
(d) illiquidity of properties;
(e) any acquisition fees payable to the Manager and the expected incremental
     income and fees payable to the Manager; and
(f) any disposition fees and how the disposal would be in the interests of
     participants.

[E]   Registration Procedures

[1]   *Preparatory Measures*

[a]   *REIT Constituted in Singapore*

For a REIT constituted in Singapore, the MAS may grant the requisite authorization if   **21**
it is satisfied that the following key conditions are met:

(a) the REIT is constituted in Singapore;
(b) the REIT, its Manager and Trustee have complied with the SFA and require-
     ments of the Code;
(c) the Trustee of the REIT is one approved by the MAS;
(d) the Manager of the REIT has met the following key requirements under the
     SFA and the Code:
         (i) it is the holder of a capital markets services licence;
        (ii) it is a corporation with a physical office in Singapore and with
              minimum shareholders' funds of SGD 1 million;
       (iii) it has a resident CEO;
        (iv) it has at least three full-time professional employees (who may
              include the CEO) engaged in investment/asset management, financ-
              ing, marketing and investor relations activities;

(v) the Manager, as well as its CEO, directors and professional employees meet the 'fit and proper' criteria set out in guidelines issued by the MAS; and

(vi) it has a minimum of five years' experience in managing property funds or has appointed advisers or employed persons with at least five years' experience in investing in and/or advising on real estate.

(e) the Manager and the Trustee of the REIT have entered into a trust deed constituting the REIT, and the deed contains covenants that comply with the SFA and the Code.

[b]   REIT Constituted Outside Singapore

22 The MAS may recognize a REIT constituted outside Singapore if it is satisfied that the following key conditions are met:

(a) the REIT is constituted outside Singapore;

(b) the laws and practices of the foreign jurisdiction under which the REIT is constituted and regulated afford investors in Singapore protection equivalent to that provided to them under Singapore laws and regulations applicable to REITs;

(c) the REIT has appointed a Singapore representative who is able to carry out certain statutory functions;

(d) the Manager of the REIT:
  (i) is licensed or regulated in its home jurisdiction; and
  (ii) meets the MAS 'fit and proper' criteria.

(e) the REIT, its Manager and the Trustee (where applicable) have complied with the SFA and requirements under the Code.

[2]   Obtaining Authorization

23 A Singapore REIT has to submit the following key documents to the MAS along with the application for authorization:

(a) Annex 2A to the Code (information requests on the property fund manager, shareholders, the property fund, etc.).

(b) Form 1 of the Securities and Futures (Offers of Investments) (Collective Investment Schemes) Regulations and the documents (e.g., draft prospectus) and information (e.g., information on the Collective Investment Scheme, the relationship between the Manager and Trustee) requested therein.

(c) The trust deed.

[3]   Other Requirements for the Incorporation of a Company

With effect from 1 August 2008, REIT managers (including REIT management compa-   24
nies) are subject to licensing requirements under the SFA. This regime sets admission
criteria and imposes several key requirements on the conduct of REIT managers. *See*
section §1.02[E][1] above for other key requirements of a REIT management company.

[4]   Obtaining Exchange Listing

Some of the key requirements a REIT denominated in SGD (S$) must comply with   25
when seeking a listing on the SGX are that it:

(a) must have a minimum market capitalization of SGD 300 million based on the
     issue price and post-invitation issued share capital;
(b) must ensure that at least 25% of its units are to be held by at least five
     hundred public Unitholders;
(c) must limit its investments in companies related to its substantial Unitholders'
     investment managers or management companies to a maximum of 10% of
     gross assets;
(d) must restrict investments in unlisted securities to 30% of gross assets; and
(e) must abide by the investment and borrowing restrictions prescribed by the
     Code.

Some of the key requirements a REIT denominated in a foreign currency must comply   26
with when seeking a listing on the SGX are that it:

(a) must have a minimum market capitalization of SGD 300 million based on the
     issue price and post-invitation issued share capital (or equivalent in other
     currencies);
(b) must ensure that at least 25% of its units are to be held by at least 500 public
     Unitholders; and
(c) must have facilities for the transfer and registration of securities in Singapore
     if it is established in a foreign country.

[a]   Other Requirements

In addition, the listing exchange also imposes other requirements; for instance, it   27
requires that a new REIT not change its investment objectives or policies in the first
three years unless approval is obtained by a special resolution of the shareholders in a
general meeting. Furthermore, the investment manager of the REIT must be reputable
with an established track record of managing investments for at least five years.

28   The following documents must be submitted to the SGX in conjunction with the listing application:

        (a) prospectus;
        (b) compliance checklist;
        (c) trust deed;
        (d) memorandum and Articles of Association, if applicable; and
        (e) annual accounts for the last five financial years, if applicable.

    [b]   *Costs*

29   The initial fee to list units on the SGX Mainboard is between SGD 100,000 and SGD 200,000 with effect from 1 July 2013, depending on the size of market capitalization admitted.

    [c]   *Time*

30   The SGX typically takes around three weeks to grant an in-principle approval upon submission of an application. Thereafter, additional documents have to be lodged before the REIT is admitted to the Official List.

[F]   Requirements and Restrictions

[1]   *Capital Requirements*

31   There are no specific regulatory minimum capital requirements for a Singapore REIT. A listed REIT must still achieve the above minimum asset size threshold prescribed by the SGX in order to maintain its listing on the Exchange (*see* section §1.02[E][4] above).

32   A single-tier leverage limit of 45% for a Singapore REIT's deposited property was introduced in 2016, following which there was no longer a requirement for the Singapore REIT to obtain a credit rating to enjoy a higher leverage limit. To provide Singapore REITs greater flexibility to manage their capital structure amid the challenging environment created by the coronavirus pandemic, the Singapore REIT leverage limit has been raised to 50% with effect from 16 April 2020.

[2]   *Marketing/Advertising*

33   Mandatory requirements and restrictions for REITs in respect of advertising content (e.g., forecasts, past performance data, etc.) are prescribed in the SFA.

[3]   Redemption

A listed REIT is allowed to redeem its units from the open market. However, the **34**
redemption procedures are governed by the SGX rules for redemptions and must be
carried out in accordance with the relevant provisions as provided under the trust deed.

[4]   Valuation of Shares/Units for Redemption and Other Purposes

A full valuation of each real estate asset held by a REIT must be carried out by a **35**
professional valuer at least once a financial year, in accordance with any applicable
Code of Practice for such valuations.

If the REIT's real estate assets were valued more than six months prior to the issue of **36**
new units for subscription or redemption, the Manager has to decide whether a desktop
valuation of the assets is necessary. A desktop valuation means a valuation based on
transacted prices/yields of similar real estate assets without a physical inspection of the
property.

[5]   Investment Restrictions

The scope of investments that a REIT is allowed to make is restricted to the following **37**
classes of 'permissible investments' under the Code and the PFG:

    (a) real estate in or outside Singapore;
    (b) real estate-related assets;
    (c) listed or unlisted debt securities and listed shares of, or issued by, local or
        foreign non-property corporations;
    (d) securities issued by the Government, supranational agency or a Singapore
        statutory board; and
    (e) cash and cash equivalents.

A REIT may invest in local or foreign assets, subject to the terms of its trust deed. **38**
Where an investment in foreign real estate is made, the Manager should ensure that the
investment complies with all the applicable laws and requirements of that foreign
country.

A REIT is also subject to restrictions on its investment activities, including the **39**
following:

    (a) At least 75% of the deposited property should be invested in income-
        producing real estate.

   (b) The fund should not undertake property development activities or invest in unlisted property development companies unless it intends to hold the developed property upon completion.

   (c) The fund should not invest in vacant land or mortgages (except for mortgage-backed securities).

   (d) The total contract value of property development activities and investments in uncompleted property developments should not exceed 10% of the value of deposited property, but this limit can be increased to 25%, subject to certain conditions.

   (e) For investments in 'permissible investments' (c), (d) and (e) above (except for deposits placed with eligible financial institutions and investments in high-quality money-market instruments or debt securities), not more than 5% of the REIT's deposited property can be invested in any one issuer's securities or any one Manager's funds.

40   In addition, a REIT should not derive more than 10% of its revenue from sources other than:

    – rental payments from the tenants of the real estate held by the REIT; or
    – interest, dividends, and other similar payments from special purpose vehicles (SPVs) and other permissible investments of the REIT.

41   A REIT may acquire from or sell assets to interested parties or invest in securities of or securities issued by interested parties, provided certain conditions are met.

[6]   *Distribution/Accumulation*

42   To qualify for tax transparency treatment, a REIT is required to distribute at least 90% of its taxable income (primarily Singapore sourced income) in a financial year. For a REIT that derives income from real estate investments outside of Singapore, this distribution policy is not relevant, but nevertheless, it is usually explicitly stated in the REIT's offering prospectus, which would also serve to enhance the marketability of the public offering.

[7]   *Reporting Requirements*

43   A REIT is not required to lodge its audited financial statements with the Accounting & Corporate Regulatory Authority annually. However, a listed REIT is required to prepare audited accounts as part of the listing requirements. SGX listing rules mandate the announcement of interim financial results on a half-yearly basis.

44   The Manager of a REIT has to prepare an annual report disclosing the following:

(a) Details of all real estate transactions during the year (including the identity of the buyers/sellers, purchase/sale prices, and their valuations, including methods used, etc.).

(b) Details of all of the REIT's real estate assets (including their locations, purchase prices and latest valuations, rentals received, occupancy rates, remaining terms of leasehold properties, etc.).

(c) The tenant profiles of real estate assets (including the total number of tenants, top ten major tenants and their percentage of total gross rental income, trade sector mix of tenants, lease maturity profiles, etc.).

(d) Top ten holdings of other assets.

(e) Details of exposure to financial derivatives.

(f) Details of investments in other property funds.

(g) Details of borrowings.

(h) Details of deferred payment arrangements.

(i) Total operating expenses, including all fees & charges paid to the Manager, adviser and interested parties, and taxation incurred in relation to the REIT's real estate assets.

(j) Performance of the property fund.

(k) Net Assets Value per unit at the beginning and end of the financial year.

(l) Where the REIT is listed, the unit price quoted on the exchange at the beginning and end of the financial year, the highest and lowest unit price, and the volume traded during the financial year.

[8] *Accounting*

A REIT is required to prepare audited financial statements in accordance with   **45**
Singapore Financial Reporting Standards. These are largely aligned with International Financial Reporting Standards.

§1.03 TAXATION

[A] Taxation of the REIT

[1] *Corporate Income Tax*

[a] *Tax Accounting*

The income of a trust (including a REIT) derived from Singapore or income derived   **46**
outside Singapore and received or deemed received in Singapore is subject to Singapore income tax unless otherwise exempted.

If the REIT obtains the necessary approvals from the IRAS, it can enjoy tax transpar-   **47**
ency treatment for its Specified Income (as defined in section §1.03[A][1][b] below)

that is distributed to its Unitholders. Under the tax transparency rules, the Trustee is not taxed on the income of the REIT, but rather, tax (if any) is levied only at the level of the Unitholders. The Trustee is taxed on any portion of the income not distributed ('Retained Income'). The Trustee is also taxed on sources of income that do not qualify for tax transparency treatment (i.e., 'other taxable income'). Retained Income and other taxable income received by the REIT are taxed at the Trustee level at the prevailing Singapore corporate tax rate (17% for income earned in the financial year ending 2021).

48 In order for a REIT to qualify for the tax transparency treatment, the Trustee is required to distribute at least 90% of the REIT's Specified Income to Unitholders in the same year in which the income is derived by the Trustee, and for both the Trustee and Manager to jointly comply with certain administrative requirements. If the requirements for tax transparency treatment are not met, all the Specified Income is subject to tax at the Trustee level. The Trustee/Manager of a REIT or its sponsor needs only to submit an application form to the IRAS to apply for the tax transparency treatment.

49 The tax transparency treatment granted by the IRAS is usually conditional on compliance with certain terms and conditions stated in the approval letter. This tax transparency treatment is critical to the marketability of a REIT.

50 Distributions to the Unitholders may be in the form of cash or units in the REITs. Distributions to Unitholders in the form of units have to satisfy certain conditions.

51 Singapore does not impose a tax on capital gains. However, profits arising from the sale of real property or Singapore SPVs could be regarded as trading gains if they are derived from a trade or business that deals in investments (including real property). In addition, the tax transparency treatment does not extend to profits realized from the sale of real property or SPVs. As a result, these profits, if taxable, will be subject to tax in the hands of the Trustee at the prevailing corporate tax rate. Gains derived during the period 1 June 2012 to 31 December 2027 (both dates inclusive) from the disposal of ordinary shares in an investee company will not be taxable if immediately prior to the disposal, the divesting company owns at least 20% of the ordinary shares of the investee company for a continuous period of twenty-four months subject to conditions. However, the following exclusions apply:

(a) For disposal before 1 June 2022, the disposal of shares in a company which is in the business of trading or holding Singapore immovable properties (excluding property development), where the shares are not listed on a stock exchange in Singapore or elsewhere.

(b) For disposals on or after 1 June 2022, disposals of unlisted shares in investee companies that are in the business of trading, holding or developing immovable properties in Singapore or abroad, except when the property developed is used by the company to carry on its trade or business, and the company did not undertake any property development in Singapore or abroad for a period of at least sixty consecutive months before the disposal.

Whether a gain realized from the disposal of real property or SPVs is considered to be   **52**
capital in nature is determined by reference to the transaction, as well as the REIT's
overall business characteristics and investment intentions. The 'badges of trade' to be
considered are:

- motive for the acquisition;
- nature of subject matter;
- length of ownership;
- frequency of transactions;
- supplementary work in connection with the property realized;
- mode of financing of the acquisition;
- circumstances of the realization; and
- any other factors.

Further, in determining whether any gain arising from the deemed disposal is capital in   **53**
nature, a factor that may be relevant is whether the REIT is taxed under section 10E of
the Income Tax Act (ITA). In particular, if the IRAS has confirmed that the company is
in the business of making investments, and the company is taxed under section 10E of
the Act, the gains from the subsequent sale of investments are generally not subject to
tax. However, taxation under section 10E does not expressly preclude the IRAS from
treating the gain as revenue in nature.

[b]   Determination of Taxable Income

The taxable income of a REIT is determined in accordance with the provisions of the   **54**
ITA. In addition, the rental and related income derived by a REIT is treated as income
derived from the business of the making of investments, and as such, certain
restrictions under the provisions of section 10E of the ITA will apply. Specifically, these
provisions do not allow the carry forward of any tax losses or unutilized tax depreciation (on plant and machinery only) for a particular year of assessment (YA). Further,
any tax losses or unutilized tax depreciation (on plant and machinery only) cannot be
set off against any other sources of income.

To secure a tax deduction, an interest expense has to be incurred in connection with an   **55**
income-producing purpose. Interest expenses incurred by a REIT on loans to finance its
rental property investments are deductible for the purposes of computing its Specified
Income (*see* section below). Like other taxpayers carrying on a business or trade, a
REIT is entitled to claim tax depreciation on qualifying assets such as industrial
buildings, plant and machinery.

As mentioned above, a REIT can apply for tax transparency. However, the tax   **56**
transparency will only apply to certain income derived by the REIT known as 'Specified
Income'.

The Specified Income of a REIT is: **57**

(i) rental income or income from the management or holding of immovable property, but not including gains from the disposal of immovable property;

(ii) income ancillary to the management or holding of immovable property, but not including gains from the disposal of immovable property;

(iii) income that is payable out of rental income or income from the management or holding of immovable property in Singapore, but not out of gains from the disposal of such immovable property;

(iv) rental support payment in relation to any immovable property that is on open market value basis and is paid to the Trustee on or after 29 December 2016 by:

   (a) the seller who sold to the Trustee the property or any interest in the owner of the property;

   (b) a person who wholly owns (directly or indirectly) the seller; or

   (c) any other person approved by the Comptroller.

(v) distributions from an approved sub-trust of the REIT out of income referred to in (i), (ii) and (iv) above.

[c]   Taxation of Income from Taxable/Non-taxable Subsidiaries

58   In order to qualify for the tax transparency treatment, a REIT must hold its Singapore properties directly (instead of holding through a subsidiary company). As a result, it is not common for REITs to own Singapore properties through a Singapore SPV.

59   Tax transparency is also accorded to the distributions of a REIT made out of specified distributions received from an approved sub-trust, which in turn holds the underlying properties, subject to the sub-trust meeting certain conditions.

[d]   Taxation of Foreign Income

60   Foreign-sourced dividend income received by the REIT or its SPVs is, in most cases, exempt from tax under section 13(8) of the ITA if certain qualifying conditions are met. If the foreign-sourced dividend income does not qualify for the section 13(8) exemption, or if the foreign income is not dividend income (e.g., interest income on shareholders' loans, trust distribution), the REIT can apply for tax exemption under section 13(12) of the ITA for qualifying foreign-sourced income that is received in Singapore on or before 31 December 2025. Section 13(12) exemption is subject to the approval of IRAS, which can impose conditions on that approval. Any foreign withholding taxes paid on foreign income are not credited against other REIT taxes or refunded.

61   The tax exemption under 13(12) will apply to foreign income received by the Trustee of a REIT or its wholly owned SPV in respect of any overseas property which:

(a) is acquired, directly or indirectly, by the Trustee of the REIT or its wholly owned SPV on or before 31 December 2025; and

(b) continues to be beneficially owned, directly or indirectly, by the Trustee of the REIT or its wholly owned SPV.

The REIT's foreign income received in Singapore after 31 December 2025 will be **62** granted the section 13(12) tax exemption so long as the above qualifying conditions, among others, for the tax exemption are met.

[2]   *Value Added Tax*

A REIT can be registered for GST (Singapore VAT) in Singapore. Once registered, the **63** REIT has to charge GST (at the prevailing rate of 7%) on the rental and related income derived from its property holding, property management and related activities unless the supply made can qualify for zero rating (i.e., GST at 0%) under section 21(3) of the GST Act or is an exempt supply under the Fourth Schedule to the GST Act (the sale and lease of residential properties are an exempt supply). The GST charged is termed as Output GST, which the REIT has to collect and remit to the IRAS, net of any Input GST. Input GST refers to GST incurred by a REIT on its expenses such as management fees, statutory audit and tax fees, property maintenance expenses, IPO-related expenses. Input tax attributable to the making of exempt supplies is generally not claimable unless certain exceptions are met (e.g., the value of exempt supply is below a certain threshold).

REITs that primarily derive dividends or distributions which are not taxable supplies **64** for GST purposes from SPVs or sub-trusts may not be able to register for GST and thus are not able to claim input tax on their business expenses. As a concession, these REITs will be able to claim GST incurred on business expenses incurred (this concession was extended to 31 December 2025). This is subject to meeting certain conditions, but the concession is available regardless of whether the REIT can be registered for GST. The GST concession has been enhanced to include SPVs set up solely to raise funds for the REITs and that do not hold qualifying assets of the REITs, whether directly or indirectly. The enhanced concession will apply to GST on expenses incurred from 1 April 2015 to 31 December 2025 to set up the SPVs as well as the GST on the business expenses of such SPVs. The amount of input tax claimable will be subject to apportionment rules where applicable. Whether the above concession will be extended will typically only be announced nearer the expiry date.

Singapore REITs will also need to note that Singapore implemented the reverse charge **65** for business-to-business (B2B) services with effect from 1 January 2020. Under the reverse charge mechanism, a GST registered entity will need to perform reverse charge on 'in-scope' imported services (i.e., self-account for GST on services procured from abroad) where the entity is not able to recover its input tax in full. A non-GST registered entity (including a REIT and its Singapore SPVs) will have to register for GST if the value of 'in-scope' imported services exceeds SGD 1 million in a year and the entity is not able to recover its input tax in full (e.g., the entity is partially exempt).

[3]   Withholding Taxes

66   No withholding applies to distributions to Qualifying Unitholders. The Trustee and the Manager of a REIT have to deduct tax on distributions out of the REIT's Taxable Income (as defined in section §1.03[A][1][b] above) to any other Unitholders. Where the Unitholders are Qualifying Foreign Non-Individual Unitholders, the Trustee and Manager must deduct Singapore income tax at a rate of 10% (final tax) on distributions made on or before 31 December 2025.

67   A 'Qualifying Unitholder' is a Unitholder who is:

- an individual;
- a Singapore-incorporated company which is tax resident in Singapore;
- the Singapore branch of a foreign company;
- a body of persons incorporated or registered in Singapore, including a charity registered under the Charities Act or established by any written law, a town council, statutory board, registered cooperative society, registered trade union; or
- an international organization that is exempt from tax on such distributions by reason of an order made under the International Organisations (Immunities and Privileges) Act; and
- REIT exchange-traded funds (REIT ETFs) which have been accorded the tax transparency treatment. For income tax purposes, a REIT ETF refers to a trust that is constituted as a collective investment scheme authorized under section 286 of the SFA and listed on the Singapore Exchange and that only invests or proposes to invest in REITs as its underlying investment portfolio.

68   A 'Qualifying Foreign Non-Individual Unitholder' is a person, other than an individual, who is not a tax resident in Singapore, and either does not have a permanent establishment in Singapore or, where he does carry on operations in Singapore through a permanent establishment, the funds used to acquire the units are not obtained from that operation.

69   Qualifying Unitholders and Qualifying Foreign Non-Individual Unitholders are required to disclose their tax status on a prescribed form provided by the Trustee.

70   Certain funds which are managed by Singapore-based fund managers in Singapore would similarly be subject to the above-mentioned 10% withholding tax instead of the 17% tax rate.

[4]   Other Taxes

The sale or transfer of immovable property located in Singapore is usually subject to   **71**
3% Singapore stamp duty (4% if the immovable property is or deemed to be residential
property for Singapore stamp duty purposes). This stamp duty is generally referred to
as Buyer's Stamp Duty (BSD) because the buyer is liable to pay the stamp duty unless
otherwise contractually agreed between the buyer and the seller. In addition to BSD,
Additional Buyer's Stamp Duty (ABSD) and Seller's Stamp Duty (both introduced as
measures to cool the Singapore property market) may also apply to the transfer of
certain types of immovable properties.

In certain situations, ABSD may be imposed in addition to the BSD that a buyer of   **72**
residential property has to pay ABSD for entities (i.e., non-individuals) and this is
imposed at rates between 10% and 35%, depending on the date of the transaction.
Housing developers may apply for remission of the 35% ABSD. However, an additional
5% ABSD (non-remittable) will apply to property developers.

Seller's Stamp Duty (SSD) is payable by the seller of a property and may apply to the   **73**
transfer of residential and industrial property located in Singapore. SSD is imposed at
5% to 15% (depending on how long the seller has held the property) for transfers of
Singapore industrial properties, acquired by the seller on or after 12 January 2013 and
sold/disposed within three years. For transfers of Singapore residential property, SSD
of between 4% and 12% (depending on when the seller acquired the property and how
long the seller held it for) generally applies for properties acquired on or after 11 March
2017 if a property is held by the seller for three years or less. It is important to ensure
that the seller has paid any applicable SSD. This is because if the seller is liable but did
not pay the SSD, the Agreement between the buyer and the seller for the purchase of
the property would not be considered as duly stamped even if the buyer paid the BSD
and applicable ABSD.

The conveyance, assignment or sale of shares in a Singapore-incorporated company is   **74**
also subject to Singapore stamp duty of 0.2% of the purchase consideration or market
value of the Singapore shares, whichever is higher.

Additional conveyance duties (ACD) may apply to buyers (ACDB) or sellers (ACDS) of   **75**
shares or other equity interest in property-holding entities (PHEs) that own prescribed
immovable property (primarily residential properties) in Singapore directly or indirectly. With effect from 16 December 2021, an ACDB rate of 44% may apply on an
instrument, while an ACDS flat rate of 12% applies. The ACD provision applies to the
purchase or sale of equity interests by persons or entities who are significant owners of
the PHE or who become one after the purchase.

The transfer of REIT units listed on the SGX effected through the scripless settlement   **76**
system operated by the Central Depository is not subject to Singapore stamp duty.

[5]   Penalties Imposed on REIT

77   If the REIT's profit distribution obligation is not regularly met, the REIT's tax transparency status could be withdrawn. Moreover, if the REIT does not comply with the requirements set by the SGX and the REIT is delisted, all tax concessions will cease to apply. As with all Singapore taxpayers, REITs are subject to penalties for failure to report and pay taxes.

[B]   Taxation of the Investor

78   Unless an exemption applies, as described below, Unitholders are assessed to income tax on any distributions from a REIT in the YA corresponding to the year in which the Specified Income of the REIT was derived. For example, if a distribution is made in 2020 out of Taxable Income of the REIT earned in the financial year ended 31 December 2018 (YA 2019), the Unitholders will be taxed on this distribution in YA 2019, regardless of when the distribution is actually made.

79   If for any accounting year end, a REIT's Specified Income, which has been agreed with the IRAS, is higher or lower than the Specified Income of that accounting year as determined by the Manager and distributed to Unitholders, the difference ('rollover income adjustments') will be added to or deducted from the Specified Income as determined by the Manager for the next distribution immediately after the difference has been agreed with the IRAS.

80   Distributions made by a REIT to Unitholders who are individuals beneficially entitled to them out of the REIT's Specified Income, regardless of their nationality or place of residence, are generally exempt from Singapore income tax if the distribution is regarded to be arising from investment (rather than trading in securities) income, and the distribution is not received through a partnership in Singapore or from the carrying on of a trade, business or profession dealing in investments in Singapore.

81   Individuals who hold units as trading assets or through a partnership in Singapore are subject to income tax on the gross amount of the distribution from the REIT. These gross distributions are taxed at the Unitholder's applicable personal income tax rates, ranging from 0% to 22% (and up to 24% for personal income derived for the YA 2024). Whether the distributions received by the Unitholders are considered to be trading income or investment income is a question of fact, determined by the IRAS after a review of their personal circumstances.

82   The following distributions to Unitholders are not subject to or are exempt from Singapore tax:

   (a) Distributions made by the REIT out of income previously taxed in the hands of the Trustee, such as Retained Income and trading income from the disposal of properties, but no tax credit is available for the tax paid by the Trustee.

(b) Distributions made by the REIT out of gains arising from the disposal of properties that are agreed with the IRAS as capital in nature.

(c) Distributions made by the REIT out of income exempt from tax under section 13(8) or 13(12) of the ITA or one-tier exempt dividends from Singapore SPVs.

Any gain derived by Unitholders from the sale of their units is not subject to tax as long **83** as the gain is regarded to be capital in nature. Unitholders who trade or deal in investments are subject to regular income tax on any gain derived from the disposal of the units.

Distributions made to non-individual Unitholders, other than Qualifying Foreign **84** Non-Individual Unitholders (*see* section §1.03[A][3] above), are subject to Singapore income tax on the gross amount of distributions made out of the Specified Income of the REIT. Distributions are taxed at the prevailing corporate tax rate.

Distributions made out of the Specified Income of the REIT to Qualifying Foreign **85** Non-Individual Unitholders (e.g., foreign corporations without any business presence in Singapore) are subject to a final 10% withholding tax (*see* section §1.03[A][3] above).

Distributions made to institutional investors out of income previously taxed in the **86** hands of the Trustee (such as Retained Taxable Income and trading income from the disposal of properties) and gains that are capital in nature will be exempt from Singapore tax in the hands of all Unitholders, regardless of their tax status. However, no tax credit will be available for the tax paid by the Trustee.

Unitholders receiving distributions made by the REIT out of income exempt from tax **87** under section 13(8) or 13(12) of the ITA or one-tier exempt dividends from the SPVs will not be assessable to Singapore income tax on the distributions received.

[1]   Taxation of Capital Gains (From Disposal of Units)

Any gain derived by institutional Unitholders from the sale of their units is not subject **88** to tax as long as the gain is not derived from the carrying on of a trade or business in Singapore. Unitholders who trade or deal in investments from the carrying on of a trade, business or profession in Singapore will be subject to tax on any gain derived from the disposal of the units.

Distributions made by the Trustee of the REIT out of non-income (e.g., operating cash **89** flows, unrealized revaluation gains, etc.) are regarded as 'return of capital' in the hands of the Unitholders. The return of capital will be applied towards reducing the cost of the investment of the Unitholders in the REIT. For a Unitholder who is trading in REIT units, the cost of the units to him will be computed by reference to the cost reduced by any return of capital, and the excess will be subject to tax as trading income of the Unitholders. For other Unitholders who are not trading in REIT units, the adjustment to the cost of the units arising from distributions that are regarded as return of capital is of no consequence.

[a]   Penalties Imposed on Investors

90   There are no penalties imposed on investors that are specific to REIT investments. General penalties apply for failure to report taxable distributions or to pay tax on those distributions.

[C]   Tax Treaties

[1]   Treaty Access

91   Although Singapore has concluded a wide network of tax treaties with its trading partners, a REIT can find it difficult to access the benefits the treaties provide. The IRAS, as a matter of policy and practice, has been reluctant to certify a REIT as a bona fide Singapore tax resident for tax treaty purposes, and a written certification is typically required by the foreign tax authority before granting treaty relief.

[2]   WHT Reduction

92   The ITA does not regard distributions made by a REIT as dividends. In this regard, any reduced dividend withholding tax rates under the double tax agreements which Singapore has concluded with other countries do not apply.

[D]   Exit Tax/Tax Privileges/Concessions

93   There are no specific exit taxes or privileges for a Singapore REIT. The GST concessions are discussed in section §1.03[A][2] and §1.03[A][4] above, respectively.

[E]   Taxation of Foreign REITs

[1]   Taxation of Foreign REIT Holding Assets in Country

94   A foreign REIT which holds Singapore properties is taxed in Singapore on its net rental income derived in Singapore. The tax is imposed at the prevailing tax rate (17% for income earned in the financial year ending 2021). The amount of income subject to Singapore tax will be determined in accordance with the provisions of the ITA.

[2]   *Taxation of Investors Holding Units in a Foreign REIT*

Usually, Singapore imposes taxation on distributions made by a foreign REIT (foreign   **95**
source income) remitted or deemed remitted into Singapore. However, Unitholders
who are individuals (except where the units are held by the individual through a
partnership in Singapore or from the carrying on of a trade, business or profession in
Singapore) are not taxed in Singapore on foreign REIT distributions. All other Unitholders are taxed on the distributions if the income is remitted or deemed remitted into
Singapore. Usually, the Unitholder can claim a tax credit for any foreign taxes paid on
the distribution.
Any gain derived by Singapore investors from the sale of their units in the foreign REIT
is not subject to tax, as long as the gain is not derived from the carrying on of a trade
or business dealing in investments in Singapore. Unitholders who trade or deal in the
units from the carrying on of a trade, business or profession in Singapore are subject to
tax on any gains derived from the disposal of the units if the gains are regarded as
Singapore sourced; that is, the buying and selling decisions are made in Singapore.

South Africa

KYLE MANDY

Kyle Mandy is Head of National Tax Technical at PwC South Africa. As part of that role, he is responsible for formulating PwC's position on matters of tax policy and tax design. Kyle has over twenty years of experience in tax and has advised numerous large corporates on all aspects of tax, including with respect to mergers and acquisitions, debt and capital markets, capital gains tax, international tax, share incentive schemes and dispute resolution.
E-mail: kyle.mandy@pwc.com

South Africa

Kyle Mandy

§1.01 BACKGROUND

[A] Key Characteristics

With effect from 1 May 2013, a formalized Real Estate Investment Trust (REIT) regime **1**
commenced in South Africa, bringing a sense of familiarity to foreign investors owing
to the fact that the South African REIT regime attempts to mirror international best
practice.[1] The South African REIT regime is mainly based on the National Association
of Real Estate Investment Trust (NAREIT)[2] in the United States (US) and European
Public Real Estate Association (EPRA)[3] in Europe.[4]

A South African REIT refers to a South African resident company (as defined in the **2**
Income Tax Act No. 58 of 1962 (the Income Tax Act)) that owns and operates
income-producing immovable property and the shares of which are listed on an
exchange as defined in section 1 of the Financial Markets Act No. 19 of 2012 (the
'Financial Markets Act') and is licensed under section 9 of the Financial Markets Act.
Furthermore, the shares must be listed as shares in a REIT as defined in the listing
requirements of the exchange and approved in consultation with the Minister of
Finance and published by the Prudential Authority in terms of section 11 of the
Financial Markets Act.[5]

---

1. *JSE Reveals New Listings Requirements for SA REITs*. [Online] Available from: www.
   sacommercialpropnews.co.za.
2. National Association of Real Estate Investment Trust.
3. European Public Real Estate Association.
4. *SA REIT Association – Frequently Asked Questions* [Online] Available from https://sareit.co.za/
   resources/.
5. C. Miller, *Analysis: REIT South African Real Estate Investment Trust Structured Introduced*. July
   2014. [Online] Available from: https://www.accountancysa.org.za/analysis-reit-south-african-
   real-estate-investment-trust-structure-introduced/. Read together with s. 1 of the Income Tax Act
   No. 58 of 1962.

3   The regime is essentially designed to provide for a 'flow-through' structure[6] that results in taxable income arising from distributions accrued or received in the hands of a shareholder.

4   In order to achieve this 'flow-through structure', section 25BB of the Income Tax Act regulates the taxation of South African REITs and provides for the deduction of dividends declared by a REIT or interest incurred in respect of debentures on linked units issued by a REIT, including an exemption from capital gains tax in certain instances.

5   The dividends distributed by a REIT do not qualify for the dividend exemption[7] in the hands of the shareholder unless it is distributed to a non-resident (in which case, such dividends are subject to a dividend withholding tax as a final tax). Consequently, a South African tax resident shareholder is generally taxed on the dividends received from a REIT (in which case, no dividends tax is imposed on such distribution).

6   Furthermore, a REIT does not qualify for capital allowances on fixed property.

7   It should also be noted that certain income (e.g., income from financial instruments) will still be taxed as ordinary revenue in the hands of the REIT unless the REIT is able to distribute a matching amount that qualifies as a deduction for income tax purposes.

[B]   History of South African REITs

8   Prior to the introduction of section 25BB of the Income Tax Act, South Africa had two forms of publicly traded investment entities, namely property loan stock (PLS) companies and property unit trusts (PUTs).

9   PLS[8] and PUTs[9] were both funds that invested in property. These funds, however, were unevenly regulated and subjected to different tax treatments and were also regulated under different legislative frameworks. PLS were regulated in terms of the Companies Act No. 71 of 2008 (the 'Companies Act'), while PUTs were regulated in terms of the Collective Investment Schemes Control Act No. 45 of 2002 (the 'Collective Investments Schemes Act'). Furthermore, a degree of uncertainty prevailed over whether PLS were legitimately entitled to deduct interest on the debenture component of linked units issued to investors.

---

6. M. Stiglingh et al., *Silke: South African Income Tax*. Lexis Nexis: Johannesburg. 2014.
7. Dividends distributed from South African resident companies to South African resident companies is exempt from dividends tax.
8. PLS are public companies that issue share capital, a share of which is linked to a debenture, and as such it pays interest rather than dividends.
9. A PUT is a scheme which consists of immovable property, property shares and other property related assets as prescribed by the Registrar of Collective Investment Schemes, in terms of the Collective Investment Schemes Act. In terms of the Collective Investment Schemes Act, a manager (being a company) together with the Trustee would establish a scheme by way of a trust deed. The scheme enables a person (an investor) to purchase a participatory interest in the fund of the scheme and through the investment has an interest in the underlying property assets comprising the fund. The underlying assets are held by the Trustee on behalf of the investor.

South Africa's need for a tax regime for the listed-property sector was further sustained **10** by the considerations of the South African Revenue Service to deny a deduction for all distributions made to the shareholders of PLS.[10]

In August 2006,[11] a two-day conference was convened by the PLS Association in order **11** to discuss the broad implications of a REIT structure for South Africa.

Consensus was reached on the key characteristics of the REIT regime as well as which **12** elements would require regulation. This culminated in the introduction of section 25BB of the Income Tax Act and the development of the Johannesburg Stock Exchange (JSE)[12] Listings Requirements for REITs which provide for the necessary regulation.

Both PLS and PUTs may now adopt the new South African REIT regime as determined **13** by the regulatory framework of the JSE, it being noted that following the introduction of certain amendments, failure to qualify as a REIT would typically result in an inability to enjoy any meaningful 'flow-through' treatment for income tax purposes.

[C]   SA REIT Market

The South African REIT Market is still in its infancy, having only commenced on 1 May **14** 2013. Currently, there are forty-two REITs listed on the JSE, one on the 4AX (4 Africa Exchange) and three on the A2X (A2X Markets).[13]

As described above, the South African REIT regime is similar to internationally **15** recognized REIT models, and the tax certainty attaching to the regime should contribute to encouraging sector growth.

Recent new listings have been attracted to the sector, and this growing attractiveness **16** has resulted in South Africa's listed real estate sector outperforming local and international equities, bonds and cash and REITs in the developed world.[14]

§1.02   REGULATORY ASPECTS

[A]   Legal Form of South African REITs

There are two types of South African REITs, namely Company REITs and Trust REITs. **17**

Key characteristics of a Company REIT are:[15] **18**

---

10. E. De Klerk, *South Africa's Seven-Year Road To REITs*. 20(3) Retail Property Insights (2013–2014).
11. 'PLSA T Host Groundbreaking Conference' eProp, 19 Jul. 2006.
12. JSE Ltd.
13. http://expert.inetbfa.com/ as accessed on 2 Jul. 2020.
14. E. De Klerk, *South Africa's Seven-Year Road To REITs*. 20(3) Retail Property Insights (2013–2014).
15. *SA REIT Association –Types of SA REITs*. [Online]. www.sareit.com.

- the name will end with 'Limited' or 'LTD', and it will also have a company registration number;
- the shareholders are active participants and enjoy the full protection of the Companies Act and Takeovers Regulations Panel;
- the shareholders can vote on specific issues in a general meeting;
- shareholders vote for the company to qualify as a REIT;
- the company has the REIT structure recorded in its memorandum of incorporation;
- the company directors are responsible for its ongoing compliance with the Listings Requirements of the relevant stock exchange and the Companies Act; and
- the company can have external or internal management and/or property administration.

19   An existing PUT will become a REIT upon application to the relevant stock exchange. In this regard, it will need to evidence its compliance with the Listings Requirements of such stock exchange and that it is registered with the Registrar of Collective Investment Schemes.

20   The key characteristics of a Trust REIT are:[16]

- investors' interests are protected by a trust deed and the Trustee, whose role it is to ensure compliance with the Collective Investment Schemes Control Act and to safeguard investors' assets;
- a Trust REIT is required to meet the listing requirements of the relevant stock exchange;
- a Trust REIT is not subject to Takeover Regulations;
- trustees report to the Registrar and must meet all the requirements of the Collective Investment Schemes Control Act; and
- in terms of the Collective Investment Schemes Control Act, a Trust REIT must have an external asset and property manager.

[B]   Regulatory Authorities

21   Company REITs need to comply with the Companies Act, and the Takeover Regulations Control Panel, while Trust REITs need to comply with the Collective Investment Schemes Act. Both would need to comply with the Listings Requirements of the relevant stock exchange (by definition, a REIT must be listed.)

---

16. *SA REIT Association –Types of SA REITs*. [Online]. www.sareit.com.

[C]   Legislative and Other Regulatory Sources

From a tax perspective, South African REITs will be governed by section 25BB of the   **22**
Income Tax Act. As stated above, the Companies Act, the Collective Investments
Schemes Control Act and the Listings Requirements of the relevant stock exchange
must also be taken into consideration to ensure that all compliance matters are adhered
to.

[D]   Exchange Controls and Reporting Requirements

South African REITs must comply with reporting requirements imposed on listed   **23**
companies. Furthermore, South Africa imposes exchange control, and this needs to be
considered for all proposed transactions.

[E]   Registration Procedures

[1]   Preparatory Measures

There are no preparatory measures applicable.   **24**

[2]   Obtaining Authorization

If a company is desirous of receiving REIT status, an application must be made to list   **25**
as a REIT on a stock exchange. The stock exchanges have certain requirements for
listing as well as additional requirements that must be met in order to achieve REIT
status.

The requirements to list a REIT on a stock exchange may be summarized as follows.   **26**

A REIT must: **27**

- own at least ZAR 300 million of property;
- maintain its debt below 60% of its gross asset value;
- earn 75% of its income from rental or from property owned or investment income from indirect property ownership;
- have a committee in place to monitor risk;
- not enter into derivative instruments that are not in the ordinary course of business; and
- distribute at least 75% of its taxable earnings available for distribution to its investors each year.

[3]   Other Requirements for the Incorporation of a Company

28   There are no other requirements in connection with the incorporation of a Company REIT. Aside from the requirements set out in the Collective Investment Schemes Act, there are no additional requirements for the incorporation of a Trust REIT.

[4]   Obtaining Listing Exchanges

[a]   Costs

29   Listing fees, documentation fees, professional advisor fees and other (i.e., transfer secretary) fees must be paid to list shares.

30   After listing, the company will also be liable for an annual listing fee in February of each year. It should also be noted that an additional Issuer Regulation annual documentation fee is payable for entities who have been granted REIT status on the JSE. This fee should be paid when the annual REIT compliance declaration is submitted.

[b]   Time

31   According to the 'JSE – Guidelines to listing on the JSE' listing may take up to nine to thirteen weeks depending on the method of listing, the correspondence of the professional advisors and the complexity of the listing. Other stock exchanges may vary in the time it takes to list a REIT.

[F]   Requirements and Restrictions

[1]   Capital Requirements

32   A REIT must have at least ZAR 300 million of gross assets as reflected in its financial statements. Furthermore, the REIT SA must have debt below 60% of its gross asset value.

[2]   Investment Restrictions

33   There are no specific investment restrictions for REITs; however, there are certain restrictions in terms of activities which are discussed in more detail under §1.02[F][4] below.

[3]   Marketing/Advertising

Any company that wants to list its shares must prepare and make available a   **34**
prospectus in accordance with the provisions of the Companies Act as well as a
pre-listing statement in accordance with the provisions of the relevant stock exchange
the REIT will list on. The pre-listing statement must contain the following information:[17]

- general information regarding the company and its capital;
- information regarding the directors and management of the company and the
  company's advisers;
- information regarding the securities to be listed;
- information on the company's/group activities; and
- information on the company's financial position and profits and losses.

[4]   Activities Restrictions

In accordance with section 13 of the JSE Listings Requirements, a REIT must derive   **35**
75% of its revenue as reflected on the statement of comprehensive income from rental
revenue. Other stock exchanges will have similar requirements. This is a requirement
that must be upheld in order for the REIT to retain its REIT status. Rental income is
defined in section 25BB(1) of the Income Tax Act to be:

- an amount received or accrued in respect of the use of immovable property,
  including any penalty or interest in respect of late payment of any such
  amount;
- a dividend from a company that is a REIT at the time of distribution of that
  dividend;
- a qualifying distribution[18] from a company that is a controlled company at the
  time of distribution;[19]
- a dividend or a foreign dividend from a company that is a property at the time
  of distribution[20] company;
- any capital allowances on buildings that are recovered or recouped; and
- the total foreign exchange gains that arise on the amounts listed above, or any
  forward exchange contract or foreign currency option contract that serves as a
  hedge on these items.[21]

---

17. 'JSE Limited – Guideline to Listings on the JSE'.
18. A qualifying distribution includes dividends paid or payable, or interest incurred in respect of
    linked by a REIT or a controlled company.
19. A controlled company is a subsidiary of a REIT as contemplated in terms of the IFRS.
20. A property company is a company in which a REIT or a controlled company owns at least 20%
    of the shares and where in the previous year of assessment, at least of 80% of the value of that
    company's assets was attributable to immovable property.
21. The definition of 'rental income' was amended by s. 32 of the Tax Laws Amendment Act of 2019
    to include foreign exchange gains to enable REITs, who have significant exposure to foreign

36 Consequently, the main activity of a REIT will be to produce rental income or to invest in companies that predominantly own property.

[5]   Distribution/Accumulation

37 To benefit from the rules set out under section 25BB of the Income Tax Act, 75% of a REITs taxable earnings must be distributed to its investors on an annual basis.

[6]   Reporting Requirements

38 Recommendations and guidelines have been provided in the context of International Financial Reporting Standards (IFRS), JSE Limited's Listing Requirements, commonly use financial and operating ratios, and the treatment of specific accounting and financial reporting matters in the SA REIT sector.[22]

39 These guidelines should be used, *inter alia*, for guidance in terms of auditing, accounting, risk and corporate governance.

[7]   Accounting

40 REITs must complete annual accounts in accordance with IFRS, as required by the relevant stock exchange.

§1.03   TAXATION

[A]   Corporate Income Tax

[1]   Determination of Taxable Income

41 The Income Tax Act deals with the taxation of South African REITs as well as so-called controlled companies[23] in relation to REITs.

42 Both a REIT and a controlled company may deduct 'qualifying distributions' for purposes of determining its respective taxable income for the year of assessment.

43 A qualifying distribution is defined as the interest incurred by virtue of a debenture on a linked unit or dividends paid or payable by a REIT or a 'controlled company' if the amount thereof is determined with reference to the financial results of the company as

---

exchange fluctuations as a result of investing in real estate outside of South Africa, to satisfy the 75% rental income requirement, and not lose their REIT status.

22. *SA REIT Association – Best Practice Recommendations* (2nd edition: November 2019). [Online] Available from: https://sareit.co.za/financial-reporting-and-regulations/.

23. A 'controlled company' is a company that is a subsidiary, as defined in the IFRS, of a REIT.

reflected in the financial statements for that year of assessment and 75% of the gross income of the REIT or controlled company is attributable to rental income[24] in the preceding year of assessment (if it is the first year of assessment for the REIT or the controlled company, then the 75% test is to be applied in respect of the current year of assessment).

If one bears in mind that at least 75% of the taxable earnings of a REIT must be **44** distributed each year, then a REIT will invariably claim a deduction of a significant amount from its income.

However, the deduction of the 'qualifying distributions' may not exceed the income of **45** the REIT before taking into account:

- the qualifying distribution itself;
- any assessed loss bought forward; and
- any taxable capital gain.

This means that the deduction of a 'qualifying distribution' may not in itself create an **46** assessed loss for either a REIT or a 'controlled company'.

Furthermore, a REIT or a 'controlled company' may deduct the following in the **47** determination of its taxable income:

(a) foreign taxes paid by a foreign vesting trust that is attributable to the vested interest of a REIT or a 'controlled company';
(b) foreign taxes paid by the REIT or a 'controlled company'; and
(c) tax deductible donations.

[2] Capital Gains Tax and Capital Allowances

Capital gains (or loss) will be disregarded for both a REIT and a 'controlled company' **48** in terms of the disposal of any:[25]

(1) immovable property;
(2) a share or a linked unit in a company that is a REIT on the day of disposal; or
(3) a share in a company that is a property company at the time of the disposal.

---

24. Rental income is defined as: in respect of immovable property, a penalty or interest in respect of late payment of any such amount, a dividend from a company that is a REIT, a qualifying distribution from a company that is a controlled company, a dividend or a foreign dividend from a company that is a property company and any capital allowances on buildings that are recovered or recouped.
25. M. Stiglingh et al., *Silke: South African Income Tax 2016*. South Africa, LexisNexis (Pty) Ltd (RD. 2014:500).

49 Furthermore, the following capital allowances may not be deducted in respect of immovable property:

(1) deductions in respect of leasehold improvement;
(2) deductions in respect of buildings used in a manufacturing process;
(3) deductions in respect of building used by hotel keepers;
(4) deductions in respect of the erection or improvement of buildings in the urban development zones;
(5) deductions in respect of commercial buildings; and
(6) deductions in respect of certain residential units.

50 In the Taxation Laws Amendment Act 2017, the corporate reorganization rules (which facilitate tax-neutral transfers of assets between groups of companies in the absence of group tax) were amended so that REITs can benefit from the tax relief provided by these rules.[26] A REIT can now also be a party to a transaction that utilizes the corporate reorganization rules and benefits from transferring assets in a tax-neutral manner within a group of companies.

[B]   Value Added Tax

51 There are no specific Value Added Tax (VAT) rules for South African REITs. Therefore the standard VAT rules are applicable.

[C]   Withholding Taxes

52 Dividends paid by a REIT or a 'controlled company' to a non-resident investor will be subject to 20% dividends withholding tax. The dividends withholding tax may be reduced by an applicable double taxation agreement (DTA).

53 South African investors will be exempt from the 20% dividends withholding tax; however, they will be taxed in accordance with their marginal income tax rate in relation to amounts accrued or received as a dividend from a REIT.[27]

[D]   Other Taxes

[1]   Securities Transfer Tax

54 No securities transfer tax is levied on the transfer of shares in a REIT.

---

26. The Corporate Rules are contained in ss 41–47 of the Income Tax Act No. 58 of 1962.
27. E. De Klerk, *South Africa's Seven-Year Road To REITs*. 20(3) Retail Property Insights (2013–2014).

[E]   Taxation of the Investor

[1]   *South African Private Investors (Individual or Company)*

There is no exemption from income tax in relation to the dividend received from a   **55**
REIT. Consequently, the tax consequences fall in the hands of each shareholder and
will depend on the nature and profile of the shareholder concerned.

Therefore, if the shareholder is not an exempt entity, such as a pension fund, the   **56**
dividend received from the REIT will be included in the shareholder's income which
will be taxed at 28% (if the shareholder is a company) or at the marginal rate applicable
to the individual.

[2]   *Taxation of Capital Gains (Individual or Company)*

Individuals disposing of shares in a REIT will be liable for capital gains tax at that   **57**
person's personal marginal position to a maximum effective tax rate of 18%. Companies will be liable for capital gains tax at an effective rate of 22.4%.

[3]   *Institutional Investors*

Certain institutions such as pension funds are exempt from tax and will therefore not   **58**
be taxed on the dividends received from a REIT.

[4]   *Foreign Investors*

Foreign investors will be exempt from income tax on dividends received from a REIT   **59**
or a controlled company but will be subject to dividends tax.

Non-residents may be subject to capital gains tax on the disposal of shares in a REIT   **60**
where that person held (directly or indirectly and together with any connected person)
at least 20% of the shares in the company and at least 80% of the gross assets of that
company were attributable to immovable property. South Africa's ability to impose
capital gains tax in these circumstances may still be subject to the allocation of taxing
rights by an applicable DTA.

[F]   Forfeiture of REIT Status

Section 25BB(7) of the Income Tax Act determines that when a company ceases to be   **61**
a REIT or a controlled company in relation to a REIT, its year of assessment is deemed

to end on that day and the first day of the next year of assessment commences on the following day. In the following year, the company will then be liable for tax in terms of normal company tax, and the REIT tax regime will no longer apply.

South Korea

TAEJIN PARK

Taejin Park is a tax partner of the tax transaction structuring team, which is part of PwC Korea's Financial Services Group, and especially specialized in real estate transaction structuring advisory.

He has over nineteen years of experience in providing tax transaction structuring advisory services for international clients. He mainly deals with clients who make cross-border and international real estate transactions.

He has extensive experience in real estate transactions made by several core funds, opportunistic funds or investment banking based in the US, Europe and Asia.

The clients include sovereign wealth fund, Angelo Gordon, Invesco, AEW, M&G, GIC, Ascendas, Carlyle, etc.

E-mail: taejin.park@pwc.com

LEE JAE-DOK

Lee Jae-Dok is a tax director who worked in the PwC Korean office for seventeen years, including the period of secondment in PwC Singapore in 2009 and 2010.

He was involved in various advisory projects from the international tax and regulatory perspective for foreign clients making investments into Korean assets, including real estate and financial products. He also was involved in the structuring service to maximize the cash flow in a tax-efficient manner for cross-border transactions.

During his secondment in PwC Singapore, he advised foreign clients to make investments in Korea using the Singapore platform.

E-mail: jae-dok.lee@pwc.com

HANNA KIM

Hanna Kim is a manager in PwC Korea's Global Tax Services Group.

Prior to joining PwC Korea, he worked at the PwC LA office for eight years, advising global asset managers/institutional investors investing in the US.

E-mail: hanna.k.kim@pwc.com

SUNG YEOL KIM

Sung Yeol Kim is a senior associate in PwC Korea's Corporate and International Tax team. Prior to joining PwC Korea, he worked in PwC Atlanta office for two years providing US income tax compliance and income tax provisions to privately held businesses and high net worth individuals.

E-mail: sungyeol.s.kim@pwc.com

South Korea

Taejin Park, Lee Jae-Dok, Hanna Kim & Sung Yeol Kim

§1.01   BACKGROUND

[A]   Key Characteristics

There are three types of Real Estate Investment Trusts (collectively the 'REIT') in South   **1**
Korea available in relation to real estate transactions.

K-REITs make their investment decisions and manage their assets by themselves. For   **2**
this purpose, they employ real estate professionals. P-REITs and CR-REITs, however,
are not allowed to hire employees. Therefore, investment decisions and asset management duties are assigned to an asset management company (AMC).

K-REITs and P-REITs invest in real estate. CR-REITs invest in corporate recovery-   **3**
related real property, such as real property that is sold by a company in order to repay
its debts.

[B]   History of REIT

K-REITs and CR-REITs were introduced by the Real Estate Investment Company Act   **4**
(REICA), enacted in April 2001. In October 2004, the REICA was amended, extending
the CR-REITs corporate income tax (CIT) exemption to P-REITs as well.

In order to develop the Korean REIT market, the Korean Ministry of Land, Infrastruc-   **5**
ture, and Transport (MLIT) amended the REICA again in October 2007. The 2007
amendments simplified the two-step REIT approval process, combining the preliminary approval and the incorporation approval into a single approval operation. The
amendments which have been made in 2010 also lowered the minimum capital
required to form a REIT. So as to boost the foreign investment in the Korean REIT
market, MLIT amended the REICA in March 2013 by specifying the subordinate
regulation.

[C]   REIT Market

6   As of December 2021, there were 20 CR-REITs, 291 P-REITs and 4 K-REITs with a total asset value of KRW 75,560 billion.

§1.02   REGULATORY ASPECTS

[A]   Legal Form of REIT

[1]   Corporate Form

7   The REIT is incorporated as a type of regular stock corporation which, in Korea, is referred to as a general stock corporation.

[2]   Investment Restrictions

8   K-REITs and P-REITs must publicly offer more than 30% of the total issued shares within two years from the date of operation approval. They must list their stock on the securities market of the Korea Stock Exchange or register them with the Korea Stock Exchange or in the association brokerage market of the Korea Securities Dealers Association (KOSDAQ) if certain conditions are met. But, K-REIT and P-REIT are not allowed to publicly offer before the date of operation approval. CR-REIT is not restricted by this public offer rule.

9   One shareholder and anyone who is specially related to the shareholder shall not possess in excess of 50% of the total shares issued by a REIT after the minimum capital preparation period. The provision does not apply within the minimum capital preparation period. CR-REIT is not subject to this restriction.

[B]   Regulatory Authorities

10   The REICA stipulates that REITs are to be regulated by the MLIT and the Korean FSC.

[C]   Legislative and Other Regulatory Sources

11   REITs are governed by both the REICA and the Commercial Code. Moreover, a REIT is regulated by the Capital Market Act if its shares are listed on the Korean Stock Exchange. REITs are subject to the Foreign Exchange Transaction Act if the REITs' investors are residents in a foreign country.

[D]   Exchange Controls and Reporting Requirements

REITs must list their shares on the securities market of the Korea Stock Exchange or   **12**
register them with the KOSDAQ for trading either in the securities market or in the
association brokerage market. Listed and registered REITs are required to provide the
public with an electronic file of their annual business reports and to provide an
electronic file of their simplified business reports on a quarterly basis. The files are
published on the internet.

[E]   Registration Procedures

[1]   Preparatory Measures

In contrast to the K-REIT, which must employ real estate personnel, P-REIT and   **13**
CR-REIT are paper companies that cannot have employees. Therefore, P-REIT and
CR-REIT must assign their management and trust duties to a qualified entity which is
called an AMC. The AMC is required to manage the property held by the REIT. The
AMC has to be approved by the MLIT. The AMC requirements for approval include the
following:

- The AMC must have a minimum capital (referring to the amount of total assets
  minus total liabilities) of KRW 7 billion.
- The AMC must employ at least five professional asset managers.
- The AMC must provide a conflict prevention system and computerized
  equipment/material equipment for conflicts of interest between the AMC and
  investors.

According to Article 35 of the REICA, the K-REIT, P-REIT and CR-REIT should trust   **14**
cash, securities and real estate to a trust company as follows:

- Cash and securities: The custody should be assigned to a trust company as
  defined by the Financial Investment Services and Capital Market Act (FIS-
  CMA) or a financial institution that operates a trust business.
- Real estate: The property should be assigned to a trust company as defined by
  the FISCMA, a financial institution that operates a trust business, Korea Land
  & Housing Corporation, Korea Asset Management Corporation or Korea
  Housing & Urban Guarantee Corporation.

[2]   Obtaining Authorization

In order to obtain approval, a REIT must file an application for approval with the   **15**
minister of MLIT. The application for approval includes the following:

- type of REIT;

- name and address of head office;
- capital;
- promoters and directors;
- target real estate and management method (detailed plan of asset management); and
- profile regarding asset management professionals.

[F]   Requirements and Restrictions

[1]   Capital Requirements

16 P-REIT and CR-REIT have to be incorporated with a minimum capital of KRW 0.3 billion, and K-REITs have to be incorporated with a minimum capital of KRW 0.5 billion. However, REITs must increase their capital up to KRW 7 billion for K-REIT and 5 billion for P-REIT and CR-REIT within the minimum capital preparation period.

17 The REIT borrowings (including the issuance of bonds) shall not exceed two times the capital and 5 billion for P-REIT and CR-REIT within the minimum capital preparation period. In the case of a special resolution at the general shareholder's meeting, the REIT borrowing may be issued to the extent the amount does not exceed ten times the capital.

[2]   Marketing/Advertising

18 When a REIT makes a public offering, the REIT is required to provide an investment memorandum that includes the following:

- name of the corporation, the purpose of establishment and address;
- investment target, investment plan and method of asset valuation;
- investment risk; and
- details of any AMC and asset custody company.

[3]   Investment Restrictions

19 REITs shall only engage in the following business activities:

- leasing and letting of real estate;
- acquisition, management and disposition of the real estate and the right to use real estate, such as surface rights and leasing rights;
- real estate development;
- purchase and sale of marketable securities; and
- holding deposits.

At least 80% of a K-REIT and P-REIT's assets must be invested in real estate, real   **20**
estate-related securities and cash as of the end of each quarter after the minimum
capital preparation period. In addition, at least 70% of K-REIT and P-REIT's assets must
be invested in real estate (including housing and buildings under construction).

Investments in real estate development projects are only allowed to the listed REIT in   **21**
the Stock Exchange Market, and the investments that (in total) exceed 30% of the
REIT's total assets have been prohibited.

REITs shall not acquire more than 10% of the voting shares in other companies, except   **22**
for the following cases:

(a) acquisition of shares in a special purpose company which is temporarily
     incorporated for the real estate development project;
(b) merger of a business;
(c) acquisition of a business; and
(d) other cases to be necessary in the ordinary course of business (e.g., in the case
     that additional ownership is necessary in order to exercise the rights of the
     REIT). A REIT may temporarily acquire more than 10% of the outstanding
     voting shares in another company due to the reasons listed above in (b), (c)
     or (d). In either case, the REIT has to reduce the voting shares it owns to less
     than 10% within six months from the share acquisition date.

REITs are not allowed to invest more than 5% of their total assets in marketable   **23**
securities that are issued by the same entity. In case of a breach, the excess market
securities should be disposed of within a six-month period from the acquisition date.

[4]   *Distribution/Accumulation*

K-REITs, P-REITs and CR-REITs have to annually distribute 90% or more of their   **24**
distributable income from the current fiscal year. Generally, a company should
accumulate a reserve of retained earnings in accordance with the Commercial Act, but
the REITs do not have to accumulate a reserve of retained earnings. P-REIT and
CR-REIT can declare dividends in excess of the distributable income, and the excess
amount is limited to the REIT's depreciation expenses in the respective fiscal year in
which the distribution was made.

[5]   *Reporting Requirements*

The K-REIT and AMCs have to submit the year-end investment report and the quarterly   **25**
investment report to the minister of MLIT and FSC and disclose it within ninety days
from the end of the previous fiscal year and forty-five days from the end of the previous
quarter, respectively.

26 REITs are required to report the following events to the MLIT within ten days from their actual occurrence:

     – contributions in kind;

     – replacements of directors;

     – transactions with directors of a REIT, related parties and shareholders that own at least 10% of the REIT shares;

     – other critical matters in the REIT relate to the course of business as defined in the Presidential Decree (e.g., a pending litigation, an application for liquidation).

[6] Accounting

27 A REIT that is required to prepare audited financial statements is as follows:

    (1) a listed REIT or a REIT which will be listed in the following fiscal year;

    (2) total asset amount in the prior fiscal year is at least KRW 50 billion;

    (3) sales in the prior fiscal year are at least KRW 50 billion; and

    (4) a REIT which meets more than two among the following conditions:

       (i) total asset amount in the prior fiscal year is at least KRW 12 billion;

      (ii) total liability amount in the prior fiscal year is at least KRW 7 billion;

     (iii) sales in the prior fiscal year is at least KRW 10 billion;

     (iv) the number of employees in the prior fiscal year is at least hundred persons.

28 Audited financial statements have to be prepared in accordance with K-IFRS for listed REITs or K-GAAP for other non-listed REITs.

§1.03 TAXATION

[A] Taxation of the REIT

[1] Corporate Income Tax

[a] Tax Accounting

29 As a general corporation, a REIT is a taxable entity. Under the Corporate Income Tax Act (CITA), taxes on domestic and foreign-sourced gains are all levied and paid at the REIT level.

[b]   *Determination of Taxable Income*

Taxable income of a REIT is calculated the same as for other general corporations. **30** There are no special rules that apply to the calculation of distributable income. Under Article 51-2 of the CITA, if a CR-REIT or a P-REIT declares 90% or more of its distributable income as dividends, the amount declared as dividends can be deducted from the REIT's taxable income. REITs do not have to set up legal reserves of retained earnings, so income derived by a CR-REIT or a P-REIT is effectively exempt from CIT to the extent a CR-REIT or a P-REIT declares 90% of the income as a dividend.

K-REIT are not entitled to a deduction for declared dividends. K-REIT are fully subject **31** to CIT at a rate of 11% (including Resident Surtax) up to the first KRW 200 million of taxable income, 22% for taxable income ranges from KRW 200 million to KRW 20 billion, 24.2% for taxable income ranges from KRW 20 billion to KRW 300 billion and 27.5% for taxable income exceeding KRW 300 billion, respectively.

[2]   **Value Added Tax**

The disposal of VATable goods and the delivery of VATable services to REITs within **32** South Korea are subject to Value Added Tax (VAT) at a rate of 10% (on the sales price). REITs are eligible for input tax relief on the VATable services and goods received. The transfer of land is VAT exempt. Therefore, when a CR-REIT or a P-REIT receives services that relate to the transfer of real estate, input VAT attributed to land is not deductible.

The VAT treatment of building transfers depends on how the buildings were used **33** before sale. If a building was used for a VATable business, the transfer of the building is subject to VAT. If a building was (partially) used for a VAT-exempt business (e.g., financial services), the transfer of the building is not subject to VAT on the portion of the building that was formerly used for a VAT-exempt business.

Generally, the regular VAT returns should be filed by 25 July and 25 January **34** respectively for the first half and second half of the year. The preliminary filing, which is for the regular filing of VAT, shall be completed by 25 April and 25 October respectively for the first half and second half of the year. However, where a company tries to get an early refund of VAT on facility investments (such as buildings) by submitting a 'statement of facility investment' along with the VAT return, the company can file at any time, which is the twenty-fifth day following the month of facility investment. The refund shall be made within fifteen days after the due date for filing each final return.

[3]   Withholding Taxes

35   For the REIT, the interest paid on a loan from a non-financial institution or foreign entity and dividends paid to a foreign entity are subject to withholding tax.

[4]   Other Taxes

[a]   Acquisition Tax

36   The acquisition of Korean real estate by a company in Korea is subject to Acquisition Tax.

[i]   Tax Base

37   The tax base is defined as the actual acquisition price reported by the real estate purchaser when the purchaser acquires the real estate. However, if the acquisition price is not declared, or if the acquisition price is below the statutory standard price as set annually by the local government, the statutory standard price is deemed to be the tax base (to be abolished as of 31 December 2022). Transaction costs that are directly related to the acquisition are subtracted from the tax base.

[ii]   Tax Rate: Standard

38   Acquisition Tax is levied at a rate of 4.6% (including Agricultural and Fishery Tax and Education Surtax).

[iii]   Tax Rate: Heavy (Seoul Metropolitan Area)

39   If the company is a Korean company incorporated in the Seoul metropolitan area, a heavy tax rate of 9.4% applies to the acquisition of real estate acquired within five years from incorporation. However, the REIT established on or before 31 December 2024 is not subject to the triple tax rate.

[b]   Capital Registration Tax

40   Capital Registration Tax is levied on the formation of the REIT or the issuance of new shares in the REIT. Capital Registration Tax is imposed at a rate of 0.48% (including Educational Surtax) on the par value of the issued shares. If a company is headquartered in the Seoul metropolitan area, the rate may be tripled to 1.44%. However, the

P-REIT and CR-REIT established on or before 31 December 2024 are not subject to the triple tax rate.

[c]   *Real Estate Holding Tax (Local Taxes and Surcharges)*

Local Taxes paid by REIT are composed of property tax on buildings and land **41** (including Education Surtax), Regional Resource and Facility Tax, and Comprehensive Real Estate Holding Tax.

Property tax on buildings is levied at a rate of 0.3% (including Education Surtax of 20% **42** of the property tax on buildings) of 70% of the statutory standard price as of 1 June of each year. Property tax on land arranging from 0.24% to 0.48% (including Education Surtax of 20% of the property tax on land) is levied on 70% of the statutory standard price as of 1 June of each year. A person who benefits from facilities such as fire safety facilities is liable to pay the Regional Resource and Facility Tax at a rate ranging from 0.04% to 0.12% for 70% of the statutory standard price of a building.

After the Local Tax Law amendment, Comprehensive Real Estate Holding Tax will also **43** be levied on the real estate owned by REIT starting in 2021. Comprehensive Real Estate Holding Tax ranging from 0.6% to 0.84% (including Agricultural and Fishery Surtax) is levied on 100% of the statutory standard price (KRW 8,000 million is deducted from the statutory standard price before computing tax base) as of 1 June of each year.

[B]   Taxation of the Investor

[1]   Individual Investors

[a]   *Taxation of Current Income (i.e., Dividend from REIT in Holding Phase)*

Dividends paid by a REIT to non-resident individual shareholders are subject to **44** withholding tax at a rate of 22% at maximum. In case a double tax treaty applies, the withholding tax rate will be reduced.

[b]   *Taxation of Capital Gains (From Disposal of REIT Shares)*

Capital gains arising from the disposal of REIT shares by non-resident individual **45** shareholders are subject to Korean withholding tax. Withholding tax is levied at the lesser of 22% on the capital gain or 11% on the gross proceeds. In the case of non-listed REIT shares, an individual income tax return will be required, and then the total tax burden will be 6.6% to 46.2%, depending on the tax base. Withholding taxes can be credited against the capital gains tax.

The disposal of the REIT shares by non-resident individual shareholders is not subject **46** to capital gains tax, and no tax is withheld if the respective REIT is listed on the Korean

Stock Exchange or registered with KOSDAQ and the non-resident individual share-holder (including related parties to him) holds or has held less than 25% of the REIT shares at any time during the year of disposal, and the preceding five calendar years.

[2]   Institutional Investors

[a]   Taxation of Current Income (i.e., Dividend from REIT in Holding Phase)

47 Foreign companies that do not have a permanent establishment are subject to withholding tax at a rate of 22%. If a tax treaty applies, the withholding tax rate can be reduced.

[b]   Taxation of Capital Gains (From Disposal of REIT Shares)

48 Capital gains arising from the disposal of REIT shares by foreign corporations that do not have a permanent establishment in Korea are subject to Korean withholding tax at the lesser of 22% on the capital gain or 11% on the gross proceeds, unless it is exempt under the applicable treaty.

49 In addition, the foreign corporation shareholders are obliged to file a tax return on the capital gains if the capital gains result from the disposal of 50% or more of the shares in a Korean company that invests more than 50% of its total assets in real estate, and the Korean company is neither listed on the Korean Stock Exchange nor registered with KOSDAQ. Then, the final tax burden will be up to 27.5%, depending on the tax base, with the withheld amount being deducted.

[C]   Tax Treaties

[1]   Treaty Access

50 Korea had entered into a wide network of tax treaties with ninety-four countries. Also, Korea has agreed with eight countries of signatories. Whether a REIT is eligible for treaty relief depends on the particular treaty.

[2]   WHT Reduction

51 The reduced withholding tax (WHT) rate on dividends paid is generally 10% or 15% under the tax treaties concluded between Korea and other nations.

Spain

ANTONIO SÁNCHEZ

Antonio Sánchez is a tax lawyer and tax partner at PwC. Antonio holds a Bachelor of Laws from Universidad Complutense de Madrid, Spain. He joined PwC Spain in 1996 and became a partner in 2007. He has also worked as an in-house tax advisor for two major companies in the construction and telecom sectors. He currently leads the Spanish tax practice for construction, engineering and real estate. He is working with the top companies within the real estate, engineering and construction industries, including national and international real estate investment funds, institutional and private, domestic and foreign investors, providing local and international tax services. Antonio is a usual lecturer in postgraduate and executive programmes and seminars with regard to taxation for construction and real estate.
E-mail: antonio.sanchez.recio@pwc.com

JAVIER MATEOS

Javier Mateos is a qualified attorney. He received a Bachelor's in Law from Universidad Pontificia de Comillas-ICADE and a Master's in Political Sciences from Universidad Complutense de Madrid. He is a legal partner at PwC. He joined PwC in 2014 after working in different leading Spanish and English law firms. He specializes in major transactions involving mergers, reorganizations, tender offers, corporate LBOs, securities issues and public offerings, and regulatory matters concerning listed companies. He regularly advises on major M&A deals and is actively involved in real estate transactions (overall, in SOCIMIs).
E-mail: javier.mateos.sanchez@pwc.com

CARLOS BRAVO

Carlos Bravo is Director of the TLS Tax Team in Madrid and is a member of the International Real Estate Tax Network of PwC, having over seventeen years of experience in leading transactional works, particularly for real estate investment funds and private equity houses on complex deals.

Carlos started his professional career at Garrigues, a Spanish law firm, and joined PwC in 2005. While working for PwC, he was involved in establishing part of the Real Estate Tax business team.

He has a great deal of experience in the real estate sector, with deep knowledge in the SOCIMI regime, serving both national and international clients. He provides tax services to (listed) real estate companies, asset managers and construction companies. This includes mergers, contributions and assisting clients in setting up regional-, country- or property-specific real estate investment funds, among others.
Carlos holds a Bachelor's in Law (Granada University) and a Master's in Taxation (Garrigues Study Centre).
E-mail: carlos.bravo.gutierrez@pwc.com.

Spain

Antonio Sánchez Recio, Javier Mateos & Carlos Bravo Gutiérrez

§1.01 BACKGROUND

[A] Key Characteristics

The Spanish Real Estate Investment Trusts (REITs) vehicle is known by its Spanish **1** acronym SOCIMI for *Sociedades Anónimas Cotizadas de Inversión en el Mercado Inmobiliario*.[1] SOCIMIs are listed corporations whose main activity is the direct and indirect investment in real estate for lease. They enjoy a corporate income tax (CIT) rate of 0% subject to the standard REIT requirements, mainly asset and income tests and dividend distribution. As of 1 January 2021, the SOCIMI will be subject to a special tax of 15% on the profits obtained and not distributed in the part that originates from income that has not been taxed at the general corporate income tax rate or that does not constitute income subject to the reinvestment period.

Especially interesting is the fact that qualifying Spanish subsidiaries of certain foreign **2** listed companies, including REIT vehicles, may be eligible for the SOCIMI regime for their Spanish rental income.

[B] History of REIT

Aiming at stimulating and revitalizing the competitiveness of the Spanish real estate **3** market, Spain initiated the first steps to join the expanding list of European Union (EU) countries with REIT regimes after most of the major EU countries had already implemented a REIT regime, France in 2003, the United Kingdom (UK) and Germany in 2007.

In October 2008, the Spanish Ministry of Finance published the first draft of the SOCIMI **4** regime. The draft provided for the typical REIT features, including a CIT exemption of qualifying rental income and dividends, as well as of related gains. The critical point

---

1. Listed corporations investing in the real estate market.

was that qualifying profits corresponding to shareholdings equal or higher than 5% were proposed to be subject to the standard CIT rate according to their proportionate ratio as opposed to the exemption derived from the SOCIMI status. This mechanism was clearly considered as an indirect restriction for shareholders (5% individually held or at a group level at any time during the tax year or on distribution), leading to certain taxation but not forfeiting the regime. Shareholders with less than 5% should be compensated in the dividend distribution process; that is, standard taxation on qualifying income should be borne only by 5% or more shareholders.

5   The controversies and complexities created by the taxation linked to those shareholders holding 5% or more of the SOCIMI led to a second draft dated November 2008 where the taxation at the entity level changed significantly: Flat 18% CIT rate on qualifying income as opposed to CIT exemption, with no specific restrictions on shareholding (other than those regulated by the stock exchange laws). A 20% exemption of income on the residential lease was available if the assets were mainly residential. Dividends were not subject to withholding tax (WHT) at source.

6   Finally, on 26 October 2009, the SOCIMI Act 11/2009 was enacted by the Parliament under the 18% taxation scheme, including also several amendments regarding the second draft.

7   The State Budget Act for 2010 increased taxation at the entity level from 18% to 19% as a consequence of a general increase in tax rates in the context of the economic crisis.

8   However, the economic turmoil, the severe real estate market crisis and the stringent requirements were to be blamed for the poor record of entrants to the SOCIMI regime so far. In this context, significant amendments to the existing SOCIMI regime were passed on 27 December 2012 with effects for tax periods starting on or after 1 January 2013. The reform seeks to turn the SOCIMI into a more standard and attractive REIT vehicle mainly through the reduction of the CIT from 19% to 0% in the REIT vehicle as well as the relaxation of many of the existing requirements.

[C]   REIT Market

9   As stated above, mainly the market conditions together with the configuration of the old SOCIMI regime contributed to the null implementation of the REIT route as a real alternative to investing in Spanish real estate as opposed to other EU countries.

10   The measures introduced in late 2012 were oriented to make some of the requirements more flexible and the regime more attractive overall. As a result, the new SOCIMI may be considered now as a competitive alternative vehicle from a tax perspective when investing in Spanish real estate for lease. The change of the SOCIMI rules marked a turning point in the short history of the Spanish REIT.

11   From a market perspective, we can differentiate between the 'listed REIT' and the 'non-listed REIT' where the listing requirement is met by the shareholder/s, a foreign listed REIT or REITs, or foreign listed companies with the corporate activity, income

and asset tests, and dividend distributions as of a SOCIMI. The reality shows that in the period 2013–2022 (January), we have seen the setting up of a growing number of listed REITs in both the Spanish stock exchange and the Spanish alternative stock market, as well as non-listed REITs. In particular, we have currently four Spanish REITs on the Spanish stock exchange and seventy-seven Spanish REITs on the Spanish alternative stock market. Additionally, there are other Spanish REITs that are exploring other European alternative stock markets, such as Euronext Access, where they may comply with the listing requirement (we have currently twenty-six Spanish REITs duly listed on Euronext Access). There is no official information on the total number of REITs in place, as there may be some applicants taking advantage of the two-year period available to meet the listing requirement. In addition, there are some SOCIMIs already in place under the non-listed format.

In 2021, the Law on Measures to Prevent and Combat Tax Fraud (Law 11/2021 of 9   **12**
July) established a new corporate income tax rate of 15% on SOCIMIs' non-distributed profits. Generally, SOCIMIs' profits are taxed at a 0% corporate income tax rate but are subject to a mandatory dividend distribution policy. SOCIMIs are entitled to distribute the full amount of profits obtained in a specific tax year, in which case the new 15% CIT on non-distributed profits would not apply. This measure entered into force for tax periods starting from 1 January 2021.

§1.02   REGULATORY ASPECTS

[A]   Legal Form of REIT

[1]   Corporate Form

The only legal form that is admitted under Spanish law for a SOCIMI is a joint-stock   **13**
corporation *Sociedad Anónima* or S.A.. However, the legal form of a Sociedad Limitada or S.L. has been accepted by the Ministry of Finance, Industry and Competitiveness for the non-listed REITs.

Both the statutory seat established in its by-laws and the place of management must be   **14**
in Spain.

[2]   Investment Restrictions

SOCIMIs must be listed on an organized stock market in either Spain, the EU or the   **15**
European Economic Area (EEA), as well as in countries with an effective tax information exchange with Spain. In addition, the listing is also possible on a multilateral trading system in Spain, the EU or the EEA.

There are no specific provisions for shareholders' requirements established by the   **16**
SOCIMI regulations. Therefore, the corresponding stock exchange regulations shall

apply. In particular, in Spain, a listed entity must have at least 25% of its voting share capital duly allocated among the public (or a lower percentage may apply to the extent that such lower percentage enables a minimum lower percentage of liquidity to be reached).

17   In the case of the Spanish multilateral trading system, called BME Growth (previously known as *Mercado Alternativo Bursátil* or MAB), there is no minimum of shareholders either. However, BME Growth requires SOCIMIs, at the time of their inclusion on the BME Growth, to have a minimum number of shareholders holding less than 5% of the share capital. Such shareholders must hold: (a) shares with EUR 2 million of market value, or (b) 25% of the share capital (the lesser of which will apply).

18   It is worth noting that the BME Growth regulations do not set out a minimum number of minority shareholders (although, in practice, BME Growth usually requires around twenty minority shareholders), neither do these establish general criteria for the determination of those shareholders that may be considered as 'minority' for the compliance with the minimum free float requirement (as an example, regulations of other multilateral trading facilities similar to BME Growth exclude shareholders with a close link to the issuer or its core shareholders). On the basis of the foregoing, both parameters will be evaluated case by case by BME Growth based on its accumulated experience.

[B]   Regulatory Authorities

19   Since SOCIMIs must be listed on an organized stock market or a multilateral trading system in Spain or abroad, those listed on the Spanish stock exchange are subject to supervision by the *Comisión Nacional del Mercado de Valores* (CNMV), and those listed on BME Growth are subject to supervision by BME Growth itself.

[C]   Legislative and Other Regulatory Sources

20   SOCIMIs are subject to SOCIMI Act 11/2009, as amended on 27 December 2012. They are also subject to the general rules for stock corporations, that is, the Capital Companies Act and the Spanish Commercial Code. Moreover, due to their listing, SOCIMIs are subject to the Spanish Securities Trading Act 4/2015 and different regulatory rules depending on the stock exchange or multilateral trading facility where they are admitted to official trading. In a scenario where trading on a multilateral trading facility is chosen, this choice implies a reduction in the regulatory requirements to be met by SOCIMIs compared to trading on a regulated market. It is worth noting, by way of example, that the companies admitted to trading on BME Growth are not subject to Spanish corporate governance rules, which apply only to companies admitted to official trading on a regulated market. This significantly reduces the level of corporate bureaucracy needed for companies incorporated on BME Growth.

Market Abuse regulation shall apply to any SOCIMI, the shares of which are listed on   **21**
a regulated market or a multilateral trading facility.

[D]   Reporting Requirements

SOCIMIs are subject to certain obligations arising from admission to a stock exchange,   **22**
including:

- ad hoc disclosure requirements regarding insider information;
- provision of reports for the financial year and half-year;
- announcement of the convening of the shareholders' meeting; and
- disclosure of significant quotas.

Additional obligations may apply; for example, companies listed on the Spanish stock   **23**
exchange must fulfil further transparency requirements. For example, some corporate
governance requirements must be complied with by these SOCIMIs, such as to appoint
an audit committee within its board of directors, to approve internal rules for their
general shareholders' meetings and board of directors meetings and to publish every
year corporate governance and remuneration annual reports.

However, when SOCIMIs opt for trading on BME Growth, they are subject to more   **24**
flexible ongoing information requirements than those required for trading on a
regulated market.

[E]   Registration Procedures

[1]   Preparatory Measures

It is required that the corporate name contains the term Sociedades Anónimas   **25**
Cotizadas de Inversión en el Mercado Inmobiliario or the acronym 'SOCIMI S.A.', and
the corporation has to be registered in the commercial register. Typically, an existing
stock corporation is already registered in the commercial register. Therefore, the
SOCIMI applicant needs only to change its name.

For the registration of a SOCIMI, the following main requirements should be met: **26**

- stock corporation with a minimum share capital of EUR 5 million;
- registered shares;
- by-laws including the corporate activity and the dividend distribution according to the SOCIMI law;
- licence to trade on an organized stock market or a multilateral trading system;
- minimum number of shareholders and free float as required by the rules governing the relevant, organized stock market or multilateral trading system where the relevant SOCIMI applies to admit its shares to official trading. Note

that this requirement must be complied with at the time of admission to official trading; As previously anticipated, the incorporation to BME Growth requires a certain degree of distribution of ownership, so that, from the beginning, shareholders with less than 5% of the share capital must hold shares of the SOCIMI, which: (i) have an estimated market value of €2 million or, alternatively; (ii) represent 25% of the issued shares;

– base prospectus in respect of SOCIMIs to be listed on the Spanish stock exchanges, or 'Information Document for Inclusion on BME Growth' in respect of SOCIMIs to be listed on BME Growth.

27 There is a two-year period to meet the listing requirements.

28 The election to the SOCIMI status should be approved by the General Shareholders Meeting.

29 The option to the SOCIMI tax regime must be formally communicated to the tax office corresponding to the tax domicile of the company before the last three months of the tax year. The tax regime shall be applicable in the tax period with closing after the option and in the successive tax periods unless a waiver is filed or the removal from the SOCIMI status occurs.

[2]   Obtaining Authorization

30 There is no specific authorization apart from the registration described above (*see* section §1.02[E][1] above).

[3]   Other Requirements for the Incorporation of a Company

31 For the constitution of a stock corporation, the following documents must be filed with the relevant register:

- notarial deed of incorporation;
- by-laws of the stock corporation;
- certificate of the registered name of the company;
- certificate of the appointment of the management board and the board of directors.

32 As a listed entity, SOCIMIs must appoint statutory auditors (in accordance with the listing rules). Additionally, in respect of SOCIMIs listed on the Spanish stock exchange, these are subject to the applicable corporate governance requirements (*see* section §1.02[D] above).

[4]   *Obtaining Listing Exchanges*

[a]   *Costs*

The costs for a listing at the Spanish stock exchange or at BME Growth will depend on   **33**
a number of factors, such as the offering proceeds, the advisors, and the circumstances
of the market, so a case-by-case analysis is necessary.

[b]   *Time*

The time required to list the SOCIMI will depend on several factors, including the size   **34**
and complexity of the transaction, whether or not it is necessary to restructure the
relevant SOCIMI or its group beforehand, the type of financial information to be
included in the listing documentation, the state of the market and how quickly funds
are received from investors. As a general rule, the Initial Public Offering process
requires six to nine months. Less time-consuming is the listing process in BME Growth
(between three and four months).

[F]   Requirements and Restrictions

[1]   *Capital Requirements*

The nominal capital of a SOCIMI must amount to at least EUR 5 million, and all shares   **35**
must be of the same class. The law requires the securities to be registered shares.
Non-monetary contributions for the incorporation or increase of capital made in real
estate must be appraised at the time of their contribution.

There are no debt restrictions for SOCIMIs.   **36**

[2]   *Marketing/Advertising*

According to the Spanish Securities regulations, SOCIMIs that seek a listing on an   **37**
organized stock market in Spain must issue a base prospectus. The prospectus is
subject to approval by the CNMV. If the SOCIMI is additionally listed on a stock
exchange abroad, foreign law may require the issuance of a separate base prospectus
as well.

In the case of BME Growth, SOCIMIs must prepare a prospectus titled 'Information   **38**
Document for Inclusion on BME Growth' with a scope and content more reduced than
that required for trading on Spanish stock exchanges. Under BME Growth rules,
SOCIMIs must also submit a valuation report of the company prepared by an
independent expert in accordance with international valuation standards (copy of this
report shall be attached to the relevant prospectus). Said valuation shall not be

necessary if, in the six months prior to the application for admission, SOCIMIs have conducted a share placement or financial operation to determine the initial listing price of their shares.

[3]   Redemption

39   There is no statutory right to redeem shares in a SOCIMI. A SOCIMI may buy back its own shares. The share buyback is subject to the general provisions for stock corporations. The share buyback must be approved by a resolution at the SOCIMI's Shareholders General Meeting.

[4]   Valuation of Shares/Units for Redemption and Other Purposes

40   As aforementioned, there is no statutory redemption right. Therefore, the shares are not valued for redemption purposes.

[5]   Investment Restrictions

[a]   Primary Corporate Activities

41   The primary corporate activities of the SOCIMI must be the following:

(a) The acquisition and development of urban real estate for lease, including the refurbishment of buildings.
(b) The holding of shares in other SOCIMIs or foreign companies with the same corporate activity as SOCIMIs and subject to the dividend distribution requirements.
(c) The holding of shares in Spanish or foreign companies with the same corporate activity and similar dividend distribution obligations as SOCIMIs. The entities referred to in this paragraph (c) may not hold shares in other entities. The capital of these entities shall be fully held by other SOCIMIs, similar foreign REITs or qualifying foreign entities.
(d) The holding of shares or units in Spanish-regulated real estate collective investment institutions.

42   Qualifying assets must be held for a minimum period of three years.

[b]   Asset Structure Requirements

43   At least 80% of the value of the assets must consist of qualifying real estate assets and shares.

The asset structure requirements shall be calculated according to their average of the **44** individual financial statements or consolidated if applicable. The SOCIMI may opt to take market values into account for calculation purposes.

If the SOCIMI is the head of a mercantile group, the asset structure requirements are **45** determined based on the consolidated financial statements of the SOCIMI and those subsidiaries described in letter (c) of section 41 above.

A minimum of only one property is required to incorporate SOCIMIs; thus, they can be **46** created in real estate projects where the existence of a company per project (and one asset per company) is essential for the purposes of liability, management, risks and licences.

[c] Immovable Property

The term 'immovable property' requires the legal ownership of property. Certain legal **47** rights in real property also qualify if registered with the land registry. Properties acquired under financial lease agreements as regulated by the CIT legislation are valid as well.

Immovable properties qualifying as special characteristics for cadastral purposes are **48** non-eligible assets. Those assets are leased to third parties under financial lease as regulated by the CIT legislation neither.

Immovable property must be held leased for at least a three-year period. For holding **49** period purposes, the period when the asset is under a 'for lease' status shall be taken into account only up to a maximum of one year.

Land for development is permitted as long as the construction is initiated within the **50** three-year period following the date of the acquisition.

There are no restrictions on foreign assets assuming that they are similar to the Spanish **51** qualifying assets and they are located in a jurisdiction with tax information exchange with Spain.

[d] Auxiliary Activities

Auxiliary activities are permitted as long as they represent less than 20% of the total **52** earnings of the company on a yearly basis.

[e] Yield Structure Requirements

At least 80% of SOCIMI's earnings must relate to rents and dividends from qualifying **53** assets and shares. The disposal of properties or shares is excluded from this ratio in so far as the disposed assets already met the applicable holding period.

54   If the SOCIMI is the head of a mercantile group, the yield structure requirements are determined based on the consolidated financial statements of the SOCIMI and those qualifying subsidiaries.

55   Earnings derived from leases to entities of the same mercantile group do not qualify for the purposes of the 80% test.

[6]   Distribution/Accumulation

56   Once all the company law obligations are met, the SOCIMI is obliged to distribute profits in the following amounts:

   – 100% of profits derived from dividends received from other SOCIMIs, foreign REITs, qualifying subsidiaries and collective investment institutions.
   – At least 50% of capital gains derived from qualifying real estate assets and shares. The remaining gain shall be reinvested within a three-year period or fully distributed once the three-year period has elapsed and no reinvestment has been made.
   – At least 80% of profits derived from income other than dividends and capital gains, i.e., including rental income and ancillary activities.

57   Distribution of dividends shall be agreed upon within the six-month period following the end of the financial year and be paid within the month following the date of the distribution agreement.

58   The legal reserve cannot exceed 20% of the share capital of the SOCIMI. The by-laws cannot create any type of non-disposable reserve different to the legal reserve.

[7]   Reporting Requirements

59   SOCIMIs are subject to the general reporting requirements that apply to stock corporations.

60   In addition, according to the SOCIMI Act, entities that have chosen to apply the SOCIMI special tax regime must create a section in the report of their Annual Accounts entitled 'Information requirements derived from SOCIMI status, Law 11/2009', in which the following information shall be included:

   (a) Reserves from years prior to the application of the tax regime established in this Law.
   (b) Reserves from fiscal years in which the tax regime established in this Law has been applied, differentiating the part that comes from income subject to a tax rate of 0%, 15% or 19%, with respect to those that, as the case may be, have been taxed at the general tax rate.

(c) Dividends distributed with a charge to profits for each year in which the tax regime established in this Law has been applicable, differentiating the part that comes from income subject to a tax rate of 0%, 15% or 19%.

(d) In the case of distribution of dividends charged to reserves, designation of the year from which the reserve was applied and whether they have been taxed at the 0%, 15%, 19% or general tax rate.

(e) Date of agreement to distribute the dividends referred to in letters (c) and (d) above.

(f) Date of acquisition of the real estate intended for lease.

(g) Identification of the assets that compute within the 80% of the value of the assets in urban real estate intended for lease, in land for the development of real estate to be used for such purpose or shares in other real estate entities.

(h) Reserves from fiscal years in which the special tax regime has been applicable, which have been disposed of in the tax period, other than for distribution or to offset losses, identifying the fiscal year from which said reserves originate.

61 Failure to comply with the above-mentioned requirement constitutes a serious infringement and entails pecuniary penalties (penalties may vary depending on the piece of missing information – lack of specific information or lack of set of data is sanctioned with different amounts of penalties).

2 In addition, at the request of the tax authorities, the companies must provide detailed information on the calculations to determine the result of the distribution of expenses among the different sources of income.

[8]   *Accounting*

62 SOCIMIs are obliged to prepare financial statements. As listed entities, SOCIMIs may prepare their financial statements under Spanish Generally Accepted Accounting Principles or International Financial Reporting Standards financial statements. Financial statements are subject to statutory audit.

63 The lease and development activities shall be subject to a separate accounting per property so that a profit breakdown per asset is available. Other activities shall be booked separately as well.

§1.03 TAXATION

[A] Taxation of the REIT

[1] *Corporate Income Tax*

[a] *Tax Filings*

64 As a taxable entity, the SOCIMI needs to prepare the applicable tax accounts and returns, as well as any accounting and supporting documentation.

65 The yearly tax return is due within the twenty-five-day period following the sixth month after the closing of the tax period, that is, between 1 and 25 of July if the tax period coincides with the calendar year.[2]

[b] *Determination of Taxable Income*

66 The CIT regulations are fully applicable to SOCIMIs for the computation of the taxable base with the particularities included in the SOCIMI Act. This means that the taxable base takes the accounting profit according to Spanish GAAP as a starting point. This is then adjusted by tax law to determine the taxable income. Worldwide income should be included in the taxable base.

67 The SOCIMI regime is not compatible with other special tax regimes regulated by the CIT laws, with the exception of those applicable to reorganizations, Controlled Foreign Company (CFC) rules, and certain financial lease contracts. It is worth mentioning that the SOCIMI is not eligible for tax consolidation purposes.

68 The SOCIMI is subject to Spanish CIT at 0%. However, it is not eligible to carry forward tax losses as well as to generate tax credits.

69 However, income and capital gains derived from investments that do not respect the three-year holding period will be taxable at the level of the SOCIMI at the standard CIT rate (25%) under the general CIT regime rules, plus the corresponding delay interest.[3]

70 On the other hand, the SOCIMI will be required to pay a 19% 'special tax' on dividends distributed to shareholders holding an interest of at least 5% that are either tax exempt or subject to an effective tax rate below 10%. This special tax will not be triggered if the

---

2. The return corresponding to the 19% Special CIT levy must be filed within two months as from the date in which the dividend distribution is approved by the SOCIMI. The new special tax of 15% on undistributed dividends, which will form part of corporate income tax, will accrue on the date on which the distribution of the dividend is approved by the General Shareholders' Meeting or equivalent body. It is subject to self-assessment and payment must be made within two months from the date of accrual.
3. Rental income from previous years needs to be regularized and standard 25% CIT tax (plus delay interests) paid.

recipient of the dividends is a foreign REIT or a foreign entity with corporate activity, investment requirements and dividend distribution policy similar to a SOCIMI as long as those dividends are subject to a minimum effective tax rate of 10% at the level of shareholders holding 5% or more of the share capital. The investor's effective tax rate of at least 10% must be communicated to the SOCIMI in order to avoid the special tax.

In addition, as from 1 January 2021, the SOCIMI will be subject to an additional 'special tax' of 15% on the profits obtained and not distributed in the part that originates from income that has not been taxed at the general corporate income tax rate or that does not constitute income subject to the reinvestment period.

[c]   Applicability of the SOCIMI Regime

The SOCIMI regime may be applicable not only to a SOCIMI itself but also to those **71** Spanish resident entities with the same corporate activity, dividend distribution obligations, asset and income tests as SOCIMIs, whose total share capital is held by a SOCIMI, other SOCIMIs, or foreign REITs or qualifying foreign entities.

These qualifying Spanish subsidiaries may also opt for the SOCIMI regime. It should be **72** noted that these entities are not permitted to hold shares in other entities.

[d]   Taxation of Foreign Income

SOCIMIs are taxed on their worldwide income. However, they are not entitled to **73** recognize a foreign tax credit on taxes paid (including WHT) in a foreign jurisdiction.

[2]   Value Added Tax

Spanish Value Added Tax (VAT) system does not provide for any specific rule **74** regarding SOCIMIs. This means that SOCIMIs are subject to general VAT regulations. The standard rate currently stands at 21%.

The acquisition and transfer of properties are subject either to VAT or to Real Estate **75** Transfer Tax, both regimes being mutually exclusive. VAT is refundable as long as the activity carried out is subject to and not exempt from VAT. Option to VAT may be implemented for those transactions which initially may be exempt from VAT: Under this scenario, the self-charge rule would be applicable. If the transaction qualifies as a going concern transfer, Real Estate Transfer Tax would be applicable with no recourse to VAT.

The lease of commercial or industrial property by a VAT person is subject to and not **76** exempt from VAT, irrespective of the status of the tenant. However, the lease of residential is, in principle, VAT exempt.

77   On the other hand, transfers of shares are VAT and real estate transfer tax (RETT) exempt as a general rule unless the share deal is purported to avoid the indirect taxation of an asset deal.

[3]   Withholding Taxes

78   Dividend distributions by the SOCIMI follow these rules:

(a) Spanish resident individuals: Standard 19% WHT is applicable.
(b) Spanish resident entities/non-resident entities with a Spanish permanent establishment: 19% WHT is applicable.
(c) Non-resident investors: WHT as per applicable Double Tax Treaty or EU Parent-Subsidiary Directive (as implemented in Spain), although the application of EU Parent-Subsidiary Directive exemption could be debatable.

[4]   Other Taxes

79   SOCIMIs are subject to the general rules with regard to other taxes. However, a couple of specific tax benefits may be found:

– Incorporation, increases of share capital, and contributions in kind are exempt from Capital Duty.
– SOCIMIs are eligible for a 95% rebate on the Real Estate Transfer Tax or Stamp Duty charge due on acquisition of residential for lease and the acquisition of land for residential development and lease. In both cases, the holding periods (i.e., three years) should be respected.

[5]   Penalties Imposed on REIT

80   A loss of the SOCIMI status occurs under the following circumstances:

– delisting;
– substantial non-compliance with reporting requirements;
– non-compliance with dividend distribution obligations;
– any other breach of SOCIMI requirements, unless remedied in the following period;
– waiver of the SOCIMI regime.

81   The company is subject to the standard tax regime in the same period when any of the above circumstances happen.

82   The removal from the SOCIMI regime prevents the option to apply for the regime at least in the three-year period following the last period in which it was applied.

[B]   Taxation of the Investor

[1]   *Private Investors*

[a]   *Taxation of Current Income (i.e., All Income Derived from REIT in Holding Phase)*

Dividends derived from SOCIMI shares distributed to resident individuals are subject to   **83**
general personal income tax rules.

Dividends derived from SOCIMI shares distributed to non-resident individuals not   **84**
acting through a Spanish permanent establishment are subject to general non-resident
income tax rules as well as treaty provisions.

[b]   *Taxation of Capital Gains (From Disposal of REIT Shares)*

Capital gains derived from the disposal of SOCIMI shares are subject to general   **85**
personal income tax rules for resident individuals, and to non-resident income tax rules
as well as to treaty provisions, generally with no recourse to domestic exemptions, for
non-resident individuals not acting through a Spanish permanent establishment.

[2]   *Institutional Investors*

[a]   *Taxation of Current Income (All Income Derived from REIT in Holding Phase)*

Regarding the tax treatment of dividends (deriving from profits taxed at the 0% rate) at   **86**
the level of resident corporate shareholders, it should be noted that dividends are
subject in their entirety to CIT at the general rate (25%) with no recourse to the
domestic participation-exemption.

Dividends obtained by non-residents acting through a Spanish permanent establish-   **87**
ment are subject to the same rules described above for resident corporate shareholders.

However, if dividends are obtained by non-resident entities without a permanent   **88**
establishment, they will be subject to general non-resident income tax rules as well as
treaty provisions.

[b]   *Taxation of Capital Gains (From Disposal of REIT Shares)*

Capital gains obtained by resident entities derived from the disposal of SOCIMI shares   **89**
shall be subject to the general income rate, that is, 25%, with no recourse to the
domestic participation-exemption.

90 The same rules described above for resident corporate shareholders are applicable to gains obtained by non-residents acting through a Spanish permanent establishment.

91 Under a scenario of capital gains obtained by non-resident entities without a permanent establishment, they will be subject to non-resident income tax rules as well as to treaty provisions, generally with no recourse to domestic exemptions.

[C]   Tax Treaties

[1]   Treaty Access

92 Since SOCIMIs are CIT taxpayers, they are eligible for treaty relief. Some treaties entered with Spain already include specific provisions for dividends and capital gains with regard to SOCIMI.

[2]   WHT Reduction

93 As stated above, dividend distributions by the SOCIMI to non-resident shareholders are generally subject to Spanish WHT according to the domestic legislation as well as to treaty provisions.

[D]   Exit Tax/Tax Privileges/Concessions/Transitional Period

94 New or existing companies and collective investment institutions can opt to join the SOCIMI regime by notifying the Tax Administration. The regime applies retrospectively from the beginning of the financial year in which the SOCIMI has validly applied to join the tax regime.

95 As a general rule, mergers, spin-offs, contributions in kind and exchange for shares may be tax neutral if such corporate restructurings are business-driven. The law assumes that those corporate transactions are based on valid economic grounds if implemented to set up one or various SOCIMIs or to convert pre-existing companies into SOCIMIs.

96 On the other hand, there is no entry tax charge established for the transition to the SOCIMI regime.

97 A number of rules should be observed by those entities converted into SOCIMIs, in particular regarding tax losses generated before conversion, latent capital gains of assets, and pending tax credits. In particular, capital gains derived from assets held before the conversion into a REIT would be allocated on a straight-line basis over the whole holding period, unless otherwise proven: Those gains allocated to the period prior to the conversion will be taxed according to the standard CIT rate and rules.

In order to be eligible for the special tax regime, the SOCIMI must continuously meet **98** the investment, distribution, regulatory requirements described above. However, a transitional period of two years starting from the date of filing the option is available to meet some of the requirements. In the meantime, the SOCIMI tax regime is applicable subject to compliance of all the requirements by the end of the two-year period. However, if the requirements are not met after the two-year period, the taxpayer will be treated as a regular taxpayer for CIT with retrospective effects, i.e., paying CIT at the standard rate on the income filed as REIT plus the corresponding surcharges and delay interest. Penalties may also be imposed.

[E] Taxation of Foreign REITs

[1] Taxation of Foreign REIT Holding Assets in Country

Real estate income obtained in Spain directly by a foreign REIT is in principle taxable **99** in Spain.

Those resident subsidiaries of foreign entities listed in the EU or the EEA or countries **100** with exchange of information with Spain with corporate activity, investment requirements and dividend distribution policy similar to a SOCIMI are eligible for the SOCIMI tax regime for their Spanish real estate investments. The Spanish resident subsidiary must be fully held by the foreign entity directly (or other SOCIMIs). In order to be eligible for the SOCIMI status, corporate activity, distribution obligations, and investment requirements regulated in the SOCIMI law must be met by the subsidiary.

[2] Taxation of Investors Holding Shares in Foreign REIT

Dividends and capital gains obtained on a worldwide basis by individuals or corporate **101** investors resident in Spain are subject to taxation according to Individual Income Tax and CIT rules and taking into account the specific features of the foreign REIT vehicle. If the foreign REIT qualifies as an exempt vehicle, the access to domestic participation-exemption will need to be carefully assessed.

Turkey

ERSUN BAYRAKTAROGLU

Ersun Bayraktaroğlu is a tax partner and territory real estate leader of PwC Turkey. He has been a tax practitioner for about thirty-five years and has been providing advisory services to several domestic and international clients in the real estate area for years. He obtained his Master of Arts in Economics at Western Michigan University in the USA. Mr Bayraktaroğlu is the author of several articles in business dailies and real estate magazines. Also, he is a speaker in several domestic and international panels, discussions and conferences and a lecturer in several seminars on tax issues.
E-mail: ersun.bayraktaroglu@pwc.com

BARAN AKAN

Baran Akan is a tax director at PwC Turkey. He has been with the firm for twenty years and has gained experience in various fields, particularly in real estate taxation and international tax planning for multinational companies. He is working as a senior advisor rendering tax audit consultancy and international tax planning services, both to international investors and to respectable local companies.
E-mail: baran.akan@pwc.com

BIRIM SARAN

Birim Saran is a senior tax manager at PwC Turkey. She has been with the firm for more than ten years and has been providing tax advisory services to several domestic and international clients in the real estate area.
E-mail: saran.birim@pwc.com

Turkey

Ersun Bayraktaroğlu, Baran Akan & Birim Saran

§1.01 BACKGROUND

[A] Key Characteristics

The concept of a 'trust' does not exist in Turkey, so REICs are structured as Real Estate **1**
Investment Companies (REICs).

REICs are defined by the Turkish Capital Markets Board (CMB) as capital market **2**
institutions that invest in real estate and that invest in capital market instruments based
on real estate, real estate projects and rights based on real estate.

At least 25% of the REIC shares have to be offered to the public on the Borsa Istanbul **3**
A.S. (BIST) within three months.

REICs are fully exempt from Turkish Corporate Income Tax and subject to 0% dividend **4**
withholding tax.

[B] History of REIC

The REIC was first introduced to the Turkish law system by the Capital Markets Law **5**
and Tax Laws in 1992. On 22 July 1995, the publication of the Communiqué on the
Principles regarding REIC in the Official Gazette set forth regulations on the establishment, operation and rules and public offering of shares of the REICs. In Turkey, the first
REIC was established and listed on the BIST in 1996.

As of February 2022, Turkey had thirty-seven REICs; thirty-six are listed on the BIST. **6**

[C]   REIC Market

7   REICs offer easy access to the profits of huge real estate portfolios, and they have attracted the attention of both local and foreign investors. The thirty-six listed REICs' total assets are approximately EUR 5,548 million as of September 2021.

8   In the years to come, it is anticipated that the number and portfolios of REICs will simultaneously grow with the completion of planned initial public offerings (IPO).

§1.02   REGULATORY ASPECTS

[A]   Legal Form of REIC

[1]   Corporate Form

9   An REIC has to be a stock corporation. Either an REIC can be a new joint-stock company (an immediate establishment) or an existing joint-stock corporation can convert to an REIC by amending its Articles of Association with the Trade Registry. The amended articles have to change the name, scope and activities of the company.

[B]   Regulatory Authorities

10   Irrespective of whether they are listed or not, REICs are regulated by CMB, and CMB supervises all kinds of REIC operations.

[C]   Legislative and Other Regulatory Sources

11   REICs are regulated under Communiqué number III-48.1 issued by CMB on Principles Regarding Real Estate Investment Companies (hereinafter referred to as 'Communiqué') on 28 May 2013. REICs are also subject to the Turkish Commercial Code (TCC) regulations.

12   Starting from the beginning of 2009, CMB announced another type of CMB-regulated company as Infrastructure Real Estate Companies (IREICs) and issued a communiqué for IREICs. However, there has not been any amendment until the beginning of 2014. Under Communiqué number III-48.1-a issued by CMB on 23 January 2014, the regulations related to IREICs are integrated into Communiqué number III-48.1. Therefore, REICs, which are incorporated to manage portfolios composed of infrastructure investment and services and other infrastructure-related market instruments under the provisions of Communiqué, can operate as IREIC. Please note that, in accordance with Corporate Income Tax Communiqué number 13, IREICs cannot benefit from the corporate income tax exemption. IREICs may offer share certificates to the public like

REICs; they can also offer share certificates to qualified investors without having an IPO.

One of the major amendments to the Communique was published in the Official **13** Gazette on 17 January 2017 as Communiqué number III-48.1-b. The provisions on Communique number III-48.1-b mainly focus on activities, structure and portfolios of IREICs. In addition to these provisions, there are a number of amendments regarding the management structure of REICs, principles on investments and activities, prohibited activities, principles on valuation and distributions, which are elaborated in the following sections. Furthermore, a new amendment to extend the period of the temporary clause was published on 10 May 2018.

On 2 January 2019, the Communiqué numbered III-48.1-ç was published in the Official **14** Gazette, amending many provisions. One of the major amendments is that portfolio limitations of IREICs are expanded, and new exemptions regarding IREICs that have not yet made IPO or been sold to qualified investors are introduced. Also, obtaining services from portfolio management companies for REICs that have more than 10% of their portfolio invested in money and capital market instruments has been introduced as a requirement. The scope of the purposes of enabling an REIC to become a subsidiary to other companies is expanded. The provision regarding the determination of real estate appraisal companies has been amended.

On 27 September 2019, the Communiqué numbered 48.1-d was published in the **15** Official Gazette, making a small amendment in the activities REICs may perform relating to real estate projects of the government.

On 09 October 2020, the Communiqué numbered 48.1-e was published in the Official **16** Gazette, amending some of the provisions. Amendments have been made in the provisions regarding decisions of the board of directors that must be disclosed to the public, investment activities and restrictions on investment activities, prohibited activities, portfolio restrictions, establishment of mortgage, pledge and limited rights in rem, construction services, use of expertise value, and public disclosure. Furthermore, in accordance with the amendment made in the relevant provision of Communiqué 48.1-e, the limitation regarding profit distribution in cash before the public offering or sale to qualified investors will not be applied to IREICs until 31/12/2023.

[D] Exchange Controls and Reporting Requirements

Important developments concerning listed REICs and their portfolio tables, including **17** their assets and net asset value per share, are announced to investors in the bulletin of the CMB.

The CMB Communiqué on Material Circumstances numbered II-15.1 provides for **18** disclosure of important events and developments which may impact the value of the BIST traded capital market instruments or be influential on the investment decisions of, or the exercise of the rights by, the investors. Therefore, listed REICs have to report such events to BIST and CMB as soon as they occur or are discovered by Public Disclosure Platform.

19   Articles 38, 39 and 40 of the Communiqué set forth the following reporting and disclosure requirements which apply to all REICs.

Important Principles Regarding Financial Reports and Reports of Board of Directors

20   Article 38 states that REICs must comply with the CMB Communiqué on Principles of Financial Reporting in Capital Markets numbered II-14.1 in preparation and disclosure of the financial statements to the public.

21   In addition, Article 39 states that REICs are required to include the following to the activity reports of the board of directors that are quarterly prepared and disclosed to the public:

  (i)   A summary of an expert report which is prepared in relation to the assets in the portfolio.
  (ii) A summary of the developments realized within the last three months.
  (iii) Actual situation of the projects along with the additional explanations such as their completion ratio and period and the issues.
  (iv) Detailed information in relation to the leased assets in the portfolio.
  (v)   Comparative financial statements of the relevant fiscal year.
  (vi) Information regarding controlling portfolio restrictions.

22   REICs must submit their annual financial statements and the related independent audit reports to the CMB and BIST, as well as their interim financial tables. Such statements and tables must also be disclosed to the public on Public Disclosure Platform. The annual financial tables must be submitted within sixty days as of the end of the accounting period for the REICs that are not required to prepare consolidated financial tables, while the time period is stipulated as seventy days for the ones that are subject to such requirement. However, the time period for the submission of the interim financial tables is foreseen as thirty days for the REICs that are not subject to prepare consolidated financial tables, whereas the time period is foreseen as forty days for the ones which must prepare consolidated financial tables.

Disclosure

23   Article 40 of the Communiqué states that REICs must submit the following documents to the CMB within three business days following execution or delivery date of such, as may be applicable:

  (i)   The appraisal reports issued optionally or pursuant to provisions of the Communiqué.
  (ii) Agreements which were signed within the context of Article 22 of the Communiqué and for the ratio of the mortgage amount to the value of the property (determined by the latest revaluation report) and to the total assets

regarding the latest financial statements that disclosed to the public if the project land is mortgaged.

The valuation reports stated in Article 34 of the Communiqué must be disclosed to the **24** public at Public Disclosure Platform within three days following their delivery. Moreover, financial reports stated in Article 38 of the Communiqué must be disclosed to the public at the Public Disclosure Platform.

Please note that in addition to the above-mentioned disclosure principles, there are **25** further requirements to be fulfilled in relation to other important events. Moreover, there are a number of minor additions to these requirements as stipulated under Communique No. III-48.1-e.

In addition to the announcements described above, Turkish REICs' annual and **26** semi-annual financial statements have to be audited by a certified external auditor and published in the bulletin of the BIST. Turkish REICs are required to prepare audited financial statements in accordance with the standards of the CMB, which are very similar to International Financial Reporting Standards.

[E]   Registration Procedures

[1]   *Preparatory Measures*

An REIC can be created by the establishment or by conversion of an existing company **27** into an REIC. New and existing joint-stock corporations that will operate as an REIC have to meet the requirements of the founders and shareholders of an REIC.

Article 7 of the Communiqué mandates the following qualifications for shareholders: **28**

(a) natural and legal person founders cannot be bankrupt, go bankrupt or have any postponement of bankruptcy;

(b) the real person shareholders should not have responsibility for events that lead to the cancellation of one or more Certificate of Authorities of companies or temporary or permanent extraction of companies from the Stock Exchange Market;

(c) there must be no bankruptcy decision, liquidation or composition of debts announcement regarding the shareholder or any institutions in which the shareholder is an unlimited partner;

(d) the natural person shareholders cannot have been imprisoned for more than five years for a crime committed on purpose, or have been found guilty of certain crimes, including terror financing, on purpose crime, bribery and fraud;

(e) the real or legal founders must provide the required resources for the incorporation of REIC from their own commercial, industrial and other legal activities as free from any debt;

(f) the real or legal founders must have a good reputation as required by their status;

(g) natural and legal person founders cannot have any tax liabilities;

(h) the person shall not be condemned for the crimes regulated under Law No. 6415 on the Prevention of the Financing of Terrorism dated 7 February 2013; and

(i) the person shall not be transaction banned according to Article 101/1(a) of the Capital Market Law.

[2]   Obtaining Authorization

29   Whether an REIC is a new corporation or an existing corporation, the founders have to apply for approval from the CMB.

30   In the case of an establishment, the CMB considers whether the applicant corporations conform to the provisions of Capital Markets Law (CML) and the Communiqué. Specifically, the CMB looks at whether:

(a) prospective REICs have the necessary corporate structure;

(b) REICs have sufficient registered capital. Registered capital is the maximum amount of capital for which companies can issue shares by a resolution of the board of directors without being subjected to the regulations of TCC. A statutory registered capital amount does not exist as all companies can determine their own registered amounts;

(c) prospective REICs meet initial offering requirements;

(d) the initial capital of the REIC is sufficient (*see* section §1.02[F][1] below);

(e) the phrase 'REIC' is included in the commercial title;

(f) an application for providing portfolio management services has been filed with the CMB;

(g) REIC founders and directors are qualified (*see* section §1.02[E][1] above);

(h) the Articles of Association of the prospective REIC are in conformity with the provisions of CML and the Communiqué.

31   In the case of an already existing joint-stock company that is converted into an REIC, the CMB considers whether the company meets the above-described qualifications. In case of both establishment and conversion of an existing company, CMB considers whether the applicant corporations conform to the provisions of CML and the Communiqué.

[3] *Obtaining Listing Exchanges*

[a] *Costs*

Companies listed on BIST mainly have two kinds of costs. For securities that provide **32** partnership rights, a quoting fee is calculated as 0.1% of the nominal price of the total shares. For publicly offered shares, the registration fee is calculated as 0.2% of the price of shares.

[b] *Time*

The time required to list an REIC will depend on several factors, including the size and **33** complexity of the transaction.

REICs are obligated to offer share certificates representing 25% of their capital to the **34** public within three months.

The time period to make a public offering begins upon the registration of incorporation **35** or the amendment of the Articles of Association.

[F] **Requirements and Restrictions**

[1] *Capital Requirements*

The minimum capital requirement for an REIC is TRY 64,500,000 for the year 2022. The **36** amount may be amended annually by the CMB.

If the initial capital is less than TRY 129 million, at least 10% of the shares representing **37** the initial capital have to be issued for cash. If the initial capital is TRY 129 million or more, at least TRY 12.9 million of the shares, and if it manages a portfolio consisting of exclusive infrastructure investment and services, at least TRY 21 million of the shares have to be issued for cash. The shares can be issued in registered or bearer form.

[2] *Marketing/Advertising*

Turkish REICs have to prepare a prospectus for shares that are publicly offered. The **38** prospectus covers financial, managerial and operational information and other information regarding REICs and their publicly offered shares.

[3] Redemption

39 CMB allows companies, which are listed on BIST, to buy their own shares if they meet conditions stated by the CMB decision.

[4] Valuation Principles

40 The assets and rights of Turkish REICs are subject to valuation on a yearly basis.

41 REICs have to employ an asset valuation company to value assets mainly in the following situations:

- purchase or disposal of assets or projects which exist in the portfolio of REIC;
- lease of assets;
- renewal or time extension of lease agreements;
- acceptation of an asset mortgage;
- determination of the legal conformity of projects in order to start the construction; and
- contribution of in-kind capital to the REIC;
- determination of the year-end values of the assets in the portfolio whose values are not determined due to any reason within the last three months of the accounting period;
- amendment to the type or quality of the assets indicated in the first item of this paragraph.

42 REICs can only work with the asset valuation companies which are on the list provided by the CMB, and REICs cannot work with a specific asset valuation company for more than three consecutive years. In order to work with the same company after three consecutive years, REICs should wait at least two years.

[5] Investment Restrictions

43 According to the Communiqué, REICs can invest in real estate and capital market instruments based on real estate, real estate projects, real estate related rights capital market instruments. Capital market instruments have to be traded on the stock exchange or an organized market. The purchase and sale of capital market instruments have to be made on the exchange.

44 In case an REIC is established with the purpose of operating in certain areas, or investing in certain projects, at least 75 % of the REICs total assets must consist of assets mentioned in its title and/or Articles of Association.

45 Specifically, the following diversification requirements apply:

- REICs are required to invest in real estate, rights supported by real estate and real estate projects participation units of Real Estate Investment Funds, companies within the scope of subparagraph (ç) of the first paragraph of Article 28 of the Communiqué, in which REICs participate 100% in the capital at a minimum rate of 51% of their portfolio;
- REICs may invest in time deposits and demand deposits in TRY or any foreign currency for investment purposes at a maximum rate of 10% of their total assets;
- REICs may invest in foreign real estate and capital market instruments backed by real estate at a maximum rate of 49% of their portfolio; and
- the rate of lands and registered lands which have been in the portfolio for a period of five years and which have not been administrated for any project cannot exceed 20% of the total assets.

REICs cannot aim to control the capital and management of the companies that they invest in, and the REIC cannot own more than 5% of the capital and voting rights in any company. However, REICs can establish ordinary partnerships to realize a project. **46**

REICs are mainly prohibited from the following types of investments: **47**

- capital market instruments which are not traded on a stock exchange or on other markets, except for investment funds;
- assets and rights that are subject to any kind of restrictions on transfer;
- short-term real estate purchasing and selling operations;
- gold or precious metals;
- commodity futures or commodities;
- short sales and lending securities or loan securities;
- transactions in derivative instruments exceeding the purpose of hedging; and
- transactions with commission fees and similar expenses exceeding 3% of the asset purchase value or sale value.

REICs are only allowed to participate in the below companies: **48**

- management companies;
- other REICs;
- companies which are established for the build-operate-transfer model of projects;
- foreign companies which are established for acquiring specific real estate, real estate projects or rights based on real estate in the portfolio or special purpose companies which are established in or outside of Turkey just for the purpose of investing in these foreign companies;
- Turkish companies with assets or rights based on assets that constitute 75% of their financial assets as of the acquisition date;
- companies that are established because of legal necessities only to provide infrastructure services to specific real estate projects of REICs.

49   Shares of REICs in management companies cannot exceed 10% of their total assets declared in their last quarter financial statements disclosed to the public. For other allowable companies listed above, the 5% general shareholding limitation does not apply.

[6]   Distribution/Accumulation

50   The CMB sets out specific rules with respect to the timing, procedures and limits of profit distributions. As REICs are public companies, profit distributions of REICs are subject to the general regulations of the CMB regulating the profit distribution of public companies. According to the communiqués regarding dividend distributions, public companies are free to determine their own profit distribution politics. The distributable profit is calculated in line with both CMB and TCC regulations.

51   In order to secure the capital position of the REIC, the lesser of the net distributable profit calculated in line with the statutory accounts or in line with CMB regulations should be distributed.

52   The public companies may freely determine their dividend distribution policy under the CMB's new Dividend Distribution Communiqué numbered II-19.1 through their general assemblies. General assemblies should determine their policy on whether to distribute any dividend, the rate and type (i.e., in cash) of the dividend, the time of the dividend payment and whether to pay an advance dividend. The general assembly of the company must determine the time of the dividend payment provided that the distribution payment process is initiated no later than by the end of the relevant financial year of that general assembly meeting.

53   Also, based on the CMB Communiqué numbered II-19.1, public companies may freely decide to:

- distribute dividends entirely in cash;
- distribute dividends entirely as shares;
- distribute dividends partially in cash and partially as shares and keep the remaining as reserves;
- keep all the profits as reserves.

54   However, the public companies whose shares are not traded in the exchange have to distribute the dividend fully and in cash. Also, the rate of the dividend for those companies cannot be less than 20% of the net distributable profit calculated under the Communiqué.

55   REICs are entitled to make advance dividend distributions quarterly. Such advance dividend distributions are subject to CMB regulations as well. Advance dividend distributions can only be realized in cash. Advance dividend distributions shall not exceed half of the net interim profit remaining after subtracting the legal reserves and accumulated losses.

Besides, the advance dividend distribution amount shall not exceed the lower one of **56**
the following amounts:

(a) The half of the previous year's net profit amount.
(b) The total amount of other distributable sources, except the net profit amount
    stated in the financials of the corresponding interim period.

In addition to the above-mentioned provisions, a temporary clause concerning profit **57**
distribution is stipulated for the IREICs under Communique No. 48.1-b and amended
by Communique number 48.1-c to extend the period. The period specified in Communiqué number 48.1-c has been extended further with Communiqué number 48.1-e.
Article 45 of the Communique regulating prohibition of the cash profit distribution
before the public offering of shares or sales to the qualified investors will not be
applicable for the IREICs until 31 December 2023.

§1.03 TAXATION

[A] Taxation of the REIC

[1] Corporate Income Tax

[a] Tax Accounting

Taxable income is determined in accordance with the Tax Procedural Law. In **58**
accordance with Turkish tax legislation, regular corporations in Turkey are subject to
corporate income tax at a rate of 20% of their taxable income (25% for 2021 and 23%
for 2022), while REICs are exempt from corporate income tax. Dividend distributions
to resident and non-resident individual and corporate shareholders of an REIC do not
trigger a dividend withholding tax burden.

[b] Determination of Taxable Income

The determination of the REIC's taxable income is no different than the determination **59**
of taxable income for ordinary companies in Turkey. Fiscal profit is adjusted for the
deductible and non-deductible expenses, and exemptions are applied. Although REICs
are exempt from corporate income tax, they still have to submit an annual corporate
income tax return.

[c] Taxation of Income from Taxable/Non-taxable Subsidiaries

The dividend income of Turkish resident companies derived from taxable Turkish **60**
resident subsidiaries is exempt from corporate income tax. Dividends received from

non-taxable subsidiaries are taxable in Turkey. However, dividends received by REICs, in general, are tax exempt due to REIC exemption status.

[d]   *Taxation of Foreign Income*

61   The foreign corporate income of REICs is exempt from corporate income tax.

[2]   *VAT*

62   Most transactions carried out by REICs are subject to 18% Value Added Tax (VAT). The purchase and sale of land or any other real estate by an REIC to or from a Turkish resident company are accounted for as input VAT.

63   Some transactions that are not subject to VAT include:

 – if the seller of the real estate is an individual who is not constantly engaging in real estate trading, the sale of real estate is not subject to VAT;
 – the acquisition of real estate from banks and insurance companies is not subject to VAT, but it is subject to banking and insurance transaction tax (BITT) at a rate of 5%. BITT cannot be offset from other BITT payable as in the input VAT system, but rather is taken into account as a deductible cost in determining the corporate income tax base; and
 – the acquisition of real estate from companies whose main activity is not real estate trading is exempt from VAT if the seller company has held the real estate for at least two years at the time of sale.

64   Input VAT can be offset against output VAT calculated on the sales or the rental income of the REIC. Input VAT that cannot be offset against output VAT is not a deductible expense for the determination of the corporate income tax base.

65   Effective VAT rate to be applied on the sale of residential units which are holding their building licence as from 1 January 2013 with a net area of less than 150 sq.m. will be 1%–8%–18% based on some certain conditions stated in the corresponding legislation.

[3]   **Withholding Taxes**

66   In addition to dividend withholding taxes, REICs are subject to other types of withholding taxes applicable to certain payments. Under the Turkish tax system, certain taxes are collected through withholding by the payers in order to secure the collection of taxes. The table below details the types of payments on which tax is withheld and the applicable withholding tax rates:

Corporate Withholding Tax	Rate (%)
Independent professional service fee payments to non-residents	20
Royalty, licence payments to non-residents	20
Income Withholding Tax	
Income tax on salaries of employees	15–40
Lease payments to individual landlords	20
Progress payments made for construction work spanning more than one calendar year	5
Independent professional service fee payments to resident individuals	20

[4]   Other Taxes

[a]   Title Deed Fee

The acquisition of the legal title to Turkish property and any re-registering of the legal   **67**
title to the property are subject to a 2% title deed charge on the higher of the sales price
or the real estate tax base. The real estate tax base is the higher of the value on which
the property tax is based or the transaction value. The title deed fee applies to the buyer
and the seller separately. Therefore, the total title deed fee is 4%. Additional title deed
fees may also apply depending on the type of title deed transaction.

[b]   Stamp Tax

Stamp tax applies to a wide range of documents, including but not limited to   **68**
agreements, financial statements and payrolls. Almost every original signed agreement
that states a monetary value is subject to stamp tax at a general rate of 0.948%. Lease
contracts are subject to stamp tax at a rate of 0.189% of the yearly rental amount.
Agreements signed by REICs regarding the acquisition and the disposal of real estate
and promises to buy or sell real estate are exempt from stamp tax.

Stamp duty rate to be applied on several agreements which are specifically related to   **69**
the real estate industry was reduced to 0% in 2017.

The corresponding agreements are as follows: **70**

- Officially drafted construction agreements on flat for land basis or revenue
  sharing.
- Construction and contracting agreements drafted among building contractors
  and subcontractors within the scope of officially drafted construction agreements on flat for land basis or revenue sharing.

- Advisory service agreements with respect to the construction work on flat for land basis or revenue sharing.
- Service agreements of building inspection.

71 Stamp tax is capped at TRY 4.814.234 (approximately EUR 310,600) under the current foreign exchange rate, subject to annual revaluation for the year 2022. All signatory parties are jointly held liable for the stamp tax payment. In practice, the parties come to a mutual agreement regarding the stamp tax payment.

[c]   Property Tax

72 An annual property tax (real estate tax) of between 0.1% and 0.3% is levied on the owner of buildings and land in Turkey. The rates double for property located within the borders of metropolitan areas.

73 For Turkish corporate income tax purposes, property tax is immediately deductible.

[d]   Environmental Tax

74 Annual environmental tax, which is determined by Municipality Income Law, is collected on water consumption and on business places and buildings used for other purposes. The tax amount varies from TRY 62 to TRY 7,500 for the year 2022 according to the degree and the group that the buildings fall into, as specified in the tariff.

[5]   Penalties Imposed on REIC

75 If an REIC does not comply with all CMB conditions and restrictions, the REIC loses the right to operate as an REIC. The CMB informs the Ministry of Finance, and the company loses its tax-exempt REIC status.

[B]   Taxation of the Investor

[1]   Private Investors

[a]   Taxation of Current Income (i.e., All Income Derived from REIC in Holding Phase)

76 Resident individual shareholders are obliged to declare half of the dividends received from REICs as income, provided that half of the dividends received exceed the declaration limit (approximately EUR 4,516 for the year 2022). If the dividend amount received by the individual shareholder does not exceed the aforementioned limit, the shareholder is not required to declare the related income.

Declared income is subject to income tax at a progressive rate between 15% and 40%.   **77**

Dividend distributions to non-resident shareholders by REICs currently do not trigger   **78**
dividend withholding tax in Turkey, and there is no further Turkish taxation for
non-resident individuals. However, the taxation of dividends at the level of non-
residents depends on the tax treatment in the shareholder's country of residence.

[b]   *Taxation of Capital Gains (From Disposals of REIC Shares)*

Capital gains derived from the sale of shares on the BIST, which are acquired after 1   **79**
January 2006 by non-resident individuals, are subject to 0% withholding tax. This
withholding tax is the final tax on capital gains for non-resident individuals, and there
is no further taxation.

Capital gains derived from the sale of shares on the BIST by resident individuals are   **80**
also subject to 0% withholding tax, and this withholding tax is the final tax.

[2]   ***Institutional Investors***

[a]   *Taxation of Current Income (i.e., All Income Derived from REIC in*
          Holding Phase)

For Turkish shareholders of REICs, local participation exemption does not apply.   **81**
Therefore, dividends received from REICs by corporate resident investors are subject to
a 20% corporate income tax (25% for 2021, 23% for 2022).

As the dividend distribution by REICs to non-resident corporations is subject to 0%   **82**
withholding tax, and there is no further Turkish taxation on dividends distributed to
non-resident corporations, their tax treatment depends on the tax laws of the country
of the investor's residence.

[b]   *Taxation of Capital Gains (From Disposals of REIC Shares)*

The capital gains derived from the sale of REIC shares by resident legal entities are   **83**
included in corporate income and are subject to corporate income tax at 20% (25% for
2021 and 23% for 2022). However, there is a special partial exemption available for
75% of the gains derived from the sale of shares that are held for at least two years, with
certain further conditions.

Capital gains derived from the sale of shares on the BIST by non-resident legal entities   **84**
that do not have a permanent establishment in Turkey are not subject to withholding
tax or corporate income tax.

Capital gains derived from the sale of unlisted Turkish company shares (such as REIC   **85**
shares that have not been offered to the public yet) by non-resident corporations that

do not have a permanent establishment in Turkey may have to be declared within fifteen days following the sale of shares. The capital gains are taxed at the regular corporate income tax rate of 20% (25% for 2021 and 23% for 2022), and dividend withholding tax may also apply. However, Turkey's taxation right can be restricted by the provisions of double tax treaties. Generally, under applicable treaties, Turkey's taxation right on capital gains depends on the holding period of the Turkish company shares.

[3]   Penalties Imposed on Investors

86   Penalties are imposed on REIC investors if the investors do not fulfil the tax declaration requirements.

[C]   Tax Treaties

[1]   Treaty Access

87   Turkey has a wide and expanding treaty network covering eighty-five countries. Since REICs are stock corporations, they are eligible for treaty relief.

[2]   Withholding Tax Reduction

88   Tax treaties eliminate or reduce Turkey's withholding taxation right on the income of foreign companies derived from independent professional service, licence and know-how payments in Turkey. These tax treaty rules are also applicable to the aforementioned payments of REICs.

[D]   Taxation of Foreign REICs

[1]   Taxation of Foreign REICs Holding Assets in Country

89   Direct ownership of real estate properties by non-resident entities is not possible in Turkey. Foreign companies, including REICs, can only acquire real estate properties through companies established in Turkey.

90   Dividends received by foreign companies (including REICs) from Turkish companies are taxed in Turkey through withholding. Local dividend withholding tax rate is 10% (15% dividend withholding tax rate has been reduced to 10% as of 22.12.2022), but this rate may be reduced to 5% by virtue of tax treaties.

[2]   *Taxation of Investors Holding Shares in Foreign REIC*

Dividend income derived by Turkish investors holding shares in foreign REICs is   **91**
taxable in Turkey, except for treaty protections. Capital gains from the sale of shares in
foreign REICs are also taxable in Turkey, with few exceptions.

United Kingdom

JONATHAN CLEMENTS

Jonathan Clements leads the UK Real Estate Tax Network of PwC LLP.

He specializes in the provision of property taxation advice to a broad spectrum of clients, including Real Estate Investment Trusts (REITs), property investors (both direct and via indirect vehicles) and real estate funds.

E-mail: Jonathan.clements@pwc.com

United Kingdom

Jonathan Clements

§1.01   BACKGROUND

[A]   Key Characteristics

A United Kingdom (UK) Real Estate Investment Trust (REIT) is a UK tax resident listed **1** company (or the UK tax resident listed parent of a group of companies) which carries on a property investment business and elects to become a REIT. The legislation is complex, but this chapter provides an overview of the key features.

The UK REIT regime was initially governed by a combination of legislation enacted in **2** the Finance Act (FA) 2006 and guidance published by Her Majesty's Revenue and Customs (HMRC), the UK's tax authorities. There have been a number of subsequent changes, the most recent being relaxations in the rules which are due to take effect in April 2022.

Since 1 January 2007, a principal company of a property investment group listed on a **3** recognized stock exchange (or a similarly listed single property investment company) can make an election to enter the REIT regime (*see* section §1.02[E][2] below).

At the point of entry to the REIT regime, each group company's activities are **4** characterized as either 'property rental business' or 'residual business'. Rental income generated by the property rental business and gains arising from the disposal of assets relating to that business are not subject to corporate or income tax if the REIT meets certain tests. Income from other activities such as interest and development gains comprises the residual business and may be subject to tax depending on the tax residence of the company. There are limitations on corporate shareholdings, gearing and the nature of a group REIT's activities.

Similar provisions apply to a single company which may become a REIT. **5**

The UK government's intention is that a REIT should replicate direct ownership of **6** property; therefore, while the REIT itself is exempt from corporate or income tax on its rental income, it is required to distribute most of this income (i.e., 90%) to its investors.

This distribution is called a Property Income Distribution (PID). Shareholders may be chargeable to tax (subject to their tax status and any applicable tax treaty) on the PID.

7 Where a UK REIT invests in another UK REIT, the distribution of rental profit from one REIT to another is tax exempt so long as the recipient REIT distributes 100% of that dividend to its shareholders.

8 REITs are also exempt from corporation tax on sales of shares in UK property-rich companies (i.e., which derive at least 75% of their value from UK land). *See* further below.

[B]   History of the UK REIT

9 There were a number of past attempts to introduce a REIT-like investment vehicle in the UK, including the failed Housing Investment Trust of the 1990s. In 2005, the UK government decided to improve liquidity in the property market through the introduction of a new property investment vehicle, the Property Investment Fund (PIF). While the PIF was like a REIT, it suffered from too many restrictions to be commercially viable. However, after representations from the market about the need for a vehicle like REITs in other countries, a dialogue was opened with HMRC and HM Treasury that led to the successful launch of the UK REIT regime on 1 January 2007.

10 There have been a number of changes since the regime was introduced.

[C]   REIT Market

11 The UK REIT sector includes some of the UK's largest real estate companies, such as British Land, Derwent London, Hammerson, Land Securities and Segro.

12 Top five REITs are as follows:*

Company Name	Mkt Cap (EUR Million)	One Year Return (EUR) %	Div Yield	% of Global REIT Index
Segro	15,285	28.96%	2. 02%	1. 17%
Land Securities	5,834	30.73%	4.00%	0.4 3%
British Land	5,343	38.49%	3.04%	0.41%
Unite Group	4,982	24.30%	1.19%	0.31%
Derwent London	4,338	23.35%	2.24%	0.3 0%

* All market caps and returns are rebased in EUR and are correct as of 30 June 2021. The Global REIT Index is the FTSE EPRA Nareit Global REITs Index. EPRA, July 2021.

13 Since the UK REIT regime was originally established, changes to the UK REIT legislation have made the regime more attractive. Entry to the REIT regime is now cheaper – the entry charge has been abolished, new REITs can list on Alternative

Investment Market (AIM), and there is a three-year grace period for REITs to become widely held and not 'close'.

Certain institutions have been encouraged to invest in REITs as a result of a relaxation   14
in the rules which treat their shareholdings in a REIT as widely held.

FA 2013 and 2014 introduced amendments in relation to UK REITs investing in other   15
UK REITs. The measure allows the income from UK REITs investing in other UK REITs
to be treated as the income of the investing REIT's tax-exempt property rental business,
and REITs shareholders to be ignored when considering 'close' status.

As a result of these regulatory changes and the relative attractiveness of real estate to   16
global investors, the REIT sector is increasingly diverse. UK REITs cover an increasingly broad range of real estate activities ranging from mainstream traditional sectors
(office, retail, industrial) to alternative real estate sectors like student accommodation
and healthcare.

These companies include internally and externally managed REITs, REITs with a   17
premium listing, AIM-listed REITs, REITs registered under the Alternative Investment
Fund Managers Directive (AIFMD).

More recently, we have seen the introduction of residential REITs and a social housing   18
REIT. The emergence of residential REITs is noteworthy as much of the political
momentum behind the UK government's drive to introduce REITs was focused on the
benefits that REIT could bring via the professionalization of the UK private rented
sector.

FA 2019 introduced an exemption for REITs from corporation tax on sales of shares in   19
UK property-rich companies (i.e., which derive at least 75% of their value from UK
land). *See* further below. There are also further relaxations in the rules which are due
to take effect in April 2022.
    A number of UK REITs are listed on the International Stock Exchange in the
Channel Islands, and their shares are not publicly traded. As a result of the changes due
to take effect in April 2022, it is likely that there will be a number of unlisted UK REITs.

§1.02   REGULATORY ASPECTS

[A]   Legal Form of REIT

The UK REIT regime is determined by tax legislation rather than through corporate law.   20
A UK REIT has to be a limited liability company which is admitted to trading on a stock
exchange 'recognized' by the UK tax authorities (which now includes AIM and similar
markets) and either listed on the London Stock Exchange (LSE) (or foreign equivalent
main market exchange) or traded on a recognized stock exchange. While there are a
certain number of non-fiscal requirements which have to be met by a REIT in order to
preserve its tax status as a REIT, most requirements are based on UK tax law.
Therefore, we will consider both listing and fiscal requirements in this section.

[1]   *Corporate Form*

21   A REIT can be either a single company REIT or a group REIT. To be a single company REIT, the company would have to be a property investment company; to be a group REIT, there would need to be a property investment group of companies.

22   The principal company of a group REIT or a single company REIT must be a public limited company and not an Open Ended Investment Company. The principal company has to be resident in the UK for tax purposes, and it cannot be resident in another jurisdiction. The Isle of Man and Jersey have introduced special rules that allow certain companies incorporated in their jurisdiction to meet the residence requirements.

23   A group REIT consists of a parent company plus all of its 75% subsidiaries, regardless of their tax residence, where the ultimate parent has an economic benefit of more than 50% in each subsidiary. For example, if a parent company X owns 75% of company A, which in turn owns 75% of company B, which in turn owns 75% of company C, then X, A and B form a group for REIT purposes. C is not part of X's group because X has an interest of 42% (75% × 75% × 75%), which is less than the required economic interest being greater than 50%.

24   The REIT must be admitted to trading either on the main LSE or recognized stock exchange as defined in section 1177 Corporation Tax Act (CTA) 2010 (which includes AIM) and either listed on the LSE (or foreign equivalent main market exchange) or traded on a recognized stock exchange. There is also a three-year grace period for listing of new REITs. HMRC have recently updated their guidance on REITs, and it is now contained in the Investment Funds Manual. It provides examples and commentary on the interpretation of the REITs legislative regime. There is a link from the REIT section of the Investment Funds Manual to a list of worldwide 'recognized' stock markets.

25   There is however a proposed relaxation of the listing requirement, due to take effect for accounting periods beginning on or after 1 April 2022. The requirement that the company's ordinary share capital be admitted to trading on a recognized stock exchange and the further condition relating to listing or trading on a recognized stock exchange are to be removed where at least 70% of the REITs ordinary shares are directly or indirectly owned by one or more of certain institutional investors (*see* below).

   To determine whether the 70% requirement is met, ownership can be traced through companies, partnerships and other types of entity including unit trust schemes and contractual co-ownership schemes.

   A person who is acting on behalf of a collective investment scheme partnership, which also meets the genuine diversity of ownership requirement, is also to be treated as an institutional investor in its own right when establishing the 70% requirement, and is therefore not traced through for these purposes.

   A REIT can only issue one class of ordinary shares. However, it can issue convertible non-voting fixed-rate preference shares as well as non-voting fixed-rate preference shares and convertible loan stock (limited voting rights are permitted for the fixed-rate preference shares if those rights are contingent on the non-payment of a dividend).

A REIT is allowed to incur debt, but there are a number of detailed restrictions. Some **26** of the more important restrictions include the following:

- Interest cannot be a disguised dividend. No relief for interest is allowed in calculating the PID where that interest is dependent upon the results of the business (except interest which falls with improving results or increases as performance deteriorates).
- Interest cannot exceed a reasonable commercial rate.
- Any sum paid together with the repayments of the principal amount of the debt cannot exceed a market rate.
- The interest cover ratio, which must be met, requires that income cannot be less than 1.25 times the interest cost. The ratio is measured on a group basis. For the purposes of calculating the ratio, 'income' is rental income after adding back financial costs and capital allowances. 'Finance costs' are limited to interest costs and amortization of discounts relating to financing.

[2] Investment Restrictions

There are fiscal restrictions on shareholder investment. The REIT must satisfy the **27** non-close test, and corporate shareholders are discouraged from owning 10% or more of the shares. In addition, there are restrictions on investments undertaken by REITs.

The non-close test will be satisfied where the shares in the REIT are widely held, and **28** the REIT is not a 'close company'. A 'close company' is a company which is under the control of five or fewer 'participators'. The term 'Participators' covers shareholders, directors or other parties (together with related parties) who can exercise control over the majority of the shares, voting rights, income or assets (either through rights held or rights they may be able to obtain). Lenders who are not lending in the ordinary course of business (known as loan creditors) are included when determining who is exercising control.

Investment partnerships which qualify as collective investment schemes can be **29** 'looked through' to the individual partners for the purpose of this test. A company will not be treated as close for REIT purposes if it is only close by taking into account shares held by 'Institutional Investors'. The HMRC list of Institutional Investors includes pension funds, charities, registered housing providers, sovereign wealth funds, certain insurance companies, the managers of UK authorized funds, and other REITs (including both UK and foreign equivalents to a UK REIT). HMRC guidance has not been published as to whether HMRC regards all overseas REIT regimes as equivalent to the UK regime for these purposes. However, a relaxation of the definition of 'overseas equivalent' of a UK REIT for this purpose has been proposed, which removes the requirement for it to be resident in a jurisdiction with a law equivalent to the UK's tax regime for UK REITs (including a 'non-close' test), and instead requires the investor itself to be equivalent to a UK REIT. The relaxation is due to take effect for accounting periods beginning on or after 1 April 2022. There are still 10% corporate shareholding restrictions for Institutional Investors.

30   However, a REIT is not a close company if at least 35% of the shares are held by members of the public (defined as individuals, close and non-close companies who own 5% or less of the voting power and those pension funds which are not for the benefit of the REIT's employees and other investors) and the principal members, together hold less than 85% of the voting power of the REIT's shares.

31   Both the 'non-close' and 'public holdings' tests are complex, with many detailed provisions not mentioned here. In practice, they require a comprehensive review before concluding that a company with a given shareholder structure can become a REIT.

32   If a REIT becomes close, then it will lose its REIT status unless it takes corrective action (*see* section §1.03[A][5] below). There is, however, a three-year grace period on being close for new REITs, allowing a new REIT to be set up with cornerstone investors. If it remains close at the end of three years, it leaves the REIT regime at the end of year three.

33   While the existence of a large corporate shareholder (holding 10% or more of the shares, called a Holder of Excessive Rights (HoER)) in a REIT will not cause a loss of REIT status, the REIT is required to take reasonable steps to ensure that no distribution of the PID is made to any corporate shareholder that owns 10% or more of the ordinary shares. The limit on distributions to large corporate shareholders is designed to discourage offshore corporate investors from taking large stakes in UK REITs and benefiting from treaties which would reduce the withholding tax (WHT) payable to the UK tax authorities. Therefore, payment of a PID to a HoER could lead to penalties levied on the REIT.

34   To fulfil its obligation to take reasonable steps to ensure that no PID is paid to a HoER, investors must be required by the REIT to disclose their status (corporate or otherwise) and their level of shareholdings to the Board of the REIT. The REIT's governing rules (Articles of Association) should also prohibit the distribution of a PID to a HoER (*see* section §1.03[A][5] below).

There are however proposed changes, which are due to take effect from 1 April 2022. The changes mean that investors in UK REITs who are entitled to payment of PIDs without tax being deducted, such as UK companies, will not be treated as holders of excessive rights. Consequently, no charge will arise on the UK REIT when a PID is paid to such an investor holding 10% or more of the shares in the REIT.

[B]   Regulatory Authorities

In the UK, the REIT regime is very much a fiscal regime rather than a financial **35** regulatory regime, and compliance with the REIT regime is overseen by HMRC.

The parent company of a group REIT must be a company which is admitted to trading **36** on a recognized stock exchange and either listed on the LSE (or foreign equivalent main market exchange) or traded on a recognized stock exchange and is subject to the regulations of the stock exchange on which it is admitted (*see* section §1.02[D] below). Previously, the company had to be listed on a recognized stock exchange, so the additional alternative of 'admitted to trading' allows a REIT to be quoted on more junior markets, such as AIM (which did not previously qualify as listed under previous rules). These facilities generally have less regulation than the main stock market. As referred to above, however, there is a proposed relaxation of the listing requirement, due to take effect for accounting periods beginning on or after 1 April 2022, where at least 70% of the REITs ordinary shares are directly or indirectly owned by one or more Institutional Investors.

Whether or not AIFMD applies to UK REITs would need to be considered on a **37** case-by-case basis.

[C]   Legislative and Other Regulatory Resources

The REIT legislation is set out in the Corporation Tax Act 2010 sections 518–609 and **38** limited statutory instruments. HMRC have produced a guidance within the Investment Funds Manual which provides examples and commentary on the interpretation of the REIT legislative regime and which has recently been updated for the rewrite set out in the Corporation Tax Act 2010.

Significant amendments to the regime came into effect on 17 July 2012 following the FA **39** 2012. Minor amendments were introduced in 2013 and 2014 to assist in allowing REITs to invest in other REITs, by allowing PIDs to flow through UK REITs and enabling REITs to take a larger percentage of shares in other REITs without making it close (and, therefore, causing it to leave the REIT regime). *See* section on Restriction on Investors for further information on 'close' rules.

Further amendments were made by FA 2019 to exempt a REIT from corporation tax on **40** sales of shares in UK property-rich companies (i.e., which derive at least 75% of their value from UK land). *See* further below.

There are also further relaxations in the rules contained in Finance Bill 2021–2022 **41** which are due to take effect in April 2022.

[D]   Exchange Controls and Reporting Requirements

42 A UK REIT must be admitted to trading on the main LSE or another recognized stock exchange and either listed on the LSE (or foreign equivalent main market exchange) or traded on a recognized stock exchange (*see* section §1.02[A][1] above). There is a link from the Investment Funds Manual to a list of worldwide 'recognized' stock markets. Current UK REITs are listed on the LSE, Luxembourg Stock Exchange, The International Stock Exchange (formerly the Channel Islands Stock Exchange), and the Aquis Stock Exchange (formerly the NEX Exchange). Trading on the UK's AIM and other similar platforms qualifies for this purpose. There is no tax requirement for the shares to be traded in the period where the company is formally listed on the LSE (or equivalent non-UK stock exchange), although listing requirements will need to be met. As referred to above, however, there is a proposed relaxation of the listing requirement, due to take effect for accounting periods beginning on or after 1 April 2022, where at least 70% of the REITs ordinary shares are directly or indirectly owned by one or more Institutional Investors.

43 There are no exchange control provisions currently in force in the UK, but UK REITs can be dual listed or solely listed on other stock exchanges, and they are subject to the rules of the relevant listing exchange(s).

44 There are no specific reporting requirements for a REIT under the LSE rules; instead, they have to adhere to the same requirements as other listed companies. For example, for a UK listing, a trading company usually needs three years of audited financial information prepared in accordance with the International Financial Reporting Standard (IFRS) as adopted by the European Union (or specified equivalent standards for overseas companies). The financial information must not be older than six months. Any acquisitions which have contributed to over 25% of the company's business during the three-year period require additional audited financial information for the period prior to acquisition.

45 REITs may be eligible to be treated as investment companies. In this case, less onerous financial information requirements apply. There is no minimum operating history requirement and no requirement for information to be less than six months old. To list on the LSE as an investment company, an existing company only has to file accounts that contain a clean audit opinion.

46 Similarly, a UK REIT listing on a non-UK exchange would need to comply with the local regulatory requirements in other jurisdictions.

47 For a new REIT, there is a grace period of three accounting periods (up to three years) for the shares to be admitted to trading and either listed on the LSE (or foreign equivalent main market exchange) or traded on a recognized stock exchange. If the company or group is not admitted to trading/listed/traded at the end of the third accounting period, it is deemed to have left the REIT regime at the end of the second accounting period.

[E]   Registration Procedures

[1]   *Preparatory Measures*

There are two types of registration – existing companies that convert to a REIT and **48**
newly listed companies that enter the REIT regime.

Before an existing property investment group can convert to a REIT, the company **49**
shareholders have to hold a General Meeting (GM) and approve an amendment to the
Articles of Association of the company. The articles are amended to give the REIT
authority to enforce the restriction on distributions to a HoER (*see* section §1.02[A][2]
above). The necessary circular, which is submitted to shareholders prior to voting at
the GM, may need to be cleared in advance with the UK Listing Authority where the
REIT is to be listed on the LSE, and it has unusual features.

A newly formed company seeking to list as a REIT typically needs to develop a business **50**
strategy and to identify the type and source of property which it will seek to buy with
the cash raised on the listing in order to satisfy shareholders that it will perform as a
property investment company. It has to produce a prospectus and ensure that the
company has similar restrictions in its articles to prevent corporate shareholders from
obtaining 10% or more of its shares.

In respect of REITs listed on exchanges other than the LSE, the requirements will
be subject to the particular listing requirements of the specific exchange. In addition,
following changes due to take effect from April 2022 under which all REITs will not
need to be listed, different requirements may apply.

[2]   *Obtaining Authorization*

To become a REIT, an existing group of companies or a newly formed group of **51**
companies has to be sure that they can meet the REIT requirements. There is no entry
charge.

Once in the REIT regime, a REIT has to monitor its activities to ensure that it continues **52**
to comply with the REIT legislation. Existing listed property investment companies and
newly formed companies make a REIT election under section 523 (group) or section
524 (single company) CTA 2010 before the beginning of the accounting period in which
they wish to become a REIT. The election is made by submitting a written notice to
HMRC. The notice has to contain the following:

- the date from which the REIT regime will apply to that group/company;
- a statement that the conditions in section 528 CTA 2010 are reasonably
  expected to be satisfied by the group/company throughout that accounting
  period; and
- other data as required by HMRC.

53   Sometimes, a newly formed group/company seeking registration as a REIT does not meet the requirements for a REIT. For example, the prospective REIT may not initially hold any property assets (because it is awaiting financing raised from the listing to purchase the property). The REIT may fail the balance of business test at the time of entry (*see* below). HMRC will approve the REIT election of a newly formed company with effect from its proposed date of entry, so long as there is a reasonable expectation that the REIT will meet the investment requirements at the end of the accounting period.

54   If the REIT fails to meet all the statutory requirements by the end of the accounting period, and HMRC believe that there has been a serious breach of the rules to gain a tax advantage, then the company will be deemed never to have entered the REIT regime.

[3]   Other Requirements for the Incorporation of a Company

55   The formation of a group/company is a straightforward process in the UK but may differ in other jurisdictions. If an existing company is used as the principal company of a REIT, for an LSE listing, it may need to be re-registered as a public limited company, and there are company law capital and reserves restrictions which need to be met, for example, a requirement to have at least GBP 50,000 issued ordinary share capital.

      In respect of REITs listed on exchanges other than the LSE, the requirements will be subject to the particular listing requirements of the specific exchange. In addition, following changes due to take effect from April 2022 under which all REITs will not need to be listed, different requirements may apply.

[4]   Obtaining Listing Exchanges

[a]   Costs

56   The fee to list a company on the LSE is minimal – ranging from GBP 11,500 for a company with a market capitalization of up to GBP 5 million, up to GBP 595,000 for the very largest companies with a market capitalization of GBP 500 million and upwards. The other costs of listing depend on the type of company being listed, that is, a property trading company or property investment company, and on the size and complexity of the company being listed. The company will need to appoint advisers, including a sponsor, reporting accountants, legal counsel and potentially underwriters, brokers and property valuers. Sponsors will generally require companies to commission appropriate due diligence.

57   A review of recent Initial Public Offerings indicates costs between 1% and 10% of market capitalization. Stock market entrants should budget at least GBP 1 million to GBP 2 million for listing costs. Other exchanges have different fees and costs for listing, and AIM admission fees are lower than the LSE Main Market fees, ranging from GBP 10,500 to GBP 120,000, depending on the market capitalization of the company.

In respect of REITs listed on exchanges other than the LSE, the fees may vary. In addition, following changes due to take effect from April 2022, not all REITs will need to be listed.

[b]   Time

It will generally take around six months from the appointment of advisers for a company to obtain a listing on the Main Market of the LSE.   **58**

In respect of REITs listed on exchanges other than the LSE, this may vary. In addition, following changes due to take effect from April 2022, not all REITs will need to be listed.

[F]   Requirements and Restrictions

[1]   Capital Requirements

To be listed on the LSE, the company must have a minimum market capitalization with equity of GBP 700,000 (shares and depositary receipts). Other exchanges have different   **59**
capital requirements. There is no minimum market capitalization for AIM.

In addition, following changes due to take effect from April 2022, not all REITs will need to be listed.

[2]   Marketing/Advertising

All companies looking to list on the LSE must produce a prospectus that includes, *inter*   **60**
alia, a statement on the sufficiency of working capital, an operating and financial review (for companies with an operating history) and a statement as to whether there has been any significant change since the last published accounts. Property companies (trading and investment) must include a valuation report where they already own or are contracted to acquire properties at the time of listing. Investment companies must include information on investment policies. The prospectus has to be approved by the UK Listing Authority. The requirements are less onerous for AIM. In respect of REITs listed on other exchanges, the requirements may vary. In addition, following changes due to take effect from April 2022, not all REITs will need to be listed.

[3]   Redemption

In the UK, a listed REIT is a close-ended vehicle, and the ordinary shares are not   **61**
redeemable. Companies can buy back shares if certain company law requirements and financial hurdles are met (e.g., the REIT has distributable reserves available at least equal to the amount to be redeemed).

[4]   **Valuation of Shares**

62   Shares are typically valued at open market value (i.e., the price which would be agreed between a willing buyer and seller) for redemption purposes.

[5]   **Investment Restrictions**

63   The REIT is required to meet the following key investment conditions throughout its accounting period:

- it carries on a property rental business that excludes letting to other members of the group or letting certain types of property (e.g., caravan sites and mobile phone masts);
- it acts predominantly as a landlord and does not use land and buildings in its trade. For example, the REIT cannot run a hotel, but it can let a hotel building to a hotel operator with whom it has no connections;
- the property rental business must own at least three properties. For this purpose, units that can be separately let (such as shops in a shopping centre) are classified as individual properties. For the purpose of the three properties test, such interests have to be held directly, and therefore exclude interests held via partnerships and certain unit trusts;
- no one property can represent more than 40% of the value of the REIT assets (using IFRS) for valuation purposes and ignoring any secured debt.

Furthermore, the REIT has to meet two 'balance of business tests' as follows:

(1) At the start of the accounting period, at least 75% of the REIT's assets have to be used in the property rental business. These assets ('qualifying assets') include land and buildings, as well as cash. Cash for these purposes includes all money held on deposit and stocks or bonds of any description. This helps where cash is raised from the capital markets via either share issues or debt issuance before rental properties have been acquired.

(2) Throughout the accounting period, at least 75% of the REIT's income has to be derived from the property rental business.

There are proposed changes to the Balance of Business test, due to take effect for accounting periods beginning on or after 1 April 2022. The first modifies rules that require provision of financial statements to demonstrate that a REIT has met the balance of business tests. They provide for simplified requirements for group REITs which, if met, remove the need to perform certain calculations and provide full financial statements for each group member.

The second change provides that profits of the (taxable) residual business resulting from compliance with planning obligations under section 106 of the Town and Country Planning Act 1990 entered into in the course of the property rental business are to be disregarded when performing the balance of business profits test and the assets excluded from the Balance of Business assets test. Certain other assets will also be excluded from the Balance of Business asset test where they are held solely in connection with other items which are also excluded from the Balance of Business profits test.

[6]   *Distribution/Accumulation*

Another fiscal requirement is that a REIT must distribute 90% of its property rental   **64** income within twelve months of its year end.

A single company REIT can determine the rental income to be distributed by taking   **65** 90% of the rental income calculated as set out below.

However, a parent company of a group REIT has to distribute 90% of the group's   **66** aggregate property rental income. The group must prepare financial statements in accordance with section 532 CTA 2010, which will include the property rental income for each subsidiary together with the group's share of the property rental income from any partnership, unit trust and joint venture. For an explanation of the calculation of group property rental income, *see* section §1.03[A][1][b] below. Note that there is no requirement to distribute gains or other income such as interest income. Where such other income is distributed, this is treated as a normal dividend from a UK company, and it is not subject to WHT. However, where there is a distribution of gains from the property rental business, such a distribution is treated in the same way as a distribution of property rental income and may be subject to WHT (*see* further below). There are complexities within groups REITs where dividends are paid from non-UK tax resident subsidiaries to a UK parent (*see* further below).

Neither a company nor a group REIT is required to pay a PID where the company or   **67** group has insufficient distributable reserves and is therefore prevented from making a distribution under UK company law (including Northern Ireland and Scottish legislation). There are provisions to allow the extension of this relief to other jurisdictions, but so far, no legislation has been passed to apply this extension (section 530 CTA 2010).

A REIT is required to monitor and submit annual details of its reserves with reconcili-   **68** ation between accounting profits and those amounts which have to be distributed.

Stock dividends can be used to satisfy the PID distribution. New shares can now be   **69** issued to investors equal to the amount of the PID due to them (after deducting WHT, where appropriate) if they agree to take shares instead of cash (it is not mandatory). WHT would then be paid to HMRC, and the investor would receive shares.

An additional three months is allowed for distributions to be made where there are late   **70** adjustments to tax returns. This relief is extended to six months, where there is an unexpected shortfall in stock dividends due to price movements of the shares.

[7]   Reporting Requirements

71   REITs listed on the LSE have to file an annual report and a half-yearly report. The filing of interim management statements (quarterly reporting) has been voluntary since 7 November 2014. Preliminary statements are not required, but if companies choose to issue them, they must be agreed upon with the auditors. The AIM requires annual and half-yearly reports, and there are requirements to disclose certain corporate transactions.

[8]   Accounting

72   REIT accounting has to comply with international accounting standards that are full IFRS for certain tests, for example, consolidated figures for balance of business. In addition, assuming the REIT is listed on an EU-regulated stock exchange, it will be required to prepare consolidated accounts in accordance with IFRS (as adopted by the European Union). The PID is calculated based on the tax results of the property rental business for each individual subsidiary and therefore uses the accounting standard of the entity company (IFRS).

§1.03   TAXATION

[A]   Taxation of the REIT

[1]   Corporate Income Tax

[a]   Tax Accounting

73   The REIT's property rental income, gains arising in the property rental business and property income dividends received from other REITs are not taxed in the REIT but are taxed at the investor level. The REIT is subject to corporation tax, currently 19% (but rising to 25% from April 2023), on all other income and non-property gains. Similar tax treatment applies to UK tax resident subsidiaries of a REIT group. Non-UK tax resident subsidiary companies of a group REIT are not subject to UK tax on gains or interest income, but their income from trading in the UK is taxable. Income and gains may be subject to local taxes.

74   Where a REIT has an interest of 40% or more in a joint venture company (measured by assessing the amount of income which would accrue to a REIT if a distribution of income were made) which invests in UK rental property, the REIT can serve a notice to enable its share of the property rental income to be exempt from corporation tax. The joint venture company then is exempt from tax to the extent of the REIT's share of the rental income; however, the exempt share of profits is included within the PID distribution calculation for the REIT.

[b] *Determination of Taxable Income*

The REIT is required to segregate profits into six pots: **75**

  (i) 100% PID distributions from other UK REITs;
  (ii) property rental business income up to 90%;
  (iii) taxable income (e.g., interest income);
  (iv) the remaining 10% of the property rental income;
  (v) property rental business gains;
  (vi) any other income and gains.

Property rental business income comprises rental income from the letting of UK **76** property, whether the property is held by a single company REIT or by partnerships or joint ventures held by members of a group REIT (including both UK and non-UK tax resident subsidiaries). This income is tax exempt in the REIT. Where a UK tax resident company owns a non-UK investment property, that income is also exempt from UK tax. Property rental business income is calculated as follows: gross rental income less allowable expenses, tax depreciation and finance costs. Gross rental income can include car parking income (if previously taxed as rent) and reasonable recharges for security and maintenance.

Allowable expenses include expenses such as management, maintenance, security and **77** insurance costs. Capital allowances (tax depreciation) are deductible when calculating the property rental business income out of which the PID has to be paid. The full amount of capital allowances must be claimed; it is not possible to make an election to reduce the capital allowances claim. REITs are subject to the finance cost restriction rules introduced in the UK in line with the Organisation for Economic Co-operation and Development's Base Erosion and Profit Shifting action 4 recommendations, subject to certain modifications to take into account the REIT regime. The starting point of the new rules is to restrict finance cost deductions to 30% of tax earnings before income tax, depreciation and amortization. There is also a GBP 2 million *de minimis* per group and the option of using an alternative group ratio or a Public Infrastructure Exemption if this will provide a better result.

The property investment business is ring-fenced, and expenses from the property **78** investment business can only be used to offset income from the property investment business.

Generally, capital gains arising from the disposal of real estate used in the property **79** rental business have not been subject to tax for one of two reasons. Either the gain is realized by a UK tax resident subsidiary (it is exempt from tax by virtue of the specific tax exemption in the REIT legislation at section 535 CTA 2010) or because the company is a non-UK tax resident subsidiary or unit trust. Non-UK tax residents were not, until April 2019, subject to tax on their gains.

80   However, a charge to tax could arise where a recently developed building is sold; the cost of development exceeds 30% of the value of the building on the date of acquisition or entry to the REIT regime, if later; and the property is sold within three years of completion (section 556 CTA 2010). The property is deemed never to have been in the REIT regime, and the disposal is subject to UK tax. These provisions apply regardless of the intention of the REIT, so a major redevelopment followed by a sale would be subject to these provisions even if disposal was not contemplated when the redevelopment took place.

81   Tax can also arise where an asset, which was previously used in the residual business, is transferred to the property rental business. For example, if property had been let by one group company to the parent company for use as a head office, and the property is subsequently let to a third party, there is a deemed disposal at market value, and tax is chargeable at the higher rate of corporation tax (currently 19% but increasing to 25% from April 2023).

82   A REIT is exempt from corporation tax on sales of shares in UK property-rich companies (i.e., which derive at least 75% of their value from UK land). The exemption applies to the proportion of the gain which relates to the company's property rental business assets. The exemption will not be available where the company being sold has, within the previous three years, completed the development of a building where the cost of development exceeded 30% of the value of the building at the date of acquisition or entry of the company to the REIT regime, if later.

   [c]   *Taxation of Income from Taxable/Non-taxable Subsidiaries*

83   In the UK REIT regime, companies may have property rental business income (e.g., rent) which is not taxable and residual income (e.g., interest) which is taxable. A dividend of taxable income paid by a UK tax resident subsidiary to the REIT parent is treated as an ordinary UK dividend which is not subject to WHT. Similarly, a distribution of property rental income from a non-UK tax resident subsidiary is treated as an ordinary dividend from a UK company and is not subject to WHT for UK tax purposes (although the local tax authorities could levy WHT).

84   A dividend from a non-resident subsidiary may not be subject to tax (note that there are complex anti-avoidance rules which will need to be considered).

85   Similar provisions apply to non-UK joint ventures investing in UK property where the REIT is entitled to 40% or more of the income available for distribution.

   [d]   *Taxation of Foreign Income*

86   Income, other than from UK rental profits of the non-UK tax resident subsidiaries, may be subject to tax with relief for WHTs and underlying tax if the REIT has a significant interest in the investment. The UK legislation with respect to foreign companies is a complex area. Distribution of such income by a REIT is treated as an ordinary dividend by that REIT and is not subject to WHT.

[e]   Taxation of Income from Other REITs

If a REIT invests in another REIT, then the PID distribution received by the investing   **87**
REIT has to be disclosed in a separate pot and distributed in full to the investing REIT. The PID distribution received is then tax exempt for the investing REIT. Distributions of residual income do not have to be distributed but may be distributed as ordinary dividends.

[2]   Value Added Tax

There are no special Value Added Tax (VAT) provisions; a REIT has to comply with   **88**
general legislation, case law and practice as it relates to VAT and property. For example, a REIT subsidiary can choose to 'opt to tax' (charge VAT on rents) when leasing commercial property and recover VAT on its letting expenses. Where a REIT subsidiary buys residential property to let, it cannot charge VAT to its tenants, and therefore, only part of the VAT cost can be recovered from HMRC.

[3]   Withholding Taxes

REITs can pay a gross PID to a shareholder who is a UK company, UK charity, UK   **89**
pension fund or a UK government body if that party gives the REIT a notice that it can be paid gross and the REIT has reasonable grounds for believing this. For all other investors, such as an individual or partnership (wherever resident) or a non-UK tax resident corporate investor, WHT, currently 20%, is withheld. The same rules for withholding apply to deductions from annual interest, but with one key exception: it is not possible for a non-UK tax resident investor to apply to receive the PID gross. Instead, non-UK tax resident investors have to apply to the Centre for Non-Residents (a department of HMRC) to make a claim for a refund under the dividend article of the relevant treaty. Taxpayers are provided with vouchers showing the makeup of the distribution, together with any WHT deducted. Such WHTs have to be accounted for on a quarterly basis by the REIT.

[4]   Other Taxes

REITs are only exempt from a direct tax on rental income and certain types of gain.   **90**
They remain subject to UK Stamp Duty Land Tax (SDLT) at up to 5% on acquisitions of commercial property with a UK situs. For residential property, the rate of SDLT applying will be up to 15%.

91   Stamp duty reserve tax is charged on the transfer of shares listed on the LSE but is not charged on the transfer of eligible AIM-listed shares.

92   Other taxes also apply to a REIT, including VAT, business rates (local tax), landfill tax, and social security and employee taxes.

[5]   *Penalties Imposed on a REIT*

93   There are various penalties that can be levied on a REIT. Some are financial penalties, and others are the disapplication or even termination of the REIT regime.

94   Where a REIT becomes 'close' through the actions of others (e.g., as the result of a bid where the public owns less than 35%) and is unable to rectify the position before the end of the next accounting period, then the group leaves the REIT regime at the end of the accounting period in which the company became close.

95   Where a REIT is taken over by another group which is a REIT, there is no penalty. However, if a REIT is taken over by a non-REIT, then it is deemed to have left the REIT regime at the end of the previous accounting period, with the result that income and gains arising after that date are taxed. It is understood that HMRC would not object to parties bringing forward the end of an accounting period before the takeover takes place.

96   For the following two breaches – number or value of properties and balance of business tests – HMRC has additional powers. While the legislation permits multiple breaches without a requirement for termination of REIT status, HMRC has the power to serve a notice of termination of REIT status if they believe that the breach in the number of properties or the balance of business is serious.

97   Where a REIT fails to have three or more properties, or it has one property that has a value greater than 40%, then it is technically in breach. While up to two failures of each condition are not fatal, a series of three successive repetitions within a ten-year period could lead to a loss of REIT status.

98   While there is a requirement for a REIT to meet the balance of business tests, whereby 75% of the income and 75% of the total assets must relate to the rental business, it is possible for these requirements to fall to 50% for income and assets. Multiple breaches are limited to a maximum of two of each condition in a ten-year period starting with the first breach. Three or more successive breaches will lead to the termination of REIT status.

99   Where a REIT fails to pay the 90% PID due within twelve months of the year end (unless there is a legal impediment, that is, insufficient distributable reserves), the REIT will suffer corporation tax at the highest rate (currently 19% but increasing to 25% from April 2023) on the amount of the PID which has not been paid. There are provisions which prevent HMRC from levying this charge if the REIT pays a PID within three months of the time that an amended PID should have been paid (or longer for stock dividends).

A penalty may be levied on a REIT where a PID is paid to a corporate shareholder who owns 10% or more of the REIT's shares. This applies where the REIT has failed to take reasonable steps to prevent payment of a PID to such a shareholder. The penalty is an amount equal to the WHT of 20%, applicable to the full PID paid to such a shareholder. **100**

Where the finance cost ratio is less than 1.25:1 (being external finance costs divided by rental income net of expenses but before tax relief for finance costs or depreciation), a corporation tax charge is levied on the REIT equal to the excess finance costs (currently 19% but increasing to 25% from April 2023). **101**

In response to a number of UK REITs making representations about their struggle to comply with the finance cost ratio test during the credit crunch, HMRC may waive a charge arising on such a breach where a REIT can demonstrate that: **102**

(i) it is in severe financial difficulties at a time in the accounting period;
(ii) the breach of the finance cost ratio arose out of unexpected circumstances; and
(iii) in those circumstances, the REIT could not have reasonably taken action to avoid the breach.

The external finance costs in the test are currently limited to the interest element of financing costs and break costs on bank debt, or interest rate swaps are no longer included. **103**

[B]   Taxation of the Investor

[1]   *Private Investors*

[a]   *Taxation of Current Income (i.e., All Income Derived from REIT in Holding Phase)*

Where a REIT investor is an individual, the PID will be paid under deduction of WHT. A UK tax resident individual is taxed on the gross distribution (including the WHT paid) as if the income was rental income. The distribution is taxed in the UK at up to 45%, with credit for the WHT suffered. REIT shares can, however, be held in an Individual Savings Account. A non-UK tax resident individual investor may be able to reclaim some or all of the WHT deducted from the PID under a relevant double taxation treaty and may also be subject to tax on that income under the laws of the investor's country. Ordinary (non-PID) dividends from a UK REIT are paid gross but may be subject to tax in the investor's country. **104**

Where gains are distributed by the REIT, the distribution is also a PID and is treated in the same way as set out above. **105**

[b]   *Taxation of Capital Gains (From Disposal of REIT Shares)*

106   Where the shares are sold by a UK tax resident individual, the investor is subject to tax on gains, reduced by his personal allowance, capital losses, etc. The resulting net gain is taxed at a rate of up to 20%. Where the individual investor is not a UK resident, the investor has not generally, until April 2019, been subject to UK capital gains tax but may have been subject to tax under the laws of his own country. However, the disposal of shares in a UK REIT by a non-UK resident individual investor has been within the scope of UK capital gains tax since April 2019 as a result of the 2019 immovable property gains rules. A UK company REIT or, from 10 April 2020, the principal company of a group UK REIT, falls within the definition of 'Collective Investment Vehicle', and so if the UK property-rich condition is met, the investor will be within the scope of the 2019 immovable property gains rules even where the shareholding is less than 25%. The provisions of any relevant double tax treaty, however, need to be considered.

[2]   Institutional Investors

[a]   *Taxation of Current Income (i.e., All Income Derived from REIT in Holding Phase)*

107   Where a REIT investor is a UK resident corporate, the PID is paid gross, without any withholding of tax. This income is taxed as if it were rental income at the corporate investor's tax rate. A non-UK tax resident corporate investor would be paid under deduction of WHT (currently 20%) and may be able to reclaim some of the WHT under a double tax treaty. The investor may then be subject to tax on that income under the laws of the investor's country.

108   Certain investors, including a UK gross fund, local government body and a UK resident charity, can be paid gross and may not be taxed on the income from a REIT. However, it is the responsibility of the investor to notify the REIT that it can be paid gross: otherwise, the REIT must withhold tax on PIDs. A non-UK institutional investor would be paid under deduction of WHT and may be able to reclaim some of the WHT under a double tax treaty. The investor may then be subject to tax on that income under the laws of the investor's country.

109   Where gains are distributed by the REIT to an institutional investor, the distribution is a PID and is treated in the same way as a distribution of net rental income, as set out above.

[b]   Taxation of Capital Gains (From Disposal of REIT Shares)

The taxation of gains realized from the sale of shares depends upon the nature of the **110** UK tax resident institution. A UK corporate is subject to tax at 19% (increasing to 25% from April 2023), whereas a UK gross pension fund or a UK charity is not subject to tax on gains. Where the corporate investor is not a UK resident, it has not, until April 2019, been subject to UK capital gains tax, but it may have been subject to tax under the laws of the investor's own country. However, the disposal of shares in a UK REIT by a non-UK resident investor has been within the scope of UK capital gains tax since April 2019 as a result of the 2019 immovable property gains rules. A UK company REIT or, from 10 April 2020, the principal company of a group UK REIT, falls within the definition of 'Collective Investment Vehicle', and so if the UK property-rich condition is met, the investor will be within the scope of the 2019 immovable property gains rules even where the shareholding is less than 25%. Existing capital gains reliefs and exemptions are, however, available to non-UK residents, with modifications where necessary. These include the Substantial Shareholdings Exemption and exemptions for reasons other than being a non-UK resident (e.g., overseas pension schemes (as defined) and certain charities). The provisions of any relevant double tax treaty also need to be considered.

[3]   Penalties Imposed on Investors

There are no penalties levied on investors. **111**

[C]   Tax Treaties

[1]   Treaty Access

HMRC accept that a distribution of a PID is a distribution of the profits of a company, **112** and therefore, an investor may be able to make a claim under the dividend article of a double tax treaty to reclaim the WHT.

[2]   WHT Reduction

HMRC will not permit a dividend to be paid under a reduced rate of WHT; any reclaim **113** has to be dealt with through the Centre for Non-residents at HMRC.

[D]   Exit Tax/Tax Privileges/Concessions

There is no exit tax. A REIT is required to value its assets used in its property rental **114** business at the point of entry into the REIT regime.

115   On a takeover by a non-REIT, HMRC would require that any distribution out of the reserves of the REIT relating to property rental income and gains be paid under deduction of WHT. Furthermore, before agreeing to the winding up of the tax affairs of a REIT in liquidation, HMRC states that they expect all property business profits to have been distributed as a PID to shareholders of the REIT.

[E]   Taxation of Foreign REITs

[1]   Taxation of Foreign REIT Holding Assets in Country

116   There are no special rules for the taxation of foreign REITs, and they are treated like any other investor. Whether the UK assets of the foreign REIT are held by a UK resident company which is a subsidiary of a foreign REIT, or a non-UK resident company, then income and gains are subject to tax at corporation tax rates (currently 19% but increasing to 25% from April 2023). If the investment vehicle is a non-UK resident, however, the UK corporation tax position on gains on the direct and certain indirect disposals of UK property will be subject to the application of any applicable double tax treaty.

[2]   Taxation of Investors Holding Shares in Foreign REIT

117   The taxation of shares in foreign REITs depends on the tax status of the owner. If the owner is a UK resident individual, tax applies to the dividend income at the investor's marginal rate of up to 45%, with tax relief for WHTs. Gains on the sale of shares are subject to UK capital gains tax at up to 20%. UK companies are subject to tax on income and gains on the sale of shares at 19% (but increasing to 25% from April 2023), with relief for WHT and possibly underlying tax. UK gross pension funds and charities may suffer local WHT on distributions, but they are not subject to tax on the income.

118   If the owner is a non-UK resident, UK tax could apply to gains on the sale of shares if the foreign REIT were UK property rich.

United States

TOM WILKIN

Tom Wilkin is PwC LLP's U.S. REIT Leader. Tom has over thirty years of experience serving clients in the real estate industry, including public/private real estate investment trusts (REITs), real estate investment advisory firms, opportunity funds, hotel operators, commercial developers and residential homebuilders, as well as extensive transactional real estate investment and acquisition due diligence experience in connection with both property and corporate M&A transactions. Over the span of his career, Tom has been responsible for some of PwC LLP's most complex real estate engagements with a significant focus on public transactions.

In addition to directly serving our traditional real estate clients, Tom also leads our 'Real Estate Life Cycles' initiative, Real, which is designed to help us seamlessly deliver our ever-broadening range of real estate-related services to meet emerging client needs for both our traditional real estate clients and significant users of real estate. These services go way beyond traditional audit and tax services. They also focus on difficult or emerging areas such as nontraditional REIT conversions/IPOs/spin-offs, mortgage REITs and products like single-family rentals.

Tom has a Bachelor's from Tulane University, Louisiana, and an EMBA from Columbia University, New York City.

E-mail: tom.wilkin@pwc.com

DAVID GERSTLEY

David Gerstley is a partner with PwC in the New York office with twenty years of experience serving audit and non-audit clients in the asset management and real estate industry. He works on both public and private REITs, works with asset managers, developers and institutional investors and has extensive experience with real estate investment transactions, including acquisition due diligence, REIT conversions, mergers & acquisitions and initial public offerings. David has been a consultant in PwC's National Office in the SEC Services Group, where he consulted with clients in the real estate industry on matters of accounting, auditing and financial reporting. David also assists clients with capital raising activities, including initial public offerings, quarterly and annual reports, SEC comment letters and comfort letters.

David received a Bachelor of Science in Accounting from the Sy Syms School of Business of Yeshiva University, New York, U.S. He is a CPA licensed in New York and New Jersey and is a member of the New York State Society of Certified Public Accountants and the American Institute of Certified Public Accountants.

E-mail: david.gerstley@pwc.com

ADAM FEUERSTEIN

Adam Feuerstein, a principal in the Washington National Tax Services practice, is PwC LLP's National Real Estate Tax Technical Leader. Adam's experience includes a broad cross-section of product types and owners, including real estate investment trusts (REITs), real estate investment funds, institutional investors, sovereign wealth funds and tax-exempt entities. Prior to joining PwC, Adam was a partner at a large international law firm where he worked for over a decade advising REITs and other clients on a variety of tax matters. Adam's experience covers the life cycle of public and private REITs from formation to operation and through liquidation, including due diligence and structuring for mergers and acquisitions of REITs. Adam has served as an adjunct professor at the Georgetown University Law Center and the Villanova University Law School and is coauthor of the treatise on REITs in RIA's Catalyst series. Adam graduated from Harvard Law School, *cum laude*, has a Master's in Public Policy from Harvard University's John F. Kennedy School of Government and received his BS with honors from Cornell University.

E-mail: adam.s.feuerstein@pwc.com

JULANNE ALLEN

Julanne Allen is a principal in PwC LLP's National Tax Service practice, and in that role, she advises REITs and brings her unique perspective from her time at the Internal Revenue Service (IRS) to help REITs navigate the complicated myriad of rules that they are required to follow.

Julanne began her career working at a large international law firm where she advised clients on a myriad of tax issues relating to the formation and operation of REITs and real estate funds. After several years of advising clients on tax matters, she entered the public sector, where she brought her practical knowledge and business understanding to the IRS' Office of Chief Counsel.

While at the IRS, she drafted, reviewed, and commented on most REIT issues addressed in published guidance, private letter rulings, and taxpayer conferences. She authored the regulation defining real property for REIT qualification purposes as well as many seminal private letter rulings addressing REIT tax and compliance matters. After many years of working in the public sector, she joined PwC, where she synthesizes her experience representing and advising clients with her unique understanding of the IRS' outlook.

Julanne has a Master of Laws in Taxation from New York University School of Law, graduated from the Catholic University of America School of Law, *magna cum laude*, and earned her BBA and BA from the College of William and Mary.

E-mail: julanne.allen@pwc.com

DAVID VOSS

David Voss is a tax partner in PwC LLP's New York office. He focuses on the taxation of real estate investors, including public and private REITs, real estate funds and inbound real estate investors, including sovereign wealth funds and other institutional investors. He advises investors and investment sponsors with respect to tax-efficient ownership structures and real estate transactions for U.S. and non-U.S. investors as well as tax-exempt institutions. He advises public and private REITs on investment structures, ongoing REIT qualification matters, partnership arrangements, cross-border transactions, and mergers and acquisitions.

David has a BA from Manhattanville College and a JD from Emory University School of Law. He is a member of the New York State Bar and a licensed Certified Public Accountant in New York.

E-mail: david.m.voss@pwc.com

STEVE TYLER

Steve Tyler is a tax partner in PwC LLP's Atlanta office. He focuses on the taxation of real estate companies, including private and public REITs and other real estate owners and investors. He has focused on tax-efficient structuring of real estate transactions and ownership structures for U.S. and non-U.S. investors as well as tax-exempt institutions. He advises public and private REITs on investment structures, ongoing REIT qualification, partnership arrangements, cross-border transactions, debt workouts, and mergers and acquisitions.

Steve received a Bachelor's in Accounting and a Master's in Taxation from the University of North Texas. He is a licensed, Certified Public Accountant in New York, Texas and Georgia and is a member of the AICPA and NAREIT.

E-mail: steve.tyler@pwc.com

JORDAN ADELSON

Jordan Adelson is a director currently on tour in PwC's National Professional Services—Accounting Services Group, a group that focuses on global consultations with domestic and international clients and engagement teams on a wide range of technical accounting matters. Jordan focuses primarily on real estate, leasing, consolidation and various transactional-related accounting issues. He is also actively involved in following standard-setting projects (i.e., leasing, consolidation, etc.) and authoring industry and firm through leadership. In his role, Jordan directly assists and serves clients in the real estate industry on accounting issues and complex transactions.

Prior to his tour in the Accounting Services Group, Jordan was a member of the New York real estate assurance practice of PwC from October 2009 to June 2018. His clients included both public and private REITs, large institutional real estate investment advisors and funds, real estate owners/developers and residential/commercial property managers. Jordan is also the cocreator and editor of *Current Developments for the Real Estate Industry*, a nationally distributed publication providing perspective on the latest market and economic trends, regulatory activities and legislative changes affecting the real estate industry, as well as informed views on the most current developments in operations, business strategy, taxation, compliance and financing.

Jordan has a Bachelor of Science in Accounting and a Master's in Accounting and Information Analysis from Lehigh University, is a licensed Certified Public Accountant, and is a member of the American Institute of Certified Public Accountants.

E-mail: jordan.y.adelson@pwc.com

CINDY MAI

Cindy Mai is a director currently on tour at PwC's National Quality Organization—Accounting Services Group, specializing in the new lease standard and complex accounting issues and transactions related to the real estate industry.

Prior to her tour, she was a director of PwC's New York real estate assurance practice, and her clients included both public REITs and private real estate investment funds.

She has experience working on real estate funds reporting at fair value, as well as historical GAAP, REIT compliance, SEC reporting, Sarbanes-Oxley 404 compliance, etc.

From 2005 to 2013, she worked in PwC's Guangzhou Office, where she provided a broad range of assurance services, including annual audits, IPO transactions and bond offerings for leading real estate development companies in China, whose shares were listed on The Stock Exchange of Hong Kong Limited.

Cindy received an MBA from Fordham University's Gabelli School of Business in 2015. She is a licensed Certified Public Accountant in New York, New Hampshire and China. She is also a CFA charter holder.

She has in-depth knowledge of U.S. GAAP, China GAAP and IFRS.

E-mail: qiyan.mai@pwc.com

United States

Tom Wilkin, David Gerstley, Adam Feuerstein, Julanne Allen, David Voss, Steve Tyler, Jordan Adelson & Cindy Mai

---

§1.01   BACKGROUND

[A]   Key Characteristics

In the United States (U.S.), a real estate investment trust (REIT) is primarily a creation **1** of the federal tax law. A REIT achieves a quasi-pass-through tax status as a result of a deduction for dividends paid to its shareholders. To qualify for this favorable tax treatment, an entity must elect to be taxed as a REIT and file annual tax returns as such. The entity must also meet several tests regarding: (i) its organization and ownership (*see* section §1.02[A] below), (ii) the nature of its assets and source of its gross income (*see* section §1.02[F][5] below) and (iii) minimum distributions to its shareholders (*see* section §1.02[F][6] below). In most other ways, a REIT computes its taxable income in the same manner as a regular corporation, and the tax rules that apply to corporations also generally apply to a REIT (*see* section §1.03[A][1] below). Failure to satisfy the REIT requirements may result in the entity being subject to tax as a regular corporation or incurring a financial penalty if a mitigation provision applies.

A REIT may be publicly held (either listed on an exchange or unlisted) or privately **2** held. Some private REITs are open-ended, offering periodic opportunities for the redemption of shares.

A REIT may hold mortgage loans as well as domestic and foreign real property. Assets **3** may be held directly or indirectly through subsidiaries. A qualified REIT subsidiary (QRS) is a wholly owned corporate subsidiary that is disregarded for income tax purposes. A taxable REIT subsidiary (TRS) is an entity that is treated as a corporation for income tax purposes, and it makes a joint election with the REIT to be subject to special rules regarding intercompany transactions (*see* section §1.03[A][5] below). Stapling a REIT to a non-REIT corporation is effectively prohibited because the requirements to qualify as a REIT are applied on a combined basis.

4   A REIT is permitted to operate or manage its own properties and, with some restrictions, it can provide "customary services" to its tenants (*see* section §1.02[F][5] below). Although some nonpublic REITs are externally advised, many public REITs are self-managed.

5   A number of different types or categories of REITs are used to describe nuances in how they raise capital, invest proceeds, operate, or are managed. These descriptors include the following:

- Publicly traded REITs—These entities are fully registered with the Securities and Exchange Commission (SEC) and listed on a publicly recognized exchange, such as the New York Stock Exchange (NYSE) or National Association of Securities Dealers Automated Quotations. Although these shares are listed, their real liquidity depends on market action or trading volume with respect to a particular stock.
- Private REITs—These are privately owned REITs that may have issued shares pursuant to one of several securities exemptions. Frequently, they are subsidiaries of larger private equity funds or other corporate entities.
- Registered but not traded REITs—These are fully registered with the SEC but are not listed on any exchange. These entities must comply with all the SEC reporting requirements in general (e.g., quarterly and annual reporting, Form 8-K reporting, proxy filings, and reporting on internal controls by management). However, because these entities lack a "public" float (as defined by the SEC to be traded equity), they are usually considered to be non-accelerated filers, have later filing deadlines, and do not require external auditor opinions on SOX 404.
- REIT roll-up—These REITs are formed in conjunction with an initial public offering (IPO), whereby preexisting operating entities/properties are combined into a single operation under one new public company. The mechanisms for completing this combination can vary significantly among transactions and are generally driven by tax planning or marketing strategies. Frequently, the transactions involve the use of an umbrella partnership REIT (UPREIT) format to defer tax consequences to the existing owners (*see* "Tax structuring" section for more information).
- Blind-pool REITs—These are newly formed entities that raise capital to be invested after the offering at the discretion of the sponsor pursuant to a predefined investment strategy as outlined in the prospectus. Blind-pool transactions avoid certain issues such as historical financial information of predecessor operations but may have certain incremental reporting requirements, including "prior performance" information on similar investments by the sponsor.
- Internally versus externally managed REITs—Another distinction is how management is involved with the entity. Generally, REITs are either "internally managed," with management as employees of the REIT/operating partnership, or "externally managed" pursuant to a management contract

with no direct employees. Usually, private REITs and registered but not traded REITs are externally managed on a for-fee basis by a related party manager. The related party fees for these types of vehicles can be significant and will vary based on the underlying investment premise and effort involved (i.e., "core" investment portfolio strategies typically have lower fee arrangements than those of more "opportunistic" vehicles).

Publicly traded REITs can be managed either internally or externally. Frequently, **6** externally managed public REITs that reach a certain size will "internalize" their management through an exchange of stock with the owners of the advisor. This internalization generally occurs several years subsequent to formation once the platform has grown and stabilized, operating to better align management and the shareholders by limiting the enterprise value growth going solely to management.

[B]   History of REITs

Prior to the enactment of the REIT Act in 1960, investment in commercial real estate in **7** the U.S. was the domain of wealthy individuals and institutions having the financial resources necessary to finance large-scale capital projects. The REIT Act enabled small investors in the U.S. to pool their capital by investing in a REIT, which in turn would use the proceeds to acquire a diversified portfolio of income-producing properties.

The REIT Act was intended to provide substantially the same tax treatment for REITs **8** that existed for mutual funds investing in equity securities. In particular, REITs would not be required to pay federal income tax so long as they distributed their taxable income to their investors in the form of dividends. As a result, REIT investors would avoid the double taxation that generally applies to investors in regular corporations. Notwithstanding these benefits, three decades would pass before the REIT format succeeded in gaining wide acceptance among investors in the U.S. Initially, REITs were intended as passive investment vehicles and were therefore restricted from actively managing the properties they owned. As a result, early REITs were advised and managed by third-party contractors whose interests often conflicted with those of the REIT. Later legislation, designed to pull the U.S. economy out of severe recession in the early 1980s, deregulated the savings and loan industry and strongly encouraged the proliferation of real estate tax shelters. By the mid-1980s, the ensuing flood of capital from savings and loan institutions and tax-advantaged real estate limited partnerships triggered a tremendous boom in new construction. REITs, which could not pass through tax losses to investors, attracted little attention.

Following the enactment of the Tax Reform Act of 1986, banks, S&Ls and life insurance **9** companies saw the value of their real estate collateral, no longer propped up by noneconomic tax incentives, drop below the balance on their loans. When foreclosures were enforced, the real estate was eventually sold, often at fire sale prices. By the end of the 1980s, the real estate industry was in the grips of its worst depression ever. Many private developers were caught in a liquidity squeeze, the value of their real estate holdings was depressed, they were facing large balloon loan payoffs, and their lenders backed away. In the meantime, REIT activity remained limited as the real estate industry struggled to regain its footing.

10   During these early years, several key changes to the tax laws governing REITs would help set the stage for a REIT renaissance in the early 1990s. In 1976, the corporate form became allowed for a REIT's legal entity type; the definition of qualifying rental income was expanded to include income from "customary services" and the rental of incidental personal property, and the restriction on owning dealer property was changed from disqualification of the REIT to a penalty tax of 100% of the gain on sale. The Tax Reform Act of 1986 enabled REITs to become self-managed for the first time and to provide customary landlord services to tenants.

[C]   REIT Market

11   By most accounts, the IPO of Kimco Realty Corporation (Kimco) in late 1991 marked the "dawn of the modern REIT era." In 1992, the UPREIT structure, pioneered by Taubman Centers, Inc. (Taubman), further propelled the movement during this period. In a UPREIT, the REIT holds substantially all of its assets through an operating partnership. In exchange for Operating Partnership Units (OPU), owners can transfer property to the partnership on a tax-deferred basis, while a transfer directly to the REIT in exchange for more liquid assets would usually be taxable. The property owner receives OPUs that receive distributions equal to the dividends paid to REIT shareholders, and the units are convertible into publicly traded REIT shares, providing the unit holders with the liquidity of the public markets. Another important change to the REIT tax regime came in 1999 with the enactment of provisions allowing REITs to provide noncustomary services to tenants through TRSs (*see* section §1.03[A][5] below).

12   The success of the Kimco and Taubman IPOs provided hope to private developers that the public equity markets could provide an alternative source of financing to recapitalize their credit-starved businesses. These offerings unleashed a wave of 156 REIT IPOs, which raised over USD 100 billion of new equity between 1991 and 1999. Also, during this decade, approximately 100 REITs achieved investment-grade ratings and accessed the public debt market for USD 60.4 billion. After seeing the positive effects of the REIT model on the U.S. real estate market, many other countries adopted their own REIT regimes.

13   Throughout the better part of the 1990s, favorable market conditions and the oversupply of properties on the market created an unusual opportunity for REITs to grow by acquiring properties at net operating income (NOI) yields exceeding their nominal cost of capital. REITs dominated the market for acquisitions during these years as investors poured money into REITs. By the end of the decade, the total equity market capitalization of the REIT sector expanded nearly 15 fold to USD 124.3 billion and 203 companies. By the end of the 1990s, however, investors had shifted their attention from REITs to the emerging "dot-com" boom.

The period 2000 through 2006 was characterized by declining yields in the capital markets as the U.S. Federal Reserve Bank slashed interest rates to boost the economy following the dot-com bust. Plummeting capitalization rates translated into a stunning increase in the value of the real estate and REIT stocks. By the end of 2006, the value of public REITs grew to USD 438.1 billion. **14**

While investors in public REIT stocks benefited immensely, private real estate inves- **15** tors saw the value of their holdings increase even more. REITs, trading at significant discounts to their underlying net asset values as the period began, became the target of frenzied bidding wars by private equity funds pursuing arbitrage strategies. Real estate merger and acquisition activity surged during this period, fueled by cash-rich private equity investors, plentiful debt, and low-interest rates. In 2007, by the time the turmoil in the debt markets put a halt to the buy-out action, forty-one public REITs were taken private in transactions totaling USD 150 billion. As a result, the total equity market capitalization for REITs fell back to USD 312 billion as of the end of 2007.

The U.S. credit crisis intensified throughout 2008; REITs were pummeled by the **16** combination of falling property values and soaring leverage. REIT stocks, in turn, plunged amid investor fears as maturing debt loads could not be refinanced. By the time they bottomed in early 2009, REIT stocks had given up over two-thirds of their 2007 peak values, and total equity market capitalization dropped below USD 200 billion for the first time since 2002.

As 2009 progressed, REITs found the equity markets receptive to a new round of **17** offerings, which re-equitized the sector and set the stage for a new round of prosperity. By the end of 2013, REITs had raised close to USD 200 billion in fresh equity, REIT stocks had regained over half of their post-bottom losses, and total equity market capitalization rose to USD 670.3 billion.

Beginning in 2013, with the Federal Reserve Bank's ongoing commitment to keeping **18** interest rates at rock-bottom levels, U.S. commercial real estate prices have continued to rise, and REIT investors have been rewarded with share price increases totaling 25%. The favorable environment has likewise benefited REIT sponsors and existing REITs, who brought 35 IPOs and over 450 secondary equity offerings to market during 2013–2016. Against this backdrop, REITs' total equity market capitalization had surpassed USD 1.0 trillion by year-end 2016.

Since 2016, the types of assets for which the REIT structure has been expanded to cover **19** include many nontraditional asset classes such as golf courses, cell towers, billboards, power transmission and many others. Further, many large asset managers have begun to offer non-traded REIT products targeted at smaller retail investors that invest in core real estate with redemption features (effectively acting like open-ended funds). With these new additions to the REIT universe, the REIT's total equity market capitalization surpassed USD 1.3 trillion by the end of 2019. It is not yet clear what impact the COVID-19 pandemic will ultimately have on the REIT market. Many property sectors have been dramatically impacted by the global health crisis and related shutdowns, most drastically, the hospitality and retail sectors. In addition to the immediate impacts, there may also be long-term implications on changes in consumer behavior, such as an increase in remote working impacting the office rental market (*source*: NAREIT).

§1.02   REGULATORY ASPECTS

[A]   Legal Form of REIT

[1]   *Corporate Form*

20   A REIT can be organized as a corporation, trust, limited liability company or partnership. Regardless of its legal structure, the entity must be taxable as a regular corporation. The majority of public REITs are organized as corporations or trusts. A REIT must be managed by trustees or directors as opposed to its shareholders or beneficiaries. Regardless of the legal form, references herein to "shares" are to the ownership interests in the REIT, and references to "shareholders" are to the owners of interests in the REIT.

21   A REIT can issue common and preferred shares and voting and nonvoting shares. A bank or similar financial institution or an insurance company cannot qualify as a REIT.

22   A REIT election is made when the entity files its first REIT tax return (Form 1120-REIT), and the election remains in effect until revoked or terminated for failure to meet the requirements for qualification. Filing the REIT election is deemed to be an election to be treated as an association taxable as a corporation for an entity that is not otherwise taxed as a corporation. Since 1976, electing REIT status has required adopting the calendar year as the taxable year of the entity.

[2]   *Investment Restrictions*

23   Beginning with its second taxable year, a REIT must have at least one hundred persons as shareholders for 335/365th of its taxable year; there is no explicit requirement that any shareholder owns a minimum value of the REIT. The diversification of ownership requirement is governed according to the "five or fewer" test: five or fewer individuals (natural persons and certain tax-exempt entities) cannot own 50% or more of a REIT at any time during the last half of its taxable year beginning with a REIT's second taxable year. If a REIT complies with the regulations for ascertaining stock ownership and does not know and would not reasonably know that it violates the "five or fewer" test, then the REIT should not be disqualified as such. A broad set of constructive ownership rules applies to attribute ownership among family members and from entities to their owners under the "five or fewer" test; these attribution rules do not apply to the hundred-shareholder requirement.

"Captive" REITs have been formed where one entity with diversified ownership holds **24** all or substantially all of the common shares, and one hundred or more other persons each acquire preferred or common shares. A captive entity remains eligible for REIT status, although some states limit the income tax advantages of captive REITs.

REIT's shares must be evidenced by transferable shares, although the directors or **25** trustees may refuse to recognize transfers that would violate the ownership requirements to qualify as a REIT. The IRS has issued private letter rulings approving restrictions to prevent: (1) violations of requirements of the securities laws; (2) loss of favorable status as a domestically controlled REIT; or (3) concentration of ownership in the hands of U.S. pension funds that would subject pension fund shareholders to adverse tax consequences.

[3] Regulatory Authorities

The Board of the Financial Accounting Standards Board, along with various organiza- **26** tions and committees, provides accounting principles for publicly traded REITs. For most publicly traded REITs, the rules and interpretive releases of the SEC govern accounting policy and/or disclosure, and the Public Company Accounting Oversight Board provides REIT auditing standards. The SEC also administers the Investment Company Act of 1940, which governs certain entities that invest primarily in securities. A listed REIT is subject to the requirements of the stock exchange on which it is traded. States generally have securities departments that regulate the sale of securities in the state.

Taxation of REITs in the U.S. is defined by the Internal Revenue Code of 1986, and the **27** IRS administers these provisions. The Employee Retirement Income Security Act (ERISA) imposes fiduciary responsibility and prohibits certain transactions with respect to pension funds. The Department of Labor administers ERISA.

On July 21, 2010, President Obama signed the Dodd-Frank Wall Street Reform and **28** Consumer Protection Act (Dodd-Frank Act). The Dodd-Frank Act is comprehensive in scope and significantly reshaped regulation of the financial markets with broad implications for all public companies, especially those in the financial services industry. The Dodd-Frank Act mandates a variety of changes to the governance, disclosure, and compensation practices of all public companies. Many of the provisions of the Dodd-Frank Act require further SEC rulemaking.

[B] Legislative and Other Regulatory Sources

Public REITs are subject to rules and regulations that were created by the following **29** Acts:

- The Securities Act of 1933 requires that investors receive financial and other significant information concerning securities being offered for public sale and prohibits deceit, misrepresentations, and other fraud in the sale of securities.
- The Securities Act of 1934 created and empowered the SEC with broad authority over all aspects of the securities industry, including the power to regulate the various U.S. stock exchanges and to require periodic reporting of information by companies with publicly traded securities.
- The Sarbanes Oxley Act of 2002 mandated a number of reforms that were designed to enhance corporate responsibility, enhance financial disclosures, and combat corporate and accounting fraud.
- The Jumpstart Our Business Startups (JOBS) Act was signed into law in April 2012 with the principal goal of encouraging job creation and economic growth by making it easier for private companies to access the public capital markets. The JOBS Act created a number of special accommodations under the U.S. securities laws intended to make it easier for a group of companies, known as emerging growth companies, to complete an equity-IPO and to operate in the SEC reporting system.

30   The legal entity selected by the REIT is formed under and governed by state law regarding corporations, business trusts, or other entities.

[C]   Exchange Controls and Reporting Requirements

31   To register a REIT as a public company, a registration statement on Form S-11 must be filed with the SEC, part of which includes the prospectus that is used to sell the shares to the public. Form S-11 also contains extensive information about a REIT, including risk factors, financial data, investment policies, and a description of the REIT's investment interests, including detailed property operating data. The financial statements required to be included depend on the size of the REIT initiating the offering, the formation structure of the REIT, and the timing of the filing.

32   Once the Form S-11 is filed, it is reviewed by the SEC to ensure compliance with the applicable disclosure and accounting requirements. When all SEC comments have been satisfactorily addressed, the SEC can declare Form S-11 as effective. At that point, the REIT may begin selling its shares to the public. Most public REITs are listed on the NYSE.

33   After a REIT's securities are sold to the public, the REIT is subject to the following ongoing filing and disclosure requirements, including:

(a) *Form 10-K*: This is the REIT's annual report that is filed with the SEC, and it provides a comprehensive overview of the REIT's business and financial condition. The report includes financial statements audited by an independent registered public accounting firm.

(b) *Form 10-Q*: The Form 10-Q is filed with the SEC for each of the first three quarts of a REIT's fiscal year, and it includes *unaudited* financial statements, an overview of the results of operations, and information about other significant events that occurred during the period. Prior to filing, interim financial statements included in quarterly reports on Forms 10-Q must be reviewed by an independent accountant using appropriate professional standards and procedures.

(c) *Form 8-K*: The Form 8-K is filed with the SEC to disclose certain material corporate events, such as entering into a material agreement, the acquisition or disposition of a significant business or the public reporting of operations and financial condition. A Form 8-K is generally required to be filed or furnished within four business days after the occurrence of the specific event. For significant acquisitions as defined by the SEC regulations, a REIT may also be required to include pre-acquisition financial statements in its filing.

(d) *Form S-11/A:* Non-traded REITs must file a sticker supplement describing each significant property that was not identified in the prospectus whenever a reasonable possibility exists that it will be acquired during the distribution period. Every three months during the distribution period, the company will need to file a post-effective amendment to the S-11 to consolidate all of the stickers and include or incorporate by reference audited financial statements for all significant consummated property acquisitions for periods prior to acquisition. Depending on the type of property or properties acquired and how significant the transaction is to the REIT, a company may need to file pre-acquisition audited financial statements in accordance with U.S. Generally Accepted Accounting Principles (GAAP) or an audited modified statement of operations in accordance with SEC regulations.

Beneficial owners of more than 5% of a listed REIT's outstanding common stock are **34** required to file their name, address, type and percentage ownership with the SEC under a Schedule 13G within forty-five days after the end of the REIT's first calendar year. Subject to certain exceptions, a person or entity who acquires more than 5% of the common stock of the REIT must file similar information with the SEC using a Schedule 13D within ten days after the acquisition.

Most public REITs must also follow SEC standards as they relate to composition and **35** disclosure rules for their Audit Committees.

A public REIT is required to include an internal control report in its annual report, **36** which states management's responsibility for establishing and maintaining an adequate internal control structure and procedures for financial reporting. The internal control report also contains an assessment, as of the end of the company's most recent fiscal year and the effectiveness of the company's internal controls and the procedures for financial reporting. Depending on the size of the REIT, an independent auditor may be required to audit and issue a report on the effectiveness of internal controls over financial reporting.

[D]   Registration Procedures

[1]   Preparatory Measures

37   In order to qualify as a REIT, an entity must meet the organization, income, asset, and distribution requirements. It must also satisfy the ownership tests after its first year as a REIT.

[2]   Obtaining Authorization

38   A U.S. corporation, business trust, limited liability company or limited partnership (in certain cases) may be eligible to be taxed as a REIT. The REIT election is made by filing Form 1120-REIT with the IRS; generally, this tax return, or extension thereof, must be filed by April 15th. An eligible entity is not otherwise taxed as a corporation is deemed to have made an election to be taxed as a corporation by filing a Form 1120-REIT.

39   No advance approval by the IRS is required to be classified as a REIT, but the return is subject to subsequent examination by the IRS. REITs often request private letter rulings from the IRS with respect to complex issues such as the eligibility of the REIT to provide specific services to its tenants (*see* section §1.02[F][5] below). A favorable private letter ruling serves as a kind of insurance against IRS audit with respect to the requested issues to the requesting REIT.

40   If a REIT voluntarily revokes its REIT status or fails the qualification requirements to be treated as a REIT and mitigation provisions, the REIT generally must wait for a period of five years before it may re-elect REIT status. Earlier reelection may be permitted by the IRS following disqualification if the REIT establishes that failure to qualify as a REIT was due to reasonable cause and not willful neglect or fraud with intent to evade tax.

[3]   Other Requirements for the Incorporation of a Company

41   In order to qualify as a REIT, the entity must be organized in one of the fifty states or the District of Columbia. In the case of a corporation, for example, a certificate of incorporation would be filed with appropriate jurisdiction. A business trust would be created by filing a declaration of trust.

[4]   Obtaining Listing on Exchanges

[a]   Costs

42   The costs associated with registering a REIT with the SEC depend on several factors, such as whether the associated capital raising is underwritten. As a general rule, a REIT should allow for costs between 4% and 7% of funds raised.

[b]   Time

The time required to register a REIT with the SEC will depend on several factors, **43** including the size and complexity of the transaction (e.g., blind pool versus previously established private REIT) and the state of the markets. As a general rule, the REIT should allow at least six to twelve months for any registration.

[E]   Requirements and Restrictions

[1]   Capital Requirements

A publicly traded REIT is required to meet certain minimum capital requirements. For **44** an IPO of a REIT to be listed on the NYSE, the REIT must have minimum shareholder equity of USD 60 million, and the value of the shares held by the public, excluding certain insiders, must be at least USD 40 million. A REIT that fails to maintain a minimum market capitalization of USD 15 million for thirty consecutive days is subject to delisting. There are additional requirements for listing based upon income, number of shareholders, trading volume, share price and other factors.

[2]   Marketing/Advertising

When a public REIT seeks to raise equity, other than through a continuous offering, it **45** prepares and files a prospectus with the SEC. REITs must also comply with Regulation Fair Disclosure, which mandates that material information be disclosed to all investors at the same time.

Some REIT offerings fall within an exemption to federal securities laws. While such **46** exemptions provide relief from SEC registration requirements, REITs must still disclose specific information in connection with the offering.

[3]   Redemption

Governing documents for a REIT often provide that the REIT cannot redeem securities **47** if the redemption causes a violation of the shareholder and ownership requirements (*see* section §1.02[A][2] above). A redemption is governed by the REIT's organizational documents (certificate of incorporation, by-laws, declaration of trust, etc.).

An open-ended REIT places limitations on redemptions based upon the availability of **48** cash to fund the redemption. If the REIT does not have cash available, it may establish a queue for shareholders requesting redemption.

The SEC accounting rules for classification of redeemable securities need to be **49** considered for redemption of stock in a public REIT. In addition, if a public REIT chooses to purchase some of its outstanding common stock, it is advised to follow certain safe harbor rules to provide protection from market manipulation and fraud claims.

[4]   Valuation of Shares/Units for Redemption and Other Purposes

50   Shares in public REITs are valued at market value. Shares in an open-ended private REIT or registered but not traded REITs may be sold or redeemed in some cases based upon the appraised value of net assets adjusted for offering or acquisition expenses as defined in the offering document.

[5]   Investment Restrictions

51   Restrictions on a REIT's investments result primarily from asset and income tests provided in the tax law (described below) and exposure to various penalty provisions (*see* section §1.03[A][5] below). A REIT investing primarily in securities, including mortgage securities, will generally operate in a manner to avoid regulation under the Investment Company Act of 1940.

52   At the close of each quarter, a REIT must satisfy the following tests related to its assets:

   (a) At least 75% of the value of a REIT's total assets must be represented by real estate assets including mortgage loans and interests in mortgages secured by real property, shares in U.S. REITs, debt instruments of publicly offered REITs, personal property (where the fair market value of the personal property under the lease is less than 15% of the total fair market value under the lease), stock or debt attributable to the investment of certain new capital for the one-year period after the REIT received the new capital, cash and cash items (including receivables), and U.S. Government securities.
   (b) Not more than 20% of a REIT's assets may be securities of TRSs.
   (c) Securities (excluding mortgage loans, shares in other REITs, securities issued by a TRS of the REIT, and U.S. Government securities) are limited to: (i) not more than 5% of the value of a REIT's total assets of any one issuer; (ii) not more than 10% of the total voting power of any one issuer; and (iii) not more than 10% of the total value of the outstanding securities of any one issuer.
   (d) Debt instruments of publicly offered REITs that are not mortgages secured by real property cannot exceed 25% of a REIT's total assets.

53   A TRS is a corporation in which a REIT holds stock and makes a joint election to be treated as a TRS. The TRS framework allows a REIT to hold interests in corporate entities that engage in activities that would either result in nonqualifying REIT income, exceed the permitted ownership thresholds under the 5% and 10% asset tests, or otherwise cause the REIT to recognize an adverse tax consequence.

When applying the 10% value test, the following items generally will not be considered   **54**
securities: (1) "straight debt" loans where the interest rate and interest payment dates
are not contingent on profits, the borrower's discretion, or similar factors, and there is
no convertibility (directly or indirectly) into stock; (2) loans to individuals or estates;
(3) certain rental agreements; (4) obligations to pay rents from real property; (5)
certain securities issued by foreign or domestic state or local governments or political
subdivisions; and (6) securities issued by other REITs.

Market value of the securities should be used if market quotations are available. For   **55**
other securities and assets, fair value, as determined in good faith by the REIT's
directors or trustees, should be used.

When applying the REIT asset tests, a REIT is treated as directly owning the assets of   **56**
any wholly owned subsidiaries for which TRS elections have not been made. In
addition, a REIT takes into account its proportionate share of each of the assets of any
partnership in which it holds an interest. A real estate mortgage investment conduit
(REMIC) is a vehicle for the securitization of mortgage loans, which is generally treated
as a real estate asset. If less than 95% of the assets of the REMIC are real estate assets,
then the REIT looks through the REMIC to its underlying assets and income for the REIT
tests.

If the REIT fails to satisfy any of the asset tests at the end of a quarter, the result may   **57**
be a disqualification as a REIT unless a mitigation provision applies. If an investment
qualifies for REIT purposes when acquired, a subsequent change in the value of that
security alone does not cause a violation. If a discrepancy results from an acquisition
during a quarter and the discrepancy is eliminated within thirty days after the close of
the quarter, the REIT will be considered to have satisfied the asset tests. For other asset
test failures, mitigation provisions allow REIT status to be maintained provided the
failure to satisfy the test was due to reasonable cause and not willful neglect; certain
information related to the failure is filed with the IRS within a specified period of time;
the asset causing the failure is disposed within a specified period of time; and in some
cases, a penalty tax is paid (*see* section §1.03[A][5] below).

In order to maintain its tax-favored status, a REIT must annually satisfy two gross   **58**
income tests meant to ensure that a significant source of a REIT's gross income is
generated from rental real estate, mortgage loans or other passive activities. Accordingly, these tests limit the amount of income that a REIT can derive from nonpassive
sources.

At least 75% of a REIT's gross income must come from specific sources, including rents   **59**
from real property, interest on obligations secured by mortgages on real property or on
interests in real property, gain from the sale or other dispositions of real property or
mortgage loans that are not dealer property or that satisfy a safe harbor provision,
dividends and gain from the sale or other disposition of shares in other REITs, refunds
and abatements of taxes on real property, income and gain derived from foreclosure
property, fees for entering into agreements to make or purchase mortgage loans or to

purchase or lease real property and income attributable to the "temporary investment of new capital."

60   At least 95% of a REIT's gross income must be derived from the same items of gross income that qualify for the 75% gross income test, as well as dividends, interest and gain from the sale or other disposition of stock or securities. The REIT income tests are based on the gross income of the REIT during the year determined under federal income tax principles. Certain items of income are excluded from consideration in the gross income tests (e.g., income from certain hedging transactions and cancelation of indebtedness income). For purposes of the tests, the gross income of the REIT is not reduced by any losses sustained during the year.

61   If a REIT fails to satisfy either the 75% or 95% gross income test during a year and the failure is due to a reasonable cause and not willful neglect, and the REIT discloses the failure on its tax return, it will be subject to a penalty tax on the income that caused the failure instead of being disqualified (*see* section §1.03[A][5] below).

62   A major source of income for many REITs is "rents from real property." In addition to amounts received for the use of real property, rents from real property also include charges for services customarily furnished or rendered in connection with the rental of real property, whether or not separately stated (i.e., utilities are a common service furnished to tenants of certain properties). Services furnished to the tenants of a particular building will be considered as customary if they are customarily offered in the geographic market in which the building is located to tenants in buildings that are of a similar class (i.e., such as luxury apartment buildings). Certain customary services may need to be furnished by a TRS or a third-party independent contractor. To qualify as a service customarily furnished, the service must be furnished or rendered to the tenants of the REIT or, primarily for the convenience or benefit of the tenant, tenant's guests, customers, or subtenants of the tenant. Most of the guidance issued on qualifying services is in the form of private letter rulings requested by individual REITs. Although the substance of the guidance is disclosed to the public, the private letter ruling only applies with respect to the REIT that requested the ruling.

63   Rents from real property also include rents attributable to personal property that is leased in connection with a lease of real property, but only if the value of the personal property does not exceed 15% of the property's total value. If the rent attributable to personal property exceeds 15%, then an apportionment is required and the entire rent attributable to personal property is disqualified.

64   Rents from real property do not include the following: (i) rent from a lease where any portion is contingent on the net income or net profits of any person; (ii) any amounts received from certain related parties based upon a 10% relationship (with certain exceptions for a TRS) or (iii) any "impermissible tenant service income."

65   Impermissible tenant service income accrues when a REIT provides noncustomary services other than through an independent contractor from whom the REIT does not receive any income or through a TRS. A classic example of an impermissible tenant service would be a REIT directly providing maid service to residents in an apartment building. If the amount of impermissible tenant service income received by a REIT with respect to an individual property exceeds 1% of all amounts received from that property in a particular tax year, then all amounts received from the property will be disqualified. The amount of impermissible tenant service income is deemed to be at least 150% of the direct cost of providing the service.

Interest income does not include fees received or accrued by a lender that are **66** considered charges for services performed for a borrower rather than a charge for the use of borrowed money. Similar to the rule for "rents from real property," interest does not include amounts with respect to an obligation if the amount depends on the net income or profits of any person, but unlike the rule for "rents from real property," there is no tainting of interest received from a related person.

Interest income for purposes of the 75% test includes interest with respect to a **67** mortgage obligation or other obligation with respect to real property. All of the income is considered mortgage interest where the amount of the loan is less than the fair market value of the real property (and personal property that does not exceed 15% of the fair market value of the real and personal property securing the loan). If, however, the amount of the loan exceeds the fair market value of the real property, then the interest amount apportioned to the real property will be based on the percentage that the fair market value of the real property bears to the entire amount of the loan. The treatment of interest income from distressed debt under this rule raises several questions. While some guidance has been provided by the IRS, questions remain.

For income that is not listed as qualifying for either the 75% gross income test or the **68** 95% gross income test, the IRS and Treasury Department have the authority to exclude or treat as qualifying such income for one or both of those tests. The Treasury Department and the IRS issued guidance that provides that certain income attributable to a REIT's investment in a non-U.S. subsidiary is treated as qualifying income for purposes of the 95% gross income test.

Because REITs were historically intended to generate primarily passive income, a **69** punitive 100% tax is imposed on net income from "prohibited transactions," and such gains are excluded from the income tests. A prohibited transaction generally applies to the sale or other disposition of "dealer" property (i.e., any property held by the REIT primarily for sale to customers in the ordinary course of its business) except for property qualifying under a safe harbor or the foreclosure property regime (*see* section §1.03[A][5] below).

[6]   *Distribution/Accumulation*

To maintain REIT status, a REIT must annually distribute at least 90% of its ordinary **70** taxable income, with certain adjustments. The 90% distribution requirement is computed on the following: taxable income, excluding net capital gains and the dividends paid deduction, plus 90% of net income from qualified foreclosure property net of tax imposed on such income and certain noncash income (e.g., original issue discount in excess of payments received and cancelation of indebtedness). A REIT deducts the dividends paid to shareholders and must pay tax on any income it retains in the same manner as a regular corporation (*see* section §1.03[A][1][b] below regarding the distributions that qualify for the deduction for dividends paid). These tax rules limit the REIT's ability to accumulate capital and place a premium on tax planning by the REIT.

[7]   *Reporting Requirements*

71   For a REIT that has registered shares with the SEC, there are basic reporting requirements required by the Securities Exchange Act of 1934 (*see* section §1.02[D] above). For an unregistered REIT, the reporting requirements are generally dictated by any agreements the REIT has entered into, such as debt agreements. There are additional reporting requirements required by the Securities Act of 1933 for debt or equity offerings (*see* section §1.02[D] above).

72   Similar to non-REIT corporations, a REIT provides tax information to its shareholders and also reports the character of distributions made throughout the year (*see* section §1.03[B] below).

[8]   *Accounting*

73   The accounting and reporting for REITs are subject to GAAP, which is often complex and requires a careful analysis of all facts and circumstances. Some of the key accounting issues REITs generally face relate to areas such as acquisitions, consolidation, leasing, impairments, and dispositions. Funds from Operations (FFO), which is considered a non-GAAP measure, is the industry norm for measuring the operating performance of REITs. GAAP net income includes a deduction for the depreciation of real estate assets, which presupposes that the value of such assets diminishes over time. FFO is generally defined as a REIT's net income (or loss), excluding depreciation and amortization related to real estate, gains and losses from the sale of certain real estate assets, gains and losses from the change in control, and impairment write-downs of certain real estate assets and investments in entities when the impairment is directly attributable to decreases in the value of the depreciable real estate held by the entity. REITs may have different interpretations and policies for computing FFO, as well as computing Adjusted FFO (AFFO). AFFO are defined individually by each company and often adjust FFO for certain income (gain) and expense (loss) items that are not provided for in the definition of FFO. Further, non-traded REITs often report Modified FFO, which, similar to Normalized FFO and AFFO, is another derivation of FFO. Refer to the discussion below involving Regulation G.

74   Regulation G imposes three conditions on companies that use non-GAAP measures such as FFO in any public disclosures (including press releases). These conditions are: (1) the non-GAAP financial information must not contain a material misstatement or omission; (2) the disclosure must include the most directly comparable GAAP financial measure; and (3) the disclosure must provide a quantitative reconciliation between the non-GAAP measure and the most directly comparable GAAP measure.

The SEC has also imposed other requirements for companies that use non-GAAP **75** measures in their SEC filings. These requirements include: (1) an equally or more prominent presentation of the most directly comparable GAAP financial measure; (2) explanation of why management believes the non-GAAP measure provides useful information to investors; and (3) if material, a statement disclosing any other purposes for which management uses the non-GAAP measures. The SEC also has various restrictions and prohibitions on the use of certain non-GAAP measures in SEC filings.

§1.03 TAXATION

[A] Taxation of the REIT

[1] Corporate Income Tax

[a] Tax Accounting

A REIT typically adopts (and is usually required to use) the accrual method of **76** accounting for tax purposes. The requirements for financial accounting of a REIT differ from the REIT's tax accounting requirements in many ways. For example, interest income may be reported for tax purposes under "original issue discount" provisions based upon yield-to-maturity principles when interest payments are deferred, the interest rate increases during the term of the loan, or the interest is contingent based upon the income of the borrower. In many cases, prepaid rent is recognized as taxable income when received, or rental income may be recognized under a different "rent leveling" principle than used for financial accounting. Allocation of the cost of an acquired property for tax and financial accounting differs, as does the method of depreciating the assets. The like-kind exchange provisions allow the deferral of tax gain on the disposition of a property, even though the gain may be recognized for financial accounting.

[b] Determination of Taxable Income

A REIT generally computes its taxable income in the same manner as a regular **77** corporation but receives a deduction for dividends paid to shareholders. In addition to deducting dividends paid during the taxable year, dividends declared in October, November, or December of any calendar year payable to shareholders of record in such months are considered received by shareholders and, likewise, paid by the REIT on December 31st of the prior year if the dividends are actually paid during January of the following calendar year in which they are declared. A REIT can also avail itself of a separate election to "throwback" dividends paid in one year to the prior tax year for purposes of the dividends paid deduction. A shareholder may elect to treat the REIT as having distributed a dividend and then having recontributed the amount to the REIT (a "consent dividend"). In the case of a consent dividend, the REIT obtains the dividends paid deduction, and the shareholder recognizes dividend income. This election has limited application to public REITs but is often used by private REITs. If after filing its return, or upon examination by the IRS, the REIT is found to have under-distributed its taxable income, the REIT may pay a deficiency dividend in the following year (*see* section §1.03[A][5] below).

78   To qualify for the dividends paid deduction, a distribution generally must be paid from current or accumulated earnings and profits to be a "dividend." Certain distributions paid in the liquidation of the REIT may also qualify for the deduction. A dividend distribution from a REIT, other than a REIT required to make periodic reports under the Securities and Exchange Act of 1934, must be pro rata to shareholders within a class, and without preference to one class of shares over another, except to the extent that one class is entitled to a preference properly authorized in the REIT's organizational documents.

79   If a REIT distributes 100% of its ordinary income and capital gains, the REIT can avoid most taxes at the entity level. Any undistributed income is taxed at the REIT level. In addition to cash dividends, the REIT may distribute a combination of cash and its shares. The IRS published guidance under which its distributions of stock by a publicly offered REIT would be eligible for the dividends paid deduction where the shareholders have an option to receive as little as 20% in cash (or 10% in cash for distributions made in 2020).

80   A REIT may pass through the character of its capital gains to its shareholders, but it cannot pass through net losses, the foreign source of income, foreign tax credits or other tax credits. A REIT can retain its long-term capital gains, pay the corporate income tax and pass through the capital gain and credit for the tax to the shareholders. States have not adopted this treatment.

81   References to "capital gains" herein generally refer to the excess of long-term capital gains over short-term capital losses. Long-term gains are gains on the sale of property held for more than one year. Short-term gains are generally treated the same as ordinary income except that they may be offset by capital losses—either long or short term. Short-term capital gains are treated as ordinary dividends when distributed to shareholders.

82   A REIT that does not have more than 10% of its assets in real property financing assets may elect to be a real property trade or business and, accordingly, can fully deduct its interest expense without limitation. The rules relating to interest expense of a REIT's underlying partnership interest expense are complex, and in certain circumstances, the interest expense of lower-tiered entities may be limited.

83   A net operating loss (NOL) can be carried forward indefinitely but is limited to 80% (100% for tax years beginning before 2021) of the taxable income of a REIT (prior to the

NOL deduction and the dividend paid deduction) in any particular year, but these losses cannot be carried back to a prior year of a REIT. The dividends paid deduction generally cannot create or increase an NOL for the year but can be used to offset the taxable income for the current year so that a loss from a prior year can be carried over to subsequent years. Also, a capital gain dividend can be paid that would otherwise be offset by an ordinary loss or NOL carryover to pass through the generally favorable treatment of capital gains and preserve the ordinary loss as a carryover.

A REIT may be subject to tax or penalties on various types of special income or   **84**
violations of the REIT requirements (section §1.03[A][5] below).

[c]   *Taxation of Income from Taxable and Nontaxable Subsidiaries*

A REIT is permitted to have wholly owned corporate subsidiaries (referred to as   **85**
"qualified REIT subsidiaries" or a QRS). A QRS is disregarded as a separate entity for tax purposes, and thus, its assets, liabilities, and items of income are treated as the REIT's.

A REIT may own shares in a corporation that elects to be treated as TRS, shares in   **86**
another REIT, or minority positions in other corporations. A TRS is taxed as a regular corporation, and distributions of its income are taxed as dividends to the REIT to the extent of the earnings and profits of the TRS. Dividends from a TRS or a non-REIT corporation are included in the taxable income of a REIT, and a dividend received from the REIT by a corporation is not entitled to the deduction for dividends received that is generally available to a corporation. A dividend received from another REIT generally retains its character as ordinary income or capital gain.

A REIT's ownership of an entity that is treated as a partnership for federal income tax   **87**
purposes is treated as if the REIT directly owned its share of the underlying assets and earned its share of the partnership's gross income. The assets and income are attributed to the REIT based upon its capital interest in the entity, regardless of the way income is shared.

[d]   *Taxation of Foreign Income*

Income from foreign sources is includable in a REIT's taxable income unless it is   **88**
generated by and taxable to a TRS (or another entity treated as a corporation that is neither a TRS nor a QRS). Income of a TRS may be subject to anti-deferral regimes causing the REIT to currently recognize income or be subject to adverse taxation, without regard to whether the REIT receives cash from the TRS associated with such taxable income. No distinction is made between foreign and U.S.-sourced income for the dividends paid deduction or upon distribution to the shareholders. No credit for foreign taxes paid by the REIT passes through to the REIT shareholders. The foreign taxes are deductible by the REIT and reduce its distribution requirement.

[2]   Value Added Tax

89   The U.S. does not impose Value Added Tax, but most states and many local jurisdictions impose sales and use taxes. A sales tax is imposed upon the buyer of goods other than for resale. A use tax is imposed when goods are purchased outside the jurisdiction and brought into the jurisdiction for use. A use tax generally allows a credit for a sales tax paid in the other jurisdiction.

[3]   Withholding Taxes

90   Income received by a domestic REIT is generally not subject to U.S. withholding tax. A REIT that holds an interest in a partnership, however, may be subject to withholding state income tax. The withholding tax would be applied against the REIT's income tax in that state, if any, or the REIT may file a return to claim a refund.

91   Distributions paid by the REIT to non-U.S. shareholders are subject to federal withholding tax. *See* section §1.03[C][1] below regarding withholding taxes and application of treaties with the U.S.

[4]   Other Taxes

92   While most states recognize REIT status, many states have disallowed the deduction for dividends paid by captive or nonpublic REITs. In addition, many states have imposed requirements for combined reporting and implemented tax regimes that diverge from the federal tax rules involving NOLs, built-in gains, or are based on items other than net taxable income. Many states now impose franchise or capital taxes, taxes based on gross receipts, transfer taxes, sales and use, and realty and personal property taxes. These taxes are determined and administered at the state and local level, and the tax rates vary widely from one jurisdiction to another. In addition, transfers of interests in entities owning real property may result in a tax being imposed as if an interest in the underlying real property had been transferred, or the transfer may cause a property tax reassessment of the property. Such taxes generally apply to REITs regardless of their special income tax status.

[5]   Penalties Imposed on REIT

93   Failure to meet requirements to maintain REIT status can lead to disqualification of the REIT or financial penalties. A REIT can often avoid disqualification under mitigation provisions if the REIT can demonstrate that the failure to comply is due to reasonable cause and not willful neglect and certain other requirements are met.

94   In the case of a violation of an income test, the penalty is a tax of 100% on the amount by which the REIT failed the test, less expenses apportioned to the income under a formula intended to represent the overall profitability of the REIT—not its profits from the specific income causing the violation.

If a REIT violates the asset tests and does not cure the violation within thirty days **95** following quarter-end, the violation must then be cured within six months of discovery of the failure. The amount of the financial penalty depends upon the magnitude of the violation. If the securities violating the value limit of the 10% asset test do not exceed the lesser of 1% of the total value of the REIT's assets at the end of the quarter or USD 10 million (a *"de minimis"* violation), there is no penalty. For other violations, the penalty equals the greater of USD 50,000 or an amount equal to the net income generated by the assets multiplied by 21%, the highest corporate tax rate.

If a REIT fails requirements relating to the organization, ownership or distribution **96** requirements, a mitigation provision may be available to retain REIT status that requires payment of a USD 50,000 penalty.

A REIT is subject to a 100% tax on net income from a prohibited transaction (the sale **97** of property held by a REIT primarily for sale to customers in the ordinary course of its business) unless a safe harbor applies. Whether the property is held by a REIT primarily for sale to customers in the ordinary course of its trade or business is a question of fact that depends on all the facts and circumstances with respect to the particular transaction. Failure to meet the safe harbor is not determinative that a prohibited transaction has occurred. The determination of whether the property is considered held primarily for sale to customers or for investment is a highly contested area, and courts will typically look at various factors including a REIT's intent to hold the property for the production of rental income or for investment with a view to long-term appreciation, the duration of property ownership, the extent of development activities with respect to the property and the number, extent, continuity and substantiality of the sales.

The safe harbor generally requires that a REIT holds the real estate asset for at least two **98** years, and if the asset is real property, that it be held for rent for at least two years. In addition, the aggregate cost of any improvements made by a REIT during the two years prior to the date of sale cannot exceed 30% of a property's net sales price. A REIT must either: (i) make no more than seven sales of property during the year in question; (ii) the aggregate adjusted bases (or value) of property sold during the taxable year does not exceed 10% of the aggregate bases (or value) of all of the assets of the REIT as of the beginning of the taxable year; or (iii) the aggregate adjusted bases (or value) of property sold during the taxable year does not exceed 20% of the aggregate bases (or value) of all of the assets of the REIT as of the beginning of the taxable year and the average of the aggregate bases (or value) of all of the assets of the REIT over the three-year period ending with the year being evaluated does not exceed 10%. If the REIT made more than seven sales of property during the year, then substantially all of the marketing and development expenditures are made through an independent contractor from whom the REIT does not derive or receive any income or a TRS. There are a number of additional rules that apply to special situations involving safe harbor.

99   A tax of 100% applies to any excessive amount of deductions allocated to a TRS based upon standards applicable to the allocation of expenses among commonly controlled entities. The penalty may apply deductions to payments (including for interest, rent or services) made from the TRS to a REIT. The penalty also applies to rental income received by a REIT to reflect services performed by its TRS for the REIT's tenants ("redetermined rents"). Certain safe harbors are available to avoid the 100% tax on redetermined rents.

100   A REIT is subject to an excise tax of 4% if it fails to distribute its taxable income within the calendar year. The nondeductible 4% tax is imposed on the excess of the "required distribution" over the dividends paid during the current year, including certain dividends deemed paid and received by the shareholders in the prior year. The required distribution is generally defined as the sum of 85% of a REIT's ordinary income, plus 95% of the REIT's net capital gain adjusted for any under-distribution, adjusted for any over- or under-distribution from the prior year. This provision is intended to limit the use of the "throwback" dividend paid after year-end (*see* section §1.03[A][1][b] above).

101   If a REIT's taxable income is adjusted as a result of an audit by the IRS or upon discovery of an error by the REIT, the REIT is permitted to make an additional distribution. The "deficiency dividend" is subject to an additional tax on the REIT computed similarly to interest but based upon the amount of the dividend—not the amount of tax on the undistributed income.

102   A REIT must annually ascertain the actual ownership of its outstanding shares by requesting written statements from its shareholders. Failure to demand annual written statements from shareholders could result in a penalty of USD 25,000 (USD 50,000 if the violation is due to intentional disregard). No penalty will result if the REIT can show reasonable cause for failure to comply.

103   A REIT may face a wide range of other penalties applicable to corporations or other taxpayers, for example, for failure to withhold or deposit taxes, failure to report "tax shelter" transactions or failure to file information returns.

[B]   Taxation of the Investor

104   The tax consequences to an investor depend upon the nature of the: (1) distributions from the REIT during its operating phase; (2) distributions from the liquidation of the REIT; or (3) gain from the sale or redemption of the shares in the REIT. Different tax rates apply to these various types of income and may vary by type of investor.

105   Distributions during the operating phase are treated as dividends to the extent paid out of the current or accumulated tax earnings and profits (E&P) of the REIT. E&P is calculated annually, starting with the U.S. taxable income of the REIT, but with certain adjustments (most significantly, longer depreciable lives, less favorable methods of depreciation, and current recognition of gains from installment sales).

Dividends paid out of E&P can be characterized either as ordinary dividends or as   **106**
capital gain dividends to the extent that the dividends are designated as such by a REIT
during the year. Capital gain dividends may include a special class of gain: "unrecap-
tured section 1250 gain," which is gain attributable to the depreciation claimed on the
real property upon a sale of the property. To qualify as a capital gain dividend, the
dividend must be designated by the REIT in a written notice mailed to shareholders
within thirty days after year-end or in its annual report.

Distributions in excess of earnings and profits are treated as a return of capital that   **107**
reduces the tax basis of REIT shares in the hands of the shareholder and results in
additional gain when the shares are ultimately sold. Distributions in excess of basis are
treated as gains from the disposition of the shares at the time of any such distribution.

Ordinary dividends may also include "excess inclusion income" attributable to a   **108**
REIT's interest in a real estate investment mortgage conduit (REMIC) or to mortgage
loans or mortgage securities that are financed with debt having multiple maturities tied
to the maturity of the mortgage loans; these dividends may be subject to tax as business
income to U.S. tax-exempt investors and are ineligible for treaty benefits for non-U.S.
investors.

Foreign source income or foreign taxes paid by a REIT, and losses incurred by a REIT,   **109**
do not pass through to a REIT's shareholders.

A sale of shares back to the REIT is redemption and subject to special considerations.   **110**
A redemption of all shares held by an investor or a minority shareholder will generally
be treated as a sale. Other redemptions may be treated as a dividend. A distribution in
liquidation is generally treated as a sale of shares, allowing recovery of basis in the
shares prior to the recognition of any gain. Redemptions and liquidations may have
Foreign Investment in Real Property Tax Act (FIRPTA) consequences to non-U.S.
shareholders (*see* section §1.03[B][1][a] below).

[1]   *Taxation of Current Income (i.e., All Income Derived from REIT in Holding Phase)*

[a]   *U.S. Residents*

U.S. individual investors are taxed on ordinary dividends received from a REIT at   **111**
graduated tax rates up to 37% but are eligible to deduct 20% of the income for an
effective tax rate of 29.6%. Ordinary dividends may be treated as "qualified dividends"
to the extent that dividends are received by a REIT from a regular corporation,
including a TRS. Qualified dividends are subject to tax at capital gains rates for
domestic individuals, estates, and trusts. U.S. individuals, estates and trusts are taxed
on capital gain dividends at 20%. REIT dividends may be subject to a 3.8% tax on
investment income in addition to the tax rates described above.

112   U.S. corporations do not receive preferential treatment on capital gains. REIT dividends also do not qualify for the corporate dividends received deduction. U.S. corporations are subject to tax at graduated rates up to 21% on ordinary or capital gain dividends from a REIT. With some exceptions, U.S. resident tax-exempt entities (e.g., pension trusts and charitable organizations) are generally not subject to tax on either dividends received from a REIT or the gain from the sale of REIT shares.

113   U.S. investors are generally not subject to withholding taxes on distributions from REITs, although certain backup withholding provisions may apply to the extent a U.S. investor does not provide a valid U.S. taxpayer identification number and withholding exemption certificate to the REIT.

> ### [b]   Nonresidents

114   For non-U.S. investors, ordinary dividends (as well as interest and other forms of passive income) are generally referred to as "fixed or determinable annual or periodic" income (commonly called FDAP income) and are subject to withholding of U.S. tax on the gross amount of the payment at a flat 30% rate assuming that the dividends are not the U.S. effectively connected income (ECI). This rate, however, may be reduced by treaty (*see* section §1.03[C] below).

115   The FIRPTA regime is designed to tax non-U.S. persons on dispositions of interests in U.S. real property, including U.S. corporations whose U.S. real property interests comprise at least 50% of their total real property and trade or business assets. This regime treats income attributable to such dispositions as income effectively connected with a U.S. trade or business. Distributions by a REIT that are attributable to gains from dispositions of U.S. real property interests received by a non-U.S. investor are subject to FIRPTA; except with respect to certain holders of 10% or less of a publicly traded REIT's shares (where capital gain dividends are instead treated as ordinary dividends). Under FIRPTA, distributions are subject to tax at the same graduated rates applicable to U.S. persons and are not eligible for reduction under a treaty. Also, the investor is required to file a U.S. income tax return, even though its U.S. tax liability is typically satisfied through the FIRPTA withholding tax mechanism.

116   Non-U.S. corporate investors are subject to tax on distributions attributable to the disposition of a U.S. real property interest under FIRPTA at 21% and a "branch profits tax" on such income. The branch profits tax rate of 30% is often reduced (sometimes even to zero) under tax treaties. The branch profits tax is applied to the capital gain dividend less the 21% income tax so that the combined effective tax rate is 44.7% if no treaty applies to reduce the branch profits tax or the branch profits tax is not applicable for another reason, such as not having a positive balance in effectively connected E&P because of losses from sales of US real property interests or US trade or business activities.

117   Non-U.S. pension funds taxable as trusts for U.S. purposes are subject to the same tax rates on capital gain dividends as U.S. individuals.

"Qualified foreign pension plans" and "qualified controlled entities" are exempt from **118** FIRPTA (and generally would not be subject to tax on distributions that would otherwise be subject to FIRPTA). In addition, certain publicly traded entities that are "qualified shareholders" and their investors are exempt from FIRPTA with respect to distributions from REITs that otherwise would be subject to FIRPTA; however, such distributions would be treated as FDAP.

Capital gain dividends are subject to withholding tax at a flat 21% rate for corporate **119** and noncorporate non-U.S. shareholders, although there is some uncertainty regarding whether withholding is required for capital gain distributions not attributable to dispositions of U.S. real property interests. This withholding should not apply to a shareholder owning 10% or less of a publicly traded REIT, or upon the issuance of a withholding certificate from the IRS if the actual tax would be less. Withholding under FIRPTA generally cannot be reduced by treaty. A REIT generally does not designate the amount of its capital gain dividends until after year-end and, as a result, the REIT would not be required to make the FIRPTA withholding until the designation is made; this procedure causes a mismatch between the year the gains are taxable to the shareholder and the year of the withholding.

[c]   *Taxation of Capital Gains (From Disposal of REIT Shares)*

[i]   Residents

Gain on the disposition of REIT shares held by U.S. individuals, estates, and trusts as **120** an investor for over one year is treated as long-term capital gain and is eligible for a 20% rate of tax. Short-term gains are subject to tax at the same rates as ordinary income. Furthermore, gain on the sale of REIT shares may be subject to an additional 3.8% tax, which applies to investment income.

[ii]   Nonresidents

Gain on the disposition of REIT shares is treated as capital gain and is also subject to tax **121** under FIRPTA unless; (1) a REIT is not a U.S. real property holding corporation (generally because the REIT primarily holds mortgage loans as opposed to real property); (2) a REIT is a "domestically controlled" REIT; or (3) the shareholder holds 10% or less of a class of regularly traded REIT shares. The buyer of the shares of a REIT that is a U.S. real property holding corporation and is not domestically controlled or does not meet a publicly traded exception is required to withhold 15% of the gross sales proceeds under FIRPTA. In that case, the non-U.S. seller is required to file a U.S. income tax return to report the gain and may claim the withheld tax against its actual tax liability. The withholding tax may be reduced or eliminated assuming certain procedural requirements are met, including the filing of a withholding certificate with the IRS prior to the time of the sale, showing that actual tax liability on the sale would be less than the required withholding. As noted above, a foreign pension plan that is treated as a "qualified foreign pension plan" is exempt from FIRPTA and generally would not be subject to tax on a disposition of REIT stock. In addition, certain publicly traded entities that are treated as "qualified shareholders" also may not be subject to tax in connection with the disposition of REIT stock, even if it would otherwise be treated as a U.S. real property interest.

122   Redemption of shares in a REIT that is a U.S. real property holding corporation may attract an allocation of gain from the sale of U.S. real property subject to the FIRPTA.

123   Ordinary dividends received by a foreign governmental entity may be exempt from tax under domestic law assuming certain conditions are satisfied (the "section 892 exemption"), but the capital gain dividends attributable to the disposition of a U.S. real property interest remain subject to the FIRPTA regime according to a notice issued by the IRS in 2007.

[2]   *Penalties Imposed on Investors*

124   A REIT shareholder can be subject to significant penalties for underpayment or nonpayment of its taxes as well as penalties for the failure to file a complete and timely return.

125   A non-U.S. investor who claims a reduction in withholding tax by application of a relevant tax treaty and who receives amounts in excess of USD 500,000 per year is generally required to file IRS Form 8833 reporting the treaty-based position, and failure to disclose such a position could result in a penalty of up to USD 10,000 per payment.

[C]   Tax Treaties

[1]   *Treaty Access*

126   The U.S. has a large treaty network, including at least sixty countries. Although REITs generally do not pay income tax, REITs are subject to tax if their profits are not distributed to shareholders or the REIT requirements are not met. Therefore, U.S. REITs should be recognized as residents of the U.S. and should be able to claim treaty benefits where applicable.

[2]   *WHT Reduction*

127   The withholding rate for non-U.S. investors may be reduced by treaty provided various requirements are satisfied, including generally the provision of valid withholding tax certificates. U.S. taxpayer identification numbers are generally required to claim treaty benefits other than for payments to offshore accounts with respect to publicly traded securities. U.S. income tax treaties usually reduce the statutory 30% withholding tax

on dividends paid from a U.S. corporation to foreign investors eligible for treaty benefits.

The 2006 U.S. Model Tax Treaty and many U.S. treaties typically reduce dividend **128** withholding tax to 15%, with a further reduction to 5% if the beneficial owner is a company owning *directly* at least 10% of the voting stock of the company paying the dividend. However, due to the special tax status of a REIT, additional limitations apply in almost all U.S. treaties with respect to dividends paid by a REIT: (1) the reduction below 15% is generally not allowed; and (2) the 15% reduced rate is typically restricted to the following circumstances:

- the beneficial owner owns 10% or less of the REIT and is an individual or pension fund;
- the beneficial owners, other than individuals or pension funds, own 10% or less and the REIT is diversified (i.e., no single property represents more than 10% of the value of the REIT's real estate holdings); or
- the REIT is publicly traded, and the beneficial owner generally owns 5% or less.

The percentage ownership requirements and the rates discussed above may differ in a **129** particular treaty. Several treaties allow exemption from withholding for pension funds (e.g., Belgium, Denmark, Japan, Switzerland, and U.K.), or both pension funds and tax-exempt entities such as charities (e.g., Canada, Germany, Mexico, and the Netherlands).

[D] Exit Tax/Tax Privileges/Concessions

If any existing corporation elects to become a REIT, it must distribute all of its earnings **130** and profits accumulated in years before it became a REIT by the end of its first taxable year as a REIT. The distribution of these earnings takes priority over the distribution of the current year's taxable income and does not qualify for the dividends paid deduction.

In addition, a REIT is subject to corporate tax on "net built-in gains" (the value of assets **131** at the time of the REIT election in excess of their adjusted tax bases to the extent the assets were held by a corporation either directly or through a partnership) recognized from taxable dispositions of the assets within five years of becoming a REIT. The amount of the built-in gain, less the corresponding tax, must be distributed to the shareholders in order to avoid the normal tax on undistributed REIT taxable income. A REIT may avoid the built-in gains tax by holding the assets for five years and may continue to defer or avoid the tax by disposing of the assets in tax-deferred "like-kind" exchanges, in which case the replacement asset becomes subject to the built-in gains tax for the balance of the five years. Also, if an existing REIT acquires the assets of a regular corporation in a tax-free transfer, merger or reorganization, similar principles apply to the acquired assets and earnings and profits transferred to the REIT. The built-in gains tax also applies to assets acquired in a tax-free transaction from a partnership with corporate partners. An election is available to recognize the gain immediately before the conversion to REIT status in order to avoid the built-in gains tax regime.

[E]   Taxation of Foreign REITs

[1]   Taxation of Foreign REIT Holding Assets in Country

[a]   General Rules

132   The taxation of a foreign REIT investing in the U.S. is analyzed similarly to other non-U.S. investors investing in U.S. real estate. U.S. taxation of non-U.S. investors depends upon whether the foreign investor is, or is deemed to be, a corporation, trust, or an individual. In the context of foreign REITs, the analysis would be on a country-by-country basis, applying U.S. standards to the classification of the entity, including the "check-the-box" rules.

133   The taxation of income from U.S. real estate owned by a foreign investor also depends on whether the investor actually has, or is considered to have, a business in the U.S., and whether or not the income is effectively connected with this business, generating ECI. ECI income from U.S. real property is subject to tax at the regular U.S. rates applicable to U.S. taxpayers. If the NOI from the U.S. real estate is not connected with a U.S. business, such as some types of net lease arrangements, then the gross rental income is subject to U.S. tax at the rate of 30%, or lower treaty rate, of the gross income (i.e., no deduction for expenses is allowed). A foreign investor can elect to treat its U.S. real property investments as attributable to a U.S. trade or business so that it is subject to tax on a net income rather than gross income basis. FIRPTA provides that gains and losses from the sale or exchange or other disposition of U.S. real property interests are automatically to be considered ECI.

[2]   Taxation of Investors Holding Shares in Non-U.S. REIT

134   The U.S. imposes worldwide taxation on U.S. individual taxpayers coupled with a complex foreign tax credit system. Generally, income is not subject to tax in the U.S. until the income is actually repatriated. However, an anti-deferral regime exists, which imposes adverse consequences on a U.S. taxable investor holding an interest in a foreign company holding substantial passive assets or generating substantial passive income, unless the investor elects to recognize the income whether or not distributed. A foreign REIT may be required to undertake a substantial tax reporting obligation for the U.S. investor to be able to comply with the requirements of this election. In addition, a U.S. investor may also be taxed on the active income of a non-U.S. REIT to the extent it exceeds a certain return on depreciable assets.

Tax Treaty Issues Related to REITs

---

30 October 2007

TAX TREATY ISSUES RELATED TO REITs
Public Discussion Draft

The use of Real Estate Investment Trusts (REITs) has significantly expanded worldwide and more and more countries are introducing rules to facilitate the use of these vehicles. This has led the OECD to examine the cross-border tax treaty issues arising from this form of investment.

The first draft of this report was prepared by an informal technical group of tax officials and experts from the REIT sector which was mandated by the OECD Committee on Fiscal Affairs to prepare an analysis of the issues related to the application of tax treaties to REITs and to present suggestions for additions to the Commentary of the OECD Model Tax Convention, including possible alternative provisions dealing with REITs that States wishing to do so could include in their bilateral treaties. The report of that technical group was presented to Working Party No. 1 on Tax Conventions and Related Questions, which is the subgroup of the OECD Committee on Fiscal Affairs that is responsible for updating the OECD Model Tax Convention. After discussion of that report, which led to a few minor changes, the Working Party approved its public release as a discussion draft.

The Working Party invites interested parties to send their comments on this discussion draft **before 15 January 2008** so that they may be examined at the next meeting of the Working Party. Comments should be sent to:

Jeffrey Owens
Director, CTPA
OECD
2, rue André Pascal
75775 Paris
FRANCE
e-mail: **jeffrey.owens@oecd.org**

Unless otherwise requested at the time of submission, comments submitted to the OECD in response to this invitation may be posted on the OECD website. Comments should be sent in electronic form, preferably in Word format, to facilitate their posting on the OECD website and their reproduction in OECD documents.

INTRODUCTION

1. Real Estate Investment Trusts (REITs) first appeared in the United States in the 1960s **1** and are now found throughout the world. The use of that investment vehicle has significantly expanded worldwide and more and more countries are introducing rules to facilitate the use of REITs. It has been estimated that, as of June 2006, REITs listed on stock-exchanges had a market capitalisation of US $608 billion and property assets worth in excess of US $890 billion.[1] The importance and the globalisation of investments in and through REITs have led the OECD to examine the cross-border tax issues that such investments raise for tax treaties.

2. The first draft of this report was prepared by an informal technical group of tax **2** officials and experts from the REIT sector which was mandated by the OECD Committee on Fiscal Affairs to prepare an analysis of the issues related to the application of tax treaties to REITs and to present suggestions for additions to the Commentary of the OECD Model Tax Convention, including possible alternative provisions dealing with REITs that States wishing to do so could include in their bilateral treaties. The report of that technical group was presented to Working Party No. 1 on Tax Conventions and Related Questions, which is the sub-group of the OECD Committee on Fiscal Affairs that is responsible for updating the OECD Model Tax Convention. After discussion of that report, which led to a few minor changes, the Working Party approved its public release as a discussion draft.

3. For the purposes of this report, a REIT is a widely held company, trust or contractual **3** or fiduciary arrangement that derives its income primarily from long-term investment in immovable property (real estate), distributes most of that income annually and does not pay income tax on income related to immovable property that is so distributed. The fact that the REIT vehicle does not pay tax on that income is the result of tax rules that provide for a single-level of taxation in the hands of the investors in the REIT (with corresponding withholding tax obligations imposed on the REIT with respect to its distributions to foreign investors).

4. Despite these common features, there may be significant differences between **4** countries as regards how REITs are structured and how the tax exemption of the income is provided. In some countries, REITs were developed using the tax rules generally applicable to trusts and companies; in others, a specific REIT tax regime has been adopted.

---

1. Ernst & Young, Global REIT Report 2006, Australia, October 2006, available at http://www.ey. com/Global/download.nsf/International/Real_Estate_-_Global_REIT_Survey_2006/$file/EY_ REHC_GlobalREITSurvey2006.pdf. Since this report was issued, Germany, Italy and the United Kingdom have enacted REIT laws.

APPLICATION OF TAX TREATIES TO REIT INVESTMENTS

5   5. The following sections of the report discuss the application of the provisions of the OECD Model Tax Convention to income from investments in and through REITs. In some cases, the report puts forward suggestions for changes intended to allow countries wishing to do so to address in a bilateral treaty some of the issues examined in the report. It is acknowledged, however, that some of the issues and suggestions discussed in this report may raise particular issues for countries that are members of the European Union. Whilst the report describes some of these issues, it would have been beyond the mandate of the Working Party to try to deal with those. It was noted, however, that these issues were the subject of on-going work by the European Commission and Member States of the Community.

Classification of the Income of a REIT

6   6. Rental income constitutes by far the largest part of the income of REITs. It is therefore assumed that most of the cross-border income derived by REITs would be covered by the provisions of bilateral tax treaties that are similar to Article 6 (Income from Immovable Property) of the OECD Model Tax Convention. Since REITs may also derive income from businesses carried on through immovable property without directly deriving income from such property, income of a REIT may also fall under Article 7 (Business Profits). REITs also derive capital gains from immovable property or securities that would be covered by Article 13 (Capital Gains) of the OECD Model, dividends covered by Article 10 (Dividends), interest from debt instruments (mostly mortgages) covered by Article 11 (Interest) and a small proportion of other types of income.

7   7. Since provisions of tax treaties that are based on Articles 6, 7 and 13 of the OECD Model grant to the State where immovable property is located an unlimited right to tax the income and capital gains derived from that immovable property or its alienation, as well as the business profits and gains attributable to a business carried on in that immovable property if it constitutes a permanent establishment, the typical income of a REIT that invests abroad would, under these provisions, be taxable in the *situs* country, with the country of residence exempting such income or providing a credit for the foreign tax levied on such income. This summary analysis, however, raises a number of issues.

Treaty Entitlement of the REIT

8   8. A first difficulty relates to the determination of the REIT's own treaty entitlement. This is relevant not only as regards the application of the treaty provisions to the income of the REIT but also as regards the application of tax treaties to the distributions of a REIT since, for example, Article 10 (Dividends) of the OECD Model applies to dividends 'paid by a company which is a resident of a Contracting State'.

9. Since the income of a REIT is typically distributed, the REIT is not, in a purely **9** domestic context, taxed on that distributed income. As already mentioned, the tax mechanisms that ensure that result vary from country to country and can include, for example, rules that allow the deduction of REIT dividends or distributions, the tax exemption of a REIT that meets certain conditions, the tax exemption of the income of a REIT that meets certain conditions, the tax exemption of all the REIT's income, the tax exemption of only the part of the REIT's income that is distributed within a specified period of time or rules that allocate the income to the investors rather than to the REIT itself. It seems, however, that in most cases, the REIT would meet the condition of being liable to tax for purposes of the treaty definition of 'resident of a Contracting State', subject to the particular problems arising from the application of tax treaties to trusts. There are a few countries, however, where this may not be the case and this is a question that would need to be clarified on a country-by-country basis during treaty negotiations.

Treaty Entitlement of the REIT Investor

10. In most cases, the investors in a REIT will be clearly entitled to the benefits of tax **10** treaties concluded by their country of residence. It should be noted, however, that a part of investments in REITs come from pension funds and that some countries consider that pension funds are not entitled to treaty benefits absent specific treaty provisions.[2]

Who is the Relevant Taxpayer for Purposes of Tax Treaties?

11. The determination of who is the relevant taxpayer for purposes of the application **11** of tax treaties to the income derived by the REIT raises treaty interpretation issues.

12. It seems clear that absent specific provisions, the determination of whether the tax **12** treaty provisions should be applied at the level of the REIT or at that of its investors will not be uniform between countries.

13. First, differences in REIT structures produce different results. For instance, a REIT **13** may be structured as a contractual or fiduciary arrangement so that the income derived by the REIT is legally that of the investors for purposes of tax treaties and the REIT itself is merely the manager of the funds invested.

14. Second, domestic tax rules may allocate the REIT income to a taxpayer who is **14** different from the one who is the legal owner of the income. Under such rules, whilst

---

2. This issue is discussed in paras 8.1 to 8.3 of the Commentary on Article 4 of the OECD Model Tax Convention.

the REIT might be the legal owner of the income, it may be considered not to be the economic owner of the income for purposes of taxation. Also, the REIT might be considered to be simply a pass-through entity for purposes of taxation. Conversely, it may be considered that whilst the income of a REIT is simply passed-through to the investors in the form of a distribution, that distribution does not retain the tax character of the underlying income so that the REIT remains the relevant taxpayer for purposes of the application of tax treaties.

15   15. The principles developed in the OECD Partnership Report are relevant to deal with cases where REITs are treated as pass-through entities. However, in many cases, the REIT will not constitute a transparent entity as described in the Partnership Report and will be the relevant taxpayer for purposes of the application of the provisions of tax treaties to the income that it derives from other countries.

16   16. Since, however, the REIT will not pay residence State tax on that income to the extent that it is distributed, this will create difficulties with respect to the application of domestic and treaty provisions for the relief of double taxation. The Working Party considered that, as a general rule, it would be appropriate, as a policy matter, for a State to allow relief of double taxation for any source tax that has been levied on the REIT even if the residence State imposes tax on the investors rather than on the REIT itself. Where the domestic law of a country does not provide for the flow-through of relief, the Working Party considers that that country should try to find a way to provide such relief.

17   17. The Working Party also concluded that the question of the application of tax treaties to REIT income was intertwined with that of the treaty treatment of REIT distributions to foreign investors so that these two questions had to be examined together.

How Should REIT Distributions to Foreign Investors be Treated Under Tax Treaties?

18   18. The application of tax treaties to REIT distributions to foreign investors involves significant tax policy and treaty interpretation issues.

19   19. As a matter of treaty interpretation, it seems clear that where the REIT is a company that qualifies as a treaty resident to whom the underlying income is allocated for treaty purposes, its distributions to foreign investors constitute dividends covered by Article 10 of the OECD Model. This, however, will often not be the case as the REIT may be structured as a trust or as a contractual or fiduciary arrangement or may be treated as a pass-through vehicle under domestic tax law.

20   20. The Working Party therefore went beyond a strict legal analysis based on existing provisions of tax treaties to try to articulate a tax treaty policy that would be generally applicable to REITs.

21   21. The starting point of that policy analysis was that the State in which the immovable property is located should have the primary, unlimited, right to tax that income. This has been a fundamental and consistent feature of provisions based on the OECD Model Tax Convention for a long time and whilst alternative views were briefly discussed, it was quickly concluded that this approach should not be challenged.

22. The real policy question, however, is whether a distribution from a REIT should be **22** considered to be income from immovable property or income from investing in a security.

23. On the one hand, one could look at the underlying income of the REIT and. consider **23** that the distribution of that income is nothing more than the allocation of a share of that income. Under that view, it would be appropriate to treat that income as income from immovable property in the hands of each investor and require each of them to be taxed as if he/she had directly earned that income. That, however, would mean that the income would be typically subject to a high rate of tax and that the investors could be subject to filing requirements in the country where the immovable property is located.

24. On the other hand, one could consider that the investor is merely looking for an **24** income distributing security that is, or is similar to, any publicly-traded share and should obtain the same treaty treatment as is normally given to the return on shares, which is covered by Article 10 (Dividends). A small investor in a REIT has no control over the immovable property acquired by the REIT and no connection to the particular property held by the REIT. Such a small investor cannot be viewed as having made an investment in the underlying immovable property held by the REIT any more than a shareholder of a multinational company can be viewed as having made an investment in the particular assets held by the company. Rather, the small investor invested in the REIT as an entity. The small investor is looking to the distributions from the REIT and the appreciation in its REIT interest for its investment returns just as a shareholder in a multinational company is looking to corporate dividends and share appreciation for its investment return.

25. It was noted, however, that there is a fundamental difference between a REIT **25** distribution and other dividends since other dividends represent the after-tax distribution of income that has already been taxed in the country of residence of the company and/or in the country where the profits of that company arose. REIT distributions, on the other hand, represent income that has not been subjected to residence-based taxation at the entity level. To the extent that the treaty treatment of dividends takes account of the corporate level taxation, which seems clear in the case of the lower rate applicable to substantial inter-corporate shareholdings, it could therefore be argued that a different treatment is warranted for REIT distributions. There are, however, other circumstances in which a reduced rate of withholding tax is applied notwithstanding that there is no underlying corporate tax. This would be the case with respect to interest on bonds, which is another type of security where there is no underlying corporate level tax (since interest is deductible) and in respect of which tax treaties generally provide for an even lower rate of tax than that applicable to dividends. REIT distributions are, of course, more of the nature of a return on equity than on debt. Even in the case of dividends, however, the treaty rules applicable to the income from portfolio investment usually provide for lower source taxation than on income from

direct investment in immovable property, probably because the most practical, and usual, way of collecting tax from portfolio investment is through a withholding tax on the gross return that does not take account of the investment expenses of the investor (e.g. leverage costs).

26   26. The Working Party noted that immovable property is increasingly viewed by capital markets as a separate asset class with mixed attributes of both equity and debt investment. Industry participants in the Group that prepared the first draft of this report have stressed that the yields on such an investment reflect a combination of attributes of both stocks and bonds.[3] Moreover, the very high distribution rates for REITs' income mean that the source tax levied in accordance with Article 10 will be substantial even though the rate of such a tax is at the rate provided for portfolio dividends. This is in contrast to other corporate vehicles, where the taxes generated by taxing dividends paid to foreign shareholders is much less substantial because of the low level of dividend distribution. By way of illustration, for the period from 1972 to 2006, distributed income represented an average of 57.1% of the total return for U.S. REITs in the FTSE NAREIT Equity REIT Index, while distributed income represented an average of just 28.2% of the total return for the securities in the Standard and Poor's 500 Index and just 26.4% of the total return for the securities in the Dow Jones Wilshire 5000.

27   27. For these reasons, it was concluded that an appropriate treaty policy would be to treat a REIT distribution to a small investor in the same way as a portfolio equity investment. It also concluded, however, that limiting the rate of source taxation to that applicable to portfolio dividends would not be appropriate in the case of an investor holding a large investment in a REIT. For such a large investor, the investment in the REIT may be a substitute for a direct investment in the underlying property of the REIT. In this situation, limiting the source State tax on distributions from the REIT to the reduced rate applicable to portfolio dividends or the even lower rate applicable to direct dividends would seem inappropriate; such distributions should be subjected to the full tax rate provided by domestic law.

28   28. That policy could be implemented by providing that a distribution from a domestic REIT to a non-resident investor who owns an interest of less than 10% in the REIT would be subject to tax in the source-country at a rate not exceeding the portfolio dividend rate (i.e., 15%) provided in subparagraph 10(2)(b) of the OECD Model Tax Convention. Conversely, a distribution from a REIT to an investor who owns an interest of 10% or more in the REIT would not be eligible to any rate limitation under Article 10. That approach should apply regardless of the legal form of the REIT so that distributions from a REIT that are not covered by Article 10 would be treated in the same way.

---

3. See Ibbotson Associates, 'Commercial Real Estate: The Role of Global Listed Real Estate Equities in a Strategic Asset allocation' (November 2006), found at http://corporate.morningstar.com/ib/documents/MethodologyDocuments/IBBAssociates/GlobalRealEstateWhitePaper.pdf

29. The implementation of such a policy would require alternative treaty provisions **29** that could be adopted by States wishing to do so. The Working Party concluded that such alternative treaty provisions should be included in the Commentary on Article 10 of the OECD Model Tax Convention and it is therefore proposed to include the following new paragraphs in that Commentary (cross-references to that new section of the Commentary could also be added in the Commentary on Articles 6, 13 and 23).

Add the Following Heading and New Paragraphs 67.1 to 67.7 to the Commentary on Article 10

IV. DISTRIBUTIONS BY REAL ESTATE INVESTMENT TRUSTS

67.1 In many States, a large part of portfolio investment in immovable property is done **30** through Real Estate Investment Trusts (REITs). A REIT may be loosely described as a widely held company, trust or contractual or fiduciary arrangement that derives its income primarily from long-term investment in immovable property, distributes most of that income annually and does not pay income tax on the income related to immovable property that is so distributed. The fact that the REIT vehicle does not pay tax on that income is the result of tax rules that provide for a single-level of taxation in the hands of the investors in the REIT.

67.2 The importance and the globalisation of investments in and through REITs have **31** led the Committee on Fiscal Affairs to examine the tax treaty issues that arise from such investments. The results of that work appear in a report entitled 'Tax Treaty Issues Related to REITs'.[4]

67.3 One issue discussed in the report is the tax treaty treatment of cross-border **32** distributions by a REIT. In the case of a small investor in a REIT, the investor has no control over the immovable property acquired by the REIT and no connection to that property. Notwithstanding the fact that the REIT itself will not pay tax on its distributed income, it may therefore be appropriate to consider that such an investor has not invested in immovable property but, rather, has simply invested in a company and should be treated as receiving a portfolio dividend. Such a treatment would also reflect the blended attributes of a REIT investment, which combines the attributes of both shares and bonds. In contrast, a larger investor in a REIT would have a more particular interest in the immovable property acquired by the REIT; for that investor, the investment in the REIT may be seen as a substitute for an investment in the underlying property of the REIT. In this situation, it would not seem appropriate to restrict the source taxation of the distribution from the REIT since the REIT itself will not pay tax on its income.

67.4 States that wish to achieve that result may agree bilaterally to replace paragraph **33** 2 of the Article by the following:

---

4. OECD, Paris, 2008. Reproduced in volume II of the loose-leaf version of the Model at R-. . . .

34 2. However, such dividends may also be taxed in the Contracting State of which the company paying the dividends is a resident and according to the laws of that State, but if the beneficial owner of the dividends is a resident of the other Contracting State (other than a beneficial owner of dividends paid by a company which is a REIT in which such person holds, directly or indirectly, capital that represents at least 10 per cent of the value of all the capital in that company), the tax so charged shall not exceed:

> (a) 5 per cent of the gross amount of the dividends if the beneficial owner is a company (other than a partnership) which holds directly at least 25 per cent of the capital of the company paying the dividends (other than a paying company that is a REIT);
>
> (b) 15 per cent of the gross amount of the dividends in all other cases.

35 According to this provision, a large investor in a REIT is an investor holding, directly or indirectly, capital that represents at least 10% of the value of all the REIT's capital. Countries may, however, agree bilaterally to use a different threshold. Also, the provision applies to all distributions by a REIT; in the case of distributions of capital gains, however, the domestic law of some countries provides for a different threshold to differentiate between a large investor and a small investor entitled to taxation at the rate applicable to portfolio dividends and these countries may wish to amend the provision to preserve that distinction in their treaties. Finally, because it would be inappropriate to restrict the source taxation of a REIT distribution to a large investor, the drafting of subparagraph *a)* excludes dividends paid by a REIT from its application; thus, the subparagraph can never apply to such dividends, even if a company that did not hold capital representing 10% or more of the value of the capital of a REIT held at least 25% of its capital as computed in accordance with paragraph 15 above.

36 67.5 Where, however, the REITs established in one of the Contracting States do not qualify as companies that are residents of that Contracting State, the provision will need to be amended to ensure that it applies to distributions by such REITs.

37 67.6 For example, if the REIT is a company that does not qualify as a resident of the State, paragraphs 1 and 2 of the Article will need to be amended as follows to achieve that result:

38 1. Dividends paid by a company which is a resident, or a REIT organized under the laws, of a Contracting State to a resident of the other Contracting State may be taxed in that other State.

39 2. However, such dividends may also be taxed in, and according to the laws of, the Contracting State of which the company paying the dividends is a resident or, in the case of a REIT, under the laws of which it has been organized, but if the beneficial owner of the dividends is a resident of the other Contracting State (other than a beneficial owner of dividends paid by a company which is a REIT in which such person holds, directly or indirectly, capital that represents at least 10 per cent of the value of all the capital in that company), the tax so charged shall not exceed:

(a) 5 per cent of the gross amount of the dividends if the beneficial owner is a company (other than a partnership) which holds directly at least 25 per cent of the capital of the company paying the dividends (other than a paying company that is a REIT);

(b) 15 per cent of the gross amount of the dividends in all other cases.

40 67.7 Similarly, in order to achieve that result where the REIT is structured 67.7 as a **40** trust or as a contractual or fiduciary arrangement and does not qualify as a company, States may agree bilaterally to add to the alternative version of paragraph 2 set forth in paragraph 67.4 above an additional provision drafted along the following lines:

> For the purposes of this Convention, where a REIT organized under the laws of a Contracting State makes a distribution of income to a resident of the other Contracting State who is the beneficial owner of that distribution, the distribution of that income shall be treated as a dividend paid by a company resident of the first-mentioned State.

Under this additional provision, the relevant distribution would be treated as a **41** dividend and not, therefore, as another type of income (e.g., income from immovable property or capital gain) for the purposes of applying Article 10 and the other Articles of the Convention. Clearly, however, that would not change the characterisation of that distribution for purposes of domestic law so that domestic law treatment would not be affected except for the purposes of applying the limitations imposed by the relevant provisions of the Convention.

Issues Arising from this Approach

30. The Working Party also examined various technical issues related to this approach **42** as well as its possible extension to situations where a foreign REIT invests in a domestic REIT or invests directly in domestic immovable property. The following reflects the conclusion of the Working Party on these various issues.

Definition of REIT

31. A first design issue is how to define a REIT for purposes of the above rules. The **43** Working Party concluded that given the differences in domestic law concerning the structure and features of REITs, this should be dealt with bilaterally. For the purpose of the above provisions, countries would therefore be expected to include in their bilateral conventions specific definitions of REITs that would allow the application of these provisions to their own REITs. Such definitions may, for example, make reference to the relevant domestic provisions that define REITs for domestic tax purposes.

Distinction Between Large and Small Investor

44 32. A first issue related to a possible distinction between large and small investors is to what extent it would be possible to provide for different treatment of distributions, or different treatment of a REIT entity, based on the size of the shareholding. It was suggested that this involved some domestic and EU law principles. For example, it was noted that disclosure rules imposed by market regulators would typically require the disclosure of any investor owning more than a certain percentage (e.g. 5%) of a listed entity.

45 33. Clearly, a large investor should not be allowed to get the benefit of the lower rate applicable to portfolio interests in a REIT by simply dividing its investment in the REIT among a number of associated entities. This is why the provision put forward does not grant the lower rate to an investor who holds 'directly or indirectly' capital that represents at least 10% of the value of the overall capital of a REIT. Also, the lower rate should not be granted in cases of abuse of the provision, for example, where a company with a holding of 10% or more has, shortly before the payment of a distribution, transferred its interests in a REIT to a number of small investors for the purpose of securing the benefits of the lower rate, with a commitment to re-acquire these interests after the distribution. States that do not believe that they can prevent such arrangements through their domestic anti-abuse rules may find it appropriate to supplement the proposed provision by a paragraph subjecting the application of the lower rate to the condition that the interests in a REIT were not acquired primarily for the purpose of taking advantage of that lower rate.

46 34. A second issue is the determination of the level of capital ownership that would trigger the application of the 'large investor' treatment. The approach put forward in this report suggests a threshold of 10% of the value of the capital of the REIT. Countries may, however, agree bilaterally to use a different threshold.

Taxation of Distributions to Large Investors

47 35. It was accepted that, ideally, the tax levied on distributions to large investors should be commensurate with the tax levied on a return from a direct investment in immovable property. While the above provisions do not limit the tax that may be charged in the State in which the immovable property is situated, some States may provide an option to file on a net basis.

Distribution of Capital Gains

48 36. The Working Party generally agreed that it would be appropriate to provide the same treatment for distributions from capital gains and distributions from rental income derived by the REIT. For that reason, the above proposal treats distributions of both types of income in the same way. The same conclusion has generally been reached with respect to all other types of income that could be derived by a REIT. It was noted, however, that in the case of distributions of capital gains, some countries use a different threshold to differentiate between a large investor that is subject to source country tax without limitation under the Convention and a small investor entitled to taxation at the rate applicable to portfolio dividend; these countries may wish to preserve that distinction in their bilateral treaties.

Treatment of Capital Gains on Interests in a REIT

37. The Working Party examined the possible application of paragraph 4 of Article 13 **49** to gains realized on the alienation of an interest in a REIT. Given that the purpose of a REIT is primarily to hold immovable property, the conditions for the application of that paragraph would be met when shares in a REIT are alienated (in the case of REITs that are set up in a non-corporate form, the same result would follow from either paragraph 1 of Article 13, which could apply to some REITs set up as contractual arrangements, or the modified version of paragraph 4 that appears in paragraph 28.5 of the Commentary on Article 13).

38. Whilst it was agreed that applying paragraph 4 to allow the source taxation of gains **50** resulting from the alienation of a large investor's interests in a REIT would be appropriate, different views were expressed as to whether that would also be an appropriate result for gains realized by small investors in a REIT.

39. For some members of the Working Party, paragraph 4 was intended to apply to any **51** gain on the alienation of shares in a company that derives its value primarily from immovable property and there would be no reason to distinguish between a REIT and a publicly held company with respect to the application of that paragraph, especially since a REIT is not taxed on its income. These members considered that as long as a treaty does not provide an exception for the alienation of shares of companies listed on a stock exchange (as suggested in paragraph 28.7 of the Commentary on Article 13), there should not be a special exception for interests in a REIT.

40. Other members of the Working Party, however, disagreed. For them, a small **52** investor's interest in a REIT should be treated as a security rather than as an indirect holding in immovable property. They considered that this treatment of the small investor's interest in a REIT as a security was consistent with this report's conclusion regarding the appropriate treatment of such interest for purposes of the taxation of distributions. These members also indicated that, in practice, it would be very difficult to administer the application of source taxation of gains on small interests in a widely held REIT. Some of them added that since REITs, unlike other entities deriving their value primarily from immovable property, are required to distribute most of their profits, it is unlikely that there would be significant residual profits to which the capital gain tax would apply (as compared to other companies).

53 41. It was also noted that allowing source taxation of such gains could. result in a double exemption if the State of source did not exercise this taxing right and the State of residence of the investor was an exemption country (that problem, which is inherent to paragraph 4 of Article 13, is described in paragraph 28.9 of the Commentary on that Article).

54 42. The Working Party concluded that the Commentary on Article 13, which already discusses possible exceptions to paragraph 4, should be supplemented to address a possible additional exception for gains on small interests in a REIT. It therefore proposes the inclusion of the following new paragraphs in that Commentary.

Renumber Paragraph 28.9 of the Commentary on Article 13 as Paragraph 28.12 and add the Following New Paragraphs 28.9 to 28.11

55 28.9 Finally, a further possible exception relates to shares and similar interests in a Real Estate Investment Trust (see paragraphs 67.1 to 67.7 of the Commentary on Article 10 for background information on REITs). Whilst it would not seem appropriate to make an exception to paragraph 4 in the case of the alienation of a large investor's interests in a REIT, which could be considered to be the alienation of a substitute for a direct investment in immovable property, an exception to paragraph 4 for the alienation of a small investor's interest in a REIT may be considered to be appropriate.

56 28.10 As discussed in paragraph 67.3 of the Commentary on Article 10, it may 10 be appropriate to consider a small investor's interest in a REIT as a security rather than as an indirect holding in immovable property. In this regard, in practice it would be very difficult to administer the application of source taxation of gains on small interests in a widely held REIT. Moreover, since REITs, unlike other entities deriving their value primarily from immovable property, are required to distribute most of their profits, it is unlikely that there would be significant residual profits to which the capital gain tax would apply (as compared to other companies). States that share this view may agree bilaterally to add, before the phrase 'may be taxed in that other State', words such as 'except shares held by a person who holds, directly or indirectly, interests representing less than 10 per cent of all the interests in a company if that company is a REIT'. (If paragraph 4 is amended along the lines of paragraph 28.5 above to cover interests similar to shares, these words should be amended accordingly.)

57 28.11 Some States, however, consider that paragraph 4 was intended to apply 11 to any gain on the alienation of shares in a company that derives its value primarily from immovable property and that there would be no reason to distinguish between a REIT and a publicly held company with respect to the application of that paragraph, especially since a REIT is not taxed on its income. These States consider that as long as there is no exception for the alienation of shares in companies quoted on a stock exchange (see paragraph 28.7 above), there should not be a special exception for interests in a REIT.

Relief of Double Taxation in the State of Residence

43. The approach put forward in this note could require appropriate adjustments to the **58** Article on relief of double taxation. It would be necessary, for instance, to avoid the application of the exemption method in the case of distributions to small investors in a REIT. Since these distributions would be subject to limited source taxation, it would be appropriate to apply the credit method to them. Conversely, distributions to large investors in a REIT, which would be subjected to source taxation without any treaty limit, should be covered by the exemption method if this is the method generally applied by a State (see also paragraph 41 above as regards the risks of double exemption of capital gains).

Application of the Participation Exemption/ EU Parent-Subsidiary Directive

44. Another issue is to what extent domestic rules on participation exemption and, **59** more generally, the EU parent-subsidiary directive, would allow a State to tax a distribution to a large investor at a rate commensurate with the rate applicable to income from immovable property rather than at the rate applicable to a dividend to a large corporate shareholder. To some extent, the answer to that question could depend on the legal structure of the REIT and on whether or not the REIT and the investor could be considered to be tax-exempt.

Distributions to Tax-Exempts (Pension Funds)

45. Paragraph 69 of the Commentary on Article 18 (Pensions) includes an alternative **60** provision that States may use to extend the domestic exemption of income derived by domestic pension funds to income derived by pension funds established in another State. That provision allows States to achieve greater neutrality with respect to the location of capital.

46. The Working Party concluded that, as a matter of policy, distributions from a **61** portfolio investment in a REIT should be treated like other investment income of a pension fund and noted that, as drafted, the alternative provision would appropriately cover that type of income. States contemplating the inclusion of such a provision should, however, consider the policy issue of whether the provision should apply to distributions to a pension fund that holds more than a portfolio investment in a domestic REIT (i.e., 10% or more).

Potential for Base Erosion and Access to Interest Treatment

47. The OECD Model Convention provides that source taxation on interest payments **62** may not exceed 10% but tax treaties often provide that interest payments will not be

taxable in the source country. Many countries have enacted thin capitalisation rules to prevent the erosion of their tax base through interest payments that would be deductible from the tax base without being subject to source taxation.

63 48. The Working Party examined whether the tax treatment of REITs could give rise to a similar base erosion concern. One example that was discussed was that of a REIT that would offer foreign investors the possibility to invest in a combined equity and debt instrument, with the debt component representing almost all the value of the investment. In such a case, a very large part of the REIT profits could effectively be distributed to the investors as interest payments subject to no source taxation.

64 49. It could be argued that the interest payments would be subject to residence taxation in the hands of the investors, although this may not provide a satisfactory response to the source country concern, particularly in the case of tax-exempt or low-tax foreign investors. Also, various design features of a REIT regime may prevent or reduce this risk of base erosion. For example, the REIT regulatory framework or market preferences may make it difficult to highly leverage the REIT and the REIT may be prevented from issuing participating debt instruments.

65 50. Whilst it was noted that at least one country had introduced a thin-capitalization rule in its REIT regime to address the base-erosion concern, the Working Party concluded that this issue was not specific to REITs and that no REIT-specific recommendation should be made to deal with it.

Investment by a Foreign REIT

66 51. The Working Party finally examined whether and how the above proposal on the tax treaty treatment of distributions to foreign investors in a domestic REIT should be extended to a foreign REIT deriving income from domestic immovable property and to a foreign REIT investing in a domestic REIT.

67 52. The industry participants in the Group that prepared the first draft of this report stressed that in order to achieve a more efficient market for portfolio investment in immovable property, REITs established in one country need to be able to invest in foreign countries' immovable property and in REITs established in other countries. Therefore, the tax obstacles that hinder such cross-border investments should be addressed. They also indicated that the adoption of solutions that would avoid the need for the arrangements that are currently used to avoid multiple taxation of such cross-border REIT investments would be beneficial for both REITs and tax administrations.

68 53. It was suggested that EU law may require a country to extend its domestic REIT regime to REITs established in other EU States. This is obviously an important question for EU Member States and it is hoped that it will be addressed as part of the on-going work on taxation and REITs that a Working Group of the European Commission and Member States of the Community is carrying on.

54. This led the Working Party to examine whether treaty provisions based on **69** paragraph 3 of Article 24 of the OECD Model Tax Convention could be interpreted to require a country to extend its domestic REIT regime to a foreign REIT holding domestic immovable property through a permanent establishment. The Working Party concluded that such an interpretation should be rejected and noted that extending the benefit of an exemption granted to a domestic REIT (the distributions from which would be taxed) to such a permanent establishment would result in an undue advantage for the foreign REIT since the distributions of that REIT could not similarly be taxed, in particular because of paragraph 5 of Article 10, by the State where the permanent establishment is located. As explained in paragraph 20 of the Commentary on Article 24:

> . . . the wording of the first sentence of paragraph 3 must be interpreted in the sense that it does not constitute discrimination to tax non-resident persons differently, for practical reasons, from resident persons, as long as this does not result in more burdensome taxation for the former than for the latter. In the negative form in which the provision concerned has been framed, it is the result alone which counts, it being permissible to adapt the mode of taxation to the particular circumstances in which the taxation is levied.

55. As a matter of tax policy, and putting aside practical considerations regarding tax **70** administration and tax collection, the majority of the members of the Group that produced the first draft of this report considered that if an equivalent tax regime could be applied to a foreign REIT, there would be no reason for a country to treat foreign REITs differently from domestic REITs with respect to investment in domestic property. This, however, would require that country to be able to levy and collect an equivalent amount of tax on distributions of domestic income by a foreign REIT as it would levy and collect on distributions of such income by a domestic REIT that would have a similar investor base and similar levels of distributions made at similar intervals, considering that the policy rationale underlying the tax exemption for domestic REITs is that tax will be collected on the income of the REIT at the investor's level rather than at the entity's level.

56. A State wishing to extend the tax benefits of its domestic REIT regime to foreign **71** REITs would, however, face various legal, administrative and compliance issues. These would primarily include:

- the difficulty of identifying which part of the distribution by a foreign REIT would correspond to domestic income;
- the general tax treaty prohibition, found in provisions similar to paragraph 5 of Article 10 of the OECD Model, against taxing distributions by a company resident in another State;
- the practical difficulty of identifying a foreign REIT's large investors and investors who are not entitled to treaty benefits; particularly where the foreign REIT's investors include other REITs;

- difficulties related to the extension of double tax relief on a distribution received by an investor in one REIT to take account of the tax levied on a previous distribution received by that REIT.

72 57. The extension of a domestic REIT regime to foreign REITs would therefore require a trade-off between the basic policy objective of ensuring an equivalent tax treatment and the need to take account of the above issues. The Working Party examined various approaches that could be considered for that purpose, including:

- levying source tax at the time that the foreign REIT that has invested domestically makes a distribution,
- deeming the foreign REIT to be a domestic REIT for treaty purposes, and
- deeming the foreign REIT to have a permanent establishment.

73 These possible approaches and some issues that they raise are discussed in more detail in the Annex.

ANNEX TECHNICAL ANALYSIS OF VARIOUS APPROACHES PUT FORWARD FOR EXTENDING DOMESTIC REIT REGIMES TO FOREIGN REITS

1. As indicated in paragraph 57 of the note, the Working Party examined various **74** approaches that could be considered for the purposes of extending a domestic REIT regime to foreign REITS. The following describes some of these approaches and presents some of the issues that were identified with respect to them.

Subsequent Withholding Tax

2. One approach would be for a State to exempt from domestic tax the income from **75** domestic immovable property derived by a foreign REIT recognized as similar to a domestic REIT, or a distribution from a domestic REIT to such a foreign REIT, but to impose a withholding tax on the subsequent distributions by the foreign REIT to its own interest-holders.

3. Under that approach, the tax on such subsequent distributions by the foreign REIT **76** would include both the tax of the State in which the foreign REIT has been established and that of the State in which the foreign REIT invested (either directly in domestic immovable property or in a domestic REIT).

4. Whilst that approach would primarily be implemented through domestic law **77** changes, it may also require a change to tax treaties in order to avoid the prohibition, found in paragraph 5 of Article 10, against taxing distributions by foreign companies (see below).

Deeming the Foreign REIT to be a Domestic REIT for Tax Treaty Purposes

5. Another approach would be to design treaty rules that would have the effect of **78** deeming immovable property income derived from a State by a foreign REIT recognized as similar to a domestic REIT, as well as a distribution from a domestic REIT to such a foreign REIT, to be the income of a distinct company resident of that State that qualifies as a REIT in that State. That income, or a percentage thereof, would also be deemed to be distributed at regular intervals (such as annually) so as to trigger the application of source taxation rights under Article 10.

Deeming the Foreign REIT to have a Permanent Establishment

6. A third approach would be to design treaty rules that would deem a foreign REIT that **79** holds immovable property in a State, or that holds an interest in a domestic REIT in such State, to have a permanent establishment in that State to which the income from such immovable property or distributions from such domestic REIT would be attrib

utable. These rules would also deem a distribution of the income of that permanent establishment to its head office and would allow the source State to tax this deemed distribution.

Application of these Approaches to Foreign REITs Investing Directly in Domestic Immovable Property

80 7. As regards the income from a direct investment by a foreign REIT in immovable property of a given State, the three approaches described above would ensure that, as would be the case for income derived by a domestic REIT, the distributed domestic income of the foreign REIT is not taxed by that State at the time of its realisation by the foreign REIT.

81 8. A first issue that would arise under all these approaches is the determination of the rate of tax at which an actual distribution by the foreign REIT (under the first approach) or a deemed distribution (under the second and third approaches) would be taxable by the source State. The foreign REIT might have large and small investors; also, these investors might be residents of the State where the REIT is established, of the State where the immovable property is located or of third States. In order to apply to the investors in the foreign REIT an approach equivalent to the one put forward in this note as regards investors in a domestic REIT, one possibility would be to adjust the tax rate by looking through the investor REIT to determine the indirect ownership percentages of investors in that REIT. Thus, if all the investors in the foreign REIT were small investors that are residents of the State where the REIT is established, the withholding tax on the distribution to the investor REIT would be imposed at the lower portfolio dividend rate applicable to small investors. If the foreign REIT had other investors not entitled to that lower rate, the withholding tax on the distribution to the investor REIT would be imposed at a blended rate based on the proportionate interests held indirectly by the various categories of investors. For this purpose, it was suggested that the determination of whether the foreign REIT has large investors could be based on filings under rules requiring public disclosure of ownership by large investors. Such a look-through approach, however, would raise considerable administrative and compliance difficulties. The Working Party noted that some of these difficulties are currently being examined by the Informal Consultative Group on Collective Investment Vehicles with a view to addressing these issues in a broader context.

82 9. The fact that the distributions by the foreign REIT will not come exclusively from the income derived from immovable property in the source State creates an additional issue with respect to the first approach. Since, under that approach, tax would be imposed on the actual distribution by the foreign REIT, it would be necessary to identify which part of that distribution can reasonably be attributed to the income derived from the source State. Also, since losses realised outside the source State could reduce or eliminate actual distributions by the foreign REIT in a case where substantial income is derived from the source State, States would have to decide either to accept that result or to introduce rules deeming a distribution of the source-State income to have been made in such a case.

10. The second and third approaches would avoid these issues by taxing deemed **83** distributions of the income arising from the source State instead of actual distributions by the foreign REIT. By doing so, however, these approaches could be seen as maintaining a significant difference between the tax treatment of domestic REITs and foreign REITs. Also, these approaches could create difficulties as regards the elimination of double taxation in the State of residence of the investor, which would tax the actual distributions. Additional rules might therefore be needed to ensure that relief of double taxation is granted under these approaches.

11. Under paragraph 5 of Article 10 of the OECD Model Tax Convention, a State is **84** prevented from taxing distributions by a company resident in the other Contracting State. Since the first approach would have the practical effect of taxing the distributions by a foreign REIT, an exception to that treaty rule would seem to be required. A similar exception may also be required for the third approach because that approach might be considered to result in the taxation of the undistributed profits of the foreign REIT to the extent that it deems a distribution of income by the deemed permanent establishment to the head office of the foreign REIT. Since the second approach would deem a distribution to be made by a resident company, however, it would not require such an exception.

12. A related issue that could arise under the first approach, but which would probably **85** be avoided under the second and third approaches, would be the practical implementation of the taxation of the distributions by the foreign REIT. If the State of residence of the foreign REIT were required to administer the tax levied by the State of source, it may be put in the difficult position of having to apply a withholding tax agreed to between the State of source and a third State where some of the foreign REIT's investors might be residing.

13. In order for any of these three approaches to be effective, the treaty rules that would **86** be designed to implement them would need to be associated with corresponding domestic law provisions. Whilst treaty rules would seem sufficient to ensure that taxation is not levied by the source State upon the realisation of income from domestic investment by a foreign REIT, in most countries changes to domestic rules would be required in order to impose tax on the actual or deemed distributions by the foreign REIT.

Application of these Approaches to Foreign REITs Investing in Domestic REITs

14. The application of the approach put forward in this note for the tax treaty treatment **87** of foreign investors in a domestic REIT to a foreign REIT that invests in a domestic REIT raises similar issues as those examined above as regards direct investment by a foreign REIT in domestic immovable property.

88   15. One difference, however, concerns the determination of the rate applicable to the actual distribution by the foreign REIT (under the first approach) or the deemed distribution (under the second and third approaches). Since the foreign REIT may itself qualify as a small investor in the domestic REIT, the determination of the treaty rate that should apply to such distributions requires a different analysis:

- If the foreign REIT qualifies as a small investor in the domestic REIT, one could consider that the foreign REIT should be entitled to the reduced rate of dividend withholding tax applicable to small investors. Some countries, however, might be reluctant to follow that approach where the foreign REIT is not considered to be a resident entitled to treaty benefits, where there are third-country investors in the foreign REIT or where it would be possible for foreign investors to divide a large investment in a domestic REIT through a number of foreign REITs each qualifying as a small investor in the domestic REIT (if it is not possible to prevent this through the approaches discussed in paragraph 33 of the note).
- If the foreign REIT is a large investor in the domestic REIT, the reduced rate of dividend withholding tax applicable to small investors nevertheless could be applied if the State considers that administrative and compliance difficulties do not justify trying to collect the extra tax that would be payable by large investors or third-country small investors in the foreign REIT and furthermore considers that REITs typically are not a vehicle that would lend itself to investors seeking inappropriately to obtain treaty benefits.
- A country, however, may be reluctant to apply the reduced rate applicable to small investors if the foreign REIT itself had large investors. The look-through approach discussed in paragraph 8 above could be used to overcome that difficulty by looking through the investor base of the foreign REIT in order to determine the proportion of large investors (and, possibly, of third country investors).

APPENDIX B

The Granting of Treaty Benefits with Respect to the Income of Collective Investment Vehicles Public Discussion Draft 9 December 2009 to 31 January 2010 Centre for Tax Policy and Administration

9 December 2009

THE GRANTING OF TREATY BENEFITS WITH RESPECT TO THE INCOME OF COLLECTIVE INVESTMENT VEHICLES

Public Discussion Draft

This Report contains proposed changes to the Commentary on the OECD Model Tax Convention dealing with the question of the extent to which either collective investment vehicles (CIVs) or their investors are entitled to treaty benefits on income received by the CIVs. The Report is a modified version of the Report "Granting of Treaty Benefits with respect to the Income of Collective Investment Vehicles" of the Informal Consultative Group on the Taxation of Collective Investment Vehicles and Procedures for Tax Relief for Cross-Border Investors (ICG) which was released on 12 January 2009.[1] In that original Report, the ICG addressed the legal and policy issues specific to CIVs and formulated a comprehensive set of recommendations addressing the issues presented by CIVs in the cross-border context.

---

1. The January 2009 report is available at http://www.oecd.org/document/27/0,3343,en_2649_33 747_41962651_1_1_1_1,00.html.

The ICG invited the OECD Committee on Fiscal Affairs (CFA) to refer these recommendations to its Working Party 1 (WP1) on Tax Conventions and Related Questions (the CFA subsidiary body responsible for changes to the OECD Model Tax Convention) for further consideration. This Report by WP1 is the result of the subsequent work on these recommendations. The main conclusions and recommendations of the Report are similar to those in the ICG Report, with some modifications that reflect the varied experiences of the WP1 delegates. Like the ICG Report, this report therefore analyses the technical questions of whether a CIV should be considered a "person", a "resident of a Contracting State" and the "beneficial owner" of the income it receives under treaties that, like the OECD Model Tax Convention, do not include a specific provision dealing with CIVs *(i.e.* the vast majority of existing treaties). Further, the Report includes proposed changes to the Commentary on the Model Tax Convention to reflect the conclusions of the Working Party with respect to these issues.

Although these proposed changes to the Commentary will clarify the treatment of CIVs, it is clear that at least some forms of CIVs in some countries will not meet the requirements to claim treaty benefits on their own behalf. Accordingly, the Report also considers the appropriate treatment of such CIVs under both existing treaties and future treaties.

With respect to existing treaties, the Report concludes that, if a CIV is not entitled to claim benefits in its own right, its investors should in principle be able to claim treaty benefits and that countries should adopt procedures to allow a CIV to make the claim on behalf of investors.

With respect to future treaties, the Report includes proposed amendments to the Commentary on Article 1 of the Model Tax Convention to include a number of optional provisions for countries to consider in their future treaty negotiations. Inclusion of one or more of these provisions in bilateral treaties would provide certainty to CIVs, investors and intermediaries.

The Report also addresses several ancillary issues, including the procedures that could be adopted to determine the proportion of treaty-eligible investors under either existing treaties or a future treaty provision.

The Committee invites interested parties to send their comments on this discussion draft **before 31 January 2010.** It is expected that once finalised, the Commentary changes will be included in the next update to the OECD Model Tax Convention, which is tentatively scheduled for the second part of 2010. Comments should be sent electronically (in Word format) to:

Jeffrey Owens
Director, CTPA
OECD
2, rue André Pascal
75775 Paris
FRANCE
e-mail: jeffrey.owens@oecd.org

Unless otherwise requested at the time of submission, comments submitted to the OECD in response to this invitation will be posted on the OECD website.

This document is a discussion draft released for the purpose of inviting comments from interested parties. It does not necessarily reflect the final views of the OECD and its member countries.

TABLE OF CONTENTS

Executive Summary

This Report is a modified version of the Report "Granting of Treaty Benefits with respect to the Income of Collective Investment Vehicles" of the Informal Consultative Group on the Taxation of Collective Investment Vehicles and Procedures for Tax Relief for Cross-Border Investors (ICG) which was released on 12 January 2009. In that original Report, the ICG addressed the legal and policy issues specific to collective investment vehicles (CIVs) and formulated a comprehensive set of recommendations addressing the issues presented by CIVs in the cross-border context.

The ICG invited the OECD Committee on Fiscal Affairs (CFA) to refer these recommendations to its Working Party 1 (WP1) on Tax Conventions and Related Questions (the CFA subsidiary body responsible for changes to the OECD Model Tax Convention) for further consideration. This Report by WP1 is the result of the subsequent work on these recommendations. The main conclusions and recommendations of the Report are similar to those in the ICG Report, with some modifications that reflect the varied experiences of the WP1 delegates. Like the ICG Report, this report therefore analyses the technical questions of whether a CIV should be considered a "person", a "resident of a Contracting State" and the "beneficial owner" of the income it receives under treaties that, like the OECD Model Tax Convention, do not include a specific provision dealing with CIVs (*i.e.* the vast majority of existing treaties). Further, the Report includes proposed changes to the Commentary on the Model Tax Convention to reflect the conclusions of the Working Party with respect to these issues. Although the Report includes an analysis by WP1 of the application of the "beneficial owner" requirement to the specific case of CIVs, the conclusions with respect to CIVs should not be seen as pre-judging WP1's continuing work on the "beneficial owner" requirement more generally.

Although these proposed changes to the Commentary will clarify the treatment of CIVs, it is clear that at least some forms of CIVs in some countries will not meet the requirements to claim treaty benefits on their own behalf. Accordingly, the Report also considers the appropriate treatment of such CIVs under both existing treaties and future treaties.

With respect to existing treaties, the Report concludes that, if a CIV is not entitled to claim benefits in its own right, its investors should in principle be able to claim treaty benefits. The Report reflects different views regarding whether such a right should be limited to investors who are residents of the Contracting State in which the CIV is organised, or whether that right should be extended to treaty-eligible residents of third States. In any event, administrative difficulties in many cases effectively prevent individual claims by investors. Accordingly, the Report concludes that countries should adopt procedures to allow a CIV to make the claim on behalf of investors.

With respect to future treaties, the Report endorses the ICG recommendation that the Commentary on Article 1 of the Model Tax Convention should be expanded to include a number of optional provisions for countries to consider in their future treaty negotiations. Inclusion of one or more of these provisions in bilateral treaties would provide certainty to CIVs, investors and intermediaries. The favoured approach for such a provision would treat a CIV as a resident of a Contracting State and the beneficial owner of its income, rather than adopting a full look-through approach. Because different views were expressed in both the ICG and WP1 on the issue of whether treaty-eligible residents of third countries should be taken into account in determining the extent to which the income of a CIV should be entitled to treaty benefits, the proposed Commentary includes alternative provisions that adopt different approaches with respect to the treatment of treaty-eligible residents of third countries. The proposed Commentary also includes an alternative provision that would adopt a full look-through approach. The look-through approach would be appropriate in cases where the investors, such as pension funds, would have been eligible for a lower, or zero, rate of withholding had they invested directly in the underlying securities.

The Report also addresses several ancillary issues, including the procedures that could be adopted to determine the proportion of treaty-eligible investors under either existing treaties or a future treaty provision. In addition, the Report discusses a possible provision that would allow an investor in a CIV to claim foreign tax credits for withholding taxes suffered at the level of the CIV, although it does not include any changes to the Commentary on the Model Tax Convention relating to this issue.

I.   INTRODUCTION

Portfolio investors in securities frequently make and hold those investments by pooling   **1**
their funds with other investors in a collective investment vehicle (CIV), rather than
investing directly. This occurs because of the economic efficiency and other advantages CIVs provide. There are several different forms CIVs take, depending on the
country in which they are established (e.g., companies, limited partnerships, trusts,
contractual arrangements). The growth in investments held through CIVs has been
very substantial in recent years and is expected to continue. Most countries have dealt
with the domestic tax issues arising from groups of small investors who pool their
funds in CIVs. In many cases, this is reflected in legislation that sets out specific tax
treatment that may have significant conditions. The primary result is that most
countries now have a tax system that provides for neutrality between direct investments and investments through a CIV, at least when the investors, the CIV, and the
investment are all located in the same country.

One of the primary purposes of tax treaties is to reduce tax barriers to cross-border   **2**
trade and investment. Treaties do this by allocating taxing jurisdiction over a person's
income between that person's country of residence and the country of source of the
income, in order to avoid double taxation. For example, treaties typically limit a source
State's taxing rights over dividends, interest and capital gains derived by a resident of
another State from holding investment securities in the source State. At the same time,
countries generally do not want those tax treaties to create instances of unanticipated
double non- taxation. In particular, countries may want to ensure, either through
explicit provisions in their double tax treaties, or by applying anti-abuse principles in
their domestic laws, that only residents of the treaty partner are entitled to treaty
benefits. With these objectives in mind, an increasing number of countries have begun
specifically addressing at least some issues presented by CIVs in their bilateral tax
treaties. These provisions, however, are by nature bilateral and may therefore not
address the frequent situation where the investors, the investment and the CIV are
located in three or more different countries.

In 2006, the Committee on Fiscal Affairs (the "Committee") established the Informal   **3**
Consultative Group on the Taxation of Collective Investment Vehicles and Procedures
for Tax Relief for Cross-Border Investors (the "ICG"). In January 2009, the Committee
approved the release for public comment of the ICG's report with respect to the legal
and policy issues relating specifically to CIVs (i.e., the extent to which either the CIVs
or their investors are entitled to treaty benefits) as well as a second report by the ICG
on "best practices" regarding procedures for making and granting claims for treaty
benefits for intermediated structures more generally. This Report, which adopts the
ICG's report with some modifications, focuses exclusively on the legal and policy
issues relating to CIVs.

For purposes of this Report, the term "CIV" is limited to funds that are widely-held,   **4**
hold a diversified portfolio of securities and are subject to investor-protection regulation in the country in which they are established. The term would include "funds of

funds" that achieve diversification by investing in other CIVs that themselves hold diversified portfolios of investments. "Intermediated structures" relates to the holding of securities, including interests in CIVs, through layers of financial intermediaries. However, issues of treaty entitlement with respect to investments through private equity funds, hedge funds or trusts or other entities that do not fall within the definition of CIV set out in this paragraph were not considered during the preparation of this Report.

5   Section II of this Report provides background regarding the benefits of CIVs and the structure of the industry. Section III discusses the application of current treaty rules to CIVs under treaties that, like the Model Tax Convention, do not include a specific provision dealing with CIVs. Section IV describes certain considerations that countries that are negotiating new treaties may want to take into account when determining whether the results that otherwise would apply to CIVs established in their jurisdictions under the analysis of Section III are appropriate or whether they should be modified by adopting new provisions addressing CIVs. Section V consists of additions to the Commentary on Article 1 incorporating such possible new provisions.

II.   BACKGROUND

2.1   Benefits of Investing Through CIVs

6   Nearly US$20 trillion currently is invested through CIVs worldwide.[2] This number can only be expected to grow because of the numerous advantages provided to small investors who invest through CIVs.

7   A small investor who tried to by-pass CIVs and other intermediaries and invest directly would incur substantial costs. Finance theory instructs the investor to diversify his risks between equity and debt securities, real estate, and other assets. Now investors are urged to diversify across international markets as well, in order to hedge currency and market risk. In addition, they are supposed to change their allocations of assets over time to ensure their risk profile matches their age and timeline to retirement, etc. A small investor who tried to satisfy all of those demands through directing his own portfolio would spend substantial time and incur significant transaction costs that might be out of all proportion to the actual amount invested.

8   CIVs allow small investors to gain the benefits of economies of scale even if they have relatively little invested. They provide access to a number of markets that might be closed to the small investor. These benefits are provided in a form that is highly liquid, as securities issued by a CIV may be redeemed on a frequent (daily, weekly or monthly) basis at net asset value (NAV) or can be transferred with minimal restrictions. CIVs also allow for highly efficient reinvestment of income. Distributions on portfolio securities

---

2. These figures do not take account of amounts held through private equity funds or hedge funds. ICI 2009 Fact Book, http://www.icifactbook.org/pdf/09_fb_table58.pdf.

held by the CIV can be reinvested by the CIV. It would be difficult for individual investors to reinvest small distributions on an efficient basis.

In addition, investors in CIVs benefit from the market experience and insights of **9** professional money managers. The cost of these money managers is spread over all of the CIV's investors. Moreover, a small investor who buys interests in a CIV can instantly achieve the benefits of diversification that otherwise would require much greater investment. For example, an employee who puts $100 each month into his employer's retirement plan or a personal savings plan that is invested in a broad market index has diversified his risk of loss as much as if he had bought a share of stock in each company in the index, but at a substantially lower cost than if he had bought the individual stocks.

Governments have long recognised the importance of CIVs as a complement to other **10** savings vehicles in terms of facilitating retirement security. In many countries, participants in defined contribution retirement plans invest primarily in CIVs. Because CIVs allow small investments, they are ideally suited for such periodic savings plans. They are highly liquid, allowing withdrawals as needed by retirees. With ageing populations in many countries, CIVs will become increasingly important.

2.2   *Structure of the CIV Industry*

CIVs typically are organised by financial services firms (including securities firms, **11** banks and insurance companies). The organising firm often is referred to as the CIV's "manager". The CIV manager typically will have hundreds or thousands of employees. The manager provides services such as portfolio management (advisory) and transfer agency (shareholder recordkeeping). In some cases, the manager may select other firms to sub-advise part, or all, of the portfolio.[3] The manager also may decide to hire unaffiliated parties to perform other services, such as legal and audit services, tax consulting, custodial services and others.

With respect to the portfolio, the adviser decides which securities the CIV will hold, and **12** when they will be bought or sold. The adviser thus will research securities and anticipate market movements. Even in the case of "index funds" (*i.e.* funds the aim of which is to match the movements of an index of a specific financial market), the adviser must decide whether the CIV will hold all of the securities in the index, or whether some smaller sample of the relevant securities will provide essentially the same return as the index, but at a lower cost. The adviser must also ensure that the CIV's portfolio is consistent with applicable regulations. Typically, there will be regulatory requirements relating to concentration of investments, restricting a CIV's ability to acquire a controlling interest in a company, prohibiting or restricting certain types of investments, and limiting the use of leverage by the CIV.

---

3. Hereafter, the term "adviser" will be used to describe the person with portfolio-manager responsibilities, whether that person is the manager or a sub-adviser.

13 Investments by the CIV could be domestic or international. International diversification of investment portfolios is becoming more significant. For example, over 25% of all equity assets held by U.S. CIVs are issued by non-U.S. companies.[4] About 30% of the assets of U.K. CIVs are invested outside the United Kingdom.[5] More than one-third of the assets of Japanese CIVs are foreign securities.[6] Assets of Luxembourg, Swiss and Irish funds are predominantly invested outside of their home market.[7] As more investments are made cross-border, the issue of CIVs' qualification for treaty benefits is becoming increasingly important.

14 Interests in the CIV are distributed through affiliated and/or unaffiliated firms. Typically, the CIV will have a distributor related to the manager. This distributor will enter into distribution arrangements with other firms that will distribute CIV shares or units. There are two distinct types of markets for CIVs – "domestic" and "global". In this context, the term refers to the location of the investors, not the investments.

15 In the case of the domestic CIV market, the CIV and essentially all of its investors are located in the same country. This situation may arise because of securities law restrictions on the public offering of non-domestic CIVs. In other cases, tax consider-ations applicable to non-domestic CIVs or to non-resident investors in a domestic CIV may make them uneconomic (e.g. U.S. passive foreign investment company rules or local tax advantages). There also may be no identifiable reason, other than investors' preferences for the form of investment vehicle with which they are most familiar.

16 The global CIV market is one in which the CIV and a significant portion of its investors are located in different countries. The global CIV can be much more efficient – it can benefit from the economies of scale described above to a greater extent than smaller CIVs. Taken to its extreme, a manager would create a single CIV for each asset class or portfolio type. This may not be possible, for the reasons described in paragraph 15. However, regulators see the benefits of a smaller number of larger CIVs, and regulatory changes, such as the UCITS Directive within the European Union,[8] are designed to encourage global business.

17 Distribution of interests in the CIV is also highly regulated. Many jurisdictions require the delivery of a disclosure statement (i.e. prospectus), which may be reviewed by the regulator. Sales of interests in the CIV are effected through regulated entities that are subject to "know your customer" rules. However, there are a number of different

---

4. http://www.icifactbook.org/pdf/08_fb_table04.pdf.
5. Asset Management in the UK 2007", published by the Investment Management Association, UK (www.investmentuk.org).
6. Data regarding the holdings of Japanese CIVs is published by The Investment Trusts Association at http://www.toushin.or.jp/result/index.html.
7. For example, as of June 2008 approximately 70% of the assets under management of Swiss-domiciled CIVs were invested outside Switzerland (see Swiss National Bank, SNB, Monthly Statistical Bulletin, October 2008 (http://www.snb.ch/en/iabout/stat/statpub/statmon/stats/statmon).
8. The Council Directive of 20 December 1985 on the coordination of laws, regulations and administrative provisions relating to undertakings for collective investment in transferable securities (UCITS) (No. 85/611/EEC), as amended.

distribution channels. Direct share purchases are effected between the ultimate investor and the CIV or its transfer agent/paying agent. However, in almost all markets, direct purchases (and holdings) are a small proportion of the investments in the CIV. Much more common are indirect share purchases through one or more intermediaries (e.g. securities firms, banks, insurance companies and independent financial advisers).

Interests in CIVs acquired through intermediaries often are registered at the CIV level **18** through nominee/street name accounts. One reason for this is competitive – intermediaries view customers' identities as highly valuable proprietary information. Another reason is efficiency – intermediaries aggregate their customers' purchases and sales each day and effect only a net purchase or a net sale each day in the nominee account. While investments in a CIV are typically long-term, a CIV's shareholder base may change every day, as new shares are issued and existing shares are redeemed (or as shares trade on an exchange). Because of nominee accounts, the CIV's manager may not be aware of changes in its underlying investors.

CIVs thus act as both issuers of securities and investors in securities. As a result, there **19** may be layers of intermediaries both above the CIV (*i.e.* between the issuer of the security in which the CIV is invested and the CIV), and below the CIV (*i.e.* between the CIV and the beneficial owner of the interests in the CIV). In many cases, those intermediaries will not be located in the country in which the issuer is located and may not be located in the country in which the investor is located. Accordingly, CIVs present issues as regards what they can and should accept from other intermediaries in order to comply with their own withholding tax obligations, and what they can and should provide to withholding agents in order to claim the benefits of tax treaties. These issues have an important practical impact as they result in significant amounts of withholding taxes paid in excess of the amounts payable pursuant to tax treaties and in significant, sometimes deterrent, compliance costs involved in obtaining the applicable treaty relief.

Difficulties in claiming treaty benefits at the time payment are made, and delays in **20** payment of refunds, reduce the return to any investor unless, in the case of a refund, it is accompanied by interest to compensate for the delay. However, there are added dimensions to such difficulties and delays when the investor is a CIV. Investors in CIVs may change daily, making it extremely difficult, if not impossible, to track particular income streams to particular investors. For example, an investor could hold shares in a CIV on 15 June, when the CIV receives a dividend. If the investor redeems or sells those shares on 1 July, the investor generally will recognise a gain or loss. To the extent that the CIV is required to allocate income to particular investors, the remaining or future investors in the CIV generally would be credited with the dividend, even if they did not own shares in the CIV at the time the dividend was received. The difficulty in tracing of course also is compounded by the fact that interests in CIVs frequently are held through layers of intermediaries. In those cases, the CIV's records will show the names of the intermediaries through which the investors hold their interests in the CIV, rather than the names of the investors themselves.

21 CIVs typically calculate NAV every day because it is the basis for subscriptions and redemptions. In calculating the NAV, the CIV must take into account amounts expected to be received, including any withholding tax benefits provided by treaty. If the withholding tax benefits ultimately obtained by the CIV do not correspond to its original assumptions about the amount and timing of such withholding tax benefits, there will be a discrepancy between the real asset value and the NAV used by investors who have purchased, sold or redeemed their interests in the CIV in the interim. Accordingly, CIVs require certainty regarding their qualification for treaty benefits. Unfortunately, for the reasons described in the following section, certainty is in short supply.

III. APPLICATION OF CURRENT TREATY RULES TO CIVs

3.1 Can a CIV Claim the Benefits of Tax Treaties on Its own Behalf?

22 The OECD's Model Tax Convention on Income and on Capital (the "Model Convention"), which is the basis on which about 3,000 bilateral tax treaties worldwide have been negotiated, contains general provisions addressing each Contracting State's taxing rights over income derived by a person resident in the other Contracting State, but it does not have any specific provisions relating to CIVs. In the absence of specific rules applicable to CIVs, a CIV will be entitled to the benefits of a convention in its own right only if it is a person that is a resident of a Contracting State. It may also have to be the beneficial owner of the relevant income. In practice, issues have arisen with respect to each of these requirements, which are addressed in turn below.

a) *Is a CIV a "person"?*

23 The determination of whether a CIV is a person begins with the legal structure of the CIV. CIVs take different legal forms in OECD member countries. In Canada and the United States, both companies and trusts are commonly used. In Australia, New Zealand and Japan, the trust is the predominant form; this also used to be the case in the United Kingdom, but that country has recently introduced corporate vehicles. In many European countries, both joint ownership vehicles (such as *fonds communs de placement)* and companies (such as *sociétés d'investissement à capital variable)* are commonly used. In all of these countries, of course, there are also forms of custodianship arrangements that are purely contractual in nature.

24 Paragraph 2 of the Commentary on Article 3 states that the definition of the term "person" that is found in the Model Convention is not exhaustive and should be given a very wide sense. That paragraph also provides the example of a foundation *(fondation, Stiftung)* as an arrangement that may fall within the meaning of the term "person" because it is treated as a body corporate for tax purposes.

Applying this guidance to the case of CIVs, a CIV structured as a company clearly **25** would constitute a person. However, in the absence of specific provisions, a CIV that is treated merely as a form of joint ownership, and not as a person, under the tax law of the State in which it is established clearly would not constitute a person for purposes of tax treaties.

The issue may be less clear in the case of a CIV that is structured as a trust. Under the **26** domestic tax law of most common law countries, the trust, or the trustees acting collectively in their capacity as such, constitutes a taxpayer. Accordingly, failing to treat such a trust as a person would also prevent it from being treated as a resident despite the fact that, as a policy matter, it seems logical to treat it as a resident when the country in which it is established treats it as a taxpayer and a resident. The fact that the tax law of the country where the trust is established would treat it as a taxpayer would be indicative that the trust is a person for treaty purposes. In practice, it seems that few countries have denied benefits to CIVs in the form of trusts solely on the grounds that the trust is not a person. This may be because those countries in which trusts are common to make it a point to resolve this question by modifying the definition of "person" to specifically include trusts. Because some countries, particularly civil law countries, may not recognise the concept of a trust in their domestic law, negotiators may want to continue the practice of including such modified definitions in future treaties.

b)   Is a CIV a "resident" of a Contracting State?

The determination of whether a CIV that qualifies as a person is a resident of a **27** Contracting State depends on the tax treatment of the CIV in the Contracting State in which it is established. The tax treatment of CIVs varies considerably from country to country, even though a consistent goal is to ensure that there is only one level of tax, at either the CIV or the investor level. Thus, the intent is to ensure neutrality between direct investments and investments through a CIV, at least when the investors, the CIV, and the investment are all located in the same country.

In some States, a CIV established therein is treated as fiscally transparent ('flow- **28** through'); that is, the holders of interests in the CIV are liable to tax on the income received by the CIV, rather than the CIV itself being liable to tax on such income. Other States regard the CIV to a greater or lesser degree as an entity interposed between investor and investments ('opaque'). In some States, a CIV is in principle subject to tax but is exempt if it fulfils certain criteria with regard to its activities, which may involve looking at its distribution practice, its sources of income, and sometimes its sectors of operation. More frequently, CIVs are subject to tax but the base for taxation is reduced, in a variety of different ways, by reference to distributions paid to investors. Deductions for distributions will usually mean that no tax is in fact paid. Other States tax CIVs but at a special low or zero tax rate. Finally, some States tax CIVs fully but with integration at the investor level to avoid double taxation of the income of the CIV. The integration may take the form of exemption in the hands of the investor or imputation of the tax imposed at the level of the CIV.

29 Under the principles of paragraph 8.5 of the Commentary on Article 4, a CIV may be "liable to tax", and therefore a resident of a Contracting State, even if that State does not in fact impose any tax on the CIV. However, the mechanism by which neutrality is accomplished will affect the treaty analysis. A CIV that is transparent for tax purposes in the State in which it is established will not be treated as a resident because it is not liable to tax in that State, nor will a CIV that is totally and unconditionally exempt from income taxation (*i.e.* without regard to the type of income it receives or its distribution policy). However, a CIV that is treated as opaque in the Contracting State in which it is established will be treated as a resident of that Contracting State even if the specific items of income it receives are exempt from taxation, or if it receives a deduction for dividends paid to investors, or it is subject to a lower rate of tax on its income. This analysis would apply to any entity that has satisfied the "person" requirement. Accordingly, for purposes of the residence test, the legal form of the CIV is relevant only to the extent that it affects the taxation of the CIV in the Contracting State in which it is established. So, for example, with respect to those countries that, for tax purposes, treat all CIVs in the same manner, regardless of legal form, all CIVs established in that country should be treated as residents, or none of them should, for treaty purposes.

30 The preceding analysis is consistent with the interpretation of the term "liable to tax" that is found in paragraph 8.5 of the existing Commentary on Article 4 of the Model Convention. However, paragraph 8.6 of that Commentary notes that some countries would take the view that an entity that is exempt from tax would not be "liable to tax" within the meaning of Article 4. Accordingly, it would be prudent to address the issue of CIVs directly in bilateral negotiations if one of the countries adheres to the position described in paragraph 8.6.

c) Is a CIV the "beneficial owner" of the income it receives?

31 In a few cases, CIVs have been denied treaty benefits because the relevant source country has taken the position that a CIV can never be the beneficial owner of the income that it receives. Because the term "beneficial owner" is not defined in the Model, it ordinarily would be given the meaning that it has under the law of the State applying the Convention, unless the context otherwise requires. Accordingly, a Contracting State might arguably be able to decide effectively the question with respect to CIVs investing in that State, even if the country of residence would take the opposite view. Because such a position would affect an entire, significant class of investors, it is particularly important to develop a broad consensus on this issue.

32 Those taking the position that a CIV can never be the beneficial owner of the income it receives generally take the view that, because of the relationship under local law of the investor and the CIV or its managers, ownership of an interest in a CIV is the equivalent of ownership of the underlying assets. However, the position of an investor in a CIV is significantly different from the position of an investor who owns the underlying assets directly. The function of a CIV is to allow a small investor to achieve investment goals that it cannot achieve on its own. An investor betters his position by joining with other investors, and in doing so, has invested in something substantially greater than his allocable share of the underlying assets. The investor has no right to the underlying assets. While the investor in the CIV has the right to receive an amount equal to the value of his allocable share of the underlying assets, this right is not the equivalent of receiving the assets as either a commercial or tax matter. Any shareholder in a publicly-traded company can receive the then-value of his allocable share of the corporation by selling his shares on the market. Selling on the market is also the way that an investor in an exchange-traded CIV realizes the value of his investment.

An investor who owned the underlying assets directly generally could direct the sale or **33** purchase of particular securities. This is not possible with respect to the vehicles that fall within the definition of "CIV" in paragraph 4, which are widely-held, hold a diversified portfolio of securities and are subject to investor-protection regulation in the country in which they are established. In the case of such CIVs, it is the manager of the CIV that has discretionary powers to manage the assets on behalf of the holders of interests in the CIV. In general, managers exercise this authority within the parameters that they have set for themselves in the offering documents they use to gain subscribers to the CIV. Although they may have practical or legal obligations to distribute the CIV's income in order to qualify for preferential treatment, this obligation does not constrain their ability to vary investments.

In most countries, the investor's tax situation is substantially different than it would be **34** if it owned the assets directly. For example, in most countries, an investor who redeems its shares in a CIV is taxed on a capital gain, not on its share of the income earned by the CIV. Accordingly, for the reasons described in paragraph 20, income from a particular asset generally cannot be traced to a particular investor, even in those countries that purport to treat the CIV as a transparent entity.

For these reasons, a widely-held CIV, as defined in paragraph 4, should be treated as **35** the beneficial owner of the income it receives, so long as the managers of the CIV have discretionary powers to manage the assets on behalf of the holders of interests in the CIV and, of course, so long as it also meets the requirements that it be a "person" and a "resident" of the State in which it is established. This conclusion, however, relates only to those economic characteristics that are specific to a CIV. It does not suggest that a CIV is in a different or better position than other investors with respect to aspects of the beneficial ownership requirement that are unrelated to the CIV's status as such. For example, where an individual receiving an item of income in certain circumstances would not be considered as the beneficial owner of that income, a CIV receiving that income in the same circumstances could not be deemed to be the beneficial owner of the income.

3.2   *If a CIV cannot Claim Benefits, is there any Relief for the Investors?*

36   While application of the principles set out above will clarify that many CIVs are entitled to treaty benefits, other CIVs clearly will not so qualify. It therefore is necessary to consider the position of an investor in a CIV that is not able to claim benefits on its own behalf. If there were no way for an investor that is a resident of a State with which the source State has a tax treaty to claim treaty benefits, then the treaty would have failed in its purpose of eliminating double taxation. Investors who invest through a CIV would be put in a worse position than if they had invested directly. The risk of double taxation would also argue for allowing treaty benefits whether the investors were resident in the same State in which the CIV is established, or in a third State where they would be entitled to benefits under that State's tax treaty with the source State. An argument could be made, however, that allowing claims in respect of treaty-eligible investors located in third countries is inconsistent with the bilateral nature of the treaty process. In particular, there may not be a significant risk of double taxation if neither the CIV nor residents of third States currently are taxable on the income received by the CIV. This matter is further discussed in paragraphs 55 and 58 to 59.

37   In any event, administrative difficulties effectively prevent individual claims by CIVs' investors. Given the number of investments by a typical CIV, and the thousands of individual investors in the CIV, each individual claim for exemption (or refund of withheld taxes) would be for relatively small amounts. It is likely that very few, if any, individual investors would bother with such claims, particularly as avoiding such administrative burdens is one of the benefits of investing collectively. Moreover, for the reasons described in paragraph 20, investors may not be able to prove that they have paid the withholding taxes. These administrative difficulties likely would result in benefits going unclaimed in many cases. If such claims were made, however, tax administrations would be overwhelmed by the sheer number of such small individual claims.

38   Accordingly, developing a system that would allow CIVs to make claims in respect of investors appears to be in the interests of both business and governments. Such a system could allow claims by CIVs with respect to existing treaties, in line with countries' views regarding the extent to which claims should be allowed with respect to treaty-eligible investors located in third countries. Some countries currently could allow such claims, including claims in respect of treaty-eligible residents of third countries, under their domestic law. For other countries, a mutual agreement would be useful or necessary.

39   Any approach that allows claims by a CIV on behalf of its investors would rely on the development of practical and reliable procedures for determining ownership of interests in CIVs and of securities held through other intermediated structures. Whilst it would be possible to require regular determinations, the costs of such determinations would be significantly higher, and compliance likely much lower, if the testing dates were determined after the fact. By contrast, if the date or dates were known in advance, the testing requirement could be built into automatic data collection systems. Under that system, information identifying the beneficial owner would be held by the intermediary with the direct relationship with the investor, rather than passed up the chain of intermediaries. However, information identifying the beneficial owners should be available to the source state upon demand.

However, there also may be situations where even such automatic data collection **40** might not be necessary. This might be true, for example, where the CIV industry is largely domestic in nature. For example, governments may be willing to rely on the fact that the fund manager or sponsor restricted sales of interests in the CIV to specific countries for purposes of concluding that the investors are resident in such countries, although they may want to confirm that such sales restrictions are co-extensive with relevant tax criteria. Alternatively, a CIV could establish separate classes of interests for those investors entitled to treaty benefits and for those investors who are not. The CIV could then require distributors to restrict sales accordingly.

3.3   *Relief from Double Taxation for Income Received by CIVs*

Discussion of the problems faced by CIVs has tended to focus on the problem of **41** qualifying for the reduced withholding rates provided by Articles 10 (Dividends) and, to a lesser extent, 11 (Interest), and therefore on claims for benefits that are directed to the source country. In fact, an equal or even greater tax loss may result from the fact that, in most cases, neither the CIV nor the investor can claim foreign tax credits for the withholding taxes imposed by the source country after application of the treaty *(i.e.* 15% for portfolio dividends according to the Model Convention).

Because most of the income received by CIVs consists of portfolio dividends and **42** interest, the income will be subject to withholding taxes in the country of source under treaties that follow the Model Convention. Accordingly, Article 23 (Relief from Double Taxation) of the Model Convention provides for the use of the credit method for such income, even for countries that use the exemption method as the primary means of relieving double taxation. However, a theoretical right to a foreign tax credit is irrelevant to an entity that has no residence State tax liability, which is the case with respect to most CIVs. Accordingly, if the CIV is treated as a resident, then the foreign tax credit is likely to go unused unless there is a special treaty or domestic law provision that would allow the credit to flow through to the CIV's investors. Some countries do allow investors in a domestic CIV to claim the foreign tax credit, at least in some circumstances.

Alternatively, if the CIV is treated as transparent in the Contracting State in which it is **43** established, then an investor in the CIV should be entitled to claim a foreign tax credit with respect to its proportionate share of the foreign withholding taxes paid on the income of the CIV. That should be relatively straightforward (e.g., under the domestic law of the CIV's State if not under Article 23 itself) if the investor is a resident of the same Contracting State in which the CIV is established. However, it could become more difficult and may require specific legislation, if that Contracting State does not view the CIV as transparent but achieves integration in some other way, such as exempting income or providing a deduction for dividends paid. Some countries have taken a different approach, "refunding" the foreign withholding tax to the CIV (*i.e.* making a cash payment to the CIV); under that approach, relief is achieved from the double taxation that would otherwise arise if the investors are subject to tax in the Contracting State in which the CIV is established, whether because they are residents of that State or, if they are non-residents, because that State levies a withholding tax at the time the earnings of the CIV are distributed.

44   Of course, the situation may become even more difficult if the investor is located in a different State, and that third State does not view the CIV as transparent. In that case, that third State is unlikely to provide a foreign tax credit for withholding taxes imposed on income received by the CIV. Moreover, this problematic situation involves three different countries. In theory, the Contracting State in which the investor is resident should not apply its treaty (if any) with the Contracting State in which the income arises, because the first-mentioned Contracting State sees the CIV in a third State as the beneficial owner of the income. The treaty between the State in which the CIV is established and the State in which the investor is a resident could solve the problem by requiring the State in which the investor is a resident to provide a foreign tax credit for any taxes withheld on payments to the CIV.

45   Such a provision could read as follows:

> [ ]. Where a resident of a Contracting State owns an interest or interests in a collective investment vehicle established in the other Contracting State, and that collective investment vehicle derives items of income that are subject to tax in a third State, the first-mentioned Contracting State shall allow as a deduction from the tax on the income of the resident of that Contracting State an amount equal to the tax paid in the third State. Such deduction shall not, however, exceed that part of the tax, as computed before the deduction is given, which is attributable to the income derived by that resident from its ownership interest in the collective investment vehicle, as determined under the laws of the first-mentioned Contracting State.

46   Some countries may be reluctant to include such a provision in a bilateral treaty because it would constitute a two-party, and therefore incomplete, solution to a multilateral problem. As a result, a Contracting State potentially would be providing relief for taxes paid to a third State without regard to whether that third State would provide reciprocal benefits. Moreover, it potentially could require the Contracting State in which the investor is a resident to provide a greater foreign tax credit than would have been granted if the investor had invested directly. (This situation could arise if the State in which the investor is resident had negotiated with the source State a lower withholding rate on the type of income than did the State in which the CIV is established.) Finally, it was noted that the proposed provision raises fundamental questions regarding when economic double taxation arises.

47   To date, investors have not expressed an interest in making such claims with respect to CIVs located in third countries and have not demanded the information that would be necessary to make such claims. However, it may be that other changes proposed in this report could, if widely implemented, increase investors' interest in making such claims.

IV.   POLICY ISSUES RAISED BY CURRENT TREATMENT OF CIVs

As noted above, the discussion and conclusions in Section III assume that the relevant   **48** tax treaties do not include any provisions specifically addressing the treatment of CIVs. Because the principles set out above are necessarily general, their application to a particular type of CIV might not be clear to the CIV, investors and intermediaries. Section III therefore does not address the issue of whether the treaty entitlement of any particular type of CIV is appropriate or not. However, as noted above, clarity is critical for a CIV because it affects the calculation of its NAV, the basis for all purchases, sales and redemptions. For these reasons, some countries have begun to include in their tax treaties provisions that specifically address the treatment of CIVs. In some cases, the provisions merely confirm the treatment that otherwise would apply while in other cases that treatment is modified to achieve specific policy goals.

This section addresses the policy considerations that countries entering into new   **49** treaties or modifying existing treaties may want to consider in determining how to treat the specific CIVs that are common in the two Contracting States. In some cases, the Contracting States might provide a single treatment that would apply to all of the forms of CIV in common use in the two countries. However, given the continuing proliferation of new forms of CIVs, it seems just as likely that the policy considerations discussed in this section will suggest that CIVs in the two Contracting States, or even within the same Contracting State, should be treated differently. At the same time, negotiators will want to keep in mind that some countries may have difficulties with a treaty providing more than one treatment for a single type of legal entity.

4.1   *Potential for Differential Treatment of Economically Similar CIVs*

The discussion in Section III demonstrates that there could be significant differences in   **50** the treatment of CIVs that take different legal forms and are subject to different tax regimes. This is true even though the goal of all of the systems is, to the extent possible, to ensure neutrality between direct investment and investment through CIVs. Such differential treatment could be seen as violating the general policy goal of treating economically similar structures similarly. Moreover, it could in many cases result in CIVs in one Contracting State qualifying for treaty benefits while those in the other Contracting State fail to so qualify, thus possibly violating the implicit assumption of reciprocity in bilateral tax treaties. Such unbalanced situations frequently have proven to be, not surprisingly, unstable. It is politically difficult for a country to provide benefits to CIVs established in another country when that other country does not provide benefits to CIVs located in the first country. That may increase the pressure on governments to deny claims for treaty benefits made by CIVs, undermining one of the primary goals of the tax treaty – to eliminate barriers to cross-border investment.

51   On the other hand, the differences in legal form and tax treatment in the two Contracting States may mean that it is appropriate to treat CIVs in the two States differently. In comparing the taxation of CIVs in the two States, taxation in the source State and at the investor level should be considered, not just the taxation of the CIV itself. The goal is to achieve neutrality between a direct investment and an investment through a CIV in the international context, just as the goal of most domestic provisions addressing the treatment of CIVs is to achieve such neutrality in the wholly domestic context. Developing practical solutions that ensure that the CIVs that are common in each jurisdiction have access to treaty benefits, even if on different terms, is likely to be more beneficial for both countries in the long run.

4.2   Potential for Treaty Shopping through CIVs

52   Some countries are also concerned about the prospect that a CIV could be treated as meeting the technical requirements for treaty benefits, and thus claim benefits in its own right, or at least without regard to the nature of the CIV's investors. They argue that a CIV, which generally is not subject to substantial taxation in the country in which it is organised, could easily serve as a vehicle for treaty shopping. Accordingly, it may be appropriate to restrict benefits that might otherwise be available to such a CIV, either through generally applicable anti-abuse or anti-treaty shopping rules or through a specific provision dealing with CIVs.

53   Again, in deciding on the appropriate approach, negotiators will want to consider the economic characteristics of the various types of CIVs that are prevalent in each of the Contracting States. For example, a CIV that is not subject to any taxation in the State in which it is established may present more of a danger of treaty shopping than a scenario in which the CIV itself is subject to an entity-level tax or where distributions to non-resident investors are subject to withholding tax.

54   A number of countries have dealt with the possibility of treaty shopping by adopting general provisions such as those mentioned in paragraphs 13 to 21.4 of the Commentary on Article 1 of the Model Convention. Some of these provisions are quite flexible and, in some treaties, such provisions apply to all claims for treaty benefits by any person. In others, there are no general anti-treaty shopping rules, but there may be specific ones that apply to CIVs. Still others may include a general anti-treaty shopping provision but apply stricter standards to CIVs. Negotiators developing a specific provision addressing the treatment of CIVs will also want to consider the effect of, and co-ordinate the provision with, any general anti-treaty shopping provision included in the treaty.

55   In the case of CIVs, an anti-treaty shopping provision generally would seek to determine whether a CIV is being used for treaty shopping by determining whether the owners, or a specific proportion of the owners, of interests in the CIV are residents of

the Contracting State in which the CIV is organised or, in some cases, whether the owners of interests in the CIV would have been entitled to equivalent benefits had they invested directly. The latter approach would help to ensure that investors who would have been entitled to benefits with respect to income derived from the source State had they received the income directly are not put in a worse position by investing through a CIV located in a third country. The approach thus serves the goals of neutrality as between direct investments and investments through a CIV. It also decreases the risk of double taxation as between the source State and the State of residence of the investor, to the extent that there is a tax treaty between them. It is beneficial for investors, particularly those from small countries, who will consequently enjoy a greater choice of investment vehicles. It also increases economies of scale, which are a primary economic benefit of investing through CIVs. Finally, adopting this approach substantially simplifies compliance procedures. Compliance procedures could be greatly simplified, because in many cases, nearly all of a CIV's investors will be "equivalent beneficiaries", given the extent of bilateral treaty coverage and the fact that rates in those treaties are nearly always 10–15% on portfolio dividends. On the other hand, some countries have expressed concern that taking into account residents of countries other than the source country and the country in which the CIV is established changes the bilateral nature of tax treaties.

Such a provision could be structured in various ways. The simplest would provide a **56** binary application; an entity should either receive 1) full treaty benefits if the requirements for benefits are satisfied, or 2) no treaty benefits if the requirements are not satisfied. This is the standard approach under many anti-treaty shopping provisions. However, that approach would create a pure "cliff", which effectively would deny benefits to investors who otherwise would be entitled to treaty benefits. For that reason, those countries that have developed provisions to specifically address the treatment of CIVs generally have allowed a CIV to make claims in proportion to its "good" ownership, whether defined to include only residents of the same State or other treaty-entitled investors as well. Procedures could be further simplified, without significantly increasing the risk of treaty shopping, by providing that, once the CIV has passed some threshold of "good" ownership, the CIV would be entitled to benefits with respect to 100% of the income it receives. This dual approach would avoid the "cliff" effect described above. On the other hand, the "cliff" effect applies equally above the threshold, in that some investors who might not have been entitled to benefits nevertheless would benefit. This might argue for the adoption of a high threshold. A higher threshold might also be justified if a broader class of investors, such as all treaty-entitled investors, were treated as "good" owners. Because of these variables, the choice of threshold is best left to bilateral negotiations.

An alternative approach, which has been adopted in a number of treaties that include **57** general anti- treaty shopping provisions, would be to provide that a CIV that is publicly traded in the Contracting State in which it is established will be entitled to treaty benefits without regard to the residence of its investors. This provision has been justified on the basis that a publicly-traded CIV cannot be used effectively for treaty shopping because the shareholders or unitholders of such a CIV cannot individually exercise control over it.

4.3   Potential Deferral of Income

58   Some source States may be concerned about the potential deferral of taxation that could arise with respect to a CIV that is subject to no or low taxation and that accumulates its income rather than distributing it on a current basis. Their view is that benefits to the CIV should be limited to the proportion of the CIV's investors who are currently taxable on their share of the income of the CIV, similar to the approach taken with respect to partnerships. Because such an approach would be difficult to apply to widely-held CIVs in practice, for the reasons described in paragraph 20 above, countries that are concerned about the possibility of deferral may wish to negotiate provisions that extend benefits only to those CIVs that are required to distribute earnings currently.

59   Other States have less concern about the potential for deferral. They take the view that, even if the investor is not taxed currently on the income received by the CIV, it will be taxed eventually, either on the distribution, or on any capital gains if it sells its interest in the CIV before the CIV distributes the income. Those countries may wish to negotiate provisions that grant benefits to CIVs even if they are not obliged to distribute their income on a current basis. Moreover, in many countries, the tax rate with respect to investment income is not significantly higher than the 10–15% withholding rate on dividends, so there would be little if any residence-country tax deferral to be achieved by earning such income through an investment fund rather than directly. Others view the risk of deferral in these circumstances as an issue primarily of concern to the State of which the investors are resident. In fact, many countries have taken steps to ensure the current taxation of investment income earned by their residents through invest-ment funds, regardless of whether the funds accumulate that income, further reducing the potential for such deferral. When considering the treatment of CIVs that are not required to distribute income currently, countries may want to consider whether these or other factors address the concerns described in the preceding paragraph so that the type of limits described therein might not in fact be necessary.

4.4   Loss of Preferential Benefits

60   In most cases, it will be simpler to treat the CIV as a resident and the beneficial owner of the income it receives. Under this approach, the CIV would be entitled to the rates on income generally applicable to portfolio investors. This approach would provide for only one reduced withholding rate on dividends. However, there may be cases where countries would want to adopt a look-through approach with respect to the entire CIV or a class of interests in the CIV. This might be the case, for example, where pension funds are substantial investors in the CIV, since they might be entitled by treaty to a full exemption from source country tax on certain types of investment income.

In considering whether to adopt such a look-through approach, however, negotiators **61** should pay particular attention to the types of vehicles to which the rules will apply. It is intended that the provisions included in the proposed Commentary that follows would apply only to CIVs as defined in paragraph 4, and therefore be limited to funds (including "funds of funds") that are widely-held, hold a diversified portfolio of securities and are subject to investor-protection regulation in the country in which they are established. It is appropriate to provide simplified methods for determining the ownership of these types of vehicles because of the difficulty in tracing investment income received by the CIV to specific investors. Where ownership in the vehicle is sufficiently stable to allow the custodian, manager or other fiduciary to credit specific income received by the vehicle to specific investors, it should also be possible to determine the extent to which those individual investors or classes or investors are entitled to treaty benefits. Where such tracing of specific income items to specific investors is clearly possible, it would be inappropriate to apply one of the less-targeted approaches provided in the proposed Commentary.

V.   PROPOSED CHANGES TO THE COMMENTARY TO ADDRESS CIVs

The following proposed addition to the Commentary on Article 1 addresses the issues **62** discussed in this Report. It begins with the conclusions from Section III regarding the application of current treaty rules to the specific case of CIVs. That is followed by a discussion of a number of optional provisions that could be adopted in new treaties to address the concerns discussed in Section IV. Because of the various factors and policy considerations discussed in Section IV, it is not possible to propose a single approach for the treatment of CIVs that could apply in all cases.

Add the following paragraphs 6.8 to 6.34 to the Commentary on Article 1 of the Model Tax Convention:

Cross-Border Issues Relating to Collective Investment Vehicles

6.8 Most countries have dealt with the domestic tax issues arising from groups of small investors who pool their funds in collective investment vehicles (CIVs). In general, the goal of such systems is to provide for neutrality between direct investments and investments through a CIV. Whilst those systems generally succeed when the investors, the CIV and the investment are all located in the same country, complications frequently arise when one or more of those parties or the investments are located in different countries. These complications are discussed in the Report by the Committee on Fiscal Affairs entitled "Report on the Granting of Treaty Benefits with Respect to the Income of Collective Investment Vehicles", the main conclusions of which have been incorporated below. For purposes of the Report and for this discussion, the term "CIV" is limited to funds that are widely-held, hold a diversified portfolio of securities and are subject to investor-protection regulation in the country in which they are established.

Application of the Model Convention to CIVs

6.9 The primary question that arises in the cross-border context is whether a CIV should qualify for the benefits of the Convention in its own right. In order to do so under treaties that, like the Model Convention, do not include a specific provision dealing with CIVs, a CIV would have to qualify as a "person" that is a "resident" of a Contracting State and, as regards the application of Articles 10 and 11, that is the "beneficial owner" of the income that it receives.

6.10 The determination of whether a CIV should be treated as a "person" begins with the legal form of the CIV, which differs substantially from country to country and between the various types of vehicles. In many countries, most CIVs take the form of a company. In others, the CIV typically would be a trust. In still others, many CIVs are simple contractual arrangements or a form of joint ownership. In most cases, the CIV would be treated as a taxpayer or a "person" for purposes of the tax law of the State in which it is established; for example, in some countries where the CIV is commonly established in the form of a trust, either the trust itself, or the trustees acting collectively in their capacity as such, is treated as a taxpayer or a person for domestic tax law purposes. In view of the wide meaning to be given to the term "person", the fact that the tax law of the country where such a CIV is established would treat it as a taxpayer would be indicative that the CIV is a "person" for treaty purposes. Contracting States wishing to expressly clarify that, in these circumstances, such CIVs are persons for the purposes of their conventions may agree bilaterally to modify the definition of "person" to include them.

6.11 Whether a CIV is a "resident" of a Contracting State depends not on its legal form (as long as it qualifies as a person) but on its tax treatment in the State in which it is established. Although a consistent goal of domestic CIV regimes is to ensure that there is only one level of tax, at either the CIV or the investor level, there are a number of different ways in which States achieve that goal. In some States, the holders of interests in the CIV are liable to tax on the income received by the CIV, rather than the CIV itself being liable to tax on such income. Such a fiscally transparent CIV would not be treated as a resident of the Contracting State in which it is established because it is not liable to tax therein.

6.12 By contrast, in other States, a CIV is in principle liable to tax but its income may be fully exempt, for instance, if the CIV fulfils certain criteria with regard to its purpose, activities or operation, which may include requirements as to minimum distributions, its sources of income and sometimes its sectors of operation. More frequently, CIVs are subject to tax but the base for taxation is reduced, in a variety of different ways, by reference to distributions paid to investors. Deductions for distributions will usually mean that no tax is in fact paid. Other States tax CIVs but at a special low tax rate. Finally, some States tax CIVs fully but with integration at the investor level to avoid double taxation of the income of the CIV. For those countries that adopt the view, reflected in paragraph 8.5 of the Commentary on Article 4, that a person may be liable to tax even if the State in which it is established does not impose tax, the CIV would be treated as a resident of the State in which it is established in all of these cases because the CIV is subject to comprehensive taxation in that State. Even in the case where the income of the CIV is taxed at a zero rate, or is exempt from tax, the requirements to be treated as a resident may be met if the requirements to qualify for such lower rate or exemption are sufficiently stringent.

6.13 Those countries that adopt the alternative view, reflected in paragraph 8.6 of the Commentary on Article 4, that an entity that is exempt from tax therefore is not liable to tax may not view some or all of the CIVs described in the preceding paragraph as residents of the States in which they are established. States taking the latter view, and those States negotiating with such States, are encouraged to address the issue in their bilateral negotiations.

6.14 Some countries have questioned whether a CIV, even if it is a "person" and a "resident", can qualify as the beneficial owner of the income it receives. Because a "CIV" as defined in paragraph 6.8 above must be widely-held, hold a diversified portfolio of securities and be subject to investor-protection regulation in the country in which it is established, such a CIV, or its managers, often perform significant functions with respect to the investment and management of the assets of the CIV. Moreover, the position of an investor in a CIV differs substantially, as a legal and economic matter, from the position of an investor who owns the underlying assets, so that it would not be appropriate to treat the investor in such a CIV as the beneficial owner of the income received by the CIV. Accordingly, a vehicle that meets the definition of a widely-held CIV will also be treated as the beneficial owner of the dividends and interest that it receives, so long as the managers of the CIV have discretionary powers to manage the assets generating such income (unless an individual who is a resident of that State who would have received the income in the same circumstances would not have been considered to be the beneficial owner thereof).

6.15 Because these principles are necessarily general, their application to a particular type of CIV might not be clear to the CIV, investors and intermediaries. Any uncertainty regarding treaty eligibility is especially problematic for a CIV, which must take into account amounts expected to be received, including any withholding tax benefits provided by treaty, when it calculates its net asset value (NAV). The NAV, which typically is calculated daily, is the basis for the prices used for subscriptions and redemptions. If the withholding tax benefits ultimately obtained by the CIV do not correspond to its original assumptions about the amount and timing of such withholding tax benefits, there will be a discrepancy between the real asset value and the NAV used by investors who have purchased, sold or redeemed their interests in the CIV in the interim.

6.16 In order to provide more certainty under existing treaties, tax authorities may want to reach a mutual agreement clarifying the treatment of some types of CIVs in their respective States. With respect to some types of CIVs, such a mutual agreement might simply confirm that the CIV satisfies the technical requirements discussed above and therefore is entitled to benefits in its own right. In other cases, the mutual agreement could provide a CIV an administratively feasible way to make claims with respect to treaty-eligible investors. See paragraphs 36 to 40 of the "Report on the Granting of Treaty Benefits to Income Earned by Collective Investment Vehicles" for a discussion of this issue. Of course, a mutual agreement could not cut back on benefits that otherwise would be available to the CIV under the terms of a treaty.

Policy Issues Raised by the Current Treatment of Collective Investment Vehicles

6.17 The same considerations would suggest that treaty negotiators address expressly the treatment of CIVs. Thus, even if it appears that CIVs in each of the Contracting States would be entitled to benefits, it may be appropriate to include a provision confirming that reciprocal treatment or otherwise to confirm that position publicly (for example, through an exchange of notes) in order to provide certainty. For example, such a provision could read:

[ ] Notwithstanding the other provisions of this Convention, a collective investment vehicle which is established in a Contracting State and which receives income arising in the other Contracting State shall be treated for

purposes of applying the Convention to such income as an individual that is a resident of the Contracting State in which it is established and as the beneficial owner of the income it receives (unless an individual who is a resident of the first-mentioned State who would have received the income in the same circumstances would not have been considered to be the beneficial owner thereof). For purposes of this paragraph, the term "collective investment vehicle" means, in the case of [the first Contracting State], a [ ] and, in the case of [the other Contracting State], a [ ], as well as any other investment fund, arrangement or entity established in either Contracting State which the competent authorities of the Contracting States agree to regard as a collective investment vehicle for purposes of this paragraph.

6.18 However, in negotiating new treaties or amendments to existing treaties, the Contracting States would not be restricted to clarifying the results of the application of other treaty provisions to CIVs, but could vary those results to the extent necessary to achieve policy objectives. For example, in the context of a particular bilateral treaty, the technical analysis may result in CIVs located in one of the Contracting States qualifying for benefits, whilst CIVs in the other Contracting State may not. This may make the treaty appear unbalanced, although whether it is so in fact will depend on the specific circumstances. If it is, then the Contracting States should attempt to reach an equitable solution. If the practical result in each of the Contracting States is that most CIVs do not in fact pay tax, then the Contracting States should attempt to overcome differences in legal form that might otherwise cause those in one State to qualify for benefits and those in the other to be denied benefits. On the other hand, the differences in legal form and tax treatment in the two Contracting States may mean that it is appropriate to treat CIVs in the two States differently. In comparing the taxation of CIVs in the two States, taxation in the source State and at the investor level should be considered, not just the taxation of the CIV itself. The goal is to achieve neutrality between a direct investment and an investment through a CIV in the international context, just as the goal of most domestic provisions addressing the treatment of CIVs is to achieve such neutrality in the wholly domestic context.

6.19 A Contracting State may also want to consider whether existing treaty provisions are sufficient to prevent CIVs from being used in a potentially abusive manner. It is possible that a CIV could satisfy all of the requirements to claim treaty benefits in its own right, even though its income is not subject to much, if any, tax in practice. In that case, the CIV could present the opportunity for residents of third countries to receive treaty benefits that would not have been available had they invested directly. Accordingly, it may be appropriate to restrict benefits that might otherwise be available to such a CIV, either through generally applicable anti-abuse or anti-treaty shopping rules (as discussed under "Improper use of the Convention" below) or through a specific provision dealing with CIVs.

6.20 In deciding whether such a provision is necessary, Contracting States will want to consider the economic characteristics, including the potential for treaty shopping, presented by the various types of CIVs that are prevalent in each of the Contracting States. For example, a CIV that is not subject to any taxation in the State in which it is established may present more of a danger of treaty shopping than one in which the CIV itself is subject to an entity-level tax or where distributions to non-resident investors are subject to withholding tax.

Possible Provisions Modifying the Treatment of CIVs

6.21 Where the Contracting States have agreed that a specific provision dealing with CIVs is necessary to address the concerns described in paragraphs 6.18 through 6.20, they could include in the bilateral treaty the following provision:

[ ] a) Notwithstanding the other provisions of this Convention, a collective investment vehicle which is established in a Contracting State and which receives income arising in the other Contracting State shall be treated for purposes of applying the Convention to such income as an individual who is a resident of the Contracting State in which it is established and as the beneficial owner of the income it receives (unless an individual who is a resident of the first-mentioned State who would have received the income in the same circumstances would not have been considered to be the beneficial owner thereof), but only to the extent that equivalent beneficiaries are the owners of the beneficial interests in the collective investment vehicle.

b) For purposes of this paragraph:

    (i) the term "collective investment vehicle" means, in the case of [the first Contracting State], a [ ] and, in the case of [the other Contracting State], a [ ], as well as any other investment fund, arrangement or entity established in either Contracting State which the competent authorities of the Contracting States agree to regard as a collective investment vehicle for purposes of this paragraph; and

    (ii) the term "equivalent beneficiary" means a resident of the Contracting State in which the CIV is established, and a resident of any other State with which the Contracting State in which the income arises has an income tax convention that provides for effective and comprehensive information exchange who would, if he received the particular item of income for which benefits are being claimed under this Convention, be entitled under that convention, or under the domestic law of the Contracting State in which the income arises, to a rate of tax with respect to that item of income that is at least as low as the rate claimed under this Convention by the CIV with respect to that item of income.

6.22 It is intended that the Contracting States would provide in clause (b)(i) specific cross- references to relevant tax or securities law provisions relating to CIVs. In deciding which treatment should apply with respect to particular CIVs, Contracting States should take into account the policy considerations discussed above. Negotiators may agree that economic differences in the treatment of CIVs in the two Contracting States, or even within the same Contracting State, justify differential treatment in the tax treaty. In that case, some combination of the provisions in this section might be included in the treaty.

6.23 The effect of allowing benefits to the CIV to the extent that it is owned by "equivalent beneficiaries" as defined in clause *(b)(ii)* is to ensure that investors who would have been entitled to benefits with respect to income derived from the source State had they received the income directly are not put in a worse position by investing through a CIV located in a third country. The approach thus serves the goals of neutrality as between direct investments and investments through a CIV. It also decreases the risk of double taxation as between the source State and the State of residence of the investor, to the extent that there is a tax treaty between them. It is beneficial for investors, particularly those from small countries, who will consequently enjoy a greater choice of investment vehicles. It also increases economies of scale, which are a primary economic benefit of investing through

CIVs. Finally, adopting this approach substantially simplifies compliance procedures. In many cases, nearly all of a CIV's investors will be "equivalent beneficiaries", given the extent of bilateral treaty coverage and the fact that rates in those treaties are nearly always 10–15% on portfolio dividends.

6.24 At the same time, the provision prevents a CIV from being used by investors to achieve a better tax treaty position than they would have achieved by investing directly. This is achieved through the rate comparison in the definition of "equivalent beneficiary". Accordingly, the appropriate comparison is between the rate claimed by the CIV and the rate that the investor could have claimed had it received the income directly. For example, assume that a CIV established in Country B receives dividends from a company resident in Country A. Sixty-five percent of the investors in the CIV are individual residents of Country B; ten percent are pension funds established in Country C and 25 percent are individual residents of Country C. Under the A-B tax treaty, portfolio dividends are subject to a maximum tax rate at source of 10%. Under the A-C tax treaty, pension funds are exempt from taxation in the source country and other portfolio dividends are subject to tax at a maximum tax rate of 15%. Both the A-B and A-C treaties include effective and comprehensive information exchange provisions. On these facts, 75% of the investors in the CIV – the individual residents of Country B and the pension funds established in Country C – are equivalent beneficiaries.

6.25 A source State may also be concerned about the potential deferral of taxation that could arise with respect to a CIV that is subject to no or low taxation and that may accumulate its income rather than distributing it on a current basis. Such States may be tempted to limit benefits to the CIV to the proportion of the CIV's investors who are currently taxable on their share of the income of the CIV. However, such an approach has proven difficult to apply to widely-held CIVs in practice. Those countries that are concerned about the possibility of such deferral may wish to negotiate provisions that extend benefits only to those CIVs that are required to distribute earnings currently. Other States may be less concerned about the potential for deferral, however. They may take the view that, even if the investor is not taxed currently on the income received by the CIV, it will be taxed eventually, either on the distribution, or on any capital gains if it sells its interest in the CIV before the CIV distributes the income. Those countries may wish to negotiate provisions that grant benefits to CIVs even if they are not obliged to distribute their income on a current basis. Moreover, in many countries, the tax rate with respect to investment income is not significantly higher than the treaty withholding rate on dividends, so there would be little if any residence-country tax deferral to be achieved by earning such income through an investment fund rather than directly. In addition, many countries have taken steps to ensure the current taxation of investment income earned by their residents through investment funds, regardless of whether the funds accumulate that income, further reducing the potential for such deferral. When considering the treatment of CIVs that are not required to distribute income currently, countries may want to consider whether these or other factors address the concerns described above so that the type of limits described herein might not in fact be necessary.

6.26 Some States believe that taking all treaty-eligible investors, including those in third States, into account would change the bilateral nature of tax treaties. These States may prefer to allow treaty benefits to a CIV only to the extent that the investors in the CIV are residents of the Contracting State in which the CIV is established. In that case, the provision would be drafted as follows:

[ ] a) Notwithstanding the other provisions of this Convention, a collective investment vehicle which is established in a Contracting State and which receives income arising in the other Contracting State shall be treated for purposes of applying the Convention to such income as an individual who is a resident of the Contracting State in which it is established and as the beneficial owner of the income it receives (unless an individual who is a resident of the first-mentioned State who would have received the income in the same circumstances would not have been considered to be the beneficial owner thereof), but only to the extent that residents of the Contracting State in which the collective investment vehicle is established are the owners of the beneficial interests in the collective investment vehicle.

b) For purposes of this paragraph, the term "collective investment vehicle" means, in the case of [the first Contracting State], a [ ] and, in the case of [the other Contracting State], a [ ], as well as any other investment fund, arrangement or entity established in either Contracting State which the competent authorities of the Contracting States agree to regard as a collective investment vehicle for purposes of this paragraph.

6.27 Although the purely proportionate approach set out in paragraphs 6.21 and 6.26 protects against treaty shopping, it may also impose substantial administrative burdens as a CIV attempts to determine the treaty entitlement of every single investor. A Contracting State may decide that the fact that a substantial proportion of the CIV's investors are treaty-eligible is adequate protection against treaty shopping, and thus that it is appropriate to provide an ownership threshold above which benefits would be provided with respect to all income received by the CIV. Including such a threshold would also mitigate some of the procedural burdens that otherwise might arise. If desired, therefore, the following sentence could be added at the end of subparagraph *a):*

However, if at least [ ] percent of the owners of the beneficial interests in the collective investment vehicle are [equivalent beneficiaries][residents of the Contracting State in which the collective investment vehicle is established], the collective investment vehicle shall be treated as an individual who is a resident of the Contracting State in which it is established and as the beneficial owner of all of the income it receives (unless an individual who is a resident of the first-mentioned State who would have received the income in the same circumstances would not have been considered to be the beneficial owner thereof).

6.28 In some cases, the Contracting States might wish to take a different approach from that put forward in paragraphs 6.17, 6.21 and 6.26 with respect to certain types of CIVs and to treat the CIV as making claims on behalf of the investors rather than in its own name. This might be true, for example, if a large percentage of the owners of interests in the CIV as a whole, or of a class of interests in the CIV, are pension funds that are exempt from tax in the source country under the terms of the relevant treaty. To ensure that the investors would not lose the benefit of the preferential rates to which they would have been entitled had they invested directly, the Contracting States might agree to a provision along the following lines with respect to such CIVs (although likely adopting one of the approaches of paragraph 6.17, 6.21 or 6.26 with respect to other types of CIVs):

[ ] a) A collective investment vehicle described in subparagraph c) which is established in a Contracting State and which receives income arising in the other Contracting State shall not be treated as a resident of the Contracting State in which it is established, but may claim, on behalf of the owners of the beneficial interests in the collective investment vehicle, the tax reductions,

exemptions or other benefits that would have been available under this Convention to such owners had they received such income directly.

b) A collective investment vehicle may not make a claim under subparagraph a) for benefits on behalf of any owner of the beneficial interests in such collective investment vehicle if the owner has itself made an individual claim for benefits with respect to income received by the collective investment vehicle.

c) This paragraph shall apply with respect to, in the case of [the first Contracting State], a [ ] and, in the case of [the other Contracting State], a [ ], as well as any other investment fund, arrangement or entity established in either Contracting State to which the competent authorities of the Contracting States agree to apply this paragraph.

This provision would, however, limit the CIV to making claims on behalf of residents of the same Contracting State in which the CIV is established. If, for the reasons described in paragraph 6.23, the Contracting States deemed it desirable to allow the CIV to make claims on behalf of treaty-eligible residents of third States, that could be accomplished by replacing the words "this Convention" with "any Convention to which the other Contracting State is a party" in subparagraph a). If, as anticipated, the Contracting States would agree that the treatment provided in this paragraph would apply only to specific types of CIVs, it would be necessary to ensure that the types of CIVs listed in subparagraph c) did not include any of the types of CIVs listed in a more general provision such as that in paragraphs 6.17, 6.21 or 6.26 so that the treatment of a specific type of CIV would be fixed, rather than elective. Countries wishing to allow individual CIVs to elect their treatment, either with respect to the CIV as a whole or with respect to one or more classes of interests in the CIV, are free to modify the paragraph to do so.

6.29 Under either the approach in paragraphs 6.21 and 6.26 or in paragraph 6.28, it will be necessary for the CIV to make a determination regarding the proportion of holders of interests who would have been entitled to benefits had they invested directly. Because ownership of interests in CIVs changes regularly, and such interests frequently are held through intermediaries, the CIV and its managers often do not themselves know the names and treaty status of the beneficial owners of interests. It would be impractical for the CIV to collect such information from the relevant intermediaries on a daily basis. Accordingly, Contracting States should be willing to accept practical and reliable approaches that do not require such daily tracing.

6.30 For example, in many countries the CIV industry is largely domestic, with an overwhelming percentage of investors resident in the country in which the CIV is established. In some cases, tax rules discourage foreign investment by imposing a withholding tax on distributions, or securities laws may severely restrict offerings to non-residents. Governments should consider whether these or other circumstances provide adequate protection against investment by non-treaty-eligible residents of third countries. It may be appropriate, for example, to assume that a CIV is owned by residents of the State in which it is established if the CIV has limited distribution of its shares or units to the State in which the CIV is established or to other States that provide for similar benefits in their treaties with the source State.

6.31 In other cases, interests in the CIV are offered to investors in many countries. Although the identity of individual investors will change daily, the proportion of investors in the CIV that are treaty-entitled is likely to change relatively slowly. Accordingly, it would be a reasonable approach to require the CIV to collect from other intermediaries on a regular basis, perhaps at the end of each calendar quarter, information enabling the CIV to determine the proportion of investors that are treaty-entitled. The CIV could then make a claim on the basis of an average of those amounts over an agreed-upon time period. In adopting such procedures, care would have to be taken in choosing the measurement dates to ensure that the CIV would have enough time to update the self-declaration and ensure the correct withholding at the beginning of each relevant period.

6.32 An alternative approach would provide that a CIV that is publicly traded in the Contracting State in which it is established will be entitled to treaty benefits without regard to the residence of its investors. This provision has been justified on the basis that a publicly-traded CIV cannot be used effectively for treaty shopping because the shareholders or unitholders of such a CIV cannot individually exercise control over it. Such a provision could read:

[ ] a) Notwithstanding the other provisions of this Convention, a collective investment vehicle which is established in a Contracting State and which receives income arising in the other Contracting State shall be treated for purposes of applying the Convention to such income as an individual who is a resident of the Contracting State in which it is established and as the beneficial owner of the income it receives (unless an individual who is a resident of the first-mentioned State who would have received the income in the same circumstances would not have been considered to be the beneficial owner thereof), if the principal class of shares or units in the collective investment vehicle is listed and regularly traded on a regulated stock exchange in that State.

b) For purposes of this paragraph, the term "collective investment vehicle" means, in the case of [the first Contracting State], a [ ] and, in the case of [the other Contracting State], a [ ], as well as any other investment fund, arrangement or entity established in either Contracting State which the competent authorities of the Contracting States agree to regard as a collective investment vehicle for purposes of this paragraph.

6.33 Each of the provisions in paragraphs 6.17, 6.21, 6.25 and 6.31 treats the CIV as the resident and the beneficial owner of the income it receives for the purposes of the application of the Convention to such income, which has the simplicity of providing for one reduced rate of withholding with respect to each type of income. These provisions should not be construed, however, as restricting in any way the right of the State of source from taxing its own residents who are investors in the CIV. Clearly, these provisions are intended to deal with the source taxation of the CIV's income and not the residence taxation of its investors (this conclusion is analogous to the one put forward in paragraph 6.1 above as regards partnerships). States that wish to confirm this point in the text of the provisions are free to amend the provisions accordingly, which could be done by adding the following sentence: "This provision shall not be construed as restricting in any way a Contracting State's right to tax the residents of that State".

6.34 Also, each of these provisions is intended only to provide that the specific characteristics of the CIV will not cause it to be treated as other than the beneficial owner of the income it receives. Therefore, a CIV will be treated as the beneficial owner of all of the income it receives. The provision is not intended, however, to put a CIV in a different or better position than other investors with respect to aspects of the beneficial ownership requirement that are unrelated to the CIV's status as such. Accordingly, where an individual receiving an item of income in certain circumstances would not be considered as the beneficial owner of that income, a CIV receiving that income in the same circumstances could not be deemed to be the beneficial owner of the income. This result is confirmed by the parenthetical limiting the application of the provision to situations in which an individual in the same circumstances would have been treated as the beneficial owner of the income.